# The Story of the World
# Activity Book Three

## Early Modern Times

From Elizabeth the First to the Forty-Niners

Edited by Susan Wise Bauer

With activities, maps, and drawings by:
Sofie Engstrom von Alten, Peter Buffington, Sara Buffington, Terri Downing, Meghan Jamieson, Rebecca Sorge Jensen, Krista Loney, Jeannie McElrath, Justin Moore, Tiffany Moore, Shelby Otto, Charlie Park, Sarah Park, Colleen Sharpe, Kara Swanson, Elizabeth Weber Edwards, and Jeff West

*www.welltrainedmind.com*

Address requests for permissions to make copies to:
Well-Trained Mind Press
18021 The Glebe Lane
Charles City, VA 23030
support@welltrainedmind.com

Reprinted in the U.S.A. by Bradford & Bigelow, May 2021

ISBN 978-1-945841-47-7

**ALSO BY SUSAN WISE BAUER**

**The Story of the World: History for the Classical Child**
(WELL-TRAINED MIND PRESS)

Volume 1: Ancient Times (revised edition, 2006)

Volume 2: The Middle Ages (revised edition, 2007)

Volume 3: Early Modern Times (revised edition, 2020)

Volume 4: The Modern Age (2005)

**The History of the World** series
(W.W. Norton)

*The History of the Ancient World* (2007)

*The History of the Medieval World* (2010)

*The History of the Renaissance World* (2013)

**The Well-Educated Mind: A Guide to the Classical Education You Never Had**
(W.W. NORTON, revised edition, 2016)

WITH JESSIE WISE

***The Well-Trained Mind: A Guide to Classical Education at Home***
(fourth edition, W.W. NORTON, 2016)

For more on Susan Wise Bauer, visit her website
at www.susanwisebauer.com.
To find out more about The Story of the World series and
other titles published by Well-Trained Mind Press, visit our website
at www.welltrainedmind.com.

Typesetting by PerfecType, Inc., Nashville, TN

# Table of Contents



# Chapters

## PHOTOCOPYING AND DISTRIBUTION POLICY

# How to Use This Activity Book

History is the most absorbing and enthralling story you can tell a young child, because it's true. A good history narrative is as strange and wondrous as a good fairy tale. Kings, queens, mummies, wooden horses, knights, and castles can be as fascinating as giants and elves—but they *really existed!*

In classical education, history lies at the center of the curriculum. The chronological study of history allows even small children to learn about the past in an orderly way; after all, the "best way to tell a story," as the King tells Alice in *Alice in Wonderland,* "is to begin at the beginning and go on to the end." When the study of literature is linked to history, children have an opportunity to hear the stories of each country as they learn more about that country's past and its people. History teaches comprehension; young students learn to listen carefully, to pick out and remember the central facts in each story. History even becomes the training ground for beginning writers. When you ask a student to narrate, to tell back to you the information he's just heard in his own words, you are giving him invaluable practice in the first and most difficult step of writing: putting an idea into words.

How do you study history classically? Find a central text, or "spine," that tells the story of history chronologically. This activity guide is designed to go along with Volume 3 of Susan Wise Bauer's *The Story of the World: History for the Classical Child.* Think of each section in *The Story of the World* as a "springboard" into the study of world history. This book provides you with a simple, chronological overview of the progression of history. It isn't intended to be complete, but when you do history with younger students, you're not aiming for a "complete" grasp of what happened in Early Modern Times. Instead, you want to give the child an enthusiasm for history, a basic understanding of major cultures and an idea of the chronological order of historical events.

## Using this guide at home

For each section in *The Story of the World*, follow this pattern:

1) Read the child one section from *The Story of the World.* Longer chapters are divided into several sections, each section appropriate for one session of history. Good readers can read the section themselves instead.

2) For each section, ask the child the Review Questions provided. Answers given are approximate; accept any reasonable answer. You can also make up your own questions. Always allow the child to look back over the text when answering questions, especially if proper names are part of the answer. This is training in reading comprehension (and it will help you evaluate whether the child is listening with attention and whether he's really understanding what he's reading).

3) Have the child tell you in two to five sentences what the history lesson was about. You can prompt the child with the Review Questions. Encourage the child to include the major facts from the history reading, but not EVERY fact. We have supplied sample narrations simply to give some idea of acceptable answers, not to imply that your child's narration should match word for word!

4) Write down the child's narration if the child is not writing independently. Good writers can be asked to write the narration down themselves. To help with this process, listen carefully to the child's narration and repeat it back to her while she writes; this will help with "writer's block." For any given section, you can instead ask the child to draw a picture of her favorite part of the history lesson and then describe the picture to you. Write the description at the bottom of the picture. Put the narration or picture in a History Notebook—a looseleaf notebook that will serve as the child's record of her history study.

5) When you have finished all the sections of a chapter, stop and do additional reading and activities on the topic covered by that chapter. This Activity Book provides titles of books that you can find at your library for additional reading, along with maps, coloring pages, crafts, and hands-on activities. Some topics will have many more resources available than others.

When you reach a topic that has a wealth of interesting books and activities connected to it, stop and enjoy yourself and don't feel undue pressure to move on. Check your local library for titles before buying. The recommended titles range in difficulty from first grade independent reads to advanced fourth grade, with some higher. When appropriate, ask the child to draw pictures or narrate about the additional reading as well. Put these pictures and narrations in the History Notebook, which should begin to resemble the child's own one-volume World History. Don't ask the child to narrate every book, or she'll grow frustrated; use this as occasional reinforcement for a topic she finds particularly interesting.

We have provided cross-reference numbers to the appropriate pages in *The Kingfisher Illustrated History of the World, The Kingfisher History Encyclopedia* (revised 3rd edition), *The Usborne Book of World History* (2008 edition), and *The Usborne Internet-Linked Encyclopedia of World History* (2009 edition). Use these books, or other age-appropriate history encyclopedia resources, for additional supplemental reading, especially for those topics that don't have extensive lists of age-appropriate library books.

6) Choose appropriate titles from the recommended literature lists and read these with your child. Most elementary students should also be doing a phonics program and/or a phonics-based spelling program; this reading should supplement those programs. Classical philosophy discourages the use of "reading textbooks" which contain little snippets of a number of different works. These textbooks tend to turn reading into a chore, an assignment that has to be finished, rather than a wonderful way to learn more about the world. Instead of following a "reading program," consider using the "real books" from these literature lists. **(RA = read aloud; IR = independent read; for children reading on a 2-3 grade level; OOP = Out of print, but still worth finding used, or at your library, or through inter-library loan; E-Only = Currently only available on Kindle, Nook, or other electronic-book formats; LFA = Limited format availability: only available in Library Binding or other non-standard formats)**

7) Optional: You can administer written tests (available separately from Well-Trained Mind Press) if you desire a more formal evaluation or wish to develop your child's test-taking ability.

## Multilevel teaching

*The Story of the World* series is intended for children in grades 1–4, but is often used by older students: Volume 1 is written primarily for grades 1–4; Volume 2 for grades 2–5; Volume 3 for grades 3–6. The maps and many of the activities in this book are also appropriate for children in grades 5–8. Each chapter of the activity guide contains cross-reference page numbers for the *Kingfisher History Encyclopedia* and the earlier edition of this work, *The Kingfisher Illustrated History of the World.* Both are good middle-grade world history reference works. To use *The Story of the World* as the center of a multilevel history program, have your older child independently do the following: Read *The Story of the World*; follow this with the appropriate pages from the *Kingfisher History Encyclopedia* or another world history reference of appropriate difficulty; place all important dates on a timeline; do additional reading on his or her own level. For book lists and more detailed directions on classical education methods for both elementary and middle-grade students, see *The Well-Trained Mind: A Guide to Classical Education at Home,* by Jessie Wise and Susan Wise Bauer (4th edition, W. W. Norton, 2016), available from Well-Trained Mind Press (www.welltrainedmind.com) or anywhere books are sold.

## For parents

Families differ in their attitudes about potentially sensitive subjects that will come up during the study of history. We suggest that you skim through the activities in this guide, glance through the literature that we recommend, and skip anything that might be inappropriate for your own family.

## Using this book in the classroom

Although this Activity Guide was initially designed to be used by home-schooling families, it adapts well to the classroom. Here is a sample of how a chapter may be taught:

1) The teacher reads aloud a chapter section while the students follow along in their own books. When you reach the end of a section, ask the review questions provided in this book to selected students. Depending upon the length of a chapter, you may read the entire chapter in one day or break it up over two days. The children should write their summaries (narration exercises) in their history notebooks and then share them aloud.

2) Using the review questions and chapter tests as a guide, type up a list of facts that the students should memorize, perhaps employing a fill-in-the-blank format. Give one to each student to help them prepare for the upcoming test. If you would like to administer formal tests, you may purchase them separately from Well-Trained Mind Press.

3) Have the students do the maps and coloring pages in the Student Pages. To purchase a license to photocopy the reproducible pages for student use, contact Well-Trained Mind Press.

4) Select one or two activities, found in the Student Pages. Some are more appropriate for classroom use than others.

5) Each day there should be an oral or written review. You can make it fun by playing oral quizzing games such as "Around the World" or "Last One Standing."

6) On the day before the test, have the students color their chapter review card.

7) Test the students.

8) You will want to periodically review the past review cards so that the students remember history chronologically.

# Pronunciation Guide for Reading Aloud

Abbas I—ah BAHS

Abolitionist—ab oh LISH uhn ist

Aborigine—AB uh RIJ uh nee

Agustín de Iturbide—ah goos TEEN day ih TUR bih day

Ahmet—AH met

Akbar—AHK bar

Alamo—AL ah moh

Alba—ALL bah

Allegheny—al eh GAYN ee

Amsterdam—AM ster dam

Angola—ang GOH luh

Antilles—an TILL eez

Antonio Lopez de Santa Anna—an TOH nee oh LOH pez day san tah ANN ah

Archangel—AHRK ayn juhl

Assyrian—ah SEE ree uhn

Aurangzeb—ahr ahng zeb

Austria—AH stree uh

Azov—ah ZAWF

Aztec—AZ tek

Babur—BAW bur

Babylonian—bab ill OH nee uhn

Baghdad—BAG dad

Bahadur—bah HA door

Balkan—BALL kuhn

Bandar—bahn DAR

Bastille—ba STEEL

Belgium—BEL jum

Bengal—ben GAHL

Berezina—by er ZHEE nah

Boer—BOHR

Bohemia—boe HEE mee uh

Bombay—bom BAY

Bosporus—BOSS porr uhs

Bowie (Jim)—BOO ee

Boyars—BOY arzh

Braddock—BRAD uhk

George Buchanan—byoo KAN an

Calcutta—kal CUTT uh

Cap-Francais—ca frahn SAY

Catesby (Robert)—KAYTS bee

Champlain (Samuel)—sham PLAYN

Charbonneau—SHAR buh noh

Charlemagne—SHAR luh MAYN

Charles Victor Emmanuel Leclerc—leh KLAYR

Cherokee—CHAYR uh kee

Chi'en-lung—CHEHN lohn

Chia-ch'ing— Chyuh Ch ing

Coleridge—COHL er ij

Concord—KON kurd

conquistadores—kon KEE stah DOR ez

Creole—KREE ohl

croissant—krwah SAHN

czar—ZAR

Daimyo—DIE mee oh (quickly slur syllables together)

Dalai Lama—DAH lye LAH muh

Dara—DAR ah

Dauphin—doh FAN ("fan" with an "a" like "apple"; barely say the "n")

Deccan—DEK un

Defenestration—dee fen uh STRAY shun

Defoe (Daniel)—duh FOE

Delhi—DEH lee

diet—DIE ett

Dingane—dinn GAH neh

Dinwiddie—DIN wid ee

Dolores—doh LOR ess

Don Miguel—dohn mee GELL

Duc de Simon—DOOK day see MOHN

Edo—EH doh

El Dorado—ell dor AH doe

El Libertador—ell LEE behr tah DOR

Electors—eh LEC turz

Empresarios—em pres AHR ee ohs

Encomiendas—en coe mee EN duz

Farrukhisiyar—fahr rook HIS see yar

Fawkes (Guy)—Fawx

Filles du Roi—FEE duh RWAH

François Jarret—fran SWAH JAHR ay

Francis Xavier—FRAN siss ex ZAY vee uhr

Fukien—FOO jiyen

Galileo—GAL ih LAY oh

Genghis Khan—JENG iss KAHN

Ghaznavids—GAHZ nuh vidz

Gobi—GO bee

Gonzales—gun ZAHL ez

Grand Vizier—grand viz EER

Grito—GREE toh

Guanajuato—gwahn ah HWAH toh

Guangzhou—GWAHN joh

guerilla—gerr ILL uh

guillotine—GEE yuh teen

Gustavus I—guh STAY vus

Habitants—hab ih TAHN

Haiti—HAY tee

Han—HAHN

Hanover—HAN oh ver

Hassan Ali—hah SAHN AH lee

Hawaii—huh WYE ee

Henrietta Maria—hen ree ETT ah mah REE uh

Heretic—HAYR eh tik

Hidalgo—hih DAHL goh

Hidetada—HEE deh TAH dah

Hideyori—HEE deh YOH lee

Hideyoshi—HEE deh YOH shee

Ho-Shen—hoh SHEN

Hone Heke—HOH neh HEH keh

Huron—HYUHR on

Husain Ali—hoo SAYN AH lee

Ibrahim—ih bra HEEM

Iemitsu—EE yeh MEE tsoo

Ieyasu—EE yeh YAH soo

Inca—INK uh

Indentured—in DEN churd

Iran—ir AHN

Iraq—ir AHK

Iroquois—IR uh kwoi

Isaac Newton—EYE zack NEWT uhn

Ismail—ISS my eel

Jahan—juh HAN

Jahangir—juh han GHEER

Janissaries—JAN iss ayr ees

Jean-Baptiste—zhahn bap TEEST

Jean-Jacques Dessaline—ZHAN ZHAK dess ah LEEN

José de San Martín—hoh ZAY day san mar TEEN

Johannes Kepler—yoh HAHN ess KEP ler

José Joaquin—hoh ZAY wah KEEN

José María Morelos y Pavón—hoh ZAY muh REE ah mor EL ohs ee pah VOHN

Juet (Robert)—ZHOO ay

Junta—HOON tah

K'ang Hsi—KAHN shee

Kara Mustafa—KAR uh moo STAH fah

Kebec—keh BEK

Khan—KAHN

Khoikhoi—koy koy (the two "k" sounds are throat clicks, but non-native speakers find them almost impossible to reproduce)

Khurram—kuhr AHM

Kifunji—ki FUHN jee

Königsberg—KEH nigz berg

Kongo—KON goh

Koran—kuh RAHN

Kororareka—koh roh rah REH kah

Leiden—LIE den (LIE to rhyme with "sky")

Lenape—leh NAH pay

Leonardo da Vinci—lee oh NAR doh dah VIN chee

Li Tzu-ch'eng—lee ZOO chuhn

Lin Zexu—LEEN tzeh SHOO

Llaneros—yah NAY rohz

Locke (John)—rhymes with "sock"

Louis—LOO ee

Louvre—LOO vruh

Luddite—LUD dite (rhymes with "kite")

Mahmud—mah MOOD

Manchu—man CHOO

Manchuria—man CHOO ree ah

Mandan—MAN dan

Maori—MAH ohr ree

Marathas—ma RAH tahs

Marie-Antoinette—muh REE an twah NETT

Marie-Madeleine—muh REE mad LEHN

Marseillaise—mar say EZ

Mary of Guise—MAYR ee of GEEZ

Massasoit—MASS ah soyt

Matamba—mah TAHM bah

Mausoleum—mah suh LEE um

Maya—MY uh

Maximilien de Robespierre—MACK sih mill ee uhn duh ROHBZ pyair

Mazarin—MAZ uh rin

Mbandi—em BAHN dee

Mecca—MEHK ah

Medina—muh DEE nuh

Meriwether—MAYR ee weth uhr

Mestizos—meh STEE zohs

Mediterranean—MED ih tuhr AYN ee uhn

Metacom—met ah kohm

Mfecane—ummf eh KAH nay

Mir Jafar—meer ja FAHR

Moghul—MOH guhl

Mongols—MON golz

Montagnis—mon TAN yees

Montreal—mon tree AHL

Mpande—uhm PAHN day

Mtetwa—uhm TET wa

Muhammad—moo HAHM ahd

Mukumbu—muh KOOM boo

Mumtaz Mahal—mum TAHZ mah HAHL

Murad—myur AHD

Muslims—MUZ limz

Nadir—NAY dir

Nagasaki—nah guh SAH kee

Nandi—NAHN dee

Napoleon Bonaparte—nuh POHL ee uhn BOHN ah part

Narragansett—nayr ah GAN sett

Narva—NAR vah

Natal—nuh TAHL

Nawab—nuh WAHB

Ncome—en COH may

Ndomba—'n DOHM bah (the first syllable is pronounced like "en" but without the "e" sound)

Netherlands—NETH ur lands

Neva—NAY vah

New Leicestershire—NEW LESS ter sher

Notre Dame—NOH truh DAHM

Nzinga—en ZING ah

Oda Nobunaga—OH dah NOH boo NAH gah

Ohio—oh HI oh

Olaudah Equiano—oh LAH duh EK wee AH noh

opium—OH pee um

Osman—OZ mun

Ottoman—OT uh muhn

Paheka—pah KEE ha

Paraguay—PAHR uh gway

Pardos—PAR dohz

Parliament—PAR lah ment

Parthia—PAR thee uh

Pasha—PAH shuh

Pepys (Samuel)—PEEPS

Peking—PEH keen

Peninsulares—payn in soo LAHR ayz

Pennsylvania—pen sill VAYN yuh

Persia—PER zha ("zh" is like the s in "treasure")

Pinyin Jiqing—PEEN yeen jee CHING

Pocahontas—POH kuh HAHN tuss

Pompey/Pompy—POMP ee

Portuguese—POR choo geez

Potomac—puh TOH mik

Powhatan—POW uh tan

Prague—PRAHG

Principia Mathematica—prin KIP ee ah math eh MAT ic ah

Prussia—PRUSH ah

Ptolemy—TOL eh mee

Qing—CHING

Quakers—QUAY kers

Queue—KYOO (pronounced exactly like the letter Q)

Quito—KEE toh

Reich—rike (rhymes with bike)

Rejeb—REJ eb

Rembrandt—REM brant

Richelieu—reesh uh LYOO

Rowlandson (Mary)—ROW land son (ROW rhymes with "cow")

Sa'adabat—suh AH dah baht

Sacagawea—SAK ah ja WEE ah, or sah kahg ah WAY uh

Safavids—SAH FAH vidz

Saint Croix—saynt KRWAH

Saint Domingue—saynt doh MING

Saint Menehould—saynt men-eu

Samurai—SAH moo rye ("rye" is really a quick "rah-ee")

Sassanids—SASS ah nidz

Sebastian Cabot—seh BAST yuhn CAB uht

Sebastiao—seb ass tee OW (rhymes with "cow")

Seigneur—sehn YUHR

Seine—SENN

Sekigahara—sek ee gah HAHR ah

Seleucids—sel OO sidz

Seleucus—sel OO suss

Seljuk—SEL juk

Shah—SHAHH (rhymes with Fa-la-lah)

Shaka—SHAH kah

Shoshone—shoh SHOH nee

Siesta—see ES tah

Simón Bolívar—see MOHN boh LEE var

Siraj—sir AHZH (ZH is like the s in "treasure")

Shimabara—SHEE mah BAH lah

Shogun—SHOH gun

Shogunate—SHO gun ayt

Sioux—SOO

Sousa—SOO sah

Sophia—soh FEE ah

Squanto—SQAHN toh

Ssu-ku ch'üan-shu—soo koo CHWAHN shoo

Strait—STRAYT

Stuyvesant (Peter)—STY vess ant ("STY" rhymes with "sky")

Sultan—SUHL tun

Surat—suh RAT

Sydney—SID nee

Tahiti—tah HEE tee

Taj Mahal—TAHZH muh HAHL ("zh" is like the s in "treasure")

Tao-kung—tow (rhymes with "cow") KOONG

Tecumseh—tuh KUM she

Tenskwatawa—tenz kwa TAH wah

Teton—TEE tahn

Thackeray—THAK er ee

Thames—TEMZ

Tigris—TYE gris

Tippecanoe—tip eh kuh NOO

tobacco—toh BAK oh

Tokugawa—TOH koo GAH wah

Toussaint L'Ouverture—too SAN LOO ver teur

Townshend (Charles)—TOWN zund

Trafalgar—truh FAL gar

treatise—TREE tiss

Tuileries—TWEE luh reez

Turkestan—TURK es tan

Ulan Bator—OO lahn BAH toh

Ulrich—ULL rik

Ural—YOOR ul

Venezuela—venn ez WAYL ah

Verchères—vehr SHAYR

Vermeer—ver MEER

Versailles—ver SYE

Vienna—vee ENN uh

Vincente Guerrero—vin SEN tay gerr AYR oh

Voltaire—vohl TAYR

Voyageurs—vwah yah ZHUR

Wallenstein (Albert of)—VAHL ehn steyn (rhymes with "fine")

Wampanoag—WAHMP an OH uhg

Waitangi—WHY tahng gee

Westphalia—wes FAYL yuh

Wittenberg—VITT en buhrg

Xanadu—ZAN ah doo

Yangtze—YAHN zoo

Zou Fulei—joh FOO lay

Zulu—ZOO loo

# A World of Empires

## Encyclopedia Cross-References

*Usborne World History (UBWH) 140-141, 144*
*Usborne Internet-Linked Encyclopedia of World History (UILE) 297, 308, 320*
*Kingfisher Illustrated History of the World (KIHW) 320, 362-363, 366-367, 388*
*Kingfisher History Encyclopedia (KHE) 220-223*

## THE HOLY ROMAN EMPIRE

### Review Questions

Which two flags have you seen during your world travels? *The first flag has a red cross on a white background; the second flag has a two-headed eagle* OR *The Spanish flag, and the flag of the Holy Roman Empire.*

Which two kings flew these two flags? *Philip II and Ferdinand I flew these two flags.*

How many kings did Charles have in his family? *Charles had three kings in his family.*

What three thrones did Charles inherit while he was still a teenager? *He inherited the thrones of the Netherlands, Spain, and Germany.*

What title did Charles want? *Charles wanted the title of "Holy Roman Emperor."*

What major empire ruled Europe 1500 years before Charles? *The Roman Empire spread across Europe 1500 years before Charles was born.*

What is the name of the leader who brought peace to France, and who first held the title "Holy Roman Emperor"? *Charlemagne first held the title "Holy Roman Emperor."*

Why was Charlemagne called the "Holy Roman Emperor"? *He was called this because he kept the peace in a large area and because he could spread Christianity across his empire.*

Which three people (or groups of people) joined together to fight against Charles and his armies? *The king of France, the princes of Italy, and the pope fought against Charles.*

Who did Charles hire to march down and attack Rome? *Charles hired a group of Protestant Christians, called the "German Fury," to march down and attack Rome.*

Did the pope agree to crown Charles "Holy Roman Emperor"? *Yes, the pope agreed!*

Charles had many problems within his kingdom. Can you name one? *Charles was growing poorer and poorer because he fought many wars, which cost money; within his kingdoms, Catholics and Protestants were battling each other; and his Protestant subjects no longer wanted to obey his decrees.*

Who inherited Charles's lands? *Philip and Ferdinand inherited Charles's lands.*

### Narration Exercise

"Charles wanted to be called the Holy Roman Emperor, but the pope wouldn't crown him. Instead the pope and the king of France and the princes of Italy fought against Charles. So Charles hired German Protestants to attack Rome—but he pretended not to know anything about it! When the pope agreed to crown him, Charles helped the pope drive the German soldiers away. Now Charles was emperor. But finally he resigned and gave his lands to his brother and his son." OR

"Charles became king of the Netherlands, Germany, and Spain because he had three kings in his family. He wanted to be even greater—he wanted to be called the "Holy Roman Emperor," like Charlemagne. If he were emperor, he could keep the peace, like Rome, and also spread Christianity. But Charles had to fight for the title. Finally the pope agreed to crown him Holy Roman Emperor. Charles was emperor for 24 years, but he grew poorer and the people in his empire fought with each other. So Charles decided to give up his throne. He gave his empire to Ferdinand and to Philip."

## THE RICHES OF SPAIN

### Review Questions

What is one thing that makes mining difficult for the young boy? *He must carry rocks up a steep tunnel; the rocks are very heavy; he must breathe foul air.*

Which country was Christopher Columbus looking for when he sailed west from Europe? *Columbus was looking for India.*

What were Spanish adventurers called? *Spanish adventurers were called* conquistadores.

What did these conquistadores realize about this land that Columbus found? *They realized that it was not India, and that it was an entirely new land.*

What was an encomienda? *An encomienda was a special contract that gave conquistadores permission to sail to South America to take gold.*

Who was living in South America? *Native tribes called Aztecs, Mayans, and Incas lived in South America.*

How did the Spanish get gold? *They took it from native tribes, panned for it in the streams, and mined it from rock.*

How much money in gold and silver did the Spanish take from South America? *The Spanish took five hundred billion dollars worth of gold and silver from South America.*

What name was given to parts of South America because so many Spanish moved there? *Parts of South America were known as "New Spain."*

The Spanish prospered from gold in South America. Did the South Americans prosper? *No, they suffered because the Spanish forced the men, women, and children to work for them in the mines.*

### Narration Exercise

"The Spanish came to South America by accident—but when they saw gold, more and more Spaniards came! The king of Spain gave *conquistadores* special permission to take the gold, because the South Americans weren't Christians. So the conquistadores took jewelry, panned for gold, and dug mines. They forced the South Americans to work for them. They grew richer and richer. The Spanish took five hundred billion dollars worth of gold and silver out of South America! So many Spanish came to South America that it was called New Spain." OR

"When Columbus first landed in South America, he thought he was in India. But then other explorers realized that he had found a whole new land. They saw that the people in this land wore gold jewelry, and they thought that the land must be filled with gold. So they began to search for gold. They forced the Mayans, the Incas, and the Aztecs to work for them in the mines, and they brought slaves from Africa to work in the mines too. The Spanish grew richer and richer! But the Mayans, the Incas, and the Aztecs grew poorer and poorer. Many South Americans and slaves died."

## Additional History Reading

*Anno's Spain*, by Mitsumasa Anno (Philomel Books, 2004). A wordless but intricate and absorbing depiction of Spain in the past and present. This title is out of print but worth looking for at your library or as a used book. (IR 1-6) **OOP**

*The Holy Roman Empire (Empires in the Middle Ages)*, ed. Carolyn DeCarlo (Rosen Education Service, 2018). This illustrated 48-page book gives a brief, readable account of the Holy Roman Empire and its rulers, from Charlemagne through Napoleon. (RA 1-2, IR 3-6)

*The Lost Treasure of the Inca*, Peter Lourie (Boyds Mill Press, 1999). A picture book with read-aloud text, telling how the Incas hid 750 tons of gold from the Spanish conquistadores. (RA 1-3, IR 4-6)

*The Sad Night: The Story of an Aztec Victory and a Spanish Loss*, Sally Schofer Mathews (Clarion Books, 1994). A picture book account of the conflict between the Spanish and the Aztecs. (RA 1-2, IR 3-4)

*The Amazon: River in a Rain Forest*, by Molly Aloian, (Crabtree Publishing, 2010). Covers the land and human geography of the Amazon River. (RA 2, IL for a stronger 4th grade reader)

*DK Eyewitness Books: Aztec, Inca & Maya: Discover the World of the Aztecs, Incas, and Mayas—their Beliefs, Rituals, and Customs*, (DK Children, 2011). Wonderful photographs and information suitable for readers of all levels. (RA 1, IR 3-7)

*Francisco Pizarro—Destroyer of the Inca Empire*, by John DiConsiglio, (Scholastic, 2008). Covers the early life of Pizarro as well as his impact on the Inca; this is for stronger readers or as a read aloud. (RA 4, IR 5)

*The Incredible Ancient History Book Box* by Fiona MacDonald, Lorna Oakes, Philip Steele and Richard Tames (Armadillo, 2012). A collection of history books where children can learn about the art, culture and inventions of ancient civilizations. Includes books on the Inca, Aztec, and Maya empires. (RA 1-2, IR 3-7)

*The Aztec Empire*, by Imogen Greenburg, Isabel Greenberg illus. (Lincoln Children's Books, 2017). A history book in the style of a graphic novel, including maps and a timeline. (RA 2 IR 3)

*The Search for El Dorado (Totally True Adventures)* by Lois Miner Huey (Random House Books for Young Readers, 2016). A nonfiction chapter book about early Spanish explorers and their search for the lost city of gold. (RA 1, IR 2-6)

*The Spanish Conquistadors Conquer the Aztecs* by Baby Professor (Speedy Publishing LLC, 2017). Along with great illustrations, this book gives a historical look at this time period. (RA 1-2, IR 3-5)

*Vanishing Cultures: Amazon Basin*, by Jane Reynolds, (Lee and Low Books, 2007). A book of photographs with text following the life of a boy whose family lives in the Amazon jungle. (RA K-4, IR 2)

*Terror on the Amazon: The Quest for El Dorado*, by Phil Gates (DK Publishing, 2000). A DK Level 3 Reader, this 48-page chapter book tells of the Spanish quest for gold in South America. (RA 1-2, IR 3-4) **E-Only.**

*The Usborne Book of Treasure Hunting*, by Anna Claybourne and Caroline Young (Usborne Publishing, 1999). General guide to gold hunting and mining, with sections referring to South America on pp. 60-61. **E-Only.**

## Corresponding Literature Suggestions

*Don Quixote: Oxford Illustrated Classics*, by Michael Harrison, illus. Victor G. Ambrus (Oxford University Press, 1999). Unfortunately out of print, this wonderful retelling with attractive illustrations is well worth a library trip or a request to interlibrary loan. (RA 3, IR 4-6) **OOP**

*Illustrated Adventure Stories*, by Lesley Sims (Usborne Publishing, 2011). Includes stories like *Don Quixote* and *The Three Musketeers* suitable to read aloud to younger children, or for older ones to read independently. Includes author biographies. (RA K, IR 2-4)

*Miguel's Brave Knight: Young Cervantes and His Dream of Don Quixote*, by Margarita Engle, Raul Colon illus. (Peachtree Publishing Company, 2017). Poems about the life of Miguel de Cervantes and the creation of Don Quixote, accompanied by lovely illustrations. (RA 2, IR 3–7)

*I, Juan de Pareja*, by Elizabeth Borton de Trevino (Farrar, Straus & Giroux, 1965). This Newbery-winning chapter book tells the story of an African slave, born in Spain in the early seventeenth century, who grows up to serve the Spanish painter Diego Velázquez. A good family read-aloud, or for strong readers; also look for the audiobook version (Blackstone Audio Books, 1998; narrated by Johanna Ward). (RA 1-4, IR 5-6)

*The Spanish Fairy Book*, by Gertrudis Segovia (Dover, 1999). Eight read-aloud fairy tales from Spain; an independent read for fourth grade and above. (RA 1-3, IR 4-6)

*Addison Cooke and the Treasure of the Incas*, by Jonathan W. Stokes (Puffin Books, 2017). An exciting, adventure-filled read about the search for Incan treasure. (RA 1-2, IR 3-7)

*The Chocolate Tree: a Mayan Folktale*, by Linda Lowery, Richard Keep, Janice Lee Porter illus. (First Avenue Editions, 2009). A poetic version of a folktale about the origins of chocolate. (RA K, IR 2)

*The Rain Player*, by David Wisniewski (Clarion Books, 1995). In this traditional Mayan tale, a young boy challenges the Rain God to a game of ball in order to keep drought away. Picture book format, easy text. (RA 1, IR 2-4)

*Secret of the Andes*, by Ann Nolan Clark (Puffin Books, 1976). Another Newbery award winner, this novel for advanced readers tells the story of a young Incan boy and his ties to the past. (IR 4-6)

*Stories from the Amazon*, by Saviour Pirotta, illus. Becky Gryspeerdt (Raintree/Steck Vaughn, 2000). A collection of traditional South American tales for reading aloud or independently. (RA 1-2, IR 3-5)

*Treasure Hunters: Quest for the City of Gold*, by James Patterson and Chris Grabenstein (Jimmy Patterson, 2018). A story of two young treasure hunters who find a treasure map which leads them to the Amazon jungle in a quest for lost treasure. (RA 1-2, IR 3-7)

## MAP WORK

### Charles's Inheritance in Europe and South America *(Student Page 1, answer 320)*

1. Charles inherited the thrones of the Netherlands, Spain, and Germany. Outline the borders of these countries in purple, then lightly shade each country in purple.
2. Charles hired the "German Fury," which marched down to Rome and burned it. Draw a purple circle around Rome.
3. From Charles, Philip inherited Spain, the Netherlands, and the Italian lands. Use a pen and draw a black **P** in the center of each of those three countries. (The Italian lands were on the same peninsula as Rome. Draw a **P** on the Italian peninsula.)
4. From Charles, Ferdinand inherited France and Germany. Draw a black **F** in the center of those two countries.
5. Philip II wanted gold from South America. With a yellow crayon, trace the path that the Spanish took to South America (from Spain to South America). Then outline South America with yellow.

## Coloring Pages

Charles V had many titles. Can you remember two of them? (See p. 2 of *The Story of the World.*) The image next to him is his royal symbol. *(Student Page 2)*

*Conquistadores* were the Spanish adventurers who followed Columbus's route to "India." *(Student Page 3)*

## PROJECTS

### Math Activity — Five Hundred Billion—How Much Is That?

The Spanish took about five hundred billion dollars worth of gold from South America. Five hundred billion pennies, laid side-by-side, would wrap the earth 700 times! This activity will show you that five billion of something can not only take you around the world, it can take you to the moon—and beyond! Note: The distance from the earth to each planet is an average; distance changes all the time because of planetary orbits.

*Materials:*
- □ Ruler (with mm and cm)
- □ Student Page 4: Space Chart
- □ Tape measure
- □ Colored pencils

*Directions:*
1. Using your ruler, find an object around the house that is about 1 millimeter in length. This is extremely tiny! In fact, it is smaller than most of the letters on this page! If you lined up five hundred billion of these objects, you could stretch a line from your house to the moon.
2. Using your ruler, find an object that is about 16 cm in length. If you lined up five hundred billion of these objects, you could stretch a line from your house to the planet Mars.
3. Using a tape measure, find an object 4 feet, 2 inches long. If you lined up five hundred billion of these objects, you could stretch a line from your house to Jupiter.
4. Using a tape measure, find an object about 8 feet, 5 inches long. If you lined up five hundred billion of these, you could stretch a line from your house to the planet Saturn.
5. Now pick four colors and outline each of the boxes in the key with a different color (for example, outline the box next to the moon with blue). Then draw a picture of the object you found for step 1 in the box next to the moon. Then draw a picture of the object you found for step 2 in the box next to Mars. Continue until you have drawn all four objects.
6. Then, using the same colored pencil you used to outline the box next to the moon, draw a line from the picture of the earth to the picture of the moon. Use the same colored pencil you used to outline the box next to Mars, and draw a line from the picture of the earth to the picture of Mars. Repeat this procedure for Jupiter and Saturn.
7. When you are finished, color the picture. Next time you are looking up at a starry sky (the planet Mars looks like a tiny red dot), think about how five hundred billion of an ordinary object can go such a long way. It is a very large number indeed!

### Craft Activity — Make Spanish Doubloons

Spanish ships loaded with gold from South America would sail back to Spain. The gold was often melted and formed into Spanish coins, called doubloons. Make your own doubloons, and use twelve of them to play the game "Steal the Spanish Treasure" (see below).

*Materials:*
- □ Jar lids, biscuit cutters, or a compass
- □ Pennies
- □ Gold or aluminum foil
- □ Cardboard (cereal boxes are good)
- □ Scissors
- □ Pencil

Directions:

1. Using a pencil, trace the lids or biscuit cutters (or use a compass) to make circles on the cardboard.
2. Cut out the circles. Use the pennies for smaller coins.
3. Cover the circles and pennies with gold or aluminum foil.
4. Draw designs on the cardboard coins using the pencil (the pennies will have to be plain). Be careful—don't pierce the foil!

## GAME ACTIVITY Steal the Spanish Treasure

The Spanish took gold from South America, and pirates took gold from Spanish ships! A Spanish ship laden with gold doubloons could make a crew of pirates wealthy men indeed. Play a game to see if you can safely navigate your way back to Spain or if your ship will be captured by pirates!

Materials:

- ☐ Checkerboard
- ☐ Paper
- ☐ Scotch tape
- ☐ 12 doubloons from previous project (or any coins)
- ☐ 7 checkers: 6 red, 1 black
- ☐ Pencil
- ☐ Two dice

Directions:

1. This is a two-player game. One player is the Spanish (red) and the other is the pirate (black).
2. Using a paper and pencil, number the red checkers 1 though 6. Tape the numbers on the tops of the checkers so you can see them.
3. The Spanish player should then take a piece of paper, turn it sideways, and make six columns, numbering them 1 through 6.
4. Then, **out of the sight of the pirate**, the Spanish player should place the 12 doubloons in any arrangement under the columns. Column 1 could have one doubloon, column 2 could have four doubloons, column 3 could have no doubloons, etc.
5. The Spanish player and the pirate player should now sit on opposite sides of the checkerboard. Each player will line up his checkers (ships) on any combination of spaces in the last row on the board (closest to where he is sitting).
6. The Spanish player will start first. A Spanish ship can move forward one space or sideways one space (but not backward or diagonally). The pirate ship can move one space forward, to the side, *or* backward (but not diagonally). The players should each take turns moving one space. The Spanish ships are trying to make it safely to Spain (the other side of the board). The pirate ship is trying to intercept all Spanish ships and raid them for gold.
7. To attack a Spanish ship, the pirate ship must be on a space next to the ship (not diagonal from the ship, but behind, in front, or beside it). If there are two Spanish ships next to a pirate ship, the pirate must specify which ship he is attacking. When attacking a ship, the pirate player should yell, "Give us all your gold!" The players then each roll one die. If the Spanish player rolls the higher number, he has successfully warded off the pirate attack—until challenged again! If the pirate rolls the higher number (or ties) the pirate gets all the doubloons that ship holds and the ship is removed from the board. The Spanish player gathers all the doubloons from that column and gives them to the pirate. A Spanish ship may not be attacked in his first row or on the farthest row (closest to the pirate player).
8. Each player must move on each turn. A pirate ship cannot sit in one space and challenge a ship twice; the pirate ship must move between each challenge.

9. The game is over when all the Spanish ships on the board are safely docked in Spain (in the row closest to the pirate player) OR when the pirate has all the doubloons. The player with the most doubloons wins the game.

## ACTIVITY PROJECT Make a Mine Shaft

Mining for gold was a very dangerous job. Miners worked long hours in deep tunnels with little light and little air. The tunnels, or shafts, were not very stable. There was always the risk that the shaft would collapse and the miner would be trapped inside. The miners would build a wooden framework inside the tunnels to keep the walls of the shaft from caving in. Dig your own mine shaft. See if you can devise a framework that will keep the walls of the shaft intact so you can reach gold at the bottom.

*Materials:*

- ☐ A bucket (or small plastic trashcan)
- ☐ Flour (about 10 lbs. or enough to almost fill your bucket)
- ☐ 3 pieces of "gold" (small doubloons, yellow M&Ms, etc . . .)
- ☐ Paper
- ☐ Scissors
- ☐ Craft sticks
- ☐ Clear tape

*Directions:*

1. Put the three pieces of gold at the bottom of the bucket.
2. Dump the flour on top.
3. Dig a narrow shaft down and try to reach the gold. Be careful of collapsing walls! To reinforce the walls, cut and tape the paper into rings and attach them to the craft sticks with tape. See if you can make a framework that will get you to the bottom of the bucket. Did you dig in the right spot to find gold?

# Protestant Rebellions

## Encyclopedia Cross-References

*UBWH 134-135, 144, UILE 304, 310*
*KIHW 318, 377, 386-387, KHE 228-229, 246*

## THE DUTCH REVOLT

### Review Questions

In addition to the land he inherited from Charles, Philip also inherited a problem. What was it? *Philip inherited a rebellious nobleman—William the Silent.*

Where did Philip grow up? What faith was he taught? *He grew up in Spain and learned Catholicism.*

Where did William grow up? What faith was he taught? *He grew up in Germany and learned Protestantism.*

What did William inherit when he was only eleven years old? *William inherited two provinces, or pieces of land, when he was eleven. One was in France and the other was in the Netherlands.*

Name two things that William learned at royal court. *William learned how to speak French, plan battles, run a country, and be a good Catholic.*

The people of the Netherlands often spent time fighting—but not fighting other countries. What did the people of the Netherlands spend much of their time fighting against? *The people of the Netherlands spent much of their time battling the tides of the sea.*

How did the Low Country people keep the sea away from their land? *They built dikes out of the earth.*

The way that Philip ruled the Netherlands upset William. What did Philip do that William found upsetting? *Philip passed laws for the people without asking the leaders of the people what would be good for them.*

When he was visiting the court of the French king, William heard a horrifying secret. What was it? *William heard that Philip intended to destroy Protestantism and massacre Protestants in the Netherlands.*

Several of William's subjects sent a petition to Philip's court. What did the petition ask? *The petition asked Philip to lift his ban on Protestantism.*

What did the Duke of Alba do to crush the revolt? *The Duke of Alba beheaded two of William's leaders and spent the next ten years killing Protestants and burning their towns.*

Did William go to see the Duke? *No, William went to Germany instead.*

What did William's soldiers call themselves? *They called themselves the Sea Beggars.*

What did seven northern provinces of the Netherlands decide to do? *They made William their king and said that they were independent from Spain.*

How did Philip finally rid himself of William? *He hired a man to assassinate William.*

### Narration Exercise

"Philip became king of the Netherlands. He gave William the job of governing the Netherlands for him. But William didn't like the way Philip ruled. Philip didn't let Protestants worship in their own way, and he made decisions without asking the people what they wanted. When William found out that Philip planned to destroy Protestants, he didn't say anything. He just went back to the Netherlands and tried to think of ways to keep Protestants safe. So he was called 'William the Silent.' William fought against Philip for many years. Finally he became king of the Netherlands." OR

"The Netherlands were also called the Low Countries because the land was below the ocean. The people there spent time building walls and dikes to keep the water out! They also fought against Spain. The Spanish king, Philip, wanted to wipe out Protestants. But William and the Protestants of the Netherlands rebelled. Philip sent the Duke of Alba to crush the rebellion. But the people fought back! Finally they made William their king. He was the first king of the Netherlands. But Philip sent an assassin to kill him!"

## THE QUEEN WITHOUT A COUNTRY

### Review Questions

Besides Holland, where were Protestants and Catholics disagreeing with each other? *Catholics and Protestants were disagreeing with each other all through Philip II's kingdom, through the Holy Roman Empire, and even in Scotland.*

When Mary, Queen of Scots, was very young, who ruled in her place? *Mary of Guise, Mary's mother, ruled in Mary's place when she was very young.*

Why did Mary of Guise send young Mary to France? *She was Catholic and was afraid that the Protestant lords would try to make her daughter a "good Protestant."*

Which preacher believed that no woman should have the right to sit on the throne? *John Knox believed that no woman should have the right to sit on the throne.*

Mary disagreed with John Knox. How old was she when she returned to Scotland to claim her throne? *Mary returned to Scotland to reclaim her throne when she was eighteen years old.*

What did Mary intend to do with the Protestants in Scotland? *Even though she was Catholic, Mary planned to allow the Protestants to worship freely in Scotland.*

How did the Protestant lords greet Mary when she arrived in Scotland? *The Protestant lords met her and told her that she was welcome.*

Who did Mary marry? *Mary married a Protestant called Lord Darnley.*

What did Lord Darnley and the Protestant lords secretly plan to do with Mary? *They planned to shut her up as a prisoner and put him on the throne.*

How did Lord Darnley die? *He was found strangled in his garden.*

How did the Protestant Lords take control of the throne from Mary? *The Lords took her away to a lonely spot and held her arm, forcing her to sign a paper making thirteen-month-old James king.*

Which country did Mary flee to when the Protestant lords took control of the throne? *Mary fled to England, hoping that her cousin Elizabeth would help her.*

Did Elizabeth help Mary? *No, Elizabeth kept her a prisoner.*

Do you remember how long Mary was a prisoner? *She was a prisoner for nineteen years!*

Who ordered that Mary be killed? Why? *Her cousin Elizabeth had Mary beheaded for treason.*

### Narration Exercise

"Mary, Queen of Scots, grew up in France. When she was eighteen years old, she came back to Scotland and claimed her throne. She married Lord Darnley, but he did not treat her very well. Then Lord Darnley was killed! Some people thought Mary had done it. She became less popular. Finally Mary had to escape to England. Queen Elizabeth put her in jail and then had her beheaded." OR

"Protestants and Catholics were fighting with each other in Scotland. Mary became Queen of Scots and fought with the Protestant lords over power in Scotland. The Protestant lords forced her to give her throne to her son James. Mary escaped to England. She hoped that her cousin Elizabeth would help her. But Elizabeth put her in jail and then beheaded her."

## Additional History Reading

*The Awful End of Prince William the Silent: The First Assassination of a Head of State with a Handgun* by Lisa Jardine (Harper Perennial, 2007). Although geared for an older audience, this book shows how the assassination of William the Silent changed the world for people who were heads of state. (IR 5-7)

*Holland/1000 Things about Holland* by Jesse Goossens and illustrated by Charlotte Dematons (Lemniscaat USA; Pck Har/Pa edition, 2013). A great pictorial overview of Holland along with accompanying guide. (RA 1-2, IR 3-7)

*Rembrandt and 17th Century Holland: The Dutch Nation and Its Painters*, by Claudio Pescio, illus. Sergio (Peter Bedrick Books, 2001). A gorgeously illustrated guide to the art of Holland. (RA 2-3, IR 4-6) **LFA**

*Rembrandt (Getting to Know the World's Greatest Artists)*, by Mike Venezia (Children's Press, 1988). Much simpler than the Pescio book listed above, this is a good independent read for young students. (RA 1, IR 2-4)

*Herstory: Women Who Changed the World*, ed. By Ruth Ashby and Deborah Gore Ohrn (Viking Books, 1995). A collection of read-aloud two-page biographies of many famous women, including Mary, Queen of Scots (also recommended for use in other chapters). **OOP**

*Mary Queen of Scots,* by Emily Hahn (Random House, 1953). Sadly out of print, the only good, readable biography of Mary Queen of Scots suitable for younger scholars is this Landmark Books version. Look for a used copy, or try your library. (RA 2, IR 3-6) **OOP**

*Ladybird Histories: Tudors and Stuarts* by Ladybird Books (Ladybird UK edition, 2013). A thoroughly-illustrated book with lots of information about the royalty and everyday life of this time. (RA 2-3, IR 4-7)

*John Knox*, by Simonetta Carr and illustrated by Matt Abraxas (Reformation Heritage Books, 2014). A concise biography of a key figure in Scottish and religious history. (IR 2-7)

*You Wouldn't Want to be Mary Queen of Scots* by Fiona MacDonald (Franklin Watts, 2008). Traces the life of the Scottish queen in an entertaining, well-illustrated way. (RA 2-3, IR 4-6)

## Corresponding Literature Suggestions

*The Boy Who Held Back the Sea*, by Thomas Locker, retold by Lenny Hort (Puffin, 1993). Beautiful paintings illustrate this picture-book tale about a small boy who finds a leak in the dikes. (IR 2-4)

*The Boy at the Dike: A Dutch Folktale* by M. J. York and illustrated by Laura Freeman (Childs World Inc., 2012). A more recent version of the story of a young boy who single-handedly held back the sea. (RA 1-2, IR 3-4)

*Hans Brinker and the Silver Skates*, by Mary Mapes Dodge (Aladdin, 2002). This marvelous tale, first published in 1865, tells of a skating race on frozen Dutch canals. Young readers may find its length too difficult. Try it as a family read-aloud; look for the unabridged audiobook version narrated by Flo Gibson (Audio Book

Contractors, 2001); or try the *Great Illustrated Classics* adaptation for independent reading (Abdo 2002). (Note: the original is much richer than the adaptation.)

*Katje the Windmill Cat*, by Gretchen Woelfle, illus. Nicola Bayley (Candlewick Press, 2001). In this picture book, a cat rescues a baby from floods when a fifteenth-century Dutch dike breaks. Beautiful illustrations and details about dikes and windmills. (RA 1, IR 2-4) **OOP.**

*The Wheel on the School*, by Meindert DeJohn, illus. Maurice Sendak (HarperTrophy, 1972). This Newbery-winning novel for slightly older readers is set in a Dutch fishing village; look for the unabridged audiobook published by American School (1985) and read by Ann Flosnik. **OOP**

*Always Room for One More*, by Sorche Nic Leodhas, illus. Nonny Hogrogian (Henry Holt, 1965). This Caldecott-winning picture book tells of a Scottish family's hospitality to strangers passing by. (RA 1-2, IR 3-4)

*Katie in Scotland* by James Mayhew (Orchard Books, 2014). A book for young readers telling of the landmarks and legends of Scotland. (IR 1-2)

## MAP WORK

### Philip's Inheritance from Charles V: The Netherlands and Spain *(Student Page 5, answer 320)*

1. Philip inherited Spain and the Netherlands from Charles V. Color both countries red.
2. William inherited land in the Netherlands and France. Draw a black **W** in the Netherlands and in France.
3. The Netherlands were called the Low Countries because they were below the level of the ocean. Draw three blue arrows that come from the sea and point toward the Netherlands.

### Coloring Pages

Mary, Queen of Scots, lost her power to the Protestant lords of Scotland. *(Student Page 6)*

## PROJECTS

### Craft Project The Sea Beggars Save Leyden

When William the Silent and the other noblemen of the Netherlands made a stand against Spanish rule, they wrote down and signed a document swearing to resist the Spanish. Margaret of Parma, who had been appointed by the Spanish to be governess of the Netherlands, read the document and exclaimed, "These beggars!" When the noblemen heard of Margaret's insult, they decided to take this name as their own. They called their navy the "Sea Beggars." The Sea Beggars helped to break the Spanish control of the Netherlands by sailing between the dikes into the waterways of the Netherlands and attacking the Spanish from the water.

When the Spanish surrounded the city of Leyden and cut off all food supplies to the city, the citizens of Leyden began to starve! They were about to give in when the *burgomaster*, or mayor, stirred them to continue their resistance. "Here is my sword!" he cried. "Plunge it, if you will, into my heart, and divide my flesh among you to appease your hunger; but expect no surrender as long as I am alive." But before the people starved to death, the Sea Beggars sailed into the waterways nearby and hacked away at the dikes. The water rushed inland, carrying the Sea Beggar ships with it. Fighting on water, the Sea Beggars routed the Spanish and saved the city! William later honored the citizens' bravery and fortitude by establishing a university there.

*Materials:*
- ☐ Metal or glass casserole dish (may use a smaller or larger cooking pan)
- ☐ Non-drying modeling clay (Play-Doh is fine)
- ☐ Pitcher of cool water

- ☐ Small piece of Styrofoam (the grocery store may give you an unused meat tray or a "to-go" salad container for free)

*Directions:*

1. Make waterways in the pan with the modeling clay. The waterways should have built-up sides, creating the dike effect needed to keep water away from the cities of the Netherlands. Make sure the dikes are as deep as half of your index finger.
2. Pour water into the waterways. Make sure that it stays in the channels you've built! Reinforce the waterways with more modeling clay if necessary.
3. Choose a dry area that can be your city of Leyden. Roll a rope of clay to be your city wall; if you want to, mold houses to go inside the city.
4. If you have a small plastic boat, use it to represent the Sea Beggar boats. Or cut pieces of Styrofoam small enough to float in your waterways.
5. Now breach the dike near the city with your finger or a table knife! At first, the winds were blowing against the Sea Beggars, but when the wind shifted around behind their fleet, the ships were able to sail right up to Leyden. If your boats don't sail through the dike, blow from behind them and help drive them towards your city!

## CRAFT PROJECT **Scottish Nationalism**

Scottish families were known as *clans*. Each clan had its own family colors, which were woven into *tartans*, which were six-foot-long plaid cloths that men wrapped around their bodies and tightened with a belt. These later became plaid skirts called *kilts*. Each clan had its own tartan, whose colors depended on the plants and dyes available to the weavers. You're going to create a tartan for your family; choose colors that reflect your surroundings (either natural or the colors in your house).

*Materials:*

- ☐ A section of sheet or white cotton cloth, six feet long and two feet wide
- ☐ Three or four different colors of fabric paint (at a craft store)
- ☐ Two sponge brushes, one for thin lines (3/4" to 1½" wide) and one for thick lines (3 to 4" wide)
- ☐ One or two large safety pins

*Directions:*

1. Decide what pattern of lines your tartan will use. You can choose one of the following: two thin lines and then a thick line; a thin line between two thick lines; a thick line between two thin lines; or another pattern that you choose. The spaces between the lines should be 1" wide. Between each pattern of lines, leave 3 inches of space.
2. Once you've chosen your pattern, decide what color each line in the pattern will be. For example, you might choose to have a thin yellow line, an inch of space, a thin blue line, an inch of space, and then a thick red line; you would then leave 3 inches of space open and start the pattern again.
3. Lay the white cloth out on the floor and paint in your vertical lines, as in the top illustration.
4. Let the paint dry. Then paint the same pattern in horizontal lines, as in the bottom illustration.

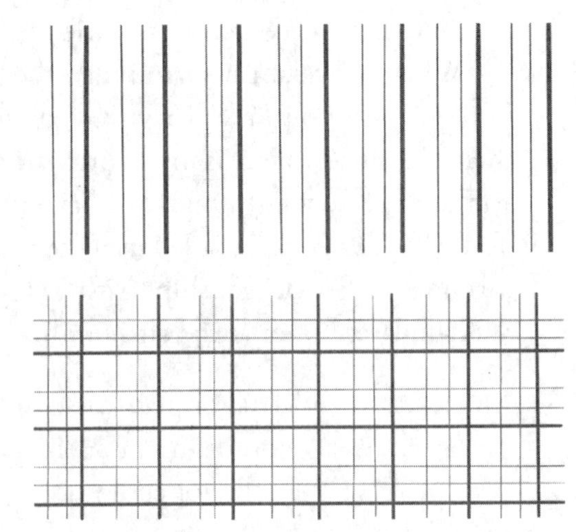

5. When the paint is dry, wrap the tartan around your waist and safety-pin it at the waist. Toss the extra material over your shoulder and wear your "Scottish" tartan proudly!

## ART PROJECT Mary Stuart Needlework Octagon

Mary Queen of Scots first learned the art of embroidery and needlework after her mother sent her to France for her formal education. Later she learned even more about needlework from her mother-in-law, who was very skilled in the art. Once back in Scotland, Mary sometimes embroidered as she attended her Council meetings but had little time for elaborate projects. But during the years that she was kept captive by Elizabeth I, she spent many hours embroidering and designing gifts. Many pieces of her embroidery and needlework had small secret messages in them!

*Materials:*

- ☐ Student Page 7: Marian Hanging
- ☐ Colored pencils, crayons, or markers
- ☐ Tracing paper

*Directions:*

1. The Student Page shows an octagon that was part of a larger work called the "Marian Hanging." The Marian Hanging had 37 different squares. Many contained hidden meanings. This octagon, called "Mary Stuart," has the letters of "MARY S." designed together. The letters have Mary's favorite flowers, thistle flowers, on both sides of them and the royal crown at the top. Color the thistle flowers and the crown on the page.
2. See if you can find all the letters in "MARY S" on the page and color them in. (Note to parent: The letter "y" is formed by a large "v" with a tiny tail.)
3. Now lay your tracing paper over the Marian Hanging page and trace out the shape of the octagon. Instead of the thistle flowers, draw your favorite flowers. Instead of the letters "MARY S," mix up the letters of your name. Instead of drawing a crown overtop the letters, draw something that symbolizes you (for example, a sun if you are a cheerful person, a bee if you are always busy, etc.).

# James, King of Two Countries

## Encyclopedia Cross-References

*UBWH 148-149**, *UILE 306, 322*
*KIHW 406-408, 414 margin KHE 246-248, 281 (picture)*
**Page 148 of the UBWH contains the legendary, but historically inaccurate, portrayal of John Smith being saved from death by Pocahontas.*

## JAMES AND HIS ENEMIES

### Review Questions

What did James's tutor, George Buchanan, teach him about a king's right to rule? *James's tutor taught him that a king had to listen to his people, because the people gave him the right to rule them.*

What did James come to believe instead? *James believed in "divine right"—that the king ruled because it was a right given by God* OR *James believed that the king's power comes from God, so the king's will is the same as God's will.*

When Elizabeth died, what two countries did James rule? *When Elizabeth died, James ruled both England and Scotland.*

What two titles did James have? *James was called James I of England and James VI of Scotland.*

What was the name of the terrible sickness plaguing London when James went to his coronation? *The Black Death was spreading through London when James went for his coronation in London.*

What three groups of Christians were in England when James was crowned king? *The three groups of Christians in England were the Catholics, the English Protestants (called Anglicans), and another group of Protestants (called the Puritans).*

How did James make the English Catholics angry? *James made the English Catholics angry when he made them pay a fine for not going to an Anglican church service.*

Did James agree to do what the Puritans wanted? *No, James refused to change the English church, and he also made Puritan worship against the law.*

What did Robert Catesby and Guy Fawkes plan to do to the Parliament building? *They planned to blow it up.*

When Parliament refused to do exactly what James ordered, what did he do? *He announced that all kings are above the law; then he sent all of Parliament home and ruled without their help.*

For what accomplishment is James most famous? *James is most famous for the King James Version of the Bible.*

### Narration Exercise

"James became king in Scotland. His tutor told him that the people gave him the right to rule, but James insisted on his 'divine right' (he said God gave him the power to rule). His relative Elizabeth died, and James became the king of England, too. Catholics wanted James to give them privileges, and Puritans wanted James to change the English church. But James refused. He also refused to listen to Parliament. Finally, he sent Parliament home. Everybody was angry with James. Two of James's angry subjects even tried to blow up Parliament!" OR

"James inherited the thrones of England and Scotland. He became James I of England and James VI of Scotland. But James had a hard time ruling. When James went to London for his coronation, not many people came because they were afraid of the Black Death. He made Puritans, Protestants, and Catholics all angry with him. He refused to listen to Parliament and told them that his words were like God's words! But James did something right—he made a new translation of the Bible, called the King James Version. People still read this Bible today!"

## KING JAMES'S TOWN

### Review Questions

James saw Philip searching for gold in South America. On which continent did James search for gold? *James gave some wealthy Englishmen permission to search for gold in North America.*

What three ships set off for North America? *The ships were called the* Susan Constant, *the* Godspeed, *and the* Discovery.

On what date did the ships arrive in North America? *The ships landed on May 13, 1607.*

When the Englishmen finally arrived, what did they name their town? *They named it Jamestown.*

At first, how did they spend most of their time? Why did this frustrate John Smith? *The colonists spent most of their time searching for gold. This frustrated John Smith because he saw that they needed to do other work before their food supplies were going to run out.*

What did the first Indian attack finally persuade the colonists to do? *After the Indian attack, the colonists finally built a log fort to protect themselves, and they cleared land on which they would grow crops.*

Why didn't the crops grow? *There was a terrible drought, and water was scarce.*

After he was captured, which great Indian chief did John Smith meet? *John Smith met with the great Indian chief Powhatan.*

When Powhatan asked John Smith why he was so far into his territory, what did John Smith say? *Smith said that he had intended to attack Powhatan's enemies, who lived up the river.*

Who married Powhatan's daughter, Pocahontas? *John Rolfe, another Jamestown leader, married Pocahontas.*

### Narration Exercise

"King James allowed some wealthy Englishmen to buy three ships so they could search for gold in North America. The colonists sailed for five months and then reached land in 1607. They named their colony Jamestown. The colonists should have been building houses and farming the land, but they spent most of their time looking for gold. They realized their mistake, but it was too late; many of them died from cold and hunger. John Smith helped the surviving colonists by making friends with the Indians." OR

"King James saw how rich Spain was and wanted gold for himself. He sent three ships to North America. Colonists who signed up for the voyage hoped for land and riches, but they faced a long and dangerous voyage. They finally reached North America and built a settlement. John Smith warned them that winter was coming, but not many men listened and many died; they were too busy looking for gold! Finally the Indians attacked John Smith and took him to their leader. Smith made friends with the chief, Powhatan, and Powhatan agreed to make peace with the Jamestown colony."

## Additional History Reading

*The National Archives: The Gunpowder Plot Unclassified* by Nick Hunter (A & C Black, 2014). Filled with photographs and original documentation, this book tells readers about Guy Fawkes and the plot to kill James I and the leaders of Parliament. (RA 1-2, IR 3-6)

*You Wouldn't Want to Be Guy Fawkes!*, by Fiona MacDonald, (Scribblers, 2016). A fun account of the Gunpowder Plot for younger readers. (RA 2, IR 3)

*1607: A New Look at Jamestown*, by Karen Lange, (National Geographic Children's Books, 2007). An examination of the archaeological evidence at Jamestown. Includes photographs of artefacts and re-enactments. (RA 2, IR 4)

*Jamestown Storybook*, by Carole Marsh (Gallopade International, 2006). A story-filled book about the founding of America. Stories of hard work, determination and adventure. (RA 1-2, IR 3-7)

*New Beginnings: Jamestown and the Virginia Colony 1607-1699*, by Daniel Rosen, (National Geographic Children's Books, 2005). This book looks at the Jamestown colony from the perspective of asking what motivated settlers and kept them going, and how this impacted the character of the new colony. (RA 2, IR4)

*You Wouldn't Want to be an American Colonist,* by Jacqueline Morley (Children's Press, 2013). A humorous book on what life was like as an American colonist. (RA 1-2, IR 3-6)

*The Powhatan: The Past and Present of Virginia's First Tribes*, by Alesha Halvorson, Danielle Smith-Llera, (Capstone Press 2017). This book covers the history and culture of the Powhatan people from first contact with Europeans to the present day. (RA 3, IR 4)

*Pocahontas (Rookie Biographies)*, by Joanne Mattern (Children's Press, revised edition 2015). A beginner biography for reluctant readers or younger siblings. (RA 1, IR 2-3) **OOP**

*Pocahontas: Young Peacemaker*, by Leslie Gourse, illus. Meryl Henderson (Aladdin, 1996). One of the wonderful "Childhood of Famous Americans" series for young readers. (IR 3-5)

*The Double Life of Pocahontas,* by Jean Fritz (Puffin, 2002). Award-winning biographer Fritz highlights the strain Pocahontas must have felt as she was trapped between two cultures. For slightly stronger readers. (IR 3-6)

*Pocahontas: In Their Own Words*, by George Sullivan, (Scholastic Reference, 2002). Uses contemporary writings to tell the story of the life of Pocahontas. (RA 2 IR 4)

*The True Story of Pocahontas*, by Lucille Recht Penner (Random House, 1994). A Step Into Reading biography for very reluctant readers or younger siblings. (IR 1-3)

## Corresponding Literature Suggestions

*Mr. Fawkes, the King and the Gunpowder Plot* by Tom and Tony Bradman (Wayland, 2016). This book for young readers tells the story of a spymaster and his assistant who try to foil the plot to kill the King. (RA 1-2, IR 2-4)

*The Lord Is My Shepherd: The Twenty-Third Psalm*, illus. Tasha Tudor (Puffin, 1999). Text from the King James Bible, with gentle rural illustrations. (RA 1, IR 2-4) **OOP**

*1607: Jamestown's Uncovered Treasures*, by Judy Brown, (Dietz Press, 2005). This book of short stories is based on real people who lived in the colony.

*Blood on the River: James Town, 1607*, by Elisa Carbone (Puffin Books, 2007). This novel for stronger readers is about a boy who comes from difficult circumstances in England, and finds himself in the colonies. (RA 2 IR 4)

*Our Strange New Land: Elizabeth's Jamestown Colony Diary*, by Patricia Hermes (Scholastic, 2002). An engaging fictional diary, kept by a young girl who came to Jamestown in 1609; part of the *My America* series. (IR 3-6) **OOP**

*Poetry for Kids: William Shakespeare* edited by Marguerite Tassi and illustrated by Merce Lopez (Moondance Press, 2018). A fully illustrated selection introducing some of Shakespeare's most popular works, some of which were written during the reign of James I and the era of Jamestown. It includes explanations of the poems and definitions of important words. (RA 1-2, IR 3-6)

## MAP WORK

### Britain and Jamestown *(Student Page 8, answer 320)*

1. King James ruled in Scotland. Trace the border of Scotland in purple, then shade the whole country lightly in purple.
2. After Elizabeth died, James ruled England, too. Trace the borders of England in purple, and then shade England in.
3. King James wanted to expand his rule to North America. Trace the path the colonists took from England to Jamestown in purple.
4. The trip took five months. Use a pen or pencil and draw a line (or a hatch mark) after each arrow. Realize that it took over a month to cover each section of the journey!
5. Jamestown became a royal colony of England. Draw a royal crown above Jamestown. (Be creative!)

**COLORING PAGE** The *Susan Constant* was one of the three ships that King James sent to North America to search for gold. *(Student Page 9)*

## PROJECTS

### MEMORY ACTIVITY "Remember, Remember, the Fifth of November . . ."

This is a popular rhyme in England. Impress your family and friends by reciting this catchy poem. Make it part of a Guy Fawkes celebration (see the following activity). Hints for memorization: Ask the child to read 2 stanzas out loud five times every day. Within a few days, the child should be able to recite most of those lines from memory. Then add another stanza and follow the same procedure until the whole poem is memorized.

Remember, remember, the fifth of November,
The gunpowder treason and plot.
I see no reason why gunpowder treason
Should ever be forgot.
Guy Fawkes, twas his intent
To blow up the king and parliament.
Three score barrels were laid below
To prove old England's overthrow.
By God's mercy he was catched
With a dark lantern and a lighted match.
Holler boys, holler boys, let the bells ring,
Holler boys, holler boys, God save the King.

## ACTIVITY PROJECT Celebrate Guy Fawkes' Day

In England, the foiling of the Gunpowder Plot is still remembered in a celebration called Guy Fawkes' Day (and also Bonfire Night). Celebrate your own version of the festivities. Here are some things you can do:

1. Make a "guy." English children make a guy (a doll) and go around begging for money and candy, saying "A penny for the guy!" Make your own guy from a balloon with a face on it, attached with duct tape or masking tape to an old pair of shorts and a shirt that you have stuffed with dishtowels. Use safety pins to hold the clothing together and to keep the armholes and legholes closed!
2. Deliver a sermon. Sermons were often preached stating how fortunate it was that the king was spared from death. The plotters were strongly condemned. Give your own speech to your family. Tell them the story of the Gunpowder Plot and let everybody cheer loudly when you get to the part about the plan failing and Guy Fawkes' arrest.
3. Celebrate with music and food. Musicians are hired and play throughout the night. Turn on the stereo and eat a special supper. Or play your own music after the meal. For dessert, make traditional Guy Fawkes' Day recipes: gingerbread men, caramel apples, or parkin (see recipe below).
4. Hold a bonfire. After all, it is Bonfire Night! Children tossed their "guy" dolls on to the wood and lit a giant fire. You don't have to light a real fire, but you can also march torches (okay, flashlights) around the house and announce to everyone you are taking your guy to be burned! You can recite the poem "Remember, Remember" from the previous activity.

### Parkin (a traditional cake from the north of England)

*Ingredients:*

2 cups flour
2 tsp. ground ginger
1 cup oats
⅓ cup butter or margarine
½ cup honey
2 tsp. baking powder
½ cup sugar
1 cup milk
½ cup molasses

*Directions:*

1. Soak oats in milk for 30 minutes.
2. Mix together flour, baking powder, ginger, and sugar in a large bowl.
3. Melt margarine or butter in the microwave and add molasses and honey.
4. Add oats and milk to molasses mixture.
5. Add the oat-molasses mixture to the dry ingredients.
6. Pour into a greased 9" x 13" pan.
7. Bake at 325 degrees for 45 minutes, or until the parkin pulls away from the sides of the pan.

## GAME ACTIVITY Become the Wealthiest Stockholder

Wealthy men joined together to buy the three ships that sailed to America. If gold were found in this new land, each of the wealthy men would get a share of it. The men formed a company called the London Company. Each man who put money in was called a stockholder. The London Company worked a little bit like this: Imagine that you get together with a group of your friends to buy a box with a mystery prize inside. No one knows exactly what the prize is. And none of you have enough money to buy it outright. But each one of you has *some* money. You have five dollars, your little brother has two dollars, and your friend who lives down the road has seven dollars. Now all three of you can buy the mystery prize together. Whatever it is, you'll get a medium-sized part of it because you put five dollars in; your little brother will get a small part because he put in two dollars; and your friend will get the biggest part because he put in the most money. That's how the stockholders in the London Company worked. Each one spent a certain amount of money on the expedition to the New World—and each one expected to get back a piece of the treasure discovered there. Play a game with another person and see who makes the most money as a stockholder!

*Materials:*
- ☐ 4 "ships": medium to large containers with lids that you cannot see into (coffee cans, small boxes, bowls with plates on top, etc. . . .)
- ☐ many pieces of "wealth" (a box of elbow macaroni, tiny LEGOs, M&Ms, Cheerios, pennies, etc. . . .)
- ☐ 16 "dollars" in single bills (make your own with paper or use playing cards)

*Directions:*
1. Each player is a stockholder in the London Company. The London Company is planning to fund four expeditions to the New World. As a stockholder, you decide how large of a share you want in each expedition. Some expeditions could find gold—and you could be rich. Other expeditions might not find anything at all—in which case you've wasted all your money!
2. Each player takes turns setting things up. Player 2 leaves the room. Player 1 takes the pieces of wealth and puts them in each of the four ships. You don't need to divide the wealth evenly; one ship could have nearly all the wealth if you like. Set the four ships up on the table. You should not be able to see the contents of any ship!
3. Player 2 comes back in the room. Players 1 and 2 each get eight dollars. Player 2 can now choose how much money he wants to invest in each expedition. Each ship needs a total of four dollars to sail. Player 2 may put zero, one, two, three, or four 4 dollars beside each ship. He must use all his money.
4. Player 1 may try to influence Player 2. Player 1 already knows which trip will be the most successful (she put the wealth in the box). Player 1 can try to talk Player 2 in or out of investing. Player 1 could say, "I hear this ship is not that sturdy," or "I know that captain is very experienced." Player 1 tries to confuse Player 2!
5. After Player 2 has invested all his money, Player 1 uses his money to make up the difference. Each ship needs a total of four dollars to sail. So if Player 2 put down one dollar on the first ship, Player 1 must put down the other three dollars. If Player 2 put down all four dollars on the second ship, Player 1 does not put any money down, and so on.
6. Once all the money has been placed, Player 1 reveals the contents of each ship. How successful was each investment? Each stockholder gets a portion of the pieces of wealth. If Player 1 put down all four dollars on a ship, he gets all the wealth inside that box. If Player 1 put down three dollars and Player 2 put down one dollar on a ship, Player 1 gets ¾ of the wealth inside (and Player 2 gets the rest). If Player 1 and Player 2 each put down two dollars, each player gets half the wealth. If Player 1 put down one dollar and Player 2 put down three dollars, Player 1 gets ¼ of the wealth and Player 2 gets the rest. You don't have to count out the pieces of wealth, just do your best to divide the portions.
7. The winner of the game is the player who has the most pieces of wealth. Play again and let Player 2 set up the game.

## Cooking Activity **Colonial Pottage**

Pottage is a thick and hearty soup of vegetables or meat. This is a recipe from a 1615 cookbook entitled *The English Huswife* (the spelling is as it appeared in the book):

*Take mutton, veal or kid, break the bones but do not cut up the flesh, wash, put in a pot with water. When ready to boil, and well skimmed, add a handful or two of small oatmeal. Take whole lettuce, the best inner leaves, whole spinach, whole endive, whole chicory, whole leaves of colaflorry or the inward parts of a white cabbage, with two or three onions. Put all into pot until done. Season with salt and as much verjuice as will only turn the taste of the pottage; serve up covering meat with whole herbs and adorning the meat with sippets.*

Can you imagine following this recipe? The new residents of Jamestown probably made pottage with any ingredients they had on hand. Here is a modern version of this pottage. Enjoy this authentic recipe!

## Pottage with Whole Herbs

*Ingredients:*

1 lb. cubed veal (or beef)
1 ½ cups oatmeal
3 ½ oz. lettuce (two large handfuls)
1 ½ oz. spinach (one large handful)
1 small endive (substitute chopped broccoli or cabbage if you don't have endive) (2 oz.)
2 oz. chicory (use additional spinach if you can't find chicory)
5 flowerets of cauliflower (this is *colaflorry*)
2 small onions, coarsely chopped
2 tsp. salt
1 Tbs wine vinegar (this is *verjuice*)
6 slices of toast (these are the *sippets*)

*Directions:*

1. Brown veal cubes on all sides. Put in a big soup pot. Cover with water. Bring to a boil.
2. Add oatmeal, lettuce, spinach, endive, chicory, cauliflower, and onion.
3. Cook approximately 1 hour or until veal is tender. If you used beef, you may need to cook it longer.
4. Add salt and vinegar.
5. Serve in soup bowls and top with sippets (toast)!

# Searching for the Northwest Passage

CHAPTER 4

## Encyclopedia Cross-References

*UBWH 150, UILE 321*
*KIHW 407 margin, 408, 410-411, KHE not covered*

## THE FRENCH IN THE NEW WORLD

### Review Questions

What was the "Northwest Passage" that many explorers searched for? *The Northwest Passage was a river that would run all the way through North America and out to the Pacific Ocean.*

Why did explorers want to find the Northwest Passage? *They thought they could get to China and India and trade for silks and spices.*

Whom did Henry IV hire to find the Northwest Passage for France? *Henry IV hired Samuel Champlain to find the Northwest Passage for France.*

Name two things Champlain saw in the beautiful new land of Canada. *Champlain saw fresh water, beautiful trees, good farmland, and friendly native people.*

What did Champlain convince Henry IV to do? *He convinced the king to let him start a French colony in Canada.*

When he returned to Canada, Champlain faced some problems on the island on which he and his men landed. What were two of the problems Champlain and his colony had? *The land was too salty for crops; the water was too foul to drink; and the cold, harsh winter was too difficult for the settlers to withstand. During this harsh winter, the men could not get to land for fresh food, so they got scurvy.*

What saved the men at St. Croix? *A ship arrived from France with more colonists, tools, and seeds.*

Champlain moved the colony to Port Royal. Why did they have to return to France when things were going well? *The king decided he had spent enough money on the colony and asked them to return to France.*

On his third attempt, Champlain faced a struggle he had faced before. What was it? *Champlain and his men suffered through another cold winter.*

What was the name of the city that Champlain founded on his third trip to New France? *Champlain founded the city of Kebec, or Quebec.*

How did Champlain make friends with the Montagnis people? *He shared the colony's food with them. He also encouraged the French and the Indians to marry each other.*

Can you remember two things that Champlain did to make Kebec a prosperous colony? *He wrote books about New France; he travelled back to France twenty-three times to convince new colonists to come to Kebec; he cleared land; he built new buildings; he encouraged the French and the Indians to marry each other.*

What is Champlain called today? *He is called the "Father of New France."*

### Narration Exercise

"The king of France wanted to find the Northwest Passage, so he hired Samuel Champlain. Champlain didn't find the Northwest Passage, but he found the land of Canada. When he returned, he told the king the French should settle there. The first colony almost froze to death and had to move. The second colony did better, but the king of France told the settlers to come home. Finally Champlain established a colony called Kebec. He spent 32 years in Canada. When he died, Kebec still had only a hundred settlers!" OR

"Explorers had been looking for the Northwest Passage for a long time, so that they could get to China and India. Samuel Champlain went looking for it, too. He didn't find it, but did find the beautiful land of Canada. Champlain and other French colonists tried to establish a 'New France' in Canada. Their first two colonies didn't last. But finally the colony of Kebec was built. Champlain worked hard to make Kebec prosperous. Today it is the capital of the province of Quebec, and the people still speak French. Champlain is called 'The Father of New France.'"

## HENRY HUDSON'S QUEST

### Review Questions

Henry Hudson wanted to find a path to which country? *Henry Hudson wanted to find a route to India.*

What route did Henry Hudson take on his first attempt at finding India? *Hudson tried to sail "up" through the North Pole.*

Did he succeed? *No, floating ice and cold weather forced his ship to turn around.*

What route did Henry Hudson take on his second attempt at finding India? *Hudson sailed northeast along the coast of Russia, hoping to go around China.*

Did this attempt succeed? *No, he ran into land, ice started to form, and his crew begged him to turn back.*

Did Henry Hudson go back to England? *No, he decided to head for North America.*

What happened when the crew found out Hudson was not heading home to England? *The crew threatened to mutiny under Robert Juet.*

Why was the "Furious Overfall" dangerous? *Treacherous rocks, swirling, sucking whirlpools, and floating cakes of ice made the channel almost impassable!*

Hudson and the men thought they'd reached the Pacific Ocean, but they soon found out they were wrong. What troubles did they encounter soon after this? *The weather grew cold and icy. They ran out of food and had to eat frogs!*

What happened to Henry Hudson? *His crew tied him up and left him in the lifeboat before they sailed back to England.*

What name was given to the large body of water Hudson discovered? *It was called Hudson Bay.*

### Narration Exercise

"Henry Hudson wanted to sail to India so he could get rich. Instead of looking for the Northwest Passage, he decided to sail up to the North Pole. The journey failed. He tried two other routes and failed again. Hudson was determined to find the Passage, so he hired another crew and sailed to North America, through Furious Overfall. He thought he had found the Pacific Ocean—but he was trapped in Hudson Bay! Finally, Hudson's crew tied him up, put him in a lifeboat, and went back to England without him." OR

"Henry Hudson was determined to find a short route to the East. He decided to try to sail over the North Pole, but it was too icy and he had to come home. He tried another route that went around Russia and China. When this didn't work, he wanted to go toward North America, but his crew wouldn't let him. A third attempt also failed. On the fourth trip, Hudson and his crew went to North America and got trapped in

Hudson Bay. Then Hudson's first mate led another mutiny and took over the ship! The Northwest Passage was never found."

## Additional History Reading

*The Big Book of Canada*, by Christopher Moore, illus. Bill Slavin (Tundra Books, revised edition 2017). A lovely reference book, revised and updated in 2017, with details on history, geography, and politics of Canada's provinces; many illustrations and maps. (RA 2-3, IR 4-6) **OOP**

*Canada: The Culture*, by Bobbie Kalman (Crabtree Publications, 2001). Gives French, English, and Native American perspectives on life in Canada. (RA 2, IR 3-5)

*The Kids Book of Canadian History*, by Carlotta Hacker and illustrated by John Mantha (Kids Can Press, 2009). Together with high-quality illustrations, this is an informative overview of the people, places and events that shaped Canada. (RA 1-2, IR 3-7)

*The Kids Book of Aboriginal Peoples in Canada*, by Diane Silvey and illustrated by John Mantha (Kids Can Press, 2012). An in-depth look at the cultures, struggles and triumphs of Canada's first peoples. (RA 1-2, IR 3-7)

*Samuel de Champlain*, by Claude Hurwicz (Powerkids Press, 2003). A beginning biography of the French Canadian hero. (RA 2, IR 3-4)

*Samuel de Champlain: From New France to Cape Cod*, by Adrianna Morganelli, (Crabtree Publishing Company, 2005). This book, for strong readers, covers all kinds of historical and cultural elements of Champlain's explorations. (RA 4, IR6)

*Explorers of the New World: Discover the Golden Age of Exploration with 22 Projects*, by Carla Mooney, (Nomad Press, 2011). Includes short biographies of explorers, information on sailing and navigation, the spice trade, and other topics related to exploration. (RA 2-3, IR 3)

*Beyond the Sea of Ice: The Voyages of Henry Hudson*, by Joan Elizabeth Goodman (Mikaya Press, 1999). Beautiful pictures and fold-out maps in this picture book; fairly advanced text. (RA 1-3, IR 4-6)

*Henry Hudson: Seeking the Northwest Passage*, by Carrie Gleason (Crabtree Publishing Company, 2005). This book describes Hudson's exciting voyages and the many hardships encountered in his quest to find a passageway to the Far East. (RA 1-2, IR 3-7)

*Hudson*, by Janice Weaver, (Tundra Books, 2010). A biography of Henry Hudson, containing maps and other supporting material, and information on navigation and culture. (RA 3, IR 4)

*Buried in Ice*, by Owen Beattie, John Geiger, and Shelley Tanaka (Scholastic, 1993). An intriguing account of a slightly later attempt to find the Northwest Passage; in 1845, Sir John Franklin and his crew sailed from England into the waters of the Arctic and froze to death. Wonderful illustrations include drawings and photographs, including those of three sailors whose bodies were preserved perfectly by the cold. (RA 2-3, IR 4-6) **OOP**

## Corresponding Literature Suggestions

*The Flying Canoe (La Chasse-Gallerie): A Christmas Story*, by Eric A. Kimmel, illus. Daniel San Souci (Holiday House, reprinted 2011). Six French-Canadian fur trappers promise a mysterious stranger that they won't speak until they reach their homes in this picture-book tall tale. (RA 2, IR 3-5) **OOP**

*Anne of Green Gables*, by Lucy Maud Montgomery (Skylark, 1984). Yes, we know, it isn't set in Quebec in the seventeenth century, but every child should read this classic Canadian tale—the sooner, the better. Also investigate the unabridged audio edition, narrated by Shelly Frasier (available on Audible.com and other online retailers).

*The Broken Blade*, by William Durbin (Yearling Books, 1998). For good readers, or as a family read-aloud. The thirteen-year-old son of French Canadian fur traders has to make a wilderness trip alone after his father's injury. (RA 3-4, IR 5-7)

*Champlain and the Silent One*, by Kate Messner (North Country Books, 2008). A novel depicting early explorers and New France. The Innu Indian called Silent One must overcome his reluctance to speak, and trust Samuel de Champlain and his Frenchmen. (RA 2-3, IR 4-6)

*Mystery in the Frozen Lands*, by Martyn Godfrey (James Lorimer, 2015). A tale of a young boy who joins a sea mission to solve the mystery of the disappearance of the later Arctic explorer, Sir John Franklin. (IR 3-7)

*I Am Canada: Graves of Ice: The Lost Franklin Expedition*, by John Wilson (Scholastic Canada, 2014). This novel is about a 14-year-old boy aboard Sir John Franklin's ship, *Erebus*, and what happens when their ship gets trapped in ice during their nineteenth-century quest to discover the Northwest Passage. (IR 3-7)

*Northwest Passage*, by Stan Rogers, Matt James illus. (Groundwood Books, 2011). A beautifully illustrated version of the Stan Rogers song about the search for the Northwest Passage over the centuries. Includes some historical information as well as the song lyrics. Suitable for all ages. (RA K, IR 3)

*Of Kings and Fools: Stories of the French Tradition in North America*, by Michael Parent and Julien Oliver (August House, 1996). Read-aloud legends and fairy tales from the French-Canadian tradition, filled with French words and phrases. (RA 3-4, IR 5-6)

*The Thundermaker*, by Alan Syliboy (Nimbus Publishing, 2018). A mythological story in both English and Mi'kmaw, illustrated by First Nations artist Alan Syliboy. Or also try other titles by the same author. (RA K, IR 2)

*Under a Prairie Sky*, by Anne Laurel Carter, illus. Alan Daniel (Orca Books, 2002). A young boy rescues his little brother, lost on the Canadian prairie during a thunderstorm. (RA 2, IR 3-4)

## MAP WORK

### Champlain's Exploration *(Student Page 10, answer 320)*

1. Champlain sailed into the St. Lawrence River. Trace the lower arrow and color the river in blue.
2. Champlain and his men tried to settle at St. Croix, but they became ill and the settlement failed. Draw a purple circle around the dot that represents St. Croix.
3. Champlain and his men moved the settlement to Port Royal and stayed warm enough to survive the next winter. Draw a large orange circle around the dot that represents Port Royal.
4. Champlain eventually settled Quebec. Quebec became the capital of the whole Canadian province. Draw a small capitol building over Quebec.
5. Trace Hudson's journey through the Furious Overfall in blue.
6. Draw a small symbol for Hudson's ship, the *Hopewell,* somewhere along the line of Hudson's path.

**Coloring Page** Samuel Champlain and his men sailed down the Saint Lawrence River. *(Student Page 11)*

## PROJECTS

### Science Project — No Sunset in the Summer in the North Pole!

Henry Hudson thought he could reach Asia by sailing over the top of the globe. He knew that in the summer, the sun shines twenty-four hours a day in the North Pole. He thought the sun would melt all the icebergs and he could sail straight through. He didn't know that the North Pole only gets to 32 degrees Fahrenheit in the warmest month, July (it's around –25 degrees Fahrenheit in February).

Use a lamp and a globe to see why it stays sunny in the winter on the north pole (and why the sun still rises and sets over England, where Henry Hudson was from).

*Materials:*
- ☐ Floor or table lamp with shade that can be completely removed
- ☐ Globe

*Directions:*
1. The planet Earth rotates on its axis. Dim the room, if possible. Turn on the lamp; remove the shade. Hold the globe so that England faces the lamp. Slowly spin the globe, but do not move the light. As England moves into the shadow, it is nighttime there. As England moves back into the light, it is daytime. It takes 24 hours for the earth to rotate all the way around. This is one day.
2. In the summer, the North Pole is tilted toward the sun. Now tilt the globe at a slight angle so that the North Pole is closer to the lamp and the South Pole is further away. Spin the globe slowly. England still moves from light into dark—but the North Pole stays in the light for all 24 hours of the day!
3. What's happening at the South Pole? That's right—when it's summer at the North Pole, it is winter at the South Pole—and is dark for 24 hours of the day.

### Game Project — The Inuit of Canada

Explorers looking for the Northwest Passage met the native peoples of northern Canada—the Inuit. Other peoples who lived nearby called the Inuit "Eskimos," or "eaters of raw meat." The Inuit lived by hunting and fishing; they used seal skins for clothes, tents, and boats; they ate their meat all raw and ate ice instead of drinking water; they traveled by training huskies to pull sleds over ice. Their children played active games—maybe to keep warm! Play some traditional Inuit games with your siblings or parents—or by yourself.

**Nauktak**

*Nauktak* is a jumping game. Lie on the ground with your feet flat against a wall and your legs straight. Mark the place where the top of your head touches the ground. Get up, crouch by the wall, and try to leap out to the mark on the ground. The person who gets out to his or her own mark first wins!

**Qijumik Akimitaijuk Itigaminak**

*Qijumik Akimitaijuk Itigaminak* is another jumping game. It is best played on the grass or on a very soft rug. Hold your toes and jump as far as you can—while still holding your toes! Mark the spot where you land. Who can jump the farthest? Or play by yourself. Can you beat your own record?

**Illukitaq**

*Illukitaq* is a juggling game played by the Inuit on Holman Island in Canada. The purpose of this game is to keep as many objects in the air as possible. Light objects work best; knot dishtowels into balls, or crumple paper into paper balls. Play with a friend, sibling, or parent; see which one of you can get the furthest through the steps below.

1. One Object: Hold the ball in your right hand. Toss it upwards so that it reaches the level of your hairline before beginning to fall. Catch it in your left hand—without looking! Now toss it back. Can you do this ten times without dropping the ball?
2. Two Objects: Hold a ball in each hand. Toss the right-hand ball up. When the ball reaches your hairline, toss the left-hand ball up as well. Catch the right hand ball with your left hand—and then catch the left hand ball in your right hand.
3. Three Objects: Put two balls in your right hand and one in your left hand. Throw one right-hand ball (Ball 1) up. Throw the left-hand ball (Ball 2) up. Throw the other right-hand cloth (Ball 3) up. Catch Ball 1 with your left hand. Catch Ball 2 with your right hand. Catch Ball 3 with your left hand. Did you do it? Try it again! Then, see if you can continue juggling by tossing each ball back up as it reaches your hand!

## ACTIVITY PROJECT Add a Little Spice . . .

Before the days of refrigerators and freezers, food spoiled quickly! Spices like cloves, pepper, and nutmeg masked the flavor and texture of food that was partly spoiled. This put spices in high demand. The English were anxious to find the Northwest Passage because they needed these spices—and the Portuguese and Italians controlled the route to India. The English had to pay extra for the spices they got.

See how spices mask the flavor of food. You don't want the "slightly spoiled" food to be dangerous—don't eat anything with fuzz on it! Be ready for some wacky flavor combinations!

*Materials:*

- ☐ 1 overripe banana
- ☐ 1 carrot (leave it out on the counter for a day or two so it gets rubbery)
- ☐ 1 apple (cut an apple in half and leave out overnight until it is brown and slightly shriveled)
- ☐ 1 large leaf lettuce (leave out overnight until it is floppy and quite wilted)
- ☐ Spices (as many as you can get):
- ☐ Ground cinnamon and cinnamon stick
- ☐ Whole and ground cloves
- ☐ Allspice
- ☐ Cloves
- ☐ Mustard
- ☐ Coarsely ground sea salt
- ☐ Coarsely ground pepper

*Directions:*

1. Cut up the carrot, apple, banana, and lettuce into bite-sized bits. Taste each one plain. Describe the flavor of each item to your parent.
2. Now experiment with adding a different spice to each piece. Does the spice change the flavor or the texture of the food? For example, how does cinnamon change the flavor or the texture of the apple? How does mustard change the flavor or the texture of the carrot?
3. Does this old, slightly spoiled food taste better plain—or all covered up with spices?

## SCIENCE PROJECT Fool's Gold

Twenty-five years before Samuel Champlain arrived in Canada, an Englishman named Martin Frobisher sailed along the coast of North America, past the wide mouth of the St. Lawrence River, and found the mouth of another body of water. When he sailed into it, he found himself in a wide body of water. He couldn't see the horizon in front of him. He was certain that he had found the mysterious passageway to the northeast! He named his passageway "Frobisher's Strait." Martin Frobisher might have gone on to explore his strait, but when he went ashore with his men to explore, he found strange black rocks with traces of gold-colored metal running through it. He took these rocks back to England, where mining experts told him that he had discovered gold! So instead of trying to sail on through Frobisher's Strait to reach the east, Martin Frobisher put all his energy into collecting this "gold." He made two more trips through Frobisher's Strait—but both times, he collected tons of rock and took it back to England.

But then the experts, with more of this "gold" to look at, discovered that they had made a mistake. It wasn't gold at all! It was a mineral called pyrite, which looks like gold, but is worthless. Another name for pyrite is "fool's gold." Martin Frobisher had certainly been fooled! He had spent all his time and energy collecting rocks instead of exploring his new route east. If he'd gone further in, Frobisher would have realized that Frobisher's Strait led, not into a passage to the east, but into a landlocked bay.

Why was Martin Frobisher fooled? Maybe he didn't know the four properties of a metal like gold: *luster* (the way it shines), *malleability* (it can be flattened), *conductivity* (electricity can run through it), and *ductility* (it can be rolled into a wire). If you had a piece of gold and a piece of pyrite, you would see that gold can be hammered flat and rolled out into a wire—while pyrite just shatters! Instead, pretend that you're trying to distinguish gold from pyrite.

*Materials:*
- ☐ Yellow Play-Doh
- ☐ Yellow rock candy (or any hard candy, such as peppermint)
- ☐ Hammer

*Directions:*
1. Roll the Play-Doh into a ball and set it beside the candy. Imagine that you're trying to tell which is gold and which is "fool's gold." Imagine that both of these gold finds have *luster* (both shine in the sun). Now, find out which one is *ductile.* Try rolling each into the shape of a wire.
2. Now, test for *malleability.* If you hit both with the hammer, the gold will mash into a soft plate; the "fool's gold" will shatter.

Which one is gold? The Play-Doh! If this were *really* gold, you could attach wires to it and pass an electrical current through it as well. But unless you have access to real gold, you'll just have to go on pretending.

## CRAFT PROJECT **The Floating Galleon**

When Henry Hudson sailed off into the west, looking for the Northwest Passage, he used a *galleon.* Galleons were sturdier and easier to steer than *caravels,* ships which had once been popular with English sailors. The English admiral Sir John Hawkins (1532–95) popularized the galleon, which had slightly lower masts than the caravel. These lower masts made the ships easier to steer in rough seas. The galleon also had a "v" shaped stern that cut through the water faster then the rounded stern of the caravel. While the forecastle of the ship still held additional space for the officers' quarters and the ramming weapon which extended beyond the ship's bow, the galleon's foremast was also strengthened. Henry Hudson's galleon was called the *Discovery.* Make your own *Discovery,* or name this galleon something from your own imagination!

*Materials:*
- ☐ Student Page 12: Sail Template
- ☐ 1 1-quart cardboard carton (milk or orange juice)
- ☐ 1 half-pint carton (whipping cream or other small dairy product)
- ☐ 2 sheets of brown craft foam (11 ½ x 17 ½)
- ☐ Scissors

- ☐ Hot glue gun and glue sticks
- ☐ Stapler
- ☐ 3 skewers
- ☐ 5 large coffee filters
- ☐ Sharpened pencil
- ☐ Coin (if needed)

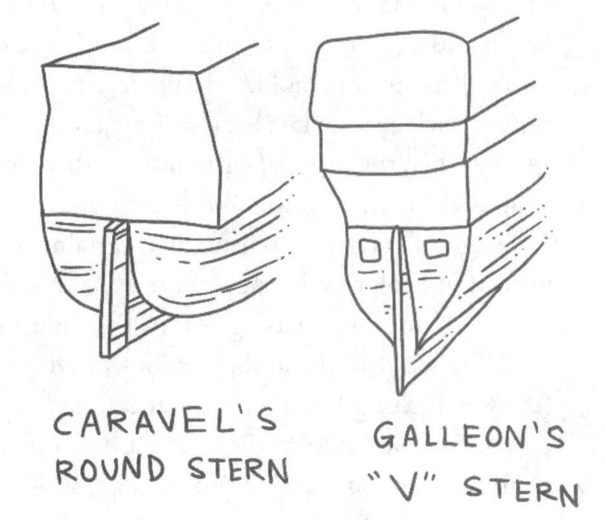


*Directions:*

1. Clean out cartons and let them dry.
2. Gently crush the half-pint carton top into a square.
3. Lay the quart carton on its side so that the top of the carton forms the bow of the ship. Glue the half-pint carton on to the end of the quart carton, opposite the pointed end. See figure 1.
4. Using the boat carton as a guide, cut out a long strip of the brown craft foam, making sure it is the width of the carton and the length of the foam. Starting from the bow of the ship (front), glue the strip down on to the top of the boat carton. You'll stick it down in one continuous strip, up and over the cabin (half-pint carton) and then down the backside of the stern all the way to the bottom of the back end. Make sure you hot glue the foam at each bending point. Trim the front point so that the brown foam covers the carton lid at the pointed opening of the carton.
5. Insert the pencil into the opening of the carton, which is now the bow of the ship. Make a hole with the sharp end, then flip the pencil so that the eraser part is secured into the carton. The pointed end reflects the battering ram.

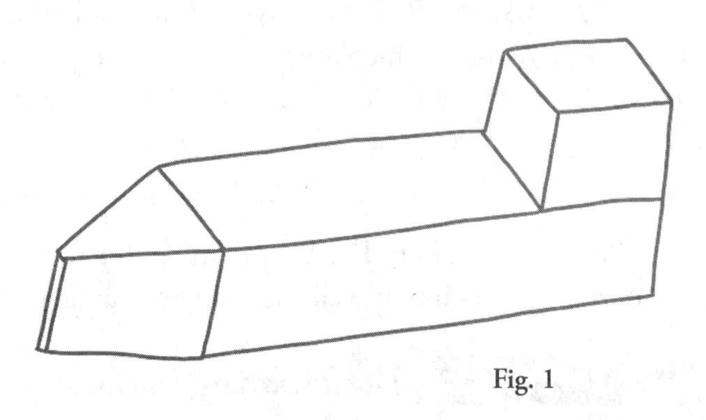

**Fig. 1**

6. Using the second foam sheet, set the boat in the center. Wrap the brown foam up the sides of the boat. Glue it onto the cartons securely, starting with one side. Continue gluing around the bottom of the boat and up the other side. Trim the long excess of the brown foam to the top of the ship so it is easier to work with.
7. Pull the front piece to a point at the bow. Staple the two edges together forming a covering at the point and locking the battering ram in position. Trim the excess foam at the point and then at the bottom side of the point and glue down the tip to the underside. See figure 2.
8. Cut around the ship, leaving a ledge around the deck for any plastic friends that may be enjoying a journey! Note the shape of the forecastle in figure 3. Go through and glue any parts of the craft foam that are not tacked down.

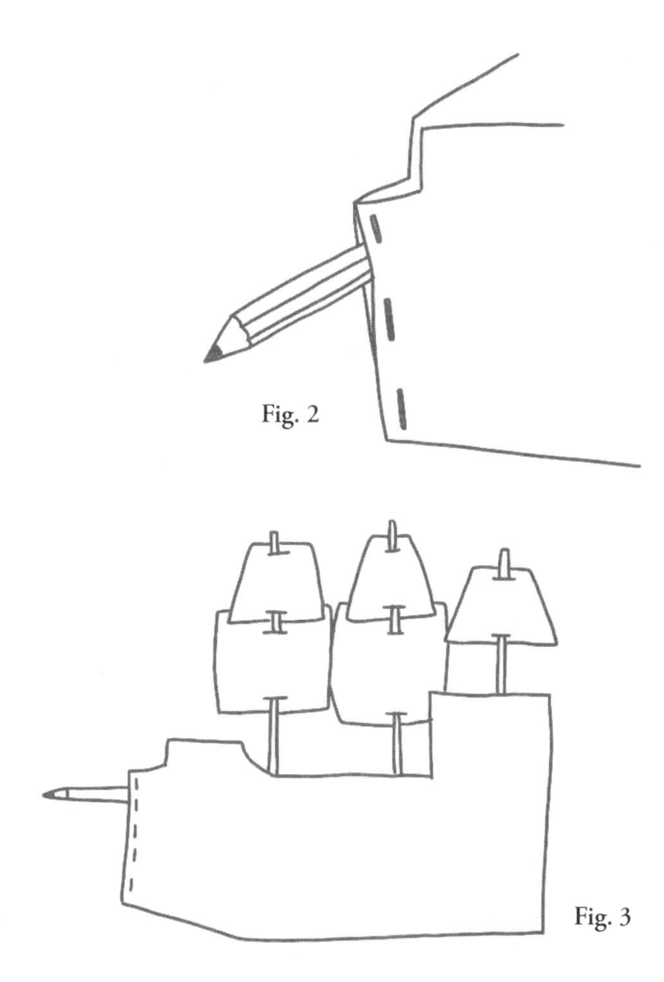

Fig. 2

Fig. 3

9. Making the masts: Use templates to cut out the sails from the coffee filter. Notch the sails in the center, then slip them over the skewers. Using a skewer tip or the point of a pair of scissors, punch in two holes for the tall masts into the boat carton; see figure 3 for approximate location. Break off 1/3 of the third skewer and fit it into the center of the cabin in the back. If your sails get wet during a voyage, they will dry. Consider using tape or hot glue if you cut your notches too big and a sail is slipping down the skewer.
10. Your ship is ready to take a trip around the world, or at least across the Atlantic in search of the Northwest Passage! If the ship is tipsy, use a coin to settle the leaning side. You may also make bigger ships with half-gallon cartons, if desired. If they're floating too high in the water, add sand to the bottom of the ship to act as ballast. Make sure it's evenly distributed, or it'll cause your galleon to capsize!

# Warlords of Japan

## Encyclopedia Cross-References

*UBWH 121, 154-155, UILE 356*
*KIHW 255, 392-393, 402-403 KHE 232-233, 244*

## HIDEYOSHI, JAPAN'S GREAT LEADER

### Review Questions

What was a daimyo? *A daimyo was a warlike nobleman who ruled a section of Japan.*

What is the name of the group of people who fought for the daimyos? *Samurai, or roving bands of Japanese knights, fought for the daimyos.*

What was Hideyoshi's job—how did he make his living? *Hideyoshi was a peddler who made his living walking from place to place, selling goods.*

Hideyoshi didn't want to remain a peddler all of his life. What did he decide to do? *Hideyoshi joined the army of Nobunaga.*

How did Nobunaga try to unify Japan? *He hired the samurai warriors and killed anyone who opposed him.*

What special position did Nobunaga give to Hideyoshi? *He gave Hideyoshi the position of sandal-bearer.*

When Nobunaga died, who wanted to rule Japan? *Four different samurai announced that they would help Nobunaga's grandson rule—but they really wanted to rule themselves!*

When Hideyoshi became the leader of Japan, he did not kill his enemies like Nobunaga did. How did he deal with his enemies? *Hideyoshi forced enemies to take oaths of loyalty to him. Those who refused had to surrender their swords.*

What large country did Hideyoshi plan to add to his empire? *Hideyoshi wanted to add China to his empire.*

What country did Hideyoshi have to cross through to get to China? *Hideyoshi had to cross through Korea to get to China.*

How did the Koreans respond to Hideyoshi's plan to march through their country? *The Koreans fought back and, with the help of the Chinese, pushed back the Japanese.*

What did the Korean navy use to fight against the Japanese? *They used "tortoise boats" with iron plates and sharp iron spikes.*

Did Hideyoshi conquer China? *No, he grew ill and died before he could attack again.*

### Narration Exercise

"At first, Hideyoshi made his living selling goods. But then he joined Nobunaga's army. First he was a sandal-bearer, but later he became a general. When Nobunaga died, four samurai tried to take power—but Hideyoshi won and took control. People in Japan had to swear loyalty to Hideyoshi or give up their swords. Hideyoshi wanted to make Japan a huge empire, so he tried to invade China—but he failed." OR

"The daimyos of Japan fought with each other until Nobunaga united the country. After he died, his general Hideyoshi became ruler of Japan. Hideyoshi wanted to make Japan larger, so he decided to invade China. But to get to China, he had to go through Korea. The Chinese and the people of Korea fought back. Their 'tortoise boats' rammed the Japanese ships! Hideyoshi tried again to invade Korea, but he grew sick and died before he could direct the attack."

## THE FIRST TOKUGAWA RULER

### Review Questions

When Hideyoshi died, to whom did he leave his power? *When Hideyoshi died, he left his power to his son, Hideyori.*

Who was supposed to help Hideyori rule? *Hideyori's five guardians were supposed to help him rule.*

Did the five guardians do their job? *No, they fought with each other over the throne!*

Eventually, the five guardians and their daimyos divided into two armies. To whom did the Western army pledge loyalty? To whom did the Eastern army pledge loyalty? *The Western army pledged loyalty to Hideyori; the Eastern army pledged loyalty to Ieyasu.*

Who won the battle between the Western and Eastern armies (the Battle of Sekigahara)? *The Eastern army and Ieyasu won the battle.*

How did Ieyasu make sure that he would win the battle? *Ieyasu bribed the daimyos of the Western army, promising them land and money in exchange for their loyalty.*

What is a shogun? Who was Japan's shogun? *A shogun is a military ruler. Ieyasu was Japan's shogun.*

What one obstacle stood in the way of Ieyasu's sons one day ruling Japan? *Hideyori was still alive, and he was the rightful heir.*

What were two of the ways that Ieyasu continued to build his own family's power? *He destroyed castles that were not lived in by the daimyos. He forced the daimyos to swear loyalty to him and to his family, while forcing the daimyos's families to live in the capital city (where Ieyasu himself lived). He also gave the samurai new jobs, encouraging them to wrestle rather than to fight with swords.*

What city did Ieyasu make the capital of Japan? What do we call it today? *Ieyasu made Edo the capital. Today we call it Tokyo.*

What happened to Hideyori and his family when Ieyasu finally attacked his castle? *Hideyori killed himself, and Ieyasu had Hideyori's son and heir put to death.*

### Narration Exercise

"Hideyoshi died and left the power to his son, Hideyori. Five regents were supposed to help Hideyori rule, but instead they fought with each other over power. Ieyasu and his Eastern Army beat Hideyori and the Western Army, and Ieyasu became the shogun of Japan. Ieyasu moved the capital city to Tokyo and continued to build up his army for the final assault on Hideyori. When Ieyasu finally broke into Hideyori's castle, Hideyori killed himself and Ieyasu killed Hideyori's family." OR

"After Hideyoshi died, Ieyasu was determined to gain control of Japan. He got his Eastern Army ready to battle with Hideyori's Western Army. Ieyasu won and declared himself the military ruler of Japan. Ieyasu made changes that made it easier for him to rule. He took away the swords of the samurai, and he encouraged them to read, study, and wrestle. Ieyasu defeated Hideyori and killed his heir, and his family became the rulers of Japan."

## Additional History Reading

*All About Japan: Stories, Songs, Crafts and Games for Kids*, by Willamarie Moore, Kazumi Wilds illus. (Tuttle Publishing, 2017). Appropriate for younger readers, this book is an introduction to the culture, language, and geography of Japan. (RA 2, IR 3)

*Eyewitness: Castle*, by Christopher Gravett, illus. Geoff Dann (DK Publishing, rev. ed. 2008). Gorgeous illustrations and brief but detailed text describe castles in France, Germany, Spain, and Japan, showing the parallels between them. (RA 2-3, IR 4-6) **OOP**

*How to Be a Samurai Warrior*, by Fiona MacDonald (National Geographic Children's Books, 2005). A "how-to" type book about becoming a samurai warrior. (RA 2, IR 3)

*Hands-On History! Ancient Japan*, by Fiona MacDonald (Armadillo, 2014). This book is full of projects which relate to ancient Japan. Great for younger or more hands-on learners. (RA K, IR 3)

*Japan ABCs*, by Sarah Heiman (Picture Window Books, 2003). Nice illustrations and brief, readable paragraphs about the history, culture, and geography of Japan. (RA 1-2, IR 3-4)

*Japan: The Land*, by Bobbie Kalman (Crabtree, 2000). A simple reader about Japan's geography, with photographs and descriptions of the terrain. (RA 2, IR 3-4)

*Japanese Traditions: Rice Cakes, Cherry Blossoms and Matsuri: A Year of Seasonal Japanese Festivities*, by Willamarie Moore and Setsu Broderick and illustrated by Setsu Broderick (Tuttle Publishing, 2010). Filled with colorful illustrations, this book looks at Japanese culture, celebrations, language and history. (RA 1, IR 2-6)

*Life in Ancient Japan* by Hazel Richardson (Crabtree Pub. Co., 2005). This book examines the politics, daily activities, art, religion, economy, traditions and social structures of ancient Japan. (RA 2-3, IR 4-7)

*My First Book of Japanese Words: An ABC Rhyming Book of Japanese Language and Culture* by Michelle Haney Brown, illus. Aya Padron (Tuttle Publishing, 2017). A beautifully illustrated book that focuses on familiarizing children with the sounds and structure of Japanese speech, as well as introducing them to the core elements of Japanese culture. (RA 1-2)

*Ninjas and Samurai—Magic Tree House Fact Tracker* by Mary Pope Osborne and Natalie Pope Boyce (Random House Books for Young Readers, 2014). This book answers lots of questions about ancient Japan as well as what it meant to be a ninja or samurai. (IR 2-7)

*Origami and Haiku: Inspired by Japanese Artwork*, by Nosy Crow, the trustees of the British Museum (Nosy Crow, 2018). In this book each piece of art is accompanied by instructions for creating an origami inspired by the picture. (RA1, IR 4)

*Samurai Castle, by Masayuki Miura* (Shogakukan, 2017). A bilingual work showing historic castles of Japan. Though it's not really a children's book, the illustrations make it an excellent book to share together. (RA 3, IR 6)

## Corresponding Literature Suggestions

*The Ghost in the Tokaido Inn*, by Dorothy and Thomas Hoobler (Philomel Books, 1999). For advanced readers, this engaging middle-grade novel tells the story of a fourteen-year-old boy who lives in eighteenth-century Japan and wants to become a samurai. (IR 3-6)

*Heart of a Samurai*, by Margi Preus, (Amulet Paperbacks, 2012). A novel for strong readers about a Japanese boy who comes to America and then returns to Japan. (RA 4, IR 5)

*How to Live Like a Samurai Warrior* by John Farndon and illustrated by Amerigo Pinelli (Hungry Tomato, 2016). Historical fiction about a young boy who trains in a Samurai castle to be a noble fighter. (RA 1-2, IR 3-6)

*Manjiro: The Boy Who Risked His Life for Two Countries* by Emily Arnold McCully (Farrar, Straus and Giroux (BYR), 2008). This is a tale of a fourteen-year-old boy who is shipwrecked, rescued and taken to live in America. He later uses his knowledge of two countries to play an important role in the opening of Japan to Western trade and ideas. (RA 1-2, IR 3-6) **E-only.**

*Night of the Ninjas: Magic Tree House #5*, by Mary Pope Osborne (Random House, 1995). In this beginning chapter book, the Magic Tree House takes two children back to the days of the samurai. (IR 2-4)

*Once Upon a Time in Japan*, by Japan Broadcasting Corporation, trans. Roger Pulvers and Juliet Carpenter (Tuttle Publishing, 2015). Japanese fairy tales paired with beautiful illustrations. The book comes with a CD of the stories read aloud. (RA K, IR 3)

*The Perfect Sword* by Scott Goto (Charlesbridge, 2010). A wonderfully illustrated book about a Japanese master sword maker and his apprentice who craft the perfect sword and then search for the samurai worthy of it. (RA 1-2, IR 3-6)

*The Samurai's Tale*, by Erik C. Haugaard (Houghton Mifflin, 1990). Set in sixteenth-century Japan, this chapter book for good readers tells the story of a young samurai who loses his fortune and position and is forced to serve a warlord. (IR 4-6)

*The Strongest Boy in the World* by Jessica Souhami (Frances Lincoln Children's Books, 2014). A re-telling of a thirteenth-century Japanese tale in which a young girl trains Kaito—a boy who longs to win a sumo wrestling championship. (RA 1, IR 2-4)

*Tales of Old Japan: Folklore, Fairy Tales, Ghost Stories and Legends of the Samurai*, by A.B. Mitford, (Dover Publications 2005). Suitable for stronger readers or as a read-aloud. Written by an English diplomat living in Japan in the late 19th century, it includes stories he collected from many sources as well as cultural information. (RA 3, IR 6)

*The Turtle Ship* by Helena Ku Rhee and illustrated by Colleen Kong-Savage (Shens Books & Supplies, 2018). A wonderfully illustrated tale about a young Korean boy who, along with his pet tortoise, designs a sailing vessel to defend his country from invaders. (RA 1-2, IR 3-6)

*Wabi Sabi*, by Mark Reibstein, (Little, Brown Books for Young Readers, 2008). An illustrated story of a cat called Wabi Sabi who explores the meaning of his name, an idea in Japanese philosophy and aesthetics. (RA K, IR 2)

## MAP WORK

### Hideyoshi in East Asia *(Student Page 13, answer 321)*

1. Hideyoshi wanted to conquer China. He took his army into Korea, hoping the Koreans would move toward China. Draw an arrow from the coast of Japan to the coast of Korea.
2. The Chinese helped the Koreans push back the Japanese. Color China orange, then draw two orange arrows from China, down through Korea.
3. After Hideyoshi died, two armies fought for control of Japan. Color the territory of Ieyasu's Eastern Territory red (the eastern, or right-hand, half of the main island of Japan). Color the territory of Hideyori's Western army yellow (the western, or left-hand, half of the main island of Japan).

## Coloring Pages

The samurai were the knights of Japan. *(Student Page 14)*

When the Japanese tried to invade Korea, the Koreans fought back with armored "tortoise boats" like this one. *(Student Page 15)*

## PROJECTS

### Cooking Project **Hold a Japanese Tea Ceremony**

In Japan, green tea was first drunk by the Zen Buddhist monks, as a way of keeping them awake during long hours of meditation. Eventually, drinking tea evolved into an elaborate ceremony that was meant to create a relationship between host and guest. Hold your own Japanese tea ceremony and invite one or more guests.

Items you should have prepared:

Salad
Hot white rice
Chicken broth with either cooked mushrooms or spinach in it
Grilled fish (the main course)
Hot water with lemon slices
Food served on a tray—bite sized pieces that resemble a mountain or the sea.
For example:
Hershey kisses (mountain) and unrolled fruit roll-up (sea)
Orange or apple slices (mountain) and ruffled potato chips (sea)
Rolls or biscuits (mountain)and flat pile of blue Skittles or raisins
Pickles, accompanied by more white rice
Sweets that represent the current season (these are served in small boxes; prepare one box for each guest)
For example:
*Spring*: mini-marshmallows stuck with toothpicks to a tootsie roll which represents a branch with budding cherry blossoms.
*Summer*: Vanilla wafers to represent the yellow disk of the sun.
*Fall*: Pretzels surrounded with Life Savers or Fruit Loops (tree bark and fallen leaves)
*Winter*: Popcorn or pecans sprinkled with powdered sugar which represents a snowy landscape.
A thick, savory tea (black tea) served in a medium-sized bowl
A thin green tea served in individual cups (check at the grocery story for green tea in tea bags)

Directions:

1. Your guests should arrive promptly. Ask them to remove their shoes and provide them with slippers. Lead your guests to a room that is restful with comfortable seating. This place is called the *mizuya* (or preparation room).
2. Once the meal is ready, lead your guests into the *chashitsu*, the room where the tea ceremony will take place.
3. Serve your guests each course of the light meal, called the *kaiseki*. The host does not eat with the guests, but attends to them. The host should snack while he or she is in the kitchen.
First: bring in the salad and some white rice for each guest.
Second: serve the broth with mushrooms or spinach (called the *Nimono* course)
Third: serve the grilled fish (called the *Yakimono* course)
Fourth: bring cups of the hot lemon water to refresh the guests (*Hashiarai*)
Fifth: bring in the "mountain" and the "sea" on the tray (the *Hassun* course)

Sixth: Serve the pickles and more white rice (this is the end of the meal)

4. Give your guests the box with the seasonal sweet treat inside. Lead them back to the *mizuya* (preparation room), where they may eat the treats and wait for you to call them.
5. Prepare the thick, savory tea (the black tea, *koicha*). Pour it into a large decorative bowl and use a wire whisk to beat the tea until it is frothy. (If you prefer, whip the tea in a blender or food processor, and reheat in the microwave. Bring the guests back to the *chashitsu* (tea ceremony room). They should pass the bowl to one another, each taking time to admire the bowl before taking a sip.
6. Then serve the guests the thin green tea (*usucha*) in individual cups.
7. Once everyone is finished, the host and guests silently and respectfully acknowledge one another. Show your guests from the room and take them back to the place they entered (and give them back their shoes!).

## Activity Project **Sumo Wrestling**

How do you cope with noblemen who keep wanting to fight each other with swords? Give them a new way of fighting—a way without weapons, where no one will get killed! The practice of sumo wrestling allowed Japanese warriors to fight without blades or bloodshed. You can act out some of the rituals of sumo wrestling with your brother, sister, friend—or even your mom or dad!

*Materials:*

- ☐ Masking tape
- ☐ Four sheets of construction paper: blue, red, white, and black
- ☐ One silk scarf or sash, preferably white, for each competitor
- ☐ Two bed pillows for each competitor
- ☐ A glass of water for each competitor
- ☐ A small bowl of salt
- ☐ Compass (not necessary if you know where to find the east)

*Directions:*

1. Outline a ring with masking tape on the floor. In Japan, the sumo wrestling ring is called the *dohyo* and is 14' 10" across. You may not want to make your ring quite so large! When you have laid out your ring on the floor, put a line of tape about 3 feet long right in the center.
2. A *dohyo* ring has a blue pillar on the east, a red pillar on the south, a white pillar on the west, and black on the north. Use your compass to place the correct piece of construction paper at the east, south, west, and north ends of the ring. These will symbolize the colored pillars.
3. Prepare yourself by placing the pillows on your front and back and tying the sash around both pillows and your waist. If you were a real sumo wrestler, you'd be wearing a sumo belt and a white apron, symbolizing purity—and you wouldn't need the pillows! If your hair is long enough, put your hair up in a knot on top of your head. This *mage* is the formal Sumo hairdo.
4. Parade into the ring. Each competitor should have two assistants, one walking ahead and one walking behind.
5. The competitors should squat at opposite ends of the ring, stretch out their hands, and clap once—this is the *chiri-chozu* ritual.
6. Now, perform the *shiko* ritual—exaggerated foot stamping on each leg to drive away bad spirits.
7. Now, each competitor should sip water to purify themselves.

8. Each competitor should reach into the salt and toss a handful into the ring.
9. Both should stride the marked white line in the middle of the ring, clench fists, crouch down, and glare at each other. The goal is to break the opponent's focus. The "glare-off" cannot last more than four minutes! At some point during the four minutes, the competitors lunge at each other and make their opening moves. This is called *shikiri.*
10. The goal is to push your opponent out of the ring. Remember: No hair pulling, punching, eye-gouging, or kicking vital areas! You can push the opponent out (*yori kiri)* or pull on him and then step out of his way so that he stumbles out (*oshi dashi).*

If you don't feel like full-body sumo wrestling, remember that—according to some experts—thumb wrestling is a form of "mini-sumo"!

## Craft Project **Wind Poem**

At the time of the Star Festival, *Tanabata* (July 7), it was traditional to decorate a bamboo branch with strips of paper, put poems and wishes on the strips, and then hang it outside. Participants in the Star Festival hoped that these wishes would come true!

*Materials:*
- ☐ Long stick or dowel
- ☐ Ribbon for hanging the dowel
- ☐ Three strips of colored paper, of unequal lengths

*Directions:*
1. On each strip of paper, write vertically a short poem or wish.
2. Tape or glue the strips of paper to the dowel, so that they hang down like streamers.
3. Attach the two ends of the ribbon to the two ends of the dowel.
4. Hang your "wind poem" outside, so that the wind can carry your poem or wishes away!

# New Colonies in the New World

CHAPTER 6

## Encyclopedia Cross-References

*UBWH 148-149, UILE 322-323*
*KIHW 408-409, 427 KHE 248-249, 259*

## STRANGERS AND SAINTS IN PLYMOUTH

### Review Questions

What did a Puritan want to happen to the Church of England? *A Puritan wanted the Church purified of candles, incense, altars, priests, prayer-books, and anything else borrowed from the Catholic church.*

What did Separatists think about the Church of England? *They didn't think the church would ever be pure, so they separated and held their own services.*

Which king made the Separatists pay high taxes and kept them from using church buildings? *King James made them pay high taxes and kept them from using church buildings.*

When the Separatists fled England, which country did they go to first? *They first went to Holland (the Netherlands).*

What was the name of the ship the Separatists used to travel to America? *The ship was named the* Mayflower.

Who were the "Strangers"? *Strangers were colonists who were not Separatists.*

What new name did William Bradford give to the two groups of colonists (the Strangers and the Saints)? *William Bradford called them all Pilgrims.*

What did the Mayflower Compact say? *It said that all colonists must agree together before a law could be passed, and that every colonist must obey the laws.*

What happened to the Pilgrims during their first winter? *They ran out of food, and started to die from fever, scurvy, and starvation.*

What was the name of the Wampanoag warrior who taught the Pilgrims how to grow crops? *His name was Squanto.*

What name did the Pilgrims give to their colony? *They called it Plymouth Plantation.*

Whom did the Pilgrims invite to the first Thanksgiving? *They invited Massasoit and other Wampanoag Indians.*

What was the purpose of the Thanksgiving Feast? *The Pilgrims wanted to thank God for their survival.*

What other colony soon formed near Plymouth Plantation? *The colony of Massachusetts Bay soon formed.*

### Narration Exercise

"William Bradford and other Separatists left England and sailed to Holland. But in Holland, the children of the Separatists forgot English and left their beliefs. So the Separatists joined with other colonists and went to North America. They established a colony in Massachusetts, called Plymouth Bay. At first, the colonists nearly starved, but they made friends with the Wampanoag and Massasoit Indians, who helped them grow food. Soon, more Puritans came to Massachusetts and built a colony called Massachusetts Bay." OR

"Puritans wanted to purify the Church of England. Separatists left the Church of England and had their own services. King James made Separatists pay high taxes and wouldn't let them use church buildings, so some

Separatists decided to find a new place to live. First, they tried Holland. Then they sailed to North America and tried to establish a colony in Massachusetts. The Indians took pity on the Pilgrims and helped them survive. The Pilgrims held the first Thanksgiving to thank God for their survival. They invited the Indians to celebrate with them."

## THE DUTCH IN THE NEW WORLD

### Review Questions

What were the English, French, and Spanish settlements in the New World known as? *The settlements were known as New England, New France, and New Spain.*

What goods did the Dutch captains bring back from the countries of Asia? *They brought back silks, spices, tea, and coffee.*

What was the name of the company that sent Dutch families to settle near the Hudson River? *The company was called the Dutch West India Company.*

What city did the Dutch West India Company build on Manhattan Island? *They built the city of New Amsterdam on Manhattan Island.*

According to stories, how did the Dutch get the island for themselves? *The Dutch bought Manhattan Island from the Lenape tribe for twenty-four dollars.*

What problems did the governors of New Amsterdam have? *The town began to fall apart, and no one fixed the houses; pigs and cows were in the streets, eating garbage; settlers and traders got drunk; the fort was collapsing; the church fell down.*

What strong governor did the Dutch West India Company finally send to fix New Amsterdam? *They sent Peter Stuyvesant.*

What unusual physical feature did Peter Stuyvesant have? *He had a wooden peg leg.*

Name two laws that Peter Stuyvesant made to improve New Amsterdam. *Colonists had to pay more for wine and beer; pigs and goats had to be kept in fences; pubs had to close at night and on Sundays; ministers had to preach more sermons.*

What was Peter Stuyvesant afraid of? *He was afraid that the English might invade.*

What did the new king of England, Charles II, declare about the Dutch land in New Netherland? *He said that New Netherland was his, and he gave it to the Duke of York for a present.*

Who captured New Amsterdam from Peter Stuyvesant, and what did they rename the town? *The English captured it and named it New York.*

### Narration Exercise

"The English and the French were settling in the New World, and the Dutch also wanted some land. They wanted to build a settlement on Manhattan Island, but to do that, they had to buy the land from the Lenape Indians. Peter Stuyvesant helped organize the new colony, called New Amsterdam. But the English came and took over, renaming the colony New York. This was the end of the Dutch settlement in this part of North America." OR

"The Dutch wanted to settle in the New World, so they organized their merchants into one company—the Dutch West India Company. The Dutch merchants visited the New World, especially the Hudson River area. They built a settlement called New Amsterdam, which was out of control until Peter Stuyvesant came.

The English eventually conquered New Amsterdam and renamed it New York. Peter Stuyvesant loved New York so much that he wanted to stay. Even though he was no longer in charge, he retired to his farm in New York."

## Additional History Reading

*The Adventurous Life of Myles Standish and the Amazing-but-True Survival Story of Plymouth Colony: Barbary Pirates, the Mayflower, the First Thanksgiving, and Much, Much More*, by Cheryl Harness, (National Geographic Children's Books, 2007). For stronger readers, this book contains all kinds of information about the *Mayflower* voyage. (RA 4, IR 6)

*. . . If You Sailed on the Mayflower in 1620*, by Ann McGovern, illus. Anna DiVito (Scholastic, 1991). A beginners' book about life on the *Mayflower* and in early colonial days. (IR 2-4)

*The Landing of the Pilgrims*, by James Daugherty (Random House, 1981). For good readers, this classic story of the Pilgrim journey uses the journal entries written by the Pilgrims themselves. (IR 4-6)

*The Library of the Pilgrims*, by Susan Whitehurst (Powerkids Press, 2002). An easy-reader series covering different aspects of Pilgrim history and daily life; good for second and third grade readers, as well as reluctant fourth graders.

*The Pilgrims Before the Mayflower*

*The Mayflower*

*Plymouth: Surviving the First Winter*

*The First Thanksgiving*

*A Plymouth Partnership: Pilgrims and Native Americans*

*William Bradford and Plymouth: A Colony Grows*

*The Massachusetts Colony* by Kevin Cunningham (Scholastic, 2011). A brief history of Massachusetts' indigenous peoples, daily life, exploration and settlement by Europeans. (IR 2-4)

*Mayflower 1620: A New Look at a Pilgrim Voyage*, by Plimoth Plantation, (National Geographic Children's Books, 2007). This book includes first-person accounts of life on the *Mayflower*, and photographs from a re-enactment of the voyage. (RA 3, IR 4)

*The Mayflower Compact: Documenting U.S. History* by Elizabeth Raum (Heinemann, 2012). A well illustrated book about one of the most significant documents in U.S. history—outlining the governance of Plymouth Colony. (RA 1-2, IR 3-6)

*Squanto, Friend of the Pilgrims*, by Clyde Robert Bulla (Scholastic, 1990). A classic first chapter book, telling about Squanto's life from childhood until the arrival of the Pilgrims. (IR 2-4)

*William Bradford: Pilgrim Boy* by Bradford Smith and illustrated by Robert Doremus (Beautiful Feet Books, 2003). A biography of William Bradford's early life growing up in England and eventual settling in America's first colony. (RA 1-2, IR 3-6)

*Life in New Amsterdam*, by Laura Fischer, (Chicago Review Press, 2012). A history of New York beginning in the days of New Amsterdam. Includes a timeline, maps, and activities. (RA 2, IR 3)

*Peter Stuyvesant: New Amsterdam and the Origins of New York*, by L.J. Krizner, Lisa Sita, (Powerplus, 2002). Plenty of illustrations accompany the text in this book about New Amsterdam and Peter Stuyvesant. (RA 3, IR 5)

*The New Americans: Colonial Times, 1620-1689*, by Betsy Maestro and Giulio Maestro (HarperCollins, 2004). Short informative paragraphs and plenty of full-color illustrations, for less advanced readers. (IR 2-5)

## Corresponding Literature Suggestions

*An Early American Christmas*, by Tomie dePaola (Holiday House, 1992). A German family in colonial New England prepares for Christmas: making candles, stringing dried apples, baking, making paper ornaments, and more. (IR 2-4). **E-Only.**

*Finding Providence: The Story of Roger Williams*, by Avi, illus. James Watling (HarperTrophy, 1997). In this chapter book, Roger Williams' little daughter tells about Williams' departure from the Massachusetts Bay Colony because of his dissension. (RA 2, IR 3-5)

*Peter and the Pilgrims*, by Louise A. Vernon (Herald Press, 2002). For advanced readers, a novel about a ten-year-old orphan who joins the Separatists and journeys with them, first to Holland and then to America. (IR 5-7)

*The Pilgrims of Plimouth*, by Marcia Sewall (Atheneum, 1986). Fictionalized first-person accounts of different Plymouth residents, based on original sources; for strong third grade readers or older (some difficult vocabulary). (RA 1-3, IR 3-6)

*Sarah Morton's Day: A Day in the Life of a Pilgrim Girl*, by Kate Waters, illus. Russ Kendall (Scholastic, 1989). A young Plymouth villager describes her life; illustrated with photographs of re-enactors at Plimouth Plantation. (RA 1, IR 2-4)

*Thanksgiving on Thursday*, by Mary Pope Osborne (Random House, 2002). The Magic Tree House takes Jack and Annie back to 1621 in this beginning chapter book. (IR 3-4)

*Three Young Pilgrims*, by Cheryl Harness (Simon & Schuster, 1992). In this advanced picture book, three Pilgrim children (based on real figures) suffer through one difficult year in the Plymouth colony. (RA 2, IR 3-4)

*On the Day Peter Stuyvesant Sailed Into Town*, by Arnold Lobel (HarperTrophy, 1987). Out of print, but well worth a library trip. The governor of Amsterdam arrives and starts issuing orders to clean up the dingy city—all in rhyming verse! (RA 1, IR 2-4) **LFA**

## MAP WORK

### Separatists in England, Holland, and Plymouth Plantation *(Student Page 16, answer 321)*

1. William Bradford and the Separatists lived in England. Color England orange.
2. The Separatists left England for Holland. Using a pen or pencil, draw an arrow from England to Leiden, Holland. Draw an orange circle around the dot that represents Leiden.
3. The Separatists began to forget their English customs in Holland. So they left and sailed to North America. Use a pen or pencil and draw an arrow from Leiden to the dot that represents Plymouth Plantation, in North America. Draw an orange circle around the dot that represents Plymouth Plantation.
4. European countries were establishing colonies in the New World. Color France red. Then underline "New France" in red.
5. Holland was also establishing a colony in North America. Color Holland purple (but don't color over your orange circle around Leiden), and then underline "Manhattan Island" in purple.

**COLORING PAGE** Squanto was a Wampanoag man who taught the Pilgrims how to grow crops so that they could have enough food. *(Student Page 17)*

## PROJECTS

### ACTIVITY PROJECT Make Your Own Mayflower Compact

When the Saints and Strangers landed on the shores of North America, they agreed that they would govern their colony together and that they would all obey the same rules. This agreement was called the Mayflower Compact. Here are the words of the Mayflower Compact, with the names of the signers beneath:

*In the name of God, Amen. We, whose names are underwritten, the Loyal Subjects of our dread Sovereign Lord, King James, by the Grace of God, of England, France and Ireland, King, Defender of the Faith, etcetera.*

*Having undertaken for the Glory of God, and Advancement of the Christian Faith, and the Honour of our King and Country, a voyage to plant the first colony in the northern parts of Virginia; do by these presents, solemnly and mutually in the Presence of God and one of another, covenant and combine ourselves together into a civil Body Politick, for our better Ordering and Preservation, and Furtherance of the Ends aforesaid; And by Virtue hereof to enact, constitute, and frame, such just and equal Laws, Ordinances, Acts, Constitutions and Offices, from time to time, as shall be thought most meet and convenient for the General good of the Colony; unto which we promise all due submission and obedience.*

*In Witness whereof we have hereunto subscribed our names at Cape Cod the eleventh of November, in the Reign of our Sovereign Lord, King James of England, France and Ireland, the eighteenth, and of Scotland the fifty-fourth. Anno Domini, 1620.*

*Mr. John Carver*
*Mr. William Brewster*
*John Alden*
*James Chilton*
*Joses Fletcher*
*Mr. Christopher Martin*
*Mr. Richard Warren*
*Digery Priest*
*Edmund Margesson*
*George Soule*
*Francis Cooke*
*John Ridgdale*
*Richard Gardiner*
*Edward Doten*
*Mr. William Bradford*
*Isaac Allerton*
*John Turner*
*John Craxton*
*John Goodman*
*Mr. William Mullins*
*John Howland*
*Thomas Williams*
*Peter Brown*
*Edward Tilly*
*Thomas Rogers*
*Edward Fuller*
*Mr. John Allerton*
*Edward Liester*
*Mr. Edward Winslow*
*Myles Standish*
*Francis Eaton*
*John Billington*
*Mr. Samuel Fuller*
*Mr. William White*
*Mr. Steven Hopkins*
*Gilbert Winslow*
*Richard Britteridge*
*John Tilly*
*Thomas Tinker*
*Richard Clark*
*Thomas English*

Now, make up your own Mayflower Compact for your home, your co-op group, or your school classroom.

*Materials:*
- ☐ Student Page 18: Our Mayflower Compact
- ☐ Pencil
- ☐ Scratch paper

*Directions:*

Write down together the answers to the following questions.

1. Who is your "top official"—parent, teacher, principal? List that person's official position or title.

2. What is that person's name?
3. What "realm" does that "official" rule over? Home, classroom?
4. What project, task, or undertaking are you all gathered together into? (A family, a co-op class, or what?)
5. Why are you gathered together into a group? What is your purpose?
6. What is your group name for yourself?
7. What town and state are you in?
8. What is the day?
9. What is the month?
10. What is the year?

Now fill these into the blanks in "Our Mayflower Compact" (Student Page 18). Read it out loud. You have just promised to obey the rules that your group makes for the general good of all! Don't forget to sign the compact.

## COOKING PROJECT Thanksgiving Feast—With Wampanoag Dishes

When you think of Thanksgiving Day, you probably think about turkeys and Pilgrims. The Pilgrims did cook turkeys for their first Thanksgiving—but the Wampanoag Indians brought food too! As a matter of fact, the Wampanoag gave us some of their food words. "Pumpkin," "squash," and "succotash" are all Wampanoag words. (So are "skunk" and "moose"!) Cook these traditional Native American dishes and add them to turkey for a real First Thanksgiving feast!

### Traditional Wampanoag Cornbread (With Modern Ingredients)

*Ingredients:*
½ stick of butter, melted
1 egg
1 ¼ cup milk
1 ¼ cup corn meal
1 cup regular flour
1 ½ tsp salt
1 ½ Tbs baking powder
½ cup sugar

*Directions:*
1. Beat melted margarine, egg, and milk together into a bowl.
2. Add dry ingredients on top of the wet ingredients. (Be sure to sprinkle the baking powder over the dry ingredients last). Beat together vigorously until smooth.
3. Pour into a greased 8" x 8" or 9" x 9" pan.
4. Bake at 350° for 35 minutes.

### Traditional "Indian" Pudding

*Ingredients:*
¼ cup brown sugar
1 tsp salt
½ cup cornmeal
1 Tbs cinnamon
⅔ cup raisins
4 eggs
3 cups milk
½ cup molasses
2 Tbs butter

*Directions:*

1. Stir the cornmeal into the milk. Microwave for 2 minutes. Stir again. Microwave for an additional 2 minutes. Stir again. Microwave for 1 minute. Stir until smooth. (You can also do this on the stovetop; it will take 10-12 minutes over low heat)
2. Add the butter and stir until it melts.
3. Add the sugar, molasses, cinnamon, and salt. Stir until smooth.
4. Add the eggs and stir until smooth.
5. Add the raisins.
6. Pour into a greased pie plate or 8" x 8" casserole dish.
7. Bake at 325 for 50 minutes. Eat while it's warm!

### Sixteenth-Century Succotash

*Ingredients:*

2 cups sweet corn (shelled—frozen or canned)
2 cups beans (lima or canned kidney beans, or mixed)
2 Tbs oil (in the 16th century, this would be bear or moose fat!)
1 small chopped onion or ½ cup chopped green onions or scallions
4 slices uncooked bacon (in the 16th century, this would be salted fat meat from a bear, pig, or other wild animal)
¼ cup cornmeal

*Directions:*

1. In a heavy saucepan, cook the onion in the oil until it is slightly browned.
2. Add the corn and beans. Stir the cornmeal into the mixture.
3. Add enough water to cover the corn and beans.
4. Add the uncooked bacon. Simmer until the bacon is cooked. Add more water as necessary. The succotash will have a thickened broth, flavored with the bacon.

### Stewed Pompion

Sixteenth-century English men and women called both pumpkins and squash "pompions"—until the Wampanoag taught them the word "squash." At the first Thanksgiving, there probably weren't any pumpkin pies, but there was most likely a dish of "pompion"!

*Ingredients:*

3 cups of cooked squash (mashed) or canned pumpkin
3 Tbs butter
2 tsp cider vinegar
1 ½ tsp ground ginger
1/2 tsp salt

*Directions:* In a heavy saucepan, stir all the ingredients together over medium heat until hot. Serve while still warm. (Don't expect pumpkin pudding; this is *not* a sweet recipe!)

## ART PROJECT The Manhattan Letter

Many historians have suggested that the story about the Dutch buying Manhattan Island for $24 is inaccurate. The only document hinting at such a purchase is a letter written by a Dutchman named Pieter Jansen Schagen to the government of the Netherlands, on November 5, 1626. Pieter was in Amsterdam, in Holland. In this letter, he explains that a ship has just arrived from North America with furs and wood from New Netherland.

Here is the exact text of this letter. The "Mauritius" is the Dutch name for the Hudson River. (Note to parent or teacher: read this letter out loud to the student, since it contains colloquial spellings)

*High Mighty Sirs:*

*Here arrived yesterday the ship the* Arms of Amsterdam, *which sailed from New Netherland out of the Mauritius River on September 23; they reported that our people there are of good courage, and live peaceably. Their women, also, have borne children there, they have bought the island Manhattes from the wild men for the value of sixty guilders, it is 11,000 morgens in extent. They sowed all their grain in the middle of May, and harvested it in the middle of August. Thereof being samples of summer grain, such as wheat, rye, barley, oats, buckwheat, canary seed, small beans, and flax.*

*The cargo of the aforesaid ship is:*
*7246 beaver skins, 178.5 otter skins,*
*675 otter skins, 48 mink skins,*
*36 wild-cat skins, 33 mink, 34 rat skins.*
*Many logs of oak and nut-wood.*

*Herewith be ye, High Mighty Sirs, commended to the Almighty's grace, in Amsterdam, November 5, Anno 1626.*
*Your High Might.'s Obedient,*
*P. Schagen*

Materials:
- ☐ Student Page 19: Pieter Schagan's Letter
- ☐ Colored pencils or crayons

Directions: Imagine that you are Pieter Jansen Schagen, anxious to show the government of the Netherlands all the riches of the New World. Draw pictures around the margins of the letter, showing the different animals, grains, and trees mentioned in the letter. Sign the letter with Pieter's signature!

## Activity Project **Play Old Silvernails**

Peter Stuyvesant was known for his wooden leg. Play Peter Stuyvesant for the day!

Materials:
- ☐ Toilet plunger (carefully washed in hot soapy water! Or buy a new one)
- ☐ Aluminum foil
- ☐ Duct tape

Directions:
1. Tear the aluminum foil into narrow strips. Wrap three strips around the handle of the toilet plunger at varying intervals.
2. Turn the toilet plunger upside down. Stand on one foot and hold your other heel against your bottom with your free hand. Place your knee in the bowl of the plunger. Use the duct tape to attach the plunger to your knee (loop the tape underneath the bell of the plunger and then bring it up over the back of your bent knee). BE SURE THAT YOU ARE WEARING LONG PANTS!
3. Now try to walk. Pretend you are Peter Stuyvesant, walking on his silver-banded peg leg. Is it difficult? How much noise does the wooden leg make as you stalk around the house?

# The Spread of Slavery

## Encyclopedia Cross-References

*UBWH 141, 149-151 UILE 324-325*
*KIHW 409, 414 margin, 450-451, KHE 270-273*

## TOBACCO—AND UNWILLING COLONISTS

### Review Questions

Were the English able to find any gold or jewels in Virginia? *No, they were not.*

What did John Rolfe plant in Virginia? *He planted some seeds of Spanish tobacco.*

What did the young men of England think about smoking? *They smoked constantly, and some even had servants to carry their tobacco equipment.*

What did King James think about smoking? *He thought it was a dangerous and disgusting habit.*

What did people in England think of the new type of tobacco? *They loved to smoke it, and they bought all that the colonists could grow!*

Name three of the activities that made growing tobacco such hard work. *Seeds had to be hand-planted, hand-weeded, and hand-pruned; caterpillars and worms had to be picked off; leaves were taken off one at a time and hung to dry; stems were removed; leaves were packed into barrels.*

At first, whom did the tobacco farmers hire to work in their fields? *They hired indentured servants.*

What did the indentured servants get in exchange for six years' work? *They got food and a place to live, and at the end of their time they received some clothes and money to help them get started on their own.*

Whom did the Jamestown colonists start using to work on their farms in 1619? *They started using African slaves.*

Who brought these slaves to the New World? *European traders brought slaves to North America and South America.*

What do we call the slave trade that went from Africa to Central America, to Europe, and back to Africa again? *We call it the Triangular Trade.*

### Narration Exercise

"The Native Americans in Virginia grew their own tobacco, but the colonists didn't like the taste of those tobacco leaves. John Rolfe planted some Spanish tobacco seeds, and the tobacco from those seeds was popular among the colonists and among people in London, England. The Virginia tobacco became so popular that the colonists were soon growing tobacco everywhere they could. But farmers needed many workers to grow tobacco. The Virginia colonists relied on slaves to do much of the hard work involved in growing tobacco. They bought the slaves from European traders."OR

"The colonists in Virginia learned to grow tobacco. This made England happy because it could get tobacco from someone other than their enemy, Spain. As the tobacco fields grew larger and larger, they required more and more work. At first, farmers used servants. Then, after a Dutch ship sold some slaves to Virginia planters, the colony used many slaves to do the hard work involved in growing the tobacco. These slaves were brought to Virginia in the Triangular Trade. They were unwilling colonists, and they could never return home to Africa."

### Review Questions

Besides the Dutch, what other European nation had been taking slaves from the west coast of Africa? *The Portuguese had been getting slaves from West Africa.*

Who was Nzinga? *She was a princess, a daughter of the ruler of Ndomba on the western coast of Africa.*

Why were the Portuguese friendly to the African kings who lived near the coast? *They wanted to receive prisoners of war that they could sell as slaves.*

How did the Portuguese change their methods during the reign of Nzinga's father? *Instead of buying prisoners as they had been doing, they tried to conquer a piece of Africa to keep, so that they could have a steady supply of slaves.*

What did Nzinga's brother Mbandi do as soon as he became king? *He drove Nzinga out of the kingdom.*

After Nzinga's brother Mbandi had become king and had fought the Portuguese for a few years, what did he ask Nzinga to do? *He asked Nzinga to meet the Portuguese in order to make a peace treaty with them.*

When the Portuguese leader tried to make Nzinga sit on the floor for their meeting, what did Nzinga do? *She used one of her servants as a human chair!*

Did the peace treaty with the Portuguese last? *No, the Portuguese invaded Ndomba again.*

What happened to Mbandi? *He died. Maybe Nzinga poisoned him!*

What did Nzinga spend the rest of her life doing? *She spent the rest of her life fighting the Portuguese.*

What happened after Nzinga's death? *The Portuguese took her kingdom and two others and named their new colony Angola.*

### Narration Exercise

"The Portuguese made friends with powerful African kings on the coast of Africa. They wanted the many prisoners that these kings had captured, so that they could sell them as slaves. But soon the Portuguese wanted some of Africa for their own. Nzinga's brother would not stand up to the Portuguese. But Nzinga did. She spent her life fighting against the Portuguese. The Portuguese finally gave up—but after Nzinga's death, they took her country and named it Angola." OR

"The Portuguese had taken slaves from the African coast for many years. They wanted a place that was all their own, so they tried to take over a place called Ndomba. Nzinga's father fought hard against the Portuguese. When Nzinga's father died, her cowardly brother took over and sent Nzinga away. But he asked her to come back and help him fight! Nzinga finally gained control and fought against the Portuguese for the rest of her life. When she died, the Portuguese took over and ruled the area for the next 300 years."

## Additional History Reading

*Tobacco (Drugs in Real Life)*, Carol Hand, (Essential Library, 2018). Explores health aspects of smoking and tobacco, as well as its history. (RA 2, IR 3)

*The Asante of West Africa*, by Jamie Hetfield (Powerkids Press, 1996). A simple, easy-reader book about the history of the Asante of Ghana, with many illustrations. (RA 1, IR 2-3)

*The Benin Kingdom of West Africa*, by John Peffer-Engels (Powerkids Press, 1996). A simple, easy-reader book about the history of the Edo people of Benin, with many illustrations. (RA 1, IR 2-3)

*The Dogon of West Africa,* by Christine Cornell (Powerkids Press, 1996). A simple, easy-reader book about the history of the Dogon people, with many illustrations. (RA 1, IR 2-3) **LFA**

*The Yoruba of West Africa,* by Jamie Hetfield (Powerkids Press, 1996). A simple, easy-reader book about the history of the West African tribe, many of whom came to America as slaves. (RA 1, IR 2-3) **LFA**

*Hard Labor: The First African Americans* by Patricia C. McKissack, Fredrick L. McKissack and illustrated by Joseph Daniel Fiedler (Aladdin, 2003). An account of the first Africans who came to Jamestown as indentured servants and their hopes for a future. (IR 3-6)

*If You Lived When there Was Slavery in America,* by Anne Kamma, (Scholastic, 2004). An overview of slavery in America, what it was like and how it worked. (RA 1, IR 3)

*The Middle Passage: White Ships, Black Cargo,* by Tom Feelings (Dial Books, 1995). Although this is a picture book, the illustrations of the Middle Passage voyage are disturbing and violent; highly recommended for adults, but preview every picture for young students; you may wish to show them only one or two illustrations as you discuss slavery. (RA 3-6)

*The Strength of These Arms: Life in the Slave Quarters,* by Raymond Bial (Houghton Mifflin, 1997). Although it describes a slightly later period, this photograph-filled book illustrates the difference between the lives of free whites and enslaved blacks in America. (RA 2-3, IR 4-6)

*100 Great African Kings and Queens (Vol. 1)* by Pusch Commey (CreateSpace Independent Publishing Platform, 2014). This book chronicles the amazing exploits of various monarchs of the African continent, including Queen Nzinga. (RA 1-2, IR 3-6)

## Corresponding Literature Suggestions

*Africa is My Home: A Child of the Amistad* by Monica Edinger and illustrated by Robert Byrd Candlewick, 2015). A well-illustrated story of a child who arrives in America aboard the slave ship *Amistad* and eventually makes her way home to Africa. (IR 4-6)

*Amistad Rising: A Story of Freedom,* by Veronica Chambers, illus. Paul Lee (Harcourt, 1998). This detailed picture book is beginning historical fiction, told from the point of view of Joseph Cinque, the historical leader of the African slaves who seized their slave ship and asked for freedom. (RA 2, IR 3-5. For good readers, consider Walter Dean Myers' paperback *Amistad: A Long Road to Freedom,* written for advanced 5th through 7th grade readers.) **OOP**

*Amistad: The Story of a Slave Ship* by Patricia McKissack and illustrated by Sanna Stanley (Penguin Young Readers, 2005). Another story of the brave young African captives who took over their captors' ship in an attempt to win their freedom. (RA 1-2, IR 3-5)

*Africa Dream,* by Eloise Greenfield (Harpercollins, 1992). A young American girl dreams of her ancestral village in Africa long ago. (RA 1, IR 2-4)

*Circle Unbroken,* by Margot Theis Raven, (Square Fish 2007). This story links a girl in America and a boy in Africa weaving traditional baskets. (RA Pre-school IR 3)

*In the Time of the Drums,* by Kim Siegelson (Jump Sun, 1999). A plantation slave in Georgia tells her young grandson an old Ibo legend about the coming of freedom. (RA 1, IR 2-4)

*The Village That Vanished,* by Ann Grifalconi, illus. Kadir Nelson (Puffin Books, 2004). A marvelous and evocative picture book about an African community that wipes out all traces of its village to deceive Arab slave traders. (RA 1-2, IR 3-4)

*Heart and Soul: The Story of America and African Americans,* by Kadir Nelson, (Balzer + Bray, 2013). Through the voice of an elderly woman, tells the story of the history of African Americans. (RA1, IR 4)

*Mumbet's Declaration of Independence,* by Gretchen Woelfle, (Carolrhoda Books, 2014). A fictionalized version of the life of Mumbet, a slave who challenged the legality of slavery. (RA K, IR 2)

*The People Could Fly,* by Virginia Hamilton, Leo Dillon illus. Diane Dillon (Knopf Books for Young Readers, 1993). This classic anthology of African-American folk tales contains many different kinds of stories. (RA 1, IR 3)

*Unbound* by Ann Burg (Scholastic Press, 2018). This book, written in verse, is about a nine-year-old girl and her family who must endure trials and tribulations on their road to freedom. (RA 2-3, IR 4-6)

*Virginia Bound* by Amy Butler (Clarion Books, 2003). A young teenager and his friend are kidnapped from the streets of London and sold to work in Jamestown as indentured servants where they must endure great hardships. (IR 4-7)

*Nzingha, Warrior Queen of Matamba: The Royal Diaries,* by Patricia McKissack (Scholastic, 2000). This fictionalized account of Nzinga's childhood ends before she begins her rule, but supplies details of daily life in her tribe and includes a brief historical essay at the end. For stronger readers. (IR 4-6)

## MAP WORK

### Triangular Trade Route *(Student Page 20, answer 321)*

1. The English bought tobacco, or "green gold," from Virginians. Trace the dotted arrow in green from Virginia to England. Write "tobacco" on the arrow.
2. Draw the three arrows of the Triangular Trade Route in blue. Trace the first arrow from Portugal to Ndomba, on the west coast of Africa.
3. Trace the second arrow from Ndomba to the West Indies.
4. Trace the third arrow from the West Indies back to Portugal, in Europe.
5. Above each arrow, write one of the "products" that was on the ship as completed that leg of the journey. Above the arrow that points from Africa to the West Indies, write "slaves." Above the arrow that points from the West Indies to Portugal, write "sugar," "molasses," or "cotton." Above the arrow that points from Portugal to Ndomba, write "European goods."
6. Ndomba remained under Portuguese control. Color Portugal purple, and then draw a purple box around Ndomba.

### Coloring Page

When Queen Nzinga came to meet with the Portuguese who were invading her country, they didn't give her a chair to sit in. So she sat on one of her own servants instead. *(Student Page 21)*

## PROJECTS

### Art Project — King James's Anti-Tobacco Poster

Tobacco was used in America long before the English arrived. When Columbus first landed on the Central American island of San Salvador, the natives who came out to meet him offered him dried tobacco leaves. They rolled up these leaves and smoked them, chewed them, and sniffed the dried powder up their noses!

Smoking in England probably began around 1586, when Sir Francis Drake rescued English settlers from a failing colony on Roanoke Island (in present-day North Carolina) and brought them back to England—along with a shipload of tobacco. Sir Walter Raleigh, the famous courtier who lived in Queen Elizabeth's day, made smoking even more popular. He showed other courtiers how to smoke, and tried to grow tobacco on his own lands, both in the New World and in England. Smoking caught on at once!

When James became king, he wanted Englishmen to stop smoking. So he wrote his famous essay *Counterblaste to Tobacco*—and gave it to everyone at court! In King James's time, there weren't advertisements or public service announcements or posters. Instead, people wrote essays if they wanted to change the way others acted.

A long portion of King James's essay is printed below. (The ellipses [. . .] show where words have been left out. Words in brackets are not in the original.)

*Materials:*

- ☐ Poster board
- ☐ Markers or crayons
- ☐ Pictures of tobacco (plants or cigarettes) cut out of magazines
- ☐ *Counterblaste to Tobacco* essay (below)

*Directions:*

1. Read the three paragraphs above to the student, so that he understands the background of tobacco smoking in England.
2. Read the *Counterblaste to Tobacco* essay below out loud (or have the student read it).
3. Help the student choose 1-3 sentences (or parts of sentences) from the essay below. Give the student any necessary assistance in writing those sentences onto the poster board as the slogan of "King James's Anti-Smoking Poster."
4. Illustrate the poster with drawings or cut-out pictures from magazines.

**Counterblaste to Tobacco**

. . . I am now therefore heartily to pray you to consider, first upon what false and erroneous grounds you have first built the general good liking [of tobacco]; and next what sins towards God, and foolish vanities before the world you commit in the detestable use of it. . . . It is thought by you . . . that the brains of all men being naturally cold and wet, all dry and hot things should be good for them, of which nature this stinking suffumigation is, and therefore of good use to them. Of this argument both the proposition and assumption are false . . . For as to the proposition that because the brains are cold and moist, therefore things that are hot and dry are best for them; it is an inept consequence. . . . The application [to the brains] of a thing of a contrary nature is . . . hurtful to the health of the whole body; as if a man, because the liver is as the fountain of blood, and as it were an oven to the stomach, would therefore apply and wear close upon his liver and stomach a cake of lead. . . . And as if because the heart is full of vital spirits, and in perpetual motion, a man would therefore lay a heavy pound stone on his breast for staying and holding down that wanton palpitation. I doubt not but his breast would be more bruised with the weight thereof than the heart would be comforted with such a disagreeable and contrarious cure. And even so is it with the brains, for if a man, because the brains are cold and humid should therefore use . . . things of hot and dry qualities, all the gain that he could make thereof would only be to . . . run mad.

. . . Tobacco is not simply of a dry and hot quality but rather hath a certain venomous faculty joined with the heat thereof which makes it have an antipathy against nature. . . . [Those who smoke argue that] this filthy smoke, as well through the heat and strength thereof, as by a natural force and quality, is able and fit to purge both the head and stomach of rheums and distillations as experience teaches by the spitting and voiding phlegm immediately after the taking of it. But the fallacy of this argument may easily appear. . . . This stinking smoke, being sucked up by the nose and imprisoned in the cold and moist brains, is by their cold and wet faculty turned and cast forth again in watery distillations, and so are you made free and purged of nothing, but that wherewith you wilfully burdened yourselves, and therefore are you no wiser in taking Tobacco for purging you . . . than, if for preventing [stomach aches], you would take all kind of windy meats and drinks. . . . and then, when you were forced to void much wind out of your stomach . . . that you should attribute the thank, therefore, to such nourishments.

. . . How easily the mind of any people wherewith God hath replenished this world may be drawn to the foolish affection of any novelty! . . . Such is the force of that natural self-love in every one of us, and such is the corruption of envy bred in the breast of every one as we cannot be content unless we imitate every thing that our fellows do, and so prove ourselves capable of every thing whereof they are capable, like apes counterfeiting the manners of others to our own destruction. . . . The general good liking and embracing of this foolish custom doth but only proceed from that affectation of novelty and popular error whereof I have already spoken.

. . . [But what of its use] by able, young, strong, healthful men? . . . Let a man, I say, but take as often the best sorts of nourishments in meat and drink that can be devised, he shall with the continual use thereof weaken both his head and his stomach. All members shall become feeble; his spirits dull; and in the end, as a drowsy, lazy belly-god, he shall fade away in a lethargy. And from this weakness it precedes that many in this kingdom have had such a continual use of taking this unsavory smoke, as now they are not able to forbear the same no more than an old drunkard can abide to be long sober without falling into an incurable weakness and evil constitution. For their continual custom hath made to them *habitual alter am natural* ["Habit changes nature itself."] So, to those that from their birth have continually nourished upon poison, and things venomous, wholesome meats are only poison.

. . . It rests only to inform you what sins and vanities you commit in the filthy abuse thereof: First, are you not guilty of sinful and shameful lust, that . . . you can neither be merry at an ordinary [feast] . . . if you lack tobacco to provoke your appetite to any of those sorts of recreation, lusting after it as the children of Israel did in the wilderness after quails. Secondly: it is as you use, or rather abuse, it a branch of the sin of drunkenness, which is the root of all sins; for as the only delight that drunkards take in wine is in the strength of the taste, and the force of the fume thereof that mounts up to the brain, for no drunkards love any weak or sweet drink. So are not those (I mean the strong heat fume) the only qualities that make tobacco so delectable to all the lovers of it? And no man likes strong heady drink the first day (because *nenia repentefit turpissimus* ["No man becomes a villain all at once"]) but by custom is piece and piece allured. . . . So is not this the very case of all the great takers of tobacco which therefore they themselves do attribute to a bewitching quality in it? Thirdly: Is it not the greatest sin of all that you, the people of all sorts of this kingdom who are created and ordained by God, to bestow both your persons and goods for the maintenance both of the honor and safety of your king and commonwealth, should disable yourselves in both? In your persons having, by this continual vile custom, brought yourselves to this shameful imbecility—that you are not able to ride or walk [a single hour] . . . but you must have a reeky coal brought to you from the next poor house to kindle your tobacco with. . . . To take a custom in any thing that cannot be left again is most harmful to the people of any land.

. . . And for the vanities committed in this filthy custom, is it not both great vanity and uncleanness that at the table, a place of respect, of cleanliness, of modesty, men should not be ashamed to sit tossing of tobacco pipes and puffing of the smoke of tobacco one to another, making the filthy smoke and stink thereof to exhale athwart the dishes and infect the air, when very often men that abhor it are at their repast? . . . Herein is not only a great vanity but a great contempt for God's good gifts, that a man's breath, being a good gift of God, should be wilfully corrupted by this stinking smoke. . . . Have you not reason then to be ashamed and to forbear this filthy novelty, so basely grounded, so foolishly received and so grossly mistaken in the right use thereof? In your abuse thereof, sinning against God, harming yourselves both in person and goods, and raking also thereby the marks and notes of vanity upon you. . . . making yourselves to be wondered at by all foreign civil nations, and by all strangers that come among you to be scorned and held in contempt; a custom loathsome to the eye, hateful to the nose, harmful to the brain, dangerous to the lungs, and in the black stinking fume thereof nearest resembling the horrible stygian smoke of the pit that is bottomless.

## Activity Project Growing "Tobacco"

Tobacco wasn't an easy crop to grow! First, the seeds were sown in beds. After they sprouted, they were transplanted and set out on hills, made four feet apart in cultivated fields. The fields had to be continually weeded to keep strong native grasses from choking the young plants. Then, the young plant had to be "topped" (the small tender top growth, including the bud, was removed, so that the leaves would continue to grow). Suckers—small growths between leaf and stem—had to be continually removed. Flies, caterpillars, and worms had to be continually shooed and removed by hand. When the plants were ready to be harvested, the leaves had to be picked by hand and hung on pegs to dry for six weeks. Then the leaves had to be taken down, the stems removed, and the leaves bound together. The bundles were packed into enormous barrels that weighed almost 500 pounds, and the barrels were rolled along to the docks and loaded onto tobacco ships! Get some feel for the difficulties of growing tobacco.

*Materials:*

- ☐ Seeds: raw peanuts (check your local grocery store), marigold seeds, kale seeds, or dried beans (soak for 24 hours before planting)
- ☐ 2 baking pans
- ☐ Potting soil
- ☐ Yard or garden dirt
- ☐ Thread or fine string
- ☐ Clothespins
- ☐ 2-3 small bottles or jars (baby food jars or pill bottles)
- ☐ Small scissors
- ☐ Fork

*Directions:*

1. Prepare your seeds for planting. Marigold or kale seeds need no preparation; dried beans should be soaked for 24 hours first. If you're using peanuts, make sure they are raw and not roasted!
2. Fill one of the baking pans with potting soil. Sow the seeds into it (NOT in rows, but scattered over the surface). Cover with a thin layer of potting soil; keep moist until plants sprout.
3. When plants are about ½ inch high, fill the second baking pan with yard or garden dirt. After the bottom of the pan is covered, make 6-8 small hills in the dirt. Transplant 6-8 of the young plants into the second pan, placing one in the center of each hill.
4. Over the course of 6-8 weeks, raise these plants to be as high as possible. Keep the dirt moist. "Cultivate" the dirt with a fork (it should sprout plenty of weeds!). Snip the tops out of the plants when they are 4-5 weeks old, to encourage them to bush out.
5. When the plants are about eight weeks old, "harvest" them. Carefully snip off the leaves. Hang the leaves to dry in a warm place (string a line of thread or string and clip the leaves on the string with the clothespins).
6. When the leaves are completely dry (5-7 days), take them down. Strip off the stems without crumbling the leaves. Tie the leaves together with thread or string into bundles of 5-6 leaves each.
7. Pack the leaves into your jars or bottles. How much "tobacco" has all of your labor yielded?

## CRAFT PROJECT Traditional West African Stamp Patterns

Angola was located in the western part of Africa. Tribes in this part of the country often used a traditional technique to decorate clothing and other items. This technique, called *adinkra,* separated the item to be decorated into squares and then stamped patterns onto each square.

*Materials:*

- ☐ White paper (several sheets, so that you can experiment!)
- ☐ Poster paint
- ☐ Sponge
- ☐ 1 large raw potato
- ☐ Small toys or items that might make interesting patterns if dipped in paint (should not be wider than 1")

*Directions:*

1. Divide the paper into 1" x ½" rectangles. You should have 8 columns and 11 rows.
2. Now, use the potato, sponge, and other items to make patterns in these squares. Cut the sponge into 1" squares, dip it into the paint, and press it down; cut the potato in half, mark a simple shape on the cut surface, and then cut away the potato from around the shape to make your own "stamp"; or dip the toys or other small items into paint and press them down on the surface of the squares. You might consider using some of the following shapes:

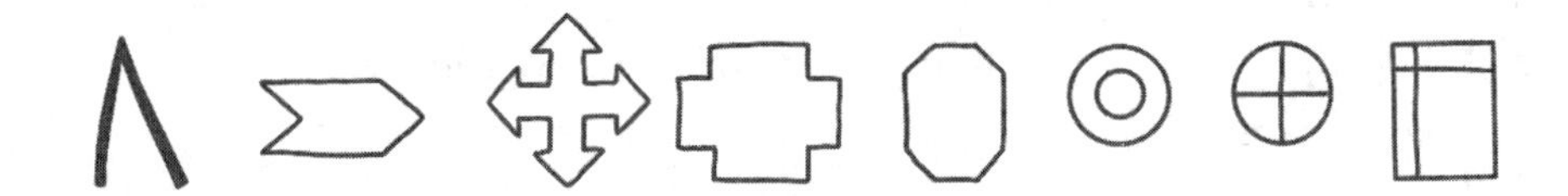

3. In *adinka,* you repeat your shapes in a pattern that runs diagonally, horizontally, or vertically. Alternate shapes, or place the same shape in a pattern of lines as illustrated below:

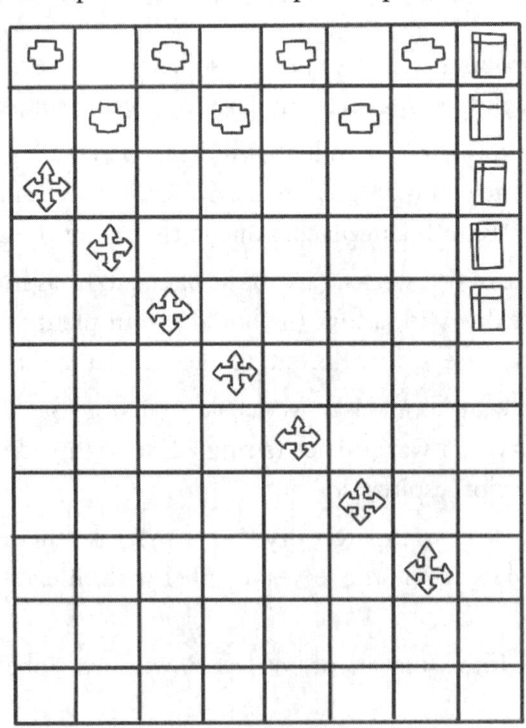

4. After you have decorated your paper, allow it to dry. Now you can use the blank side to make a greeting card, or to write a letter.

# The Middle of the East

## Encyclopedia Cross-References

*UBWH 142-143, UILE 298-299*
*KIHW 346-347, KHE 266*

## THE PERSIAN PUZZLE

### Review Questions

Instead of asking the student questions about the complicated history of the Middle East, try chanting together, in chronological order, the nations which have occupied this part of the world.

Assyria, Babylon,
Persia, Alexander the Great!
Seleucids, Parthians,
Sassanids, Islamic Empire!
Ghaznavid Turks, Mongols,
Safavids—now we've come to Abbas the Shah!

### Narration Exercise

"Many different nations claimed Persia! Finally the Safavids ruled over Persia. Their ruler was called the *shah.* Abbas I was the greatest Shah. He defeated the Ottoman Turks and made Persia into a great country. But he thought that his noblemen and his brothers, and even his son, were plotting against him." OR

"Today, we call Persia *Iran.* The greatest ruler of Iran was Abbas I. He made Persia prosperous and built roads, bridges, and a port. His port, Bandar Abbas, is still an important place in Iran!"

## THE OTTOMAN TURKS

### Review Questions

When the Ottoman empire grew weaker, which great and cruel ruler rescued it? *The Sultan Murad rescued it.*

Which group of people had founded the Ottoman empire? *The Seljuk Turks* OR *the Ottoman Turks, followers of Osman, had founded the empire.*

What two great empires of the Middle East were ruled by Turks? *The Persian empire and the Ottoman empire were both ruled by Turks.*

What two great cities did the Ottoman Turks conquer? They renamed one of the cities. *The Turks captured Baghdad and Constantinople. They renamed Constantinople Istanbul.*

Why did the kings of Europe begin to get nervous? *They were nervous about how far the Ottoman empire would spread.*

What was the condition of the empire when Murad came to the throne? *It was too large; the sultans were spending too much money on feasts and palaces; Spanish gold was making Ottoman coins worthless; the Ottomans had lost control of Baghdad.*

How old was Murad when the Ottoman army rebelled? *Murad was twenty-three years old.*

What did Murad do to Rejeb after he found that Rejeb was the ringleader of a revolt? *He had Rejeb's head cut off.*

How did Murad keep rebels from forming new plans? *He closed all the taverns so the rebels wouldn't have a place to meet.*

Once Murad had frightened his people into obeying him, what did he set out to do? *He started recapturing the land that the Ottoman empire had lost, including Baghdad.*

How old was Murad when he died? *Murad was only twenty-eight years old when he died.*

### Narration Exercise

"When Murad became king of the Ottomans, he was only eleven years old. He waited and grew stronger and older. When he was twenty-three, his army rebelled. Murad found out that his Grand Vizier was a ringleader of the rebellion. He ordered the Grand Vizier killed and then started to make the empire larger again. He was cruel, but he succeeded. When he died, the Ottoman Empire was strong again." OR

"The Seljuk Turks were a tribe that took control of part of the Muslim empire. But they were nomads, so they didn't do a good job of keeping their empire together. One of the Seljuk Turks was named Osman. He gathered followers around him and started his own empire—the Ottoman Empire. The Ottoman Empire spread all the way over into Europe. But then it grew too large and started to become weak. A sultan named Murad came to the throne and made the Ottoman Empire strong again."

## Additional History Reading

*Ancient Iran,* by Massoume Price (Anahita Productions, 2008). Filled with pictures of ancient art, pottery and other artifacts, this volume provides comprehensive coverage of ancient Iran and leaves the reader with a richer perspective on Persia during the time period discussed in chapter 8. (IR 4-8)

*Dining at the Safavid Court: 16th Century Royal Persian Recipes*, by M.R. Ghanoonparvar (Mazda Publishers, 2017). This book is based on a cookbook by the chef to Shah Abbas. It's written to adults, but parents and kids could have fun comparing the old recipes to the modernized versions (and possibly trying them!). Colorful illustrations. (RA 1-4)

*Iran,* by Joyce Markovics (Bearport Publishing, 2017). An easy introduction to the history and modern life of Iran with vivid pictures and interesting facts (RA 1-3, IR 1-3)

*Iran,* by G.S. Prentzas (Cherry Lake Publishing, 2013). Written in narrative style and supplemented with photos, this book gives some history of Iran along with information about the people and their culture. Interspersed throughout are activities, including a map-copying exercise. (RA 1-2, IR 2-4)

*Iran,* by Vijeya Rajendra (Cavendish Square, 2015). With numerous full-color photos and links to relevant web content, this comprehensive overview of Iran includes sections on its geography, history and people. (IR 4-6)

*Iran: The People*, by April Fast (Crabtree Publishing Company, 2010). This book contains more information than the one above, at a slightly more advanced reading level. The last two-page spread contains a story about a little girl on her older sister's wedding day. (RA 1-3, IR 3-4)

*Rumi: Whirling Dervish*, by Demi (Marshall Cavendish Corporation, 2009). Rumi was the popular name of a Persian poet whose family settled in Turkey after Mongols were invading their homeland. Demi writes and illustrates a very engaging biography about him. (RA 1-3, IR 3-4)

*T is for Turkey,* by Nilufer Topaloglu Pyper and Prodeepta Das (Frances Lincoln Unlimited, 2010). A lovely, accessible introduction to Turkey with information on the country's history, culture and modern life. (RA 1-4, IR 3-5)

*Turkey*, by Vicky Franchino (Cherry Lake Publishing, 2013). Contains basic information about Turkey and its history. Talks about the people, celebrations, and foods of Turkey; and contains some fun activities for kids to do. (RA 1-2, IR 2-4)

*Turkey,* by Joanne Mattern (Cavendish Square, 2018). Interestingly written overview of the history, geography, lifestyle, religion, and culture of Turkey. Filled with photos and fact boxes that provide supplementary information. (RA 2-4, IR 3-6)

*Turkey,* by Joanna Robinson (The Child's World, 2016). With full-color photos, this introduction to Turkey's history, culture and topography will orient the reader and help them better understand the lasting influence of the Ottoman Empire. (RA 1-3, IR 3-6)

*Mosque*, by David Macaulay (Houghton Mifflin, 2003). Detailed pictures and fascinating read-aloud text tell the story of a mosque constructed by the Ottoman Turks. (RA 1-4, IR 4-6)

*The Ottoman Empire* (Life During the Great Civilizations), by Lucille Davis (Blackbirch Press/Gale Group, 2003). For advanced fourth graders and above, or as a read-aloud. (RA 3-4, IR 4-6).

*The Ottoman Empire,* by Adriane Ruggiero (Benchmark Books, 2003). A comprehensive junior-level history of the Ottoman Empire from the early nomads to the enduring influence of the Ottomans. (RA 4+, IR 5-8)

## Corresponding Literature Suggestions

*A Donkey Reads*, by Muriel Mandell, illus. Andre Letria (Star Bright Books, 2010). A story about a poor family who offers a donkey to their king. The king threatens to kill the father, until a wise man steps in and convinces the king that the donkey can read. (RA 1-2, IR 2-4)

*Goha the Wise Fool*, by Denys Johnson-Davies, illus. Hany El Saed Ahmed and Hag Hamdy Mohamed Fattouh (Philomel Books, 2005). A collection of stories, originating around the late Medieval period, about Goha and his antics. These stories are gorgeously illustrated by hand-sewn *khiyamiyas* from the tentmakers' souk in Cairo. (RA 1-3, IR 2-4)

*The Green Musician*, by Mahvash Shahegh, illus. Claire Ewart (Wisdom Tales, 2015). When Barbad the musician gets thwarted by a rival from playing before the king, he devises another plan. This story is taken from the Shahnameh ("Book of Kings"), an epic poem from medieval Persian culture. (RA 1-2, IR 3-4)

*The Kind Old Lady*, by Meimanat Mirsadeghi, trans. Nazanin Mirsadeghi, illus. Roya Sadeghi (Bahar Books, 2017). Based on a Persian folktale, this is a story of an old woman who takes in stray animals from a rainstorm during the night. The colorful illustrations are charmingly painted and depict patterned textiles from clothing to bedding. (RA 1-2, IR 2-4)

*The Knight, the Princess, & the Magic Rock: A Classic Persian Tale*, retold by Sara Azizi, illus. Alireza Sadeghian (Wisdom Tales, 2012). Another story from the Shahnameh, this is a tale of love between two people from enemy nations. This particular version is based on commentary from a mystic from the early seventeenth century. Very engaging and lavishly illustrated. (RA 1-3, IR 2-4)

*Pea Boy and other Stories from Iran,* by Elizabeth Laird and Shirin Adl (Frances Lincoln Limited, 2009). This book contains a variety of short folktales alongside whimsical illustrations—perfect for short read-aloud sessions. (RA K-6, IR 4-6)

*The Persian Cinderella,* by Shirley Climo (Harper Collins, 1999). Fans of the traditional Cinderella story will recognize a similar storyline in this beautifully-illustrated picture book. (IR 2-4, RA K-4)

*The Rich Man and the Parrot* retold by Pippa Goodhart (Tiny Owl Publishing, 2017). Young children will enjoy this Persian folktale of a parrot who tricks a wealthy merchant. (RA 1-4, IR 2-4)

*Shahnameh: The Persian Book of Kings*, retold by Elizabeth Laird, illus. Shirin Adl (Francis Lincoln Children's Books, 2012). This is a collection of stories retold from the epic poem by Ferdowsi, a Persian poet. The stories capture the imagination and are gorgeously illustrated. (RA 1-3, IR 3-4)

*The Hungry Coat* by Demi (Margaret K. McElderry Books, 2004). With beautiful full-color traditional Turkish paintings, this humorous tale of Turkey's most famous folk hero teaches an important lesson about appearances. (RA K-4, IR 3-6)

*A Treasury of Turkish Folktales for Children*, by Barbara K. Walker (Linnet Books, 1998). Read-aloud folktales from the land of the Ottoman Turks. (RA 2-4, IR 5-7) **OOP**

*Some of My Ancestors are Ottomans and Turks*, by Judy Light Ayyildiz, illus. Dr. Vedii Ayyildiz (Yeni Yasam Yayinlari, 2005). An American boy learns about his Turkish heritage from the stories his grandfather tells him. Book is beautifully illustrated with watercolor paintings. (RA 1-3, IR 2-4)

## MAP WORK

### Map of Persia *(Student Page 22)*

#### The Persian Puzzle

*Materials:*
- ☐ Student Page 22: Map of Persia
- ☐ Multi-colored tissue paper (or construction paper, but tissue paper is better)
- ☐ Wrapping paper, contact paper

*Directions:*

1. You will make a pattern, approximately the same size, for each of the following twelve countries. (The pattern must fit on the part of the map labeled Persia. You might consider using a pattern a little larger than a half dollar, or a mason jar lid.) Choose a color for each country. If necessary, you can make a pattern on different colors of construction paper to differentiate them (so that red might represent Persia, but red with blue spots might be Alexander the Great.) Make them all roughly the same shape, about the size of a half dollar (this does not have to be exact).
   - A. Assyrian empire
   - B. Babylonian empire
   - C. Persian empire
   - D. Alexander the Great's empire
   - E. Seleucids
   - F. Parthia
   - G. Sassanid dynasty of Persia
   - H. Islamic empire
   - I. Turks
   - J. Ghaznavids
   - K. Mongols
   - L. Safavids
2. These twelve peoples ruled Persia at different times throughout history. Assyria ruled the area of Persia first. So, glue your pattern for Assyria down on Persia. After the Assyrians, the Babylonians ruled. Glue the pattern for Babylonians on the map, partly covering the Assyrian pattern (you can cover as much or as little of the previous pattern as you want, as long as it fits in Persia).

3. You will then glue "Persia" over "Babylonians." You will continue to do this with each of the following patterns, until you finally glue the "Safavids" pattern.

**Coloring Page** When Murad inherited the throne of the Ottoman Empire, he was a quiet, weak boy. But he trained and exercised and became a strong, fierce ruler who took back the lands that the empire had lost to its neighbors. *(Student Page 23)*

## PROJECTS

### Art Project Persian Writing

*Materials:*
- ☐ Pencil
- ☐ Scratch paper
- ☐ Item to be decorated (book cover, art paper, etc.)
- ☐ Markers

*Directions:* In ancient times, the language of the Persians was written in cuneiform—like the language of the ancient Sumerians. Sometimes the cuneiform signs stood for letter sounds, like "t":

Or like "m":

Sometimes the cuneiform signs stood for words, like "king":

Or like "god":

The two signs are similar; the Persian king thought of himself as a son of the gods!

After the Muslim army invaded Persia, Persia became an Islamic nation. The Persians still spoke their own language—but they began to use the Arabic alphabet when they wrote their words down. Here is a line of Persian, written in Arabic letters:

تمام افراد بشر آزاد به دنیا می آیند و از لحاظ حیثیت و

حقوق با هم برابرند، همه دارای عقل و وجدان می باشند و

باید نسبت به یک دیگر با روح برادری رفتار کنند.

In English, this means, "All human beings are born free and equal in dignity and rights. They are endowed with reason and conscience and should act towards one another in a spirit of brotherhood." Would you like to hear how the first part of this saying sounds in Persian? Try pronouncing it as follows. Do you see the (ch)? When you pronounce this letter, say an "h" sound, but gargle a little bit in your throat when you say it. (You won't sound exactly like a Persian speaker when you read this, but it will give you some idea of how Persian sounds!)

"Tah-maim-eh ah-fraid-eh bah-shar aiz-aid beh-don-yay mih-yay-ahnd vah ahz leh-(ch)aze-eh (ch)ee-shee-yat-oh (ch)oh-kook bay-hahm bar-aye-rand."

Now try writing down some Persian letters. Remember to start at the right hand edge of your page and work to the left! If you were really learning how to write Persian, you would use different forms of the letters when you wanted to hook letters together into a long flowing line. But for right now, just practice the individual letters.

| ذ | د | خ | ح | چ | ج | ث | ت | پ | ب |
|---|---|---|---|---|---|---|---|---|---|
| Z | D | X | H | CH | J | S | T | P | B |
| ق | ف | ی | ه | و | ن | م | ل | گ | ک |
| GH | H | W | N | M | L | G | K | Q | F |

Because most Muslims don't draw pictures of animals or people, the Persians often used letters of the alphabet to decorate flat surfaces. Use your pencil and scratch paper to design a border, using the letters of the Persian alphabet. Then, use your markers to draw this border onto the paper, book cover, or other item that you have chosen to decorate.

Ager, Simon. "Omniglot - writing systems and languages of the world." www.omniglot.com Accessed on October 23, 2019. Used with permission.

## SCIENCE PROJECT The Bridge of Thirty-Three Arches

Shah Abbas was known for his building projects. He built roads and bridges, the most famous of which was called the "Bridge of Thirty-Three Arches." The Zayandeh-Rood river flowed beneath this great bridge. The thirty-three arches were arranged in two layers; large arches along the bottom supported smaller arches above. High walls kept wind from blowing pedestrians off the high bridge. Shah Abbas ordered frescoes (paintings on fresh plaster) painted along the walls to entertain people as they walked. You can still walk across this bridge today; it stands in present-day Iran.

Test the strength of an arched bridge like the Bridge of Thirty-Three Arches by making your own "arched bridge" out of paper. Even paper becomes strong when bent into an arch. Imagine how strong an arched bridge of stone must have been!

*Materials:*
- ☐ Three sheets of typing paper
- ☐ Scissors
- ☐ Ruler
- ☐ Tape

*Directions:*
1. Using the first sheet of typing paper, cut four strips along the long edge so that each strip is 11" long and 2" wide.
2. Using the second sheet of typing paper, cut four strips 6" long and 2" wide.
3. Bend each long strip of paper into an arch. Tape a shorter strip of paper to the bottom of each arch to hold it in place. Each arch should look like this:

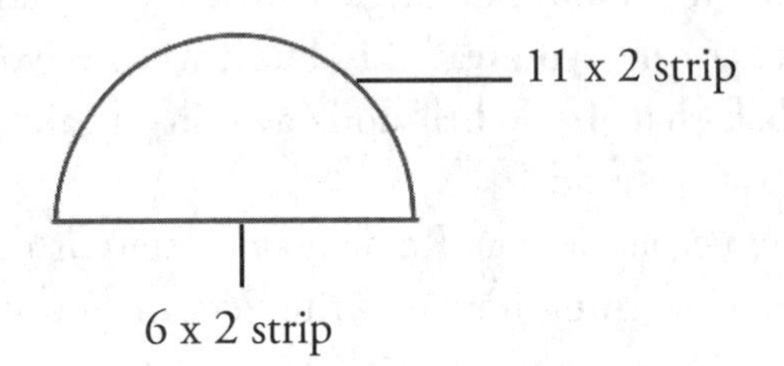

4. Set the four arches side by side. Use the tape to fasten them together into a row, placing the tape about 1" high on the sides of the arches, like this:

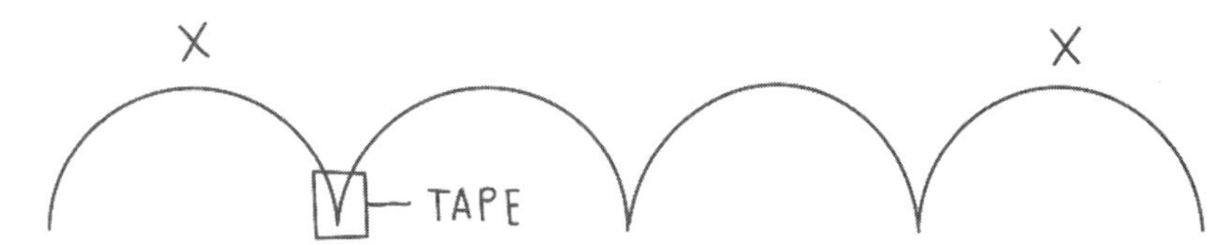


5. Now, cut one 11" x 2" strip and one 7" x 2" strip from the third sheet of paper. Tape them together to create one 18" x 2" strip. This will be the roadway of your bridge. Tape it across the top of the arches so that the ends attach at the center of the end arches (where the x's are marked above).
6. Set a heavy book on end at each end of your paper bridge to keep the bridge upright. Now try placing small items on your bridge: small stones, Hot Wheels cars, etc. How much weight can your "Bridge of Four Arches" support?

## LITERATURE PROJECT The Poems of the Ottoman Turks

The Ottoman Turks respected poetry so much that almost every sultan wrote poems! These poems were short but complicated. The Turks thought that poems should be like flowers, complex and small, rather than long epics that went on for pages and pages.

Sultan Murad's chief advisor, Hafiz Pasha, once wrote to the Sultan asking him to send soldiers to help with a battle. He wrote his request as a poem—and Sultan Murad wrote back in another poem! You will find both of these poems on Student Page 24. (Note to instructor: the language in these poems has been slightly simplified, and both poems have been condensed.)

*Materials:*
- □ Student Page 24: Poems of the Ottoman Turks
- □ Paper and two envelopes (for Option #1)
- □ Crayons or markers (for Option #2)

*Directions:*
1. Read both of the poems. What is Hafiz Pasha asking for in his poem? Does he get it from Sultan Murad?
2. Notice that the poems use two different *metaphors*—word pictures that stand for something else. Hafiz Pasha talks about his men as chessmen on a board, in a game that is about to be checkmated. He also talks about them as swimmers who are about to get sucked into a whirlpool. Both of these metaphors show that he is afraid his men will lose the battle!
3. Notice that there is a repeated line in the poem. What is it?
4. Option #1: Write a poem to your parents, asking them for something that you want. This poem can be very short. It doesn't have to rhyme unless you want it to. But try to think of a *metaphor* to use in the poem. If you want something very badly, you might be like a flower needing water, or like a dog hungry for its supper! Also, try to think of a line that you can repeat after each part of the poem, just like Hafiz Pasha does. Put the poem in an envelope and give it to your parent. Then, ask them to write a short poem back to you, telling you whether or not your request is granted. Tell them that they need to use the same metaphor, and repeat the same line! OR

5. Option #2: Illustrate Student Page 24. Try to draw pictures of the images in the poem: the chess queen and knight, the whirlpool, the swimmer, and any other illustrations that seem to suit the poems.

## ART PROJECT — Color an Ottoman Design

This is an Ottoman design that represents the spots and stripes of leopard and tiger skins. It comes from seventeenth-century Damascus!

*Materials:*
- ☐ Student Page 25: Ottoman Design
- ☐ Markers or watercolor paints

*Directions:* Decide what colors you will use on your seventeenth-century design, and go to work!

# The Western War

## Encyclopedia Cross-References

*UBWH not covered, UILE 308*
*KIHW 414-419, KHE 215, 250-255*

## THE THIRTY YEARS' WAR, 1618-1648

### Review Questions

What did Charles V, the Holy Roman Emperor, do with his empire? *He divided it between his brother Ferdinand and his son Philip.*

When Ferdinand died, he left his lands to his son Maximilian, and then they went to Maximilian's son Matthias. Who did Matthias leave the lands to? *He left the lands to his cousin, Ferdinand II.*

What did Ferdinand II do that made many German princes angry? *He tried to get rid of Protestant worship in Germany.*

How did the Protestants in the part of Germany called Bohemia react? *They gathered together in Prague to protest Ferdinand's laws.*

What did the Protestant people of Prague do to two of Ferdinand's officials? *They threw them out of a castle window!*

Ferdinand II was the king of Germany, but he wanted another title as well. What was it? *Ferdinand II wanted to be the Holy Roman Emperor.*

Who had to elect the Holy Roman Emperor? *Seven German princes, or electors, had to elect the Holy Roman Emperor.*

What two countries sent soldiers to help Ferdinand defeat the Protestant rebellion? *Spain and Austria sent soldiers to help him.*

Ferdinand defeated the rebels and became Holy Roman Emperor. Did this stop the rebellion? *No, more Protestants rebelled!*

Two more Protestant countries sent their own armies to help the Protestants fight Ferdinand. What were they? *England and Denmark sent armies to help the German Protestants.*

What was the name of Ferdinand's scary general? *His name was Albert of Wallenstein.*

Albert of Wallenstein led the German forces against the English and the Danish armies and defeated them. Another Protestant nation decided to get involved in the conflict. What was the nation, and why? *Sweden decided to get involved because the Swedish were afraid that Ferdinand might decide to attack their country, too!*

What was the name of the Swedish king whose army pushed Ferdinand's men out of Denmark and back to their own capital? *The king's name was Gustavus II.*

What was different about the way that Gustavus's soldiers fought? *They fought in small groups instead of a long line, and they all wore the same blue and yellow uniform.*

What two countries formed the Protestant Union? *Sweden and Protestant Germany formed the Union.*

When did the Protestant Union start to fall apart? *The Protestant Union started to fall apart after Gustavus was killed.*

What did the peace treaty say about Protestants and their religion? *It said that every German prince could decide what religion his region would follow.*

After a peace treaty was signed, which nation restarted the war? *France restarted the fighting by declaring war on Ferdinand.*

What was the name of the final peace treaty signed by Europe? *The final peace treaty was called the Peace of Westphalia.*

How many years did the Thirty Years' War actually last? *Fighting actually went on for 41 years!*

What happened to the people of Germany because of this long war? *Thousands of Germans died (in some places, half of the population); the countryside was full of unburied bodies; soldiers robbed the people; many of the citizens nearly died of starvation.*

## Narration Exercise

Since the Thirty Years' War is such a complicated event, use "directed narration"; ask the student to answer one of the following questions; answers given are simply suggestions, meant to illustrate an appropriate level of detail.

*Question:* Can you tell me why the Thirty Years' War began and how it ended?

*Suggested answer:* The Thirty Years' War began because the king of Germany, Ferdinand II, tried to stamp out Protestantism in Germany. The German princes who were Protestants wanted to make the decisions about what religions would be followed in their own lands, so they fought back. The Thirty Years' War ended when the Peace of Westphalia was signed. Sweden and France both got some German land, and other parts of Germany were allowed to rule themselves.

*Question:* Can you tell me about three of the men who led the Thirty Years' War?

*Suggested answers (choose three)*: Ferdinand II was the king of Germany. He wanted to get rid of Protestantism in Germany, and he wanted to become the Holy Roman Emperor. He began the war by making strict laws against Protestantism. He managed to become the Holy Roman Emperor, but he died before the war was over.

Christian IV was the king of Denmark. He joined his army with the English army and marched into Germany to defend Protestantism. He was forced to flee for his life when his army met the German army in battle.

Albert of Wallenstein was Ferdinand's general. He loved war; he was tall and thin; and he was a violent, frightening man. He led the German army against the Danes, but he lost when the Swedish army attacked Ferdinand's soldiers. Ferdinand had him assassinated.

Gustavus II was the king of Sweden. He decided to attack Ferdinand because the German army invaded Denmark and was camped right on his borders. His soldiers fought in small groups and wore blue and yellow uniforms. He pushed Ferdinand's army back into Germany and invaded Germany, but he was killed in battle.

Cardinal Richelieu was the prime minister of France. He attacked Ferdinand because he wanted the king of France to be the Holy Roman Emperor. The Thirty Years' War didn't end until after the cardinal died.

*The Holy Roman Empire,* by Carolyn DeCarlo, editor. (Rosen Education Service, 2018). Beginning with Charlemagne and ending with Napoleon, this overview of the Holy Roman Empire will orient students and provide context for the Thirty Years' War. (RA 3-5, IR 3-6)

*Germany,* by Mary Colson, (Barnes and Noble, 2011). Includes information on the wildlife, geography, and culture of Germany. (RA 2, IR 3-4)

*Germany: The People,* by Kathryn Lane (Crabtree Publications, 2001). Focuses on the history of the different regions of Germany, including Bavaria and Prussia. For advanced third grade and older. (RA 2-3, IR 3-5)

*National Geographic Countries of the World: Germany,* by Henry Russell, (National Geographic Children's Books, 2001). An overview of the history, culture, geography, and natural history of Germany. (RA 3, IR 4-5.)

*It's Cool to Learn About Countries: Germany,* by Vicky Franchino (Cherry Lake Publishing, 2012). Filled with photos, this book contains engaging narrative text about the history, geography, people, celebrations, and food of Germany. (RA 1-3, IR 4-5)

*The Rhine: Europe's River Highway,* by Gary G. Miller (Crabtree Publishing Company, 2010). The Rhine River was significant during the Thirty Years' War. Learn more about this European river and its history. (RA 1-2, IR 3-4)

*10 Fascinating Facts About Castles,* by Jessica Cohn (Children's Press, 2017). Information about Prague Castle, where the Defenestration of Prague occurred, is mentioned in this book. (RA 1-2, IR 3-4)

*13 Bridges Children Should Know,* by Brad Finger (Prestel, 2015). What is now known as the Charles Bridge is where Ferdinand hung the heads of the Prague rebels. Read about the bridge (and other historic bridges!) and see photos in this book. (RA 1-3, IR 4-6)

*Denmark* by R. Conrad Stein (Children's Press, 2017). With detailed information on Denmark's history, culture and people, this volume will give the older elementary student a better understanding of the context of the Thirty Years' War as well as the place of modern Denmark in today's world. (RA 3-5, IR 4-7)

*Sweden,* by Joanne Mattern (Cavendish Square Publishing, 2018). Part of the Exploring World Cultures series; this book contains color photos and short narratives about the history, customs, and language of Gustavus's country. (RA 1-3, IR 4-6)

*Sweden* by Julie Murray (Big Buddy Books, 2015). Filled with photographs of modern Sweden, this book also covers the country's rich history and culture. (RA 1-4, IR 3-6)

*Cardinal Richelieu (World Leaders Past & Present),* by Pat Glossop (Chelsea House, 1990). Although this is out of print, it is worth checking your library for; written for fourth grade and above, it describes Richelieu's life and includes his involvement with the Thirty Years' War. Includes many portraits of European leaders in the seventeenth century. (RA 3-4, IR 4-7) **OOP**

*Johannes Kepler* by Daniel Harmon (The Rosen Publishing Group, 2018). Part of the series Leaders of the Scientific Revolution, this biography of the astronomer Johannes Kepler (who lived in Bohemia and Germany during the time of the Thirty Years' War) covers his childhood and scientific accomplishments. (RA 4-6, IR 4-6)

## Corresponding Literature Suggestions

*Complete Grimm's Fairy Tales*, by the Brothers Grimm (Pantheon, 1976). These original German tales are often gory, generally dark, and uniformly fascinating. For reading aloud (at your discretion). (RA 3-4, IR 5-7)

*The Glass Mountain*, by Diane Wolkstein, illus. Louisa Bauer (Morrow, 1999). There are many picture-book versions of the German fairy tales collected by the Brothers Grimm, but this retelling of a little-known story is vivid and particularly fascinating. (RA 2, IR 3-5)

*The Bremen Town Musicians*, by Brian Wildsmith (Star Bright Books, Inc., 2012). Wildsmith also illustrated this Grimm story in colorful detail. A donkey leaves his farm and collects animal friends along the way to join a band in Bremen. (RA 1-2, IR 3-4)

*The Pied Piper of Hamelin*, by Robert Browning, illus. Kate Greenaway (Dover, 1997). This classic poem is set in a German town filled with rats; read the story aloud while children look at the 36 watercolor illustrations. (RA 2-5, IR 6-7)

*Princess Sophie and the Six Swans,* retold and illustrated by Kim Jacobs (Wisdom Tales, 2017). One of the lesser-known but nonetheless worthwhile Grimm fairy tales, this story tells the tale of Sophie, whose loyalty to her brothers goes too far and lands the whole family in trouble. (RA K-3, RA 2-4)

*Rapunzel*, by Paul O. Zelinsky (Dutton, 1997). This Caldecott-winning adaptation of a German folktale is illustrated in Renaissance style. (RA 2, IR 3-5)

*Snow White and Rose Red*, by Kallie George, illus. Kelly Vivanco (Simply Read Books, 2014). Beautiful paintings in this retelling of the story of two very different but loving sisters. From the Brothers Grimm. (RA 1-2, IR 3-4)

*The Golem's Latkes*, by Eric A. Kimmel, illus. Aaron Jasinski (Marshall Cavendish, 2011). Based on a narrative about Rabbi Judah of Prague from just before the time of the Thirty Years' War. Basha, Judah's housemaid, instructs the Golem do her tasks while she is out—until disaster strikes. (RA 1-2, IR 3-4)

*The Golem of Prague*, by Irene Cohen-Janca, illus. Maurizio A.C. Quarello (Annick Press Ltd., 2017). A darker version of the golem narrative: preview before reading aloud. A boy named Frantz decides to secretly investigate the attic where the smashed golem supposedly is hidden. (RA 3-4, IR 4-6)

*Hans in Luck,* retold by Felix Hoffmann (North South, 2017). This compilation of seven stories by the Brothers Grimm includes traditional favorites like Rapunzel and Sleeping Beauty as well as lesser-known tales like Hans in Luck and King Thrushbeard. (RA 1-6, IR 4-6)

*Kristina, The Girl King*, by Carolyn Meyer (Scholastic, Inc., 2003). From the *Royal Diaries* series, this book depicts what life might have been like for Gustavus Adolphus's daughter who was raised to become a ruler. (RA 3-4, IR 5-7)

## MAP WORK

### Protestant and Catholic Europe *(Student Page 26, answer 321)*

1. Fill in the key in the upper left corner of the map. Color the "against Ferdinand" box red. Color the "for Ferdinand" box blue.
2. England, Sweden, Denmark, and the Netherlands had many Protestants who were willing to fight against Ferdinand. Color these lands red (down to the dotted line below Prague.)
3. Ferdinand had control of Germany, and he had allies in Spain. Outline the borders of the Empire and Spain in blue, then shade them lightly in blue.

4. Ferdinand and his forces pushed back the army led by Christian IV. Draw three blue arrows from the Empire up into the Netherlands.
5. In Sweden, Gustavus II saw what happened to Christian IV's army and decided to attack. Draw two black arrows from Sweden down into "The Empire."
6. Richelieu in France saw that Ferdinand had been weakened by the war, and he also decided to fight against Ferdinand. Outline the border of France in red. Then draw three red arrows from France into the Empire.
7. Even after the peace treaty, Spain and France continued to fight. Draw two red arrows from France into Spain (which should have blue borders).

**Coloring Page** Many countries became involved in the Thirty Years' War. These soldiers from Sweden are wearing blue and yellow uniforms because their king, Gustavus Adolphus, wanted them to be able to recognize each other during battles. *(Student Page 27)*

## PROJECTS

### Activity Project: The Thirty Years' War Game

*Materials:*
- ☐ Student Page 28: Thirty Years' War Game Board
- ☐ One die or spinner
- ☐ Two game pieces
- ☐ *The Story of the World, Volume 3*

*Directions:*
1. This game is for two players. Each player should choose a path and place his or her piece at "Start."
2. Take turns rolling the dice or spinning the spinner. Move ahead the number of squares shown.
3. Each time you reach a square with a question, you must answer this question before moving on (even if your roll would take you past the square). If you are unable to answer the question, your turn is over. At the beginning of the next turn, you will have one more chance to answer. If you answer correctly, you may roll and progress forward. If you still can't answer the question, look up the answer in *The Story of the World* and read it out loud. You may then place your piece on the square directly after the question square. You may roll again at the beginning of your next turn.
4. The first person to reach the last space and answer the question wins!

### Craft Project: Uniforms of the Thirty Years' War

During the Thirty Years' War, armies used uniforms to identify each other for the first time!

*Materials:*
- ☐ colored pencils or crayons
- ☐ Scissors
- ☐ Scotch Removable Double-stick Tape
- ☐ Student Pages 29, 30, and 31: soldiers of The Thirty Years' War
- ☐ White cardstock

Directions: 1. *Note: You might want to make copies of the figures and uniforms before coloring and cutting them, so you can create a whole army.* Color the paper dolls and the uniforms. The Swedish soldier is a musketeer, who carries gunpowder in little wooden bottles on a belt around his chest. The German cavalryman wears heavy armor and might carry a long pistol that he can shoot with one hand while riding a horse. The Spanish soldier carries a long spear called a "pike." Remember: the Swedish uniforms are bright blue and yellow! A Spanish soldier might have different colors in his uniform, depending on his position, but the most common color in Spanish uniforms was a rich deep red. The armor of the German cavalry soldier could be gray or silver or black, and his sash and pants could be green or red.

2. Glue the paper doll onto thick cardstock. Cut to size. Laminate if possible (you'll be happier with the results and the paper doll tends to last longer.) If laminating at a professional site (such as Office Depot or copy stores), opt for the thicker grade of plastic cover.
3. Use the double-stick tape to attach uniforms.

## ACTIVITY PROJECT Celebrate St. Martin's Day—And Martin's Day.

Before the sixteenth century, Sweden—like most of Europe—was a Catholic country. The people of Sweden celebrated "saints' days," holidays honoring saints recognized by the Catholic church. November 11th was St. Martin's Day. This holiday honored St. Martin of Tours, a bishop who was best known for giving his cloak to a beggar to keep the beggar from freezing to death.

But then Protestantism spread into Sweden! By the time of Gustavus II, Sweden was a Protestant country. As a matter of fact, Gustavus II joined the Thirty Years' War because he was afraid that Ferdinand would invade his country and force the Swedes to become Catholic again!

But Gustavus II and his people still celebrated St. Martin's Day. Why did they still keep this Catholic holiday? For two reasons. This holiday had become the traditional "first day of winter." And St. Martin's Day also happened to be just one day after the birthday of Martin Luther, the father of the Protestant reformation! So St. Martin's Day was moved from November 11 to November 10, Martin Luther's birthday, and became known as Martin Day. Martin Day is still celebrated in the south of Sweden on November 10.

However, in Germany, which had so many Catholic states, St. Martin's Day was still celebrated on November 11. Today, children celebrate this holiday by parading through the streets with lanterns and singing as they approach a bonfire. After the bonfire, they go door to door and sing or recite verses and are rewarded with candy and treats by those who hear them.

You can celebrate St. Martin's Day or Martin Day—just choose one set of instructions from below!

**St. Martin's Day Celebration (November 11)**

In Germany, this celebration begins on the eleventh day of the eleventh month, at 11 minutes past 11 in the morning! Your celebration may not be on November 11, but you can still begin it at 11:11. Make the lantern below and parade around your house, singing or chanting. Here is a popular verse you might try chanting out loud as you go:

I'm coming with my lantern
And my lantern with me
There, over the light are the stars,
Here, under the light are we
My light is out, we're going home

You can also sing this song, honoring Martin of Tours, to the tune of "My Bonnie Lies Over the Ocean":

Saint Martin once saw a beggar
Who needed some food and some clothes

So he ripped his cape in two pieces
And eased some of the beggar's woes.
Martin, Martin
He always helped those in need, in need
Martin, Martin
He showed his goodness in deeds.

If you can, build a small bonfire outside; if you don't have room for a bonfire, you can light a candle and pretend!

Then, take your lantern and sing a song or recite a short poem for your parents or neighbors. Remind them that you need a piece of candy in return!

***Make a St. Martin's Day Lantern*** **(requires adult supervision)**

Materials:
- ☐ A square box, preferably narrower and taller than a shoebox, with the lid cut off.
- ☐ Two candles, one long taper and one smaller candle, just tall enough to stand in the box but still be at least 2 inches below the top
- ☐ Candleholder or self-hardening clay
- ☐ Cookie cutters (moon, star, apple, angel, or anything else you have on hand)
- ☐ Tissue paper, white or colored
- ☐ Tape
- ☐ Knife or large scissors (for adult to use)

Directions:
1. Choose your favorite cookie cutters and place them on the four sides of your box. Trace each cookie cutter. Cut out the cardboard on the lines.
2. Wrap the sides of the box with tissue paper, as though you were wrapping a present. Try to use only one layer of the tissue paper. Tape the paper into place. Remember, the top of the box should remain open.
3. Place the smaller candle into the box, either using the candleholder or the self-hardening clay to hold the candle into place.
4. Light the smaller candle using the long taper. CAUTION: THE TOP OF THE BOX MUST REMAIN OPEN. DO NOT PUT A LID OR PAPER OVER THE TOP OF THE BOX. The candlelight should shine out through the cutouts, covered with tissue paper.

**Martin's Day Celebration (November 10)**

The traditional Martin Day celebration in the south of Sweden is a big feast: roast goose; soup made with wine, goose stock, and a generous cupful of goose's blood; applecake; and *spettekaka*—cake baked on a spit! You probably can't roast a goose for this feast—so we'll skip the goose and the blood soup. Instead, serve chicken or turkey at your feast, along with Swedish apple cake. And if you're feeling very adventuresome, try the *spettekaka!*

## Swedish Apple Cake

*Ingredients:*

1 cup sugar
⅓ cup shortening or margarine
2 eggs
¼ tsp salt
1 tsp vanilla
2 large or 3 small apples

3 Tbs butter
3 Tbs milk
1 ½ cups brown sugar

1¼ cup flour
1 tsp cinnamon
1 tsp nutmeg
1 tsp baking soda
¼ tsp cloves

*Directions:*

1. Chop or grate the apples without peeling.
2. Cream the sugar and margarine or shortening together. Add eggs and vanilla.
3. Add flour, spices, soda, and salt. Mix.
4. Add grated or chopped apples. Mix thoroughly.
5. Pour into an 8" x 8" greased baking dish. Bake for 20 minutes at 350 degrees.
6. While the cake is baking, melt 3 Tbs of butter. Add 3 Tbs Milk and 1 ½ cups of brown sugar, and stir into a smooth paste. Keep warm.
7. Take cake from the oven when the 20 minutes are up and spread the topping on the surface. Bake for an additional 25 minutes.

## Spettekaka

*Ingredients:*

1 ½ sticks of butter, softened
1 ½ cups of sugar
7 eggs (two separated)
1 cup flour
1 Tbs grated lemon peel
1 Tbs crushed almonds.
¼ tsp cardamom
½ cup vegetable oil
confectioners' sugar
(optional) flowers

*Directions:*

1. Beat the sugar and butter until creamy. Add the 5 eggs one at a time. Add the 2 egg yolks (reserve the whites).
2. Add flour, lemon peel, almonds, and cardamom. Beat until smooth.
3. Beat egg whites until stiff. Fold into batter.
4. Heat oil in medium frying pan until it sizzles when you drop cold water into it. Drip spoonfuls of the batter into the pan until the pan is filled with a thin latticework of dough (like a funnel cake). Cook until golden brown. Remove from pan with a fork or spatula and drain on a paper towel. Continue until all batter is used.
5. Stack the layers on a plate. Shake confectioners sugar over each layer before adding the next. Decorate with fresh flowers!

# Far East of Europe

CHAPTER 10

## Encyclopedia Cross-References

*UBWH 153-155, UILE 352-353, 356*
*KIHW 402-403, 430 margin, 432-433, KHE 232-233, 244-245, 262-263*

## JAPAN'S ISOLATION: CLOSED DOORS IN THE EAST

### Review Questions

What religion did most of the Japanese people belong to? *Most of the Japanese were Buddhists (or, they belonged to the Buddhist faith).*

What missionaries were coming to Japan at this time? *Christian missionaries, mostly Jesuit Catholics, were coming to Japan.*

What did Ieyasu's advisor William Adams say to Ieyasu about the Jesuits? *He said that missionaries would be followed by the Spanish army so that Spain could invade Japan.*

What laws did Ieyasu make against Christians? *First he said that no Japanese could become Catholic Christians. Then he ordered all foreign missionaries to be driven from the country.*

What two actions did Ieyasu's son, Hidetada, take against Christians? *He ordered Japanese Christians executed. He threw Catholic priests who wouldn't leave the country into jail.*

How did the shogun Iemitsu try to keep foreign religions and ideas out of Japan? *He decreed that Japanese could not travel any further away than Korea, and then he said that no ships could enter or leave Japanese ports.*

How did the Christians at Shimabara react to Iemitsu's orders? *They tried to fight, but they were driven into a castle and put to death.*

Which nation was allowed to send one ship per year to Japan? *The Dutch could send one ship per year.*

Were the Dutch allowed to come ashore? *No, they had to dock at an artificial island in the harbor of Nagasaki.*

What kind of Buddhism flourished in Japan. *Zen Buddhism flourished in Japan.*

Where did Zen Buddhists look for truth? *They looked inside their own souls.*

### Narration Exercise

"Catholic missionaries came to Japan, and many Japanese became Christians. The shogun, Ieyasu, asked his advisor about the missionaries. His advisor told him that the Spanish army would come after the missionaries and conquer Japan! Ieyasu made a law driving the missionaries out. His son made other laws against Christianity. And *his* son, Iemitsu, closed Japan to outsiders! No one could leave Japan, and no one could come to Japan from a foreign country. Only one Dutch ship a year could come to Japan, and they couldn't come ashore. Japan was closed to the rest of the world." OR

"The shoguns of Japan were suspicious of Christianity. Ieyasu ordered the Japanese to stop becoming Christians and sent all missionaries away. Hidetada executed Christians and threw missionaries in jail. And his son, Iemitsu, made even more laws. He wanted to keep foreign ideas out of the country, so he ordered that no ships could come into or go out of Japan, and shipbuilders couldn't make large ships. He wanted anyone trying to come into or leave the country executed! Japan was closed to the rest of the world, so the Buddhist faith flourished."

## Review Questions

The Ming dynasty was from the south of China. What were the people in the south of China called? *People in the south of China were called Han Chinese.*

What group from the north of China decided to attack the Ming? *The Manchus, who came from Manchuria (northern China), decided to attack the Ming in the south.*

Besides the Manchu invasion, name two other problems China was having. *The emperors had spent too much money fighting the Japanese; there were too many people and not enough farm land to grow food for them; cold weather had killed the crops; soldiers were deserting the army and robbing and destroying cities.*

Were the Han Chinese pleased with the Ming emperors? *No, they complained that the emperor was doing nothing to help them!*

A postman named Li Tzu-ch'eng decided to set up his own government. What did he do next? *He gathered up other discontented men and marched to Peking. Then he took over the Ming palace.*

Why didn't the Ming army fight back? *The plague had killed many of them!*

Did Li Tzu-ch'eng get to be emperor? *No, he did not.*

Why not? What did the remaining Ming generals ask the Manchu to do? *They asked the Manchu to come down from the north and help them beat the rebels.*

What did the Manchu do instead? *They came down and beat the rebels, but then they kept the throne for themselves.*

What name did the Manchu call themselves to show that they were better than their Han (southern) subjects? *They called themselves Qing, which meant "pure."*

What did the Manchu force the Han to do to their hair? *They made them wear it in the Manchu style (shave the fronts of the head and grow a pigtail in the back).*

When K'ang-hsi became emperor, how did he treat his subjects? *He treated them more fairly and lessened their taxes; he treated Han Chinese and Manchu the same.*

## Narration Exercise

"The Ming emperors, who ruled over China, were Han Chinese. But up north, the Manchu people were about to attack them. China had other problems. People were hungry and dissatisfied! One postman decided to attack the Ming emperor. His army marched right into Peking! So the Ming asked the Manchu to come help them out. The Manchu came right down into China and took over the throne! At first, the Manchu treated the Han Chinese unkindly. But then the second Manchu emperor, K'ang-hsi, changed this. He treated the Han Chinese and the Manchu the same and lowered their taxes. Because of this, his empire grew larger and stronger." OR

"There were two kinds of Chinese in China—the Manchu and the Han Chinese. The Manchu swept down and took over Peking because the Han Chinese dynasty, called the Ming dynasty, asked them for help. The Manchu called themselves "pure" because they thought they were better than the Han Chinese. The first Manchu emperor was cruel to the Han Chinese. He forced them to shave the fronts of their heads and wear pigtails, and he treated them like servants. But the second emperor, K'ang-hsi, knew that he would have to treat the Han Chinese kindly to keep power. He gave them positions at court and told them that he had freed them from the Ming emperors. Because of this, K'ang-hsi had a long and prosperous rule."

## Additional History Reading

*For additional books on Japan, see the reading lists in Chapter Five.*

*Buddhism* by Katie Marsico (Cherry Lake Publishing, 2017). This book includes easily understandable explanations of the historical roots of Buddhism and how geography influenced its spread. (RA 2-6, IR 3-6)

*The Children of China: An Artist's Journey*, by Song Nan Zhang (Tundra Books, 1995). Beautiful paintings and read-aloud text show the children of the nomadic cultures of China. (RA 1-3, IR 4-6)

*China: The Land*, by Bobbie Kalman (Crabtree Publications, 2000). Many photographs and simple text describe the landscape and the different cultures of China. (RA 2, IR 3-5)

*China* by John Perritano (Mason Crest, 2016). Targeted at the middle grades, this comprehensive overview of China also includes vocabulary words, comprehension questions and research project ideas. (RA 3-6, IR 4-6)

*Eyewitness: Ancient China*, by Arthur Cotterell, illus. Alan Hills and Geoff Brightling (DK Publishing, 2000). Double-page spreads with many illustrations and brief but relatively difficult text cover multiple topics of Chinese history, including the ruling dynasties. (RA 2-3, IR 4-6)

*Japan: The Culture*, by Bobbie Kalman (Crabtree Publications, 2000). Many photographs and simple text describe Japanese customs and feasts, with some attention to their history. (RA 2, IR 3-5)

*Life in Old Japan Coloring Book*, illus. John Green (Dover Publications, 2008). A classic Dover coloring book, depicting people (such as Ieyasu) and scenes from seventeenth and eighteenth century Japan. Scenes include all sorts of cultural activities people did during this time period. (RA 1-3, IR 3-4)

*Shipwrecked: The True Adventures of a Japanese Boy*, by Rhoda Blumberg (HarperCollins, 2001). The true story of a Japanese boy, shipwrecked off his country's coast during Japan's isolation and not allowed to return. Read-aloud text set in a slightly later time period (1800s), but good for reinforcing Japan's status as a closed country. (RA 1-4, IR 5-6)

*Grass Sandals: The Travels of Basho*, by Dawnine Spivak, illus. Demi (Atheneum Books, 2009). Tells of the travels of Basho, who was a famous poet in Japan in the seventeenth century. He is recognized as the greatest master of haiku. (RA 1-2, IR 3-4)

*Saint Ignatius of Loyola*, by Donna Giamo and Patricia Edward Jablonski (Pauline Books & Media, 2000). Part of the "Encounter the Saints" series, this biography from a Catholic press is definitely not nonsectarian, but will be useful for curious students who are good readers and want to know more about the Jesuit order. (IR 4-8)

*Samurai: Warlords of Japan* by Patricia Dawson (Cavendish Square, 2015). Simple chapters, large text and interesting illustrations and photographs. (RA 1-3, IR 1-3)

*What's Inside the Forbidden City?*, by Professor Beaver (Speedy Publishing Canada, 2017). Excellent introduction to the layout and history of the Forbidden City, the palace complex used by emperors of the Qing dynasty in China. (RA 1-2, IR 2-4)

## Corresponding Literature Suggestions

*For additional fiction set in Japan, see Chapter Five.*

*The Boy from the Dragon Palace,* retold by Margaret Read Macdonald (Albert Whitman & Company, 2011). This lively retelling of a traditional Japanese folktale—and its vibrant illustrations—will delight students. (RA 1-4, IR 1-3)

*The Boy of the Three-Year Nap,* by Dianne Snyder, illus. Allen Say (Houghton Mifflin, 1988). In this picture-book retelling of an old story, a lazy boy must get busy in order to win the girl he loves. The illustrations reflect Japan of the seventeenth century. (RA 2, IR 3-4)

*The Cat Who Went to Heaven,* by Elizabeth Coatsworth, illus. Lyn Ward (Aladdin, 1990). This Newbery-winning chapter book is set in Buddhist Japan and tells how a cat helps his artist master win recognition. (RA 2-3, IR 4-6)

*The Crane Girl,* adapted by Curtis Manley (Shen's Books, 2017). Also based on various traditional Japanese folktales, this more advanced picture book will expose students to haiku, a form of Japanese poetry. (RA 2-6, IR 3-6)

*Yuki and the One Thousand Carriers,* by Gloria Whelan, illus. Yan Nascimbene (Sleeping Bear Press, 2008). Yuki's father is summoned to Edo, so the whole family travels the Tokaido Road during Japan's isolationist period. This story is told from Yuki's perspective; she also writes a haiku each day at the request of her teacher who is left behind. (RA 1-3, IR 2-4)

*The Great Race,* by Christopher Corr (Frances Lincoln, 2018). This gorgeous picture book tells the story of the Chinese zodiac—a way of measuring time—with large, colorful illustrations. (RA 1-4, IR 2-4)

*Liang and the Magic Paintbrush,* by Demi (Henry Holt, 1988). Beautiful illustrations and simple text; this story tells of a young boy who must keep his magic paintbrush out of the hands of a tyrannical emperor in China. (RA 2, IR 3-4)

*Little Monk and the Mantis: A Bug, A Boy, and the Birth of a Kung Fu Legend,* by John Fusco, illus. Patrick Lugo (Tuttle Publishing, 2012). Based on the legend of Wong Long from the seventeenth century, this tells of a boy who was taken in by Chinese monks and taught Kung Fu. He ends up starting the practice of Praying Mantis Kung Fu. (RA 1-3, IR 3-4)

*Moonbeams, Dumplings & Dragon Boats: A Treasury of Chinese Holiday Tales, Activities, & Recipes,* by Nina Simonds and Leslie Swartz, illus. Meilo So (Gulliver Books, 2002). Produced by the Children's Museum of Boston, this beautiful book offers read-aloud folk tales, recipes, and plenty of crafts focused around four major Chinese holidays (RA 2-3, IR 4-6)

*The Paper Dragon,* by Marguerite W. Davol, illus. Robert Sabuda (Atheneum, 1997). In this fantastic tale, a dragon appears during the days of the Manchu (the story is set during the Qing dynasty—look for the hero's pigtail!) and must be defeated by a painter. (RA 2, IR 3-5)

*Sky Sweeper,* by Phillis Gershator, illus. Holly Meade (Farrar, Straus, and Giroux, 2007). This story of a boy named Takebori is beautifully written and illustrated. Takebori takes a job sweeping and tending flowers for monks in a Buddhist temple, and does this work happily for his entire life. Includes a translation of a short poem from the early 1500s. (RA 1-2, IR 3-4)

## MAP WORK

### China and Iemitsu's Japan *(Student Page 32, answer 322)*

1. Iemitsu was the ruler of Japan. Color Japan orange.
2. Iemitsu disliked foreign ideas, so he closed the country. Draw a dotted line around Japan in brown.

3. Find the key in the upper left corner of your map. Color the Manchu/Qing box green, and the Han/Ming box, blue. Next, find the Manchu area, the northern part of China, and color it green. Color the Han region, the southern part, blue. (Peking is within the southern part of China.)
4. Peking was the capital city. Draw a star over the dot that represents Peking.
5. The Manchu swept down from the North. They helped the Han drive Li Tzu-ch'eng out of Peking. But instead of putting the Ming dynasty back in control, they put themselves on the throne. Draw two green arrows from Manchuria south, down into Han territory. Make sure one of the arrows goes right through Peking!

**COLORING PAGE** In the teachings of Zen Buddhism, people can find inner wisdom by meditating quietly in small, simple places. This Japanese Zen garden is a place for peaceful meditation. It has trees that have been specially grown, and rocks surrounded by gravel with carefully shaped patterns in it. *(Student Page 33)*

## PROJECTS

### CRAFT PROJECT Make a Zen Garden

The Japanese had been Buddhists for many hundreds of years. But Japan was also influenced by Zen, an Indian practice that travelled from India to China and then from China to Japan. Zen told its followers that wisdom and enlightenment came not from ideas, doctrine, or the intellect, but from the inside. So Zen practitioners didn't study books or make long pilgrimages. Instead, they meditated, waiting for enlightenment. A Zen garden was the perfect place to meditate. The regular patterns of sand and rock helped the Zen practitioner to focus on the inside. No bright flowers or unruly bushes would distract the eye!

*Materials:*

- ☐ Tray or box top
- ☐ Enough clean sand to fill the tray or box top
- ☐ Large serving fork or miniature garden rake
- ☐ Three stones, about half the size of your clenched fist

*Directions:*

1. Fill the tray or box top with sand. Level the sand and make it perfectly even. Break up any clumps; remove any sticks or debris.
2. Use the serving fork or miniature rake to rake the sand, leaving perfectly straight horizontal lines along the sand.
3. Place the stones in the box. Place one in the center of one short side, the second along one of the long sides, and the third towards the center of the box.
4. Use the serving fork or miniature rake to rake the sand around each rock in a circle. The circles should be the width of two fork or rake widths.
5. Your finished garden might look like the illustration below. If you were sitting in this garden, would you find it easy to focus on your inward thoughts, instead of on the garden itself? If you walked into the garden, you would rake your own footprints away behind you, so that not even a footprint would distract your eyes!

## Science Project The Little Ice Age

During the years described in this chapter of *The Story of the World,* China and Europe were entering into a time sometimes called "The Little Ice Age." For years, the weather was colder than usual. The Thames River in England froze. Near Marseille, in France, the sea itself froze over! Frosts killed the orange trees in the Kwangsi province of China. Because of this cold weather, crops didn't grow as well. The growing season itself was reduced by one month. So crops yielded less food and had a shorter time to grow. The price of grain in China quintupled! No wonder so many Chinese went hungry.

See how cold weather affects crop growth, using a Growing Journal and three different kinds of beans.

*Materials:*
- ☐ Growing Journal (two or three sheets of paper, stapled together)
- ☐ pencil or pen
- ☐ lima beans (uncooked)
- ☐ dry kidney beans
- ☐ dry black-eyed peas
- ☐ six styrofoam cups

*Directions:*
1. Soak the dry beans in water for 24 hours at room temperature.
2. Write "lima" on two cups, "kidney" on two cups, and "peas" on two cups. Put two beans of the appropriate kind in each cup.
3. Fill each cup with water so that the beans are submerged.
4. Place one lima, one kidney, and one pea cup in a warm place, such as a windowsill or kitchen counter. Make sure that the three cups will get sunlight for at least four hours during the day.
5. Place one lima, one kidney, and one pea cup in a large bowl next to the other three cups. Fill the bottom of the bowl with ice.
6. Each morning and evening, check all six cups. Replace the ice in the large bowl both morning and evening. Record your observations in your Growing Journal. Which beans sprout first? Do the warm beans or the cold beans sprout earlier? How quickly do the sprouts grow?

## Craft Project Make a Bonkei Garden

Zen also taught that universal truth could be found even in the smallest, most miniature setting—so Zen practitioners often cultivated *bonsai* (dwarf trees) and *bonkei* (miniature landscapes made on trays). Make your own *bonkei* garden on a plate.

*Materials:*

- ☐ large round plate
- ☐ 2 cups potting soil or garden dirt
- ☐ jar lid (mayonnaise or peanut butter)
- ☐ alfalfa sprouts (check your local grocery store)
- ☐ twig, about 6 inches high, with several branches
- ☐ green and yellow construction paper
- ☐ scissors
- ☐ tape
- ☐ small pebbles
- ☐ moss from outdoors along with any other collected small plants (optional)

*Directions:*

1. Fill the plate with the potting soil, leaving a border of about ½" around the edge. Water the potting soil until damp.
2. Place the jar lid in the center of the soil. Push it down so that it is completely sunk into the potting soil. Arrange the pebbles around the edge of the jar lid, pushing them down into the dirt. Fill the jar lid with water. Now your garden has a pond!
3. Make a path with the remaining pebbles from the jar lid. Your path can lead directly from the pond to the edge of the plate, or can spiral around.
4. Cut small leaves from the construction paper. Tape the leaves to the branches of the twig. Place your miniature tree in your garden. If necessary, use pebbles around its base to keep it upright.
5. Decide where your "flower patch" will stand. Gently loosen the dirt. Push the bottoms of the alfalfa sprouts into the potting soil and arrange dirt over them. Water the sprouts.
6. Gently press patches of moss into the potting soil in a pattern that you devise.
7. Optional: Plant other small collected plants in the potting soil.
8. Water your garden frequently!

# The Moghul Emperors of India

## Encyclopedia Cross-References

*UBWH 152, UILE 300-301*
*KIHW 360-361, 440-441, KHE 234 (picture), 265*

## THE MOGHUL EMPERORS OF INDIA: WORLD SEIZER, KING OF THE WORLD, AND CONQUEROR OF THE WORLD

### Review Questions

What was the name of the dynasty, descended from the Mongols, which ruled India? *This dynasty was called the Moghul dynasty.*

What nickname was the emperor Jahangir given? *He was called World Seizer.*

Was he a gentle and humble king or ruthless? Support your answer by telling me one thing that he did. *He was a ruthless king: he ordered his father's best friend killed; he sentenced lawbreakers to be crushed by elephants or beheaded; he put their heads on towers along the roads.*

Why did Jahangir sign a trade treaty with James I? *He wanted English traders to come and buy silks and spices.*

Who did Jahangir invite to India? *Jahangir invited an English ambassador.*

Why did Jahangir invite the English ambassador to come to India? *He invited the ambassador so that the two countries could be friends and could trade with each other.*

What name was given to Jahangir's son Khurram when he became king? *He was now called Shah Jahan, or King of the World.*

How did Shah Jahan protect his claim to the throne? *He put all his rivals to death—including his own brothers!*

What was the name of Shah Jahan's wife, who traveled with him and helped him rule? *His wife's name was Mumtaz Mahal.*

When his wife died, what did Shah Jahan do to show the world how much he loved her? *He decided to build her a tomb, or mausoleum.*

What do we call the beautiful mausoleum that Shah Jahan built? *We call this building the Taj Mahal.*

Who ruled India while Shah Jahan built his beautiful buildings? *Shah Jahan's four sons ruled India.*

Who was Shah Jahan's favorite son? What was he like? *Shah Jahan's favorite son was Dara. He lounged around the court!*

Which of Shah Jahan's sons rebelled and took over the kingdom? *His son Aurangzeb rebelled and took over the kingdom.*

What happened to Shah Jahan when Aurangzeb took over? *Aurangzeb kept Shah Jahan in prison until he died.*

What name did Aurangzeb give himself? *He called himself Conqueror of the World.*

### Narration Exercise

Since there is a lot of information in this chapter, use "directed narration." Say to the student, "There were three emperors in this chapter. Can you tell me the name of each emperor, and one important thing that each emperor did?" If necessary, help the student remember and pronounce the Indian name, as well as the title, of each emperor. Acceptable answers include:

Jahangir, World Seizer: Signed a trade treaty with England so that English traders would come to India; invited an English ambassador to the Indian court.

Kurram, or Shah Jahan, King of the World: Put all rivals for the throne to death; built the Taj Mahal for his wife; allowed his four sons to rule India while he worked on his building projects.

Aurangzeb, Conqueror of the World: Defeated his brother Dara and his father Shah Jahan to claim the throne; kept his father imprisoned in his own fortress.

## AURANGZEB'S THREE DECISIONS

### Review Questions

How many years did Aurangzeb rule? *Aurangzeb ruled for almost fifty years.*

Many of India's people followed the Hindu religion. Which religion did Aurangzeb follow? *Aurangzeb was a Muslim, a follower of Islam.*

Other Moghul emperors had been Muslims. How had they behaved towards their Hindu subjects? *They allowed their Hindu subjects to worship in their own way.*

What kind of law did Aurangzeb try to apply to all of his subjects? *He tried to make them obey the law of the Muslim faith (the Shari'ah).*

How did Aurangzeb treat the Hindus in his country? Give at least two examples. *Aurangzeb refused to give Hindus positions at court; he forced them to pay extra taxes; he destroyed Hindu temples; he made wine illegal; he ended music at his court; he made festivals illegal.*

What part of India did Aurangzeb spend so much time trying to conquer? *He tried for years to conquer the south of India.*

What is the name of this southern part of India? *The south of India was called the Deccan.*

What was the Deccan like? *The Deccan was covered with jagged hills, rough country, and thick brush* OR *The Deccan was mostly Muslim and it wasn't under Aurangzeb's control.*

Who helped the kingdoms of the Deccan fight against Aurangzeb? *Hindu tribes called Marathas helped the Deccan kingdoms fight against Aurangzeb.*

What is the name for bands of soldiers who fight in sneak attacks rather than as an organized army? *We call them guerilla warriors.*

While Aurangzeb was fighting in the Deccan, what was going on in the rest of his empire? *He ignored the rest of his empire; his administrators were spending money freely, neglecting the people, allowing crime to flourish.*

Who built a new city and factory in Bengal, on the eastern coast of India? *English merchants built a new city and factory in Bengal.*

What was the name of the new city that the English built? *The city was called Calcutta.*

How did Aurangzeb feel about his reign at the end of his life? *He was weary and sick, and he knew that the end of India's greatness was coming.*

### Narration Exercise

As with the first section of this chapter, used "directed narration." This "directed narration" has two parts. First, ask the student:

"What were Aurangzeb's three decisions?" (If necessary, you may prompt the student by hinting, "One had to do with religious faith; the second, with attacking part of India; the third, with foreign merchants.")

Acceptable answers include:

*First.* Aurangzeb decided to make Muslim law the law of India OR Aurangzeb decided to make Hindus obey Muslim law.

*Second.* Aurangzeb decided to attack the south part of India OR Aurangzeb decided to conquer the Deccan.

*Third.* Aurangzeb allowed the English to build a new city in India OR Aurangzeb let English merchants settle down on the eastern shore of India.

Now ask the student, "Can you give me one or two important details about each of these decisions?"

Acceptable answers include:

*First.* Aurangzeb's ancestors allowed Muslims and Hindus to live together in peace, but Aurangzeb wanted to spread the Muslim faith and make India into a Muslim country; he only allowed Muslims to have power in the country; he refused to give Hindus positions at court; he forced Hindus to pay extra taxes; he destroyed Hindu temples; he made wine illegal; he banned music, festivals, art, and parties; Muslims and Hindus began to quarrel with each other.

*Second.* Aurangzeb spent over twenty-five years conquering the Deccan; he couldn't expand his empire to the north, east, or west, so he decide to move south; the Deccan leaders were Muslim, but didn't want to be ruled by the Moghuls; the Deccan leaders made alliances with the Hindu tribes called the Marathas; the Marathas were Hindus who resented the ways Hindus were treated in India; Aurangzeb conquered the kingdoms of the Deccan, but they were never really loyal; guerilla warriors in the Deccan kept fighting against Aurangzeb's rule; Aurangzeb ignored the rest of his empire while he was fighting in the Deccan.

*Third.* Aurangzeb's grandfather had signed a trade treaty with England; English merchants could build trading posts in India; the English wanted to build a trading post in Bengal, on the eastern coast; the trading post became known as Calcutta; Calcutta had a factory, soldiers, and gunpowder; Calcutta looked more like an English colony than an Indian city.

## Additional History Reading

*Captain Kidd: 17th-Century Pirate of the Indian Ocean and African Coast,* by Aileen Weintraub (Powerkids Press, 2002). An English pirate troubles the Indian coast during Moghul days. Simple text, plenty of color pictures. (RA 1-2, IR 3-4)

*India* by Jim Bartell (Bellwether Media, 2011). An ideal first book on India—its geography, culture and people—for early elementary students. (RA 2-5, IR 3-5)

*Letters Home from India,* by Marcia S. Gresko (Gale Group, 1999). This guide to India describes visits to New Delhi, Bombay, the Taj Mahal, and other historical sites. (RA 2-3, IR 4-5)

*Nur Jahan of India,* by Shirin Yim Bridges, illus. Albert Nguyen (Goosebottom Books, 2010). Nur Jahan was Jahangir's wife. This book describes her work, her clothing, her work with her husband, and her influence on India through her husband. Contains photos, drawings, and maps. *Preview (for items such as a definition of "eunuch") before reading aloud or handing over for independent reading.* (RA 1-4, IR 3-6)

*Taj Mahal* by Grace Hansen (Abdo Kids, 2018). With big, beautiful photographs and simple text, this book is written at an early elementary level yet would be a good supplement for most elementary students. (RA 1-4, IR1-4)

*Taj Mahal: A Story of Love and Empire*, by Elizabeth Mann, illus. Alan Witschonke (Mikaya Press, 2008). Definitely for reading aloud, but full of beautiful illustrations of the Taj Mahal. The text and explanatory captions are also very engaging and give the sense of story behind the building. (RA 1-4, IR 5-7)

*Where is the Taj Mahal?*, by Dorothy Hoobler and Thomas Hoobler (Grosset & Dunlap, 2017). Tells about Shah Jahan's childhood, of meeting his future wife, and of their life together. Contains beautiful black and white illustrations, maps, and close-up photos of sections of the Taj Mahal. (RA 1-3, IR 3-5)

*Diwali*, by Hannah Eliot, illus. Archana Sreenivasan (Little Simon, 2018). Not your usual board book! This account of the Hindu festival Diwali explains quite a bit about the reasons for celebrating. It is intricately illustrated and colored for eye-popping enjoyment. (RA 1-2, IR 2-4)

*Hinduism* by Rita Faelli (AV2 by Weigl, 2016). This basic introduction to the most common religion in India includes all of the information you would expect on Hindu beliefs as well as interactive elements available online. (RA 2-6, IR 3-5)

*Visiting a Mandir*, by Jean Mead and Ruth Nason (Evans Brothers Limited, 2005). This photo-filled book contains explanations about a Hindu place of worship, or *mandir*. It describes some of the objects, ceremonies, and symbols found in a *mandir*. Great introduction. (RA 1, IR 2-4)

*A World of Food: India* by Anita Ganeri (Clara House Books, 2010). With introductory chapters on India's history and role in world history, this book also includes information on Indian culture and food—including several recipes to give a hands-on approach to your study of the country. (RA 4-6, IR 2-4)

## Corresponding Literature Suggestions

*The Adventures of Rama*, by Milo Cleveland Beach (Mapin Publishing, 2011). This adaptation from the Indian epic poem *The Ramayana* is illustrated with twenty-three reproductions of lavish paintings from a late-sixteenth century Mughal manuscript. (RA 1-3, IR 3-4)

*The Elephant's Friend and other Tales from Ancient India* retold by Marcia Williams (Candlewick Press, 2012). Written in a graphic novel format with colorful, whimsical illustrations, this collection of Indian folktales will appeal to a wide variety of readers. (IR 2-5)

*Folktales from India*, A. K. Ramanuijan (Pantheon Books, 1994). Over a hundred folktales, from one to ten pages long, coming from twenty-one different Indian languages. Some can be read independently by strong third-grade readers or above. (RA 2-3, IR 3-7)

*Good Night India*, by Nitya Mohan Khemka, illus. Kavita Singh Kale (Good Night Books, 2017). Board book for preschoolers following along, or for young elementary students to practice reading aloud from. The very colorful pages take the reader on a journey through India, stopping at festivals, buildings, and geographical destinations. (RA 1, IR 2-4)

*How Ganesh Got his Elephant Head* by Harish Johairi and Vatsala Sperling (Bear Cub Books, 2003). Ganesh, one of the most beloved characters in Indian folklore, is known for his elephant head. This advanced picture book tells the tale of how he became the elephant-headed God. Character traits such as dedication and compassion are emphasized. (RA 2-4, IR 3-6)

*Monsoon*, by Uma Krishnaswami, illus. Jamel Akib (Farrar, Straus & Giroux, 2003). Set in modern India, but reflecting a centuries-old reality of Indian life, this lovely picture book shows a child waiting for the beginnings of the rainy season in northern India. (RA 2, IR 3-4) **E-Only.**

*Ramayana* by Arshia Satter (Restless Books, 2016). This illustrated retelling of the famous Indian tale is both entertaining and exciting. (RA 2-6, IR 4-6)

*Stories From India*, by Anna Milbourne, illus. Linda Edwards (Usborne Publishing, 2005). Not to be confused with Usborne's *Illustrated Stories From India.* This older edition has the stories printed on the illustrations which are gorgeously patterned, colored, and drawn. The stories are engagingly written. This book is out of print, but seems to be fairly easily located through secondhand sellers (or local libraries or interlibrary loans). **OOP**

*Tales from India* by Jamila Gavin (Templar Books, 2011). Ideal for read-alouds. Each chapter includes a traditional Indian myth of how things came to be. The illustrations are quite remarkable. (RA 2-6, IR 4-6)

*Tigers at Twilight*, by Mary Pope Osborne, illus. Sal Murdocca (Random House Books, 1999). Not much information about Indian history, but Magic Tree House fans will enjoy Jack and Annie's adventures in the jungles of India. (RA 2, IR 3-4)

## MAP WORK

**India** *(Student Page 34, answer 322)*

1. Aurangzeb focused his energy on trying to conquer the southern parts of India, including the Deccan. Draw a large circle around "Deccan" and color it brown.
2. The Marathas were Hindu tribes who helped the people of the Deccan fight Aurangzeb. Make a small symbol for the Marathas. (You might choose to use an "M".) In the key in the upper left hand of the map, draw your symbol for the Marathas in the correct box. Then, draw the symbol in three places outside of the brown circle around the Deccan. Draw arrows from the symbols toward the brown circle to show that the Marathas attacked Aurangzeb.
3. The British established a trading post in Calcutta. From here, they eventually took over India! Draw a blue and red box around Calcutta. After you've drawn the box, draw six blue and red arrows from Calcutta into India.

**COLORING PAGE** When his wife Mumtaz died, Shah Jahan decided to build a tomb, or mausoleum, that would show the whole world how much he loved her. Twenty thousand craftsmen labored for twenty years to build the Taj Mahal. *(Student Page 35)*

## PROJECTS

### ART PROJECT Decorate the Taj Mahal

The two most distinctive decorative features of the Taj Mahal are Arabic calligraphy (sayings from the Koran) and *pietra dura*. Pietra dura is a craft where precious gems are inlaid into a geometric or floral design. The Taj Mahal does not have any pictures of animals or people because Muslims did not draw pictures of them. Make your own decoration in the style of the Taj Mahal.

*Materials:*
- ☐ piece of paper
- ☐ colored pencils

*Directions:*

1. Write a message in your best cursive handwriting on the piece of paper.
2. Along the lines of your handwriting, draw and fill in small circles, diamonds, and triangles. These represent gemstones, inlaid along your writing.
3. Decorate the rest of the piece of paper with fruit, vines, flowers, and geometric designs. Use lots of colors to show how you would use gemstones in the design.

## Activity Project Guerilla Warfare

Aurangzeb spent twenty-six years in the Deccan, fighting off guerilla warriors. Guerilla warriors are soldiers who fight in sneak attacks and from under cover. Use the techniques of guerilla warfare to see if you can catch your parent by surprise.

*Materials:*

- ☐ three ribbons
- ☐ three clothespins

*Directions:*

1. The parent should attach three ribbons to the back of his or her shirt with clothespins.
2. Over the course of the day, the child should hide "under cover" (under a table, for example). The child must sneak up to the parent and try to get a ribbon without being caught by the parent. If the parent nabs the child, the child must give back the ribbon or try again. If the child makes it safely back under cover, the ribbon belongs to the child. Point out to the child that when one side (the parent) is stronger than the other side (the child), guerrilla warfare is a better strategy than frontal attack. After all, the parent would definitely catch the child if the child walked up to the parent and said, "Hi! I am going to try to take the ribbon from you now."

## Activity Project Khurram's Birthday Celebration

The English ambassador wrote to James I about the riches in Jahangir's court. He described in amazement the enormous celebration held on the birthday of Khurram, the emperor's favorite son. On this day, Khurram was dressed in gold and jewels and was seated on one side of an enormous pair of golden scales. Courtiers heaped bags of gold, jewels, spices, corn, and butter on the other side of the scales until they had measured out the weight of the prince in goods. Then the goods were given away to the poor. You can stage your own version of Khurram's birthday celebration. See if you can measure out items that will weigh the same as one of your stuffed animals!

*Materials:*

- ☐ a stuffed animal (not light-weight)
- ☐ 2 grocery plastic bags (with handles)
- ☐ masking tape
- ☐ long wooden rod like a mop or shop-broom handle (preferably the kind that unscrews at the base)
- ☐ goods (like popcorn kernels, sticks of butter, costume jewelry, spice containers)
- ☐ paper and pencil

*Directions:*

1. Put the stuffed animal in one plastic bag. If the stuffed animal doesn't fit, find a smaller animal.
2. Hang the handles from one end of the rod.
3. Tape the handles in place.
4. Tape the empty bag to the opposite end of the rod.

5. Balance the rod on the back of a chair or stool. The center of the rod should rest on the chair or stool. The stuffed animal should cause the rod to tip in its direction.
6. Fill the empty bag with goods until the rod balances.
7. Write on the piece of paper the contents of the bag (i.e. "2 sticks of butter," or "2 cups popcorn kernels," or "ten strings of beads").
8. Fill the bag with different kinds of things. Get creative!

## Craft Project The Peacock Throne

Shah Jahan's throne, the Peacock Throne, cost five million dollars! The Peacock Throne was covered with emeralds, rubies, diamonds, and pearls. It was covered by a canopy held up by twelve pillars made of emerald. On top of the canopy, a peacock sat. It had a gold body, a tail made out of sapphire, and a huge ruby on its chest with an enormous pearl hanging from it. The Peacock Throne was large enough to lie down in! Turn your own bed into the Peacock Throne and sit back and think about what it would be like to be emperor of all of India!

*Materials:*

- ☐ Student Page 36: Peacock Template
- ☐ paper plate
- ☐ scissors
- ☐ glue stick
- ☐ glitter, sequins, craft jewels, markers
- ☐ two sheets of colored construction paper
- ☐ "step" (an upside-down laundry basket or plastic crate, a stool)
- ☐ fabric (like a pretty blanket or sheet)

*Directions:*

1. Color and decorate the peacock template with the markers, glitter, sequins, or craft jewels.
2. Cut out the template and paste it to the paper plate.
3. Decorate the two sheets of construction paper with the markers, glitter, sequins, or craft jewels.
4. Set up the step at the base of the bed. Drape the step with fabric.
5. Hang up the two pieces of decorated construction paper on the footboard or along the side of the bed. Hang the peacock on the headboard (or the wall above the bed).

# Battle, Fire, and Plague in England

CHAPTER 12

## Encyclopedia Cross-References

*UBWH 158-159, UILE 306-307*
*KIHW 430-431, 442, KHE 260-261*

## CHARLES LOSES HIS HEAD

### Review Questions

Who inherited the throne of England after James I? *James's son Charles became king after James.*

What was the name of the French Catholic princess who became King Charles's wife? *Her name was Henrietta Maria.*

How did most English Protestants feel about Catholicism? *They hated and feared Catholicism.*

Why did Charles cancel his big coronation parade? *He was afraid that Puritans might shout insults at him along the way.*

Name one or two of the things that went wrong during Charles's coronation. *Henrietta refused to come to the Protestant ceremony and punched her fist through a glass window; the royal barge went aground; Charles tripped at the threshold of the church and nearly fell; a jewel fell out of his coronation ring and disappeared; the crowd didn't hear the Archbishop tell them to shout "God Save the King"; there was an earthquake!*

Charles and Parliament had different ideas about who should make the laws in England. What did Charles think? What did Parliament think? *He thought the king had a divine right to rule—that God had put him on the throne, and his subjects should obey without question. Parliament thought that its members should make laws because they represented the people of England.*

Why did King Charles dismiss Parliament? *He dismissed Parliament because the members would not give him the money he wanted.*

What did Puritans do during Charles's rule? *Hundreds left England and went to the American colonies.*

Why did Charles have to call Parliament back into session after eleven years? *He was running low on money and needed to ask them for more.*

What do we call this parliament, which went on meeting for eight years? *We call it the Long Parliament.*

What did the members of the Long Parliament start bickering about among themselves? *The Puritans and non-Puritans were arguing over whether the Church of England was pure enough.*

Why did Charles bring five hundred soldiers to Parliament one day? *He was trying to arrest the five Puritans who were his fiercest enemies.*

How did the people of England react to the news that Charles would use the English army against other Englishmen? *More Englishmen turned against Charles, and a rebellion started to form.*

During the civil war, what were the nicknames given to the two sides? *Those who supported King Charles were called Cavaliers, and those who supported Parliament were called Roundheads.*

Whom did the Roundheads find to lead their New Model Army? *Oliver Cromwell led the New Model Army.*

What happened at the battle of Marston Moor? *The Roundheads defeated Charles's army because twenty thousand Scotsmen came to help out.*

After the war between Cavaliers and Roundheads was won, whom did Oliver Cromwell drive out of Parliament? *He drove out everyone who still had sympathy for Charles.*

After this, Parliament only had sixty members left. What do we call this Parliament? *We call it the Rump Parliament.*

Charles was put on trial for treason. At the end of the trial, what did the court decide to do to him? *They decided to have him put to death.*

How was Charles executed? *His head was cut off by an executioner.*

What year did Charles's execution happen? *Charles was executed in 1649.*

## Narration Exercise

Since there is a lot of information in this chapter, use "directed narration." Say to the student, "This chapter covered three big events. Charles became king of England, a civil war broke out, and Charles was executed. Let's talk about these events one at a time. First, can you tell me three important things that happened during Charles's reign, but before the Civil War?"

Acceptable answers include: *Charles married a Catholic princess, and his people resented and feared her; many bad things happened at Charles's coronation; Charles believed that he had a divine right to rule, so when Parliament wouldn't obey him, he dismissed Parliament; Charles forced Puritans to leave England and forced the Scottish church to use the English prayer book; Charles had to reassemble Parliament because he was running out of money; the Long Parliament met for eight years; the Long Parliament bickered with itself over the purity of the English church; Charles marched his army into Parliament to arrest some of its members.*

"Second, let's talk about the Civil War. What event set off the Civil War?" *Charles marched his army into Parliament to arrest some of its members.*

"Tell me about the two sides during the Civil War and describe how one of the sides won the war."

Acceptable answers include:

*The Cavaliers were on the king's side, and the Roundheads were on the side of the Puritans. The Roundheads had an army called the New Model Army. Oliver Cromwell was its commander. The Scots joined the New Model Army, so the Roundheads defeated the Cavaliers.* OR

*Charles's army, the Cavaliers, fought against Oliver Cromwell's army, the Roundheads. The war went on for six years. Finally it ended at the Battle of Marston Moor. Charles was put in jail, and the Roundheads were in charge.*

"Third, let's talk about Charles's execution. Can you tell me why Oliver Cromwell and his followers decided to put Charles on trial, and what happened? Try to remember the year that Charles was executed!"

Acceptable answers include:

*Cromwell was afraid that Charles's supporters would put him back on the throne. Parliament thought that England would only be peaceful if Charles were put to death. So they put him on trial. Charles wouldn't answer any questions, but he was declared guilty. He was beheaded in 1649.* OR

*Parliament didn't really know what to do with Charles, but Cromwell wanted him gone for good. He drove everyone who had sympathy for Charles out of Parliament. Then Parliament put Charles on trial because he attacked his own people. Charles was convicted and put to death. It was 1649.*

## Review Questions

What is a monarchy? *A monarchy is a country ruled by a king or a queen.*

Now that Charles was dead, England was to be a country where the people rule by electing their own leaders. What was such a country called? *It was called a commonwealth.*

What part of English society did many men and women want to see reformed? *They wanted to see the courts changed for the better.*

During this time, why were the rich people the only ones in England who could make use of the courts? *The laws were complicated, and the lawyers who understood them cost a lot of money.*

Did the Rump Parliament act quickly to make the English laws better? *No, they moved very slowly.*

When Oliver Cromwell became frustrated with the Rump Parliament, what did he use his soldiers to do? *He drove the Rump Parliament out.*

Why did Oliver Cromwell think that it was all right to use the army against other Englishmen? *Cromwell believed that his use of force pleased God.*

Who picked the members of the new Nominated Assembly? *The Nominated Assembly members were picked by Cromwell and his army generals.*

What nickname was this new Parliament, the Nominated Assembly, given? *It became known as the Barebones Parliament.*

What title did Parliament give to Cromwell? *Parliament gave him the title Lord Protector of England.*

Can you name two things Cromwell did that were kinglike? *He moved his family into the royal palace; his advisors called him "Your Highness"; he had a ceremony that looked like a coronation ceremony; he told Parliament that he was speaking for God; he dissolved Parliament.*

Can you name two things that Oliver Cromwell did that made him unpopular? *He ordered his soldiers to destroy royal regalia; he allowed them to wreck churches that seemed too "Catholic"; he made card playing illegal; he ordered the theaters closed; the only songs allowed were hymns.*

After Oliver Cromwell died, who claimed the title of Lord Protector? *His son Richard claimed the title of Lord Protector.*

How did the English react when Richard became Lord Protector? *They were tired of the protectorate* OR *They started to argue about who should rule England next.*

Who did the new Parliament invite to come and rule England? *They invited Charles I's son, Charles II, to come and be the king.*

In what year did Charles II return to England? *He returned in 1660.*

## Narration Exercise

Say to the student, "Can you tell me three important things that happened during Oliver Cromwell's protectorate, and then can you tell me how the protectorate ended? Be sure to give the date!"

Acceptable answers for the first part of the question include:

"Many English wanted Parliament to reform the courts, but Parliament never did."

"Oliver Cromwell replaced Parliament with his own Parliament, called the Barebones Parliament (The Nominated Assembly)."

"Oliver Cromwell was supposed to ask Parliament for permission to rule, but he dissolved Parliament when it disagreed with him."

"Cromwell acted like a king—he moved his family into the palace, his advisors called him 'Your Highness,' and he said that he spoke for God."

"Cromwell's soldiers broke up the royal regalia and any churches that seemed too 'Catholic'."

"Cromwell made it against the law to play cards, go to plays, or sing songs other than hymns."

"Someone tried to assassinate Cromwell because he was so unpopular."

Acceptable answers for the second part of the question include:

"Cromwell grew sick and died. His son wanted to become Lord Protector, but instead the English invited Charles's son back from France to become king. He came back in 1660."

"After Cromwell died, his son Richard claimed the title Lord Protector. But the English were tired of the Protectorate. Noblemen argued about who could become king. So a general helped invite Charles II back to England in 1660."

## PLAGUE AND FIRE

### Review Questions

What is the Restoration? *The Restoration is the period of Charles II's reign, when the monarchy was "restored."*

What was England's largest city during the reign of Charles II? *London was the largest city in England. It had nearly half a million people.*

What was London like? *It was crowded and dirty—houses were close together, and there was water, sewage, and trash in the streets.*

What disease began to spread through London just four years after Charles II's triumphant return? *The plague, also called the Black Death, began to spread through the city.*

Where did Londoners try to go? Why didn't this work? *People in London tried to flee into the country, but villagers drove them off because they were afraid of the plague.*

What animals did the people of London kill in order to stop the plague? *They killed all the dogs and cats, thinking that these animals were carrying the plague.*

Which animals were really to blame for carrying the plague? *The fleas who lived on rats were the ones carrying the plague.*

For how long did the Black Death afflict London? *It lasted for a year, killing more than two hundred thousand people.*

Nine months after the plague, there was a great fire in London. How did it get started? *A coal fell out of a baker's oven and started a fire in some brushwood.*

Was the Lord Mayor of London worried about the fire? *No, he said that a woman could put it out.*

What enormous stone church was destroyed by the fire? *Saint Paul's Cathedral was destroyed by the fire.*

How many days did the fire burn? *The fire burned for three days.*

How did soldiers manage to stop the fire? *Soldiers blew up houses in front of the fire with gunpowder, and pulled away the wreckage so that the fire wouldn't have fuel.*

How much of London was burnt? *Four-fifths of London had been burnt.*

### Narration Exercise

"Two terrible things happened to London. First, the Black Death started in London, It spread all over the city, because it was carried by the fleas on rats. People tried to flee to the country, but the villagers drove them away. The churches ran out of room to bury the dead! Finally, the Black Death died down. But then a fire started in 1666. A coal fell out of a baker's oven. The fire spread all though London. People ran to the churches, but even the churches burned down. Finally, soldiers blew up houses in front of the fire and stopped it. But four-fifths of London had burned down." OR

"The Restoration was the time when Charles II ruled. In the Restoration, life in England seemed to be back to normal. But then the plague started to spread through London. Thousands of people died every week. People stayed in their houses—and grass started to grow in the streets! Two out of five people died in London. When the plague died down, something else horrible happened. A fire started in a baker's shop and spread all over London. The fire even burned stone buildings. It burned for three days! By the time the fire burned down, houses, churches, jails, and post offices were all gone."

## Additional History Reading

*England,* by Amy Rechner (Bellwether Media, 2018). With vibrant photos, interesting text and eye-catching sidebars, this volume will help students better understand modern England in light of the country's history. (RA 2-4, IR 3-5)

*The United Kingdom,* edited by Jeff Wallenfeldt (Britannica Educational Publishing, 2014). A weighty text with perhaps more information than anyone will ever need to know about the history of the United Kingdom, portions of this book would nonetheless be useful to older students looking to supplement their reading on certain historical periods. (IR 6+)

*Anthony van Dyck,* by Alix Wood (Windmill Books, 2015). Van Dyck was the court painter for King Charles I, and is best known for the portraits he made of Charles and his family. This biographical book contains photos of some of his paintings, as well as a bit of guidance on some art techniques. (RA 1-2, IR 2-4)

*Oliver Cromwell (British History Makers)*, by Leon Ashworth (Cherrytree, 2015). From a London publisher, a rare juvenile biography of the Lord Protector. Not always easy to find in the U.S., but there are many used copies available. Excellent for struggling readers. (IR 2-5)

*Tudors and Stuarts,* by Brian and Brenda Williams, illus. Carlo Molinari and Clive Goodyer (Ladybird, 2013). This book covers a longer period of time than just the English Civil War; but it has short chapters about the Roundheads and the Cavaliers, as well as about the Great Fire and the plague. (RA 1-3, IR 2-4)

*London: From Roman Capital to Olympic City* by Richard Platt (Kingfisher, 2009). This unique book shows illustrations of London as it might have looked at various points throughout history—including during the plague and the Great Fire. (RA 2-6, IR 4-6)

*A Journal of the Plague Year,* by Daniel Defoe (Dover, 2001). First published in 1722, this account of the Plague of 1664-1665 was reconstructed by Defoe from letters, journals, and eyewitness accounts. Read selected portions out loud. (RA 3-5, IR 6-8)

*The Bubonic Plague,* by Kevin Cunningham (ABDO Publishing, 2011). A comprehensive overview of the plague and its effects in Europe throughout history. Chapter 8 specifically addresses the second pandemic and would be excellent supplementary material. (RA 3-6, IR 4-6)

*You Wouldn't Want to be Sick in the 16th Century!* by Kathryn Senior, illus. David Antram (Franklin Watts, 2002). Although this entertaining guide covers medical practices a few years before the Plague, medicine hadn't advanced much further by the middle of the seventeenth century; this will provide a good overview of what doctors were able to do in the face of the Black Death. (RA 2, IR 3-5)

*The Great Fire of London,* by Susanna Davidson (Usborne, 2015) With larger text and short paragraphs, this chapter book is ideal for young readers looking for more information on the Great Fire. (RA 1-3, IR 2-4)

*The Great Fire of London of 1666,* by Magdalena Alagna (Rosen Publishing, 2004). Readable and brief, this book tracks the day-by-day progress of the terrible fire. (RA 2-3, IR 4-6)

*You Wouldn't Want to Be in the Great Fire of London!,* by Jim Pipe, illus. David Antram (Book House, 2016). Another great book in the *You Wouldn't Want to* series. In a humorous but factual way, this book covers the events of the Great Fire of London. (RA 1-3, IR 3-5)

*Samuel Pepys,* by Izzi Howell (Wayland, 2016). This simple biography about Samuel Pepys gives facts about the diarist who recorded the Great Fire of London and the Plague. Great for beginning readers. (RA 1-2, IR 1-4)

*William Harvey: Discoverer of How Blood Circulates,* by Lisa Yount (Enslow Publishers, 2008). Harvey was a court physician to James I and Charles I. This book recounts his life and his discoveries. Good for reading aloud to young children who are curious about science, anatomy, and seventeenth-century medicine. (RA 1-4, IR 3-6)

## Corresponding Literature Suggestions

*Ghosts, Rogues, and Highwaymen: 20 Stories from British History,* by Geraldine McCaughrean, illus. Richard Brassey (Orion Publishing, 2002). Contains some fictional and/or debunked stories from the English Civil War. McCaughrean is a wonderful storyteller; it would be worth finding this on the used book market or through library/interlibrary loan. **OOP**

*The Great, Smelly, Small-Toothed Dog: A Folktale from Great Britain,* retold by Margaret Read McDonald (August House Little Folk, 2007). Young students will enjoy this British variant of Beauty and the Beast. (RA 1-3, IR 2-3)

*Jack and the Beanstalk,* illustrated by Nina Towe (Michael Neugebauer Publishing, 2017). The classic English fairy tale is lavishly illustrated—a delightful read aloud experience for all ages! (RA 1-6,IR 3-5)

*The Loathsome Dragon,* retold by David Wiesenthal and Kim Kahng (Clarion Books, 2005). With familiar elements like a wicked stepmother, a beautiful princess and a dragon, this English fairy tale (and its illustrations) will enchant readers of all ages. (RA 1-4, IR 3-5)

*Rex and the Royal Prisoner,* by Kate Sheppard, illus. Kate Sheppard (Walker Books Ltd., 2015). This quirkily illustrated book follows a dog named Rex who goes back in time, meets King Charles I's dog, and tries to rescue the king from being imprisoned. (RA 1-3, IR 2-4)

*The Great Plague: A London Girl's Diary, 1665-1666,* by Pamela Oldfield (Scholastic, 2001). This chapter-book novel, part of the *My Story* series, follows the adventures of a thirteen-year-old girl who lives in London during the days of the plague and the Great Fire. May be accessible to some advanced third-grader readers. (IR 4-6) **OOP**

*At the Sign of the Sugared Plum*, by Mary Hooper (Bloomsbury USA, 2003). Written for fifth-graders, this historical novel tells of a young girl who comes to London in 1665 to help her sister run a candy shop—just as the plague begins. (IR 5-8) **E-Only.**

*The Baker's Boy and the Great Fire of London*, by Tom and Tony Bradman (Wayland, 2018). Young Will believes he must stop the fire from spreading from his family's bakery to the rest of the city. This book is a short overview of the fire and features an appearance by Samuel Pepys. (RA 1-2, IR 2-4)

*Raven Boy,* by Pippa Goodheart (Catnip Publishing, 2007). Exciting historical fiction from the United Kingdom covering the era of the Great Fire of London and the plague. (RA 3-5, IR 4-6)

*Toby and the Great Fire of London,* by Margaret Nash (Franklin Watts, 2008) This book is ideal for new readers to help them build up their confidence while learning about an important historical event. (RA 1-2, IR 1-2)

*Vlad and the Great Fire of London* by Kate Cunningham (Reading Riddle, 2016) Aimed at younger students, this book is an entertaining introduction to a somber topic, told from the perspectives of a flea and a rat! (RA 1-3, IR 1-3)

## MAP WORK

### Charles I's England *(Student Page 37, answer 322)*

1. Charles I planned to get to his coronation in London by sailing down the Thames River. Trace the Thames River in blue.
2. Charles made the Puritans and Parliament angry. When he realized a rebellion might break out, he fled London and went to the north of England. Draw a red arrow from London into the northern part of England.
3. Parliament gained control of the southeastern part of England. Draw a circle in the southeastern part of England (on the peninsula), and color it in yellow.
4. Charles lost an important battle to Cromwell at Marston Moor. Marston Moor is in the northern part of England. Find the dot, and label it Marston Moor. Then, draw a blue circle around the dot that represents Marston Moor.

### Coloring Page

The Great Fire of London burned for three days. Four-fifths of old London burned down! *(Student Page 38)*

## PROJECTS

### Activity Project: A City Too Close

How could an entire city go up in flames? The buildings of London were so crowded that fire leapt easily from one house to the next. Cut out this London City street model to see how crowded London's buildings were.

*Materials:*
- ☐ Student Page 39: London City Street Template
- ☐ colored pencils
- ☐ glue
- ☐ toothpicks
- ☐ duct tape or electrical tape
- ☐ scissors
- ☐ jumbo craft sticks (optional)

Directions:

1. Paste the London City Street Template onto thin cardboard. If you can photocopy the template and make more than one street of buildings, you can build a larger cityscape; also, you may wish to enlarge the London City street template to fit onto 11" x 14" white cardstock.
2. Color in the buildings. London buildings were usually wood and cob (hay and mud), white-washed into a grayish white color. But your street buildings can be any color you like!
3. Cut out the building strip, being careful not to break up the four connected buildings.
4. The growing city of London had tailor shops where a man could get a finely made suit, shoe shops, millinery shops (for hats and bonnets), bakeries, butcher shops, inns, pubs, and more. Using the blank signs on the top of the enlarged cardstock copy, design different business signs for your shops. Poke a small hole in the top of the shop roofs and insert a toothpick into each hole so that the toothpicks are perpendicular to the ground. Tape the signs onto the toothpicks. A small piece of duct tape on the backside will serve to hold the toothpicks in place.
5. Score the two end edges on the dotted lines and bend them back to create a stand. If a larger stand is needed, cut out the scraps from the white cardstock and enlarge the edges. Cut the extra pieces wider by the same height. Glue jumbo craft sticks behind the last buildings on either side. This will add strength, if needed.
6. Create a street at least eight buildings long, gluing the edges together in the middle. If desired, you can build the other side of your street with another row of eight houses. There was typically enough space for one carriage to drive through and a little walking space on either side. This made the streets very narrow. When the city of London caught on fire, the connected roofs made of flammable material caused the city to go up quickly in flames.
7. If you want to burn your city down, give it a try! Wait until the paper and cardboard is completely dry. Make sure you put the city in a very safe place (outdoors, or in a fireplace) before lighting it. If the buildings weren't connected, would your fire burn as quickly?

## Craft Activity Project **Roundheads and Cavaliers!**

English Puritans, who fought for Parliament and against Charles, were called Roundheads because of their Puritan haircuts. Below is a Roundhead wig that would help you blend in to the New Model Army, commanded by Oliver Cromwell. Or would you prefer to wear a Cavalier badge, showing your allegiance to King Charles? Pick a side!

### ***Roundhead Wig***

Materials:

- ☐ one skein of any shade of brown yarn
- ☐ cardboard side of a box
- ☐ measuring tape
- ☐ brown felt rectangle 7" x 1"
- ☐ brown thread (optional)
- ☐ sewing machine or hot glue and hot glue gun

Directions:

1. Measure from the center of your head to your shoulders and double the number. Cut your cardboard that length and 15 inches wide.
2. Wrap the yarn around the cardboard lengthwise until the yarn is all used. Make sure your yarn is evenly dispersed along the width of the cardboard.
3. Once finished, carefully clip the two ends of the yarn. Lay the yarn on the table.

4. Place the brown felt strip in the center of the thick yarn mass. *If hot gluing* the wig together, place the hot glue on the first inch of the brown felt strip and press the yarn to it. Continue to apply glue to the felt strip one inch at a time. *If sewing*, place the strip down and sew over the yarn pieces, down the center, making sure each piece is tacked securely onto felt strip. Flip wig over so felt strip is lined up with the center of your head. Trim any side that is uneven.

***Cavalier Badge***

Materials:
- ☐ Crayola Model Magic or air-drying clay, one package, yellow, blue or red
- ☐ toothpick
- ☐ large safety pin or craft mounting pin (available at craft stores)
- ☐ black or blue marker

Directions:
1. Mold a golf ball size amount of the Model Magic or Sculpey into a flat star that fits into the palm of your hand.
2. On the backside, secure the safety pin or craft pin by adding extra clay over the non-open side of the pin.
3. Turn over the star to the front. Using the toothpick, engrave into the star the first letters of the following Latin phrase, from a medal King Charles I gave to soldiers who came to the aid of the Cavaliers in their fight against the Roundheads:

**INVICTAE FIDELITATIS PRAEMIUM**
Reward for faithfulness unconquered

4. After your star badge dries, go over the inscription with a black or blue marker to outline the letters. Write the interpretation on the back if you would like.

## COOKING PROJECT A Loaf That Measures Up

You're down to your last few pennies. You feel hungry but can only afford a penny loaf. Here in the growing city of London, the government has decreed that every penny loaf should weigh the same amount. The price of bread changes according to the price of a bushel of wheat. Bread prices are adjusted weekly by a jury of townsmen appointed to the task.

But which baker in the city will give you a loaf the fair and legal weight? The baker down the first street, so the neighbor whispers, is known to pinch off a bit of dough from the loaf. His weights are faulty. What about the baker a couple of streets over? It's a ways to walk, but that baker is said to be a fair man. Especially since he paid a fine last year of six shillings and two pence for selling a three-penny loaf two ounces short! He says it was an honest mistake. But how can you be sure that *your* penny loaf measures up to the proper weight? See if your loaf measures up!

Materials:
- ☐ favorite bread recipe, or store-bought bread mix
- ☐ scale of any kind, preferably an ounce scale

Directions:

1. Mix up a batch of bread using your favorite bread recipe or a premixed recipe—or use the recipe provided below (this is Susan's favorite easy bread recipe). Shape the mixed dough into a large round loaf and place on an oiled cookie sheet. Cornmeal may be sprinkled over the oil on the cookie sheet before placing the round loaf of dough; this helps the loaf slide off the cookie sheet after baking and adds chewiness to the bottom crust.
2. To weigh your bread, using a standard bathroom scale, step on the scale without the bread and note your weight. Now step on the scale holding your bread and note the difference. Subtract your first weight amount from your second and the difference is the weight of your bread. If you have an ounce scale, this will show the weight more accurately. (Alternately, you can use a kitchen scale if you have one.)
3. Experiment with other loaves of bread. How much does a store-bought loaf of bread weigh? A box of doughnuts? Other baked goods?

Optional: Look at the price on a loaf of bread and turn it into pennies ($2.65 = 265 pennies). See how heavy the bread is in ounces. Now divide the cost by the number of ounces. How much does your store-bought bread cost per ounce?

## Bread Recipe:

*Directions:*

1. Melt ½ stick of margarine in the microwave.
2. Dump 1 Tbs quick-rise yeast, ¼ cup sugar, ½ Tbs salt, and two cups of flour into the bowl of a food processor.
3. Add 1 cup of water and 1 egg to the margarine. With the blade running, pour water, egg, and margarine mixture into flour mixture.
4. Add flour until dough rolls up into a soft ball.
5. After shaping dough, allow to sit in pan for 1 hour on the back of the stove (or in another warm place).
6. Bake at 350 degrees for 35 minutes.

# The Sun King

## Encyclopedia Cross-References

*UBWH 158-159, UILE 312-313*
*KIHW 436-439, KHE 254-255, 264, 284*

## THE SUN KING OF FRANCE

### Review Questions

Who was Louis XIV's father? *His father was Louis XIII.*

How old was Louis XIV when he became the king of France? *He was four years and eight months old when he became king!*

When the French called their king a "visible divinity," what did they mean? *They meant that he was God's representative on earth.*

What did the king's minister, Cardinal Mazarin, continually remind him of? *He continually reminded the king that he should be treated like a god and rule with a strict hand.*

When Cardinal Mazarin died, what surprising announcement did the young king make? *He announced that he would rule without any ministers to advise him.*

What did Louis choose as his emblem, to represent his power? *He chose the Sun as his emblem and was called the Sun King.*

What was the name of the enormous palace that Louis ordered to be built? *The palace was known as Versailles.*

Can you remember two details about the palace at Versailles? *Versailles had a Hall of Mirrors with seventeen mirrors, a solid silver throne, hundreds of statues of Greek gods with Louis' face, and a Grand Canal that ran through the grounds.*

Why did Louis XIV bring his noblemen to Versailles? *He wanted to increase his power and keep his eye on them.*

How did Louis XIV treat the noblemen who joined his court at Versailles? *He forced them to pay attention to court manners; he encouraged them to spend too much money.*

Can you remember one of the catastrophes that Louis faced, late in his life? *His son died of smallpox; his grandson and his grandson's wife died; another grandson was killed falling from a horse; Louis got gangrene.*

What problems did Louis XIV leave behind him? *His wars and his extravagant lifestyle had cost much money and thousands of French lives.*

### Narration Exercise

"Louis XIV inherited the throne when he was only four years old. At first, he had a First Minister to help him reign. But then he announced that he would rule all alone. He called himself the Sun King because of his greatness. He built a huge fancy palace and spent many years fighting wars to make France larger. But when he died, the people of France were angry because Louis's wars and building projects had forced them to pay too many taxes and work too hard." OR

"Louis XIV wanted to make France great. He fought many wars and made France the largest country in Europe. He also built a huge palace at Versailles with a solid silver throne and statues of Greek gods, all with Louis' face. He forced his noblemen to live at the palace and obey him without question. But many French peasants died building Louis's palace and fighting in his wars. By the end of his reign, the people of France were angry with the king."

## Additional History Reading

*Welcome to France*, by Merdith Costain and Paul Collins (Chelsea House, 2001). Written on a third-grade level, this introduction to France gives a brief history as well. (RA 2, IR 3-4) **LFA**

*Brick City: Paris* by Warren Elsmore (Lonely Planet, 2018). A fun, hands-on supplement to your study of French history. Includes information on French history and instructions to make famous French landmarks out of Legos. (RA 2-4, IR 3-6)

*E is for Eiffel Tower: A France Alphabet*, by Helen L. Wilbur, illus. Yan Nascimbene (Sleeping Bear Press, 2010). This poetic and intricately illustrated book outlines some of the history, culture, and geography of France. In addition to the poetic parts is well-written supplementary text that adults can read to children to give even more background of the history and culture mentioned on each page. (RA 1-3, IR 3-6)

*France* by Bitsy Kemper (The Child's World, 2016). A broad overview of modern day France—its geography, government, people and daily life. Understanding the modern country will help students better understand historical context. (RA 2-6, IR 3-6)

*France* by Adam Markovics (Bearport Publishing, 2018). With simple text and large, vibrant photographs, this book is an ideal introduction to France for new readers. (RA K-3, IR 1-3)

*Good Night Paris*, by Adam Gamble and Mark Jasper, illus. Cooper Kelly (Good Night Books, 2019). A colorfully illustrated board book that takes young children on a tour of famous historical sites in and around Paris, including the Palace of Versailles. The text makes a delightful read-aloud for younger children, or easy reading practice for older readers. (RA 1-2, IR 2-4)

*How They Became Famous Dancers: A Dancing History*, by Anne Dunkin, illus. Christy Little (CreateSpace Independent Publishing Platform, 2015). This book of well-written biographies of dancers includes one about Louis XIV. It richly describes his childhood, his surroundings, and his love of dance and theatrical living. Would make a great read-aloud for young children. (RA 1-4, IR 4-7)

*The King's Day: Louis XIV of France*, by Aliki (HarperCollins, 1991). Step-by-step watercolors show every stage of King Louis's three-hour morning dressing ritual. (RA 1, IR 2-4) **OOP**

*French Baroque and Rococo Fashions*, by Tom Tierney (Dover Publications, 2002). For kids who want to know more about Louis XIV's fashion choices, this classic Dover coloring book is a wealth of information and drawings. Each illustration is captioned by descriptions of the featured costume in the time period. (RA 1-4, IR 3-6)

*Palace of Versailles: France's Royal Jewel*, by Linda Tagliaferro (Bearport Publishing Company, 2005). This is a great read-aloud introduction to the home that Louis XIV had built: full of facts about his early life, his lifestyle in the palace, and what happened to the palace after his death. (RA 1-3, IR 2-4)

*The Palace of Versailles* by James Barter (Lucent Books, 1999). While this book is quite detailed and likely too advanced for early elementary students, sections read aloud may enhance the study of the Sun King. (RA 4-6, IR 5+)

*Visitors to Versailles* by Danielle O. Kisluk-Grosheide (Metropolitan Museum of Art, 2018). While the text in this book is certainly beyond most elementary students, the paintings of Louis XIV's life and times and palace at Versailles are beyond compare and the book is worth a look for them alone. (RA 2-6)

*Haunted Houses Around the World,* by Joan Axelrod-Contrada (Capstone, 2017). The Palace of Versailles is included in this book of two-page spreads about why particular locations are considered haunted. Each spread features just one photo and an interestingly written narrative. (RA 1-3, IR 2-4)

*A World of Food: France* by Kathy Elgin (Clara House Books, 2010). Learning about a country's culture—especially its food—is a fun way to enhance any history study. Simple recipes, ideal for cooking with children, are included. (RA 2-5, IR 4-6)

## Corresponding Literature Suggestions

*The Man in the Iron Mask,* by Alexandre Dumas. This classic tale of intrigue during the reign of Louis XIV is available in a variety of translations. The 2003 one by Joachim Neugroschel (published by Penguin) is unabridged and very long; for a read-aloud or as an independent reading project for an advanced reader. Also consider the unabridged audio versions read by Geoffrey Sherman or Simon Vance. The *Great Illustrated Classics* abridgment (Waldman, 2008; IR 3-6) is an excellent choice for an independent reading project.

*Back in Time: The Second Journey through Time* by Geronimo Stilton (Scholastic, 2015). A lighthearted story of a mouse's time travels—including to the age of the Sun King, where he plans a party and finds a missing royal medallion case. (RA 1-3, IR 3-5)

*The Fly on the Ceiling,* by Dr. Julie Glass, illus. Richard Walz (Random House Books, 1998). A humorous and simple account of the life of Rene Descartes. Descartes was a mathematician from France who was once awarded a pension by nine-year-old King Louis XIV (though it was never paid). (RA 1-2, IR 2-4)

*King Louie's Shoes,* by D. J. Steinberg (Beach Lane Books, 2012). This picture book is a gem—not only does it include important facts about the Sun King, but it does so in a humorous way. Targeted to the younger elementary range but valuable for all ages. (RA 1-6, IR 2-6)

*The Last Musketeer,* by Stuart Gibbs (Harper Collins, 2011). Using the original Three Musketeers as a jumping-off point, this story of time travel weaves together fact and fantasy into an adventure that will appeal to a wide age range. (RA 3-6, IR 4-7)

*Mister Descartes and His Evil Genius,* by Jean Paul Mongin, trans. Anna Street, illus. Francois Schwoebel (Diaphanes, 2016). For confident readers or as a read-aloud, this funny picture book depicts some of the events of French philosopher Rene Descartes' life in a breezy manner. (RA 1-3, IR 3-6)

*The Orange Trees of Versailles,* by Annie Pietri, trans. by Catherine Temerson (Yearling Books, 2005). Talented Marion takes a job blending exquisite perfumes for Louis XIV's mistress. However, after credit is given to someone else, Marion starts sensing danger in the palace. **Parents should preview;** the nature of Louis' relationship to his "mistress" is not discussed in depth, but it is clear that he is having children with a woman other than his wife—a scenario which may prompt awkward questions. (RA 1-3, IR 3-6)

*The Story of Cyrano de Bergerac,* by Stefano Benni, trans. Howard Curtis, illus. Miguel Tanco (Penguin Random House, 2017). Story based on a play by Edmond Rostand, about French poet Cyrano de Bergerac who lived during the first part of King Louis XIV's reign. Cyrano is fictionally cast here as a man in love and in possession of a big nose. Quirky and colorful illustrations capture the imagination in this read-aloud. (RA 1-4, IR 3-6)

*Beauty and the Beast,* retold by Cynthia Rylant (Disney Hyperion, 2017). With lovely illustrations and a simplified storyline, this is an ideal introduction to the classic French tale for younger students. (RA K-3, IR 2-4)

*The Cat Who Walked Across France*, by Kate Banks, illus. George Hallensleben (Frances Foster Books, 2004). A cat returns to his home by the sea in a long journey through the French countryside. (IR 2-4)

*Cinderella,* adapted by Gilda Francis (Sterling Children's Books, 2013). A fresh look at the classic French fairy tale, this volume is beautifully illustrated and ideally suited as either a read-aloud for early elementary students or an independent reader for slightly older children. (RA K-4, IR 3-5)

*The Complete Fairy Tales*, by Charles Perrault, trans. Christopher Betts (Oxford University Press, 2009). For reading aloud to young children, this compilation of fairy tales Perrault collected during King Louis XIV's reign is fascinating. The originals are not like the Disney versions; they contain darker themes and endings. (RA 1-4, IR 4-7)

*Puss in Boots,* by Paul Galdone (Houghton Mifflin Harcourt, 2016). The classic French fairy tale of the ingenious cat Puss is delightfully told and illustrated in this edition. (RA 1-4, IR 3-5)

## MAP WORK

**France** *(Student Page 40, answer 322)*

1. France has many rivers. Find the rivers, which are indicated by the small dots on your map, and trace them in blue.
2. Louis XIV lived a lavish courtly life at Versailles. Draw a purple circle around Versailles, and color in the circle with purple.
3. The peasants of France became poorer and poorer. They had to pay heavy taxes to pay for Louis's rich life. Outline the border of France in orange. Then widen, or thicken, the orange band around the edge of the country until it is a thick orange band.
4. Because of the heavy taxes, the peasants became angry. Draw four orange arrows from the border (the thick orange band) of the country toward Versailles.

**COLORING PAGE** Louis XIV chose the sun as his symbol, and was called "The Sun King" by his servants. He wanted to seem as important to France as the sun is to the Earth. He was an excellent dancer, and in one ballet he played the part of Apollo the sun god in this beautiful golden costume. *(Student Page 41)*

## PROJECTS

### ACTIVITY PROJECT Medicine of the 1600s

Since the king held all the power in France, his health was very important. People thought that the country might be ruined if he got sick and died. So Louis had several doctors who kept a daily record of his health. Whenever he got sick, they tried all the best remedies for illness that they knew. In the 1600s, some of the treatments for illness were very strange: drinking tea made with pearls and bones, shaving your head and putting a pigeon on it, putting a split chicken on your back, and other odd things.

Try some of the remedies that King Louis' doctors used. They won't cure you of anything, but they are fun to try!

***Sip Bone and Pearl Tea***

Crush some "bone" (use a peppermint candy or a sugar cube) and place it in a cup filled with hot water. Add some "pearls" (miniature marshmallows). If you want to make a tasty beverage, add some hot cocoa mix (although Louis' doctors probably didn't do this for him!).

***Cut a Pigeon Over Your Shaved Head***

*You will want to do this outside or in the bathtub.* Unless your hair is quite short, cut a piece of pantyhose and slide it over your head. Then cut open a honeydew melon, a cantaloupe, or a big, juicy tomato (this will be the "pigeon") and let someone else set it on your head and mush it to get all the juice out. (Do you feel better now?)

***Split Chicken on Your Back***

*Again, do this outside or in the bathtub.* The idea was that the warm chicken would dry out the evil "humors" in the body. Cook some spaghetti (let it cool some—it should not be scalding). Lie on your stomach and have someone put the warm, dripping spaghetti noodles on your back and let them sit. Do you feel the "evil humors" drying up inside your body?

## ACTIVITY PROJECT Get Dressed like Louis XIV

As befitted a "god on earth," Louis XIV had literally thousands of servants and attendants who waited on him hand and foot. His morning routine alone took hours—and hundreds of people! With the help of your parents, siblings, or friends, act out a morning in the life of Louis XIV. Follow these steps (everyone may need to play more than one part):

1. Louis's First Valet of the Chamber slept on a cot in the king's room, so that Louis would never need to call a servant. The First Valet got up each morning before the king and woke him precisely at 8 AM. Make up a bed with blankets on the floor for your parent, brother, sister, or friend to act out the part of First Valet. Then curl up comfortably and wait to be awakened.
2. As soon as the king was awake, his First Physician, First Surgeon, and his old nanny would come into the room to check his health. Someone should now take your temperature, peer into your eyes and ears, check your teeth, flex your elbows and knees, and ask you if you are feeling well.
3. Next, the king's favorite courtiers (whoever was in favor that week) would be allowed a special privilege: watching the king dress! Louis would order these fortunate favorites admitted to his room. Decide who will have the privilege of watching you dress, and let them come into your room.
4. The valet would hand the king's shirt to the courtier with the highest rank. That courtier would then be given the privilege of handing the shirt to the king—who would then put it on! Choose a Most Important Courtier. Your valet should give your shirt to this courtier, who should then bow deeply and hand it to you. The rest of your clothes should also be given, piece by piece, to this courtier, who will then hand it to you.
5. Next, the king would shave and adjust his wig, while his valet held a mirror in front of him. Have your valet hold a mirror in front of you so that you can brush your hair.
6. The king would now pray. All of his courtiers would wait silently until he was done! When he was finished, he would go to mass. (You may act out these steps, or skip them if you feel it would be disrespectful.)
7. Finally, Louis would get to eat his breakfast. He was served ten to twelve dishes of food. No one ate with the king; everyone stood and watched him eat. Make sure your "courtiers" watch you finish your food before they have any themselves!

## GAME PROJECT Who Is the Man in the Iron Mask?

There was a man kept as a prisoner during the reign of Louis XIV. The identity of the man was a secret; he always wore a black velvet mask (although some believe the mask was made of iron). The French call him *L'homme Au Masque De Fer* (the Man in the Iron Mask). He was kept under the watch of the prison governor; so he was obviously a very important prisoner. Every Frenchman had a theory about who the man in the mask was: the son of Louis XIV and another woman (not his wife); an elder brother of Louis XIV (who, therefore, would be the rightful king of France); or the author Moliére who wrote a shocking play, *Tartuffe*. Today, most historians agree that the Man in the Iron Mask was Eustache Dauger.

Eustache Dauger served as the valet (a gentleman's personal servant) to a man named Nicholas Fouquet. Fouquet was an enemy of Louis XIV's chief minister. The minister had Fouquet and his valet Dauger arrested for an unknown reason. Even after Fouquet died in prison, Dauger was kept in jail because the minister was worried that Fouquet had told Dauger his secrets. If anyone found out who Dauger was, and what secrets he knew, the minister could be ruined. Dauger died a prisoner in 1703, after spending over thirty years as a prisoner and wearing a mask.

Play a game in which you, like the French people, guess at the identity of the Man in the Iron Mask.

*Materials:*
- ☐ paper
- ☐ pencil
- ☐ a piece of dark cloth

*Directions:*

1. Write a list of people that both players know. These can be friends, family members, even characters from books or movies.
2. Player One chooses a person from the list and writes the name on a piece of paper (Player Two must not see who it is). Player One slides the name under a piece of dark cloth (this will be the Mask).
3. Player Two can ask Player One a question a "yes" or "no" question about the "person in the iron mask." If Player One does not know the answer, Player Two may ask another question. Suggestions for questions:

   Does the person live in our town?
   Is the person a woman?
   Is the person in our own family?
   Is the person older than 18?
   Do I see this person at least once a week?
4. Player Two may ask up to ten questions. When Player Two thinks he knows the identity of the person in the iron mask, he may guess. If he guesses wrong, the Player Two gets no points. If Player Two guesses correctly, he gets points.

   Scoring:
   If Player Two guesses correctly after the first question, he gets ten points.
   after the second question, he gets nine points
   after the third question, he gets eight points
   after the fourth question, he gets seven points
   after the fifth question, he gets six points
   after the sixth question, he gets five points
   after the seventh question, he gets four points
   after the eighth question, he gets three points
   after the ninth question, he gets two points
   after the tenth and final question, he gets one point
5. Now Player One and Player Two switch roles. After three rounds each, the player with the most points wins!

## CRAFT PROJECT A Masked Ball at Versailles

Louis XIV kept himself and his court entertained at Versailles with elaborate parties, theatrical productions, music performances, and ballets (Louis XIV even danced in a few). Masked balls were another popular form of entertainment. All the guests wore decorative masks. Create your own mask. You can even make a sun mask in honor of the Sun King.

*Materials:*

- ☐ colored paper plates with raised sides
- ☐ Student Page 42: Mask Template
- ☐ unsharpened pencil
- ☐ strong tape
- ☐ scissors and craft glue
- ☐ yellow or gold construction paper (optional)
- ☐ gold glitter, ribbon, beads, or other decorative items.

*Directions:*

1. Draw mask pattern onto plate. Cut it out.
2. Cut out eyeholes.
3. Tape the end of the pencil to the right edge of the mask. You can use this pencil to hold the mask in front of your eyes, the way courtiers did at the masked balls of Versailles. (The masks didn't really hide your identity!)
4. Decorate the mask. You can hang curls of ribbon from the bottom edge, put gold glitter around the eyes, or cut triangles of construction paper to make rays around the top edge if you want a Sun King mask.

# The Rise of Prussia

## Encyclopedia Cross-References

*UBWH not covered, UILE 319*
*KIHW 483 (map), KHE 292*

## THE RISE OF PRUSSIA

### Review Questions

In the years after the Thirty Years' War, how many little states was Germany divided into? *Germany was divided into three hundred states.*

Did Germans think of themselves as "citizens of Germany"? *No, each person thought of himself as a citizen of his own little state.*

Which two German states did Prince Frederick rule? *He ruled over Brandenburg and Prussia.*

Brandenburg lay inside the borders of what empire? *Brandenburg lay inside the borders of the Holy Roman Empire.*

Was Prussia inside the Holy Roman Empire as well? *No, Prussia was outside of the Holy Roman Empire.*

What did Frederick start to call himself? *He started to call himself King Frederick I. He wanted to be the Prussian King.*

Did he have permission from the Holy Roman Emperor to call himself king? *Yes, but he could only call himself king in Prussia, not in Brandenburg.*

What did Frederick start to call his whole kingdom—both Brandenburg and Prussia? *He called the whole thing the kingdom of Prussia.*

Until this time, what two things had most Europeans given their loyalty to? *They were loyal either to a piece of land (like the island of Britain) or to one ruler (like Philip II of Spain).*

What did Frederick want his people to be loyal to? *He wanted them to be loyal to a state, to the idea of a German kingdom ruled by a German king.*

What was "the first *Reich*"? *The first Reich was the first German kingdom.*

Can you name some things that Frederick did to make his people think of themselves as citizens of one country? *He founded a Prussian university, a Prussian Academy of the Arts, and a Royal Prussian Academy of Sciences. He had this academy teach people how to speak the German language properly. Also, he acted like a great king with elaborate feasts and parties.*

What did Frederick's son, Frederick William I, do to strengthen this Prussian kingdom? *He announced that Prussia and Brandenburg were both part of the Prussian kingdom; he made the army stronger.*

What did Frederick's grandson, Frederick the Great, do to make the Prussian kingdom stronger? *He fought to add land to Prussia and built a palace in Brandenburg.*

What modern country had its beginnings in the Prussian kingdom? *The country of Germany had its beginnings in Prussia.*

### Narration Exercise

"Prince Frederick ruled two German states—Brandenburg and Prussia. Brandenburg was inside the Holy Roman Empire, but Prussia was outside it. The Emperor gave Frederick permission to call himself the king *in* Prussia. But Frederick behaved like the king of both states. He wanted his people to think of themselves as citizens of Prussia, not citizens of different German states. His son and grandson made the Prussian kingdom even stronger." OR

"Once, the people who lived in Germany didn't think of themselves as Germans. They thought of themselves as citizens of the different little German states. Frederick wanted to change this. He called himself the king of Prussia and built a university and an academy of sciences. He founded the first German kingdom. His son made the army stronger. His grandson was Frederick the Great. Frederick the Great had real power over Prussia."

## Additional History Reading

*Berlin: A 3D Keepsake Cityscape,* by Candlewick Press, illus. Sarah McMenemy (Candlewick Press, 2014). This is a foldout book for young children. It features famous landmarks, including the Brandenburg Gate, around the city of Berlin. (RA 1-3, IR 3-4)

*Germany ABCs,* by Sarah Heiman (Picture Window Books, 2003). Nice illustrations and brief, readable paragraphs about the history, culture, and geography of Germany, the country that rose from Prussian roots. (RA 1-2, IR 3-4)

*Germany: The Land,* by Kathryn Lane (Crabtree Publications, 2001). Some mention of Germany's history, but the primary focus of this well-illustrated book is Germany's varied geography and many different regions. For advanced fourth grade readers and older. (RA 2-3, IR 3-5)

*Germany,* by Susan Hoskins Miller (The Child's World, 2016). Written at a middle-grades reading and interest level, this volume includes information on Germany's people, cultures and history. (RA 3-5, IR 4-6)

*Germany,* by Sarah Tieck (ABDO Publishing 2015). With large, simple text and colorful photos and illustrations, this book will help students better understand modern-day Germany in light of its history. (RA 2-4, IR 3-5)

*Becoming Bach,* by Thomas Leonard (Roaring Brook Press, 2017). This picture book is an imaginative look at the genius of young Johann Sebastian Bach, ideal for young elementary students. Bach lived in Germany during the reigns of Frederick William I and Frederick the Great. (RA K-3, IR 2-4)

*Johann Sebastian Bach,* by Mike Venezia (Scholastic, 2017). This volume is an approachable and fun introduction to J.S. Bach for elementary students. (RA 1-4, IR 3-6)

*George Handel,* by Mike Venezia (Children's Press, 1995). This biography of the composer who lived during the reigns of all three Fredericks belongs to the third-grade level series "Getting to Know the World's Greatest Composers." (RA 2, IR 3-4)

*Professor Kant's Incredible Day,* by Jean Paul Mongin, trans. Anna Street, illus. Laurent Moreau (Diaphanes, 2016). A very funny picture book depicting daily events in the life of eighteenth century German philosopher Immanuel Kant who lived in Konigsberg, Prussia. Great for a read-aloud to younger children or an independent reading by skilled readers. (RA 1-3, IR 3-6)

*Her Majesty: An Illustrated Guide to the Women Who Ruled the World,* by Lisa Graves (Xist Publishing, 2015). Queen Louise, wife of Frederick the Great, is one of the historical women featured in this beautiful book.

She is depicted in a full-page painting, and a page is devoted to a biography of her life. The book makes a great resource for reading about other women in history, too. (RA 1-3, IR 3-4)

*The King of Prussia and a Peanut Butter Sandwich,* by Alice Fleming (Atheneum, 2009). This easy-to-read book tells about the Mennonite response to Frederick the Great's decree that all young men must serve in the army—they went first to southern Russia, and ultimately to the midwestern United States. (IR 2-5)

## Corresponding Literature Suggestions

*For additional literature from Germany, see Chapter Nine.*

*The Adventures of Bella & Harry: Let's Visit Berlin!*, by Lisa Manzione, illus. Kristine Lucco (Bella & Harry, 2015). Follow these cute sibling dogs as they trot their way through Berlin, seeing the sights. One stop they make is at the Brandenburg Gate (built on the orders of Frederick William I), where Bella explains its history to Harry. (RA 1-2, IR 3-4)

*Clara: The (Mostly) True Story of the Rhinoceros who Dazzled Kings, Inspired Artists, and Won the Hearts of Everyone . . . While She Ate Her Way Up and Down a Continent,* by Emily Arnold McCully (Schwartz & Wade, 2016). An account of a rhinoceros who toured mid-eighteenth-century Europe with her owner for seventeen years. Frederick the Great was one of the people whom she met. Engagingly told on colorful watercolor and ink drawings. (RA 1-3, IR 3-5)

*The Potato King* by Christopher Niemann (Owl Kids Books, 2013). According to legend, Frederick the Great helped popularize the potato in Europe. Young students will enjoy this tale of trickery along with the potato-print illustrations. (RA 1-2, IR 1-2)

*Bird Boy: A Grimm and Gross Retelling,* by Benjamin Harper, illus. Timothy Banks (Stone Arch Books, 2019). A hilarious (and disgusting, in an entertaining-to-a-kid sort of way) retelling of the Grimms' story "The Foundling Bird." Elementary students with a penchant for this kind of humor will be delightedly yelling, "Eeeeewwww!" Just don't read it right before lunchtime! (RA 1-4, IR 3-6)

*Dwarf Nose* by William Hauff (Michael Neugebauer Publishing, 2016). A delightful retelling of a classic German children's story. Although this is a picture book (and the illustrations are equally delightful), the text is long. Best as a read-aloud or independent read for older students. (RA 3-6, IR 4-6)

*The Elves and the Shoemaker* adapted by Mara Alperin (Tiger Tales, 2014). With simplified text and bright, beautiful illustrations, this adaptation is a great way to introduce younger students to the Grimms' fairy tales. (RA 1-3, IR 2-3)

*German Hero-Sagas and Folk-Tales,* by Barbara Leonie Picard, illus. Joan Kiddell-Monroe (Oxford University Press, 1994). Excellent for slightly older readers who want to explore the shared literary tradition of the German states. (RA 3-4, IR 5-7) **E-Only.**

*Little Red Cap,* by Jacob and Wilhelm Grimm, trans. Elizabeth D. Crawford, illus. Lisbeth Zwerger (North South Books, 1995). Translated directly from the German, this classic folktale earned a New York Times Notable Book designation for the quality of its illustrations. (RA 2, IR 3-5) **E-Only.**

*Hansel and Gretel,* illustrated by Francesca Cosanti (White Star Kids, 2017). The illustrations in this retelling of the classic German story are simply mesmerizing! (RA 2-4, IR 3-5)

*Illustrated Grimm's Fairy Tales* by Ruth Brockelhurst (Usborne, 2010). An ideal choice for read-alouds with beautiful stories alongside mesmerizing illustrations. (RA 1-5, IR 3-5)

*The Original Folk and Fairy Tales of the Brothers Grimm: the Complete First Edition,* by Jacob Grimm and Wilhelm Grimm, trans. Jack Zipes, illus. Andrea Dezso (Princeton University Press, 2014). The "first edition" contains two volumes of the 156 German tales the brothers collected from diverse sources and put into writing in 1812 and 1815. This book is the first to put them all together in English. The translations reflect the diversity, and the illustrations are detailed and compelling. (RA 1-4, IR 3-6)

*Twelve Dancing Princesses* by Alison Jay (Little Bee Books, 2016). A sweetly illustrated version of the classic German folktale. Early elementary students will especially enjoy this! (RA 1-4, IR 2-4)

## MAP WORK

### The German States and Prussia *(Student Page 43, answer 323)*

1. Remember that people in countries like England and Spain thought of themselves as English or Spanish. Color England red.
2. People in Germany did not think of themselves as German. They thought of themselves as citizens of the small German state they belonged to. Brandenburg was one of those small states. Draw an orange circle around Brandenburg, and color it in orange.
3. Prince Frederick ruled Brandenburg, which was part of the Holy Roman Empire. He also ruled Prussia, which was outside of the borders of the Holy Roman Empire. Draw a purple circle around Prussia. The circle should go all the way up and around Konigsberg. Color the circle in purple.
4. Frederick wanted to be an absolute monarch of both Brandenburg and Prussia, but he knew the Holy Roman Emperor would not give it to him. So he *behaved* like an absolute monarch and called both territories "Prussia." Draw a purple circle that goes around both territories—Prussia and Brandenburg.

**Coloring Page** Frederick declared himself to be the King of Prussia. Berlin became one of the most important cities of this new kingdom. The pathway in Berlin from Frederick's palace to his hunting-forest had beautiful linden trees on either side and was called "Unter den Linden" *("Under the Linden Trees")*. You can still walk this path in Berlin today. *(Student Page 44)*

## PROJECTS

### Art Project — Color a Prussian Flag

Materials:
- ☐ Student Page 45 (top half): Prussian Flag
- ☐ Yellow, black, and red markers, colored pencils, or crayons

Directions:
1. Color these parts yellow: the beak of the eagle, the letters **FR** on the breast of the eagle (for "Frederick Rex"), the scepter and the orb in the eagle's claws (the orb symbolizes the earth), and the "spokes" of the crown.
2. Color the "cloth" portion of the crown red.
3. The body of the eagle is black.

### Foreign Language Activity — Speak German

Prussians spoke the German language. Learn some common German words and phrases!

| English | German | Pronunciation |
|---|---|---|
| Yes | Ja | *yah* |
| No | Nein | *nine* (rhymes with **mine**) |
| Hello | Guten Tag | *GOO ten tahg* |

| | | |
|---|---|---|
| Goodbye | Auf Wiedersehen | *owf VEE dur zane* |
| Please | Bitte | *BIT tuh* |
| Thank you | Danke | *DAHN kuh* |
| Excuse me | Entschuldigung | *ent SHOOL dee guhng* |
| I'm sorry | Es tut mir leid | *es TOOT mer lide* ("lide" rhymes with **hide**) |
| Help! | Hilfe! | *Hil fuh* |
| Milk | die Milch | dee *MEELKH* (kh sounds more like the "h" in **hue**) |
| Cookies | die Plätzchen | *dee PLETS khen* (again, the kh sounds like **hue**) |
| Brother | der Bruder | *dare BROO der* (roll the r's) |
| Sister | die Schwester | *dee SHVES ter* |
| Father | der Vater | *dare FAH ter* |
| Mother | die Mutter | *dee MOO ter* |
| Car | das Auto | *dahs OW toe* |
| America | Amerika | *ah MAYR ih ka* (roll the r) |
| Germany | Deutschland | *DOITCH lahnd* |

## CRAFT ACTIVITY PROJECT Prussian Royal Seal

The Holy Roman Emperor agreed to let Frederick call himself King of Prussia, but only in Prussia itself and not in the other part of his kingdom. Once Frederick was coronated, he had to have a seal—a special symbol which he stamped onto his royal orders to show that they came from the King. Use the symbol below, which was used on the early Prussian flags, or make up your own.

*Materials:*

- ☐ Sculpey, color of your choice
- ☐ Toothpick
- ☐ Popsicle stick broken in half
- ☐ Sealing wax sticks (found in craft stores) or stamp pad
- ☐ Cookie sheet or smaller baking pan

*Directions:*

1. Mold your Sculpey block into a thick square 1" by 1". Make it as thick as your pinky finger.
2. Gently turn the block over so you can carve on the flattest side. If you are using the above symbol, cut it out and lay it gently on top of the flat square. Using the toothpick, carve around the outline of the crown. Lift the template. Now carefully cut away the clay around the outline, leaving a raised crown symbol about ⅛" high at the center of the block.
3. Carefully turn over seal on to an ovenware pan, carved side down. Stick the halved Popsicle stick into the middle of the Sculpey square on the top but do not allow it to go all the way through. This will act as the handle to your seal.
4. Bake your seal block at about 225 degrees for 20 to 30 minutes. Let it cool before touching.
5. Use the stamp pad or sealing wax to make stamps! If using sealing wax, follow the directions on the package and stamp your crown in the center of the warm wax. Try to find wax that is "Prussian Blue" when you seal your orders!

## CRAFT ACTIVITY Frederick the I's Order of the Black Eagle

On the eve of his coronation, Frederick I established the Order of the Black Eagle, Prussia's highest honor. Any person who received the Star of the Order of the Black Eagle automatically became a member of Prussian nobility (if he wasn't already). Knights, princes, and officers who distinguished themselves in battle were among those who received the star. Frederick the Great (Frederick I's grandson) had a portrait of himself painted wearing the Star of Order of the Black Eagle. The Star is worn over the heart, on an orange sash called the Grand Cordon. The motto of the Order is written near the center of the star: SUUM CUIQUE (which means "to every one his own"). Make your own order of the Black Eagle and wear it over your heart. Remember, if you are a member of the Order, you are a Prussian noble! You can either color the Star, or follow the directions below to give it a wild "marblized" effect.

*Materials:*

- ☐ Student Page 45 (bottom half): Star of the Order of the Black Eagle
- ☐ red, blue, or green acrylic paint
- ☐ water
- ☐ plastic spoon and knife
- ☐ paper cup
- ☐ liquid starch
- ☐ a pan or plate
- ☐ scotch tape
- ☐ large safety pin

*Directions:*

1. Mix two tablespoons of paint with two tablespoons of water in the cup. The mixture should be thick but liquid, about the consistency of buttermilk.
2. Pour starch into the pan until it is about one inch thick.
3. Sprinkle drops of the paint-water mixture into the starch. If the paint sinks to the bottom of the pan, it's too thick; add a little water to the mixture. It should float on the surface of the starch.
4. Swirl designs into the starch with your knife.
5. Lay your star paper, face down, on the surface of the starch mixture. The center should touch the starch first. Smooth the star over the starch from the center out, but don't let it sink down into the starch.
6. Leave the star on top of the mixture for 15 seconds. Remove the star and set it, face up, on paper towels.
7. Gently lay another paper towel on top of it; blot to remove excess paint. Take the paper towel off. Repeat until excess paint is removed.
8. When dry, cut out star. Attach safety pin to the back of the star with tape, and wear proudly!

# A New World in Conflict

## Encyclopedia Cross-References

*UBWH 149-150, UILE 321-323*
*KIHW 410-411, 460-461 (pictures), 474-476, KHE 280-281, 302*

## WAR AGAINST THE COLONIES: KING PHILIP'S WAR

### Review Questions

As the Massachusetts colony grew larger, it spread into the lands of which Native American tribe? *It spread into the land of the Wampanoag tribe.*

Who was the king of the Wampanoag tribe? *Metacom was the king of the tribe.*

Why did Metacom become unhappy with the English? *The English were fishing in his streams and hunting his deer* OR *Metacom saw that his kingdom was vanishing.*

What did John Sassamon try to warn the governor of Plymouth about? *He tried to warn him that King Metacom was raising an army to fight the English.*

Did the governor, Josiah Winslow, believe John Sassamon's warning? *No; he claimed that Plymouth was safe from attack* OR *he said that he couldn't believe an Indian.*

What did the English do to the three warriors who were supposed to have killed John Sassamon? *They tried them for murder, convicted them, and executed them.*

What did Metacom and his warriors do in return? *They attacked a Plymouth settlement and burned its houses.*

During the war between the Native Americans and the English, what did the Native Americans do with the colonists they captured? *They released them in exchange for money and weapons.*

At what kind of place did the English colonists attack Metacom's warriors and the Naragansetts? *They attacked them in the middle of a swamp.*

Do you remember what this battle was called? *It was called the Great Swamp Fight.*

What did the English do to Metacom after he was killed? *They cut off his head and put it up on a pole in their settlement.*

How many Native Americans and how many English had died in the war? *Over three thousand Native Americans, and one in every sixteen men among the colonists, had been killed in the war.*
What was this war known as? *The English called it King Philip's War.*

### Narration Exercise

"More and more English colonists came to the New World, and moved into Indian land. One tribe, the Wampanoag, decided to fight back. A young Indian man tried to warn the colonists, but they didn't listen. The young man was killed! The colonists arrested three Indian warriors and executed them. The war was on! It was called 'King Philip's War,' and it went on for months and months. When it was over, thousands of Indians had died, and the English went on spreading across their land." OR

"King Philip's War started when the king of the Wampanoag, Metacom, attacked a settlement in Plymouth. Metacom was afraid that the English would take over his kingdom, and he was angry because the English had put three of his warriors on trial and then executed them. The war went on for months. The Indians took English settlers captive and traded them for money and weapons. But then the English banded together and beat the Indians in the Great Swamp Fight. Eight months later, Metacom was captured and put to death."

## WAR AGAINST THE COLONIES: LOUIS XIV SAVES NEW FRANCE

### Review Questions

How had Samuel Champlain tried to make friends with the Huron tribe? *He had given them presents, slept and ate in their villages, and helped them to fight against their enemies.*

What disease did the French accidentally pass on to the Huron tribe? *They passed along a disease called smallpox, which killed more than half of the Hurons.*

When the nearby Iroquois saw that the Huron were weakened by disease, what did they do to the Huron tribe? *They invaded Huron land, burned Huron houses, and killed hundreds of Huron men and women. Then they claimed the Huron land for themselves.*

After they took over the Huron land, what did the Iroquois try to do to New France? *They tried to destroy New France (by raiding farms in Quebec and laying siege to Montreal).*

What effect did this have on the colonies of New France? *The colonies shrank because more and more colonists went home!*

When King Louis XIV sent soldiers to fight the Iroquois, what did he promise these men? *He promised to give them land in the New World if they would save New France.*

Were these French soldiers ever able to defeat the Iroquois? *No, but they did force the Iroquois to stay on their own land, and they were able to protect the settlements of New France from attack.*

After the soldiers settled down on their new land, what new problem did they face? *They wanted to start families, but there were six men for every woman in New France!*

How did Louis XIV solve this problem? *He announced that he would pay young Frenchwomen large amounts of money if they would go and live in the colonies.*

### Narration Exercise

Today, give the student a choice of narration exercises. Say, "You can either tell me what problem New France faced and how Louis XIV helped solve it, or you can retell the story of Marie-Madeleine de Vercheres."

An acceptable level of detail for the first exercise would be, "The colony of New France was under attack from the Iroquois. Louis XIV sent soldiers over to fight the Iroquois. He promised them land in the New World if they would fight. Then, when the soldiers settled down, Louis XIV paid young women to go over and marry soldiers and start families."

An acceptable level of detail for the second exercise would be, "Marie-Madeleine's father was a soldier who had been given a farm. One day, he was away when the Iroquois attacked the farm. Madeleine and her little brothers shut themselves inside the fort. They fixed the walls and shot cannon at the Iroquois—for eight days! At last French soldiers came and drove off the Iroquois. Madeleine's statue stands in Quebec because of her bravery."

## Review Questions

William Penn's father commanded the ship that brought Charles II back to England. In gratitude for this, what did Charles II do for him? He *made him an admiral and a knight.*

What did William Penn's father do for Charles II? *He loaned the king sixteen thousand pounds.*

What religious group did William Penn start meeting with during his time at Oxford? *He started meeting with the "Society of Friends of the Truth," who were nicknamed the "Quakers."*

Where did the "Quakers" get their nickname? *They got this nickname because people said that they quaked, or shook, when they felt God's presence.*

Why were the Quakers often thrown into jail? *They refused to take their hats off in the presence of the king, and this seemed like a rebellious thing to do.*

When did William Penn become a Quaker? *He became a Quaker at the age of twenty-two, while sitting in a Quaker meeting.*

Why did William Penn have to give up the idea of becoming a soldier? *Quakers believed that fighting was wrong.*

Why did William Penn want the Quakers to have their own colony? *He wanted them to have a place to worship God as they pleased.*

The king of England still owed the Penn family sixteen thousand pounds. Instead of asking for money, what did William Penn ask the king to pay him back with? *He asked the king to give him land in North America.*

What did the king name the piece of land that he gave to William Penn? *He said that it should be called Pennsylvania, in honor of William's father.*

What was the "Frame of Government?" *The Frame of Government was the set of directions that told how the new colony would be run.*

How many groups of people would run the colony? *Three groups of people would run the colony.*

How did William Penn intend to treat the Native Americans? *He promised to pay them for the land the colony used, and he ordered that no one wrong the Indians.*

Why did the governor of Maryland worry about Pennsylvania's growth? *He was afraid that the colonists would take away land that belonged to Maryland.*

Why did William Penn go back to England? *He had to defend Pennsylvania's right to its own land.*

Why didn't the people of England like the new king, James II? *They were afraid that he would make England a Catholic country.*

Who did the English Protestants ask to come to England and be the king and queen? *They asked William III of Orange and Mary II ("William and Mary") to come and be king and queen of England.*

What year did William and Mary arrive in England? *They arrived in 1688.*

What did the English call this takeover? *They called it the Glorious Revolution.*

What paper did William and Mary sign? *They signed a paper promising that they would not pass any laws without Parliament's approval.*

Why did William Penn have to go into hiding? *He was suspected of loyalty to James II, the Catholic king.*

How many years did Penn stay away from his colony? *He stayed away for fifteen years!*

### Narration Exercise

Since there is a lot of information in this chapter, use "directed narration." Say to the student, "Tell me how Pennsylvania got started." An acceptable level of detail would be, "The king owed William Penn's father a lot of money, so William Penn asked for a piece of land in the New World in payment. He wanted to start a colony where Quakers could worship as they pleased, and where everyone would be equal. He wrote out directions showing how the colony would be run by three elected groups of people. Then he brought colonists over to Pennsylvania. Pennsylvania grew larger and larger. Its capital, Philadelphia, grew to be the second largest town in North America!"

Then say to the student, "Tell me how William and Mary came to England. Be sure to use the names Charles II, James II, and William and Mary, and the Glorious Revolution, and also include the date 1688." An acceptable level of detail would be, "When Charles II died, his brother James II became king. But James was Catholic. The English were afraid that England would have a whole line of Catholic kings. So they invited Mary, who was a Protestant, to come and take the throne. Mary and her husband William arrived in England in 1688. James had to flee to France! The English called this the Glorious Revolution, because the new king and queen would not be tyrants or try to seize power."

## Additional History Reading

*The Library of Living and Working in Colonial Times* (Powerkids Press, 2002). A simple illustrated series with clear, easy-to-read text, describing the livelihoods of colonial Americans. Good for second and third-grade readers as well as reluctant fourth-graders. **LFA**

*A Day in the Life of a Colonial Cabinetmaker*, by Amy French Merrill

*A Day in the Life of a Colonial Dressmaker*, by Amy French Merrill

*A Day in the Life of a Colonial Glassblower*, by J. L. Branse

*A Day in the Life of a Colonial Sea Captain*, by J. L. Branse

*A Day in the Life of a Colonial Soldier*, by J. L. Branse

*A Day in the Life of a Colonial Surveyor*, by Amy French Merrill

*A Day in the Life of a Colonial Blacksmith*, by Kathy Wilmore

*A Day in the Life of a Colonial Wigmaker*, by Kathy Wilmore

*A Day in the Life of a Colonial Silversmith*, by Kathy Wilmore

*A Day in the Life of a Colonial Printer*, by Kathy Wilmore

*A Day in the Life of a Colonial Schoolteacher*, by Kathy Wilmore

*A Day in the Life of a Colonial Innkeeper*, by Kathy Wilmore

*Horrible Jobs in Colonial Times* by Louise Spilsbury (Gareth Stevens Publishing, 2014). With large photographs, this book highlights the difficulties of life in colonial times. (RA 2-4, IR 3-5)

*A Kid's Life in Colonial America* by Sarah Machajewski (PowerKids Press, 2015). Written to kids, about kids. A fascinating book to help students understand how ordinary children lived during colonial times. (RA 2-4, IR 3-5)

*The Wampanoag*, by Kevin Cunningham (Children's Press, 2011). Part of the "A True Story" series, this simple introduction to the Wampanoag tribe is perfect for readers who are at grade level or a little below. (IR 3-6)

*Outrageous Women of Colonial America* by Mary Rodd Furbee (John Wiley and Sons, 2001). Organized chronologically, each short chapter highlights a particular influential colonial woman. A useful adjunct to your studies of colonial times. (RA 3-6, IR 6+)

*People Who Made History: Native Americans*, by Jason Hook (Steck-Vaughn, 2001). A good brief biography of King Philip, along with other Native Americans (Squanto, Pocahontas, Tecumseh, etc.) (RA 1-2, IR 3-4) **LFA**

*Colonial America (You Choose: Historical Eras)* by Allison Lassieur (Capstone Press, 2014). This entertaining book can be read several times, experiencing colonial times from the perspective of an indentured servant, a sailor or a soldier. (IR 3-5) **LFA**

*The Iroquois* by Danielle Smith-Lear (Capstone Press, 2016). This is an excellent introduction to the Iroquois, also called the Haudenosaunee. Content includes both historical importance of this group as well as the role of the modern Haudenosaunee in the United States. Parents and teachers will appreciate discussion questions and lists of additional resources for further study. (RA 3-4, IR 3-6)

*Iroquois* by Sarah Tieck (Big Buddy Books, 2015). With large, colorful illustrations and relatively simple text, this book includes interesting facts on how the Iroquois lived—what they ate, what their homes looked like, their handicrafts and their oral traditions. (RA 1-2, IR 2-4)

*Life in a Longhouse Village*, by Bobbie Kalman, (Crabtree Publishing, 2000). An illustrated book about the village life of Eastern Woodlands peoples. (RA 2 IR 4)

*Timeline History of Early American Indian Peoples*, by Diane Marczely Gimpel, (Lerner Publishing Group, 2014). A timeline-style history of the American Native peoples from 20,000 BCE. It divides them into five main groups based mainly on geography. (RA 3, IR 4)

*The Iroquois: The Six Nations Confederacy*, by Mary Enlar, (Capstone Pr INc, 2016). A history of the Iroquois, including illustrations, maps, and a timeline. (RA 2 IR 3)

*Voices from Colonial America: New France, 1534-1763*, by Richard Worth (National Geographic Children's Books, 2007). For good readers, this history of New France is told through direct quotes from the residents of the New France colonies. (IR 5-7)

*What Really Happened in Colonial Times: A Collection of Historical Biographies*, by Terri Johnson, illus. Darla Dixon (Knowledge Quest Inc, 2016). Eight short biographies of important persons of the colonial era, including Pocahontas, Lord Nelson, and James Cook. (RA 3, IR 4)

*William Penn: Founder of Pennsylvania (Graphic Biographies)*, by Ryan Jacobson, illus. Tim Stiles (Capstone Press, 2006). A biography of William Penn in graphic-novel format suitable for intermediate readers. (RA 2, IR 3-6)

*The World of William Penn*, by Genevieve Foster (Beautiful Feet Books, 2008). For stronger readers, this classic biography connects William Penn to his contemporaries the Sun King, Charles II, Isaac Newton, Peter the Great, and more. (RA 3, IR 4-7)

*Exploring the Pennsylvania Colony*, by John Micklos, Jr. (Capstone Press, 2016). Part of the "Exploring the 13 Colonies" series, this walks readers through daily life in the Pennsylvania colony as well as exploring its Quaker origins. (IR 3-6)

*The Extraordinary Suzy Wright* by Teri Kanefield (Abrams Books, 2016) There are too few accounts of the women who shaped history; this marvelous book celebrates the influence of Suzy Wright, an early Quaker who traveled from England to Pennsylvania. A fascinating read, with photographs, illustrations and snippets of Wright's own personal correspondence. (RA 4-6, IR 5-8)

*Although titles are not available in the U.S., Canadian readers may be able to find junior-level biographies of three more notable personalities: Jeanne Mance, who built a hospital in Montreal; Marguerite Bourgeoys, a teacher who taught the* filles du roi *and founded an order of teaching nuns; and Father Brebeuf, who lived with the Hurons and was executed with them during the Iroquois invasion.*

## Corresponding Literature Suggestions

*The Witch of Blackbird Pond,* by Elizabeth George Speare (Yearling, 1958). This Newbery-winning chapter book tells the story of a young Connecticut colonist in the 1680s who befriends a woman wrongly rumored to be a witch; **parents may want to preview** before assigning. A good family read-aloud, or for strong readers; also look for the audiobook version. (RA 1-4, IR 5-6)

*Tapenum's Day: A Wampanoag Indian Boy in Pilgrim Times*, by Kate Waters (Scholastic, 1996). Biographer Kate Waters follows a fictional Wampanoag boy through his day in. 1627; beautifully illustrated with photographs. from Plimouth Plantation.

*Legends of the Iroquois*, by Tehanetorens (The Book Publishing Co., 2001). Traditional stories accompanied by Iroquois pictographs that reproduce the symbols used by the Iroquois. (RA 2-3, IR 4-6)

*The Huron Carol*, by Ian Wallace, (Groundwood Books, 2013). A beautifully illustrated version of the carol written in Huron by Fr. Jean de Brebeuf in the 17th century. Versions in several languages are included, as well as the history of the carol. (RA K, IR2)

*Skywoman: Legends of the Iroquois* by Joanne Shenandoah (Clear Light Publishers, 1998). Each of nine legends are vibrantly illustrated and ideal for read-aloud sessions. Stories include Skywoman, Grandmother Moon, The Star Dancers and more. (RA 1-6, RA 4-6)

*The Birchbark House*, by Louise Erdrich, (Hyperion Books for Children, 2002). The story of a year in the life of an Ojibwa girl living on Lake Superior in the 19th century. (RA 2, IR 3)

*Hiawatha and the Peacemaker* by Robbie Robertson (Abrams Books, 2015). This advanced picture book tells the story of Hiawatha, a Native American leader whose life—as well as the lives of his Iroquois people—is transformed by a prophet known as the Peacemaker. (RA 2-4, IR 3-5)

*I Am Algonquin: An Algonquin Quest Novel*, by Rick Revelle, (Dundurn, 2013). The story of an Algonquin boy before European contact. This is a well-rounded narrative including depictions of daily life, conflicts and warfare, and cultural practices. (RA 3, IR 4)

*Ice King*, by Allison Mitcham, Serena Sock, Naiomi Mitcham illus, (Nimbus, 2013). A Mi'kmaq folktale about a hero facing the Ice King to protect his village. The text is in Mi'kmaq, French, and English. Other titles by the same author include other traditional tales. (RA 1, IR 3)

*The King's Daughter*, by Suzanne Martel, (Groundwood Books, 1994). For stronger readers, the story of one of the *filles du roi*, an orphan who comes to colonial New France to marry someone she has never met. (RA 4, IR 5-6)

*Benjamin West and His Cat Grimalkin*, by Marguerite Henry, (Alladin, 2014). A fictionalized account of the life of the painter Benjamin West, growing up in a Quaker family. For stronger readers. (RA 3, IR 4-6)

*Hornbooks and Inkwells* by Verla Kay (G.B. Putnam, 2011). This lovely picture book offers a view of life inside a colonial schoolhouse. (RA 1-3, IR 2-3)

## MAP WORK

### Colonizing North America *(Student Page 46, answer 323)*

1. More and more people moved from Europe to the colonies in New England. Draw an arrow from England over to the coast of New England.
2. These people began to colonize the east coast of North America. Draw a thick red line along the coast of New England, from Jamestown up to Plymouth.
3. The colonists wanted more land, so they started to move west. Metacom, or King Philip, and the Wampanoags fought against the English. After a deadly battle that lasted for months, the English defeated the Wampanoags, and continued their move west. Draw a red arrow that points west from Plymouth.
4. The French settlers in New France had done their best to be friends with the Native Americans nearby. But the Iroquois attacked the settlers in New France. King Louis XIV sent soldiers to protect the settlers. Color France purple, and then draw a purple arrow from France to New France.
5. The English continued to settle in New England. William Penn came from England to Pennsylvania with a hundred colonists. Color England blue; then draw a line from England to Philadelphia, the capital city of Pennsylvania.

### Coloring Pages

Fourteen-year-old Marie-Madeline de Verchères helped fight off an attack by Iroquois warriors at the settlement where she lived. *(Student Page 47)*

## PROJECTS

### Activity Project **Blending In**

Modern armies use camouflage to disguise themselves from enemies. The fierce and determined Iroquois tribe also used camouflage as they tried to push out the new settlers. To fight with success, the Iroquois appeared and then disappeared before the settlers had a chance to fight back. They knew how to blend in with the forest around them and keep themselves hidden until the time was right. Now you try to blend in with your environment!

*Materials:*

- ☐ Your backyard or a park
- ☐ Old clothes the same color as the environment (perhaps green or brown)
- ☐ Face paint, or mud
- ☐ Leaves, sticks, grass from your backyard

*Directions:*

1. Plan well! Your job is to blend in to your backyard or a park area so that no one could easily spot you! First, put on clothes that are the colors of your area.
2. Make sure no part of your skin shows if it would give you away. Cover it with face paint or mud.
3. Use the sticks, leaves and grass to add to your camouflage.
4. To truly test your camouflage, play a game of hide-and-go-seek. It is much harder to find someone when he or she blends in to the environment!

## SCIENCE PROJECT **Be a Habitant!**

The new settlers knew that they had to get some crops growing quickly or else they would starve when winter came. Plowing the land and planting the fields were top priority. See how well your crop can grow.

*Materials:*
- ☐ 2 dark, plastic seedling trays (found at plant nurseries or hardware stores)
- ☐ Potting soil
- ☐ Wheat berries (found at a whole food store) or grass seeds (from the hardware store)
- ☐ Spray-mist bottle for watering

*Directions:*
1. Fill your seedling tray halfway full of potting soil. Plant seeds as directed on back of seed package.
2. Cover seeds with the second seedling tray, forming a dome over the first tray with the dirt and seeds in it.
3. Spray seeds with water daily.
4. Remove the cover tray from the top of the seedling tray when you see the first sign of a sprout. Continue spraying the seeds with water once a day.
5. Count how many days it takes before you see sprouts. Keep notes on how long it takes to get tall blades.
6. Sometimes the Indians burned the ripe crops to discourage the settlers and try to push them back to France. But the settlers were strong and tough. Often, they would go back and replant! With a grown-up's supervision, light a match and try to set your grass on fire. Does it burn? What do you have to do to keep the flames going? Allow half the tray of seedlings to burn, and then put the fire out. How do the other seedlings look? Did they survive the fire?

## WRITING PROJECT **The Liberty Bell**

One of the famous Philadelphia landmarks is the Liberty Bell. In 1751, fifty years after William Penn made up the Charter of Privileges, the Pennsylvania Provincial Assembly commissioned the bell to be built. The bell was made in London and delivered to Philadelphia in 1752. Although it is only three feet high, the bell weighs over 2000 pounds!

While testing the bell in Philadelphia, the bell cracked. The bell was repaired and hung in the State House (now called Independence Hall). The bell is engraved with a verse from the Bible: "Proclaim liberty throughout all the land unto all the inhabitants thereof" (Leviticus 25:10).

The bell tolled for the First Continental Congress, as well as the Battles of Lexington and Concord. The bell was also rung on July 8th, 1776 after the Declaration of Independence was read to the public for the first time. When the British marched into Philadelphia, the bell was hidden in another town because people were worried the bell would be melted down for cannonballs. In 1835, back in Independence Hall, the bell cracked again when it was rung for the funeral of Chief Justice John Marshall. The bell was rung for the last time in 1846 to celebrate the birthday of George Washington. It cracked beyond repair and has not chimed a note since.

The following popular fictional story, published in *The Saturday Courier* in 1847, was very popular. From then on, the Liberty Bell was primarily associated with the Declaration of Independence. Read the story and then write your own fictional story about the bell.

**The Fourth of July, 1776**

Popularly known as "Ring, Grandfather, Ring"
Adapted from *Legends of the American Revolution*, 1847
by George Lippard

In yonder wooden steeple, which crowns the red brick State House, stands an old man with white hair and sunburnt face. He is clad in humble attire, yet his eye gleams, as it is fixed upon the ponderous outline of the Bell, suspended in the steeple there. The old man tries to read the inscription on that bell, but cannot. He is no scholar, he scarcely can spell one of those strange words carved on the surface of that bell. By his side, gazing in his face, stands a flaxen-haired boy, with laughing eyes of summer blue. . . .

And the child raised itself on tip-toe and pressed its tiny hands against the bell, and read, in lisping tones, "Proclaim Liberty to all the Land and all the inhabitants thereof." The old man ponders for a moment on those strange words; then gathering the boy in his arms he speaks, "Look here, my child? Wilt do the old man a kindness? Then haste you down stairs, and wait in the hall by the big door, until a man with a velvet dress and a kind face will come out from the big door, and give you a word for me. When he gives you that word, then run out yonder in the street, and shout it up to me."

The boy with blue eyes and flaxen hair sprang from the old Bell-keeper's arms, and threaded his way down the dark stairs.

Under that very bell, pealing out at noonday, in an old hall, 56 traders, farmers and mechanics had assembled to shake the shackles of the world. Look over the faces of these 56 men and see every eye turned to the door. There is silence in this hall—every voice is hushed—every face is stamped with a deep and awful responsibility. Why turns every glance to that door? . . . The Committee of Three, who have been out all night, penning a parchment are about to appear. The parchment, with signatures of these men, written with the pen lying on yonder table will either make a world free—or stretch these necks upon the gibbet. The door opens—the Committee appear. The three advance to the table. The Parchment is laid there. Shall it be signed or not?

Look! How they rush forward. . . . Look how the names blaze on the Parchment. . . . And now the Parchment is signed; and now let word . . . go out to all the earth. . . . Let the Bell speak out the great truth!

Meanwhile, the old man waited. "Oh," groaned the old man, "he has forgotten me! These old limbs will have to totter down the State House stairs, and climb up again—"

As the word was on his lips, a merry, ringing laugh broke on the ear. There, among the crowds on the pavement, stood the blue-eyed boy, clapping his tiny hands. And then, swelling his little chest, he raised himself on tip-toe, and shouted a single word, "Ring!"

Do you see that old man's eye fire? Do you see that arm so suddenly bared to the shoulder, do you see that withered hand, grasping the Iron Tongue of the Bell? The old man is young again; his veins are filled with new life. Backward and forward, with sturdy strokes, he swings the Tongue. The bell speaks out! The crowd in the street hear it, and burst forth in one long shout! The city hears it, and starts up from desk and work-bench, as though an earthquake had spoken! Yes, as the old man swung the Iron Tongue, the Bell spoke to all the world. That sound crossed the Atlantic—pierced the dungeons of Europe—the work shops of England—the vassal-fields of France!

## Activity Project **Speak Like a Quaker**

The Quakers had a particular way of addressing others. See if you can spend a day "speaking like a Quaker." Use "you" when addressing your parents or other adults, and use "thee" when talking to your friends or siblings. For example, if you are talking to your mother, you would say, "Mother, will **you** be going outside?" and if you are talking to your sister you would say, "Sister, will **thee** be going outside?"

# The West

## Encyclopedia Cross-References

*UBWH 133, 162-163, UILE 314-315, 336-337*
*KIHW 452-453, 488-489, 508-509, KHE 268-269, 286-287, 294-295*

## THE UNIVERSAL IDEAS OF NEWTON AND LOCKE

### Review Questions

How did Galileo's observations about the sky disagree with the ideas of Aristotle and Ptolemy? *He realized that the earth went around the sun; the sun did not go around the earth.*

What do we call the method where a person carefully observes the world and then tries to make a theory that will explain these observations? *We call this method the "scientific method."*

Which did Isaac Newton agree with—the ideas of Plato and Aristotle, or the ideas of Galileo and Copernicus? *He thought that modern scientists like Galileo and Copernicus were closer to the truth.*

What name did Newton give to the force that pulled the apple toward the ground? *He called this force "gravity."*

What did Newton's new rules, the "laws of gravity," show about motions and actions in the universe? *They seemed to show that every motion and action in the universe had a law to govern it.*

According to Newton's ideas, how was the universe like a machine? *The universe always worked in the same way.*

What do philosophers think about? *Philosophers think about ideas.*

What do economists think about? *Economists think about money and how it works.*

What do political philosophers think about? *Political philosophers think about the ways countries are governed.*

What connection did philosophers, economists, and political philosophers start to make between Newton's universal laws and the actions of people? *They started to think that if universal laws governed objects, then maybe universal laws governed people too! If these laws could be discovered, life would not be so mysterious.*

Did John Locke prefer a commonwealth government or the government of a king and queen? *He preferred a commonwealth government.*

Where did Locke go during Charles II's return to England? *Locke went to France, Holland, and other European countries.*

When did Locke return to England? *He came back to England when Mary and William took the throne.*

In a "constitutional monarchy," what do the king and queen have to obey? *They have to obey the laws passed by Parliament.*

When Locke wrote down his ideas about government, what did he call his book? *He called it Two Treatises of Government.*

According to John Locke, every person has, by natural law, the right to seek what four things? *He said that every human being had the right to seek "life, health, liberty, and possessions."*

People in a country need someone to make laws. According to Locke, what should people join together to draw up? *They should draw up contracts that give power to certain people to govern.*

According to Locke, what could happen to a king if he doesn't obey the contract, or if he tries to "destroy, enslave, or empoverish" his people? *The king could be thrown out of office, and the people could appoint new rulers* OR *He could lose his throne.*

In Locke's thinking, how many parts should a good government have? *He said that a good government should have three parts.*

What would each part do? *One part would make the laws, another part would enforce those laws, and the third would be in charge of fighting wars with other countries.*

What do we sometimes call the period when the ideas of Newton, Locke, and others became popular in Europe? *We sometimes call this period the Enlightenment.*

### Narration Exercise

Since there is a lot of information in this chapter, use "directed narration." Say to the child, "Can you tell me what kind of 'universal laws' Isaac Newton was looking for, and one law that he found?" An acceptable level of detail would be, "Isaac Newton was looking for universal laws that explained how the universe worked. If he found these laws, he could predict what would happen. The universe seemed like a machine that always worked the same way. One law Newton discovered was the law of gravity. It said that large objects like the earth have a force that pulls other objects towards them."

Now say to the child, "Can you tell me what kind of 'universal laws' John Locke was looking for, and can you also tell me two specific 'laws' that Locke suggested?" An acceptable level of detail would be, "John Locke was looking for laws that predicted how people would act. He said that all people have a right to seek life, health, liberty and possessions, and that no king could throw people in jail just because he wanted to." (Other acceptable "laws" include: people should join together and draw up a contract that gives rulers their power; if a king doesn't obey the contract, he can be thrown off his throne; a good government should have three parts.)

## SCIENTIFIC FARMING

### Review Questions

If universal laws governed the universe and people, what else could they govern, according to scientific farming? *Universal laws could also govern crops and animals.*

If farmers obeyed universal laws of farming, how would their crops and animals improve? *They could raise larger crops and healthier animals.*

What would happen to a field that was planted with wheat year after year? *It would give less grain, because the wheat would use up the minerals in the soil.*

What new kind of crop rotation did Lord Charles Townshend invent? *He invented a four-year rotation where farmers first planted wheat, then turnips, then barley or oats, and finally clover.*

Since farmers now had more grain and more cattle food, what could they afford to do? *They could afford to keep larger herds of cattle alive all year round. This meant that they could eat meat any time of the year.*

What did the "Acts of Enclosure" do? *They divided the common fields up into smaller private fields, with each one fenced off.*

What happened to farmers if they didn't have enough money to pay the enclosure fees? *They had to sell their farms to richer neighbors.*

Once farmers could keep their sheep and cows separated from other farmers' sheep and cows, what could they do? *They could choose what animals would breed and produce larger, healthier offspring.*

What machine, invented by farmer-scientist Jethro Tull, helped farmers get more of their seeds to sprout? *The seed drill helped put seeds into the ground so that more of them would sprout.*

Scientific farming produced a new kind of "revolution." What is this revolution called? *This revolution is called the "Agricultural Revolution."*

### Narration Exercise

Since there is a lot of information in this chapter, use "directed narration." Say to the child, "Can you tell me three new farming practices that became common during the Agricultural Revolution? One has to do with growing crops, one has to do with breeding animals, and one has to do with how fields are planted." An acceptable level of detail would be:

"Farmers learned how to plant different crops each year, so that minerals in the soil wouldn't be used up. This was called crop rotation. Farmers could raise more grain with crop rotation.

"Farmers kept their animals in pens instead of all together in common fields. Then they could choose which animals would mate. The calves and the lambs would be healthier and stronger.

"Farmers used a seed drill to plant their crops. The seeds fell in straight lines so that farmers could walk between the plants and care for them. The seeds also fell into furrows so that birds couldn't eat them and the sun couldn't dry them out."

## Additional History Reading

*How to Think Like a Scientist*, by Stephen P. Kramer, illus. Felicia Bond (HarperCollins, 1987). An excellent introduction to scientific thinking. (RA 2, IR 3-5)

*The History of the Scientific Method*, by Heather Moore Niver (Britannia Educational Publishing, 2018). A history of the scientific method. (RA 3, IR 4)

*Galileo for Kids: His Life and Ideas, 25 Activities*, by Richard Panchyk (Chicago Review Press, 2005). For stronger readers, this book includes biographical information, illustrations and maps, and activities and experiments related to Galileo's discoveries. (RA 4, IR 6)

*Who Was Galileo*, by Patricia Brennan Demuth, John O'Brian illus. (Penguin Workshop, 2015). A narrative account of the life of Galileo, more suitable for younger readers than the above title. (RA 2, IR 3)

*The Magic School Bus Plays Ball: A Book About Forces*, by Joanna Cole and Bruce Degen (Scholastic, 1997). The Magic School Bus classroom learns about friction and other Newtonian forces. (RA 1-2, IR 3-4) **OOP**

*Isaac Newton: Greatest Genius of Science*, by Margaret J. Anderson (Enslow Publishers, 1996). One of the "Genius Scientists and Their Genius Ideas" series, this biography for older readers explains the basics of Newton's discoveries as well as paying some attention to the politics of his times. (RA 3-4, IR 5-7)

*Isaac the Alchemist* by Mary Losure (Candlewick Press, 2017). A fascinating biography of Isaac Newton for the older student—complete with black-and-white reproductions of paintings, drawings and Newton's actual writings. (RA 4-6, IR 4-8)

*Isaac Newton and the Laws of Motion*, by Andrea Gianopoulos (Capstone Press, 2007). A **graphic novel** version of the life of Isaac Newton may appeal to a wide range of ages. (RA 2, IR 4)

*Newton and the Anti-Gravity Formula* by Luca Novelli (Chicago Review Press, 2017). This biography of the father of modern physics includes entertaining hand-drawn pencil illustrations as well as humorous text—likely to appeal to 3rd graders and up. (RA 3-6, IR 3-6.)

*World History Biographies: Isaac Newton: The Scientist Who Changed Everything*, by Philip Steele (National Geographic Children's Books, 2013). A biography more suitable for younger readers than the above title. (RA 2, IR 3)

*Haydn's Farewell Symphony*, by Anna Harwell Celenza, illus. JoAnn E. Kitchel (Charlesbridge, 2016). Joseph Haydn writes the "Farewell Sympathy" for his patron, Prince Nicholas of Austria. This book adds a bit of music appreciation to your history studies. (RA 1-2, IR 3-4)

*Joseph Haydn: The Merry Little Peasant* by Opal Wheeler and Sybil Deucher (Zeezok Publishing, 2005). This inspiring account of Joseph Haydn's life features simple line drawings and large text. (RA 2-4, IR 3-6)

*Food and Farming Then and Now*, by Bobbie Kalman (Crabtree, 2014). Suitable for younger readers, this book looks at food production today and in the past. (RA K, IR 1)

*A Farm Through Time: The History of a Farm from Medieval Times to the Present,* by Angela Wilkes, illus. Eric Thomas (Dorling Kindersley, 2001). Oversized watercolors and fold-out pages graphically illustrate the changes brought about by the Agricultural Revolution; highly recommended. (RA 1-2, IR 3-5) **OOP**

## Corresponding Literature Suggestions

*Galileo's Leaning Tower Experiment* by Wendy Macdonald (Charlesbridge, 2009). This advanced picture book has large, colorful illustrations along with an exciting story that makes Galileo's scientific findings more easily understandable for children. (RA 1-6, IR 3-6)

*Galileo's Telescope*, by Gerry Baily, Karen Foster illus. (Crabtree Publishing, 2008). This storybook tells about two modern day children who discover Galileo's telescope. (RA K, IR 2)

*I, Galileo* by Bonnie Christensen (Borzoi Books, 2012). This advanced picture book is intended for ages 9-12 and is an accessible introduction to the great scientist. (RA 2-4, IR 3-6)

*Starry Messenger*, by Peter Sis (Sunburst, 2000). This imaginative advanced picture book reproduces pages of Galileo's journal as it imaginatively retells the scientist's story. (RA 2, IR 3-5)

*Newton's Rainbow* by Kathryn Lasky (Farrah Straus Giroux, 2017). A clear, enjoyable picture. book for all ages, depicting a young Isaac Newton and his revolutionary discoveries. (RA 1, IR 2-5)

*Century Farm: One Hundred Years on a Family Farm*, by Cris Peterson, illus. Alvis Upitis (Boyds Mill Press, 1999). Descriptions of how the labor on a farm changes over a hundred-year period. (RA 2, IR 3-5)

*Farmer Boy*, by Laura Ingalls Wilder, illus. Garth Williams (HarperTrophy, 1953). This classic novel describes farm life a little later than the period under study, but gives an excellent overview of a farmer's responsibilities. Advanced third grader readers and above should be able to read it independently. (RA 2-3, IR 3-6)

*Farming* by Gail Gibbons (Holiday House, 1988). Perhaps best as a supplement for younger children tagging along with older siblings, this book would be an ideal read-aloud. (RA 1-2, IR 2-3)

*The Year at Maple Hill Farm*, by Alice and Martin Provensen (Aladdin, 2001). In this picture book, animals progress through the months one by one, showing the rhythm of the farm year. (RA 2, IR 3-4)

## MAP WORK

### England and the Netherlands *(Student Page 48, answer 323)*

1. Isaac Newton studied at Cambridge. Find Cambridge on your map. Draw a small apple to the right of the text of "Cambridge," and color it red. Then draw a red circle around the dot that represents Cambridge.
2. John Locke, who wrote about a three-part government, studied at Oxford. Draw a blue triangle around the dot that represents Oxford.
3. Isaac Newton spent the end of his life in London. Underline London in red.
4. People in England and the Netherlands began to use crop rotation and other scientific methods of farming. Outline the borders of England and the Netherlands in brown.
5. Crop rotation allowed the minerals in the soil to renew themselves, and crops in this richer soil yielded better crops. In the Netherlands, draw three green arrows that connect to form a circle (symbolizing crop rotation).

**Coloring Page** With new methods, farmers created new breeds of animals that could grow more wool or give more meat. One farmer, Robert Bakewell, created the Leicester Longwool sheep and the English Longhorn cow. *(Student Page 49)*

## PROJECTS

### Science Project: Examine John Locke's Philosophy

Most people in John Locke's time believed that everyone was born with an understanding of certain ideas: everyone can recognize the colors yellow and white, everyone knows what love is, everyone call tell that an object is hard or soft. No one has to teach you about these things—you are born with the knowledge already. John Locke did not believe that a person is born with any knowledge. He thought a person is born completely "blank." You learn through experience. You see a banana, a dandelion, and a lemon and it is only THEN that you realize what yellow is. Your experiences give you understanding. Read this excerpt from John Locke's *An Essay Concerning Human Understanding.*

1. It is past doubt that men have in their minds several ideas, such as are those expressed by the words whiteness, hardness, sweetness, thinking, motion, man, elephant, army, drunkenness, and others: it is in the first place then to be inquired, How he comes by them? I know it is a received doctrine, that men have native ideas, stamped upon their minds in their very first being. This opinion I have at large examined already; and I shall appeal to every one's own observation and experience.
2. All ideas come from sensation or reflection. Let us then suppose the mind to be, as we say, white paper, void of all characters, without any ideas: How comes it to be furnished? Whence has it all the materials of reason and knowledge? To this I answer, in one word, from EXPERIENCE. In that all our knowledge is founded; and from that it ultimately derives itself.
3. First, our Senses, conversant about particular sensible objects, do convey into the mind several distinct perceptions of things. And thus we come by those ideas we have of yellow, white, heat, cold, soft, hard, bitter, and sweet. This great source of most of the ideas we have, depending wholly upon our senses, and derived by them to the understanding, I call SENSATION.

Examine John Locke's philosophy yourself. See if, through experience, you can understand and define sweetness and selflessness.

***Sweetness***

Put four sweet items in front of you: a chocolate chip, a raisin, a marshmallow, and a teaspoon of sugar (or a sugar cube). Taste each item, one at a time. John Locke would say that only after you have tasted those items would your brain recognize what it means when something is "sweet."

***Selflessness***

When you are selfless, you do something kind for someone else without expecting anything in return. You are not thinking of yourself: you are thinking of others. A *selfless* act is the opposite of a *selfish* act, which you do only for your own benefit. Do four selfless acts today. You can pick up your sibling's room for him or her (or pick up the family room). You can set the table for the meal, or clear the dishes when it is finished. You can let a brother or sister play with one of your favorite toys. You can pick flowers or make a drawing for your mother. John Locke would say that only after you have performed these acts would you know what it means to be selfless.

## PUZZLE PROJECT Crop Rotation

Different kinds of plants use different kinds of minerals. If you plant the same crop in the same soil year after year, the soil will lose its minerals, and the crop will not be as healthy. So Lord Charles Townshend came up with a rotation of crops, alternating crops that use minerals and plants that return minerals to the soil. Crop rotation can also reduce the number of insects and plant infections in crops. So how do you figure out what to plant when? Complete this logic puzzle of an actual eight-year vegetable crop rotation used in the northeastern United States. You plant one crop each year.

*Materials:*
- ☐ Paper
- ☐ Pencil or pen

*Directions:*

1. The plants are:
   - potatoes
   - tomatoes
   - English peas
   - squash
   - carrots
   - beans
   - corn
   - cabbage
2. Construct a chart on a piece of scratch paper. Draw a large circle. On the circle, draw eight dots or stars. In between the dots, draw small arrows that indicate that the cycle is going clockwise.
3. As you read the following clues, write the name of a vegetable next to the appropriate dot. Remember to cover up the answer key at the end of this activity!

*Clues:*

1. **Potatoes** and **tomatoes** need to be the maximum distance apart because they are similar plants and require the same nutrients from the soil.
2. A crop of **potatoes** is easy to weed and therefore reduces the number of weeds in the field.
3. **Tomatoes** are cleared before winter.
4. **Tomatoes** need a nitrogen-rich soil, so it must follow a crop that returns nitrogen to the soil.
5. **English peas** need to be started early so they must follow a plant that is cleared before winter.

6. **English peas** are cleared before winter.
7. **Squash** reduces the number of weeds.
8. **Carrots** must follow TWO crops that both reduce the number of weeds.
9. **Corn**, unlike most plants, still thrives when it follows cabbage.
10. **Beans** return nitrogen to the soil.
11. **Cabbage** needs to be started early so it must follow a plant that is cleared before winter.

**Answer Key**: Starting at any place in the circle: Carrots, Beans, Tomatoes, English Peas, Cabbage, Corn, Potatoes, Squash.

## SCIENCE PROJECT The Force of Gravity

Newton figured out that the reason an apple (or any other object) falls straight down to the ground when it is dropped is because there is a force pulling it down. He called this force "gravity." Because the earth is so large, objects are pulled toward it by the earth's gravity. Even the moon is caught by the earth's gravitational pull—that is why the moon goes around the earth instead of spinning off into space. If you drop a marble off the top of the Empire State Building, the earth's gravity will pull the marble down to the ground. The marble will get faster and faster as it falls until it is "stopped" by the ground. Here is an interesting fact: if you drop a bowling ball and a marble off the top of the Empire State Building at the same time, they will hit the ground at the same time, too. All objects dropped from the same height fall at the same speed whether they are heavy or light. See this principle in action by conducting an experiment.

*Materials:*

- ☐ a basketball or soccer ball
- ☐ a ping-pong ball, golf ball, or rubber bouncy ball
- ☐ a height over ten feet you can stand on and drop and object straight down (like a staircase, a treehouse, etc. . . .)

*Directions:*

1. You will need two people to perform this experiment. One person should stand at the top of a flight of stairs (or wherever) with the basketball and the ping-pong ball.
2. The other person stands by the ground where the objects will be dropped. This person is in charge of watching the balls and deciding if they hit the ground at the same time.
3. When the person on the ground is ready, the person on the stairs holds up the two balls at an equal height off the ground. Then that person drops (not throws) the balls. The person on the ground watches the ball hits the ground and gives his observation of the results.
4. Do this experiment several times. Do you get the same results each time? Switch roles so both participants can see the result of gravity pulling on the two objects.

## SCIENCE PROJECT Isaac Newton's First Law of Motion

Isaac Newton's observations of the world produced several laws that "changed the world." Three of these laws are called "The Laws of Motion," and they explain why and how objects move. Learn about Newton's First Law of Motion and do an activity with a ball that will demonstrate this law.

***Newton's First Law of Motion:***

An object that is still will stay still unless an outside force is applied to it.

An object moving in a straight line will continue to move in a straight line unless an outside force is applied to it.

*An object that is still will stay still unless an outside force is applied to it.*
Set a ball (like a tennis or soccer ball) on a level floor. If you set it down without pushing it, the ball will remain where it is. It is in a "state of rest." The only outside force on the ball is the force of gravity. Gravity is pulling the ball straight down; that is why the ball rests on the floor. If there were no gravity pulling on the object, the ball would float in the air, just like objects in outer space. So the ball sits on the floor, at rest. The only way a ball will move is if "another force works on it." This could be a strong breeze or the force of your hand as you push the ball across the floor.

*An object moving in a straight line will continue to move in a straight line unless an outside force is applied to it.*
Now push the ball across the floor in a straight line. Newton's first law of motion states that this ball will go in a straight line "unless an outside force is applied to it." If the ball hits an object or a wall, or if there is a strong breeze, the ball will change directions; otherwise the ball will go straight. Push the ball several more times. Now push the ball toward a wall. Before the ball hits the wall, what direction is it going? It should be going straight according to Newton's law. After the ball hits the wall and is forced in another direction, which direction does it go?

*Note: Newton's First Law of Motion states that a moving object will continue to move in a straight line until an outside force is applied to it. If that is the case, why does a ball eventually stop when you push it, even if it doesn't hit anything? The answer is *friction*. A moving ball moves because energy from a force is causing it to move. If you pushed the ball, the force of your push gave the ball energy to move. As the ball rolls along the ground, it scrapes against it. This scraping, or *friction*, causes the ball to lose a little bit of energy. As the ball loses more and more energy, it slows down until it finally comes to a stop.

# Russia Looks West

## Encyclopedia Cross-References

*UBWH 145, UILE 317*
*KIHW 456-457, KHE 276-278*

## PETER THE GREAT

### Review Questions

In medieval times, did Russia seem more Eastern or Western? *It seemed more Eastern.*

What kind of power did the kings, or czars, of Russia have? *The czars had absolute power, like Chinese emperors and Japanese shoguns.*

When Peter I was a young man, who tried to take his country away from him? *His sister Sophia tried to take the throne for herself.*

Who helped Peter become the Czar of Russia? *The royal guard declared their allegiance to him and helped him take the throne.*

Did many Europeans live in Russia? *No, and those who did lived in separate colonies for foreigners.*

Why did Peter want to have a fleet of merchant ships? *He wanted to send ships to Europe with Russian honey, wax, and furs, so that they could bring back Western luxuries.*

What was the problem with Archangel, the shipping port that Russia already had? *Archangel was so cold and icy that ships couldn't reach it for most of the year—the water was frozen solid!*

How long were the days in Archangel during the winter? *The days were only five hours long!*

What warm port did Peter want to take from the Turks? *He wanted to take the port of Azov.*

Why couldn't Peter's army capture the port of Azov? *Turkish ships could sail into the city to bring food and weapons to the Turks inside the fortress.*

What did Peter have his army build, in order to stop the Turkish ships from helping the people of Azov? *He had his men build a navy of warships and barges.*

Once Peter had his port, why did he need the help of other countries in the West? *He needed them to help him fight against the Ottoman Turks, because the Turks controlled the passage into the Mediterranean Sea.*

Name two places Peter visited on his great expedition to the countries of the West. *He studied gunnery in Prussia; he worked at the docks in Amsterdam (in Holland) and London (in England); he visited the Tower of London and the English Mint. He went to a Quaker meeting in London.*

When Peter returned to Russia, what did tell his noblemen to do so that they would look more Western? *He made them cut off their beards* OR *He made them wear Western clothes.*

What Western ideas did Peter not want his people to find out about? *He didn't want them to hear about the philosophers who said that all people were equal, or that rulers shouldn't be able to do exactly as they pleased.*

### Narration Exercise

"Peter the Great became czar of Russia after his sister tried to take his throne. He wanted to be able to trade with the West, so he built ships and captured the Port of Azov. Then he took a journey to the West to see what Western countries were like. He visited Prussia, England, and Holland. When he returned to Russia, he told his noblemen to cut off their beards and wear Western clothes, so that they would look more Western. But he didn't want them to insist that men and women were equal to the czar!" OR

"Peter the Great wanted Russia to look to the west. He wanted Russian ships to carry wax and honey to Europe, and to bring back luxuries. But he needed a port, because Archangel was frozen so much of the year. So he attacked the Port of Azov. At first, he couldn't capture it because ships sailed into the port to bring food and weapons. So Peter built a whole fleet of ships. Then he was able to capture the port! He still needed help defeating the Turks, so he took a journey to the West to convince other countries to come and help him fight against the Ottomans."

## PETER'S PORT TO THE WEST

### Review Questions

Was Peter able to convince England and Holland to join him in fighting the Turks? *No, he was not able to convince them.*

What was another sea that Peter could use to trade with Europe? Which country controlled this sea? *He could use the Baltic Sea, but Sweden controlled the Baltic.*

Why did Denmark-Norway join Peter in his fight against Sweden? *The people of Denmark-Norway thought that Sweden was growing too large and powerful.*

What was the nineteen-year-old king of Sweden, Charles XII, like? *He was known for wild parties and reckless adventures, like hunting bears with wooden pitchforks.*

Peter thought that with the kingdom of Denmark-Norway on his side, his Russian army could beat Sweden quickly. Was he right? Was the war short or long? *He was wrong—the war lasted for twenty-one years.*

What weather event allowed the Swedes to beat the Russians at Narva? *A huge snowstorm blinded the Russian soldiers.*

What did Charles XII put on a medal to celebrate his victory? *The medal showed Peter the Great running away and crying.*

Peter managed to capture a little Swedish fortress on what river? *He captured a fortress on the Neva River.*

Where did Peter decide to build his new city, St. Petersburg? *He decided to build it on the banks of the Neva River, near the Baltic Sea.*

Why was it difficult to build a city on the banks of the Neva? *The land was swampy and muddy; there were no trees for wood and no stones for foundations; all the wood and stone had to be dragged from far away.*

When Charles XII invaded Russia, what happened to his army? *His army froze to death because the weather was so cold and they couldn't get into shelter quickly enough.*

Did Peter finally win the shore of the Baltic? *Yes, after four more years of battle the Swedes surrendered the eastern shore of the Baltic.*

Can you name two things that Peter did to make Russia a rich country? *Peter built canals, factories, salt works, iron mills, mines; he brought craftsmen to Russia; he turned St. Petersburg into a large city.*

How did Peter catch the illness that led to his death? *He jumped into icy water to rescue some sailors whose boat was sinking.*

### Narration Exercise

"Peter the Great attacked Sweden because he wanted to own the shores of the Baltic Sea. He thought he could defeat Sweden easily—but Charles XII of Sweden fought back for years! At first, Charles won a great victory. But then his soldiers chased the Russian army into Russia. Many froze to death when winter came, and the Russian army defeated the rest. Sweden had to give the shore of the Baltic Sea to Peter. Now Peter could sail ships to the West. Peter also built factories and mines to make Russia strong, and built a new city called St. Petersburg to be his capital." OR

"Peter couldn't convince the other nations of Europe to join with him against the Ottoman Turks. So instead, he tried to take the Baltic Sea away from Sweden. Denmark-Norway joined with him—but the war, called the Great Northern War, went on for many years. Finally, Peter won the Baltic Sea. He built a new city called St. Petersburg. All of the wood and stone had to be brought from far away! He also built factories, salt works, and iron mills. He brought craftsmen to Russia to teach the Russians how to make cloth and other things. He made Russia great. He died when he dived into icy water to save drowning sailors."

## Additional History Reading

*Cultural Traditions in Russia*, by Molly Aloian, (Crabtree Publishing, 2012). An overview of the traditions and culture of Russia. (RA K, IR 2)

*Let's Explore Russia* by Walt K. Moon (Bumba Books, 2017). Aimed at the early elementary set, this introduction to Russia includes large, vibrant photographs as well as information on Russia's geography and people. (RA K-2, IR 1-2)

*Living in Russia* by Jesse Burton (Simon and Schuster, 2018). An excellent introduction to the geography, history and people of Russia as told through the eyes of a Russian child. (IR 1-3, RA 1-2)

*Restless Empire: A Historical Atlas of Russia*, by Ian Barnes, (Belknap Press, 2015). This book is intended for adults, but is an atlas containing a chronological history of Russia through maps and illustrations, and may be of interest to a wide range of ages. (RA 4, IR 6)

*Russia*, by Andrea Pelleschi, (Essential Library, 2013). For more advanced readers, an overview of Russia, its people, geography, history, and culture. Includes a timeline. (RA 4, IR 6)

*Russia ABCs*, by Ann Berge (Picture Window Books, 2003). Nice illustrations and brief, readable paragraphs about the history, culture, and geography of Russia. (RA 1-2, IR 3-4)

*Russia: The Land*, by Greg Nickles (Crabtree Publications, 2000). Provides descriptions of Russia's huge expanse along with a brief history. (RA 2, IR 3-5) **LFA**

*Spotlight on Russia*, by Bobbie Kalman, (Crabtree Publishing, 2010). An overview of the culture, geography, and people of Russia. (RA K, IR 2)

*Peter the Great and Tsarist Russia*, by Miriam Greenblatt (Benchmark Books, 2000). One of the "Rulers and Their Times" series, this excellent elementary-grade biography has two parts: a biography of Peter the Great, and a history of Czarist Russia. Long, but simple reading level. (RA 1-2, IR 3-5) **OOP**

*Peter the Great*, by Diane Stanley (Morrow, 1989). Picture-book format with excellent illustrations and fairly detailed text. Good as a read-aloud, or as an independent read for strong third-grade readers and older. (RA 1-3, IR 3-5)

*St. Petersburg: Cities of the World*, by Deborah Kent (Children's Press, 1997). This detailed, photo-filled history of Saint Petersburg is an independent read for fourth grade and above; the sections on the founding of the city can be read aloud for younger children. (RA 2-3, IR 4-6) **LFA**

*St. Petersburg,* by Andrew Langley (Gareth Stevens, 2005). Part of the "Great Cities of the World" series, this straightforward read with contemporary photographs reviews the history. of St. Petersburg as well as its development into modern times. (IR 3-6)

*Sweden* by Rachel A. Koestler-Grack (Bellwether Media, 2011). A basic introduction to the history, geography and culture of Sweden, the country that tried to block Peter's path to the West. (IR 2-4, RA 1-3)

## Corresponding Literature Suggestions

*Baba Yaga and Vasilisa the Brave*, by Marianna Mayer, illus. Kinuko Y. Craft (William Morrow, 1994). A simple picture-book version of a classic Russian tale about a brave girl. (RA 2, IR 3-5)

*Deep in the Woods* by Christopher Corr (Frances Lincoln, 2015). A retelling of a classic Russian folktale, this book and its delightful, colorful illustrations will appeal most to younger students. (RA K-3, IR 2-4)

*Fairy Tales of the Russians and Other Slavs: Sixty-Eight Stories*, Ace G. and Olga A. Pilkington eds. (Forest Tsar Press, 2009). A broad collection of Slavic fairy tales. (RA 3, IR 5)

*Fearless Ivan and His Faithful Horse Double-Hump* by Pyotr Yershov and retold by Jack Zipes (University of Minnesota Press, 2018). This favorite Russian folktale is the story of a peasant boy who defeats the cruel tsar in a most unlikely way. (RA 3-6, IR 4-8)

*The Fool and the Flying Ship*, by Arthur Ransome, illus. Uri Shulevitz (Farrar Straus & Giroux, 1968). A classic retelling of one of the most famous Russian tales: a simple son wins the favor of the Czar. (RA 2, IR 3-4)

*The Fox and the Hare*, by Vladmir Dal, Francesca Yarbusova illus. (Rovacada Publishing, 2013). A Russian tale suitable for young or struggling readers, with excellent illustrations which were the basis for an animated version of this story. (RA K, IR 2)

*Frog Went A-Traveling* retold by Amanda StJohn (The Children's World, 2012). A retelling of a famous Russian folktale, the delightful story of Fedja the frog will appeal to younger elementary students, as will the big, bright illustrations. (RA K-3, IR 2-4)

*The Night Journey*, by Kathryn Lasky, (Puffin Books, 2005). The story of a young girl listening to her grandmother's stories of Jewish people in Russia. (RA 3, IR 4)

*The Sea King's Daughter: A Russian Legend*, by Aaron Shepard, illus. Gennady Spirin (Atheneum, 1997). This picture book for older children shares Peter the Great's obsession with the sea. (RA 2, IR 3-5)

*Shoemaker Martin*, by Leo Tolstoy, Bernadette Watts illus. (NorthSouth Books, 2018). A beautifully illustrated storybook version of this tale by Tolstoy. (RA K, IR 3)

*The Tale of Tsar Saltan*, by Aleksandr Pushkin, illus. Gennady Spirin (Dial Books, 1996). This child's tale, written by the great nineteenth-century Russia poet Pushkin, is illustrated by a well-known Russian artist.

*Vasilisa the Beautiful* retold by Anthea Bell (Michael Neugebauer Edition, 2015). Another classic Russian folktale, the story of Vasilisa is a delight, sure to please students of all ages. (IR 2-6, RA 1-6)

## MAP WORK

**Peter and the West** *(Student Page 50, answer 323)*

1. English farmers and European philosophers lived in the "West." Find the border that runs through the "O" in Poland. Trace the border from the Baltic Sea down to the Black Sea with a green crayon.
2. Peter wanted a port to the West, but his only port city was the cold and wintry Archangel. Draw a blue circle around Archangel.
3. Peter attacked the Turks and won the port city of Azov. Draw a blue circle around Azov.
4. Peter was still unable to get to the West, because the Turks kept him from getting to the Mediterranean. So Peter went "West" on land. Two of the places he visited were Great Britain and the Netherlands. Outline both of these areas in blue.
5. Denmark-Norway and Russia banded together to fight against Sweden. Color Denmark-Norway and Russia orange. Draw two arrows from Sweden into Russia.
6. The war lasted a long time, but Peter did not give up. He eventually defeated the Swedes. Draw two blue arrows from Russia toward the Baltic Sea.
7. Peter made St. Petersburg the capital of Russia. Draw a star next to the "S" in St. Petersburg.

**Coloring Page** Peter the Great planned a new city, Saint Petersburg, in a spot that had been full of swamps, reeds, and mosquitoes. He forced thousands of people to work at building it, and eventually made it his capital city. Before long, Saint Petersburg was full of magnificent buildings (like this one, the Peterhof Palace) with fountains and gardens. *(Student Page 51)*

## PROJECTS

### Craft Project Fall of Azov

Azov had a strong defense, but Peter was sure he could defeat it. So he gathered his troops and surrounded Azov. No one in Azov seemed too worried. One side of their city faced the Sea of Azov, and as long as their ships sailed in with food and ammunition, they were determined to sit the Russians out.

*Materials:*
- ☐ large plastic tub about the size of a kitchen sink
- ☐ dirt, to fill up half the tub
- ☐ plastic garbage bag
- ☐ duct tape
- ☐ water
- ☐ Student Page 52: Azov's Wall
- ☐ raisins and small pebbles
- ☐ small plastic toy boats

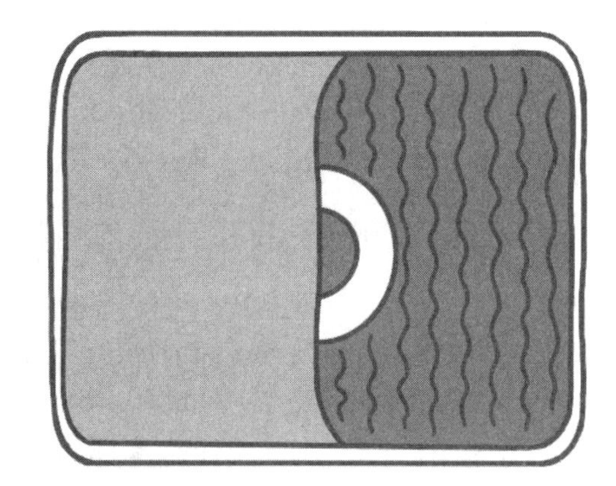

Directions:

1. Copy Azov's Wall on white cardstock, if desired, or use the paper Student Page provided. Color both sides. Fill the large tub halfway full with dirt. Add a little water to help the dirt stick together. Pull the dirt to one side of the tub and pack it down so that it stays securely. This will be the land next to the Sea of Azov.
2. Place the garbage bag into the open area next to the dirt. Cover the entire area with the bag and secure it to the top of the tub with duct tape. Make sure the bag is slick against the sides including the side against the dirt. This will keep the water from seeping in and causing the dirt to fall in. To secure the bag on the dirt side, place its edge on the top of the dirt and cover over with more dirt. Fill bag side slowly with water and make any adjustments needed.
3. Our model of Azov will sit in a semi-circle in the center of the bank, as seen in the illustration. Bend the cardstock or paper of the city walls to form a semi-circle. Press into the dirt to hold it in place.
4. Load your plastic boats with raisins (food) and pebbles (ammunition). Float them up to the walls of Azov. Can you see how Peter's army, over on the land on the other side of Azov, would find it impossible to stop the supply ships?
5. Now designate one of your plastic models a Russian ship. Act out the sea battle where Peter the Great took control of Azov!

## CRAFT PROJECT Medal of Triumph

Peter thought the Swedish King, Charles XII, would be easy to beat! After all, he was only nineteen years old and was known for doing silly things. But Charles, aided by bad weather and faulty cannons on the Russian side, led his army to victory. He was so happy with his win that he had a special medal made for those who fought beside him. Every day there are people who help us to do our best. Make this medal to show that you see what they are doing to help you!

Materials:

- ☐ craft foam in four different colors and/or patterns OR
- ☐ four different colors of construction paper
- ☐ craft tacky glue (regular glue does not keep the foam together) OR
- ☐ Elmer's glue (for construction paper)
- ☐ permanent marker (any color that stands out)
- ☐ assorted embellishments, like sequins, glitter, craft flat-back jewels (optional)
- ☐ sticky back jewelry pin (in craft stores in jewelry section) OR
- ☐ plain safety pin
- ☐ Student Page 53: Template of Medal Pieces

Directions:

1. Using the templates, cut out each part in a different foam or construction paper color.
2. Stick the pieces together with glue. Let dry.
3. Design your center using the permanent marker that focuses on the great thing your recipient did for you. On his medal, Charles XII put a picture of Peter the Great, with tears pouring from his eyes and handkerchief in his hands, riding away in retreat. You could draw a picture as well!
4. Stick the craft pin or safety pin to the back of your medal so the recipient can wear it proudly.
5. Embellish the triangle tips, center or the ribbons with sequins, jewels and glitter, if desired.
6. Add a special verbal thanks as you ceremonially give your Medal of Triumph!

## CRAFT PROJECT **Dream Up a City!**

When Peter the Great planned St. Petersburg, he could see a beautiful city in his imagination. But his city site was a muddy swamp, filled with water birds and mosquitoes. There were no trees for lumber or stones to build with. But Peter could still see St. Petersburg in his mind! If you could build a city from nothing, what would your city look like?

*Materials:*

- ☐ Graph paper or plain white paper
- ☐ Pencil
- ☐ Colored pencils
- ☐ Construction paper

*Directions:*

1. Make a list of everything you think a town would need. Did you include a grocery store, a post office, and a fire station? How about a gas station, park, or a power source? What about roads? Check your list with an adult.
2. Using your graph paper, map out your city. Think of what the people would need to have close together. For example, if the houses were within walking distance from a grocery store then they would have a convenient source for their food. Is the fire station close to the houses and businesses? What about the parks? If you add an urban train system people could get from one place to the other with more ease.
3. Color in your map and add trees, rivers and lakes, if there are any. Name your dream city. Mat your picture on to a piece of construction paper to frame it. Secure it on the wall.

# East and West Collide

## Encyclopedia Cross-References

*UBWH 142, UILE 298-299*
*KIHW 455, KHE 266-267*

## THE OTTOMANS LOOK WEST—TWICE

### Review Questions

What was the title given to the ruler of the Ottoman Turks? *He was called a sultan.*

What religion did the Turks follow? *The Turks were followers of Islam.*

Who were the Janissaries? *They were the sultan's private royal guards, who would carry out any decree he gave.*

What city did the Turks send their large army to capture? *They tried to capture Vienna.*

Why was Vienna an important city? *It was the capital of the German state of Austria, and the Holy Roman Emperor lived there.*

When the Ottoman army set up their siege camp, what did the leader, or *vizier,* do? *He put up tents with silk covers, rich rugs, and gardens planted all around them.*

How did the Turkish soldiers try to get past Vienna's wall? *They made tunnels to get underneath the walls.*

Who heard the Turks tunneling on one quiet morning? *A baker who was kneading bread heard them tunneling, and he warned the soldiers.*

In honor of the baker's warning, what kind of bread did the Viennese bakers invent? *They invented croissants, or rolls shaped like the crescent emblem on the Turkish flag.*

An army made of soldiers from three different countries finally drove the Turks away. Can you remember at least two of the countries? *The soldiers were from France, Germany, and Poland.*

What happened to the vizier, Kara Mustafa? *His head was brought to the sultan in a velvet bag!*

Twenty-five years later, there was a new sultan who admired Western culture. What particular western item did he bring back to Turkey? *He brought tulips back to Turkey.*

What nickname was given to Sultan Ahmet III? *He was called the "Tulip King."*

Ahmet III and his grand vizier, Ibrahim Pasha, tried to make the Ottoman court more like courts of the West. Can you remember two things that they did? *The Sultan's new palace was like a French palace; ambassadors went to French cities and factories; they learned more about European art and science; they brought back a printing press so that the Ottomans could print their own books.*

Which group of people were unhappy about the changes that Ahmet was making to his court? What did they do about it? *The Janissaries were unhappy. They rioted, burned down the palace, and threw the sultan in jail.*

Today, what country is the last remnant of the huge Eastern empire of the Ottoman Turks? *Today, we call this country Turkey.*

### Narration Exercise

Since there is a lot of information in this chapter, use "directed narration." Say to the child, "First, tell me about the Turkish attack on Vienna. Be sure to tell me why they attacked, the way in which they attacked, and what happened." An acceptable level of detail would be, "The Turks attacked Vienna because they wanted to make the West part of their empire (OR because it was an important city where the Holy Roman Emperor lived). They camped around the city and started to dig tunnels towards the walls and underneath them. The people of Vienna thought that the Turks would attack at any moment. But at last French, Polish, and German soldiers attacked and defeated the Turks. The Turkish empire began to shrink."

Then, say to the child, "Now tell me about Ahmet III, the Tulip King. Be sure to tell me three things he did, and how his reign ended." An acceptable level of detail would be, "Ahmet III liked the ideas and culture of the West. He brought tulips from the Netherlands back to the Turks and planted thousands and thousands of bulbs. He and his vizier made their palace to look like a Western (OR French) palace, and they brought back a printing press so that the Turks could publish books (OR they sent ambassadors to French cities and factories and learned about European art and science). But the Janissaries didn't like the new Western ideas. They threw Ahmet III into jail and put his nephew on the throne instead."

## Additional History Reading

*Armenia,* by Sakina Dhilawala (Cavendish Square, 2018). The chapter on Armenia's history, including Ottoman rule, may be useful as a supplement or for readers interested in learning more about this country. (RA 3+, IR 5+)

*Austria,* by Lisa Owings (Bellwether Media, 2015). An excellent introduction to Austria and its capital Vienna for a wide range of ages. (RA 2-5, IR 3-6)

*The Barbarossa Brothers: 16th Century Pirates of the Barbary Coast,* by Aileen Weintraub (Powerkids Press, 2002). Turkish pirates range along the Mediterranean coast, fighting against Christian ports; simple text and color illustrations. (RA 1-2, IR 3-4) **LFA**

*Cultural Traditions In Turkey,* by Joan Marie Galat, (Crabtree Publishing 2017). Cultural information about Turkey. (RA K, IR 2)

*Early Islamic Empires,* by Lizann Flatt, (Crabtree, 2013). For stronger readers, this book explores the rise of Muslim empires, including the Ottomans. (RA 4, IR 5)

*From Bulb to Tulip,* by Lisa Owings (Lerner Publications, 2015). A step-by-step description of how a tulip grows. A fun way to inject a bit of science into your history studies. (RA 1-3, IR 2-3)

*The Genius of Islam: How Muslims Made the Modern World,* by Bryn Barnard, (Knopf Books For Young Readers, 2011). This book looks at historic Muslim contributions to science, mathematics, engineering, and other areas. (RA 3, IR 5)

*Islam,* by Michael Ashkar (Mason Crest, 2018). Thorough coverage of Islam and its major tenets. Best for capable readers, or use sections as a read aloud for additional context. (RA 3+, IR 5+)

*Islam,* by Trevor Barnes (Kingfisher, 2013). Written at a slightly lower level than the previous volume, this book is a succinct introduction to the Islamic faith. (RA 3-5, IR 5-6)

*Mosque,* by David Macaulay, (HMH Books for Young Readers, 2008). An illustrated exploration of the architecture of a mosque. (RA K, IR 2)

*The Ottoman Empire*, by Carolyn DeCarlo (Rosen Education Service, 2018). Part of the "Empires in the Middle Ages" series, this book offers a readable, illustrated overview of the Ottoman Empire's high points. (RA 2, IR 3-4)

*Turkey,* by Joanna Jarc Robinson (The Child's World, 2016). A readable introduction to modern Turkey, including its history, culture and people. (RA 2-4, IR 3-5)

*National Geographic Countries of the World: Turkey*, by Sarah Shields, (National Geographic Children's Books, 2009). An overview of Turkey and the Turkish people. (RA 3, IR 5)

*Story Of Islam*, by Sue Meredith, (Usborne, 2007). An overview of the Muslim religion as well as the history and culture of Islam. RA1, IR 2)

## Corresponding Literature Suggestions

*The Two Trumpeters of Vienna*, by Hertha Pauli (Hillside Education, 2019). Four teenaged friends live through the siege of Vienna by the Ottoman Turks. This classic novel was originally published in 1961 by Doubleday, as part of the Clarion series of juvenile historical novels, and has just been republished by homeschool press Hillside; you may be able to find used copies of the original for a very low price. For strong readers. (IR 5-9)

*The Great Tulip Trade* by Beth Wagner Brust (Random House Books for Young Readers, 2005). A book for young readers set in the 1600's in the Netherlands where the value of a flower was more precious than jewels. (RA 1, IR 2-3)

*Hana in the Time of the Tulips* by Deborah Noyes (Candlewick Press, 2004). In this sweet story, the main character reminds her greedy father—who is consumed by the thought of making money selling tulips—what is really important in life. (RA 3-6, IR 4-6).

*The Contest*, by Nonny Hogrogian (Greenwillow, 1976). Two robbers discover that they are engaged to the same girl in this illustrated Armenian tale. (RA 2, IR 3-4)

*Folktales from Turkey* by Serpil Ural (Citlembik Publications, 2012). These traditional folktales will delight your elementary students. Also included are maps noting the location of each story as well as historical and cultural references. (RA 2-3, IR 3-4)

*Folk Costumes of Turkey* by Amy Chaple (Citlembik Publications, 2001). This paper-doll book will bring hands-on learning to your studies. As they put together the paper dolls, students will learn more about traditional Turkish folk dress as well as culture and traditions. (RA 2-3, IR 3-4)

*The Garden of Wisdom: Earth Tales from the Middle East*, by Michael J. Caduto ed., Odelia Liphshiz illus., (Green Heart Books, 2018). Traditional stories from the Middle East, on themes related to nature. Includes background material and activity suggestions for parents. (RA 2, IR 4)

*The Greedy Sparrow: An Armenian Tale*, retold by Lucine Kasbarian (Two Lions, 2012). The classic Armenian folktale that crime never pays is retold with fantastic illustrations. Especially note the traditional folk attire. (RA 1-3, IR 2-4)

*The Hundredth Name*, by Shulamith Levey Oppenheim, Michael Hays illus. (Boyd's Mills Press, 1997). A story about religious faith and life in a Middle Eastern village. (RA K, IR 3.)

*The Hungry Coat: A Tale From Turkey* by Demi (Margaret McElderry Books, 2004). This traditional Turkish folktale exemplifies the virtues of fairness and kindness. (RA 1-5, IR 3-5)

*My Little Lore of Light*, by Hajjah Amina Adil, Kerima Sperling adapt., illus., (Naqshbandi-Haqqani Sufi Order of America, 2009). An adaptation for children of traditional stories with origins in the Ottoman period. (RA 3, IR 5)

*The Olive Fairy Book* by Andrew Lang (Abela Publishing, 2017). In the same series as the well-known *Blue Fairy Book*, this volume contains traditional folktales from countries such as Turkey and Armenia. (RA 3-6, IR 5+)

*Once There Was, Twice There Wasn't: Fifty Turkish Folktales of Nasreddin Hodja,* by Michael Shelton, (Hey Nonny Nonny Press, 2014). Traditional stories about folk hero Mullah Nasreddin. (RA 3 IR 5)

*Snow White: An Islamic Tale*, by Fawzia Gilani, Shireen Adams illus., (The Islamic Foundation, 2013). Suitable for younger readers, an Islamic version of the fairly tale, set in Anatolia. (RA K, IR3)

## MAP WORK

### Europe and the Middle East *(Student Page 54, answer 324)*

1. Color the Arabian Sea, the Caspian Sea, the Black Sea, and the Mediterranean Sea blue. If you need help finding the borders, look at the map at the beginning of Chapter 18 of *The Story of the World: Volume 3.* (Make sure you do not color Arabia!)
2. Outline the border of the Ottoman Empire in brown, and then lightly shade it. Notice that it is "lightly speckled" on your map. (If you need help, refer to the map in Chapter 18 of *The Story of the World: Volume 3.)*
3. Vienna was seen as the heart of the West. Draw a red circle around Vienna.
4. The Ottomans wanted to conquer the "West." They began by marching toward Vienna. Draw a brown arrow from the Ottoman Empire toward Vienna.
5. France, Germany, and Poland marched toward Vienna to drive back the Turks. Draw one orange arrow from France, one from the German states, and one from Poland, toward Vienna.

### Coloring Page

Sultan Ahmet III loved tulips, and had thousands of them planted at his palace. On spring nights when the flowers were blooming, Ahmet would hold enormous parties among the flower beds, with brightly colored birds for the guests to see, and turtles swimming through the garden streams carrying candles on their backs. *(Student Page 55)*

## PROJECTS

### Art Project — Ottoman Miniature Paintings

One of the most characteristic kinds of Ottoman art was the miniature painting. Miniature paintings flourished during the sixteenth century. In the court of Suleiman the Magnificent, there were 29 instructor-masters and 16 apprentice-pupils. An instructor-master would paint the outline of the portrait or scene and then the apprentice-pupil would color it in. A miniature painter signed his work only if he had done all the work on it himself. Few miniatures were dated. Artists used paint made from powdered dyes and egg white. The most common colors in miniature painting were bright red, scarlet, green and shades of blue. You will also find some yellow, gold, black, and white in the tiny paintings. Pretend that you are an apprentice-pupil in the court of the sultan. Color in the two miniature paintings and then design your own. You can't sign the paintings you color, but you can sign the painting you design and color yourself;

*Materials:*
- ☐ Student Page 56: Miniature Paintings
- ☐ colored pencils or crayons

- ☐ construction paper
- ☐ scissors
- ☐ glue stick

*Directions:*
1. Color the two miniature paintings and then design and color your own.
2. Cut all three out and glue them on construction paper. They should be at least an inch apart.
3. Cut out the construction paper so you have three paintings each with their own construction paper frame.

## Cooking Project **Turkish Delight**

Turkish Delight (also called Lokum) is one of the oldest known confections in the world. According to legend, a sultan ordered the creation of a sweet dessert to make his wives happy. The sweetmaker labored in the kitchen: creating a sugar syrup, mixing in bits of dried fruits and nuts, and adding a sticky substance to bind the whole thing together. The sultan was so pleased with this deliciously-sweet dessert that he appointed the sweetmaker "Chief Confectioner" and ordered that Turkish Delight be served every day. Make your own Turkish Delight; it is still a sweet and tasty treat!

*Ingredients:*
5 Tbs cornstarch
½ cup cold water
½ cup hot water
2 cup sugar
½ cup orange juice
1 tsp rosewater (or lemon juice)
2 cup shelled pistachios (or other nuts)
1 cup powdered sugar

*Directions:*
1. Mix the corn starch and cold water in a small bowl, and set aside.
2. In a medium saucepan, bring hot water, sugar, and orange juice to a boil.
3. Add the corn starch mixture to the saucepan.
4. Simmer for fifteen minutes, stirring frequently.
5. Remove from heat. Add rosewater (or lemon juice) and nuts.
6. Pour into a greased 9" x 13" pan.
7. Let it cool until it thickens. This may take a while!
8. Cut into 1 inch cubes with a hot, wet knife, and roll the cubes in powdered sugar.

## Craft Project **Turkish War Camp**

Color and set up your own Turkish war camp that surrounded Vienna. Remember, the Ottomans loved bright colors and intricate patterns.

*Materials:*
- ☐ Student Page 57: Turkish Tent Templates
- ☐ scissors
- ☐ glue stick
- ☐ colored pencils or bright pastels
- ☐ hairspray (if using the pastels)

*Directions:*

1. Copy the Turkish Tent templates and enlarge if desired. You may copy the template onto regular paper or cardstock. Make as many tents as you want. There were thousands of Ottoman Turks at the siege, waiting for the fall of Vienna.
2. Color the tents bright colors. Usually the top part was a different color and pattern than the sides, and the opening flap of the tent was yet another festive color. If you are using pastels, lightly spray hairspray over your tents to set the color. This will help to reduce smearing.
3. Cut out tents and stands. Fold the tent stands at the dotted line and attach the stand to the middle of the back of each tent, gluing it on the left side only. Press the fold out to keep the tent standing up.

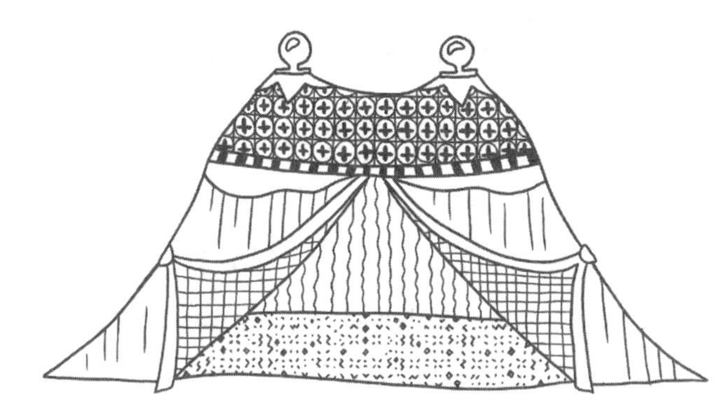

## ACTIVITY PROJECT **Shadow Theatre**

In the Ottoman empire, shadow theatre became a popular form of entertainment during the 1500s. A puppet master would move his puppets behind a cloth screen, so that the shadows acted out a story for the audience. Try to tell your own shadow-puppet story, using your stuffed animals and household objects.

*Materials:*

- ☐ Large white cotton sheet
- ☐ Lamp with shade removed and 60-watt bulb (preferably gooseneck or reading lamp that can be directed towards a particular place)
- ☐ Two chairs with tall backs
- ☐ Clothespins
- ☐ Sofa, low table, or other furniture for the child to crouch behind
- ☐ Stuffed animals
- ☐ Props (see below)

*Directions:*

1. Place the chairs 4-5 feet apart. Clothespin the sheet to the backs of the chairs to form a screen. Place the sofa, table, or other furniture in front of the sheet. The student should be able to crouch behind the sheet, keep his body behind the "shield" and lift his hands up to the level of the sheet. The "audience" will sit in front of the sheet.
2. Place the lamp behind the sheet, shining through the sheet towards the audience.
3. Decide what story the student will act out (e.g., the Three Bears with three teddy bears and a doll). Assemble whatever household objects (e.g., bowls) will be needed for props.
4. Act out the story! Hold up the "actors" (stuffed animals) so that the light casts their shadows against the sheet. The student may wish to try both acting out the story and watching from out front.

# The English in India

## Encyclopedia Cross-References

*UBWH 152, 156, 180, UILE 301, 328*
*KIHW 494-495, 440-441, 528, KHE 265, 298-299*

## THE INDIAN EMPIRE FALLS APART

### Review Questions

Who were the three great Moghul emperors that we've already read about? *They were Jahangir, Shah Jahan and Aurangzeb* OR *World Seizer, King of the World and Conqueror of the World.*

What three decisions did Aurangzeb make? *He made Islam the religion of India, spent his whole reign fighting in the Deccan, and gave the English permission to built a trading post at Bengal.*

Who fought over Aurangzeb's throne after he died? What name was given to the one who won this fight? *Three of his sons fought over the throne, and Bahadur Shah won the battle.*

Bahadur Shah only ruled for five years. Who claimed the throne? *His son claimed the throne.*

Bahadur Shah's son wasn't a very good ruler. Who decided to kill him? *Two Indian noblemen, the brothers Husain Ali and Hasan Ali, decided to have him killed.*

The Ali brothers put a young man named Farrukhisiyar on the throne. What was this new "emperor" supposed to do? *He was supposed to obey the Ali brothers.*

After putting two more "emperors" on the throne, the Ali brothers crowned Mohammad Shah. What did Mohammad Shah do first? *Mohammad Shah got rid of the Ali brothers.*

How did Mohammad Shah spend most of his time? *He spent most of his time going to animal fights.*

While Mohammed Shah was amusing himself, what were all of the officials in India doing? *They were dividing up the land and ruling it for themselves.*

Instead of an empire under one emperor, what had India become? *It had become a group of little provinces ruled by petty kings.*

Which Persian ruler attacked India, using war camels and cannons? *Nadir Shah attacked India and took away much of its wealth.*

Why did Nadir Shah become angry with the court at Delhi? *He was insulted because no one sent a messenger back to him.*

Nadir Shah left Mohammad Shah on the throne—but what did he do to India? *He burned Delhi, had its people killed, took India's wealth, plundered the Taj Mahal, and even took the Peacock Throne.*

### Narration Exercise

Since there is a lot of information in this chapter, use "directed narration." Say to the child, "First, tell me about the different emperors who became king after Aurangzeb died. List as many as you can remember!" Encourage the child to include at least three of the following emperors:

1. Aurangzeb's oldest son, Bahadur Shah, tried to make India stronger, but he only ruled for five years.
2. Bahadur Shah's son took the throne and paid more attention to his dancing girls than to ruling.

3. The Ali brothers put a cowardly, suspicious young man named Farrukhisiyar on the son.

4. The Ali brothers had Farrukhisiyar killed and put another king on the throne, but he died after four months.

5. The Ali brothers put another king on the throne, but he too died quickly.

6. The Ali brothers put Mohammad Shah on the throne, and he got rid of the Ali brothers.

Next, say to the child, "Tell me what India was like when Mohammad Shah ruled, and what happened to India during his reign." An acceptable level of detail would be, "Mohammad Shah spent more time going to animal fights than ruling, so all the officials of India divided up their land and ruled it themselves. India was weak and divided. The Persian king, Nadir Shah, wanted India to recognize his power. He invaded India, burned Delhi and killed many people, and stole India's treasure. Mohammad Shah was still emperor, but India was now poor and divided."

## THE SHOPKEEPERS' INVASION

### Review Questions

Name two of the places in India where the English had trading posts. *They had trading posts in Surat, in Bombay, and in Bengal.*

English merchants banded together to form one big company. What was this company called? *It was called the East India Company.*

Why did the English begin to worry about their trading posts and their merchants? *Hindu tribes from the south, Muslim rebels, and Persian invaders might attack them.*

What did the English do to protect themselves? *They began to build forts (in Bombay and Bengal).*

What did the ruler of Bengal, named Siraj, think when he saw the English building a fortress in Calcutta? *He began to grow suspicious and to think that the English wanted to take over Bengal.*

Who did Siraj ask for help? What did he offer them? *He asked the French for help, and he offered them land in India.*

When Siraj's men captured the English fort, what did Siraj do with his prisoners? *He ordered them all to be thrown into one small dungeon!*

According to a survivor, John Holwell, what happened to 120 of the prisoners? *He said that 120 of the prisoners died from suffocation.*

What was the name given to the dark, hot dungeon where the prisoners were kept? *It was called the Black Hole of Calcutta.*

Who decided to send an army to punish Siraj and the Indians of Bengal? *The East India Company hired its own army to attack Siraj.*

Who led the army of the East India Company? *A general named Sir Robert Clive led the army.*

What message did Sir Robert Clive send to Mir Jafar, the chief general of Siraj? *He told Mir Jafar to hold his army back from the battle, and promised to reward Mir Jafar by making him the ruler of Bengal.*

After the battle, Mir Jafar became the nawab of Bengal. But what happened when Mir Jafar resisted the orders of the East India Company? *Another army arrived and attacked him.*

What laws did Bengal follow, after this? *Bengal followed English laws and used English courts with English judges.*

What happened to the last Moghul emperor? *The English took the emperor under their "protection" (he was their prisoner).*

### Narration Exercise

Since there is a lot of information in this chapter, use "directed narration." Say to the child, "Tell me why Siraj, the ruler of Bengal, decided to attack the English trading post of Calcutta. Be sure to include his plan to get allies for his army!" An acceptable level of detail would be, "When the Indian empire fell apart, the English started to worry that they would be attacked. So they started to build forts to protect themselves. Siraj thought that the English might use the fort at Calcutta to take over Bengal. So he promised the French land in Bengal if they would help him defeat the English. The French and Siraj's army marched to Calcutta and captured it, and put all the English in a tiny dungeon called 'The Black Hole of Calcutta.' "

Next, say to the child, "What did the East India Company do in response? Be sure to include the English promise to Mir Jafar!" An acceptable level of detail would be, "The East India Company sent an army and a general to attack Siraj. The English general promised Mir Jafar, Siraj's general, that he would become ruler of Bengal if he didn't fight. So Mir Jafar didn't give his soldiers any orders. They retreated, and the English army won. Mir Jafar became the ruler of Bengal, but he had to obey the orders of the English."

## Additional History Reading

*For additional titles, see the history book list in Chapter Eleven.*

*Beasts of India*, Kanchana Arnie ed., Gina Wolf ed., (Tara Books, 2018). This book presents animals of India; each is depicted in a different tribal art tradition, and it is as much an introduction to Indian art as it is an introduction to Indian wildlife. (RA K, IR K)

*A Children's History of India*, by Subhadra Gupta, (Rupa Publications India, 2015). A history of India up to modern times. Includes activities. (RA 2, IR 4)

*The Culture and Recipes of India* by Tracey Kelley (PowerKIDS Press, 2017). Learn more about India and its history while learning to cook Indian cuisine—a fun way to add a hands-on element to your history studies. (RA 2-4, IR 3-6)

*Delhi* by Joyce Markovics (Bearport Publishing, 2018). This colorful picture book is full of big, beautiful illustrations and large text—perfect for emerging readers, or as a read aloud. (RA 1-3, IR 1-3)

*Games People Play: India* by Dale Howard (Children's Press, 1996). A unique title in which students will learn about the cultural and historical aspects of sports in India. (RA 3-6, IR 4-6)

*Hands-On History! Ancient India: Discover the Rich Heritage of the Indus Valley and the Mughal Empire, with 15 Step-by-Step Projects and 340 Pictures*, by Daud Ali, (Armadillo, 2014). A very simple introduction to premodern India; although this focuses primarily on ancient times, the activities give a general introduction to Indian culture. (RA K, IR 3)

*I See the Sun in India* by Dedie King (Satya House Publications, 2014). This bilingual English-Hindi book is a fun way to learn about Indian language, history, culture, landmarks and daily life from the perspective of a child. (RA 1-4, IR 3-5)

*India* by Darice Bailer (The Child's World, 2017). With information on India's geography, culture and history, this book will provide interested students with additional context for their history studies. (RA 2-4, IR 3-5)

*India* by Manini Chatterjee (Dorling Kindersley, 2002). A visually stunning book with a wealth of information on India's people and traditions. (RA 3-5, IR 4-6)

*India: The Culture*, by Bobbie Kalman (Crabtree Publications, 2000). Focuses on the art, music, festivals, and religions of the different people groups in India. (RA 2, IR 3-5)

*India ABCs* by Marcie Aboff (Picture Window Books, 2006). For your youngest students, a fun way to learn more about the country of India. (RA K-2, IR 1-3)

*The Ganges, India's Sacred River*, by Molly Aloian, (Crabtree, 2010). For stronger readers, this book gives a look at the sacred river Ganges, its significance and history. (RA 3, IR 5)

*True Books: India*, by Sunita Apte, (Children's Press, 2008). An overview of India, suitable for younger readers. (RA K, IR 3)

*Beginner's Bengali*, by Dr. Hanne-Ruth Thompson (Hippocrene Books, 2017). A challenging project for ambitious students: an introduction to the native language of Bengal, complete with audio CD. Bengali is the seventh most-spoken language in the world! (IR 5-up)

## Corresponding Literature Suggestions

*The Barefoot Book of Earth Tales* by Dawn Casey (Barefoot Books Press, 2009). Although this volume contains stories from several countries, the Indian tale "Amrita's Tree" would work wonderfully as a read-aloud. Includes related activities for each tale. (RA 1-4, IR 3-6)

*Cinnamon* by Neil Gaiman, illustrated by Divya Srinivasan (Harper, 2017). A tale of an Indian princess, as written by the acclaimed author Neil Gaiman and beautifully illustrated by Divya Srinivasan, this story will delight young students. (RA 1-3, IR 3-5)

*The Drum: A Folktale from India*, by Rob Cleveland, Tom Wrenn illus. (August House, 2006). For younger readers, a storybook style rendition of a folktale. (RA K, IR 2)

*The Elephant's Friend and Other Tales from India*, by Marcia Williams, (Perfection Learning, 2014). A comic-book-style selection of Indian tales. (RA1, IR 3)

*The Ghost Catcher* by Martha Hamilton and Mitch Weiss (August House, 2008). This Bengali folktale and its whimsical illustrations highlight the virtue of generosity. (RA 2-5, IR 3-5)

*Grandma and the Great Gourd* retold by Chitra Banerjee Divakaruni (Roaring Book Press, 2013). This story, based on an Indian folktale, emphasizes courage, cleverness and love. (RA 2-4, IR 3-5)

*The Monkey and the Crocodile: And Other Fables from the Jataka Tales of India*, by Ellen C. Babbitt, Ellsworth Young illus. (Dover Publications, 2015). A collection of fables. (RA 1, IR 3)

*Ramayana: An Illustrated Retelling*, by Arshia Sattar, Sonali Sorah illus., (Restless Books, 2018). A children's version of the classic Hindu story, this is suitable for stronger readers or as a read aloud. (RA2, IR 4)

*Tales Alive!*, retold by Susan Milford (Williamson Publishing, 1995). This delightful book includes folktales from a variety of countries, including India. What makes it especially unique is that it includes hands-on activity suggestions—such as craft or cooking projects—correlating with each folktale. Also look for tales from Russia, Japan and Turkey in the same volume. (RA 2+, IR 3-6)

## MAP WORK

### The Indian Kingdom *(Student Page 58, answer 324)*

1. Outline the border of all bodies of water in blue.

2. Aurangzeb's large kingdom began to collapse soon after he died. Use a red crayon and trace the dotted line—the edge of Aurangzeb's empire. Trace the borders of India that fall between the dotted lines, so that you have a continuous red line around Aurangzeb's empire.
3. After Aurangzeb died, his oldest son Bahadur Shah killed the other brothers and moved into the palace at Delhi. Underline the city of Delhi in purple. (The city of Delhi is next to the dot that represents the city.)
4. Nadir Shah marched from Persia to Delhi, burned the city, killed the people, and returned to Persia with the riches of India. Draw an orange arrow from the "P" in Persia to Delhi, and another arrow from Delhi back to Persia.
5. Siraj, his Indian army, and some French traders captured the English Fort William at Calcutta. They forced the captured English into the Black Hole. Draw a large black circle around Calcutta.

**COLORING PAGE** Siraj, the *nawab* (ruler) of Bengal, used elephants in his army. Some of them, like this one, had metal swords attached to their tusks. But even with elephants, Siraj could not defeat the army of the East India Company. (You can still see suits of elephant armor today in museums; one suit is in the Royal Armouries Museum in Leeds, England.) *(Student Page 59)*

## PROJECTS

### MATH ACTIVITY Black Hole of Calcutta

Fort William's Dungeon (nicknamed the "Black Hole") was unbelievably small for 145 men and one woman. If they were of average size, there was room enough for everyone to stand close together, but they couldn't all sit down at the same time! There was no food or water, it was unbearably hot, and people were dying all around you. To get a sense of how crammed the "Black Hole" was, measure out your own prison cell of proportional size and see how many sitting and standing people you can fit inside.

*Materials:*

- ☐ 2 1 lb. bags of plain M&Ms
- ☐ 2 1 lb. bags of peanut M&Ms
- ☐ Masking tape
- ☐ Ruler
- ☐ Plastic placemat (unless you don't mind putting tape on your table)

*Directions:*

1. Use the masking tape to make a 9 x 10 inch rectangle. (Make sure the 9 x 10 inches measures the inside box created by the tape, not the outer edge of the tape). This is proportionate to the size of the cell and the size of the people.
2. Count out 146 plain M&Ms. This is the amount of space an average person would take up standing in your cell. Can you fit all 146 inside?
3. Take off the plain M&Ms and set them aside. Now count out 146 peanut M&Ms and place as many as you can inside the cell. Can you fit all of these? How many would not fit? Keep aside the peanut M&Ms that will not fit in the cell.
4. Now, trade out 10 peanut M&Ms inside the cell for 10 plain M&Ms. This should create some extra space. Put some of the peanut M&Ms inside that would not fit before. Now trade out another 10 peanut M&Ms for 10 plain M&Ms. Keep doing this until you get the maximum number of peanut M&Ms sitting while still having a total number of 146 M&Ms overall. How many people could sit at one time in the cell? How many were left standing?

## Science Project Make a Sundial like Samrat Yantra

Jai Singh II was a scientist, architect, and political figure during Mohammad Shah's reign. Jai Singh II had a passion for astronomy. He built the Jantar Mantar in Jaipur, India. The Jantar Mantar, which means "The Formula of Instruments," is a marvel; it has fourteen towering geometric devices made of local stone and marble. The Jantar Mantar can measure time within one second, predict eclipses, track the orbits of stars, and predict the alignment and distances of the planets. One of the grandest structures there is Samrat Yantra, a giant sundial 90 feet high and 148 feet wide. It can tell the time within an accuracy of 30 seconds. Jai Singh II designed this structure himself. Make your own sundial. It may not be as large as the Samrat Yantra, but it will still tell time by the position of the sun.

*Materials:*

- ☐ Student Page 60: Sundial Base Template
- ☐ Student Page 61: Gnomon Template
- ☐ Thin cardboard or cardstock (enough for the templates)
- ☐ Scissors
- ☐ Masking tape or clear packing tape
- ☐ Glue stick
- ☐ Compass (so you can find north)

*Directions:*

1. Cut out the sundial base template and the gnomon (the "point") template.
2. Paste them onto the thin cardboard and cut around them.
3. Cut a slit into the sundial base, right down the center where it is marked "cut along this line."
4. Fold the gnomon along the bottom line.
5. Slide the gnomon into the slit in the base, making sure the longest side (the hypotenuse of the right angle) goes in first.
6. Turn the base over and tape the fold of the gnomon to the underside of the base.
7. Turn the sundial right-side up. The gnomon should stand up straight. If it does not, add more tape.
8. Go outside on a sunny day. Set the sundial in a spot without shade. Use the compass to point the compass north. The "12" line should face north exactly.
9. Check the time on your watch. Look at the place where the edge of the shadow falls *between* two of the hour lines. Is the sundial reading the correct time? How close would you say that it is?

## Activity Project Dress Up Like a Sikh Bodyguard

The Sikh religion had been founded by a holy man who taught that Hindus and Muslims were the same in God's eyes. When Aurangzeb insisted that only Muslims be given positions of power in his kingdom, he offended many Sikhs! And Aurangzeb had ordered his soldiers to destroy Sikh places of worship, called *gurdwaras.* In response, the religious leader of the Sikhs organized a group of Sikh warriors into a band called the *Khalsa.* The Khalsa were given the task of defending the Sikh faith. Their leader taught them that they must wear five symbols, called the five Ks, that would show their membership in this group of defenders of the Sikh faith. These are the symbols:

*Kes* is long hair that is never cut, to symbolize brotherhood and living in harmony with God's will;

*Kangha* is a comb with which the warrior combed his hair twice a day before tying it up into his turban to keep it clean and neat;

*Kirpan* is a sword which he was to use to defend the weak and oppressed;

*Kara* is a steel bracelet which the Sikh wore on his right wrist to remind of him of his vows and to remind him not to do any evil with his hands.

*Kachcha* are special shorts that allowed the Sikh to move more quickly than other warriors who might be wearing long, loose robes.

The religious leader who formed the Khalsa wrote a poem defining who the Khalsa were. Here is an excerpt:

*He who repeats night and day the name of Him,*
*Who has full love and confidence in God,*
*Whose enduring light is inextinguishable,*
*Who puts no faith in fasting and worshipping cemeteries and monasteries,*
*He is recognized as a true member of the Khalsa,*
*In whose heart the light of the Perfect One shines.*

The Khalsa had excellent self-defense skills; so much so, that the British in India would hire Sikh bodyguards to protect high-ranking British officials. Dress up like a member of the Khalsa. Then guard your parent for an hour. Recite the poem about the Khalsa to your parent.

*Make a Kirpan*

Materials:
- ☐ Student Page 62: Kirpan Template
- ☐ Cardstock or cardboard
- ☐ Scissors
- ☐ Aluminum foil
- ☐ Crayons, markers, or colored pencils

Directions:
1. Cut out the kirpan template and trace it onto the cardstock or cardboard.
2. Wrap aluminum foil around the blade of the kirpan.
3. Color the handle of the kirpan or leave it plain.
4. Put on a belt and carry the kirpan in your belt. You need to be ready to use it at a moment's notice!

*Make a Kara*

Materials:
- ☐ Bracelet (preferably a bangle without a clasp)
- ☐ Aluminum foil

Directions:
1. Wrap the aluminum foil around the bracelet so it looks like the bracelet is made of iron. The bracelet symbolizes God since it has no beginning and no end. The bracelet is made of iron to symbolize courage.

**Comb Your Kes with your Kanga**

Comb your hair twice with a comb, your kanga. If you have long hair, wear it pulled back.

**Wear Kachcha**

Put on a pair of boxer shorts over your clothes. The Khalsa wore the Kachcha under their clothes, so if you want to be more authentic you can do that instead.

## Craft Project Make a Puppet Ruler of India

When the British invaded, they planned to make Mir Jafar into their "puppet ruler" of Bengal. The people of Bengal would see Mir Jafar and treat him like their ruler, but the British would direct Mir Jafar's actions. So Mir Jafar's actions would actually be British actions. This is why we call him a puppet ruler.

*Materials:*
- ☐ Large wooden spoon
- ☐ Handkerchief
- ☐ Two rubber bands
- ☐ Crayons and paper

*Directions:*
1. Make a puppet "face." Either draw directly onto the spoon, or trace the oval of the spoon onto construction paper and draw a face onto the paper. Make a construction paper crown and attach it to the top of the head. (Masking tape sticks to wood; you can also tape a rubber band onto the back of the construction paper face with Scotch tape, and then slip the rubber band over the spoon.)
2. Pretend that your fingers are a gun (your index finger and thumb are extended, while your other three fingers are folded back to your palm). You should hold the handle of the spoon with your three folded fingers. Your index finger and thumb will be the arms of the puppet (the spoon handle should rise up between your finger and thumb).
3. Drape the handkerchief over your index finger and thumb. Use a rubber band to secure it around each finger.
4. Now you're ready to govern! The puppet is the Nawab of Bengal, and your hand is the British empire. Who is really controlling Bengal?

# The Imperial East

## Encyclopedia Cross-References

*UBWH 153, UILE 352-353*
*KIHW 432-433, 502, KHE 262-263, 304*

## EMPEROR CHI'EN-LUNG'S LIBRARY

### Review Questions

Where was the Forbidden Palace? *The Forbidden Palace was in Peking.*

What was Chi'en-lung doing by moonlight? *Chi'en-lung was copying a famous poem by Zou Foulei.*

Was Chi'en-lung Han Chinese or Manchu? *He was a Manchu emperor (the fourth).*

Who was his grandfather? *His grandfather was K'ang-hsi.*

Is the Chinese empire strong and powerful at the time of Chi'en-lung? *Yes, the Chinese empire at the time of Chi'en-lung was strong and powerful.*

Before the time of Chi'en-lung, the stories of China were scattered throughout the country. What did Chi'en-lung do to make the greatness of China known throughout the world? *Chi'en-lung decided to gather all of China's greatest literature together in one enormous collection.*

Did Chi'en-lung undertake the task of collecting literature alone? *No, he appointed twelve scholars to head up this task.*

Can you name two of the four categories of the most important books? *The four categories were history, literature, philosophy, and classics.*

Deciding on the list of books was the easy task. What difficult task did the scholars face after deciding on the list of books? *The works had to be copied out into a single huge set!*

What was one of the challenges of the Chinese language? *The Chinese language has many symbols for different sounds and letters—over forty thousand.*

How many copies were made of the Complete Library in the Four Branches of Literature? *Seven copies were made.*

What did Chi'en-lung do with books that made unflattering remarks about the Manchu? *He had them destroyed.*

What did Chi'en-lung love even more than books? *He loved his power.*

### Narration Exercise

"During the reign of the fourth Manchu emperor, China's poems and novels and other books were all scattered through the country. Chi'en-lung decided to collect them all. Scholars helped him find important books in four different categories. Then they copied all these books out—seven times! This was 'The Complete Library in the Four Branches of Literature.' The emperor saved these books, but he ordered other books that criticized him to be burned." OR

"Chi'en-lung was the grandson of K'ang-hsi. He ruled over a huge and powerful Chinese empire. His capital city was Peking—the largest city in the world! Chi'en-lung wanted the world to see how great China's writings were. So he hired scholars to collect books from all over China. They put the most important books together and called them 'The Complete Library in the Four Branches of Literature.' Then Chi'en-lung had copies put in his palaces and in libraries. But he ordered books that made unflattering remarks about the Manchu burned."

## THE LAND OF THE DRAGON

### Review Questions

(Note: you may want to look at a map while you answer these questions.)

What two rivers were at the center of the Chinese empire? *The Yellow and Yangtze Rivers were at the center of the Chinese Empire.*

Describe two characteristics of the imperial dragon. *The imperial dragon, the symbol of the emperor's power, had five toes on each foot. His body was long and snakelike; his tail was the tail of a fish. His head was crowned with the sharp antlers of a deer. His eyes glowed red!*

What is the name of the huge dry plain in the northern part of China? *The huge dry plain is the Gobi Desert.*

What was the name of Mongolia's capital city? *Ulan Bator was the capital city of Mongolia.*

The people of Chinese Turkestan were not Buddhists. What religion did most of them follow? *Most people of Chinese Turkestan were Muslim (or, followed Islam).*

In the country of Tibet lies the highest mountain in the world. What is its name? *The name of the mountain in Tibet is Mount Everest.*

What was special about the people of the mysterious Shangri-la? *Those who lived in Shangri-La were never hungry; no one grew old in Shangri-La, and no one died!*

What two people ruled in Tibet? *A Buddhist monk called the Dalai Lama ruled alongside a Mongol prince.*

The emperor of China sent some soldiers to "help" the Dalai Lama rule in Tibet. What were the two leaders of this group of soldiers called? *The two Chinese officials called "High Commissioners" were "helping" the Dalai Lama rule.*

What was the name of the land to the east of the Bay of Bengal? *The land to the east of the Bay of Bengal was called Burma.*

From Burma, you flew across the South China Sea. What long thin country lies along its western edge? *The country of Vietnam lies along the western edge of the South China Sea.*

What small island lies off the coast of China? *Taiwan lies off the coast of China.*

At this time in history, what proportion of the world's population lived under the flag of the Chinese imperial dragon? *At this time in the world, one-third of the world's population lived under the flag of the Chinese imperial dragon.*

### Narration Exercise

Instead of asking the child to narrate, ask him to locate the following places on the map in Chapter 20 of *The Story of the World, Volume 3.*

The Yellow River
The Yangtze River
The Gobi Desert
Mongolia
Ulan Bator

Turkestan
Tibet
The Bay of Bengal
Burma
Vietnam
Taiwan
Korea

## Additional History Reading

*Art in China*, by Craig Clunas (Oxford University Press, rev. ed. 2009). Check your library for this adult introduction to Chinese art, which includes many color photographs of Chinese poems written on scrolls and decorated; it includes a photograph of the plum branch and poem described in *The Story of the World, Volume 3*.

*China—the Land*, by Bobbie Kalman, (Crabtree, 2008). A short but broad introduction to the land and geography of China, with many photographs. (RA 1, IR 3)

*China* by Walter Simmons (Bellwether Media, 2011). An excellent overview of China's history and culture for the early elementary student. (RA 1-3, IR 2-4)

*China: Land of Dragons and Emperors: The Fascinating Culture and History of China*, by Adeline Yen Mah, (Ember, 2011). For stronger readers, the book includes historical and cultural information about China. (RA 1, IR 3)

*My First Book of Chinese Calligraphy*, by Guillaume Olive, Zihong He, (Tuttle Publishing, 2010). A lovely book examining all elements of Chinese calligraphy, including its history and meaning, and how to do it yourself. This book includes an interactive CD-ROM. (RA 1, IR 2)

*In the Forbidden City*, by Chiu Kwong-chiu, Ben Wang trans., Nancy S. Steinhardt ed., (China Institute in America, 2014). A book with fascinating illustrations of the details of the Forbidden City; even younger children will enjoy these illustrations. (RA 1, IR 4)

*You Wouldn't Want to Be in the Forbidden City!: A Sheltered Life You'd Rather Avoid*, by Jacqueline Morley, illus. David Antram (Franklin Watts, 2008). A comical look at getting a job and living in the Forbidden City. Full of interesting and odd facts about life in and around the Forbidden City. (IR 4-6)

*Mongolia*, by Guek-Cheng Pang, (Benchmark Books, 2010). An overview of the land, history, and people of Mongolia, with photographs. (RA1, IR 2)

*Boy on the Lion Throne: The Childhood of the 14th Dalai Lama*, by Elizabeth Cody Kimmel, (Flash Point, 2009). For stronger readers, or as a read aloud, this book gives a narrative account of the life of the Dalai Lama. It includes information about Tibetan culture and geography, and Buddhism, and is worth reading to learn about Tibet as well as the Dali Lama himself. (RA 2, IR 3)

*The Dalai Lama*, by Demi (Henry Holt, 1998). This picture-book biography of the present Dalai Lama also describes the history of this Tibetan institution. (RA 2, IR 3-5)

*Far Beyond the Garden Gate: Alexandra David-Neel's Journey to Lhasa*, by Don Brown (Houghton Mifflin, 2002). The true story of the first Western woman who entered the forbidden Tibetan city of Lhasa. (RA 1-2, IR 3-5) **E-Only.**

*M is for Myanmar*, by Elizabeth Rush, Khin Maung Myint illus., (Things Asian Press/Global Directions, 2011). This introduction to the country of Myanmar (called Burma in this chapter of *The Story of the World*) is told through a narrative of two sisters visiting the country. The text is bilingual. (RA 1, IR 3)

*Myanmar* by Saw Myat Yin (Marshall Cavendish, 2012). Too advanced for this age if read in its entirety, but individual chapters might be helpful in understanding Myanmar's role in the Imperial East. (RA 4-5, IR 4-6)

*Vietnam (Enchantment of the World)*, by Terri Willis (Children's Press, 2013). Covers the history, geography, and culture of Vietnam. (RA 2, IR 4)

*The People of Vietnam*, by Dolly Brittan (Powerkids Press, 1997). A simple, easy-reader introduction to the history of this southeast Asian country and the ancient influences of China on its culture. (RA 1, IR 2-3)

*Vietnam* by Max Winter (The Child's World, 2016). With colorful photos and interesting text, this is an ideal overview of Vietnam's history, culture and people. (RA 2-4, IR 3-6)

*Welcome to Taiwan*, by Vanessa Wan, (Gareth Stevens Pub Learning library, 2004). An overview of the country with photographs. (RA 2, IR 4)

*South Korea* by Patrick Ryan (The Child's World, 2008). This series is excellent for elementary schoolers with large pictures and easy-to-read text. A great introduction to South Korea—its people and culture—for a variety of ages. (RA 1-3, IR 3-5)

*Cultural Traditions in South Korea*, by Lisa Dalrymple, (Crabtree, 2016). This book focuses on the cultural and religious holidays of South Korea, with lots of photographs. (RA 1, IR 2)

## Corresponding Literature Suggestions

*A Thousand Peaks: Poems from China*, by Siyu Liu and Orel Protopopescu (Pacific View Press, 2001). Thirty-five poems, from the Tang dynasty through recent times, each presented both in Chinese and in English, with illustrations. (RA 2-3, IR 4-6) **OOP**

*Cowboy on the Steppes*, by Song Nan Zhang (Tundra Books, 1997). A teenager who lives in Beijing (Peking) is sent to herd cattle on the Mongolian steppes in the 1960s; based on a true story, this is a marvelous tale. (RA 2, IR 3-6) **OOP**

*The Last Dragon*, by Susan Miho Nunes, illus. Chris K. Soentpiet (Clarion Books, 1995). In this picture-book tale, a young boy in Chinatown restores a huge festival dragon with the help of the community. (RA 2, IR 3-4)

*Where the Winds Meet: Mongolia*, by Mi-hwa Joo, Oh Lee illus., (Big & Small, 2015). Beautifully illustrated picture-book showing traditional Mongolian life. (RA K, IR 2)

*Favorite Children's Stories from China & Tibet: (Chinese & Tibetan Fairy Tales)* by Lotta Carswell Hume, Lo Koon (Tuttle Publishing, 2018). A wide selection of folk tales from China and Tibet. (RA 1, IR 3)

*Tintin in Tibet*, by Herge (Little, Brown & Co., 1975). Okay, it's not exactly literature, but relax and have some fun. (IR 3-6)

*I See the Sun in Myanmar* by Dedie King (Satya House Publications, 2013). This bilingual picture book provides an introduction to Buddhist culture as well as the traditions of the people of Myanmar. (RA 1-4, IR 2-4)

*Children of the Dragon: Selected Tales from Vietnam*, by Sherry Garland, illus. Trina Schart Hyman (Harcourt, 2001). In this picture book for older readers, six long illustrated stories are given along with historical background. (RA 2-3, IR 4-7)

*To Swim In Our Own Pond/Ta Ve Ta Tam Ao Ta: A Book of Vietnamese Proverbs*, by Ngoc Dung Tran, illus. Xuan-Quang Dang (Shen's Books, 1998). Twenty-two Vietnamese proverbs, illustrated and given alongside Western proverbs which have the same basic meaning. (RA 2, IR 3-6)

*Vietnamese Children's Favorite Stories*, by Phuoc Thi Minh Tran, Dong Nguyen illus., Hop Thi Nguyen illus., (Tuttle Publishing 2015). A collection of folk tales from Vietnam. (RA 1, IR 3)

*Korean Children's Favorite Stories*, retold by Kim So-un (Tuttle Publishing, 2004). With a variety of traditional Korean folktales, this would be an ideal read-aloud. (RA 3-5, IR 4-6).

## MAP WORK

### The Land of the Dragon *(Student Page 63, answer 324)*

1. Chi'en-lung lived in the capital city, Peking. Find the dot near the Yellow River. Use a pen or pencil and label the dot, "Peking."
2. Find the northeastern border of India (the border that India shares with Tibet). The Himalayan Mountains divide India from Tibet. Make up a symbol for mountains. (You might use something like: /\/\.) Draw the symbol for mountain along the border between India and Tibet (under the title, Himalayas). Color your symbols for mountains brown.
3. Trace the journey of the dragon around the largest empire in the world:
   a. Using a pencil, begin at Peking. Draw an arrow through Mongolia and toward the Gobi Desert.
   b. From the Gobi Desert, draw an arrow toward Turkestan.
   c. From Turkestan, draw an arrow toward the Himalaya mountains. (Remember, the dragon flew over Mount Everest, in the Himalayas.)
   d. Draw an arrow above the Himalayas, through Tibet, through Burma, and toward Vietnam.
   e. Remember that the dragon took you out over the South China Sea. Draw an arrow from Vietnam, through the South China Sea and to Taiwan.
   f. Draw an arrow from Taiwan up into Korea.
   g. Finally, draw an arrow from Korea back to Peking.
4. Lightly trace over the arrow in red. Then shade the area within the arrow.
5. Find England, France, and Spain on the left of your map. Color them green. Compare the size of these three countries with the size of the Chinese empire.

**Coloring Page** This dragon was an imaginary animal in Chinese stories. A dragon was also the symbol of the emperor's power. It had a snakelike body, a fish's tail, and the antlers of a deer. *(Student Page 64)*

## PROJECTS

### Cooking Project Tibetan Yak-Butter Tea

Yaks are a very important animal to the people of Tibet. They warm themselves around fires of yak dung, they use yak-butter as a fuel for lamps, they eat the meat and blood from yaks, they churn yak milk into butter, cheese, and yogurt. They weave the yak hair into clothing, shelter, and even boats. So it is no wonder that the everyday beverage of Tibet is yak-butter tea. Yak-butter, hot tea, and salt are poured into a wooden churn and blended together. Then the yak-butter tea is put in a kettle over the fire so stays warm all day or until it is ready to be served. Churn your own butter and make some yak-butter tea. Perhaps you will like it so much you will want to drink it every day just like the people of Tibet!

*Ingredients:* Butter from recipe below or 1 stick butter, very softened
Hot black tea (about 3 cups)
1 tsp salt

*Directions:*
1. Put all the ingredients in a quart sized mason jar (or another container) with a screw-on lid. Shake the container vigorously for two minutes.
2. Pour the tea into a saucepan and warm. Pour it into mugs and enjoy!

*To make your own butter:* Pour ½ pint of heavy whipping cream (you need the real stuff for this) into a blender. Whip until the butter becomes a creamy solid.

## ACTIVITY PROJECT **Assemble the Complete Library of the Four Branches of Literature**

Ch'ien-lung collected a set of over 36,000 books and entitled the set "The Complete Library of the Four Branches of Literature." The books were all classified into different categories. Compile your own "Complete Library." Decide on the four categories of books you would like to include, types of books that you feel are the most important and useful (this could be "books about dinosaurs, fairy tales, books about how engines work, and schoolbooks" or "books about horses, books about pioneers, biographies, and joke or riddle books" or some other set of four categories). Now select twenty favorite books from around the house, five for each category. Make a list of the five books for each category—this is your "Complete Library in the Four Branches of Literature."

Now the child should also make a stack of books which he thinks makes his life more difficult for "burning." Remember, Chi'en-lung burned the books that made unflattering remarks about the Manchu dynasty!

## ACTIVITY PROJECT **The Extent of the Land of the Dragon**

China is called the Land of the Dragon, since the dragon is its symbol. According to legend, the great emperor Huang Di had the emblem of a snake on his coat of arms. Every time he conquered a tribe, Huang Di would add the tribe's symbol to his coat of arms. By the time Huang Di died, his symbol looked like a dragon with the body of a snake, the scales and tail of a fish, the antlers of a deer, the face of a "gilin" (a mythical creature with fire all over its body), eagle talons, and the eyes of a demon. Since the Chinese consider Huang Di to be their ancestor, they refer to themselves as the "descendants of the dragon."

The Chinese dragon also has five toes, whereas the Korean and Indonesian dragon has four toes, and the Japanese dragon has only three toes. The Chinese explain it this way: Dragons originated in China. The farther a dragon travels, the more toes it loses. Dragons only live in China because if they traveled any farther than Japan, they would have no toes at all and would not be able to walk.

Pretend that your house is the great empire of China. Label each room a different region in China. Then put a dragon's paw print over each region's name to symbolize that this place is under Chinese control.

Materials:
- ☐ 8 sheets of blank paper
- ☐ Black marker
- ☐ Clear tape
- ☐ Scissors
- ☐ Colored pencils or crayons

*Directions:*

1. Write each of the following regions on a piece of paper with black marker, one region per paper.

   Uplands of China
   Gobi Desert
   Mongolia
   Chinese Turkestan
   Tibet
   Burma
   Taiwan
   Korea

2. Tape the regions to the doors of the rooms in your house. For example, make your bedroom the "Uplands of China" and make the kitchen "Mongolia." You can also put signs on closet doors.
3. Draw large dragon pawprints (remember all five toes!) on pieces of construction paper. Cut the prints out.
4. Go back through the house, putting the dragon paws over the names of each region. All of these areas belonged to the Land of the Dragon!

## Writing Project: The Plum Branch

Chi'en-lung read Zou-Fulei's poem and painting of a plum branch. Try your own hand at a poem picture! Go outside and bring in a small tree branch. Stick the end of a branch in a container and set the container in front of a light so it casts a small shadow on the table or wall. Then trace the shadow onto a piece of paper and color it in. Then construct a four- or eight-line poem that relates to the branch. Reread Zou Foulei's poem in the chapter for inspiration!

# Fighting Over North America

## Encyclopedia Cross-References

*UBWH 150, 161, UILE 320, 321, 323*
*KIHW 470-471, 482-483, 496-499, KHE 300-303*

## THREE POINTLESS WARS

### Review Questions

Why did the first of the three wars (the war started by Louis XIV, the Sun King) begin? *The first war began because Louis XIV wanted to expand his empire in Europe.*

Can you name two of the three countries that banded together to stop Louis XIV from expanding his empire? *The Netherlands, Austria, and England banded together to stop him.*

What did these countries call the war? *They called it "The War of the Grand Alliance."*

What did the English government pay Iroquois warriors to do? *The government paid warriors to attack French settlements in Canada.*

What name did the English colonists have for "The War of the Grand Alliance"? *They called it "King William's War."*

What was the outcome of "King William's War" in Europe and North America? *France and England made peace in Europe and ordered their colonies to cease fighting in North America.*

How did the French and English colonies feel about each other? *They hated each other!*

What title did Louis XIV give his grandson? *He made him the King of Spain.*

What two countries then declared war on France and Spain together, to keep Louis's power from growing? *England and the Netherlands declared war on France and Spain.*

England and the Netherlands called their war against France and Spain the "War of Spanish Succession." What did the North American colonists call it? *They called this war "Queen Anne's War."*

What did the English gain in North America during "Queen Anne's War"? *During this war, the English managed to capture several French settlements.*

What happened to the Spanish colony of Pensacola, down in Florida? *The English marched down and burned it.*

Did the war end with either side gaining a decisive victory? *No, the war ended without either side gaining a clear victory.*

Who was given the English throne when Queen Anne died? *Parliament gave George Louis, crowned George I, the throne.*

What language did George I speak? *George I spoke only German!*

Did France and England go to war during the reign of George I? *No, they were at peace.*

Who inherited the English throne after George I died? *George II, his son, became king of England.*

What did Englishman Robert Jenkins claim the Spanish had done to him? *He claimed the Spanish had boarded his ship and when they couldn't find any stolen goods, the captain cut off his ear and claimed he would do the same if the king of England had been there.*

What did Parliament do when they heard Jenkins' story? *They declared war on Spain.*

Which countries joined England in the war against Spain? *Austria joined England in the war against Spain.*

Which countries joined Spain in the war against England? *Prussia and France joined Spain in the war against England.*

What were the other two names for the "War of Jenkins' Ear"? *This war was also called the "War of Austrian Succession" and "King George's War."*

### Narration Exercise

Because there is a great deal of information in this chapter, use "directed narration." Say to the child, "We talked about three wars in this chapter. England and France were in all three wars! I will give you the European name of the war. I want you to give me the North American name for the war, and tell me one important fact about it."

***The War of the Grand Alliance***

North American name: King William's War

Acceptable facts: The Netherlands, Austria, and England banded together against France; it began when Louis XIV tried to expand his empire; the English paid the Iroquois to attack the French settlements in North America; the war lasted eight years and had no results.

***The War of Spanish Succession***

North American name: Queen Anne's War

Acceptable facts: The war began when Louis XIV put his grandson on the throne of Spain; the English captured several French settlements, including Acadia; English soldiers burned Pensacola; peace was made after thirteen years of fighting.

***The War of Austrian Succession***

North American name: The War of Jenkins' Ear

Acceptable facts: The war started when Robert Jenkins claimed that he was insulted by a Spanish captain; the war grew bigger because the heirs of the Holy Roman Empire were fighting over his power; English colonists in Georgia attacked the Spanish colonies in Florida; the French and English colonists fought with each other.

## THE SEVEN-YEAR WAR

### Review Questions

What three countries were fighting for control of North America? *England, France, and Spain were fighting for control of North America.*

The English heard that the French were moving south into the Ohio River Valley. Why did this alarm them? *They were alarmed because they might lose this land to the French forever.*

What message did King George II of England tell Governor Dinwiddie of Virginia to deliver to the French regarding the land of the Ohio River Valley? *King George sent a message to Dinwiddie that said: Send a messenger and tell the French to leave. If they won't leave, go chase them out—and build an English fort to protect the land!*

What young Virginian carried George II's message to the French? *George Washington volunteered for the dangerous mission.*

How many rivers join together at the Ohio Fork? *Three rivers join together.*

How did the French respond to the message? *The French commander simply laughed and told Washington to go back to Virginia.*

What difficulties did Washington and his guide encounter on their journey back to Virginia? *They were running out of food, the weather was extremely cold, and they encountered hostile Native American allies of the French.*

When Washington told Governor Dinwiddie about the French refusal, what two things did Dinwiddie do? *He asked England for more soldiers; he promoted Washington to a higher rank and sent him to protect a fort at the place where the three rivers met.*

After Washington and his small army were defeated by the French, the English sent Edward Braddock and his soldiers to fight the French. What did Edward Braddock call his soldiers? *He called them "regular and disciplined."*

Early in the French and Indian War, what advantages did the French have over the English? *The French were used to fighting in the woods and the English were not; the English were easy targets with their red uniform coats.*

This North American war was also given a European name. What was that name? *In Europe, it was called the Seven Years' War.*

What was the name of the Prime Minister of England who tried to make sure that the English would triumph? *William Pitt was the Prime Minister of England.*

What did the English soldiers do to fight more effectively against the French? *They took off their red coats, turned them inside out, and covered the insides with clay. They rubbed soot and dirt on their shiny, ship-shape gun barrels so that they wouldn't glint in the sun. Then they started fighting in small groups, from behind trees.*

What was the name of the treaty that ended the Seven Years' War? *The Treaty of Paris ended the Seven Years' War.*

What city stands on the spot where the Ohio River Fort was built? *The city of Pittsburgh stands there (named after William Pitt).*

What two large French settlements did the English conquer? *They conquered Montreal and Quebec.*

Louis XV lost the empire that Louis XIV had given him. How did his people feel about him? *They hated him and poured quicklime on his body when he died.*

## Narration Exercise

Because there is a lot of information in this chapter, use "directed narration." Say to the child, "Tell me how Washington ended up trying to defend Fort Pitt!" An acceptable answer might be, "The French and the English both wanted North America. The French were building roads down into the Ohio Valley, so George Washington was sent to tell them to leave. They just laughed at him! So he went home. But he had found the perfect place to build a fort—where three rivers met. The governor of Virginia ordered George Washington to go back and defend a fort built at the three rivers. But the French defeated Washington, and he had to surrender."

Then say to the child, "Tell me how the English fought in the French and Indian War, how they changed their way of fighting, and what happened at the end of the war." An acceptable answer might be, "At first, the English soldiers marched in long lines, beat drums, and wore red coats. The Indians, who were allies of the French, found it very easy to beat them! But then the English soldiers took off their red coats, rubbed themselves with dirt, and started to fight from behind trees. The English drove the French out of North America. George Washington got the fort back. Today, it is called Pittsburgh."

## Additional History Reading

*The French and Indian War, 1660-1763,* by Christopher Collier and James Lincoln Collier (Benchmark Books, 1998). A clear account of the establishment of European colonies, the wars fought over them, and George Washington's role in the last of the wars. Better suited for slightly older readers. (RA 1-4, IR 4-6) **E-Only.**

*Struggle for a Continent: The French and Indian Wars,* 1689-1763, by Betsy Maestro and Giulio Maestro (Harpercollins, 2000). A clear but detailed picture-book account of the wars described in this chapter. (RA 1-3, IR 4-6)

*DK Eyewitness Books: Pirate: Discover the Pirates Who Terrorized the Seas from the Mediterranean to the Caribbean,* by Richard Platt, (DK Children, 2007). A fun, heavily illustrated history of piracy through the ages. (RA1, IR 2)

*The History of Pirates* by Allison Lassieur (Capstone Press, 2007). Includes information on the pirate life, how people became pirates and their ultimate fate. (RA 2-4, IR 3-6)

*Pirates: Magic Tree House Research Guide,* by Will Osborne and Mary Pope Osborne (Random House, 2001). An easy-reader guide to piracy in the seventeenth and eighteenth centuries. (RA 1, IR 2-4)

*Who Was Blackbeard?,* by James Buckley Jr., (Penguin Workshop, 2015). Written in an early chapter book style, this is a narrative account of the life of the early-1700s pirate Blackbeard. Includes some illustrations and maps. (RA 2, IR 3)

*You Wouldn't Want to Be a Pirate's Prisoner!* By John Malam, illus. David Antram (Franklin Watts, rev. ed. 2012). A sure favorite for pirate enthusiasts; vivid descriptions of the unpleasant aspects of seventeenth-century life on the high seas. (RA 2, IR 3-6)

*Meet George Washington,* by Joan Heilbroner (Random House, 2001). A Step-Up biography that covers Washington's youth and his role in the French and Indian War. (RA 1-2, IR 3-4)

*A Picture Book of George Washington,* by David A. Adler, John Walner illus. Alexandra Walner illus.(Holiday House, 1990). An account of the life of George Washington, for younger readers. (RA K, IR 2)

*Take the Lead, George Washington,* by Judith St. George, illus. Daniel Power (Puffin Books, 2005). A illustrative story of George Washington's childhood and teenage years. (RA 1-3, IR 4-6)

*If You Lived in Williamsburg in Colonial Days,* by Barbara Brenner and Jennie Williams (Scholastic, 2000). An illustrated guide to daily life in the colonial capital, with details about Williamsburg's early history. (IR 2-5)

*The French and Indian War* by Andrew Santella (Scholastic, 2012). Like the other books in the *Cornerstones of Freedom* series, this volume includes thorough age-appropriate coverage of the French and Indian War along with reproductions of period artwork and artifacts to help set the context. (RA 3-6, IR 3-6)

*French and Indian War,* by Jeremy Thornton, (PowerKids Press, 2003). Includes important events and persons in these conflicts. RA 3, IR 4)

*The French and Indian War,* by Gerry Boehme, (Cavendish Square, 2018). For older readers, primary source accounts from people involved in the Seven Years War. (RA 4, IR 6)

*Robert Rogers: Rogers' Rangers and the French and Indian War,* by Jennifer Quasha, (The Irregular Press, 2016). The story of an officer in the French and Indian Wars, drawing from first person accounts and journals.

*Who Was Daniel Boone?* By Sydelle Kramer (Grosset and Dunlap, 2006). A lively, interesting biography of the early American pioneer Daniel Boone (who was present when General Braddock was ambushed and defeated, and who explored Virginia and Kentucky during the years of the French and Indian War) written at a level ideal for elementary students. (RA 2-4, IR 3-6)

*Daniel Boone: Frontiersman*, by Janet Benge, (Emerald Books, 2004). A narrative story-style biography of Daniel Boone, suitable for reading out loud. (RA 2, IR 5)

## Corresponding Literature Suggestions

*Gulliver's Travels: Voyage to Lilliput*, by Jonathan Swift, Chris Riddell illus. (Candlewick, 2017). An illustrated version of Gulliver's journey to Lilliput, from *Gulliver's Travels*, written during the reign of King George I. (RA 1, IR 4)

*The Golden Age of Pirates* by Bob Temple (Capstone Press, 2016). A "You Choose" adventure with 3 story paths, 38 choices and 14 possible endings. (IR 3-5)

*Pirates Past Noon: Magic Tree House #4*, by Mary Pope Osborne (Random House, 1994). Two children go back to the days of pirates in this simple chapter book. (RA 1, IR 2-4)

*The Sign of the Beaver*, by Elizabeth George Speare (Yearling, 1983). This Newbery-winning chapter book tells the story of a New England family living at the time of the French and Indian war; twelve-year-old Matt becomes friends with the grandson of a Native American chief. A good family read-aloud, or for strong readers; also look for the audiobook version. (RA 1-4, IR 5-6)

*The Last of the Mohicans* retold by Deanna McFadden (Sterling, 2008). The timeless James Fenimore Cooper story, set during the French and Indian War, is retold in this edition at a level more easily enjoyed by elementary students. (RA 3-5, IR 3-6)

*George Washington's Teeth*, by Debra Chandra, (Square Fish, 2007). A humorous, poetic account of Washington's life, centered around the loss of his teeth. (RA K, IR 1)

*Malian's Song*, by Marge Bruchac (University Press of New England, 2005). A picture book told from the perspective of a young Abenaki Indian girl whose tribe is attacked by English troops led by Robert Rogers. This would make a good counterpart to the Rogers biography listed above, since it gives the perspective of his "enemies." (RA 2-4, IR 3-5)

*The Winter People* by Joseph Bruchac (Puffin Books, 2002). Another book from a Native American perspective. This chapter-book tells the story of Saxso, an Abenaki teenager who has to protect his family from the English. While historical fiction, this story helps illuminate the realities of the French and Indian War. (RA 4-6, IR 5+)

*Kaya's Escape! A Survival Story*, by Janet Shaw (Pleasant Company, 2002). Set in 1764, this chapter book (part of the American Girls Collection) tells about the adventures of two Nez Perce girls taken captive by another Native American tribe. (RA 1-3, IR 4-6) **E-Only.**

*Admiral Wright's Heroical Storicals: Daniel Boone and the Battle of Boonesborough*, by Annie Winston, (Waterside, 2007). A chapter book suitable for students who dislike reading history, involving time travel and Daniel Boone.

## MAP WORK

### Three Pointless Wars *(Student Page 65, answer 324)*

Note: The pluses (+) and minuses (–) used below are not a judgment on which side was "good" or "bad." We are using the symbols to show opposition.

1. England, France, and Spain fought three wars that began in Europe and then spread to the colonies. You will use different colors to represent the different wars. The first war was called The War of the Grand Alliance. In Europe, the English fought the French. Draw a red + (plus) in England, and a red – (minus) in France. (Make sure to leave enough room for two or three more +s in each of the countries.)
2. The War of the Grand Alliance also included fighting in North America, where it was called King William's War. The English paid the Iroquois to attack French settlements in North America. Put a red + and – up near Canada.
3. The War of Spanish Succession began when Great Britain and the Netherlands declared war on France and Spain. Put a brown + in Great Britain and the Netherlands, and a brown – in France and Spain.
4. Over in North America, the War of Spanish Succession was called Queen Anne's War. The English captured a French settlement east of Quebec, and the English marched down into Florida and burned a Spanish colony. Put a brown + near Quebec, and another one down in Florida.
5. The War of Jenkins' Ear involved more countries than the other wars you read about in this chapter. The war began between England and Spain. But soon France joined Spain, and Austria joined England. Put a blue + in England and another in Austria. Put a blue – in Spain and another in France. Prussia then joined France, so put a blue – to the east (right) of Austria.
6. Again, the fighting trickled over to the colonies. Put a blue + in Georgia, where the English colonists lived, and a blue – in Florida, where the Spanish still had colonies.

**Coloring Page** Native Americans from the Iroquois and Seneca Nations worked together with the French. Here, they are getting ready to attack some British soldiers in the forest. The Iroquois and Seneca warriors carried guns, knives, and war-clubs, and they painted their faces red and black when it was time to fight. *(Student Page 66)*

## PROJECTS

### Game Project: Name That War

*Materials:*
- ☐ 3" x 5" cards
- ☐ pencil or pen
- ☐ a partner

***Option One: Name That War***

*Directions:*
1. Write the European name for the each of the following wars on one side of a 3" x 5" card (you will use 3 cards): The War of the Grand Alliance, The War of Spanish Succession, and The War of Jenkins' Ear/The War of Austrian Succession.
2. On the other side of the cards, write the American name for the wars: King William's War (on the back of The War of the Grand Alliance), Queen Anne's War (on the back of The War of Spanish Succession), and King George's War (on the back of The War of Jenkins' Ear/The War of Austrian Succession).
3. With your three cards, play "Name That War." Hold up a card to your partner. If your partner sees the European name of the war, he should give you the American name of the war.

***Option Two: Name That Country***

*Directions:*

1. Take six cards. On each card, write an American or a European name of each of the three wars. (So, you should have six cards, each with one of the following names: The War of the Grand Alliance, The War of Spanish Succession, The War of Jenkins' Ear, King William's War, Queen Anne's War, King George's War. Remember that The War of Jenkins' Ear eventually became The War of Austrian Succession. If you want, you may use a seventh card and include The War of Austrian Succession.)
2. On the back of each card, write the name of the countries that were involved. For example, on the back of the War of Spanish Succession card, you would write, "England and the Netherlands v. France." For the same war in North America, Queen Anne's War, you would write, "French colonists v. English colonists." Below is a list of countries in each of the wars:
   a. The War of the Grand Alliance—England v. France
   b. King William's War—English paid the Iroquois to attack the French
   c. The War of Spanish Succession—England + Netherlands v. France
   d. Queen Anne's War—French colonists v. English colonists
   e. War of Jenkins' Ear—England v. Spain *but this turned into*
   War of Austrian Succession—England + Austria v. Spain + France + Prussia
   f. King George's War—French colonists v. English colonists
3. After you've made your cards, shuffle them (or mix them up). Then, with a partner, see how well you know which countries were involved in each of the wars.

## Craft Activity Project **Leaf Camouflage**

Edward Braddock and his English troops were sitting ducks! Their red uniforms made them easy targets in the forest. In order to fight well against the French and the Indians, they needed to change their uniforms. Make your own camouflage shirt.

*Materials:*

- ☐ leaves and grass from your own yard (ferns work very well for this)
- ☐ hammer
- ☐ clean, hard floor, like the garage
- ☐ old towel
- ☐ light green T-shirt
- ☐ ½ cup of salt

*Directions:*

1. Smooth out your old towel on to the floor. Place your T-shirt over the towel. Spread your leaves on your shirt to get an idea of how you want the leaf-prints to look.
2. Take one leaf at a time and place it on your shirt where you want it to stain it green. Hammer the leaf hard, so that the green leaf pigment stains the shirt. Repeat until all of your leaves are used. Try and cover your shirt as much as you can.
3. Soak the shirt in a sink full of cold water and ½ cup of salt to "set" the dye.
4. Dry in the dryer (without any other clothes in the dryer, to be safe). Wear with pride!

## Craft Activity Project **Fort Pitt**

When young George Washington found the Ohio Fork, he thought he had found a perfect place for a fort. And indeed, he did! Fort Pitt lies in the center of two major rivers merging into the great Ohio River. From Fort Pitt's guard posts you get a great view of the three rivers, and you get to see who or what may be coming your way. You also have a commanding view of the rich valley. In this project, you will build your own rendition of the Ohio Fork and Fort Pitt.

***Option One: Framed paper construction***

Materials:
- ☐ Old cookie sheet with sides (jellyroll pan)
- ☐ Blue construction paper
- ☐ Black marker
- ☐ Green construction paper
- ☐ Light green construction paper
- ☐ Brown construction paper

Directions:
1. The first option offers a bird's eye view of the Ohio Fork and Fort Pitt. Use the picture to the right as a model for your paper model. Use the cookie sheet as your frame and fill the bottom of the pan with green construction paper.
2. With light green construction paper, make the peninsula for Fort Pitt.
3. Cut out the blue construction paper and make the three rivers that form the Ohio Fork.
4. With brown construction paper, make the boundaries of Fort Pitt and the semi-trapezoidal shape of the fort's barracks.
5. Include a KEY for your framed map in the lower left hand corner OR use a marker to label each of the rivers and the fort.

***Option Two: Three dimensional model of the Ohio Fork and Fort Pitt***

Materials:
- ☐ old cookie sheet with sides (jellyroll pan)
- ☐ blue construction paper
- ☐ black marker
- ☐ dirt
- ☐ grass seeds
- ☐ spray bottle (for water)
- ☐ brown construction paper
- ☐ toothpicks
- ☐ tacky craft glue
- ☐ Brown Model Magic air-dry clay
- ☐ brown marker

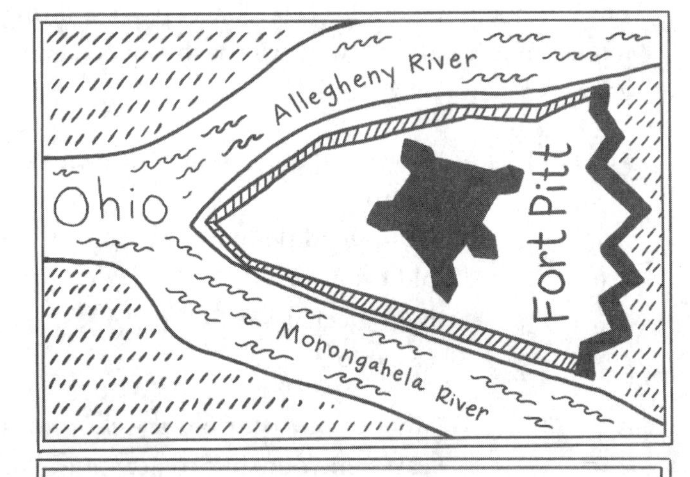


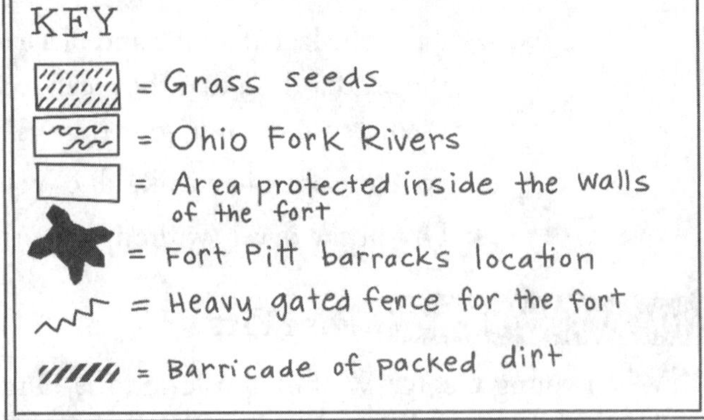


Directions:
1. Cut your blue construction paper to fit the bottom of the cookie sheet, and place it in the bottom of the pan.
2. Fill the cookie sheet with dirt up to the top of the pan. Use the Fort Pitt diagram on this page, and clear a path for the three rivers. You should be able to see the blue construction paper where you have cleared the paths for the rivers.

3. Build up the dirt sides making Fort Pitt's strong, protective, mud walls along the river sides. Use the spray mist water bottle to moisten the dirt, if you are having trouble making the walls.
4. Cut a long strip of brown construction paper to make the fort's wall on the open side of the peninsula. Make sure this strip of paper is slightly narrower than the length of a toothpick (see picture at right). Bend the paper (accordion style) to simulate the structure of the wall as seen in the map above. After you have folded the paper, smear tacky glue on the front side. Fill in these sections with toothpicks. Once you have covered the paper with toothpicks, set it in place in the dirt, simulating the spiked outside wall. Once the glue is dry, color the toothpick posts with a brown marker, if desired.

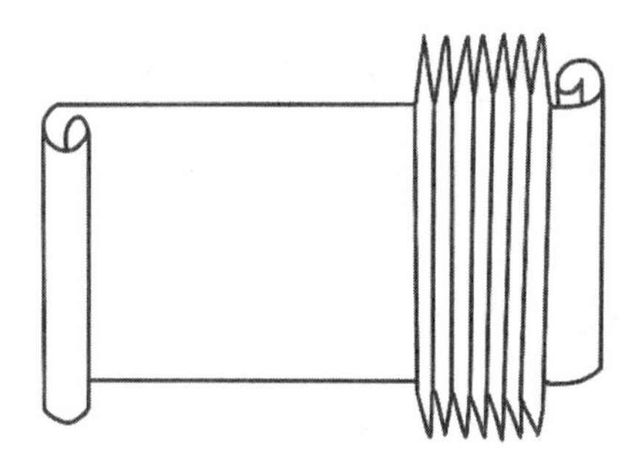

5. Using the brown Model Magic air-dry clay, make a small building to represent Fort Pitt. Place your clay model of Fort Pitt in the center of the peninsula, behind the fort's wall. The clay will dry within 24 hours.
6. Plant your grass seeds! Sprinkle them on top of the dirt outside of the fort. Water with the spray bottle every day or as directed on seed packets. Wait for Ohio Fork grass to grow!

# Revolution!

## Encyclopedia Cross-References

*UBWH 172, UILE 330-331*
*KIHW 504-505, 518-519, 520, KHE 303, 306-307, 316-317*

## DISCONTENT IN THE BRITISH COLONIES

### Review Questions

Do you remember what happened in the "Act of Union"? *The Act of Union joined Scotland and Wales to England.*

In the early eighteenth century, four different kinds of people sailed under the flag of Great Britain. What were they? *Englishmen, Scotsmen, Welshmen, and Americans all sailed under the flag of Great Britain.*

Britain had spent thousands of pounds during the Seven Years' War. How did they intend to regain some of that money? *They decided to pass laws requiring the colonists to pay taxes.*

What did the Sugar Act require of the American colonists? *American colonists had to pay extra money for all sugar and molasses that came into American ports—unless the sugar came from Britain.*

Name two things that were taxed by the Stamp Act. *The Americans were taxed for newspapers, pamphlets, dice, playing cards, and legal documents.*

What were the American colonists ordered to provide for British troops? *Colonists were ordered to provide rooms and food for British troops sent to North America—and to pay for those rooms and food themselves.*

What were General Assemblies? *General Assemblies were meetings of all the colony leaders.*

Was American colonist Patrick Henry arguing for or against the British Acts? *He was arguing against the acts.*

What was Henry's main argument against the colonists having to pay taxes? *He said that they shouldn't have to pay taxes because they did not have representatives in Parliament, which was making the laws.*

What did the new king of Great Britain, George III, agree to do in response to the colonists' protests? *He agreed to repeal some of the acts. He did not repeal the tax on tea.*

What did colony leaders name the incident in which British soldiers fired into a crowd and killed five colonists? *Colony leaders called the incident the Boston Massacre.*

What did the colonists do at the "Boston Tea Party"? *Sixty American colonists wrapped themselves up in Indian blankets and feather headdresses, marched to the wharf where three British tea ships lay at anchor, and dumped 342 chests of tea into Boston harbor.*

Can you remember two things that the Continental Congress asked Parliament to do? *This petition asked the British government to remove the British soldiers, reopen the port, and repeal the taxes; it also warned Parliament that the colonies wouldn't obey laws passed against their will.*

Who said, "Give me liberty or give me death!"? *Patrick Henry made this famous speech.*

### Narration Exercise

Because there is a lot of information in this chapter, use "directed narration." Say to the child, "Tell me three things that the British did to annoy the American colonists; then, tell me two actions that the colonists took in response." Acceptable answers to the first question include:

"The British passed the Sugar Act and taxed sugar."

"The British passed the Stamp Act and taxed newspapers, cards, and documents."

"The British made the Americans give British soldiers rooms and food."

"The British put taxes on glass, paper, paint, and tea."

"The British killed five Americans in Boston in the Boston Massacre."

"The British closed the Boston port and told the Americans they needed permission to hold town meetings."

Acceptable answers to the second question include:

"The colonists met in General Assemblies and demanded that George III repeal the taxes."

"Americans in Boston dressed up like Indians and dumped all of the British tea into Boston Harbor. This was called the Boston Tea Party."

"Colony leaders gathered in the First Continental Congress. They sent a petition to Parliament."

"Colonists started to gather up weapons and bullets in case a war started."

## THE AMERICAN REVOLUTION

### Review Questions

Who were the Minutemen? *The Minutemen were young men who practiced with weapons and were ready to fight against the British at any minute.*

What happened on April 18, 1775? *British soldiers marched to Concord, Massachusetts to seize the weapons.*

Why didn't the British surprise the Americans? *Paul Revere and William Dawes rode ahead of them, warning, "The British are coming!"*

What happened when the British soldiers met the Minutemen in Lexington? *They fired at each other, and the War of American Independence began.*

What did the Second Continental Congress do? *They made George Washington the commander of the army.*

Where did the first huge battle of the war take place? When? *The Battle of Bunker Hill took place on June 17, 1775.*

At first, many Americans were fighting for representation in Parliament. But what did Thomas Paine hope that the Americans would do? *He wrote about it in his pamphlet* Common Sense. *Thomas Paine wanted Americans to break completely from England.*

What was the first colony to declare itself free from Great Britain? *The colony of Rhode Island was the first to declare itself free from Great Britain (in May of 1776).*

Why did the Continental Congress meet again in Philadelphia? *It needed to write out the reasons why the colonies needed to form a new country.*

Who wrote the first draft of the Declaration of Independence? *Thomas Jefferson wrote the first draft.*

What did the British do in response? *They attacked Washington's army with thirty thousand men!*

What river did George Washington cross to launch his surprise attack on Christmas night, 1776? *He took his men across the Delaware River.*

The war went on for two more years. What turned the tide in America's favor in 1778? *France joined the American side against England (so did the Netherlands and Spain).*

Where did the American army corner the British in 1781? *The American army cornered the British at Yorktown, on the coast of Virginia.*

When the British army, under Lord Cornwallis, surrendered, what tune did the band play? *They played 'The World Turned Upside Down.'*

What happened in 1783? *Great Britain signed an agreement giving the colonies independence.*

### Narration Exercise

Because there is a lot of information in this chapter, use "directed narration." Say to the child, "I am going to give you six 'key words.' For each key word, tell me the important event or idea related to that word." Acceptable answers for the key words include:

1. Lexington

"The first battle of the American Revolution happened at Lexington. British soldiers were trying to march to Concord to take away the Minutemen's weapons. The Minutemen were warned by Paul Revere and met the British, ready to shoot!"

2. Bunker Hill

"The first huge battle of the war happened at Bunker Hill. The Americans were camped on Bunker Hill, near Boston. The British attacked them and took the hill. But the British lost three times as many soldiers as the Americans."

3. Common Sense

"Thomas Paine wrote *Common Sense.* He wanted Americans to break free from Great Britain and be their own country—not just to fight for representation."

4. The Declaration of Independence

"Thomas Jefferson wrote the first draft of the Declaration of Independence. It listed the reasons why the colonies [or *states*] needed to become their own country, and all the wrongs Great Britain had done to the colonies."

5. Delaware River

"On Christmas night, 1776, the American and the German troops were camped on opposite sides of the Delaware River. George Washington wanted to take the German troops by surprise. So he sent his men over, one boatload at a time, in the middle of the night. The Americans surprised the Germans and defeated them."

6. Yorktown

"At Yorktown, the Americans cornered the largest British force. Then French ships sailed up the coast so that the British couldn't retreat. The British commander, Lord Cornwallis, surrendered to the Americans!"

## Additional History Reading

*The Boston Massacre: Headlines from History*, by Allison Stark Draper (PowerKids Press, 2001). A very simple and highly illustrated account. (RA 1-2, IR 3-4)

*The Boston Tea Party: Headlines from History*, by Allison Stark Draper (PowerKids Press, 2001). A very simple and highly illustrated account. (RA 1-2, IR 3-4)

*You Wouldn't Want to Be at the Boston Tea Party!*, by Peter Cook, illus. David Antram (The Salariya Book Company, 2014). What was life like before the American Revolution? Find out who the Sons of Liberty were, how the Boston Tea Party came about, and the aftermath. (RA 3, IR 4-6)

*Can't You Make Them Behave, King George?* by Jean Fritz, illus. Tomie de Paola (Coward, McCann & Geoghegan, 1977). A lively and entertaining account of the American Revolution from George III's perspective. (RA 1-2, IR 3-5)

*. . . If You Lived at the Time of the American Revolution*, by Kay Moore, illus. Daniel O'Leary (Scholastic, 1997). Brief, readable explanations of life during the Revolution, the participants in the war, and the reasons for which they fought. (RA 1-2, IR 3-4)

*Liberty! How the Revolutionary War Began*, by Lucille Recht Penner, illus. David Wenzel. (Random House, 2002). Engaging, colorful guide to the American Revolution. (RA 1-2, IR 3-5)

*George Vs. George: The American Revolution as Seen from Both Sides*, by Rosalyn Schanzer (National Geographic Children's Books, 2007). An engaging look at the British as well as the American position during the Revolution, with many direct quotes. (RA 2-3, IR 4-6)

*African Americans and the Revolutionary War*, by Judith E. Harper (The Child's World, 2001). Wonderful account of the bravery of African American revolutionaries. (RA 1-3, IR 4-5) **OOP**

*Betsy Ross and the Silver Thimble* (Ready to Read Level 2), by Stephanie Green (Aladdin, 2002). For reluctant readers or younger siblings, the story of the girl who grew up to make the first American flag. (RA 1, IR 2-3)

*Thomas Paine: Common Sense and Revolutionary Pamphleteering*, by Brian McCartin (Powerkids Press, 2002). For advanced readers, the story of the English political philosopher who came to America and put America's ideas about freedom into print. (IR 4-6)

*Where was Patrick Henry on the 29th of May?* by Jean Fritz, illus. Trina, Schart Hyman (Coward, McCann & Geoghegan, 1997). A colorful and engaging biography of the Virginia statesman; for strong third-grade readers and older. (RA 1-3, IR 3-5)

*Will You Sign Here, John Hancock?* by Jean Fritz, illus. Trina Schart Hyman (Coward, McCann & Geoghegan, 1976). A colorful and engaging biography of the signer of the Declaration of Independence; for strong third-grade readers and older. (RA 1-3, IR 3-5)

*Those Rebels, John and Tom*, by Barbara Kerley, illus. Edwin Fotheringham (Scholastic Press, 2012). A picture book about how Thomas Jefferson and John Adams, two very different men, came together to craft the Declaration of Independence and win America's freedom. (RA 2-3, IR 4)

*Paul Revere: In Their Own Words*, by George Sullivan (Scholastic, 1999). This excellent chapter-book biography series includes plenty of quotes from the biographical subjects themselves. (RA 2, IR 3-4) **OOP**

*Nathan Hale: Patriot and Martyr of the American Revolution*, by L. J. Krizner and Lisa Sita (Powerkids Press, 2002). For advanced readers, an excellent biography of the American patriot executed by the British. (IR 4-6)

*Marquis de Lafayette: French Hero of the American Revolution*, by Gregory Payan (Powerkids Press, 2002). For advanced readers, an excellent biography of the French aristocrat who took up the American cause. Now out of print, but still available in audio format. (IR 4-6) **LFA**

*Molly Pitcher*, by Frances E. Ruffin (Powerkids Press, 2002). A simple, heavily-illustrated account of the Revolutionary War heroine who fired cannon in her husband's place during the Battle of Monmouth. (RA 1-2, IR 3-4)

## Corresponding Literature Suggestions

*Johnny Tremain*, by Esther Forbes (Yearling, 1943). This classic tale of an apprentice silversmith's role in the Revolutionary War won a Newbery Award. A good family read-aloud, or for strong readers; also look for the unabridged audiobook version read by Grace Conlin (Blackstone Audio Books, 2002). (RA 1-4, IR 5-6)

*Mr. Revere and I*, by Robert Lawson (Little, Brown & Co., 1953). This classic account of the Revolution is told by Paul Revere's horse. For fourth grade and older, but second and third graders will enjoy the unabridged audiobook version read by Davina Porter (Recorded Books, 2002). (RA 1-3, IR 4-6).

*Sleds on Boston Common: A Story From the American Revolution*, by Louise Borden, illus. Robert Andrew Parker (Margaret K. McElderry Books, 2000). A little boy sledding on Boston Common runs his sled into General Thomas Gage.

*Sam the Minuteman*, by Nathaniel Benchley, illus. Arnold Lobel (HarperCollins Children's Books, 1969). An I-Can-Read book for reluctant readers or younger siblings. (IR 1-2)

*Freedom at Any Price: March 1775-April 19, 1775* (Liberty's Kids), by Amanda Stephens (Grosset & Dunlap, 2003). A historical fiction book about the beginnings of the American Revolutionary War through the eyes of two teenagers with different perspectives, one an English girl and another an American Colonist boy. A book in a series, but can be read as a stand-alone. Also available as a PBS animated series online or on DVD (great for elementary ages). (RA 2-3, IR 4-6)

*I Survived the American Revolution, 1776*, by Lauren Tarshis (Scholastic Inc., 2017). The "I Survived . . ." books are a series; however, they are independent from each other. This instalment is about a boy's journey during the Battle of Brooklyn during the Revolutionary War. (RA 3, IR 4-6)

*George Washington's Socks,* by Elvira Woodruff (Apple, 1993). In this chapter book for good readers, five children are transported to the Delaware River in 1776, get mixed up in Washington's crossing of the Delaware, and see the battle of Trenton. (RA 2-3, IR 4-6)

*George Washington's Spy*, by Elvira Woodruff (Scholastic Press, 2010). In this sequel to *George Washington's Socks*, children travel back in time and are caught in the Battle of Dorchester. One becomes a spy for the Patriots, while two other children befriend Loyalists. (RA 2-3, IR 4-6)

*The Making of the American Flag: Betsy Ross and George Washington*, by Janet Palazzo-Craig (Rosen Publishing, 2004). Historical fiction for beginning readers. (RA 2, IR 3-4)

*We Are Patriots: Hope's Revolutionary War Diary*, by Kristiana Gregory (Scholastic, 2002). Part of the "My America" series, this young-readers chapter book takes the form of a diary kept in 1777 by a young girl in Valley Forge, Pennsylvania. (RA 1, IR 2-4)

*Chains (Seeds of America Book 1)*, by Laurie Halse Anderson (Atheneum Books for Young Readers, 2010). For older or advanced readers, a novel about an enslaved African girl, Isabel, in New York at the dawn of the Revolution, who seeks her freedom while the colonies do the same. (IR 5-9)

*Forge (Seeds of America Book 2)*, by Laurie Halse Anderson (Atheneum Books for Young Readers, 2011). The second book in the *Seeds of America* trilogy, *Forge* follows runaway slave Curzon who finds food and shelter by enlisting with the 16th Massachusetts Regiment in the Continental army. (RA 3-4, IR 4-8).

*Ashes (Seeds of America Book 3)*, by Laurie Halse Anderson (Atheneum Books for Young Readers, 2017). In the conclusion to the Seeds of America trilogy, Isabel and Curzon try to free Isabel's sister Ruth from slavery during the Battle of Yorktown.

*Gingerbread for Liberty!*, by Mara Rockliff, illus. Vincent X. Kirsch (Houghton Mifflin Harcourt, 2015). A fictional story based on the true story of an American Revolutionary War hero, Christopher Ludwick, who became the chief baker for George Washington's army. (RA 1-2, IR 3-4)

*Colonial Voices: Hear Them Speak*, by Kay Winters, illus. Larry Day (Dutton Children's Books, 2008). A story about the perspectives of persons met in a town by an errand boy in the colonial period of America that shows how many different people showed their patriotism. Told as poems from the different townspeople's perspectives. (RA 3, IR 4)

*Sophia's War: A Tale of the Revolution*, by Avi (Beach Lane Books, 2013). A chapter book that interweaves historically-accurate storylines from the American Revolution with a fictional one about a girl named Sophia who becomes a spy. (IR 4-6)

*The Scarlet Stockings Spy (Tales of Young Americans)*, by Trinka Hakes Noble (Sleeping Bear Press, 2011). A cute tale of how a brother, a soldier, and a sister, a spy for the colonists, contributed their efforts to the Revolutionary War. (RA 2-3, IR 4)

*Spies at Mount Vernon (The Virginia Mysteries Book 7)*, by Steven K. Smith (MyBoys3Press, 2018). A group of friends learn about George Washington while chasing down criminals. This book is part of a series, but can be read as a stand-alone. (RA 3, IR 4-6)

*Woods Runner*, by Gary Paulsen (Wendy Lamb Books, 2011). For older or advanced readers, a critically acclaimed novel about a thirteen-year-old boy trying to find his parents, taken captive during the American Revolution. (IR 5-9)

## MAP WORK

### Great Britain and Her Colonies *(Student Page 67, answer 325)*

1. Great Britain wanted to pay for the Seven Years' War, so they taxed the colonies. The colonists were unhappy with the taxes, so the British sent more soldiers to the colonies. Draw an arrow from Britain to the northern part of the colonies (near Boston). Above the arrow, write "taxes" and "soldiers."
2. The taxes generated much income for Great Britain. Draw a green arrow from the colonies back to Britain. Over the arrow, draw a dollar sign ($).
3. In protest to the taxes, sixty colonists in Boston dumped 342 chests of tea into the Boston Harbor. Next to Boston, draw a small tea cup.
4. Great Britain sent 30,000 more soldiers to New York. You've already drawn a line from Great Britain to the north part of the colonies. Have another arrow come from the middle of this line, toward New York. Under the arrow, write "30,000 soldiers."
5. The colonists, with the help of the French, surrounded the British troops at Yorktown. Draw a small ship at Yorktown and color it blue.

**Coloring Page** The British Parliament was furious about the "Boston Tea Party," where American colonists threw boxes of British tea into Boston Harbor. It punished the Americans by passing a series of laws which the colonies called "The Intolerable Acts." *(Student Page 68)*

## PROJECTS

### Craft Activity: Make an American Flag

The first flag of the new country had thirteen stars, one for each of the thirteen colonies.

*Materials:*
- ☐ white construction paper
- ☐ red construction paper
- ☐ blue construction paper
- ☐ glue

*Directions:*
1. Use a red piece of construction paper as the base of your flag.
2. Cut out a 4 inch blue piece of construction paper and glue it in the upper left hand corner of the red piece of construction paper.
3. Cut six white strips of paper. Each strip of white paper should be ⅔ inch wide. Three of the stripes should be 7 inches long (as these three white stripes will "stop" at the blue square), and 3 should be the full 11 inches.
4. The flag had thirteen stripes. Starting at the top, begin with a red stripe, then glue a white stripe, and so on, down the flag. You will glue on all six white stripes. (Note to parent: you have to "creatively" space the last couple stripes as you near the bottom of the flag.)
5. Make a pattern for a small, white, five-pointed star. Then make twelve more small white stars, and glue all thirteen in a circle on the blue square.

## CRAFT ACTIVITY Soldiers of the American Revolution

The British sent thousands of soldiers to America to keep the colonies part of their empire. Besides sending British soldiers, they also hired German soldiers (sometimes called "Hessians") to fight the Americans. The Americans put together an army to fight back, with men from all thirteen colonies. Here, you'll color and cut out paper dolls of a British soldier, a German soldier, and an American soldier from the colony of Virginia.

*Materials:*
- ☐ colored pencils or crayons
- ☐ scissors
- ☐ scotch removable Double-stick Tape
- ☐ Student Pages 69, 70, and 71: American, British, and German soldiers
- ☐ white cardstock

*Directions:*
1. Note: You might want to make copies of the figures and uniforms before coloring and cutting them, so you can create a whole army. Color the paper dolls and the uniforms. The redcoats had bright red coats. Their pants were red at the top, but their legs were covered with long, white leggings. The German soldiers wore blue coats with red and white trim, white pants, and black shoes and socks. The American soldiers wore many kinds of uniforms; this soldier from Virginia might wear a white or purple hunting shirt, a brown hat, and white leggings. Cut the figures out.
2. Glue the paper doll onto thick cardstock. Cut to size. Laminate if possible (you'll be happier with the results and the paper doll lasts longer.) If laminating at a professional site (such as Office Depot or copy stores), opt for the thicker grade of plastic cover.
3. Use the double-stick tape to attach the uniforms to the dolls.

4. ***Option***—Replace the soldier's head with a picture of yourself! Scan your picture into your computer and enlarge it to fit, or take a picture into an enlargement site, such as the machines at Target or Wal-Mart, and enlarge your picture to fit the soldier body. Proceed with laminating and follow the rest of the steps.

## GAME ACTIVITY The Battle of Bunker Hill

*Materials:*

- ☐ *The Story of the World, Volume 3*, chapter 22
- ☐ Student Page 72: Bunker Hill Game Board
- ☐ Student Page 73: Game Card Template
- ☐ game pieces: beans, coins, buttons or small plastic toys to serve as player markers
- ☐ one or two dice, depending on how fast you want the game to go

*Directions:*

1. Before the game:
   a. Enlarge the game board to fit on an 11" x 14" cardstock. Copy the game cards on to two different colors of cardstock, making two decks of the cards.
   b. *Optional*: Glue the game board on to cardboard or posterboard to add strength.
   c. *Optional*: Cover the game board with clear contact paper.
   d. Each player gets a game piece and a deck of the *Battle of Bunker Hill Cards*, turned face down in front of him on the letters on the board.
2. To play:
   a. All players begin by placing game pieces on the map. The oldest player gets to start the game. You may not begin the game until you roll a one. Once you roll a one, you may begin by placing your game piece on the starting square. You cannot move forward until the next turn.
   b. Roll the die/dice and after you have moved, draw a card from your pile. As you draw the cards, place the cards in order according to when they happened. Every turn, you must draw a card from your pile and place it in your ordered set of cards. You might consider using *The Story of the World* to help you while you play the game the first few times.
   c. Continue to move around the board. When you land on the end of an arrow, you may slide to the end. If you slide past another player's piece, that player is sent back to the center of the board. He must stay there until he rolls a one. He then returns to the square he was on.
   d. If you land on a square that is already occupied, the player who was there first is sent back six spaces.
   e. END SQUARE—You do not need to have the exact roll to finish on the *End Square*. Once there, choose a final card from your pile and put it in order. The winner is the first person in the end square and whose cards are correctly in order.

## MEMORY ACTIVITY

Memorize one or both of the following passages. Ask the child to read 8-10 lines out loud five times every day. Within a few days, the child should be able to recite most of those lines from memory. Then add another 8-10 lines and follow the same procedure until the whole poem or declaration is memorized.

**"Paul Revere's Ride,"**
**by Henry Wadsworth Longfellow (1860)**

Listen, my children, and you shall hear
Of the midnight ride of Paul Revere,
On the eighteenth of April, in Seventy-Five;
Hardly a man is now alive
Who remembers that famous day and year.

He said to his friend, "If the British march
By land or sea from the town to-night,
Hang a lantern aloft in the belfry arch
Of the North Church tower, as a signal light,
One, if by land, and two, if by sea;
And I on the opposite shore will be,
Ready to ride and spread the alarm
Through every Middlesex village and farm,
For the country-folk to be up and to arm."

Then he said "Good-night!" and with muffled oar
Silently rowed to the Charlestown shore,
Just as the moon rose over the bay,
Where swinging wide at her moorings lay
The *Somerset*, British man-of-war;
A phantom ship, with each mast and spar
Across the moon like a prison-bar,
And a huge black hulk, that was magnified
By its own reflection in the tide.

Meanwhile, his friend, through alley and street
Wanders and watches with eager ears,
Till in the silence around him he hears
The muster of men at the barrack door,
The sound of arms, and the tramp of feet,
And the measured tread of the grenadiers,
Marching down to their boats on the shore.

Then he climbed the tower of the Old North Church,
By the wooden stairs, with stealthy tread,
To the belfry-chamber overhead,
And startled the pigeons from their perch
On the somber rafters, that round him made
Masses and moving shapes of shade,
By the trembling ladder, steep and tall,
To the highest window in the wall,
Where he paused to listen and look down

A moment on the roofs of the town,
And the moonlight flowing over all.

Beneath, in the churchyard, lay the dead,
In their night-encampment on the hill,
Wrapped in silence so deep and still
That he could hear, like a sentinel's tread,
The watchful night-wind, as it went
Creeping along from tent to tent,
And seeming to whisper, "All is well!"
A moment only he feels the spell
Of the place and the hour, the secret dread
Of the lonely belfry and the dead;
For suddenly all his thoughts are bent
On a shadowy something far away,
Where the river widens to meet the bay,
A line of black, that bends and floats
On the rising tide, like a bridge of boats.

Meanwhile, impatient to mount and ride,
Booted and spurred, with a heavy stride
On the opposite shore walked Paul Revere.
Now he patted his horse's side,
Now gazed on the landscape far and near,
Then, impetuous, stamped the earth,
And turned and tightened his saddle-girth;
But mostly he watched with eager search
The belfry-tower of the Old North Church,
As it rose above the graves on the hill,
Lonely and spectral and somber and still.
And lo! as he looks, on the belfry's height
A glimmer, and then a gleam of light!
He springs to the saddle, the bridle he turns,
But lingers and gazes, till full on his sight
A second lamp in the belfry burns!

A hurry of hoofs in a village street,
A shape in the moonlight, a bulk in the dark,
And beneath, from the pebbles, in passing, a spark
Struck out by a steed flying fearless and fleet:
That was all! And yet, through the gloom and the light,
The fate of a nation was riding that night;
And the spark struck out by that steed, in his flight,
Kindled the land into flame with its heat.

He has left the village and mounted the steep,
And beneath him, tranquil and broad and deep,
Is the Mystic, meeting the ocean tides;
And under the alders that skirt its edge,
Now soft on the sand, now loud on the ledge,
Is heard the tramp of his steed as he rides.

It was twelve by the village clock,
When he crossed the bridge into Medford town.
He heard the crowing of the cock,
And the barking of the farmer's dog,
And felt the damp of the river fog,
That rises after the sun goes down.

It was one by the village clock,
When he galloped into Lexington.
He saw the gilded weathercock
Swim in the moonlight as he passed,
And the meeting-house windows, blank and bare,
Gaze at him with a spectral glare,
As if they already stood aghast
At the bloody work they would look upon.

It was two by the village clock,
When he came to the bridge in Concord town.
He heard the bleating of the flock,
And the twitter of birds among the trees,
And felt the breath of the morning breeze
Blowing over the meadows brown.
And one was safe and asleep in his bed
Who at the bridge would be first to fall,
Who that day would be lying dead,
Pierced by a British musket-ball.

You know the rest. In the books you have read,
How the British regulars fired and fled,
How the farmers gave them ball for ball,
From behind each fence and farm-yard wall,
Chasing the red-coats down the lane,
Then crossing the fields to emerge again
Under the trees at the turn of the road,
And only pausing to fire and load.

So through the night rode Paul Revere;
And so through the night went his cry of alarm
To every Middlesex village and farm,

A cry of defiance and not of fear,
A voice in the darkness, a knock at the door,
And a word that shall echo forevermore!
For, borne on the night-wind of the Past,
Through all our history, to the last,
In the hour of darkness and peril and need,
The people will waken and listen to hear
The hurrying hoof-beat of that steed,
And the midnight message of Paul Revere.

**The Introduction of the Declaration of Independence**

The Declaration of Independence of the Thirteen Colonies

In CONGRESS, July 4, 1776

The unanimous Declaration of the thirteen united States of America,

When in the Course of human events, it becomes necessary for one people to dissolve the political bands which have connected them with another, and to assume among the powers of the earth, the separate and equal station to which the Laws of Nature and of Nature's God entitle them, a decent respect to the opinions of mankind requires that they should declare the causes which impel them to the separation.

We hold these truths to be self-evident, that all men are created equal, that they are endowed by their Creator with certain unalienable Rights, that among these are Life, Liberty and the pursuit of Happiness.

—That to secure these rights, Governments are instituted among Men, deriving their just powers from the consent of the governed,

—That whenever any Form of Government becomes destructive of these ends, it is the Right of the People to alter or to abolish it, and to institute new Government, laying its foundation on such principles and organizing its powers in such form, as to them shall seem most likely to effect their Safety and Happiness. Prudence, indeed, will dictate that Governments long established should not be changed for light and transient causes; and accordingly all experience hath shewn, that mankind are more disposed to suffer, while evils are sufferable, than to right themselves by abolishing the forms to which they are accustomed. But when a long train of abuses and usurpations, pursuing invariably the same Object evinces a design to reduce them under absolute Despotism, it is their right, it is their duty, to throw off such Government, and to provide new Guards for their future security.

—Such has been the patient sufferance of these Colonies; and such is now the necessity which constrains them to alter their former Systems of Government. The history of the present King of Great Britain is a history of repeated injuries and usurpations, all having in direct object the establishment of an absolute Tyranny over these States. To prove this, let Facts be submitted to a candid world.

# The New Country

## Encyclopedia Cross-References

*UBWH 172, UILE 331*
*KIHW 520-521, KHE 317*

## THE AMERICAN CONSTITUTION

### Review Questions

How many American colonies became states? *Thirteen American colonies became states.*

What is a constitution? *A constitution is a set of rules explaining how a country will work.*

When the states started writing constitutions, they disagreed over basic issues. Can you remember two? *They disagreed over basic issues such as which states owned which rivers, what type of money to use, foreign treaties, navies, and how to pay back France for the money borrowed during the revolution.*

Who were two of the American leaders who saw that America was heading toward trouble? *American leaders like Alexander Hamilton from New York, James Madison from Virginia, Benjamin Franklin from Pennsylvania and George Washington himself saw that the new states would soon be in trouble.*

What is a federal government? *A federal government has the power to act for all of the states.*

Many Americans were afraid of federal government. What were they afraid might happen if they had a federal government? *They were afraid of going back to the type of rule they had been under in Britain.*

In which city did the "Constitutional Convention" take place? *The "Constitutional Convention" took place in Philadelphia.*

The delegates wanted to make sure that the new Constitution would give the United States of America the power to act together—but also to act separately. What plan did they come up with? *They agreed on a plan that would divide the government of the United States into two "houses," like the House of Commons and the House of Lords in the English parliament. These "houses" would be responsible for writing out laws and voting on them.*

What was the name of each of the "houses" of government? *The houses were called the Senate and the House of Representatives.*

What were the two houses of the government called, together? *The two houses were referred to as Congress.*

Congress would be the "legislative" part of the new federal government. What is one duty of this legislative branch of the government? *The legislative branch is able to pass laws, declare war, and make treaties with foreign countries.*

The President has the power to veto any of the laws of Congress. What does this mean? *The President is able to stop any law from being passed.*

What branch of government does the President belong to? *The President belongs to the executive branch.*

The executive and legislative branches are the first two branches of government. What is the third branch of government? Who makes up this third branch? *The third branch of government is the judicial branch, which consists of the Supreme Court.*

What was the name of the document in which the delegates wrote down the rules of government? *The document was called the Constitution.*

How many states needed to accept, or *ratify,* the Constitution? *Nine states had to ratify the Constitution.*

Patrick Henry, along with other Americans, wanted a Bill of Rights. What was this Bill? *The Bill of Rights was a list of powers that the government could never use against the people of the United States.*

What was one of the amendments in the Bill of Rights? *The Bill of Rights, ten "Amendments" (additions) to the Constitution, said that Congress could never forbid American citizens to speak their opinions, to worship God as they pleased, to assemble together in public, or to keep weapons to defend themselves. No one could ever be seized by the government and kept in jail without a public trial. The Bill of Rights said that the federal government could never behave like a king towards its people—even if there seemed to be good reasons for doing so.*

### Narration Exercise

Because there is a lot of information in this chapter, use "directed narration." Say to the child, "The Constitution describes three branches of government. Name each one of the branches of government, tell me who's in it, and then tell what that branch does. Then, tell me what the Bill of Rights does." An acceptable answer might be,

"The legislative branch makes laws, declares war, and makes treaties. It has two parts, the House of Representatives and the Senate. Together, the two parts are called Congress. The executive branch is the President. The President can veto any laws that Congress passes. The judicial branch is a court of judges who can make sure that the laws are followed. The Supreme Court is part of the judicial branch. The Bill of Rights lists powers that the government can never use against the people. It says that the government can never behave like a king towards the people."

## THE FIRST AMERICAN PRESIDENT

### Review Questions

What did George Washington want to do after the American War for Independence? *He wanted to stay on his farm in Virginia, feed his animals, work in his garden, and sit with his wife in front of the fireplace in the long quiet evenings.*

Why did the delegates want George Washington to be the leader of the new nation? *They knew he would never try to be the king.*

What was the result of the first presidential election, in 1789? *George Washington was elected unanimously.*

What city did Washington ride to when he was sworn in, or inaugurated, as president? *He had to ride to New York, the temporary capital of the United States.*

Washington hoped for a quiet ride to New York. Did he get that quiet ride? *No, he did not. All along the way, people cheered for him.*

How many men did Washington choose to help him run the country? What were they called? *He chose four men to help him run the country. They were known as the "President's Cabinet."*

Can you remember two of the four titles these men held? *They were the Secretary of the Treasury, the Secretary of State, the Secretary of War, and the Attorney General.*

Who was Washington's vice-president? *John Adams was his vice-president.*

Between what two states would the new capital city of the country lie? *The capital of the United States would be on a small piece of land between Virginia and Maryland, the District of Columbia.*

What title did Washington choose for himself? *Washington simply went by "Mr. President."*

After his terms as President, what did Washington do? *He refused to be President again.*

### Narration Exercise

"George Washington was elected unanimously to be the first President. He didn't want to be President, but he agreed because he knew it would be good for the country. He chose four men to help him run the country. They were called the President's Cabinet. Washington hired a thousand people to help run the federal government. He also chose a new capital city, the District of Columbia. But after he served for eight years, George Washington refused to be president again. He wanted the Constitution, not the president, to rule." OR

"George Washington became the first President in 1789. He rode to New York for his inauguration. Everywhere he went, there were parades and celebrations. When he took the oath of office, fireworks went off and people shouted, 'God bless Washington!' Washington seemed like a king, but he wasn't like a king—he didn't want power. He chose four men to help him run the country. He refused to be called 'His Highness.' And after he was President twice, he refused to serve for a third term. He didn't want to hold power for life!"

## Additional History Reading

*A More Perfect Union: The Story of Our Constitution*, by Betsy and Giulio Maestro (HarperCollins, 2008). Simpler than the Fritz book below, this picture book tells the story of the Constitutional Convention and provides a list of amendments. (RA 1-2, IR 3-5)

*. . . If You Were There When They Signed the Constitution*, by Elizabeth Levy (Scholastic, 1992). A simple account of the Declaration of Independence, the Constitutional Convention, and the Constitution and Bill of Rights. (RA 1-2, IR 3-4)

*Shh! We're Writing the Constitution*, by Jean Fritz, illus. Tomie de Paola (G. P. Putnam's Sons, 1987). A simple, although longish, guide to the Constitutional Convention and the Constitution; includes the text of the Constitution and the list of signers. (RA 1-3, IR 4-5)

*The United States Constitution: A Graphic Adaptation* by Jonathan Hennessey, illus Aaron McConnell. (Hill and Wang, 2008). Interesting and engaging graphic novel describes the framing of the Constitution, and the meaning and background of each article and amendment. Might be a bit much for younger readers to fully absorb but the rich illustrations lend themselves to be starting points for further conversation. (IR 4-8).

*We the Kids*, by David Catrow (Dial Books for Young Readers, 2002). A cute picture book illustrating the preamble of the Constitution to help young readers understand the preamble and what it means. (RA 1-2, IR 3)

*What Is the Constitution?*, by Patricia Brennan Demuth (Penguin Workshop, 2018). An informative chapter book with illustrations. Tells why the Constitution was needed, who helped shape it, and how it is implemented today. (RA 3, IR 4-6)

*Hail to the Chief: The American Presidency*, by Don Robb (Charlesbridge, 2010). A clear, simple introduction to the office of the presidency, its origins, and its duties and. powers. (RA 2, IR 3-5)

*Ben Franklin Thinks Big* (I Can Read Level 2), by Sheila Keenan, illus. Gustavo Mazali (Harper, 2018). A biography of Benjamin Franklin and the milestones in his life for young readers. (RA 1-2, IR 3-4)

*What's the Big Idea, Ben Franklin?*, by Jean Fritz, illus. Margot Tomes (Coward, McCann & Geoghegan, 1976). A longish but simply written biography of Franklin. (RA 1-2, IR 3-5)

*Who Was Ben Franklin?*, by Dennis Brindell Fradin (Grossett & Dunlap, 2002). A beginner's biography with diagrams of Franklin's inventions. (IR 2-3)

*Alexander Hamilton: From Orphan to Founding Father (Step into Reading)*, by Monica Kulling, illus. Valerio Fabbretti (Random House Children's Books, 2017). An inspiring story about the life of Alexander Hamilton and how he went from his humble beginnings to help shape the system of government of the new United States. (RA 2, IR 3-4)

*George Washington: First President 1789-1797* by Mike Venezia (Children's Press, 2005). The first book in the *Getting to Know the U.S. Presidents* series. The author weaves delightful illustrations and humorous anecdotes into each biography making them both factual and memorable. (RA 1-2, IR 2-4).

*New Nation Through the Eyes of George Washington* (Presidential Perspectives), by Anita Yasuda (Abdo Publishing, 2016). Insight on George Washington's presidency. This book includes websites for more information and poses thoughtful questions. (IR 3-6)

*President George Washington*, by David A. Adler, illus. John Wallner (Holiday House, 2005). A book about George Washington's life for young students that includes quotes from George Washington, a timeline, additional readings, author's notes, and sources for the information used in the book. (RA 1-2)

*George Washington: The First President (I Can Read Level 2)*, by Sarah Albee, illus. Chin Ko (Harper, 2017). An intro to George Washington's life with a timeline and additional information about life at Mount Vernon. (RA 1-2, IR 3,4)

*George Washington*, by Cheryl Harness (National Geographic Society, 2000). A wonderful picture book of George Washington's life from birth to death. (RA 2-3, IR 4-6)

*Martha Washington: America's First Lady* by Jean Brown Wagoner (Aladdin, 1986). From the Childhood of Famous Americans series, this book gives young readers a chance to picture Martha Washington as a real person who was once a kid just like them. More for background information about this famous American, the book covers only a bit of Martha's life after the Revolutionary War. (RA 1-2, IR 2-4).

*Worst of Friends: Thomas Jefferson, John Adams, and the True Story of an American Feud*, by Suzanne Tripp Jurmain, illus. Larry Day (Penguin Group, 2011). A nice picture book about the ups and downs in the relationship between John Adams and Thomas Jefferson as they helped found the United States and then lead the new nation. (RA 3, IR 4-6)

## Corresponding Literature Suggestions

*Ben and Me*, by Robert Lawson (Little, Brown & Co., 1939). A classic children's novel, narrated by Amos, a mouse who lives in Benjamin Franklin's house. For good third-grade readers and above, or as a family read-aloud. (RA 1-3, IR 4-6)

*Democracy's Signature: Benjamin Franklin and the Declaration of Independence*, by Danny Fingeroth (Rosen Publishing, 2004). Historical fiction for beginners. (RA 2, IR 3-4)

*Ben Franklin's In My Bathroom!*, by Candace Fleming (Schwartz & Wade books, 2017). Benjamin Franklin comes to the present and learns about all the new inventions that the twenty-first century has to offer.

Includes information about his personal life, his inventions, and his contributions to America, this book is a fun read for upper elementary aged students. (IR 4-6).

*Spenser's Story of the Constitution* by Paul Sleman Clark, illus Ray Driver. (Ozymandias Press, 2016). Spenser the cat, a close friend of Ben Franklin, relates the story of the drafting of the U.S. Constitution at the State House in Philadelphia. Charming story enhanced with lots of information about the framing of this historical document. (IR 3-5).

*Alexander Hamilton: Little Lion (The Treasure Chest, #2)*, by Ann Hood (Grosset & Dunlap, 2012). A brother and sister travel back in time and befriend seventeen-year-old Alexander Hamilton. Based on true events, this historical fiction will take readers back to when Hamilton was young and introduce them to the events that led him to be a great man. ((RA 3, IR 4-6)

*Duel! Burr and Hamilton's Deadly War of Words*, by Dennis Brindell Fradin, illus. Larry Day (Walker and Company, 2008). A picture book of the famous duel between Aaron Burr and Alexander Hamilton, including what led up to it and the effects afterwards. (RA 2-3, IR 4)

*Imogene's Last Stand* by Candace Fleming, illus Nancy Carpenter (Schwartz & Wade Books, 2009). Charming picture book about a little girl who loves history and who fights to keep her local Historical Society from being demolished. She discovers a connection between the house and George Washington but will it be enough to convince the town to abandon their plans for a shoelace factory to be built on the site? (RA K-3, IR 2-4).

*The President and Me: John Adams and the Magic Bobblehead* by Deborah Kalb, illus Robert Lunsford (Schiffer, 2018). In the tradition of the *Magic Tree House* books, two kids find themselves transported back in time by a magic bobblehead doll. There, they meet John and Abigail Adams and learn a bit about the early history of the U.S. firsthand. The second book in *The President and Me* series. (IR 3-4).

*Tricking the Tallyman* by Jacqueline Davies, illus S.D. Schindler (Dragonfly Books, 2014). Amusing story with clever illustrations based on the story of the first U.S. Census, in 1790. Great for discussing what a census is and what it is used for as well as for showing how the new country was growing (RA K-3, IR 2-5).

## MAP WORK

### The 13 Colonies *(Student Page 74, answer 325)*

1. The thirteen colonies were acting as independent countries, making up their own constitutions. Color the colonies different colors. Be sure to use different colors for colonies that share a border.
2. The first capital of the country was in New York. Draw a blue circle around the dot that represents New York.
3. The country moved the capital from New York to the District of Columbia, or Washington D.C. Draw a large star on top of the dot that represents Washington D.C.

**COLORING PAGE** Delegates from the American states met in Philadelphia to discuss how they could join their states into one country, and what kind of government this new country would have. Benjamin Franklin was too old to walk to the daily meetings, so he hired four prisoners from a local jail to carry him to and from Independence Hall in a chair. *(Student Page 75)*

## PROJECTS

### GAME PROJECT Play Presidential Inauguration

On April 30, 1789, George Washington was inaugurated president in New York. You are going to go through your own version of the first presidential inauguration.

*Materials:*
- ☐ Paper
- ☐ Pencil or pen
- ☐ At least one other person (to cheer you on)

*Directions:*

1. (Start this activity in your bedroom, as you will have to "travel" during this activity.) Before his inauguration, George Washington wrote in his diary, "[I begin the presidency] with a mind oppressed with more anxious and painful sensations than I have words to express." Write a short diary entry in which you explain how you feel about becoming the president.
2. George Washington had to ride to New York to be sworn in, or inaugurated. People cheered and threw flowers at every town through which he passed. New York was the temporary capital of the United States. You must travel from your room to a larger room (the kitchen or the living room). Make sure that you have someone cheering you, or throwing flowers at your feet as you make the journey!
3. When he finally arrived in New York, the people were saying, "The great Washington is here." As you arrive in the larger room, make sure that someone says, "The great (your last name) is here!"
4. George Washington was sworn in, or inaugurated, when he got to New York. He stood on a balcony, laid his hand on a Bible and said, "I solemnly swear that I will faithfully execute the office of President of the United States and will, to the best of my ability, preserve, protect, and defend the Constitution of the United States." Put your left hand on a book, and raise your right hand. Then repeat the oath that Washington took.
5. After he was sworn in, Washington gave the First Inaugural Address. Below you will find excerpts from the first and last paragraphs of that address. Washington gave the address in a low voice, so read the following paragraphs in as low a voice as you can (note to parents: you may need to help your children with some of the words):

> Fellow-Citizens of the Senate and of the House of Representatives:
>
> . . . No event could have filled me with greater anxieties than that of which the notification was transmitted by your order, and received on the 14th day of the present month. On the one hand, I was summoned by my country, whose voice I can never hear but with veneration and love, from a retreat which I had chosen with the fondest predilection, and, in my flattering hopes, with an immutable decision, as the asylum of my declining years—a retreat which was rendered every day more necessary as well as more dear to me by the addition of habit to inclination, and of frequent interruptions in my health to the gradual waste committed on it by time. On the other hand, the magnitude and difficulty of the trust to which the voice of my country called me, being sufficient to awaken in the wisest

and most experienced of her citizens a distrustful scrutiny into his qualifications, could not but overwhelm with despondence one who (inheriting inferior endowments from nature and unpracticed in the duties of civil administration) ought to be peculiarly conscious of his own deficiencies. In this conflict of emotions all I dare aver is that it has been my faithful study to collect my duty from a just appreciation of every circumstance by which it might be affected. . . .

Having thus imparted to you my sentiments as they have been awakened by the occasion which brings us together, I shall take my present leave; but not without resorting once more to the benign Parent of the Human Race in humble supplication that, since He has been pleased to favor the American people with opportunities for deliberating in perfect tranquility, and dispositions for deciding with unparalleled unanimity on a form of government for the security of their union and the advancement of their happiness, so His divine blessing may be equally *conspicuous* in the enlarged views, the temperate consultations, and the wise measures on which the success of this Government must depend.

6. Many of the bystanders shouted, "God bless our Washington! Long live our beloved President!" Have someone shout, "God bless our (your last name)! Long live our beloved President!"

## GAME PROJECT The Articles of the Constitution

Parents should refer to a copy of the Constitution. The following link is a stable link to an online version of the text: www.senate.gov/civics/constitution_item/constitution.htm. The parent should read through the articles with the child. The parent will explain the article, and the child will write the article number on the front of an index card, and a summary (given below) on the back of the index card. You will then be able to use these index cards for a game.

### Directions

*Set up:*

The following are the summaries for each of the seven articles. As you read through the original text with your child, have him write the article number on the front of the card, and the summary on the back of the card.

1. Article I—The ten sections in this article describe how the House and Senate will work.
2. Article II—The four sections of this article describe how the President will be elected.
3. Article III—The three sections of this article describe how the courts will work.
4. Article IV—This article says how the states will relate to each other and says that anyone who commits a crime in one state and then flees to another will have to be turned over to the original state; it also says how states can be added, and promises that the United States will protect each state from foreign invasion.
5. Article V—This article says that the Constitution can be amended if three quarters of the states agree.
6. Article VI—This article says that all public officials must support the Constitution.
7. Article VII—This article is signed by George Washington, and the "deputies of twelve states."

Have the child study the seven index cards until he knows the summary of each of the seven articles. When he thinks he is ready, have the student play "Last Man Standing." (This game works best with more than one child, but if there is only one child, the game is "How Long Can You Stand?")

*To play:*

1. The parent has the child stand up.
2. In early rounds (i.e. the easier option), the parent reads the summary of the article. The child tells the parent which article is being described. If there is more than one child, the parent goes around, asking each child a different question. If a child misses a question, he sits down and is out of the game. The question moves on to the next child who is standing up. (Note: If all of the players are stumped by one question and no one is left, everyone who went out on that question is back in the game.)
3. To make the game more difficult, name an article and ask the child to recite the summary.
4. Play this game throughout the week that you study this chapter, so that the child masters the seven articles.

## MEMORY GAME President Memory Game

*Materials:*
- ☐ Student Page 76: Presidential Timeline
- ☐ ruler or straight edge
- ☐ pen or pencil
- ☐ index cards (16)

*Directions:*
1. Using the Presidential Timeline, draw an upside down **V** from 1789 to 1797. From the top of the upside down **V**, use your ruler and draw a line straight up. On the line, write "George Washington, 1789-1797."
2. Continue like this, and put the rest of the dates of the presidents on the timeline. Put them on the timeline in the same way you put the dates of George Washington on the timeline.
3. After you have completed the timeline, take your index cards. On the front of the card, write the name of the president and his wife, the dates in office, and the state he is from. On the back of the card, write the interesting facts listed below.
4. Arrange the cards in order. You should learn the order and be able to chant the name, wife, dates in office. For example: George and Martha Washington, 1789-1797; John and Abigail Adams, 1797—1801; Thomas and Martha Jefferson, 1801—1809; and so on through Abraham Lincoln. The parent, or another child, can use the cards to check the child.
5. After you complete the above memorization, you may play a trivia game with the interesting facts. Have one person hold the cards, shuffle them, and then ask a question like, "Which president was the first to wear long trousers?" "James Madison was the first president to wear long trousers."

George and Martha Washington, 1789-97, from Virginia
- never went to college—studied at home
- had false teeth made of deer antlers
- had a dog named Sweet Lips

John and Abigail Adams, 1797-1801, from Massachusetts
- had a horse named Cleopatra
- there was no water or plumbing in the White House, so people had to carry water from spring five blocks away

Thomas and Martha Jefferson, 1801-9, from Virginia
- enjoyed pancakes and spoon bread
- first speleologist—(one who studies caves)
- kept a mocking bird that ate food out of his mouth during meals

- was given 1200 pound block of cheese; people started calling him "The Big Cheese"

James and Dolley Madison, 1809-17, from Virginia
- had a pet macaw
- thought we should rent Portugal's navy, not have our own
- smallest president at 5'4", weighed less than 100 pounds
- first to wear long trousers

James and Elizabeth Monroe, 1817-25, from Virginia
- first president to ride a steamboat
- no one ran against him when he ran for a second term
- the White House was painted white while he was in office

John Quincy and Louisa Catherine Adams, 1825-9, from Massachusetts
- John Quincy was the son of John Adams
- had a pet alligator
- swam naked every morning in Potomac River
- first president to be photographed

Andrew and Rachel Jackson, 1829-37, from Tennessee
- fought in war of 1812
- liked to fight duels and killed man for insulting his wife Rachel
- he was shot in the chest during the duel and the bullet was never taken out
- believed the earth was flat
- his pet parrot had to be removed from his funeral for swearing

Martin and Hannah Van Buren, 1837-41, from New York
- originated O.K. (abbreviation for his home, formed a club called OK club) to mean all correct
- presided over the senate wearing two pistols because there was so much violence in the senate
- had two tiger cubs for pets
- he and his wife spoke Dutch at home

William Henry and Anna Harrison, 1841, from Virginia
- president for 30 days
- caught pneumonia during inauguration
- his supporters pushed a paper ball covered with campaign slogans from city to city—that is where the expression "Keep the Ball Rolling" comes from
- Tecumseh placed a curse on him that he would die in office

John Tyler, 1841-5, from Virginia (1st wife, Letitia; 2nd wife, Julia)
- played violin
- was playing marbles when he found out that Harrison died and he was now president
- had 15 kids

James and Sarah Polk, 1845-9, from Tennessee
- died from exhaustion
- he felt parties were frivolous, so no refreshments were ever served at a function and his first lady banned dancing in the White house
- refused to take office on a Sunday so the president pro tempore of the Senate was sworn in for a day
- always rode his horse sidesaddle into battle

- died after eating cherries and milk on hot day
- Abe Lincoln gave the eulogy at his funeral

Zachary and Margaret Taylor, 1849-50, from Louisiana

- kept his army horse Whitey on the front lawn and visitors used to pull hairs out of Whitey for souvenirs
- he died suddenly in 1850
- in 1991 his descendants had him exhumed (dug up) to see if he had been poisoned by arsenic—and found nothing

Millard and Abigail Fillmore, 1850-3, from New York

- 8 brothers and sisters
- Abigail had the first bathtub installed in the White House

Franklin and Jane Pierce, 1853-7, from New Hampshire

- first president to have a Christmas tree
- nicknamed Handsome Frank
- first stamped envelopes were used during his presidency

James Buchanan, 1857-61, from Pennsylvania

- never married
- cabbage was his favorite food
- liked to give sauerkraut and mashed potato parties
- Jingle Bells was written during his term

Abraham and Mary Lincoln, 1861-5, from Illinois

- liked fruit salad
- was the tallest president at 6'4"
- a rival called him "two-faced" and Lincoln responded, "If I had another face, do you think I would wear this one?"
- had a turkey named Jack

## MEMORIZATION PROJECT The Preamble to the Constitution

Memorize the following passage. Ask the child to read the preamble out loud five times every day. Within a few days, the child should be able to recite the preamble from memory.

We the people of the United States, in order to form a more perfect union, establish justice, insure domestic tranquility, provide for the common defense, promote the general welfare, and secure the blessings of liberty to ourselves and our posterity, do ordain and establish this Constitution for the United States of America.

## CRAFT ACTIVITY Three Branches of Government

The Americans needed a central government that could make decisions for all of the 13 states. But how? The framers of the Constitution built a structure that reflected the needs and concerns of all of the delegates. It has made an impact on the world as a model for many new constitutions in the 20th century. Make this game to play whenever you want to challenge your memory!

*Materials:*
- ☐ red and blue craft foam
- ☐ white acrylic paint
- ☐ thin paintbrush
- ☐ black permanent marker
- ☐ scissors
- ☐ pencil

- ☐ Tacky craft glue (regular white glue does not hold together craft foam)
- ☐ craft magnets with sticky back
- ☐ sticky-back Velcro circles
- ☐ Student Page 77: 3 Branches of Government Template

*Directions:*

1. Cut out all the pieces on the template sheet. Trace one "house" on to either the blue or the red craft foam. Cut out and set aside.
2. Trace and cut out three of the small squares on the unused color. Glue the smaller paper squares with the definitions onto each larger square. Let dry.
3. Place them on the "house" shape on the bottom, as shown in the sample above. Leave some space in between each of the small squares. Once you've got them placed in the right position, attach a Velcro circle between the squares and the "house" shape. Make sure that you use the same Velcro side for the small squares and the same Velcro side for the "house" shape so that the squares will be interchangeable.

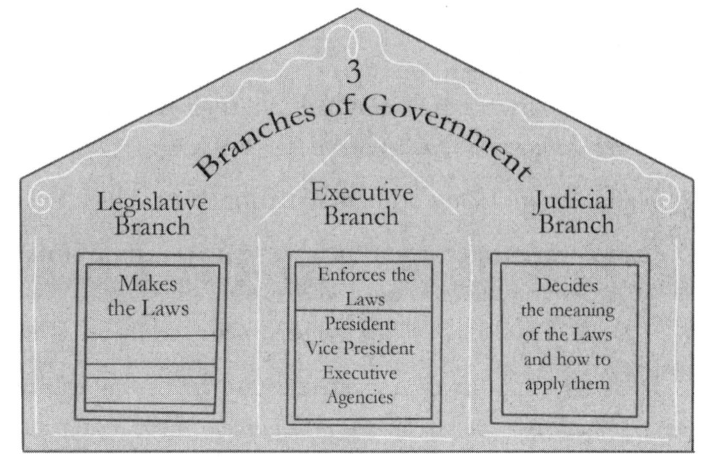


4. Using the black marker, write on the top of the "house": ***3 Branches of Government***, as seen on the sample above. Also, write the names of the three branches: ***Legislative, Executive***, and ***Judicial*** above each of the squares.
5. With the white paint, decorate around the top part and in between the three branch options. See sample above for ideas.
6. Stick the magnet on the back of the "house" and place on your refrigerator. Remove the squares, and see if you can remember which branch does what. If you don't, reread chapter 23 in *The Story of the World, Vol. 3*! Mix them up and time yourself to see how fast you can put them back together! Or mix them up and see how long it takes for someone to notice they are not in the right order.

# Sailing South

## Encyclopedia Cross-References

*UBWH 176, 181, UILE 326-327*
*KIHW 512-513, KHE 88-89, 312-313*

## CAPTAIN COOK REACHES BOTANY BAY

### Review Questions

What scientific expedition had the English government hired Captain Cook to make? *He had been hired to sail to Tahiti and look at the planet Venus.*

Had Captain Cook done much sailing in his life? *Yes, he had done much sailing.*

Venus was interesting. But what was even more interesting to Cook as he was beginning his voyage? *More interesting than Venus was the sealed envelope in the bottom of his sea chest. The envelope contained secret orders which Cook was to undertake when he finished watching Venus.*

Why were Cook's men excited about the trip to Tahiti? *The island was rumored to be full of warm beaches, fresh food, and the most beautiful women in the world.*

What was Cook's secret mission? *Cook was to sail south and find the Great Southern Continent for England!*

Cook went in search of the Great Southern Continent. What were the two islands that he first sailed around? *Cook first sailed around the islands of New Zealand.*

When Cook finally found the Great Southern Continent, he didn't realize that he had discovered it. What did he name the bay in which he first landed? *Cook named the area Botany Bay.*

What did Cook find the next year, when he went on his second voyage? *Cook found Antarctica and ice.*

What was Cook searching for on his third voyage? *He was searching for the Northwest Passage.*

Why were the Hawaiians treating Cook and his men so well? *They thought he was a god.*

When Cook and his men returned to Hawaii to repair their ship, they found a very different welcome. What was it like? *The natives were not happy to see him or the crew. They refused to feed the sailors and sabotaged Cook's ships.*

What happened to Cook? *One of the young warriors hit Cook in the head with a club. Most of the soldiers scrambled back to the ship, but Cook and three others lay dead on the beach.*

### Narration Exercise

"Captain Cook went to Tahiti to watch Venus cross the sun. But he was also supposed to look for the Great Southern Continent. He found New Zealand, and decided to go home. While he was going home, he anchored at Botany Bay. The bay was part of Australia—the Great Southern Continent. But Cook didn't know what he had discovered! He went on looking. Captain Cook was killed on his third voyage, when the natives of Hawaii grew angry with him because his sailors demanded so much food." OR

"The continent of Australia lay down to the south. The British government wanted to find it, so they sent Captain James Cook to look for it. Cook found the two islands of New Zealand and headed home. On his way home, he anchored in Australia, at Botany Bay. But he didn't realize that he had discovered a new continent! He made other voyages, searching for the Great Southern Continent and the Northwest Passage. Finally, he was killed in Hawaii."

## THE CONVICT SETTLEMENT

### Review Questions

When England lost the American colonies, where did they first send their prisoners? *They sent them to "hulks"—ancient ships that they moored in the rivers.*

What were the conditions like inside these "hulks"? *They were filthy, damp, dark, and filled with rats and insects.*

As they were running out of room on the "hulks," the English remembered another place they might send their prisoners. What place did they remember? *They remembered "New South Wales."*

What were some of the fears people had about life in Australia? *People were afraid of the Aborigines and of the wild animals. They were afraid of an area that they knew very little about.*

Why did the first governor, Arthur Phillip, want to find somewhere other than Botany Bay to settle? *Botany Bay was surrounded by swamp and had no fresh water.*

How did Arthur Phillip get around the fact that prison guards would not work beside the prisoners? *He made some of the convicts themselves colony leaders!*

Arthur Phillip and the colony of Sydney had a difficult first few years. Years later, what did an English ship bring to the colony? *An English ship brought more slaves—and more food.*

Some convicts realized that life in Australia was better than life in England. Why did they think so? *In Australia, if the prisoners worked hard, Arthur Phillip would give them a farm of their own.*

What was a squatter? *A squatter was someone who didn't buy land, but built a house on it and claimed it.*

How was life difficult for squatters in Australia? *Squatters had to fight off burning sun, drought, unexpected floods, and loneliness. There were no doctors, no stores, no towns. Squatters only got their mail two times per year, when the supply wagons came.*

What happened to the Aborigines as the English claimed more land in Australia? *As the English claimed more land, the Aborigines lost their land and the population shrank.*

### Narration Exercise

"After the American colonies rebelled, Britain couldn't send prisoners to America any more. Instead, they decided to send prisoners to Australia. They sent Arthur Phillip and eleven ships to settle in Australia. Phillip worked hard to build his colony. He tried to keep the prisoners from starving, and gave them land of their own if they worked hard. When he finally returned home, Australia had a colony of over four thousand people. Most of them were convicts!" OR

"The first English settlers in Australia were prisoners. They had to build their own houses, plant their own crops, and even pull their own plows. They almost starved to death! But the governor of the colony forced them to work hard and helped the colony survive. The colony grew. Eventually, thousands and thousands of prisoners and free people came to Australia and settled in five English colonies. But they also pushed the Aborigines off their land."

*Captain James Cook: Great Explorers*, by Enid Broderick (World Almanac, 2003). A simple, illustrated biography. (RA 2, IR 3-5)

*Captain Cook: Great Explorer of the Pacific (Great Explorers of the World)* by Stephen Feinstein (Enslow Publishers, Inc. 2010). A book about the life and voyages of James Cook with color illustrations and photos of the locations he traveled to and maps to help trace the journey. (IR 4-6)

*Explore with James Cook (Travel with the Great Explorers)*, by Lisa Dalrymple (Crabtree Publishing Company, 2016). An illustrative book of James Cook's voyages. It covers what he found, who were his crew members, how his crew defeated scurvy and how he died. (RA 3-4, IR 5-6)

*Lives of the Explorers: Discoveries, Disasters (and What the Neighbors Thought)* by Kathleen Krull & Kathryn Hewitt (HMH Books for Young Readers, 2018). Short chapters summarizing the adventures and lives of famous explorers, including Captain James Cook. (RA 2-3, IR 3-5).

*So You Want to Be an Explorer?* By Judith St. George, illus David Small (Philomel Books, 2005). Amusing and engaging illustrations make this an interesting book for kids, includes brief summaries of the exploits of famous explorers, including Captain James Cook. Ends with glossary of famous explorers along with the dates that they lived and a sentence about their adventures. (RA K-2, IR 3-4).

*You Wouldn't Want to Travel With Captain Cook!: A Voyage You'd Rather Not Make* by Mark Berlin, illus David Antram (Scholastic, 2006). Another humorous entry in the *You Wouldn't Want to Be* series, covers life on board ship more than Cook's discoveries and accomplishments. (IR 3-5).

*The Inner Planets: Mercury, Venus, and Mars*, by Sherman Hollar (Rosen Education Service, 2011). For scientifically minded students who want to find out more about Venus's transit. (RA 3-4, IR 5+)

*Hawaii*, by Angie Swanson (Capstone Press, 2016). An introduction to the history of the fiftieth state. (RA 2, IR 3-5)

*Australia (Rookie Read-About Geography)*, by Rebecca Hirsch (Children's Press, 2012). Very easy text; for reluctant readers or younger siblings. (RA 1, IR 2-3)

*Australia ABCs*, by Sarah Heiman (Picture Window Books, 2003). Nice illustrations and brief, readable paragraphs about the history, culture, and geography of Australia. (RA 1-2, IR 3-4)

*Australian Aborigines*, by World Book (World Book, 2009). A book with information and many color photos about the different tribes of the Aborigines, their cultures, beliefs, art and way of life. (RA 3, IR 4-6)

*Learning About Australia (Searchlight Books)*, by Lisa Owings (Lerner Publications, 2016). Learn about Australia's history, culture, geography, and natural resources in a book for young readers with many colorful photos and maps. (RA 3, IR 4-6)

*You Wouldn't Want to Be an 18th-Century British Convict!: A Trip to Australia You'd Rather Not Take*, by Meredith Costain, illus. David Antram (The Salariya Book Company Ltd, 2005). Times are hard in the late 18th century for the British. Find out what life is like and what happens to convicts in this humorous look at how British convicts were sent to Australia. (IR 4-6)

*Escape from Botany Bay: The True Story of Mary Bryant* by Gerald & Loretta Hausman (Irle Books, 2011) For advanced readers, the true story of a woman convicted in England of stealing a bonnet and sentenced to be sent to the penal colony of Australia. She becomes the first convict to get married there, and eventually she and her family escape back to England. (IR 6-7).

## Corresponding Literature Suggestions

*Carry On, Mr. Bowditch*, by Jean Lee Latham (Houghton Mifflin, 1955). This Newbery-winning tale of an eighteenth-century navigator paints a vivid picture of life aboard a sailing ship like James Cook's. A good family read-aloud, or for strong fourth-grade readers and older to read independently. Also available as an audiobook read by Jim Weiss (Well-Trained Mind Press, 2016). (RA 1-4, IR 4-6)

*The Mutiny on the Bounty*, by William Bligh, adapted by Deborah Kestel (Waldman, 2008) From the *Great Illustrated Classics* series, this adaptation of a classic work tells of mutiny on a British naval vessel off Tahiti during the era of Captain Cook; also consider the unabridged audio version read by Jonathan Reese (Tantor Media, 2005). (IR 3-5)

*Stowaway*, by Karen Hesse (Aladdin, 2002). A wonderful tale about a young boy named Nicholas Young who stows away on Captain Cook's ship during his historic voyage. A good family read-aloud, or for strong fourth-grade readers and older to read independently; also look for the unabridged audiobook version read by Daivd Cale (Listening Library, 2000). (RA 1-4, IR 4-6)

*Captain Cook's Christmas Pudding*, by Iris Van Rynbach (Boyds Mills Press, 1997). A granddaughter is making a Christmas pudding named after Captain James Cook with her grandmother while the grandmother tells her where some of the ingredients came from during Captain Cook's voyages. (RA1-2, IR 3)

*Cook's Cook: The Cook Who Cooked for Captain Cook* by Gavin Bishop. (Gecko, 2018). The voyage of Captain Cook as told by the ship's cook, including real recipes and engaging illustrations. (RA 1-2, IR 2-5).

*The Goat Who Sailed the World (Animal Stars #1)* by Jackie French (HarperCollins, 2019). This book recounts Captain Cook's voyage to map the transit of Venus and explore the Southern Continent from the perspective of the ship's 12-year-old servant and the grumpy resident goat, kept on board to provide fresh milk to the crew. (RA 2-3, IR 3-6).

*Sailing the Unknown: Around the World with Captain Cook*, by Michael J. Rosen, illus. Maria Cristina Pritelli (Creative Editions, 2012). A fictionalized diary of Nicholas Young, an eleven-year-old, who traveled with James Cook. (RA 3, IR 4)

*Dog of the Sea Waves* by James Rumford (Houghton Mifflin, 2004). Enchanting picture book written in both English and Hawaiian. Tells of Polynesian boys who found Hawaii long before Captain Cook came there; they encounter a strange animal (who turns out to be a seal). Includes notes about the native plants and animals described in the story. (RA 1-3, IR 2-4).

*Hawaiian Myths of Earth, Sea, and Sky* by Vivian L. Thompson, illus Leonard Weisgard (University of Hawaii Press, 1988). Chapter book of twelve myths from Hawaii, this would make a good read-aloud for younger children or an independent read for advanced readers. (RA 3-4, IR 4-7).

*Lydia and the Island Kingdom: A Story Based on the Real Life of Princess Liliuokalani of Hawaii* by Joan Holub, illus Nonna Aleshina (Simon Spotlight, 2007). Young Princess Lydia works to preserve the customs of old Hawaii by committing them to paper, for the very first time. Includes a timeline as well as a list of Hawaiian definitions and pronunciations. (RA K-1, IR 2-3).

*Where the Forest Meets the Sea*, by Jeannie Baker (William Morrow, 1988). A young boy and his father walk through the Australian jungle as he imagines the Aboriginal children who lived there long ago. (RA 1-2, IR 3-4)

*Down and Out Down Under (Geronimo Stilton #29)*, by Geronimo Stilton (Scholastic Inc., 2006). Geronimo, a mouse, takes a trip to Australia where he studies the history of Australia and meets an Aborigine. He is there with his friends to protect the wildlife. Very visually appealing book for reluctant readers. (RA 1-2, IR 3-5)

*Living in . . . Australia*, by Chloe Perkins, illus. Tom Woolley (Simon Spotlight, 2017). A cute picture book about a girl's life in Australia. The history of Australia is included in the story. (RA 1-2, IR 3-4)

## MAP WORK

### Captain Cook's Voyages *(Student Page 78, answer 325)*

1. Captain Cook took his crew south from Tahiti. He discovered New Zealand, sailed around New Zealand, and then to *Terra Australis*—Australia. Draw a blue line in the key next to "1st Voyage." Then draw a blue line from Tahiti to New Zealand, and from New Zealand to Botany Bay, Australia.
2. By this point, Cook had lost none of his crew to scurvy. Cook accomplished this feat by feeding his crew citrus fruit and sauerkraut. He traveled from Australia up to the Dutch East Indies, where many of his men contracted malaria and died. Draw a blue line from Botany Bay up around Australia toward the Dutch East Indies, and then around the bottom of Africa and up to Great Britain.
3. On his second voyage, Cook went toward Antarctica and found only ice. Find Antarctica and outline the edge of the continent in purple.
4. Cook sailed a third voyage to find the Northwest Passage by searching the western coast of North America. Find "3rd Voyage" in the key and draw an orange line in the box. Cook sailed to New Zealand, and then to the west coast of North America. He returned to Hawaii where he was eventually killed. Draw an orange line from Great Britain to New Zealand; from New Zealand, to the western coast of North America (in the upper right corner of your map); and then back to Hawaii.

**Coloring Page** When Captain James Cook and his ships first came to Hawaii, the native Hawaiians welcomed these visitors. But Cook and his men stayed too long and took too many things, and the Hawaiian people became angry with them. *(Student Page 79)*

## PROJECTS

### Science Project **Spotting Venus**

(Note: This activity will "work" some years, and will not work in others. Venus is easily visible 3 or 4 years out of every 10; also, the directions will vary if you are spotting Venus from different geographic areas.)

The transit of Venus between the Sun and the Earth has happened six times since the invention of the telescope. The seventh transit occurred in June, 2004; the eighth occurred in June, 2012. The next transit will be 105 years later—in December, 2117!

Although you may not see one of the rare transits of Venus, you may find Venus in the night sky. Besides the Sun and the Moon, Venus is the brightest object in the sky. You will have to look for Venus near sunrise or sunset, as you will (usually) not be able to see it in the middle of the night. To locate the west, remember to look outside when the Sun goes down. Venus will be near the horizon in the west (depending on the time of year, southwest or southeast), so when you go out to find Venus, you will begin facing the direction the sun goes down in.

Some interesting facts about Venus:

- it is the second planet from the Sun, and Earth's planetary neighbor
- it has the longest day of any planet—243 Earth days
- it is the only planet where the Sun rises in the west and sets in the east
- it has a poisonous atmosphere—it's full of sulfuric acid!

- the first spacecraft to soft-land on Venus, the Soviet Venera, was "cooked" 23 minutes after touchdown in the nearly 900 degree F atmosphere (in 1970)

## GAME ACTIVITY Australia Day, January 26th

Arthur Phillip started the British settlement in Australia on January 26th. Every year, Australians celebrate January 26th as a national holiday, called Australia Day. Find these words from Chapter 24 on the word search!

*Materials:*
- ☐ Student Page 80: Word Search Sheet
- ☐ pencil

*Directions:* Find and circle the words on the list! They may be up, down, diagonally, or across, backwards or forwards.

## CRAFT ACTIVITY Planting Well

The first British settlers to land in Australia were surprised by much of what they found. They were used to different weather, different plants and animals, and different ways of doing things. They soon discovered that how they had farmed in England was not going to work in this dry, sunny climate. Arthur Phillip sent for supplies from Calcutta until the new colony could become self-sufficient. Try this experiment with carrot seeds and see what the colonists discovered when it came to growing a crop.

*Materials:*
- ☐ Carrot seeds (or squash)
- ☐ Potting soil
- ☐ Sand
- ☐ Clayish dirt
- ☐ 3 Styrofoam cups or small pots
- ☐ Permanent marker

*Directions:*
1. Place the cups in a row. Using a pencil or pen, gently poke a hole in the bottom of each cup.
2. Gently fill each cup with a different type of dirt. Using the marker, label each cup with the kind of soil you used. Write the date on the opposite side to help with record keeping.
3. Following the instructions on the back of the seed packet, gently poke a hole in the top of the soil. Insert at least three seeds into the hole. Water gently.
4. Continue to water the cups. Keep a record of what happens. Which seed sprouts first? Put a star on that cup. How long does it take for the other seeds to catch up? Make a note of the date it sprouts on the cup. Write your observations. If you made a prediction, did it match what actually happened? How do you think the types of soil affected the people who started to build colonies in Australia?
5. Option for older students: On your record keeping sheet, make a prediction about what you think might happen in each of the cups.

## CRAFT ACTIVITY Message Sticks

The Aborigines had many languages and dialects, but they did not have a written language. Instead, they used painted and carved "message sticks" with pictures that reminded the messenger what the message content was. It also proved that the message and the messenger were genuine. You are going to create your own Message Stick.

*Materials:*

- ☐ Long, thick stick about half as long as your arm
- ☐ White acrylic paint
- ☐ Acrylic paints, colors of your choice
- ☐ Paint brushes, variety of widths
- ☐ Newspapers
- ☐ Hairdryer (optional)

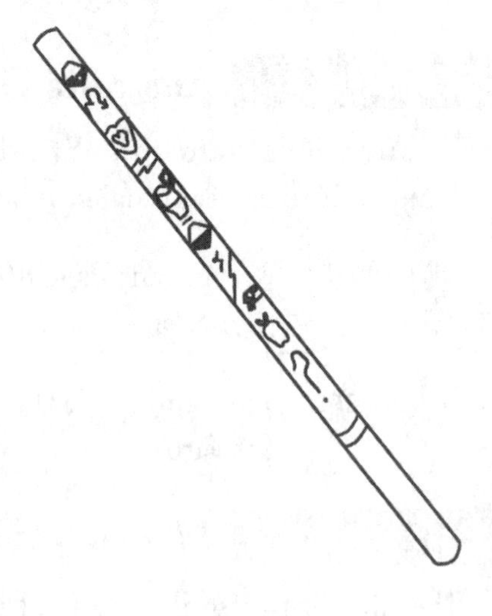

*Directions:*

1. Lay out the newspaper to keep your work area clean. Gently rub off any dirt or loose bark from your stick. Paint the stick white and let it dry, or use the hairdryer to speed up the drying. Be careful not to hold the hot dryer too close to the paint because it could cause it to bubble up.
2. While the paint is drying, draw your message on a piece of paper, to make sure you know what you want to say. Remember, you cannot use any written words—only pictures and symbols.
3. Paint the message on the white stick. Let it dry.
4. Send your message!

# Revolution Gone Sour

## Encyclopedia Cross-References

*UBWH 170, UILE 332-333*
*KIHW 522-523, KHE 318-319*

## THE STORMING OF THE BASTILLE

### Review Questions

In the years after the French helped the Americans in the American revolution, what did the French people come to think about their king? *They thought their king was wrong when he claimed he had a divine right to rule France and to do as he pleased.*

How had Louis XIV and Louis XV made themselves unpopular with the poor people of France? *The kings had made the poor people pay more and more taxes.*

The French people were divided into three estates. Which people belonged to each of the estates? *Roman Catholic priests were the First Estate. The noblemen of France were the Second Estate. All of the merchants, shopkeepers, doctors, farmers, lawyers, judges, wagon drivers, peasants, bakers, tailors, and cobblers of France belonged to the Third Estate.*

To which estate did most people of France belong? *Most people of France belonged to the Third Estate.*

What was the greatest difference between the people of the Second and the Third Estate? *The noblemen of the Second Estate were rich, while the peasants of the Third Estate were extremely poor.*

Why was Louis XVI's wife Marie-Antoinette unpopular? *She was unpopular because she was spending a lot of money, while the poor people of France suffered.*

When Louis XVI tried to make the noblemen of the Second Estate pay taxes, what did they announce? *They announced that they would only pay taxes if representatives of all three Estates met and agreed that taxes were necessary.*

Can you remember one way in which members of the Third Estate were made to feel unimportant at this meeting? *They could only wear black clothes; they could only use the side doors; there were no reserved seats for them at the special mass.*

Could the Third Estate outvote the First and Second Estates? *No—because each estate had only one vote!*

What did the Third Estate rename the meeting? *They named it the National Assembly.*

When the noblemen told Louis XVI that the Third Estate was trying to convince the First Estate to join them, what did Louis XVI do? *He locked the Third Estate out of the meeting room so they could not vote.*

What was the Tennis Court Oath? *The members of the new National Assembly met on a tennis court and swore to make a new Constitution for France.*

Why did Louis XVI fear that his soldiers would not fire on the rebellious people of Paris? *He knew that his soldiers were also part of the Third Estate.*

Where did the people of Paris go to find gunpowder? *They went to the Bastille; they then freed the seven prisoners, chopped off the keeper's head, and ran through the streets with it stuck on the edge of a pike.*

What was the date of the Fall of the Bastille? *The Fall of the Bastille occurred on July 14, 1789.*

What kind of government did the National Assembly plan to institute? *They planned to have a government in which the king followed the laws, and in which everyone was equal.*

### Narration Exercise

Because there is a lot of information in this chapter, use "directed narration." Say to the child, "Tell me about the Three Estates of France, and who belonged to each Estate—and what taxes they paid." An acceptable answer would be, "The First Estate were Roman Catholic priests, who didn't pay taxes. The Second Estate were the noblemen of France. They were very wealthy and paid very few taxes. The Third Estate were the rest of the people in France. They paid almost all of the taxes!"

Now say to the child, "Tell me what happened at the meeting of the three Estates. Be sure to mention the storming of the Bastille!" An acceptable answer would be, "The three Estates all met together at Versailles, because the noblemen said that they would only pay taxes if all three Estates agreed. At the meeting, the members of the Third Estate begged the priests to join them. They took an oath to make a new constitution for France—one that would make everyone in France equal. When the people of Paris heard about the Third Estate's revolt, they stormed the royal prison of Paris to get gunpowder. This was called the Storming of the Bastille. Now the people of the Third Estate ruled in Paris!"

## THE REIGN OF TERROR

### Review Questions

What people wanted to put Louis XVI back on the throne? *The clergy and the well-off members of the Third Estate—the doctors, lawyers, and merchants—wanted to put Louis XVI back on the throne.*

Who was the leader of the Third Estate? *The leader of the Third Estate was Maximilien de Robespierre.*

What did the Assembly decide to do with the First and Second Estates? *The Assembly outlawed the First and Second Estates.*

What title did every Frenchman receive? *Every Frenchman was known as "Citizen."*

When the king and his family tried to escape, what happened? *A man recognized the king because his face was on France's money! He warned people in the next town, and a mob stopped Louis' carriage.*

After a few years, hatred for the king was waning. What happened that renewed the people's hatred of him? *Austria and Prussia were threatening to invade France and destroy Paris if any harm came to the king.*

What type of government did France finally decide to adopt? *They decided they would be a republic.*

After the French decided to be a republic, they renamed the National Assembly. What was the new name of the governing body in France? *The new name of the National Assembly was the National Convention.*

What did Louis XVI urge his son as he was led to the guillotine? *He urged him not to seek revenge.*

Even after Louis XVI was beheaded, things did not immediately go well for the Republic. What committee did the National Convention form, and who was its leader? *The National Convention formed the Committee of Public Safety, and they put Maximilien Robespierre in charge.*

What did Robespierre do with anyone he thought disloyal? *He arrested him and put him to death.*

Why did the National Convention begin to worry about Robespierre? *They thought he had too much power, and he had put many people to death in his Reign of Terror.*

How did Robespierre die? *After he was arrested by the National Convention, he was beheaded.*

### Narration Exercise

Because there is a lot of information in this chapter, use "directed narration." Say to the child, "Tell me what happened to France after Louis XVI was executed." An acceptable answer would be, "France was a republic, but many French were afraid that the republic might fall. So they formed the Committee of Public Safety. Its head was Robespierre. He was allowed to arrest and execute anyone who might not be loyal to the Republic. Robespierre became a tyrant. He had thousands and thousands of people killed! Finally, the National Convention arrested Robespierre and executed him."

## Additional History Reading

*Getting to Know France and French*, by Nicola Wright, illus. Kim Wooley (Barrons, 1993). This simple book is excellent for younger or reluctant readers; it contains easy text about France's geography and history, along with illustrations and plenty of French words and phrases. (RA 2, IR 3-5)

*France (Horrible Histories Special)* by Terry Deary, illus Martin Brown (Scholastic Hippo, 2002). The popular Horrible Histories series tackles all the nasty bits of French history, including an excellent section on the French revolution. *Note: This series is published and available in the UK, but can be ordered through Amazon and a Kindle version is available.* (IR 3-6). **E-Only.**

*The Cartoon History of the Modern World, Part 2: From the Bastille to Baghdad*, by Larry Gonick (Harper, 2009). This comic book style of retelling of the French Revolution provides a different approach to learning the story. The French Revolution starts on page 24. (IR 5-6)

*The French Revolution (Cornerstones of Freedom)* by Josh Gregory (Children's Press, 2013). Story of the French Revolution through the rise of Napoleon. (RA 3-4, IR 4-6).

*The French Revolution Explained for Kids (The English Reading Tree)*, by Keith Goodman (Great Little Read, 2018). This well-written text explains the causes of the French Revolution and the events that transpired during it. (RA 3, IR 4-6)

*The French Revolution (Days of Change)*, by Kate Riggs (Creative Co., 2009). This illustrated book explains why the French Revolution happened, and covers the period from the early years of King Louis XVI and Marie Antoinette to the rise of Napoleon. (IR 4-6) **LFA**

*You Wouldn't Want to Be an Aristocrat in the French Revolution: A Horrible Time in Paris You'd Rather Avoid* by Jim Pipe, illus. David Antram (Franklin Watts, 2007). Another humorous entry in the *You Wouldn't Want to Be* series. Told from the point of view of a British aristocrat trapped in France during the time of the French Revolution, this book will appeal visually to younger readers but some of the grim details are better suited for older readers (IR 3-5).

*Marie Antoinette: "Madame Deficit" (The Thinking Girl's Treasury of Dastardly Dames)* by Liz Hockinson, illus. Peter Malone (Goosebottom Books, 2011). Using visual elements such as timelines, maps, and photos of key places from the time as they look today, this book helps the reader to understand who Marie Antoinette was as a ruler, and how and why the events of the French Revolution occurred. (IR 3-8).

*Marie Antoinette, Queen of France (Queens and Princesses)*, by Mary Englar (Capstone Press, 2008). A short biography from Marie Antoinette's wedding to her death. (IR 3-4)

*Who Was Marie Antoinette?* By Dana Meachen Rau, illus. John O'Brien (Penguin, 2015). Part of the popular *Who Was/What Was* series, this book covers the life of Marie Antoinette and, in grim detail, her eventual death. Great for reluctant readers because there are illustrations on nearly every page. Written at a third grade reading level, but some details may be a bit too intense for younger kids. (IR 3-7).

*Robespierre: Master of the Guillotine (A Wicked History)* by John DiConsiglio (Franklin Watts, 2008). For advanced readers or use sections as a read-aloud. This book about Maximilien Robespierre, part of the *Wicked History* series, includes his participation in the French Revolution and the Reign of Terror. (RA 3-4, IR 4-8)

*Top Ten Worst Wicked Rulers You Wouldn't Want to Meet*, by Fiona MacDonald, illus. David Antram (Sterling, 2013). Comic biographies of wicked rules throughout history. Contains biographical information on Maximilien Robespierre and short facts about the French Revolution. Maximilien Robespierre is talked about on page 18.

*Mesmerized: How Ben Franklin Solved a Mystery that Baffled all of France* by Mara Rockliff (Candlewick Press, 2015). Interesting story about how Ben Franklin helped the king and queen of France by using the scientific method to explain a mysterious force. (RA 1-3, IR 3-5).

*Who Was Wolfgang Amadeus Mozart?*, by Yona Zeldis McDonough (Grosset & Dunlap, 2003). A chapter book about Mozart, a famous composer during Marie Antoinette's life. They met when Marie Antoinette was young. (RA 3, IR 4-6)

## Corresponding Literature Suggestions

*The Bad Queen: Rules and Instructions for Marie-Antoinette* by Carolyn Meyer (Harcourt, 2010). For advanced readers, this middle-grade novelization of the life of Marie-Antoinette in the years before the French revolution is well-written and engaging. Each chapter begins with a rule or instruction for life as a queen that Marie-Antoinette sometimes struggles to follow and sometimes simply ignores outright. (IR 4-8).

*The Lacemaker and the Princess* by Kimberly Brubaker Bradley (Margaret K McElderry Books, 2009). Fast-paced tale about friendship in the time of Marie Antoinette. (RA 2-3, IR 3-5).

*Marie Antoinette, Princess of Versailles: Austria-France, 1769*, by Kathryn Lasky (Scholastic, 2000). Part of *The Royal Diaries* series, this chapter book for slightly older readers takes the form of a diary kept by the young Marie; an epilogue with engravings and other contemporary illustrations tell of Marie's execution. (IR 4-6) **E-Only.**

*Moi & Marie Antoinette*, by Lynn Cullen, illus. Amy Young (Bloomsbury Children's Book, 2006). A dog travels with young Marie Antoinette to adulthood. (RA 1-2, IR 3-4)

*Den of Thieves (Cat Royal Series)*, by Julia Golding (Frost Wolf, 2018). Follow the adventures of Cat Royal during her stay in Paris, France, where she is recruited as a spy during the French Revolution. (IR 5-6)

*The Golden Hour*, by Maiya Williams (Harry N. Abrams, 2006). Thirteen-year-old Rowan and his two friends go back in time to find Rowan's sister in Paris during the French Revolution. (IR 4-6)

*Madame Tussaud's Apprentice: An Untold Story of Love in the French Revolution* by Kathleen Benner Duble (Simon Pulse, 2014). A young artist is forced to teach drawing to the King's sister at Versailles and finds herself caught between the revolution growing in the streets, where she comes from, and the French aristocracy, not all of whom are as evil as she had been led to believe. (IR 4-7).

*Redoute: The Man Who Painted Flowers*, by Carolyn Croll (Philomel Books, 1996). A picture-book biography (with fictionalized scenes) of the French artist known as the "Raphael of Flowers;" Redoute, who lived through the French Revolution, the Republic, and the Reign of Terror, was famous for his nature paintings. (RA 2, IR 3-5)

*The Scarlet Pimpernel*, by Baroness Orczy (Puffin, 1997). The original version of this classic tale of an English nobleman who rescues French aristocrats from the guillotine is long and complicated, but consider either the abridged audiobook (Audio Holdings, 2009, read by Simon Williams) or the unabridged audiobook (Blackstone, 2005, read by Ralph Cosham). Susan strongly recommends her favorite version—the 1982 movie version with Anthony Andrews and Ian McKellen, available on DVD and on streaming formats.

*A Tale of Two Cities*, by Charles Dickens (Bantam, 1984). This classic tale of heroism and sacrifice during the French Revolution would make a very long family read-aloud; consider the audiobook versions on CD, either abridged/adapted (Well-Trained Mind Press, 2015, read by Jim Weiss) or unabridged (Page2Page, 2019, read by Jerry Trant). You can also find the *Great Illustrated Classics* version, adapted for 3rd-4th grade readers (ed. Marion Leighton, published by Spotlight, 2002).

*Time Machine 14: Blade of the Guillotine*, by Arthur Byron Cover (Ibooks for Young Readers, rev. ed. 2017). A book similar to the *Choose Your Own Adventure* series where the reader is a time traveler with a mission to find a missing diamond necklace that helped spark the French Revolution. Includes background information about events during this time period. (IR 4-6)

## MAP WORK

### Fighting in France *(Student Page 81, answer 325)*

1. Find Versailles, the site of the meetings of "The General Assembly" and "The National Assembly." Draw a purple circle around the dot that represents Versailles.
2. Paris was only twelve miles from Versailles. The commoners of Paris heard of the Third Estate's revolt and prepared to join the revolution. Find the key on your map, and color the top box orange. Draw an orange circle around the city of Paris.
3. Several cities in France supported the National Assembly and the commoners of Paris in the revolution of 1789. The following were some of those many cities: Marseille, Montpellier, Bordeaux, Rennes, Caen, Lyon, Troyes, Amien. Find these cities on the map and draw an orange circle around each dot that represents those cities.
4. Find the three areas on your map that have been marked with small dashed lines. Remember that throughout the countryside, peasants revolted, invaded the mansions of the rich, and murdered the hated noblemen of the Second Estate. Color these areas orange.
5. Many in France, called Royalists, did not support the revolution of 1789. Find the key, and color the lower box brown. Color the remaining area of France brown. (Note: The division between those who supported the revolution and those who did not was more complex than the map shows. The map has been simplified for the purpose of this activity.)

## Coloring Pages

Marie Antoinette, the Queen of France, was not a cruel woman, but she didn't pay attention to how unhappy the people of France were, and she continued to spend large amounts of money on expensive dresses and fancy things. *(Student Page 82)*

The Bastille, the royal prison of Paris, was an old fortress with eight towers and walls fifteen feet thick. Do you remember what happened to the Bastille in 1789? (See Chapter 25 of *The Story of the World*.) *(Student Page 83)*

## GAME PROJECT Storm the Bastille! Game

Materials:
- ☐ *The Story of the World, Volume 3*
- ☐ Student Page 84: Storm the Bastille Gameboard
- ☐ Student Page 85: Game Card Template
- ☐ game pieces, beans, coins, buttons or small plastic toys to serve as player markers
- ☐ die

Directions:

*Set up:*
1. Enlarge the game board to fit on an 11" x 14" sheet of cardstock. Also copy the game cards onto cardstock and cut them out.
2. Color the board and the designs around it. (optional)
3. Glue the game board onto cardboard or posterboard to add strength. (optional)
4. Cover with clear contact paper. (optional)
5. Select game pieces, one for each player.

*To play:*
1. All players begin by placing game pieces in the center of the board. The youngest player gets to start the game.
2. You may not leave the "Bastille" until you roll a 6. Once you roll a 6, you may begin by placing your game piece on the starting square. You cannot move forward until the next turn.
3. On each of your turns, roll the die. Before you move, you have to answer the question on the next card in the stack. If you don't get it right, you have to stay where you are. If you get it right, you get to move forward the number of spaces on your die. Place used cards at the bottom of the pile. (Note: Decide before you start if you want to use your *Story of the World* book to help answering the questions.)
4. Continue moving around the board. When you land on the end of an arrow, you may slide to the arrow's point.
5. If you land on a square that is already occupied, the player who was there first must answer the next question in the stack. If he cannot, he moves back to the square you started your turn on.
6. *REVOLTING*! Everyone is allowed to *Revolt* only once in the game. To *Revolt* you must declare your desire BEFORE you roll the dice. Once you call the *Revolt*, you are allowed to change places with another player and then you are done with your turn. *You cannot revolt on the last (fourth) side of the board.*
7. END SQUARE—The winner is the first one to the *End Square.*

## CRAFT PROJECT: Red Citizen Cap

The people surrounded the great Bastille. They had heard that an army was marching towards them to stop their pursuit of freedom. They needed gunpowder to fight them—gunpowder locked inside the Bastille! They loaded a cannon and aimed it at the Bastille's iron gates. Soon they were inside, and they freed the prisoners that had been locked away inside. Some of the prisoners joined the mob, still wearing their red prisoners' caps. These caps became one of the French Revolution's most powerful symbols of freedom! Soon, citizens across France wore the red cap to show their dedication to the ideals of "Freedom! Equality! Brotherhood!"

Materials:
- ☐ Student Page 86 and 87: Hat Pattern
- ☐ Red fabric (either knit, fleece, or felt; 24" x 13")
- ☐ Straight pins
- ☐ Red thread
- ☐ Needle or sewing machine or hot glue gun

Directions:

1. Measure the "revolutionary's" head.
2. Enlarge pattern piece #2 so that the bottom side measurement is half the head-width plus a one inch seam allowance for sewing. Enlarge pattern piece #1 to the same size.
3. Cut out the pattern pieces and tape them together as shown in figure 1.
4. Fold the fabric in half length-wise. Lay the pattern down with the straight side (side B in figure 2) along the fold. Pin the pattern to the fabric and cut it out. Do not cut along the folded fabric side.
5. Sew or glue along the open back edge (side A in figure 2). Finish the bottom edge of the hat opening (side C, figure 2) if needed.
6. Turn the hat right side out, so the seam is on the inside. Press the hat gently so the seam lays flat. Make a cuff on the hat opening (side C, figure 2) about 1½" wide. Tack the cuff up with glue or a few stitches at the back seam. (See figure 3.)
7. If you make a revolutionary ribbon (the last project on this page), you can pin or glue it to your revolutionary hat!

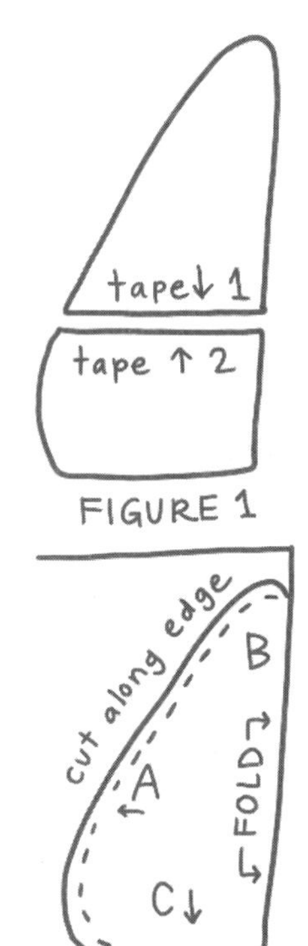


## GOVERNMENT PROJECT Two Declarations of Independence

In 1776, Thomas Jefferson drafted the American Declaration of Independence. In 1789, twelve years later, Thomas Jefferson helped the Marquis de Lafayette, a French nobleman, write out a similar declaration for France—the Declaration of the Rights of Man and of the Citizen. Like the Declaration of Independence, the Declaration of the Rights of Man tried to explain that human beings have certain rights—and that when those rights are violated, citizens of a country can revolt against the government that violated them.

In some ways, the two declarations were very similar—and in some ways, very different.

*Materials:* □ Student Pages 88–93: Two Declarations

*Directions:*

1. Read the sections of the two declarations together. The American declaration is a list of specific crimes committed by the King of England against the American colonies. The American declaration explains the principles that prove the King of England was at fault. How did the King of England violate each one of the principles laid out in the American declaration?
2. At the end of the declarations, pay special attention to the signatures. The Declaration of Independence was signed by representatives of every new state. The Declaration of the Rights of Man and of the Citizen was signed by one man, Louis XVI—but he only signed the Declaration because he was forced to. He never intended to keep any of its terms! And soon, the French Revolution and the Reign of Terror would result in the rule of Robespierre—who violated the rights of more French citizens than any king had ever done!

*Note to the Parent:* This is a difficult activity, but students who show a particular interest in government will enjoy comparing the two documents. Be prepared to read the sections out loud to the student, if necessary. Give all necessary help with vocabulary words. Feel free to paraphrase or explain any difficult sentences. Neither declaration has been rewritten, but the Articles of the French declaration have been re-ordered so that they correspond in order to the points of the American declaration.

## CRAFT PROJECT **Tricolor Revolution Ribbon**

French revolutionaries wore the tricolor ribbon to show their commitment to the revolution. Make your own Revolutionary Ribbon, using craft foam. You can stick it on the side of your hat, or you can wear it proudly pinned on your clothes.

*Materials:*
- □ blue, white and red small sheets of craft foam
- □ 3 small plates of different sizes
- □ scissors
- □ Tacky glue or hot glue gun (regular glue doesn't hold)
- □ craft jewelry pin (at craft stores in the jewelry making section)

*Directions:*

1. Place the largest plate on the blue foam. Trace around its perimeter and cut out the circle. Do the same with the medium-sized plate on the white foam and the smallest plate on the red foam.
2. Glue them together, with the smallest circle on top, then the medium-sized circle, and then the largest circle on bottom. Let it dry.
3. Using the hot glue gun, glue the pin to the center of the Revolutionary Ribbon. Once dry, pin it to your shirt or hat.

# Catherine the Great

## Encyclopedia Cross-References

*UBWH 186, UILE 318*
*KIHW 510-511, KHE 310-311*

## PRINCESS CATHERINE COMES TO RUSSIA

### Review Questions

According to the empress Catherine the Great, where did kings get the power to rule? *Catherine thought that God gave power to kings.*

From what two countries did Catherine's parents come? *Her father was German, and her mother was Swedish.*

Why did the Empress Elizabeth invite Catherine to Russia? *She thought that Catherine would be a good wife for her nephew, Peter Ulrich.*

Catherine's parents had different reactions to the prospect of her becoming a queen. Which parent was excited for Catherine? *Catherine's mother Johanna was thrilled that Catherine might one day be queen.*

What promise did Catherine's father ask her to make? *He asked her to promise that she would not leave the Lutheran church.*

What did Catherine remember about her first meeting with Peter Ulrich? *She remembered an odd, small, white-faced boy, bad-tempered and full of strange twitches. Even though he was only ten, he drank so much wine at dinner that he had to be carried away from the table. He had been unfriendly and rude to his servants, and seemed to want only to play toy soldiers with one of his servants.*

Where did Catherine go when she was to meet Peter Ulrich again? *Catherine went to St. Petersburg, the capital of Russia.*

Did Catherine like Peter more or less when she got to know him better? *The more she got to know Peter, the less she liked him.*

Can you remember two things that she disliked about Peter? *He was rude to servants and courtiers; he made unpleasant noises and loud jokes in church; he refused to speak Russian; he wanted to live in Prussia.*

What was one of Empress Elizabeth's qualities that made Catherine afraid to tell her she didn't want to marry Peter? *Elizabeth was a big, frightening woman who flew into rages at her servants.*

What happened to Peter Ulrich four months after his engagement that made him barely recognizable to Catherine? *Peter came down with smallpox.*

What subjects did Catherine read about during the nine lonely years following her marriage ceremony? *She spent the nine lonely years reading books of history and philosophy, books about military tactics, and books about the emperors of Rome and their strategies for ruling their empire.*

What was happening to Peter during this time? How was his behavior changing? *Peter was going mad and his behavior was becoming odder than ever.*

What happened to Catherine's baby right after he was born? *The Empress Elizabeth took the baby into her own room, left Catherine alone, and wouldn't let her see her baby for six weeks.*

When Catherine recovered, what did she begin to plan to do? *She started to plan to rule in place of her husband.*

Did Catherine lead a revolt as soon as the empress died? *No; she was expecting another baby, so she waited.*

### Narration Exercise

"Catherine was a princess from Germany, not a Russian princess. But she came to Russia to marry Peter Ulrich, the heir to the throne. While they were engaged, Peter Ulrich caught smallpox and became disfigured. He also grew rude and unpleasant. But Catherine was afraid to break the engagement! After they were married, Peter often ignored Catherine. She spent years reading about great rulers of the past, and wondering whether she could rule in her husband's place. But when Peter inherited the throne, Catherine was expecting a baby. She decided to wait until she was stronger before starting a revolt!" OR

"The Empress Elizabeth invited Catherine to Russia to meet the heir to the Russian throne, Peter. Catherine didn't like Peter, but she was afraid to tell the empress! So she married him—but she was very unhappy. Peter didn't treat her well, and the empress took her baby son away and raised him herself! Catherine knew that the army respected her and the Russian people liked her. She planned to take over the throne after the empress died! But when Elizabeth died, Catherine had to wait. She was expecting a baby, and she was too weak to lead a rebellion."

## CATHERINE THE GREAT

### Review Questions

After Empress Elizabeth's death, what did Catherine do to show the people of Russia how devout she was? *She went to the cathedral every day to mourn Elizabeth's death.*

While Catherine mourned Elizabeth's death, what did Peter do? *He threw huge feasts, told the court not to wear mourning clothes, and told jokes when he visited the empress's body in the cathedral.*

Peter made several changes in the army. Can you list two? *He wanted the army to be more like the Prussian army; he made the army wear the uniform of the Prussian soldiers; he planned to teach them how to march and fight like Prussians.*

What did the army think of Peter's plans? *The Russian army hated the Prussians and began to think that Catherine would be a better ruler.*

When Peter needed more money for the royal treasury, where did he decide he would get that money? *Peter decided he would get the money by selling the land of the Russian Orthodox Church.*

Did most of the army support Catherine as the new empress of Russia? *Yes, most of them supported her; few of them supported Peter's son, Paul.*

What other important Russian official supported Catherine? *The head priest of Petersburg, the Metropolitan, blessed Catherine and pronounced her Empress.*

Catherine did not let Peter go live in Prussia. What was she afraid of? *Catherine knew that if Peter went to Prussia, he might be able to convince the Prussians to invade Russia and help him take his throne back.*

How did Peter supposedly die? What was the problem with this story? *Peter supposedly died in a fight with Prince Baritainsky. The problem with the story was that Peter appeared to have been strangled.*

What were two of the Western ideas that Catherine brought to Russia? *She rewrote Russia's confusing, ancient laws so that her people would have more rights. She told her ministers of state that no one could be tortured for information. She opened new schools and started the first college for Russian women. She even made a woman the director of the Russian Academy of Sciences. Catherine opened new hospitals and brought in doctors from the West to improve the health of the Russian people.*

What did "equality" mean to Catherine? *Equality meant that Russians had to obey the same laws.*

By the end of Catherine's reign, who had more power (than when she began her reign)? Who had less power? *By the end of her reign, her noblemen had even more power over the peasants and serfs who lived on their land—and these poor Russians had grown hungrier and more ragged than ever before.*

### Narration Exercise

Since there is a great deal of information in this chapter, use "directed narration." First, say to the student, "How did Catherine become Empress?" An acceptable answer might be, "Catherine knew that the army disliked Peter because he wanted to make them more like Prussians. The Russian Orthodox Church disliked him because he sold some of their land. So Catherine dressed like an empress and asked the army and the Church to support her. Peter had to sign a paper giving up his throne. He wanted to go live in Prussia—but Catherine ordered him to stay in one of his palaces. Not long after, Peter was mysteriously killed."

Now, say to the student, "Can you tell me at least three things that Catherine did to change Russia during her years as empress?" Any three items from the answer above are acceptable.

## Additional History Reading

*Also see the history lists in Chapter Seventeen for more books about Russia.*

*Catherine the Great: Empress of Russia* by Zu Vincent (Scholastic, 2009). For advanced readers or use sections as a read-aloud, this book, part of the *Wicked History* series, covers the life of Catherine from her birth as a princess in what is now Germany, to her death in 1796. Includes a timeline and glossary. (RA 3-4, IR 4-8).

*Good Night Stories for Rebel Girls: 100 Tales of Extraordinary Women*, by Elena Favili and Francesca Cavallo (Timbuktu Labs, 2016). A quick biography of many famous women from hundreds of years ago to the present day. Catherine the Great gets her own entry.

*Herstory: Women Who Changed the World*, Ruth Ashby and Deborah Gore Ohrn, eds. (Viking Books, 1995). A collection of read-aloud two-page biographies of many famous women, including Catherine the Great (also recommended for use in other chapters). (RA 2, IR 3-5) **OOP**

*Lives of Extraordinary Women: Rulers, Rebels (and What the Neighbors Thought)* by Kathleen Krull (HMH Books for Young Readers, 2000). Short chapters summarizing the lives and accomplishments of famous women in history, including Catherine the Great. (RA 3-4, IR 3-5)

*Ten Queens: Portraits of Women of Power* by Milton Meltzer, illus Bethanne Andersen (Dutton Juvenile, 2003). Good for a read aloud or advanced reader. Does a good job of providing historical context for each queen. **Please note: there are some discussions of marital infidelity in a few chapters, including Catherine's, that parents may wish to preview.** (RA 4-5, IR 4-8).

*What Would She Do?: 25 True Stories of Trailblazing Rebel Women*, by Kay Woodward (Scholastic Inc., 2018). A great collection of one-to-two page profiles of strong female leaders. A question is posed about how each leader might handle a hypothetical certain modern-day situation, and a quotation from each leader is provided. Catherine the Great has her own entry. (RA 3, IR 4-6)

*Russia: The Culture, by Greg Nickles* (Crabtree Publications, 2000). A simple-to-read exploration of historic Russia customs, with special attention to festivals and religious holidays of the Russian Orthodox Church. (RA 2, IR 3-5)

*Russia (Country Profiles)* by Amy Rechner (Bellwether Media, 2017). Engaging book about modern Russia but includes a map, timeline, and numerous photos of well-known places in the country that can help bring a broader perspective to a historical study of the country. (RA 2-3, IR 3-5).

*Russia (Enchantment of the World)* by Nel Yomtov. (Children's Press, 2013). This book about Russia includes a chapter on Russian history with a short but thorough coverage of Catherine the Great. Also includes a timeline of Russian history alongside a world history timeline that enhances the connection between this chapter and surrounding chapters. (IR 4-6).

*The Icon Handbook: A Guide to Understanding Icons and the Liturgy Symbols and Practices of the Russian Orthodox Church*, by. David Coomler (Templegate, 1995). A little expensive if purchased new, but used copies are available for a very low price. A challenge for more advanced students: investigate the origins of Russian Orthodox icons and symbols that arose during the times of Catherine and Peter. (IR 5-up)

## Corresponding Literature Suggestions

*For more literature suggestions, see Chapter Seventeen.*

*Catherine: The Great Journey, Russia, 1743 (The Royal Diaries)* by Kristiana Gregory (Scholastic, 2005). Written from the viewpoint of Princess Sophie Augusta Fredericka of Anhalt-Zerbst, who later became Catherine the Great. Diary format makes this book easy to be read in small chunks. (IR 3-5).

*A Royal Ride: Catherine the Great's Great Invention* by Kristen Fulton, illus Lucy Fleming (Margaret K. McElderry Books, 2019). This picture book tells an embellished version of Catherine the Great's actual connection to the invention of roller coasters. (RA K-2, IR 2-4).

*When Catherine the Great and I Were Eight!*, by Cari Best, illus. Giselle Potter (Farrar, Straus and Giroux, 2003). A Russian writer tells a tale about a little girl and her Russian grandmother nicknamed Catherine the Great. Tells about Russian culture. (RA 1-3)

*How Much Land Does a Man Need?* by Leo Tolstoy, illus. Elena Abesinova (Interlink Publishing, 2001). The famous Russian novelist's fable about a greedy landowner who comes to a very bad end; this story reflects the tensions between the aristocracy and the peasants of Russia. (RA 2-3, IR 4-6) **E-Only.**

*Kashtanka*, by Anton Chekhov, trans. Ronald Meyer, illus. Gennady Spirin (Gulliver Books, 1995). An actual tale of the great Russian writer Chekhov, illustrated for children. (RA 2-3, IR 4-6) **E-Only.**

*Favorite Russian Fairy Tales*, by Arthur Ransome (Dover Publications, 1995). A classic collection of traditional Russian stories, including the story of the Firebird and the tale of Baba Yaga. Large print and excellent prose, for independent reading on an advanced third grade level and above. (RA 2-3, IR 3-6)

*The Tale of the Firebird*, trans. by Tatiana Popova, illus. Gennady Spirin (Philomel Books, 2002). A picture-book retelling of the famous Russian tale, with illustrations reminiscent of Eastern Orthodox images. (RA 2, IR 3-5)

*The Pearl: A Russian Love Story* by Nan Richardson, illus Alexandra Young (Umbrage, 2011). Beautifully illustrated story set in Russia during the time of Catherine the Great. Based on a true story of a wealthy Russian nobleman who marries a serf. (RA K-3, IR 3-4). **OOP**

*Baba Yaga*, by An Leysen (Clavis, 2016). A Russian tale about a witch trying to eat an adorable little girl and the little girl's struggle to escape the witch and make it back home. (RA 2-3, IR 4)

*The House with Chicken Legs*, by Sophie Anderson (Scholastic Press, 2018). Twelve-year-old Marinka's grand-mother (Baba Yaga) leaves the Baba Yaga position earlier than anticipated, leaving Marinka behind to be the next Baba Yaga. However, Marinka doesn't want to be the next Baba Yaga and tries to bring her grandmother back. (IR 4-6)

## MAP WORK

### European Ideas in Russia *(Student Page 94, answer 326)*

1. Peter III was born in Kiel, Germany. Draw a red arrow from Kiel to St. Petersburg.
2. Catherine was born in Germany and moved from Germany to Russia. Draw a black arrow from the German states to St. Petersburg.
3. The first time Catherine went to see Peter, she went from St. Petersburg to Moscow. Draw a black arrow from St. Petersburg to Moscow.
4. When Peter III came to the throne, he forced the Russian soldiers to become more like the Prussian soldiers. The Prussians and Russians had been fighting for years. Find the border between Prussia and Russia. Draw a thick brown line between the two countries.
5. Catherine liked some of the ideas of the West. Color France and Great Britain, the West, orange. Then draw an orange box around "Russia."

**COLORING PAGE** Catherine was crowned empress of Russia in 1762. *(Student Page 95)*

## PROJECTS

### CRAFT ACTIVITY Catherine the Great Paper Doll

One morning, when she felt it was time to become the empress, Catherine dressed in fancy clothing—the way an empress should be dressed. In this activity, you'll color different clothing fit for an empress.

*Materials:*
- ☐ colored pencils or crayons
- ☐ scissors
- ☐ Scotch removable Double-stick Tape
- ☐ Student Page 96: Catherine the Great Paper Doll
- ☐ Student Pages 97, 98, and 99: Paper Doll Dresses
- ☐ white cardstock

*Directions:*
1. Color the paper doll and her clothes. Cut them out. The first set of clothes is what Catherine wore to be crowned empress. Her dress has the royal symbol of double-headed eagles, and her crown has many diamonds. The second outfit is a more "everyday" dress she might wear at court, with a blue sash. The third outfit is an army uniform she wore to show that she was also the commander of the Russian army.
2. Glue the paper doll onto thick cardstock. Cut to size. Laminate if possible (you'll be happier with the results and the paper doll lasts longer). If laminating at a professional site (such as Office Depot or copy stores), opt for the thicker grade of plastic cover.
3. Use the double-stick tape to attach the dresses and hats.

## GAME **Be the Next Czar**

In order to be a successful czar of Russia, you had to please four different groups—the army, the Russian Orthodox Church, the noblemen, and the common people. Play this game to see if you can get enough "support" to be the next czar of Russia.

*Materials:*
- ☐ Student Page 100: Be the Next Czar Game Board
- ☐ 1 die
- ☐ game pieces (borrow from another board game)
- ☐ support pieces (dimes or paperclips)
- ☐ piece of paper

*Directions:*

*Set Up:*
1. Each player places a game piece on Start. Have a stack of support pieces nearby (allot six for each player). Have the book open to this activity (so you can read the questions and answers). Cover the answers with a piece of paper so you can't read them.

*To play:*
1. Roll to see who goes first. Player 1 rolls the die. If Player 1 lands on the double question mark place, he is read two questions. For each question he answers correctly, he gets a support piece. If he answers both questions correctly, not only does he get two support pieces, he also gets to bypass the loop on his next roll (follow the down arrow). If he answers one question correctly, he gets one support piece but must move through the loop on his next turn (follow the arrow that points left). If he does not answer either question correctly, he does not get any support pieces and must move through the loop on his next turn.
2. If a player lands on an instruction space (for example, "go back two spaces" or "lose all tokens"), he follows the instructions. If, as a result of the instruction pieces, the player lands on a double question spot, he must answer two questions (see step 1).
3. A player only needs to go around each loop once (unless he is able to bypass the loop).
4. If a player lands on a single question mark space, he is asked one question. If he answers that question correctly, he gets a support piece. Even is he answers incorrectly, he rolls again on his next turn.
5. If a player lands on a flag space, he follows the arrow to the designated space on another loop.
6. In order to win, the player must have at least four support pieces (remember, Catherine needed the support of the common people, the noblemen, the army, and the Russian Orthodox Church). If a player does not have four support pieces by the end of the game board, he must stop on the last question mark space. He is asked one question per turn until he has four support pieces in his possession.
7. The player who first reaches the crown with at least four support pieces becomes the next czar of Russia!

QUESTIONS:

1. Catherine, Empress of Russia, was known as "Catherine the ________."
   - A. Mighty
   - B. Beautiful
   - C. Tall
   - D. Great

2. True or False. Catherine's parents were both from Russia.
3. What was the name of the old Empress of Russia, Peter Ulrich's aunt?
   A. Elizabeth
   B. Anastasia
   C. Petra
   D. She was also named Catherine.
4. Who did Catherine believe gave kings and empresses power?
   A. God
   B. the previous king or empress
   C. the people; they voted for the king
   D. a council of noblemen
5. True or False. Peter Ulrich heard about Catherine's beauty and decided she would be his wife. He sent for her to visit him in Russia.
6. Although Catherine's mother was thrilled she might become a queen, her mother was worried that
   A. she would not get to visit her daughter.
   B. Catherine would not listen to her own mother's advice anymore.
   C. Catherine would become a member of the Russian Orthodox Church.
   D. Catherine would argue with Empress Elizabeth.
7. Catherine met Peter Ulrich for the first time when he was ten years old. She thought he was
   A. odd, unfriendly, and rude.
   B. a kind, sweet-tempered young man.
8. What was Russia's capital city during Catherine's time?
   A. Moscow
   B. Leningrad
   C. Constantinople
   D. St. Petersburg
9. When Catherine finally met the grown-up Peter, her first impression was that Peter was
   A. still odd, unfriendly, and rude.
   B. taller and more handsome than she remembered.
   C. quiet and nervous.
10. Peter wished he did not live in Russia but in _____.
   A. England
   B. China
   C. Prussia
   D. France
11. Catherine received the title "Russian Grand Duchess" when she
   A. got engaged to Peter.
   B. demanded it from the empress.
   C. was born.
   D. came to the throne.

12. Four months after the engagement, Peter got sick with
    A. the flu
    B. smallpox
    C. the Black Death
    D. food poisoning
13. Catherine's wedding was
    A. small and quiet; only close family were invited.
    B. held in Rome.
    C. huge and elaborate.
14. Immediately after Catherine's first baby was born, what did the Empress do?
    A. She named Catherine the sole empress of Russia.
    B. She whisked the baby away to her own room and kept him there.
    C. She told Catherine to leave the palace and never return.
15. During Catherine's first nine lonely years of marriage, what did she do with her spare time?
    A. She read books on history, philosophy, and military strategy.
    B. She spent time with her many close friends at the palace.
    C. She designed and sewed all her own gowns.
    D. She dressed up in a Prussian military uniform and spoke in German.
16. What did Peter, now Czar Peter III, do at Empress Elizabeth's funeral?
    A. He wept over the empress's body.
    B. He gave a moving speech about her life and the love he felt for her.
    C. He didn't go to the funeral.
    D. He told jokes and laughed loudly.
17. What did Peter do once he was in charge of the army?
    A. He ordered them to dress and fight more like the Prussian army.
    B. He disbanded the army and said Russia would be at peace.
    C. He trained them to be the most skilled army in the world.
    D. He appointed army officers to all the head posts in his government.
18. Peter planned to sell land for money. Whose land was it?
    A. It belonged to the army.
    B. It belonged to the noblemen.
    C. It belonged to the common people.
    D. It belonged to the Russian Orthodox Church.
19. After Catherine became Empress, what did Peter request of her?
    A. He asked to rule alongside her.
    B. He asked to go to Prussia, a country he had always loved.
    C. He wanted her to step down and make their son, Paul, the new czar.
20. Why didn't Catherine let Peter go to Prussia?
    A. She was worried he was not healthy enough to make the trip.
    B. She worried he would convince Prussia to invade Russia.
    C. He didn't ask her nicely.
21. How did Catherine say that Peter died?
    A. He was killed in a fight that took place at a dinner.
    B. She admitted that she had had Peter killed.
    C. He died of smallpox.

22. True or False. Under Catherine's reign, Russia became larger.
23. True or False. Catherine made Russia a place where everyone had the same rights and everyone had a say in government.

ANSWERS:

1. (D) Great
2. False. Catherine's mother was Swedish and her father was German.
3. (A) Elizabeth
4. (A) God
5. False. Peter's mother, the Empress Elizabeth, was the one who chose Catherine to be Peter's wife.
6. (C) Catherine was raised a follower of the teachings of Martin Luther.
7. (A) He even drank so much wine at dinner he had to be carried away from the table!
8. (D) St. Petersburg. The city is named after its founder, Peter the Great.
9. (B) He was also very friendly when she first met him.
10. (C) He even spoke German instead of Russian!
11. (A)
12. (B) It left him covered with scars!
13. (C)
14. (B) Catherine didn't get to see her baby for six weeks!
15. (A)
16. (D)
17. (A)
18. (D)
19. (B) But Catherine didn't let him go to Prussia!
20. (B)
21. (A)
22. True. The Russian army claimed the land of Alaska, took land away from the Turks and the Mongols, and seized part of Poland.
23. False.

## Art Project **Circle the Cows**

Edward Jenner took fluid from a cowpox pustule on a milkmaid's hand. He injected the fluid into a young boy. Six weeks later, he exposed the boy to smallpox, and the boy did not show any symptoms of the disease. Still, people were skeptical. English cartoonist James Gillray etched a print that depicts one of the fears that people had about the vaccine—that cows would come from inoculated people's bodies!

*Materials:*
- ☐ Student Page 101: Edward Jenner Administering Vaccinations
- ☐ Pen or pencil

*Directions:* 1. Circle all of the cows coming from different parts of people's bodies. How many cows can you find?

2. The man giving the inoculation is supposed to be Edward Jenner, the man who invented the smallpox vaccine. Draw an arrow from the top of the print to Jenner's head.

## MEMORY PROJECT Manifesto of Catherine the Great

Catherine the Great issued a manifesto in the summer of 1763. The manifesto told immigrants what they were and were not allowed to do. The following is an excerpt from her manifesto. Ask the child to read 2-3 lines (preferably ending at the end of a sentence) out loud five times every day. Within a few days, the child should be able to recite most of those lines from memory. Then add another 2-3 lines and follow the same procedure until the excerpt from the manifesto is memorized.

**Excerpt from the Manifesto of Catherine the Great:**

In order that the foreigners who desire to settle in Our Empire may realize the extent of Our benevolence to their benefit and advantage, this is our will:

We grant to all foreigners coming into Our Empire the free and unrestricted practice of their religion according to the precepts and usage of their Church. To those, however, who intend to settle not in cities but in colonies and villages on uninhabited lands we grant the freedom to build churches and bell towers, and to maintain the necessary number of priests and church servants, but not the construction of monasteries. On the other hand, everyone is hereby warned not to persuade or induce any of the Christian co-religionists living in Russia to accept or even assent to his faith or join his religious community, under pain of incurring the severest punishment of Our law. This prohibition does not apply to the various nationalities on the borders of Our Empire who are attached to the Mahometan [Muslim] faith. We permit and allow everyone to win them over and make them subject to the Christian religion in a decent way.

# A Changing World

## Encyclopedia Cross-References

*UBWH 164-165, 168-169, UILE 336-339*
*KIHW 490-491, 500-501, 534, KHE 296-297*

## STEAM AND COAL IN BRITAIN

### Review Questions

What kind of power made the machines and tools of the weaver and the blacksmith work? *Muscle power made their machines work. People in England had also learned to harness the wind and the water to help them with their work.*

What machine did James Watt perfect in 1769? *He perfected the steam engine.*

After James Watt perfected the steam engine, what were people able to use this machine for? *People were able to use the steam engine to run mills for grinding grain, engines to pull plows and heavy loads, bellows, water pumps, even ships!*

The steam engine changed the West because it could "work" longer than human muscles, windmills, or waterwheels. How long could a steam engine perform a task? *A steam engine could run as long as it had coal.*

Where did the coal for the steam engine come from? *The coal was mined from the ground by hand.*

What was one of the dangers that coal miners faced? *Miners could be killed by suffocation, explosion, or tunnel collapse.*

What happened to miners who breathed too much coal dust? *After years of breathing coal dust into their lungs, miners couldn't breathe properly any more. They died when their lungs could no longer pull in enough oxygen to keep them alive!*

In what two ways was coal transported to towns? *It was transported by barges and by trains.*

What change did steam bring to the way people travelled? *More people began to travel by train.*

### Narration Exercise

Because this chapter contains factual information about machines, rather than a story that can be narrated, use "directed narration." Ask the child to list three ways in which steam power changed life in Britain. Acceptable answers might include:

"Mills were run by steam power instead of by wind."

"Engines pulled heavy loads; cows and horses didn't have to do this any more."

"Ships and trains, run by steam, could haul heavy loads and carry more passengers."

"Steam engines used coal, so more and more coal had to be dug from coal mines."

"Railroads were built across land where cows and sheep grazed."

## Review Questions

What was one of the main crops grown in the southern United States? *Plantation owners in the southern United States grew cotton.*

How was a cotton ball from the plant different from cotton ball you buy in a store? *The cotton from the plant was filled with seeds that were covered with hooks. These seeds had to be separated from the cotton before it could be used.*

Who came up with a new way of separating the seeds from the cotton? *Eli Whitney, a college boy from Massachusetts, solved the problem of cotton seeds.*

How did Eli Whitney's new machine work? *Whitney had built a metal roller with teeth that rubbed up against a metal grill. The roller, turned by a handle, pulled up cotton and scraped it across the grill. The seeds dropped away.*

What was the name of Whitney's new machine? *This new machine was called the cotton gin.*

How many pounds of cotton could a single worker clean in one day, using the cotton gin? *He could clean fifteen to twenty pounds per day.*

How could a plantation owner make the cotton gin work even faster? *He could use a water wheel or steam engine to run the cotton gin.*

Why did it take a long time to fix a gun? *Each gun's parts only fit* that *gun, so a soldier would have to wait for a gunsmith to make a new part.*

Eli Whitney had another idea about how the army might have better guns. What was his basic idea? *Eli Whitney thought that the army might design guns that had standard-sized parts. Then if part of a gun broke, the soldier could grab a replacement part and put it in.*

We now call Eli Whitney's idea *standardization.* What is standardization? *Standardization means that parts are interchangeable.*

Was Whitney the first person to think of interchangeable parts? *No, someone in France had already thought of it. But his factory was the first that became famous for this.*

Soon, interchangeable parts were used for all sorts of goods. What was one other manufactured good that soon was using interchangeable parts? *Clocks, farm machinery, and cotton gins soon were using interchangeable parts.*

## Narration Exercise

Because this chapter contains factual information about machines, rather than a story that can be narrated, use "directed narration." Ask the child, "How did the cotton gin change cotton farming?" An acceptable answer might be, "Before the cotton gin, cotton had to be cleaned by hand. A slave might work all day and only clean one pound of cotton! But if the slave ran a cotton gin, he could clean fifteen or twenty pounds. If the gin was hooked up to a steam engine, it would work even faster. Now, plantation owners could plant larger fields and buy even more slaves."

Then, say to the child, "Can you explain what *interchangeable* parts are, and why they are convenient?" An acceptable answer might be, "Interchangeable parts will fit into any gun, or a clock, or a light-bulb holder, no matter what company makes the parts. Before interchangeable parts, a part of a gun or a clock would have to be hand-made to fit a particular gun or clock. But now, any part will fit into any gun or clock. The owner doesn't have to wait for the part to be hand-built!"

## Additional History Reading

*The New Way Things Work: From Levers to Lasers, Windmills to Web Sites, A Visual Guide to the World of Machines*, by David Macaulay (Houghton Mifflin, 1998). For the mechanically minded, hundreds of illustrations of basic machines and the ways in which they were powered and used. (RA 1-3, IR 4-6) **OOP**

*The Steam Engine: Transforming Power of Technology*, by Sara Louise Kras (Chelsea House Publishers, 2003). For advanced readers or slightly older students, this book describes how steam changed various aspects of daily life. (RA 2-4, IR 4-7) **LFA**

*1000 Inventions & Discoveries*, ed. Marie Greenwood (Dorling Kindersley, 2014). The section "Revolutionary Changes" covers the invention of steam power and dozens of other life-changing machines from 1751-1850; brief sections, easily read aloud. (RA 1-4, IR 5-6)

*Growing Up in Coal Country*, by Susan Campbell Bartoletti (Houghton Mifflin, 1996). Fairly advanced text, but photographs of actual children involved in coal mining on every page make this a good book for all ages. (RA 2-4, IR 4-7)

*You Wouldn't Want to be a 19th-century Coal Miner in England!: A Dangerous Job You'd Rather Not Have*, by John Malam, illus. David Antram (Franklin Watts, 2006). Learn that coal is what drove the steam machines and how working as a coal miner revolved throughout the years, from new machines to work with, to the struggle for improved working conditions. (IR 4-6)

*Robert Fulton and the Development of the Steamboat*, by Morris Pierce (Powerkids Press, 2002). For advanced readers, a well-illustrated account of the failed painter who became the inventor of the steamboat. (IR 4-6)

*All Aboard! Elijah McCoy's Steam Engine*, by Monica Kulling (Tundra Books, 2013). A picture book for elementary students, but worth investigating for all; the only biography of the African-American inventor who travelled to Scotland and improved on the steam engine's design. (RA 2, IR 3-5)

*Crossing on Time: Steam Engines, Fast Ships, and a Journey to the New World*, by David Macaulay (Roaring Brook Press, 2019). Distinguished illustrator-author Macaulay examines the development of the steam engine and how it changed transatlantic travel in this fascinating, meticulously illustrated book. (RA 3-4, IR 5-7)

*Steam, Smoke, and Steel: Back in Time with Trains*, by Patrick O'Brien (Charlesbridge, 2000). A picture book with numerous illustrations showing the development and advances in trains over the past 200 years. (RA 1-2, IR 3-4)

*From Cotton to T-Shirt: Start to Finish*, by Robin Nelson (Lerner, 2013). This guide to cotton harvesting has great photos of modern versions of the cotton gin. (IR 2-4)

*Eli Whitney (Jr. Graphic American Inventors)*, by Tracy J. Garcia (PowerKids Press, 2013). A great comic book about Eli Whitney and his inventions of the cotton gin and interchangeable parts for muskets. (RA 2, IR 3-5)

*The Inventions of Eli Whitney: The Cotton Gin*, by Holly Cefrey (Powerkids Press, 2003). An easy-to-read description of the cotton gin's mechanism and invention. (RA 1, IR 2-4) **LFA**

*Life on a Plantation*, by Bobbie Kalman (Crabtree Publications, 1997). Many illustrations and fairly detailed text compare the life of the plantation owner and his family with the lives of the workers in the cotton fields. (RA 2-3, IR 4-6)

## Corresponding Literature Suggestions

*Cleonardo, The Little Inventor* by Mary GrandPre (Arthur A. Levine, 2016). Endearing picture book about a girl from a family of inventors who wants to be an inventor too. Great for sparking conversations about inventions and inventing. (RA K-2, IR 3-4).

*ELFWOOD: The Shiny Silver Steam Engine*, by Nancy Trancey Buscher (TJ Press, 2012). A steam engine train stops at a small town. The children have fun trying to figure out what it does and how to revive it. (RA 3, IR 4-6)

*The Gate in the Wall* by Ellen Howard (Aladdin, 2007). Locked out of her job in the silk factory, ten-year-old Ellen ends up working on the canal boats. Engaging story set during the early Industrial Revolution in England, this book includes a glossary at the end to help readers understand the dialect used in the story. (RA 1-3, IR 3-5).

*Here's What You Do When You Can't Find Your Shoe (Ingenious Inventions for Pesky Problems)* by Andrea Perry (Atheneum Books for Young Readers, 2003). Humorous poems about imagined inventions. Great for talking with children about the inspiration for famous inventions. (RA K-2, IR 2-3).

*Hot Air: The (Mostly) True Story of the First Hot-Air Balloon Ride* by Marjorie Priceman (Atheneum Books, 2005). The story of the 1783 liftoff of a new invention—the hot-air balloon. The passengers for this flight were a duck, a sheep, and a rooster and this book tells the story from their perspective. Includes a timeline that shows the process from idea to invention. (RA K-3, IR 2-4).

*Leather Shoe Charlie* by Kyeong-hwa Kim, illus Anna Balbusso (Eerdmans Books, 2017). This picture book about a boy whose cobbler family is affected by the new factories introduces the Industrial Revolution in England to young readers. The story is left unfinished, creating opportunity for discussion about what might happen next. (RA 1-2, IR 3-4).

*Scott and the Intrepid* (Scott's Adventures Book 1), by Charlie Forrestt (The Alderbourne Press Ltd., 2018). While trying to figure out where his father has gone, Scott is obsessed with building a steam engine. (RA 3, IR 4)

*Steam Train, Dream Train*, by Sherri Duskey Rinker and Tom Lightenheld (Chronicle Books LLC, 2013). Great picture book for younger kids about a steam train carrying animals. (RA 1-2)

*Up and Away! How Two Brothers Invented the Hot-Air Balloon* by Jason Henry (Sterling, 2018). This beautifully illustrated picture book tells the story of the invention of the hot-air balloon in 1782 and King Louis XVI's visit in 1783 to see it fly. (RA K-2, IR 1-4).

## MAP WORK

### Industrial Revolution in Britain and America *(Student Page 102, answer 326)*

1. Britain was an agricultural country that relied on muscle power and machines for work. Outline England and Scotland in light green.
2. James Watt was from Scotland. Draw a black box around the word "Scotland."
3. Railroads became a new way to transport the coal. Using the following symbol, draw a railroad up the middle of Britain (England and Scotland): ++++++++.
4. The introduction of steam power changed Britain. Fill in the green outline with grey (shade lightly with a black crayon)

5. Eli Whitney made standardization popular in the United States. Draw a small symbol for a factory. Then, draw five of those symbols along the east coast of America.
6. Find the I in AMERICA. Go right until you get to the coast. Use a brown crayon and outline the coast of America from here down. This area was already a large cotton producer, and with the introduction of steam engines and the cotton gin, became an even greater cotton producer.

**Coloring Page** Once steam engines were invented, they were used for all kinds of things, like powering trains that pulled loads of coal or passengers. Farmers worried that the noise and steam from these new machines would scare their cows and chickens! *(Student Page 103)*

## PROJECTS

### Craft Project — The Cotton Gin

Note to Parent: This "cotton gin" will not actually take seeds out of cotton, but it should help the student understand how a real cotton gin works.

*Materials:*

- ☐ shoe Box (one with a lid)
- ☐ paper towel roll tube
- ☐ toothpicks
- ☐ pen, or something else sharp to punch the holes for the toothpicks
- ☐ scissors, or X-acto knife, to cut the shoe box
- ☐ straight edge
- ☐ (optional) brown spray paint
- ☐ cotton balls
- ☐ popcorn kernels

*Directions:*

1. (optional) If you want, you may choose to spray paint the shoe box with brown spray paint. (Note: If the box looks "shiny," the paint may not adhere, or it may not dry quickly.)
2. Take the lid off of the shoe box. Cut it in half (so that you have two medium-sized rectangles, not two long skinny rectangles).
3. You will use one of these rectangles to make a screen. On the cardboard side (the side you can draw on), draw what looks like a wire mesh screen. Use a ruler to draw many horizontal lines on the cardboard. Then go back and draw vertical lines. After you have made this piece of cardboard look like a screen, slide it into the shoe box so that it fits snugly against the edges of the box. Place it about ½ of the way in to the box. (As of now, do not secure it with tape or glue. You might choose to do that later.)
4. Now, you are going to fit the paper towel roll tube through the shoe box, from side to side. You may hold the tube up to the shoe box to trace the hole. Use the scissors or X-acto knife, and cut two holes for the cylinder to fit through (see diagram on the next page). Make sure that the tube is not too close to the bottom of the box, or the tube will not turn after it has the tooth picks sticking out of it. After you have put the tube through the shoe box, use a pen (or something else sharp) and punch holes through the tube. It works best to do one row (across) at a time. You may choose how many tooth pick holes to put in the paper towel tube. Put the tooth picks in the holes you've made.
5. Now put popcorn kernels in some of the cotton balls. These represent the raw cotton. Put these between the end of the box and the cylinder (the paper towel tube with tooth picks).

6. Put the clean cotton balls on the other end. In a real cotton gin, someone would turn the cylinder, which would pull the raw cotton (with seeds) next to the screen. The screen would catch the seeds, and the cotton would be pulled through without the seeds.

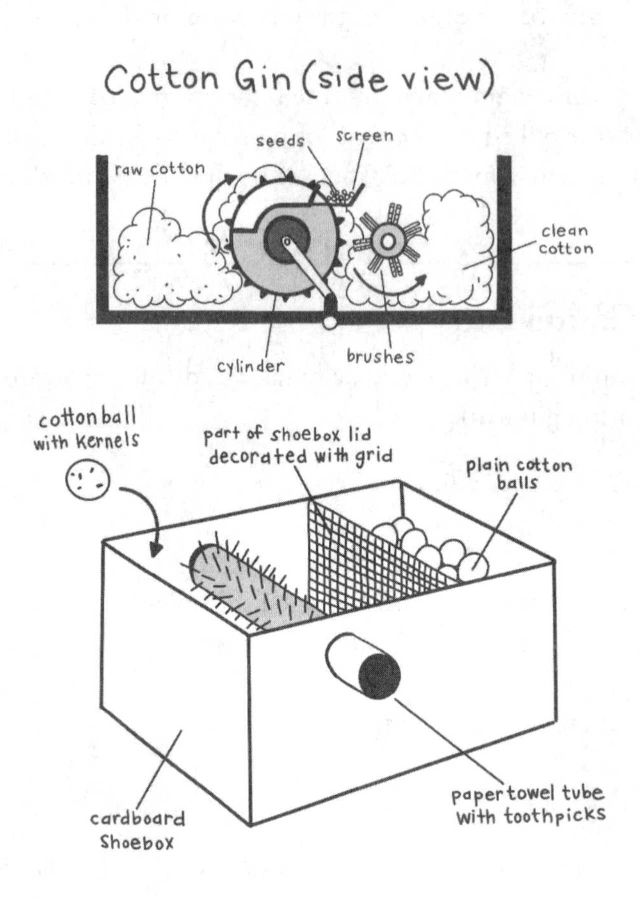


## SCIENCE PROJECT Steam Experiment

Steam power could move the parts of engines, making engines of all kinds faster and more powerful. Test the power of steam with this experiment.

*Materials:*
- ☐ kettle (with spout), stove, and water
- ☐ two playing cards, or 3" x 5" index cards
- ☐ two drinking straws (at least 8" each)
- ☐ scissors
- ☐ tape

*Directions:*
1. Start a covered kettle (with a spout) boiling on the stove.
2. Make a "paddlewheel" from two playing cards (each cut halfway, and then forming an "X" with the cuts inserted into one another).

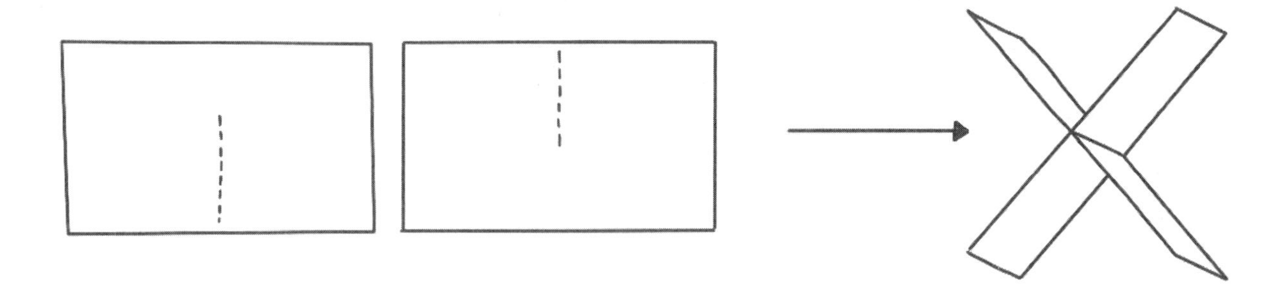

3. Cut two drinking straws into four 4" lengths. Nestle one in the crook of each arm of the X, so that each sticks out ½" from the sides of the paddlewheel. Wrap a strip of tape around each ½" set of straw-ends.
4. Use the point of two pens or sharpened pencils to pick up the paddlewheel: Stick the point into the very middle of each set of straw-ends (the center of the set of straw-ends should form a small diamond).
5. Hold the paddlewheel over the steam coming out of the boiling kettle.
6. Observe what happens to the paddlewheel.

Note: The wheel turns because of the pressure the steam is putting on the blades of the paddle. Although paddleboats don't use this specific method to turn their wheel, this shows how steam creates pressure, and how this pressure can be focused to perform work.

## GAME ACTIVITY House of Interchangeable Parts BINGO!

When in Europe, Thomas Jefferson visited a German gun maker. He saw a room full of wooden boxes, each filled to the top with a part of the gun. As a demonstration, the gun maker had his observers pick out random pieces from the boxes. Each piece fit snugly into the gun. The parts were interchangeable.

In this game, you'll look at everyday items that feature interchangeable parts.

Play this game two ways. First, try and fill up your Bingo card by finding the different machines you have in your house. Then, use the Bingo cards (or make your own) and play the traditional way.

Materials:
- ☐ Student Page 104: Bingo Card Template and House of Interchangeable Parts Pieces
- ☐ colored pencils or crayons (optional)
- ☐ tape

Directions:
1. Copy all of the templates on white or colored cardstock. Note that the *House of Interchangeable Parts Pieces* sheet has many blank squares. Those blanks can be filled in with other items, or can be used as the board covers when playing. You may want to copy them on a different color of cardstock or they can be colored a different color with the colored pencils.
2. (Optional) Color the House of Interchangeable Parts Bingo cards.
3. Cut up the *Pieces* sheet and place the squares in a large bowl.
4. Begin game by covering the "Free" space in the center of your card. Draw out an Interchangeable Part piece from the bowl and call it out. Each player should cover that piece on his card.
5. The winner is the first to get five in a row: up, down, across or diagonally.
6. Option #2: Race around the house and see who can fill their Bingo card by finding the different interchangeable parts listed on the card first!

7. Option #3: For a great travel game, copy the templates on magnetic-backed paper. ***Note*** that it is not necessary for the *Pieces* sheet to all be put on magnetic-backed paper, just the blank ones that will be used as covers for the game board. Color, cut out and keep game going on a jelly roll pan (cookie sheet with sides) while traveling or running around the house.

Once someone has won, look at each of the cards that you've pulled from the bowl. If the items written on the cards are nearby, go look at them and talk about what interchangeable parts each one has. How do interchangeable parts help keep your house running?

## Activity Project **Writing a Patent**

Eli Whitney applied for a patent for his cotton gin, but it took him a long time to get one. Until he had a patent, anyone who wanted to could make their own cotton gin. When he finally received a patent, people had to pay him to be able to make one of his machines.

You are not able to patent an idea; you must patent an invention. When you finally have an invention, you must write your own patent. Your invention must be:

1. **Non-obvious**: You cannot patent something like a wheel.
2. **Novel:** Your invention may be similar to an existing one, but it must be new to the world.
3. **Useful:** Does it serve a purpose? Your invention must do something. Otherwise, will people buy it?
4. **Workable:** It must work. If you want to patent a car that burns garbage for fuel, you must show that it works.

*Materials:* □ Student Page 105: Patent Application

*Directions:*
1. Think of something you would like to invent. If you can't think of anything, choose something that has already been invented (preferably something that you understand fairly well).
2. Follow the directions on the student page. These questions are questions that someone thinking about applying for a patent would ask himself.

# China and the Rest of the World

## Encyclopedia Cross-References

*UBWH 153, 156, 189 (top) UILE 352-354*
*KIHW 502-503, 548-549, 568, KHE 304-305*

## THE KINGDOM AT THE CENTER OF THE WORLD

### Review Questions

Why did the Chinese call themselves the "Central Civilization"? *They believed the universe was centered on China.*

While the West was trying to master nature, China was not. What did Confucius teach the Chinese about how to relate to nature? *He taught that the Chinese should accept nature and learn from it in a harmonious way, not try to master it.*

How many ports did Chi'en-lung open to the Western countries? *He opened one port, Canton, to the Westerners.*

What was the purpose of the Eight Regulations? *The Eight Regulations told foreign merchants what they could and could not do.*

Can you remember two of the Eight Regulations? *Foreign women could not visit the warehouse or dock at Canton; foreign merchants had to have Chinese merchants speak to officials for them; traders had to leave China at the end of the trading season; foreigners couldn't learn Chinese or buy Chinese books.*

What were some of the goods that England liked to buy from China? *The English loved the Chinese teas, silks, and spices.*

Who was England's ambassador to China? *George Macartney was England's ambassador.*

George Macartney brought many gifts to Chi'en-lung. What did Chi'en-lung do with the gifts? *Chi'en-lung ordered that they be left at a summer palace. He then said he had no need of Western goods.*

Did Chi'en-lung treat George Macartney like an ambassador? *No, he treated Macartney like a visitor bringing tribute.*

What did the Chinese courtiers expect Macartney to do? Did he do it? *They expected Macartney to kowtow, but he refused.*

Macartney had brought a letter from England's king, George III. Can you remember two things that this letter asked Chi'en-lung to do? *In the letter, George III explained that Britain wanted to send an ambassador to China to live in Peking. British ships wanted to sail into ports all up and down China's huge coast. The British wanted to build trading posts and settlements where English merchants could live year round.*

Did Chi'en-lung grant the requests of George III? *No, he refused every request.*

### Narration Exercise

"Countries in the West wanted to trade with China, but the Chinese believed that they had everything they needed. They called themselves the 'Central Civilization.' They made foreign traders follow Eight Regulations to keep them out of China. The king of England sent an ambassador, George Macartney, to ask Chi'en-lung to change the Eight Regulations. Chi'en-lung refused. He told the king of England that the Chinese didn't need any of England's goods." OR

"George Macartney went to China to ask Chi'en-lung to change the Eight Regulations. English merchants wanted to live in China year round, and to build ports and settlements. Macartney brought Chi'en-lung a whole shipful of presents. But the emperor of China treated the presents like tribute. His courtiers expected Macartney to kowtow, but Macartney told them he would only kowtow if they would bow to the portrait of the king of England. The Chinese refused! Chi'en-lung refused all of Macartney's requests and sent him back to England."

## THE RISE OF THE OPIUM TRADE

### Review Questions

What did England have that China wanted? *England had opium.*

What did doctors use opium for? *Doctors gave opium to patients who were in pain.*

What was the worst thing about taking opium? *The more the patients took it, the less it worked, so they needed more and more opium.*

Why doesn't Samuel Taylor Coleridge's poem about Xanadu make sense? *Coleridge was under the influence of opium while he wrote the poem.*

Where did the East India Company grow poppies for opium? *They grew the poppies and made the opium in India.*

Why did the emperor of China forbid the British to bring opium to China? *He saw that the Chinese were becoming addicted to opium.*

Did the British stop shipping opium into China when the Chinese emperor made it illegal? *No, they did not. They kept shipping the opium in secret.*

Did the English official in charge of India want the British in India to smoke opium? *No, he did not. He thought the drug was "pernicious" and should be made illegal in India.*

If the English official did not want the British in India to smoke opium, why did he keep shipping the drug to China? *He had money to gain. Opium was very valuable and brought the English a lot of money.*

### Narration Exercise

"The British grew poppies and made opium in India. Then they shipped this opium to China. More and more Chinese grew addicted to opium. The emperor of China ordered the British to stop bringing opium to China. But the British were making so much money that they refused to stop. Meanwhile, they wanted to make opium illegal in India—so that British citizens wouldn't smoke it!" OR

"Opium was made from the juice of poppies. It took away pain, made sick people feel peaceful, and gave them beautiful dreams. Many English people became addicted to opium. Then the British began to ship opium to China. Opium was poisoning the Chinese. So many of them spent their days in opium dreams that the emperor of China made opium illegal. But the British kept right on bringing opium to China. They were making too much money to stop!"

## Additional History Reading

*For more history titles, see Chapter Ten.*

*Confucius: Great Chinese Philosopher*, by Anna Carew-Miller (Mason Crest Publishers, 2002). This simple biography of Confucius includes snippets from his teachings. (RA 2, IR 3-5) **E-Only.**

*Ancient China: Discover the History of Imperial China from the Great Wall to the Days of the Last Emperor* (DK Eyewitness Books) by Arthur Cotterell (DK Children, 2005). Full of pictures and drawings portraying life in Ancient China through the end of the Qing Dynasty. Includes a detailed timeline. (RA 2-5, IR 4-6).

*China (Follow Me Around)*, by Wiley Blevins (Children's Press, 2017). Join Wang as he takes a look around China. Children will encounter the Chinese way of life, historical landmarks, and a brief timeline of all the major dynasties. (RA 2-3, IR 4)

*China: Land of Dragons and Emperors* by Adeline Yen Mah (Ember, reprint 2011). Excellent summary of Chinese history in short chapters full of pictures. Chapter 10 covers the Qing Dynasty. Excellent format for short read aloud sessions, or independent reading for older or advanced readers. (RA 1-4, IR 4-8).

*China: Land of the Emperor's Great Wall: A Nonfiction Companion to Magic Tree House #14: Day of the Dragon King* by Mary Pope Osborne and Natalie Pope Boyce, illus Carlo Molinari. (Random House, 2014). Nonfiction companion to the Magic Tree House book, includes the same engaging characters and writing as the popular fiction series. (RA 1-2, IR 3-5).

*Early Times: China's Later Dynasties* by Suzanne Strauss Art (Pemblewick Press, 2002) A good reference book for older readers, this text has maps of China and provinces as well as timelines and lists of Emperors for each Dynasty. Includes a full chapter on the Qing dynasty. (IR 4-8).

*Elephants and Golden Thrones: Inside China's Forbidden City*, by Trish Marx, photographed Ellen B. Senisi (Harry N. Abrams, 2008). Detailed color photographs and extensive text reveal how several of China's Emperors (and an Empress) lived and ruled in the Forbidden City. (IR 4-6)

*Through Time: Beijing* by Richard Platt, illus Cappon Manuela (Kingfisher, 2008). The history of the city from prehistoric time through the 2008 Olympics. Detailed artwork makes this an engaging book but some subject material may be too intense for younger readers. (IR 3-5).

*Opium,* by James Barter (Lucent, 2004). An entry in the Drug Education Library series, this book for older and more mature students explains the history of opium growing and use, the chemistry of opium addiction, and modern forms of the drug. (IR 6-up)

## Corresponding Literature Suggestions

*For additional literature titles, see Chapter Ten.*

*The Making of Monkey King*, by Robert Kraus, illus. Wenhai Ma (Pan Asian Publications, 1998). A picture-book retelling of the first chapters from the sixteenth-century Chinese novel *Journey to the West*, about the battle between the Monkey King and the Demon of Chaos. (RA 2, IR 3-5)

*Tales from Within the Clouds: Nakhi Stories of China*, by Carolyn Han, trans. Jaiho Cheng, illus. Ji Li (University of Hawaii Press, 1997). Translated from the original Chinese, these fantastic stories come from the Nakhi tribe. (RA 2, IR 3-5)

*Tales of a Chinese Grandmother: 30 Traditional Tales from China* by Frances Carpenter, illus. Malthe Hasselriis (Tuttle Publishing, reissue 2017). A collection of 30 Chinese folktales, as told by the grandmother of a 19th century Chinese family. (RA 3-4, IR 4-7).

*A Time of Golden Dragons*, by Song Nan Zhang and Hao Yu Zhang (Tundra Books, 2000). A beautifully-painted picture book that leads young readers through the place of dragons in Chinese history and myth, including the place of the dragon in the Chinese calendar. (RA 1, IR 2-5)

*The Mystery in the Forbidden City (Greetings from Somewhere Book 4)*, by Harper Paris (Little Simon, 2014). Students follow the adventures of Ethan and Ella as they get lost trying to find the statutes of dragons in the Forbidden City. (RA 1-3)

*This is the Greatest Place! The Forbidden City and the World of Small Animals*, by Brian Tse, illus. Alice Mak (China Institute in America, 2014). A story about a group of young animal friends learning how nature inspired the design and architecture of the Forbidden City. (RA 1-2, IR 3)

*Treasure Hunters: Secret of the Forbidden City (Treasure Hunters Series Book 3)*, by James Patterson and Chris Grabenstein (Little, Brown and Company, 2015). Four siblings are trying to find their parents. Their parents leave them clues which take them to different places. In this book, they travel to the Forbidden City and Munich. (IR 4-6)

*Kubla Khan: A Pop-Up Version of Coleridge's Classic*, by Nick Bantock, Barbara Hodgson, and Dennis K. Meyer (Viking Press, 1994). This original version of Coleridge's opium-induced poem looks like something you'd see in a dream. (RA 2, IR 3-6) **OOP**

## MAP WORK

### The Kingdom at the Center of the World *(Student Page 106, answer 326)*

1. China tried hard to keep Western ideas out of China. Draw a thick brown border around China.
2. The English loved the tea, silks, and spices of China, and wanted to be able to trade with them. So England sent Macartney through Canton to speak with Chi'en-lung. Color England red. Then draw a circle around the dot that represents Canton.
3. England had many trading posts along the coast of India. Outline the coast of India in red.
4. Although he kept out Western ideas, Chi'en-lung could not keep out England's opium. English traders secretly smuggled opium into China. Draw an arrow with a dotted line from the coast of India into China. (Because the map is narrow, you will have to cross over the peninsula at the bottom of the map; ships would have sailed around it.)

**Coloring Page** The meeting between the British ambassador and the Chinese emperor didn't go well. The British ambassador refused to bow down on his hands and knees, and the Chinese emperor said his country didn't need any of the things that Britain had to offer. *(Student Page 107)*

## PROJECTS

### Activity Project Eight Regulations

The Chinese tried to protect themselves by passing regulations to keep foreigners at a distance. You are going to write your own Eight Regulations and post them on the door of your room!

*Materials:*
- ☐ paper
- ☐ pen or pencil
- ☐ tape
- ☐ (optional) colored pencils or markers

*Directions:* 1. Read "The Eight Regulations." Then, read "My Eight Regulations."
2. Write "My Eight Regulations" across the top of your paper. Copy your Eight Regulations on to the paper. You may choose to decorate your paper by putting a border around the edge, or by drawing a symbol that goes with one of the rules. (For example, you might draw a butter knife with an "X" through it, next to regulation two.)
3. Hang the paper on your door. Make people follow your eight regulations for one day!

**The Eight Regulations**

1. No warships may enter the harbor.
2. No one may bring firearms to the harbor.
3. No one can communicate with Chinese officials except through designated interpreters.
4. Foreigners can only go ashore to visit the public gardens, three times a month, in groups of less than ten.
5. Foreigners who had office buildings on the shore could not enter and leave too often.
6. Foreigners can't stay in China during the summer, when the trading season is over.
7. Foreigners can't buy Chinese books or learn Chinese.
8. Foreigners can't smuggle goods into China.

**My Eight Regulations**

1. No one can enter my room wearing outside clothes—shoes, jackets, coats, or hats.
2. No one can bring play swords, water pistols, table knives, butter knives, scissors, pens, nail files, forks, sticks, rocks, or toothpicks into my room.
3. Anyone who wants to talk to me while I'm in my room has to tell Mom what they want, and then Mom will tell me.
4. You can't sit on my bed except at 11 AM, 1 PM, and 5 PM, for five minutes at a time.
5. You can only come into my room four times per day. When you've come in four times, you can't come in at all until the next day.
6. You can't enter my room at all between 2-4 PM.
7. When you are in my room, you can't read anything or borrow any books; you can't take anything with print on it out of my room.
8. Before you come into my room, you have to turn all of your pockets inside out and leave them that way.

Do these regulations make it harder for others to come into your room? That's how the English felt in China!

## ACTIVITY PROJECT Kowtow!

Remember that Chi'en-lung and his courtiers expected George Macartney to kowtow to the emperor—to get down on his hands and knees and knock his forehead against the floor nine times.

*Materials:*
- ☐ large piece of art paper (life size)
- ☐ pen or pencil
- ☐ coloring materials

*Directions:* 1. Make a drawing of yourself on big paper—life size! You may want to have a partner trace you while you lie down on the paper.
2. Color your clothes and draw in your face.

3. Hang this drawing up in a room that you visit several times during the day. Everyone who goes into the room must *kowtow* to your picture (get down on hands and knees and knock their forehead against the floor nine times).

## ART PROJECT Make a Vase from the Chi'en-lung Period

Much of the pottery from the period of Chi'en-lung's reign has survived. Some of the most common relics are the white and blue vases from the period.

*Materials:*

- ☐ Self-hardening clay (clay that does not need to be glazed and fired)
- ☐ Acrylic paints—blue and white
- ☐ Paint brush
- ☐ Needle stuck in a cork, or a craft knife
- ☐ Newspaper, or other type of paper to work on

*Directions:*

1. First, put the newspaper down so that you have a surface on which to work the clay. You may also want to have your craft knife (or needle stuck in cork) ready to cut the clay.
2. There are two ways to go about making a vase that will make the vase look like the one above on the left. The first is to roll the clay in to long, narrow strips, or rolls. Notice that the top of the vase in the above right picture has little coils. This is what your vase would look like if you use the "coil" method. If you use the "coil" method, make sure the coils are all nearly the same width, but of varying lengths. Then form them into circles. Change the length of the roll to make a larger or smaller circle, varying the length as you go so that the shape of the vase follows that of the one in the above drawing. Once you have these "coils," you may smooth out the outside of the vase, so that you do not see the seams (of the coils).
3. Or, you may also choose to flatten the clay (with a roller) and form the vase with flat sections of clay. The bottom of the vase at the above right shows what your vase might look like if you use flat sections of clay to make the vase.
4. Leave the vase to dry.
5. When the vase is dry, you are ready to decorate it. Two of the most-used colors on this type of pottery were white and blue. You might consider first painting the entire vase white. Then go back and use the blue to decorate the vase. The patterns on the vase above left are typical of the patterns of the vases of the time.

# The Rise of Bonaparte

## Encyclopedia Cross-References

*UBWH 170-171, 183, UILE 334, 350*
*KIHW 530-533, 556, KHE 319-321, 328*

## NAPOLEON COMES TO POWER

### Review Questions

After the end of the National Convention, the French removed the king and the aristocrats. France became an oligarchy. Who ruled in this type of government? *An oligarchy was a country where only some of the citizens have power to rule.*

Who was allowed to vote for leaders? *All soldiers and all Frenchmen who owned a certain amount of land were allowed to vote for leaders.*

How were these leaders organized? *These leaders were put in two "houses," like the American Senate and House of Representatives.*

Can you remember the names of these two "houses"? *In France, though, the houses were called "the Council of Ancients" and "the Council of Five Hundred."*

What was the name of the five-man committee that ruled France? *The committee was called "the Directory." The Directory ruled France.*

What was the name of the general that the Directory chose to lead an attack on Austria? *The general's name was Napoleon Bonaparte.*

When Napoleon went down to attack Italy, his troops were tired. How did he inspire them? *He promised them that they would find honor, glory, and wealth in the towns that they were going to conquer.*

After he had driven the Austrians out of Italy, what did Napoleon announce to the Italians? *He announced that he had come to set them free from their Austrian captors.*

After his victory over Austria, Napoleon had great ambition. The Directory knew that Napoleon wanted power for himself, so they gave him a difficult task. What was this difficult task? *They told him to invade Great Britain.*

How did Napoleon respond to the Directory's suggestion of invading Great Britain? *He suggested that France invade Egypt instead.*

When he captured the Egyptian cities of Alexandria and Cairo, what did Napoleon say to the Egyptians? [Hint: He said the same when he invaded Italy.] *He told the Egyptians that he was coming to set them free from the tyranny of the Turks.*

How did Napoleon escape from the British when they finally caught up with his troops at the Battle of the Nile? *He boarded a small ship and sneaked past the British navy in a fog.*

After Napoleon returned to Paris, he took control—the rule of the Directory ended. What type of rule took the place of the Directory? *Three consuls ruled, one of which was Napoleon. Soon, Napoleon was the only consul.*

### Narration Exercise

Since there is a great deal of information in this chapter, use "directed narration." You may choose to allow the student to look back at the chapter while answering.

First, say to the child, "Tell me about two countries that Napoleon invaded—and one that he was *supposed* to invade. Explain about these three countries in the same order as in *The Story of the World*." An acceptable answer might be, "Napoleon invaded Italy, and told the Italians that he would free them from the tyrants of Austria. Napoleon wanted power for himself, so the Directory told him to invade Great Britain. Instead, Napoleon invaded Egypt. He told the Egyptians that he had come to free them from the tyranny of the Turks."

Now, say to the child, "Tell me how Napoleon gained control over the government of France. Begin by explaining how the *oligarchy* of France worked. Be sure you describe the two "houses" of the French government." An acceptable answer might be, "Soldiers and Frenchmen who owned land voted for leaders. These leaders belonged to two houses, the Council of Ancients and the Council of Five Hundred. The two houses chose five men to be the Directory. After he came back from Egypt, Napoleon forced the Council of Ancients to replace the Directory with three consuls. One of the consuls was Napoleon. Soon he became the *only* consul!"

## THE EMPEROR NAPOLEON

### Review Questions

When Napoleon ruled in Paris, did the votes of the people really matter? *No, they did not matter. He had all of the power.*

How did the Napoleonic Code order that all people should be treated? *People should be treated equally by the law—but with some exceptions.*

What rights did women have under the new Napoleonic Code of law? *They had no rights at all.*

How did Napoleon get the support of the Catholic Church? *He told the pope that Catholics could worship as they pleased in France, and that France would even pay Catholic priests appointed by the Church—as long as they swore loyalty to Napoleon. The pope agreed.*

When did Napoleon's term as consul end? *Never—he was consul for life!*

Where did Napoleon get his new constitution? *He wrote it himself.*

What was one of the powers that the new French constitution gave to Napoleon? *Napoleon could make any laws he wanted, declare wars himself, and decide on France's policies all alone.*

Napoleon needed money in order to expand his empire across the rest of Europe. How did he get that money? *He sold all of France's land in North America to the United States for fifteen million dollars.*

What was this land called? *It was called the Louisiana Territory.*

What title did Napoleon proclaim for himself at his coronation ceremony? *He proclaimed himself "Emperor."*

Which country was the first that Emperor Napoleon planned to conquer? *Napoleon planned to begin with Great Britain.*

When Napoleon invaded Britain, he met an opponent that had beaten him before. What was his opponent's name? *Horatio Nelson had beaten Napoleon at the Battle of the Nile.*

Napoleon planned to drive English warships out of the English channel. What did he plan to do next? *He planned to have barges full of French soldiers row across the channel and invade England.*

Which country won this sea battle—the battle of Trafalgar? *England won the battle of Trafalgar.*

### Narration Exercise

Since there is a great deal of information in this chapter, use "directed narration." Say to the child, "Tell me four things that Napoleon did as he took control of France. Give me one detail about each act. Make sure that you include his plans to invade Britain!" You may choose to allow the student to look back at the chapter while answering. Acceptable answers include:

"Napoleon rewrote the laws of France. His new code was the Napoleonic Code OR His new laws made everyone equal OR His new laws said that employees and women didn't have the same rights as other people."

"Napoleon told the Catholic Church that Catholics could worship in France. Priests had to be loyal to him OR He added loyalty to the Emperor to the catechism."

"Napoleon had himself made consul for life. He ordered his council to do this."

"Napoleon wrote a new constitution. It said that Napoleon could make the laws and declare wars OR He ordered people to vote on the constitution, and announced that it passed."

"Napoleon sold France's land in America to the United States. It cost fifteen million dollars OR This was called the Louisiana Territory OR the Louisiana Purchase."

"Napoleon crowned himself emperor. He held the ceremony in the Cathedral of Notre Dame OR He crowned himself with laurel leaves."

"Napoleon planned to conquer Britain. He ordered British citizens arrested OR He planned to row barges filled with soldiers over to Britain."

"Britain and France met in the Battle of Trafalgar. Admiral Horation Nelson commanded the English fleet. He was killed in the battle OR The battle ended Napoleon's attempt to take England."

## Additional History Reading

*The French Revolution (Days of Change)*, by Kate Riggs (Creative Co., 2009). This illustrated book about the French Revolution also discusses Napoleon's rise to power. (IR 4-6) **LFA**

*Napoleon: Emperor and Conqueror (Wicked History)* by Kimberly Burton Heuston (Franklin Watts, 2010). This book, part of the *Wicked History* series, covers the life of Napoleon Bonaparte from his birth in 1769, to his death in 1821. Includes maps, a timeline, and glossary. For advanced readers (or you can use sections as a read-aloud). (RA 3-4, IR 4-8).

*Napoleon: The Story of the Little Corporal* by Robert Burleigh (Harry N. Abrams, 2007). A great overview of the life and adventures of Napoleon from his boyhood to the general who crowned himself emperor. (RA 2-3, IR 4-7)

*Who Was Napoleon?* By Jim Gigliotti, illus Gregory Copeland (Penguin, 2018). Part of the popular *Who Is/Was* series, this book covers the life and exploits of Napoleon. (RA 2-3, IR 3-7).

*The Louisiana Purchase*, by Michael Burgan (Compass Point Books, 2002). An excellent, simple account of Napoleon's great sale to the U.S. (RA 2, IR 3-5)

*Louisiana Purchase* by Peter Roop, illus. Sally Wern Comport. (Aladdin, 2004). A Ready-for-Chapters book about Napoleon's decision to sell the Louisiana Territory to the United States. (RA K-2, IR 2-5).

*Notre Dame (Houses of Faith)* by Shenaaz Nanji (Av2 by Weigl, 2014). This illustrated book explores the architecture, history, people and beliefs of the great cathedral where Napoleon crowned himself emperor. (RA 2-3, IR 4-6).

*Walks Through Napoleon and Josephine's Paris*, by Diana Reid Haig (Little Bookroom, 2004). This is a travel book for grown-ups, but check your library; if you can find it, the whole family will enjoy browsing through the beautiful photographs of the historical places where Napoleon and Josephine lived and ruled. (RA 2-6, IR 7-adult)

*Beethoven's Heroic Symphony* by Anna Harwell Celenza, illus. Joann E Kitchel (Charlesbridge, 2016). A lovely illustrated story of the creation of Beethoven's Third Symphony, which was originally dedicated to Napoleon, but which Beethoven angrily retitled after Napoleon made himself an emperor. (RA K-2, IR 2-5).

*Lighter Than Air: Sophie Blanchard, the first Woman Pilot* by Matthew Clark Smith, illus. Matt Tavares. (Candlewick, 2017). Delightful picture book set in 18th and 19th century France that recounts the life of Sophie Blanchard, who became the first woman to fly on her own in a hot air balloon, and who demonstrated her skills to Napoleon himself (RA K-2, IR 2-4).

*Child o' War: The True Story of a Boy Sailor in Nelson's Navy*, by Leon Garfield (HarperCollins, 1972). This book recounts the actual experiences of a British sailor who began his career on a ship in Nelson's fleet. (RA 2-3, IR 4-7) **OOP**

*The Navy that Beat Napoleon*, by Walter Brownlee (Cambridge University Press, 1980). Out of print, but worth checking your library for; this guide to the British navy and its ships helps explain the victory at Trafalgar. (RA 2-3, IR 4-6) **OOP**

*Trafalgar*, by Richard Balkwill (Silver Burdett Press, 1993). From the *Great Battles and Sieges* series, an illustrated 32-page book detailing this critical battle. (RA 3, IR 4-6) **OOP**

*Epic!: Battles* by Rob Colson (Wayland, 2017). This book covers 12 of the most significant battles in world history, including Trafalgar (from this chapter) and Waterloo (discussed in chapter 33). Well illustrated; includes a timeline of each event. (RA 2-3, IR 4-7)

*Nelson (Usborne Famous Lives)* by Minna Lacey, illus. David Cuzik (Usborne, 2006). Part of the Usborne Famous Lives series, this book details the life of Admiral Horatio Nelson who defeated Napoleon at the Battle of the Nile and the Battle of Trafalgar. (IR 3-4).

## Corresponding Literature Suggestions

*Lyrical Ballads*, by William Wordsworth and Samuel Taylor Coleridge (Oxford University Press, 1969). Published in England the year before Napoleon seized power in France, the Lyrical Ballads launched English Romanticism; read them out loud together. (RA 2-4, IR 4-adult)

*Songs of Innocence and of Experience*, by William Blake (Oxford University Press, 1977). The great English poet Blake was writing during the career of Napoleon; this edition has Blake's original paintings as illustrations. (RA 2-3, IR 4-adult)

*Who Stole Mona Lisa?* by Ruthie Knapp (Bloomsbury USA Childrens, 2010). Told from the perspective of Mona Lisa herself, this is a story about her "kidnapping" from the Louvre and being taken to where she rightfully belongs. (RA 1, IR 2-3)

*I, Crocodile*, by Fred Marcellino (Michael Di Capua, 1999). This marvelous picture-book satire is based on a nineteenth-century French work; it tells the story of an Egyptian crocodile who is disturbed when Napoleon shows up, demanding everything he sees (including crocodile pie). (RA 2, IR 3-6)

*Clang! Ernst Chladni's Sound Experiments* by Darcy Pattison, illus Peter Willis (Mims House, 2018). Charming picture book about the meeting between German scientist Chladni and Napoleon Bonaparte in 1806. Excellent tie-in between history and science. (RA K-2, IR 1-5).

*Powder Monkey: Adventures of a Young Sailor* by Paul Dowswell (Bloomsbury USA Childrens, 2012). This book geared toward older readers tells the story of one boy's life in the British navy during the Napoleonic wars. (IR 4-7)

*Battle Fleet: Adventures of a Young Sailor* by Paul Dowswell (Bloomsbury, 2008). The third book in the series that began with *Powder Monkey*. A young boy stands with Admiral Nelson on the deck of the ship *Victory* during the Battle of Trafalgar. For advanced readers (IR 4-9).

*Pip of Pengersick—My Part in Napoleon's Downfall* by Jane A. C. West (Harvey Berrick Publishing, 2012). A tale of a dog who finds important documents aboard a smashed Spanish galleon. The dog and her master must bring this information to Admiral Horatio Lord Nelson in time to avoid the perils of war. (IR 3-6)

*Peter Raven Under Fire* by Michael Molloy (Chicken House, 2005). This book is geared toward older readers as there are some explicit battle scenes. It is a seafaring adventure that takes place after the French Revolution when Napoleon is in power. (IR 4-7)

*Thunder From the Sea: The Adventures of Jack Hoyton and the H.M.S. Defender* by Jeff Weigel (G.P. Putnam's Sons Books for Young Readers, 2010). Illustrated in comic book form, this is a story about a young boy who enlists in the Royal Navy. He is assigned to a ship defending the British Isles against French emperor Napoleon and finds himself in many adventures. (RA 1-2, IR 3-6)

*Mr. Midshipman Hornblower*, by C. S. Forester (multiple editions, most recently Penguin Books, 2017). In this classic sea tale, seventeen-year-old British officer Horatio Hornblower goes to sea for the first time just as the Napoleonic Wars begin. For older or more mature readers (a great tale, but some bad nineteenth-century language, and complex character development). (IR 6-up)

## MAP WORK

### Napoleon, Europe, and North America *(Student Page 108, answer 326)*

1. Napoleon directly ruled France and part of Italy. Color France blue; color a small part of Italy blue (the area around the line from the word "Italy").
2. Members of Napoleon's family ruled Spain and the rest of Italy. Color these areas in green.
3. Find the unlabeled area just to the east (right) of France. Napoleon ruled these dependent states. Color the areas in orange.
4. Outline the Louisiana Territory, in North America, in blue. This territory belonged to France.
5. Color the American colonies (and territories) east of the Mississippi River yellow. Napoleon sold the Louisiana Territory to the United States so that he would have money to expand his empire. Color in the Louisiana Territory in yellow.
6. Find England on your map and color it purple. Napoleon tried to invade Britain, but he failed. Draw a dark line between France and England.

**Coloring Page** Three years after becoming Consul, Napoleon told his council to make him Consul for life. Later, he made himself emperor. But most of the time he still liked to wear the uniform of a soldier. *(Student Page 109)*

## PROJECTS

### Game Project: Conquer the World! Game

Materials:
- ☐ *Story of the World, Volume 3*
- ☐ Student Page 110: Conquer the World Game Board
- ☐ Student Pages 111 and 112: Game Card Templates
- ☐ game pieces, beans, coins, buttons or small plastic toys to serve as player markers

Directions:

***Before the game:***
1. Enlarge the game board to fit on an 11" x 14" cardstock. At that time, copy the BRITISH game cards on to red cardstock and the FRENCH on to blue cardstock. (Or you may use the cards as they are.)
2. Color the board and the designs around it. (optional)
3. Glue game board on to cardboard or posterboard to add strength. (optional)
4. Cover with clear contact paper. (optional)
5. Select game pieces, one for each player.

***To play:***
1. Choose your side and place your marker on the top of your country's name. Youngest player gets to start the game.
2. RED CARDS/BLUE CARDS—At the start of your turn, draw a card from your deck (French team has the blue cards and British team, the red), answer your question and if you get it right, move ahead as described. ***If you do not get it right, move back one space.*** (Note: Decide before you start if you want to use your *Story of the World* book to help answering the questions. Of course, the idea is that you can answer them without the book, but getting help the first few times around may be a great way to start.)
3. Continue to move down your squares on the board. If you land on a square with a symbol on it (the French side has the British ships and the British side has the French Imperial Eagle), you are to immediately change sides with your opponent and end your turn. You may only switch sides if either you or your opponent lands on a square with a symbol on it.
4. To *Finish*-You do not need to have the exact number to finish on the last square. Once there, you can choose a question from either your pile or your opponent's pile of game cards. The winner is the first one to the finish square who correctly answers their question.

### Activity Project: The Rosetta Stone

The Rosetta Stone was found in 1799 by scholars who accompanied Napoleon to Egypt. The Rosetta Stone is a stone with writing on it in two different languages (Egyptian and Greek), but with three different scripts. The different scripts were used so that the priests, government officials, and rulers of Egypt could read the stone. People who deciphered the stone used Greek to figure out what the other two Egyptian scripts meant.

You have a sentence below in English. The second sentence is in code. Each letter corresponds with the letter in the previous sentence. For example, the "N" in Napoleon corresponds with the "K" in the coded sentence.

Notice that the every "N" in the English sentence is represented with a "K" in the second sentence. (Note: That does not mean that the "N" in the second sentence corresponds with a "K" in the English sentence!)

Use the information that you have to decode the answers to the three questions about Napoleon on your own paper (you may have to guess on a few of the letters).

***English Sentence:*** Napoleon sold the Louisiana Territory to the United States for fifteen million dollars.

***Coded Sentence:*** Ketuiruk zuih ncr Iuodzdeke Nrmmdnumq nu ncr Okdnrh Znenrz aum adanrrk jdiiduk huiiemz.

Use the above sentences to decode the answers, written in code, to these questions about Napoleon. Write the answers on your own paper.

***Question One*:** How old was Napoleon when he became a French lieutenant?

***Answer One, in code*:** Zdvnrrk

***Answer One, in English*:** *(write on your own paper)*

***Question Two*:** When Napoleon was in Egypt, he visited the Great Pyramid. He asked to be left alone in the King's Chamber. What other famous historical figure visited the pyramid and spent time alone in the King's Chamber?

***Answer Two, in code*:** Eirvekhrm ncr Bmren

***Answer Two, in English*:** *(write on your own paper)*

***Question Three*:** Where did Napoleon make most of his battle plans?

***Answer Three, in code*:** Dk e zekhfuv

***Answer Three, in English*:** *(write on your own paper)*

## CRAFT PROJECT Napoleon's Triangle

This mathematic principle is attributed to Napoleon (that's why his name is on it). Mathematicians are skeptical—Napoleon probably didn't know enough math to figure this out!

Materials:
- ☐ Paper (2 sheets)
- ☐ Pencil
- ☐ Scissors
- ☐ Marker
- ☐ Dry spaghetti noodles (have around 5 since they break easily)
- ☐ Craft glue
- ☐ Yarn (about a foot of it)
- ☐ Ruler

Directions:
1. Make a right triangle: Take one sheet of paper. On the bottom left corner, measure 3 centimeters along the bottom, from the corner. Put a little dot along the edge of the paper to mark the distance. Then turn the ruler and measure 4 cm up the side (from the same corner). Mark the distance with a dot on the edge. Then turn your ruler on the diagonal and connect the two dots with a pencil (the line should be perfectly straight). Cut along the line with scissors. You should have a tiny triangle.
2. Color the triangle a solid color. Glue the triangle to the center of a blank piece of paper.

3. Take out your ruler and spaghetti noodles. Take one noodle and lay it along the shortest edge of the triangle, lining the end of the noodle up with a corner of the triangle. Use the marker to dot the noodle at the length of the triangle side. Break the noodle at that exact mark. Break two other noodles the same length (you should have three noodles 3 cm long).
4. Repeat step 3 for the other two sides of the triangle. All told, you should have three 3 cm noodles, three 4 cm noodles, and three 5 cm noodles.
5. Use the craft glue to stick a 3 cm noodle to the shortest side of the triangle. Then take the other two 3 cm noodles and attach them to the first noodle to make a new triangle. The glued noodle is the bottom side of this new triangle. This new triangle does not overlap with the paper triangle. Its tip should point outward. It is an equilateral triangle (all the sides are the same length), so it looks like a yield sign, not like the paper triangle you made before. Glue the other two noodles in place.
6. Repeat step 5 with each of the other sides (and their noodle counterparts). Let the glue dry.
7. When the glue is set, dot the center of each of the three noodle triangles. Be as exact as possible.
8. Use the ruler and measure the distance between two dots. Cut a piece of yarn that length and glue it to form a straight line. Do the same to connect the other dots.
9. You now have a yarn triangle. Do you notice anything special about the yarn triangle? All of its sides are the same lengths—that is what Napoleon is said to have figured out!

## COOKING PROJECT **Eat Like a British Sailor**

During the Napoleonic Wars, the sailors of the British navy sometimes lived at sea for months at a time, without ever setting foot on land. What did they eat? Salt pork, dried split peas, and hardtack! Hardtack was ship's bread, made so that it wouldn't spoil or mold. Try some—and see whether you would have enjoyed the life of a sailor!

*Ingredients:* 2 cups flour
⅔ cup plus 1 tsp. water

*Directions:*

1. Mix dough and knead by hand or in a mixer for 6-8 minutes, until the dough is elastic.
2. Roll the dough into a rectangle and cut it into squares with a knife.
3. Prick each square with a fork.
4. Bake the hardtack at 450 for 7 minutes; then turn the oven to 350 and bake another 7 minutes.
5. The hardtack should be hard—as a rock! It never spoils, so eat it any time. (A hint: soak it in cocoa or soup to soften it!)

# Freedom in the Caribbean

CHAPTER 30

## Encyclopedia Cross-References

*UBWH not covered, UILE 324-325*
*KIHW 526-527, KHE 322-323*

## THE HAITIAN REVOLT

### Review Questions

What two major crops did the people of St. Domingue grow? *The people of St. Domingue grew coffee and sugar cane.*

What country "owned" the colony on St. Domingue? *The colony belonged to France.*

Who did much of the actual labor on the island of St. Domingue? *Many African slaves labored in St. Domingue.*

What rights did slaves have in France? What right did slaves have in St. Domingue? *French law said that a slave who earned his freedom had the rights of any Frenchman. Slaves in St. Domingue had no rights at all.*

How did the planters and leaders of St. Domingue live? *They lived like French aristocrats, dressed in fancy clothes, gave parties, and spent lots of money.*

There were thirty-six thousand white Europeans in St. Domingue. How many African slaves were there? *There were half a million slaves in Saint Domingue.*

What stories did the African slaves hear during their ancient religious ceremonies? *The African slaves heard about the revolutions in France and America—revolutions that set men free.*

What happened on August 20th, 1791? *The slaves broke out of their fields and quarters, burned the mansions of the planters, killed the planters, and wrecked the fields.*

What was the problem with the slaves' first revolt? *The slaves had no strategy. They just wanted revenge.*

What was the name of the man who organized the slaves into an army? *Toussaint L'Ouverture organized the slaves into an army.*

Which country did Toussaint work for first? When did he switch loyalty? *Toussaint first worked for Spain. When he realized that the Spanish saw nothing wrong with slavery, he swore loyalty to the France of the Revolution.*

What changes did Toussaint make when he was governor of St. Domingue? *Toussaint made the planters and slaves work side by side, and he outlawed the abuse of slaves.*

Who did Napoleon send to St. Domingue to conquer it? *Napoleon sent his brother-in-law, Leclerc, to St. Domingue.*

What did Napoleon and Leclerc plan to do with the people of St. Domingue? *They planned to put them back into slavery.*

What disease killed many of the French soldiers? *Yellow fever killed four thousand French soldiers in just four weeks.*

What country helped the people of St. Domingue drive the remaining French soldiers from St. Domingue? *The English helped the people of St. Domingue drive the French from the island.*

What was the new name for St. Domingue? *St. Domingue's new name was Haiti.*

### Narration Exercise

"Saint Domingue was a French colony on an island just above South America. Rich French planters lived there—and so did half a million African slaves. The slaves worked hard, but were very badly treated. Finally, they revolted! Their leader, Toussaint L'Ouverture, organized them into an army and became the Lieutenant Governor of the island. But Napoleon sent his brother-in-law and a French army to reconquer the colony. Toussaint was captured and sent to prison—but the French caught yellow fever and had to surrender. The island was renamed Haiti." OR

"The country of Haiti used to be a French colony. The slaves of the colony grew coffee and sugar cane, but were badly treated. Finally, they revolted. Toussaint L'Ouverture became their leader. At first, he made an alliance with Spain, but when he realized that the Spanish kept slaves, he changed sides back to the French. However, Napoleon didn't want the colony to have an African governor, so he sent his brother-in-law and French soldiers to take the island back over. But the English came to the island and helped drive away the French, and Haiti became independent."

## Additional History Reading

*Haiti (Countries)*, by Kate Furlong (Checkerboard Library, 2002). The simplest overview of Haiti's history. (RA 2, IR 3-5) **LFA**

*Haiti (Exploring Countries)* by Jim Bartell (Bellwether Media, 2011). Simple book about Haiti, includes a short section on the Haitian Revolution. (RA K-2, IR 2-3).

*Haitian Creole Children's Book: Your Child's First 30 Words* by Roan White and illustrated by Federico Bonifacini (CreateSpace Independent Publishing Platform, 2018). Together with great illustrations, this book introduces simple Creole words. (RA 1-2)

*Open the Door to Liberty: A Biography of Toussaint L'Ouverture* by Anne Rockwell, illus R. Gregory Christie. (HMH, 2009). The story of Toussaint L'Ouverture and the first successful slave uprising in the Americas. The author does a good job drawing the connection between the uprising in Haiti and Napoleon's decision to sell the Louisiana Territory to the United States. (RA 1-2, IR 3-5).

*Toussaint L'Ouverture: The Fight for Haiti's Freedom*, by Walter Dean Myers, illus. Jacob Lawrence (Simon & Schuster, 1996). This picture-book biography is illustrated by the Harlem Renaissance artist Jacob Lawrence. **OOP**

*Toussaint L'Ouverture, Lover of Liberty*, by Laurence Santrey (Troll, 1994). This Troll biography may be difficult to find, but is an excellent chapter-book account of the Haitian hero's life. (RA 2, IR 3-5) **OOP**

*Haiti: The First Black Republic* by Frantz Derenoncourt (Lightning Fast Book Publishing, 2016). Along with fantastic illustrations, this book tells of the fall of Haiti and then subsequent rise again to become the first black republic. (RA 1-2, IR 3-4)

*Sélavi, A Haitian Story of Hope* by Youme (Cinco Puntos Press, 2004). A picture book story in modern Haiti about children who live on the streets but build a family among themselves. Includes afterword by Edwidge Danticat that sets the story within the history of Haiti. (RA 2-3, IR 3-5).

*An American Plague: The True and Terrifying Story of the Yellow Fever Epidemic of 1793* by Jim Murphy (Clarion Books, 2003). This book gives extensive information about yellow fever, the disease which decimated France's army in Haiti. It mentions the Sainte Domingue slave revolt, though its focus is on the epidemic's spread to the capital city of the United States. (IR 4-7)

## Corresponding Literature Suggestions

*The Magic Orange Tree and Other Haitian Folktales*, by Diane Wolkstein (Schocken Books, 1997). A collection of traditional read-aloud tales from Haiti. (RA 2-3, IR 4-7)

*Tap-Tap*, by Karen Lynn Williams, illus. Catherine Stock (Clarion Books, 1995). Set in modern-day Haiti, this beginning-readers story is good for reluctant readers or younger siblings. (RA 1, IR 2-3)

*Anacaona: Golden Flower, Haiti, 1490* by Edwidge Danticat (Scholastic Inc., 2005). This novel written in diary format reveals the story of the first European invasion of Haiti from a native Caribbean viewpoint. (IR 3-6)

*The Last Princess of Saint-Domingue* by Michelle St. Clair (May 3rd Books, 2016). Bibi is born to the queen of a small African village, but that doesn't protect her from the French slave ships that take her away to Haiti, where she becomes a slave on a sugar cane plantation in the late 1700s. (IR 4-7).

*Sugar* by Jewell Parker Rhodes (Little, Brown Books for Young Readers, 2014). This is a story of a newly freed slave girl who, though still working on a sugar plantation, finds adventure and fun while still yearning for freedom. (RA 2, IR 3-6)

*The Banza: A Haitian Story* by Diane Wolkstein, illus Marc Tolon Brown. (Dial, 1981). A Haitian folktale about a tiger and a goat who become unlikely friends. (RA K-2, IR 2-4).

*Janjak and Freda Go to the Iron Market* by Elizabeth Turnbull, illus Wally Turnbull (Light Messages, 2013). Bilingual book tells the story of two children visiting this well-known landmark in Port-au-Prince, Haiti in both English and Haitian-Creole. (RA 1-2, IR 3-5).

*Painted Dreams* by Karen Lynn Williams, illus Catherine Stock (HarperCollins, 1998). A young girl in Haiti longs to create art but lacks the supplies she needs so she uses her creativity to create her pictures. (RA K-2, IR 3-4).

*Serafina's Promise* by Ann E. Burg (Scholastic Press, 2015). This is a novel written in verse about a young, persistent Haitian girl who dreams of becoming a doctor so that she can bring healing to her people. (IR 4-6)

## MAP WORK

### North America and Western Europe *(Student Page 113, answer 327)*

1. The people of Saint Domingue heard of the revolutions in America and in France. Color those two countries red. (The north border of the United States ends around the Great Lakes. Do not color, in red, the area north of the Great Lakes.)
2. Many of the slaves in Saint Domingue came from Africa. Find Africa on the map and color it orange.
3. Spain declared war on France, and helped drive the French out of Saint Domingue. Color Spain blue and then underline "Haiti" in blue.
4. Under the leadership of Leclerc, France re-conquered Haiti. Draw a red line over the top of the word "Saint Domingue."
5. Leclerc and his men caught yellow fever. Soon after this, the British came to Saint Domingue, determined to drive France from the island. Draw an arrow from Britain to the island of Saint Domingue.

**Coloring Page** Toussaint L'Ouverture fought for the freedom of the enslaved African people of Saint Domingue. *(Student Page 114)*

## PROJECTS

### Craft Project — Palm Tree Haitian Stamp

Still a symbol found on the Haitian flag today, the palm tree has had many meanings to the Haitians through out the ages. Woven in their ceremonial robes and painted on objects of common and spiritual use, the palm frond hinted at royalty and freedom in connection with the same West African symbols. It is said that Jean-Jacques Dessaline, Haiti's first head of state and national hero, used the palm tree as his symbol.

*Materials:*
- ☐ craft foam, any color
- ☐ Tacky glue (regular household white glue does not work with craft foam)
- ☐ Student Page 115: Palm Tree Stamp Template
- ☐ tracing paper
- ☐ pencil
- ☐ clean block of scrap wood the size of the Palm Tree stamp template
- ☐ Exact-o knife or box cutter (for parent's use only)
- ☐ acrylic paint
- ☐ objects to stamp, such as a tin can, a glass jar, a canvas bag, apron, or paper

*Directions:*
1. Trace the pattern of the Palm Tree stamp on to the craft foam using the tracing paper. Make sure you trace the lines on the tree trunk. Cut out the pieces.
2. Glue the pieces on with the tacky glue, making sure that all of the edges are glued tightly down on to the wood. Let dry.
3. Get a parent to use the Exact-o knife to cut in along the lines of the tree as shown on the template. The paint will seep into these cut lines and form lines nicely on to your projects.
4. Your stamp is ready to use!

*Note-Before starting, enlarge or shrink template on copy machine if desired.

### Craft Activity — Color the Haitian Flag

According to tradition, the Haitian flag was created on March 18th, 1803 when the new congress of Haiti met at the township of Arcahaie. Dessaline picked up a French flag, which has three sections: blue, white, and red. He tore the flag into three strips and tossed aside the white section. Haiti was to have nothing more to do with white oppression. Dessalines gave the bars of red and blue to a young local girl named Catherine Flon and asked her to sew the bars together. He put the new flag on a staff and designated it the new national symbol for Haiti. The blue bar on the top of the flag symbolizes the large population of former slaves who were the overall majority in Haiti. The red bar below the blue bar symbolizes the mulattoes, or people of mixed race. After Dessalines's death, the new president Alexandre Pétion designed the coat of arms that is placed at the center of the flag. The coat of arms is a palm tree flanked by flags and cannons. Above the coat of arms is the motto is "l'Union fait la Force" which means "there is strength in unity."

*Materials:*
- ☐ Student Page 116: Flag of Haiti
- ☐ Colored pencils or crayons

*Directions:* 1. Color the Haitian flag. Remember, the upper bar is blue and the bottom bar is red.

## ACTIVITY PROJECT **Yellow Fever Remedies**

Yellow fever was a dreaded disease. Doctors tried a variety of remedies to cure the disease before a vaccine was invented to prevent it. Some of these ancient remedies included blood-letting and making patients vomit by giving them salt water and ipecacuanha bark. If the patients vomited too much, they were given a mixture of lime-water and milk to settle their stomachs. Patients were not allowed to eat much food—they were given cold drinks and had to breathe cool air when possible. Because doctors believed that a patient with a sore throat would surely die, they would try to get their patients to salivate. The doctor forced the patient to swallow mercury or rubbed mercury on their skin. Although mercury did cause the patient to salivate, it is a very poisonous liquid metal that causes muscle shakes, deafness, blindness, the loss of teeth, madness, and eventually death.

Doctors tried to break the fever by exposing the patient to temperature extremes. In addition to cold baths and cold drink, the patient was "sweated." He or she was wrapped in a blanket; then hot bricks soaked in vinegar were piled on top of him or her. "Blisters" of mustard paste were applied to the body. This paste actually burned the skin. The doctors believed this would stimulate blood flow and help the body battle the fever.

Try some of these remedies below.

***Take a Cold Bath***

Fill the bath tub with cold water and add some ice cubes. Can you even get in all the way?

***Sweat It Out***

After the bath (drink an icy drink if you couldn't manage the bath), dry off and get dressed in warm clothes. Wrap yourself in blankets and stand near a heat source (a radiator, heat vent, or bath heater). Stay there until you start to sweat. Sweat for 15 minutes. Patients were "sweated" for 6 hours at a time for five or six days in a row!

***Drink Limewater and Milk to Soothe Your Stomach***

Combine 1 Tbs of lime juice with 1 cup of milk—and drink it!

***Apply a Mustard Paste***

Don't worry—this one doesn't burn! Put some table mustard in a plastic bag and heat it up in the microwave until pleasantly warm. Seal the bag and place it on neck to get that blood flowing! (Test bag first against the inside of the wrist—make sure the mustard isn't too hot, or you'll burn yourself.)

# A Different Kind of Rebellion

CHAPTER 31

## Encyclopedia Cross-References

*UBWH 164-165, 166-167, UILE 338-339, 340-341*
*KIHW 490-491, 546-547, KHE 296-297, 327, 340-341*

## THE WORLD OF THE FACTORIES

### Review Questions

Can you remember how two or three of the different members in a weaver's family helped out with the family's work, in the days when people worked in their homes? *If the mother and father wove cloth, the children worked too; a ten-year-old sorted cotton; a teenaged daughter spun thread; an older son tended the sheep and sheared their wool. Even a toddler might help by winding thread carefully onto a roll.*

Thirty years later, what had taken the place of the cottages and gardens? *Factories had taken the place of gardens and cottages.*

How did steam power help make the production of cloth faster? *Steam power allowed the machines to spin, weave, and knit without having to stop.*

Which was cheaper—factory-made cloth, or hand-made cloth? *Factory-made cloth was cheaper.*

Weavers who worked at home could no longer get people to buy their cloth. What new job were they forced to take? *They had to go work in the factories.*

What was one way that work in factories differed from work in the home? *In factories, workers did only one task over and over again. In the home, a worker did all of the jobs, from beginning to end.*

A weaver working at home made money when he sold his goods. How did a factory worker make money? *He made money because he was paid by the hour.*

What did an "overseer" do? *An overseer made sure that factory workers spent all of their time working hard.*

How were the working conditions of the factory difficult for the children who worked there? *Children often had to work long hours while standing. They also breathed in the fine white dust from the cotton, which hurt their lungs.*

Who protested against the laws that the British government made to improve factory working conditions? *The rich men who made money from the factories objected to the laws.*

## THE WORLD OF THE FACTORIES

### Review Questions

"When people worked at home with their families, everyone did part of whatever jobs needed doing. When the workers sold their goods, they made money. But when factories were built, people had to leave their homes and go away to work. They stayed at factories all day long, and did one job over and over. They were paid by the hour, and overseers watched them to make sure that they worked hard. Women and children had to work long hours in hot, dirty factories—but the factory owners didn't want any laws passed to make the days shorter." OR

"When factories started to use steam power, goods like cloth became much cheaper. People began to buy this cheap cloth instead of the more expensive hand-made cloth. Weavers who worked at home couldn't stay in business, so they had to go and work in the factories. And factory owners could hire women and children more cheaply than they could hire men, so many men lost their jobs. Children worked long days, breathing dust and standing up for hours and hours. Finally a Factory Act said that children could only work twelve hours a day—and that they had to be at least eight before going to work in a factory!"

## THE LUDDITES

### Review Questions

What kind of workers were pushed out of jobs with the rise of factories? *Weavers, spinners, and others who were trained in a craft were pushed out of jobs.*

Why did Alexander Hamilton think that factories were good for the country? *He thought that people who hadn't been trained in a craft could still find work.*

What did some workers begin to do, in order to protest against the factories? *They began to attack factories and smash machines.*

What was the name of the man who led the underground army that opposed the rise of factories? *General Ned Ludd led the group of people opposed to the rise of factories.*

What was the name of the group that followed General Ludd? *Ludd's followers were known as the Luddites.*

What were the Luddites angry about? *The Luddites were upset that their whole way of life was changing. They could no longer make a living at home.*

What leader in the United States agreed with the Luddites? *Thomas Jefferson agreed with the Luddites, and said that factories would not benefit the country.*

What kind of men disagreed with Jefferson, and thought factories should be a part of the United States? *Businessmen could not resist the money that factories would bring to the United States.*

Near what two cities in the United States were factories built? *Factories were built at the edges of New York and Boston.*

What was one of the problems with these "worker settlements"? *So many people crowded to live there that the cities couldn't keep up with building roads or laying down pipes for fresh water. Therefore, the towns were often filthy.*

### Narration Exercise

"When more and more factories were built, more and more workers began to lose their jobs. Some of these workers began to protest by smashing machines and burning factories. They called themselves 'Luddites'. They had their own secret password, and they sang war songs while they broke into factories. They were tired of working long, hot days for very little money! Some leaders, like Thomas Jefferson, thought that factories would be bad for the United States. But others, like Alexander Hamilton, thought that factories would give jobs to people with no training. Businessmen agreed with Alexander Hamilton. Even more factories were built, especially near large cities." OR

"Some workers protested the loss of their jobs by breaking into factories and smashing machines. But factory owners knew that they could make large amounts of money with their factories. They joined with the British government and made breaking machines against the law. You could be put to death for breaking a factory machine! Over in the United States, factories were built at the edges of cities like Boston and New

York. Thousands of poor people came to these cities to work in the factories. They lived in crowded slums where the water was filled with trash and caused many people to become sick."

## Additional History Reading

*The Story of an English Village*, by John S. Goodall (Macmillan, 1989). Shows an English village from medieval times through the coming of industry, up until the present days of urban congestion. (RA 1-3, IR 4-5) **OOP**

*Kids During the Industrial Revolution*, by Lisa A. Wroble (Newbridge Educational Publishing, 1999). For reluctant readers, a survey of life in early mill towns and factory slums, with very large print and many pictures. (RA 1, IR 2-4) **OOP**

*You Wouldn't Want to Be a Victorian Mill Worker!: A Grueling Job You'd Rather Not Have* by John Malam and illustrated by David Antram (Franklin Watts, 2007). With great illustrations and humor, this book describes the many dangerous jobs performed by children in the cotton mills of industrialized England. (RA 1-2, IR 3-6)

*Kids at Work: Lewis Hine and the Crusade against Child Labor*, by Russell Freedman, photographs by Lewis Hine (Clarion Books, 1994). The text is fifth-grade and above, but dozens of historic photographs of children working in mills, factories, and fields can be appreciated by the youngest students. (RA 1-4, IR 5-7).

*In the Bag!: Margaret Knight Wraps It Up* by Monica Kulling, illus. David Parkins (Tundra Books, 2013). Fascinating picture-book biography of Margaret Knight. Witnessing an accident in the cotton mill that she worked in as a child in the mid-1800s inspired her to begin inventing items to make life easier. She is best known for her invention of the flat-bottomed paper bag, though she developed more than 80 other devices. (RA K-3, IR 2-5).

*Mill* by David Macaulay (HMH Books for Young Readers, 1989). Beautifully illustrated book about mill buildings and their role in the early Industrial Revolution in New England. Excellent for getting a close up look at how mill buildings were constructed. (RA 3-4, IR 4-8).

*New Industries, New Jobs: British Immigrants Come to America 1830's–1890's* by Jeremy Thornton (Powerkids Press, 2004). Along with detailed illustrations, this book looks at the British who left their homes to take advantage of a booming economy, plentiful jobs, and new opportunities created by the Industrial Revolution in the United States. (RA 1-2, IR 2-4)

*A River Ran Wild: An Environmental History*, by Lynne Cherry (Voyager Books, 1992). This picture book tells the story of the Nashua River, in New England, and the changes brought to it when factories and paper mills were built on its banks. (RA 1-2, IR 3-4)

*Meet Thomas Jefferson*, by Marvin Barrett (Random House, 2001). A Landmark easy-reader biography of Thomas Jefferson, who was suspicious of the new factories. (RA 2, IR 3-4)

*Thomas Jefferson*, by Cheryl Harness (National Geographic, 2004). An excellent simple biography with many quotes from Jefferson himself. (RA 2-3, IR 4-6)

## Corresponding Literature Suggestions

*Midnight Is a Place*, by Joan Aiken (Houghton Mifflin, 2002). This chapter-book novel from the author of *The Wolves of Willoughby Chase* tells the story of nineteenth-century British orphans surviving (and escaping) the factories. (RA 2-3, IR 4-6)

*Oliver Twist,* by Charles Dickens (Abdo & Daughters, 2000). This adaptation, from the *Great Illustrated Classics* series, is set in the orphanages, slums, and workhouses of London during the Industrial Revolution. (RA 2-3, IR 3-5)

*A Visit to William Blake's Inn: Poems for Innocent and Experienced Travelers,* by Nancy Willard (Harcourt Brace, 1981). Amusing poems with illustrations of 18th-century London, inspired by Blake's verse. (RA 1-2, IR 3-5)

*Factory Girl* by Barbara Greenwood (Kids Can Press, 2007). Historical facts and archival photos enhance this story about a young girl working in a garment factory. (RA 2-4, IR 3-8)

*Lyddie,* by Katherine Paterson (Puffin, 2004). By the Newbery Medal award-winning author of *Bridge to Terabithia,* this book follows 10-year-old Lyddie as she works in the textile mills in Lowell, Massachusetts. For advanced readers (IR 4-8).

*My Story: Mill Girl,* by Sue Reid (Scholastic Non-Fiction, 2015). This is a diary-type book about a young girl sent to work in the Manchester cotton mills. After watching her friends' lives get wrecked by poverty, sickness and unrest, Eliza realizes she must fight to escape life in the mills. (IR 2-6)

*So Far from Home: The Diary of Mary Driscoll, an Irish Mill Girl (Dear America),* by Barry Denenberg (Scholastic, 1997). Part of the popular *Dear America* series, this book tells the story of Mary, an Irish immigrant who finds work in the Lowell Mills in 1847. Includes details about working conditions at the time. (RA, 3-4, IR 4-7).

*Sweep: The Story of a Girl and her Monster* by Jonathan Auxier, (Harry N. Abrams, 2018). This book about a young chimney-sweep and her golem friend is set in Victorian England, a bit later than the time period covered by this chapter. However, it is an excellent story for older or advanced readers that illustrates the dangerous conditions that children worked in during this time. (IR 3-7).

## MAP WORK

### The Industrial Revolution in Britain, Ireland, and the US *(Student Page 117, answer 327)*

1. Find England on the map and outline it in brown. England was becoming more industrial. Three of the major industrial cities in England were Manchester, Leeds, and Birmingham. Find each of the cities on the map and draw a green circle around each dot.
2. The water in England was becoming dirtier. Along the outside of the coastline in England, color the ocean black.
3. Boston and New York were the early industrial centers in the United States. Draw blue circles around the dots that represent Boston and New York.
4. Many Irish came to New York to find jobs. Color Ireland purple. Draw a purple arrow from Ireland to New York.

**Coloring Page** In England, some of the weavers and spinners attacked factories and smashed the machines that were changing their lives. *(Student Page 118)*

## PROJECTS

### Memory Project William Wordsworth

William Wordsworth wrote "The Excursion" in 1814. In it, he complains that the lives of people were being sacrificed to make money. Ask the child to read 5 lines out loud five times every day. Within a few days, the child should be able to recite most of those lines from memory. Then add another 5 lines and follow the same procedure until the excerpt from the poem is memorized. (The following excerpt is from "The Excursion," Book Eighth, lines 164-184.)

Then, in full many a region, once like this
The assured domain of calm simplicity
And pensive quiet, an unnatural light
Prepared for never-resting Labor's eyes
Breaks from a many-windowed fabric huge;
And at the appointed hour a bell is heard—
Of harsher import than the curfew-knoll
That spake the Norman Conqueror's stern behest—
A local summons to unceasing toil!
Disgorged are now the ministers of day;
And, as they issue from the illumined pile,
A fresh band meets them, at the crowded door—
And in the courts—and where the rumbling stream,
That turns the multitude of dizzy wheels,
Glares, like a troubled spirit, in its bed
Among the rocks below. Men, maidens, youths,
Mother and little children, boys and girls,
Enter, and each the wonted task resumes
Within this temple, where is offered up
To Gain, the master idol of the realm,
Perpetual sacrifice.

## Cooking Project: Factory Work

The division of labor resulted in both positives and negatives in regards to the working conditions of laborers. This activity will allow your family to try dividing work into different elements, and will let you discuss the division of labor's merits and drawbacks.

Bake these cookies in as many small round cake tins as you have available. Mix up the cookies together. Then, divide the labor needed to shape, bake, and finish the cookies. Divide the following tasks among as many laborers as you have.

*Materials:*
- ☐ peanut butter cookie dough (see recipe below)
- ☐ white sugar
- ☐ cake tin
- ☐ timer
- ☐ cooling rack
- ☐ Tablespoon
- ☐ chocolate kisses (one per cookie)

*Directions:*

NOTE: Divide the following tasks among as many people as you have helping out.

1. Dip out a heaping tablespoon of cookie dough and put it onto a sheet of waxed papers in rows. NOTE: You can do this with eight people (one for each task), four people (one person should take tasks 1 and 5, the second 2 and 6, the third 3 and 7, and the fourth 4 and 8), or two people (alternate tasks).
2. Roll each tablespoon into a ball.
3. Roll the balls in sugar.
4. Take the sugared balls and place them in the cake tin, 5 at a time.
5. Put the cookies into the oven (the same person should take them out after step 6). Bake at 350 degrees.
6. Watch the cookies bake for 8 minutes each.
7. Press the chocolate kisses into the cookies.
8. Put the cookies on cooling rack.

If you are a factory worker, you don't get to eat the cookies! Only consumers can eat the cookies. But if you ask nicely (go on strike) maybe you'll get one.

### *Peanut Butter Cookie Dough Recipe*

*Ingredients:*

2 cups sifted flour
1 tsp baking soda
1 tsp salt
½ cup shortening (or margarine)
¾ cup peanut butter
½ cup brown sugar (firmly packed)
½ cup granulated sugar
1 egg
3 Tbs milk
1 tsp vanilla

*Directions:*

1. Combine ingredients in one bowl. Beat with large mixer until smooth.

# The Opened West

## Encyclopedia Cross-References

*UBWH 182-183, UILE 350, 351 (map)*
*KIHW 556 KHE 328*

## LEWIS AND CLARK MAP THE WEST

### Review Questions

How many states were originally in the United States? *Thirteen states were originally in the United States.*

The states had divided the land east of the Mississippi into territories. Can you name two of these three territories? *The three territories were the Indiana Territory, the Northwest Territory, and the Mississippi Territory.*

When could a territory join the United States? *It could join when it had the same number of settlers as a state.*

What new piece of land did Thomas Jefferson purchase from Napoleon? *Thomas Jefferson bought the Louisiana Territory from Napoleon.*

What two people did Jefferson hire to explore the land west of the Mississippi River? *Jefferson hired Meriwether Lewis and William Clark.*

What was one early obstacle that Lewis and Clark faced on their journey west? *Lewis and Clark began their journey by moving upstream, and by enduring mosquitoes and gnats.*

With what tribe did Lewis and Clark decide to build their winter camp? *Lewis and Clark decided to build their winter camp among the Mandan tribe.*

What did Charbonneau and Sacagawea offer to do to help Lewis and Clark? *Charbonneau and his wife offered to help them interpret the speech of the tribes they would meet.*

Sacagawea brought an extra person with her when the expedition left. Who was this person? *She brought her new baby Jean-Baptiste (Pompy) with her.*

How was the bear Lewis shot in the west different from the bears he was accustomed to seeing in the east? *The bear was much larger and more aggressive than the bears Lewis was used to seeing.*

What is the Continental Divide? *The Continental Divide is a ridge that runs down the middle of North America. Both sides of the Continent slope up to the Divide.*

What did Lewis hope to buy from the Shoshone Indians that would help him with the journey? *Lewis hoped to acquire horses from the Shoshone to help them across the Rocky Mountains.*

What happened during the meeting that included Sacagawea and the chief of the Shoshone tribe? *Sacagawea recognized the chief as her brother, and then explained to him that Lewis and Clark needed horses.*

What did Lewis and Clark give to the tribe in exchange for horses? *Lewis and Clark traded guns for the horses.*

What was one difficulty that the expedition faced as it made its way across the mountains? *There were no animals to shoot; there were no fish; the ground was steep and stony; there were no buffalo; they couldn't eat the horses, so they had to eat some of the hunting dogs.*

Lewis and Clark made it across the Continental Divide. They eventually found what large body of water? *Lewis and Clark finally found the Pacific Ocean.*

What did Lewis and Clark do that would help people who wanted to head west in the future? *Lewis and Clark made detailed maps of their route west.*

### Narration Exercise

"After Thomas Jefferson bought the Louisiana Territory, the United States had lots of land out west. Thomas Jefferson hired Lewis and Clark to explore this land. They sailed up the Missouri River and headed west. When they camped for the winter, they met a trader and his wife, Sacagawea, who offered to translate for them when they met Native American tribes. The expedition crossed the Rocky Mountains, went across the Continental Divide, and finally made it to the Pacific Ocean. Lewis and Clark made maps of the lands they went through. Other settlers could follow these maps." OR

"Lewis and Clark led an expedition across the western part of North America. They started out by going up the Missouri River. Then they went into North Dakota. They decided to camp for the winter with the Mandan tribe. While they were camping, they met a Canadian trader and his Native American wife Sacagawea. They offered to go with the expedition and translate. In the spring, the expedition kept going west. They met Shoshone Indians who sold them horses to ride across the mountains. One of the Indians was Sacagawea's brother! Even with the horses, the expedition barely made it across the mountains. They even had to eat some of their horses and dogs! But finally they reached the Pacific Ocean."

## TECUMSEH'S RESISTANCE

### Review Questions

How did Native American tribes react to white settlers moving farther west? *Some tribes welcomed the settlers, while others feared them.*

What was the name of the Shawnee Indian who led raids against white towns and forts in the Northwest Territory? *Tecumseh led raids against white settlers in the Northwest Territory.*

Tecumseh was angered that some of his fellow Native Americans were beginning to think like the white settlers. What was one way the two groups were beginning to think alike? *The Native Americans started to believe that you could own land, as they began to sell their land to the white settlers.*

Who was "the Prophet"? *He was Tecumseh's brother.*

What are two things that the Prophet preached to the Native Americans? *The Prophet said that the Great Spirit was angry that his children were behaving like whites. Unless the Native Americans changed their ways, they would lose their land forever. "Do not drink the white man's alcohol!" he preached. "Don't wear their wool and cotton clothes; wear the furs and skins of our people. Do not sign treaties with them, for none of us own the land. Do not marry them!"*

In which territory did Tecumseh and the Prophet settle? *They settled in the Indiana Territory.*

What did Tecumseh want the Native American tribes to do? *He wanted them to join together in a confederacy, or union, against the white settlers.*

What did William Henry Harrison want to do when he invited several chiefs to a meeting at Fort Wayne, Indiana? *He wanted to convince them to sign a land treaty—to sell their land for a very low price.*

Harrison wanted to take the Prophet to Washington, D.C. What did Tecumseh do instead? *Tecumseh took 400 armed men to the governor's headquarters.*

William Henry Harrison attacked Prophetstown before Tecumseh could return. What did the Prophet tell his warriors so that they would attack Harrison's men? *He told them that his magic had made the white man's bullets useless.*

What did Tecumseh find upon his return to Prophetstown? *When Tecumseh returned from the south, he found his town destroyed, his warriors scattered, and the word spreading to all of his allies that the Prophet was a fraud.*

### Narration Exercise

Because there is a great deal of information in this chapter, use "directed narration." Say to the student, "First, tell me how Tecumseh became a leader. Make sure you tell me what he wanted the Native American tribes to do." An acceptable answer might be, "After Lewis and Clark finished their expedition, many more white settlers went west. Some Native American tribes welcomed them, but others feared them. Tecumseh was a Shawnee warrior who fought against white settlers. He didn't want the Native American tribes to sell the whites land. He and his brother, the Prophet, joined together and tried to convince all of the Native American tribes to join in a confederacy against the whites."

Then, say to the student, "What happened to Prophetstown? Make sure you tell me what Prophetstown was, and who William Henry Harrison was." An acceptable answer might be, "Prophetstown was the settlement where Tecumseh and the Prophet lived. Many Native Americans came to join them. William Henry Harrison attacked Prophetstown while Tecumseh was away. The Prophet told the Native Americans that his magic would protect them, so they attacked—and many were killed. Harrison burned Prophetstown and even dug up bodies from its graveyard."

Now reinforce the child's knowledge by asking, "Did Tecumseh's plan to unite the Native American tribes succeed?" An acceptable answer might be, "No, after Prophetstown was burned, Tecumseh couldn't unite the tribes."

## Additional History Reading

*How We Crossed the West: The Adventures of Lewis and Clark* by Rosalyn Schanzer (National Geographic Children's Books, reprint 2002). Includes text from the actual journals kept by Lewis & Clark during their journey. (RA 1-2, IR 3-5)

*Lewis and Clark: Uncharted Lands,* by John Hamilton (Abdo & Daughters, 2003). A good, concise read-aloud account of the journey, with photographs of the countryside. (RA 1-3, IR 4-6) **LFA**

*Lewis and Clark,* by Cynthia Klingel and Robert B. Noyed (Child's World, 2002). Much briefer than the book by Kroll listed below, and very clearly written. (RA 1-3, IR 3-5) **E-Only.**

*Lewis and Clark: Explorers of the American West,* by Steven Kroll, illus. Richard Williams (Holiday House, 1994). A picture-book account of the journey, with brief text and beautiful paintings. (RA 1-2, IR 3-5)

*I Am Sacagawea* by Grace Norwich and illustrated by Anthony Vanarsdale (Scholastic Paperbacks, 2012). This book chronicles the life of one of Lewis and Clark's guides, Sacagawea. It tells her story from young childhood, through her kidnapping as a young girl and her travels with Lewis and Clark, up to her death as a young woman. (RA 1-2, IR 3-7)

*Sacajawea: Her True Story (All Aboard Reading Level 2),* by Joyce Milton (Grossett & Dunlap, 2001). For reluctant readers or younger siblings, the story of Lewis and Clark's Native American guide. (RA 1, IR 2-3)

*Sacagawea,* by Liselotte Erdrich (Carolrhoda Books, 2013). Another excellent biography, this one illustrated with large watercolor paintings. (RA 2, IR 3-6)

*Shoshone,* by Rodney Kleid (PowerKids Press, 2015). From the *Spotlight on Native Americans* series, an excellent introduction to the early history and culture of the Shoshone (Sacagawea's tribe); simple reading, but detailed. (RA 2, IR 3-6)

*American Slave, American Hero: York of the Lewis & Clark Expedition* by Laurence Pringle, illus Cornelius Van Wright & Ying-Hwa Hu. Excellent picture book biography of York, the African-American slave owned by Clark, including his contributions to the mapping of the Louisiana Territory. (RA 1-2, IR 3-5).

*My Water Comes From the Rocky Mountains* by Tiffany Fourment and illustrated by Dorothy Emerling (Taylor Trade Publishing, 2009). A beautifully illustrated book that teaches about America's watershed, the Continental Divide, and how snowmelt forms the headwater of all streams and rivers along the front range of the Rocky Mountains. (RA 1, IR 2-5)

*Native American Heroes: Osceola, Tecumseh, and Cochise* by Ann McGovern. (Scholastic, 2014). The section in this book on Tecumseh would be a good supplement to the discussion of his life in this chapter. Text is easy to read but detailed and is supplemented with maps, illustrations and photos. (RA 2-3, IR 3-5).

*Tecumseh, 1768-1813,* by Rachel A. Koestler-Grack (Blue Earth Books, 2003). Highly recommended, this wonderful biography has clear simple text, beautiful illustrations and maps, and even a recipe for Shawnee blackberry pudding. **OOP**

*Shawnee*, by Kadeem Jones (PowerKids Press, 2016). From the *Spotlight on Native Americans* series, a survey of the history and culture of Tecumseh's tribe. (RA 2, IR 3-6)

## Corresponding Literature Suggestions

*A Big Cheese for the White House* by Candace Fleming, illus S.D. Schindler (DK Publishing, 1999). Picture book based on the true story of a Massachusetts town that decided to create a gigantic wheel of cheese for President Thomas Jefferson in 1801. (RA K-2, IR 2-4).

*Jefferson's Sons: A Founding Father's Secret Children* by Kimberly Brubaker Bradley (Puffin Books, 2013 reprint). An excellent story focusing on voices not typically heard from in traditional history books. Thomas Jefferson fathered two sons with his slave Sally Hemings, and their story presents an opportunity to think about issues of family, slavery, and historical injustice. (RA 4, IR 5-6). **Parents may want to preview this book first.**

*Thomas Jefferson's Feast*, by Frank Murphy, illus. Richard Walz (Random House, 2003). Find out how much Thomas Jefferson loves food in this gastronomic tale about the foods he introduces to America such as macaroni and cheese and ice cream. Based on true facts. (RA 1-3, IR 4)

*The Crossing* by Donna Jo Napoli, illus. Jim Madsen (Atheneum Books for Young Readers, 2011). A fun-to-read book enhanced by bold illustrations, this is the story of the Lewis & Clark expedition told from the perspective of Jean-Baptiste Charbonneau, the baby that Sacagawea carried on her back throughout the journey. (RA K-2, IR 2-4).

*Lewis and Clark and Me: A Dog's Tale*, by Laurie Myers, illus. Michael Dooling (Henry Holt, 2002). The journey out west from the point of view of Lewis's dog, with excerpts from Lewis's own journals and full-page illustrations. (RA 2-3, IR 4-6)

*Tall Tails: Cross-Country With Lewis and Clark* by Donna Smith (Scholastic Paperbacks, 2004). Another telling of the Lewis & Clark expedition from the perspective of Lewis's dog. (RA 1-2, IR 2-4)

*Streams to the River, River to the Sea: A Novel of Sacagawea,* by Scott O'Dell (Houghton Mifflin, 1986). For older or advanced readers, this excellent historical novel is based on actual conversations and incidents in Sacagawea's life. (RA 3-4, IR 5-7)

*Shoshone Tales,* by Anne Smith (University of Utah Press, 1993). A rare collection of legends and myths from Sacagawea's tribe. Scholarly, but the tales themselves are very readable. (RA 3-4, IR 5-up)

*Little House on the Prairie,* by Laura Ingalls Wilder (HarperCollins, 2008). The classic series about a family moving west during Westward Expansion. (RA 2-3, IR 4-7) **E-Only.**

*The Birchbark House,* by Louise Erdrich (Hyperion, 2002). Engaging story about a young Ojibwa girl and her family. A good counterpart to the *Little House* books and their representation of Native Americans during westward expansion.

*The Devil's Highway,* by Stanley Applegate, illus. James Watling (Peachtree Publishers, 1998). For slightly older readers, this historical novel tells the story of a young boy and a half-Choctaw girl on an adventure in the new Western lands. (IR 4-7)

*Swamp Angel,* by Anne Isaacs, illus. Paul O. Zelinsky (Puffin Books, 1994). This picture-book retelling of a traditional frontier tale (about a mountain woman in the Tennessee wilds) won a Caldecott. (RA 1-2, IR 3-4)

*Mountain Men: True Grit & Tall Tales* by Andrew Glass (Doubleday, 2001). Mix of historical stories and tall tales from the time just after Lewis & Clark, when trappers made their homes in the mountains and traded furs with Native Americans and Canadians. (RA 2-3, IR 3-5).

*Westward Expansion: An Interactive History Adventure (You Choose History)* by Allison Lassieur (Capstone Press, revised edition 2016). Another book in the popular *You Choose* History series, this one gives readers the chance to explore the west and make choices from many different perspectives including exploring the west as a settler, or defending it as a member of the Lakota tribe. (RA 2-3, IR 3-5).

## MAP WORK

### US Territories *(Student Page 119, answer 327)*

1. Find the Mississippi River. It begins in the Northwest Territory and flows south to the Gulf of Mexico. Trace the river in blue.
2. The U.S. added three territories to its land. Find the Indiana Territory, the Mississippi Territory, and Northwest Territory and color them lightly in red. (Note that the western border of the Northwest Territory is the Mississippi River.)
3. President Thomas Jefferson bought the Louisiana Territory from Napoleon in 1803. Look at the size of the territory! Outline the territory in green.
4. Find St. Louis. This is where Lewis and Clark began their journey. Trace Lewis and Clark's journey to the Pacific in orange.
5. You've already traced their journey from St. Louis to the Pacific Ocean. But Lewis and Clark stopped for their first winter at a Mandan village. Find the village and draw an orange box around it.
6. Trace Lewis and Clark's route back from the west coast in orange.
7. Fort Wayne was the capital of Indiana. William Henry Harrison marched his troops down from Ft. Wayne to Prophetstown. Draw an arrow from Ft. Wayne to Prophetstown.

**COLORING PAGE** Sacagawea, a young Native American woman, and her baby son, nicknamed "Pompy," joined Lewis and Clark partway through their travels and helped them find their way across the West. *(Student Page 120)*

## PROJECTS

### ACTIVITY PROJECT Jefferson's Secret Code

President Thomas Jefferson knew that Meriwether Lewis would need to send news to the President about the progress of the expedition. Fearing that the letters may be intercepted, Jefferson devised a way to send these messages in code. Jefferson was no stranger to writing in code—he exchanged coded letters with people like James Madison, James Monroe, and John Adams. You could only decode the message if you had a "cipher" (a chart or key that enables the user to translate the code). Jefferson found ciphers useful. It was a way to "have at hand a mask for whatever may need it."

Jefferson sent a cipher to Lewis and instructed him on how to use it. See if you can decode Jefferson's sample message. Once you mastered the cipher and reading in code, you can also write in code!

*Materials:*
- ☐ Student Page 121: Jefferson's Cipher
- ☐ Pencil
- ☐ Paper (graph paper is best)

*Directions:*

1. Turn the graph paper horizontally (11" x 8"). Write the following coded message on the paper, one letter per graph square. Leave at least three spaces between lines.
   jtgkxbxqnybwipxquyoltgoamjaxolxxfvewteny
   jfysewhduzbj&amncprr
2. In order to code the message, you need a key word. Jefferson and Lewis used the key word "artichokes," so we will use the same. Write "artichokes" over the coded message (you should end up writing the word six times.) Write the "a" in artichokes over the first coded letter, "j." Then the write the "r" in artichokes over the second coded letter, "t." Continue this process until you reach the end of the coded message (you'll write "artichokes" several times).
3. Now you have "pairs" of letters. You are ready to use the cipher. Your first pair of letters is "a, j." Look at the top horizontal row of letters. Put your finger on the "a" (from artichokes) in that row. Now run your finger down the column of letters BENEATH that "a" until you get to the letter "j." Now run your finger horizontally to the column on the far left of the page. The letter in the far left column, in line with the "j," is "i." "I" is the first letter in the decoded message. Write it above the letter pair on your graph paper. Repeat this process for all the letter pairs.
4. Now you have the decoded message without capitalization, punctuation, or spaces. See if you can figure out where the words divide and read the message. You can now read in code!

***To write in code:***

1. This is the reverse of the process you used to read in code. Write out your coded message on graph paper without any spaces or punctuation. Leave at least three spaces between lines.
2. Above the message, write the key word "artichokes" over and over again until you get to the end of the message. It is not important to finish writing the word "artichokes" the last time (you can end up with "arti" or "artich" and it still works).

3. Now take out the cipher. Find the "a" in the top horizontal row of letters. Put your right index finger on it. Now find the first letter of your message in the far-left vertical column of letters. Put your left index finger on that letter. Now move your RIGHT index finger down the letters BENEATH the "a" until you get to the letter that is in the same horizontal row as the letter you are pointing to with your left index finger. This new letter is the coded letter. Write it above the letter pair on your graph paper. Repeat this process for the remaining letter pairs.
4. Now you have your coded message! Write it on a slip of paper and give it to a friend, along with the cipher. Don't forget to tell him that the key word is "artichokes."

*Note: You can change the key word to make another code. The key word should have all different letters in it. You can make up your own code with key words such as "question," "superman," "Meriwether," or "doubting."*

**ANSWER KEY. DO NOT READ UNTIL YOU HAVE DECODED THE MESSAGE!**
*Answer to the Secret Message: "I am at the head of the Missouri. All is well, and the Indians so far friendly."*

## CRAFT PROJECT Lewis and Clark Duds

By sewing a few easy seams, you can be on your way to JOINING Lewis and Clark in the fashion of the great frontiersmen of the day!

*Materials:*
- ☐ suedecloth or other fabric that is the color of deer leather (about 3 yards)*
- ☐ thread to match
- ☐ 1" elastic for pants
- ☐ tailor's chalk (optional)
- ☐ sewing machine (straight stitches are only needed)
- ☐ cloth scissors or sharp household scissors

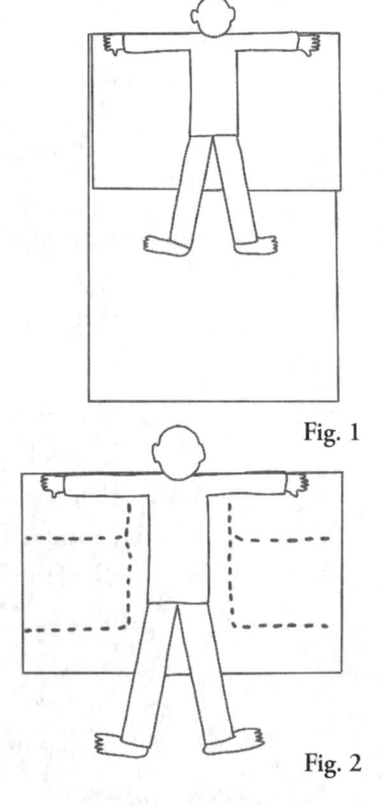
Fig. 1
Fig. 2

*Directions for Tunic Top:*

1. Fold cloth so that a third of it is over the rest and lay fabric smoothly on to a clean floor (figure 1.) Have the wearer of the frontiersman's outfit lay down in the center, with the neck just above the middle of the fold. Stretch out arms in a cross like fashion so that the fold of the fabric is along the top of the arms.
2. Giving generous space (at least 4 inches from the body), cut out the tunic along the sides up to about 4 inches above the belly button (less or more according to your tastes). Then cut out to the edge of the fabric, following along the arms from that distance. This extra amount of fabric hanging down will be your fringe. Go back and cut up along the body sides until you are 3 inches from the armpit. Repeat on the other side. See Figure 2 (bottom side not shown.)
3. Mark the center of the fabric under the head. Have wearer carefully get off the fabric and cut alongside the top edge. Trim later if it is too long, but leave the length until you see how long you want the tunic's bottom fringe. Pin the sides together.
4. Fold the tunic in half and make a small half circle cut for the neck opening. Open the tunic up and on the front cut down the center. See figure 3.

5. Sew along the arms on the right side of the fabric until you get to the side cut. Repeat on other side. See dotted lines in bottom example of figure 3. Turn tunic inside out and sew up the sides. Turn back right side out and try on the tunic. Using the cloth scissors, cut a fringe along the edge of the arms almost up to the sewed edge. Do not cut on the top. If the tunic is too long (allow for a belt), trim at this time. Then, cut the bottom to make a fringe. It's ready to wear!

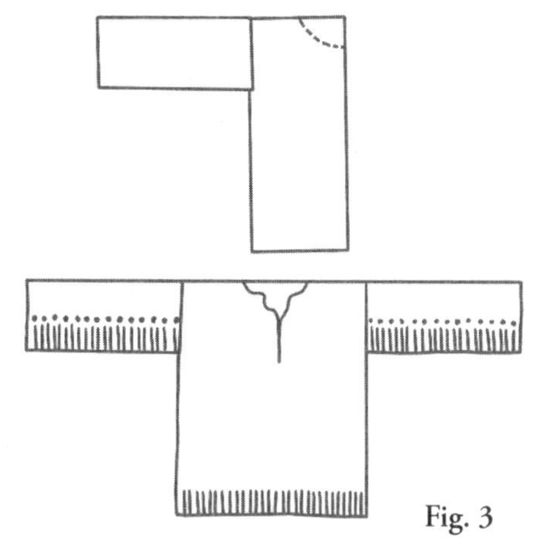

Fig. 3

*Directions for Frontier Pants to go with the Tunic:*

1. Fold pants either lengthwise or width-wise to fit the wearer. Have wearer carefully lay down on the fabric again, only this time with all of the trunk on to the fabric instead of the top. Make sure you are on the fabric up to the belly button. See figure 4.
2. Make one careful cut in the fabric in between the legs leaving about three inches from the crotch. Cut along the sides of the leg about 5 to 6 inches from the edge of the leg. Have the wearer gently get off the fabric and pin the edges. See figure 4.
3. Sew up the sides on the right side of the fabric about 6 inches from the edge. Do not cut the fringe yet. Turn fabric inside out and sew along the inside of the pant seam. Turn pants back to the right side and try on. Make any adjustments to the top of pant so it fits comfortably, though not too fitted, in the crotch.
4. Make an elastic casing for pant top by folding fabric over on the top about 1½ inches. If you have more fabric on the top, trim. Make the casing, leaving one side open to slip in the elastic. Tack down once elastic is in place. See figure 5.
5. Cut the fringe of the pants along the side. Slide on the pants and the tunic and enjoy the great outdoors! Be sure and wear your Lewis and Clark outfit when doing the other crafts in this chapter!
6. *Optional*: If you have any extra fabric, you can make an easy drawstring "provisions" bag that can attach to the belt of the Lewis and Clark outfit. Or save it to use when making the Lewis and Clark journal.

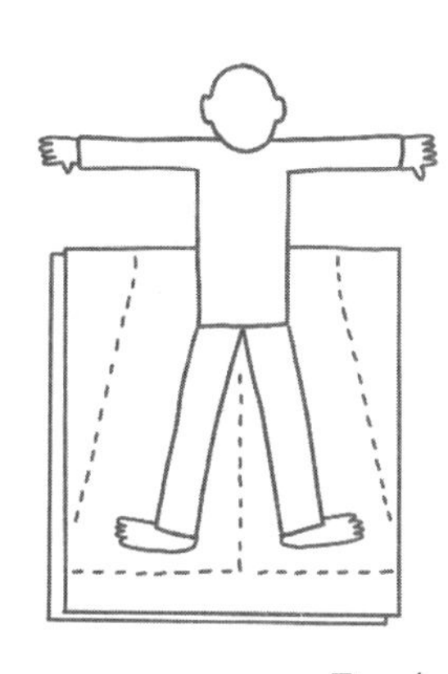

Fig. 4

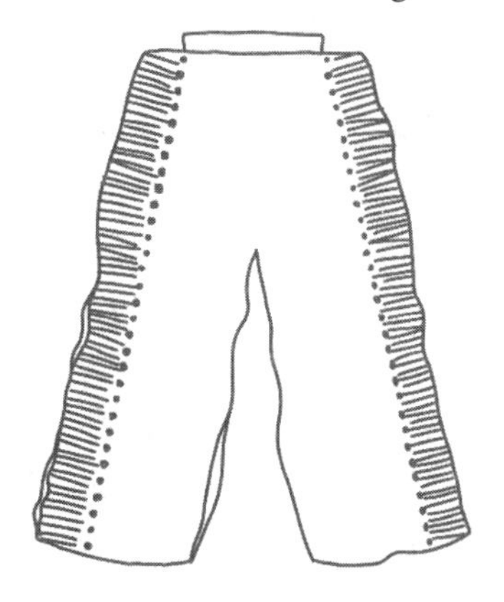

Fig. 5

**Note:* Fabric amount may need to be adjusted for your child. Measure the child from head to toe and double the measurement.

## Craft Project Mapping the Area

Thomas Jefferson and the Americans he represented were eager to discover all that the Louisiana Territory held. So, as Lewis and Clark moved down the Missouri River, they stopped and drew a map of what they saw, Indian tribes they connected with, special land formations and waterways and noted the animal and plant life they discovered. On their maps, they detailed the coastal line, waterfalls, islands, and rivers, all of which they named. Go to a park and do the same. Pretend that no one but you and those you're with have ever seen the area. Be creative with your names.

*Materials:*
- ☐ blank white paper
- ☐ clipboard (optional)
- ☐ pencil
- ☐ colored pencils (optional)
- ☐ a nearby park that you're not too familiar with

*Directions:*
1. (Hopefully you have your Lewis and Clark Frontier outfit on!) Imagine you are at a place that many others are very eager to hear about. They want all the details, but especially a map of what is before you. Using your white paper, take a walk around the area you are in and begin to draw on your map what you see.
2. If you can, add the colors to your map while you are there, then you can make a key for your map later. Or just lightly color the highlighted object's outline if you want to do a more careful job later at a table.
3. Find an unusual tree or flower, and draw a picture of it on another piece of paper. Come up with a name for it.
4. Finish your map at home and add it to your Lewis and Clark journal (below). Make sure you have a picture of yourself and all who are with you at the park to remember the day and to stick with your map. Or display your map in a frame and compare the details with the observations of Lewis and Clark.

## Craft Project Lewis and Clark Adventure Journal

Pages out of the personal journals of Lewis and Clark have drawings of plants, animals and the faces of different Indian tribes they met along the way. Along the side of these pictures are long descriptions with information for the people back home. Journals are used for all kinds of things. They keep our thoughts and dreams, or stories and poems. They act as a record of our drawings or our trips. Make your *Adventure Journal* for your own adventures, or make several to give away as gifts. Below are the general directions and then several optional ways to spice up your journal craft.

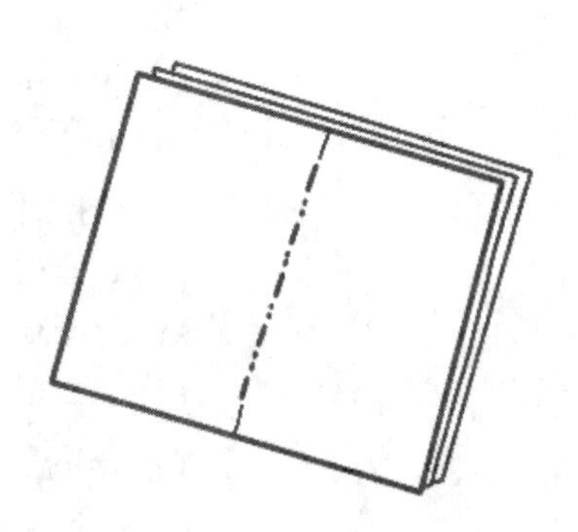

*Materials:*
- ☐ 20 sheets of white paper (8½" x 11")
- ☐ needle
- ☐ thread
- ☐ cardboard piece (10½" x 13)
- ☐ fabric piece (13½" x 16) *OR* fancy paper
- ☐ Tacky glue

*Directions:*

1. Fold the white sheets of paper in half lengthwise. Pull two sheets to the side for the final step.
2. Separate them into grouped piles of six sheets, and put them inside of each other. You should have three booklets of six folded pages in each. Hand-sew one booklet at a time in the middle, starting with the backside fold and punching in to the middle center. This assures that the knotted end of the thread is on the outside and will not be visible when the book is all completed. Repeat with the other two booklets.
3. Fold your cardboard piece in the middle. Tack each of the three booklets into the center of the cardboard, one at a time. Tack it by hand sewing the booklet at the top and bottom of the sheets, starting at the back of the booklet to keep the thread knot from showing once the book is finished. Repeat with the other two booklets, making sure they are snugly in the center of the cardboard.
4. Lay the cardboard cover open and flat on a covered work place, journal-side down. Fold the fabric or paper in half to find the center. Spread tacky glue all over the backside of the cardboard. Match the center of the fabric with the center of the cardboard cover and press down from the center towards the sides, smoothing out the covers so that no air bubbles remain. Let it dry.
5. Flip journal over and glue down the fabric or paper on to the inside covers of the cardboard. Trim the middle of the fabric or paper so it doesn't squish the journal paper. On the inside of the front cover, take one of the pieces of paper you set aside in the beginning and glue on to the cardboard cover and the other side on to the first sheet of the journal paper. See figure 4. This will finish off the book covering all of the fabric edges. Repeat in the inside of the back cover. Let it dry.
6. *Optional*: Decorate the cover with beads, stickers or paint.
7. *Other options*: To add to the look of a Lewis and Clark journal, after step one, gently rip off the edges of the paper. Then, soak all of the pages in a jellyroll pan filled with instant coffee or steeped, bagged tea (smells better). This will give the paper an aged look. Dry the paper on a paper towel, or folded over a string hung over a bathtub. Do not dry the paper in the oven or in the sun because it will cause the paper to be brittle and fragile.

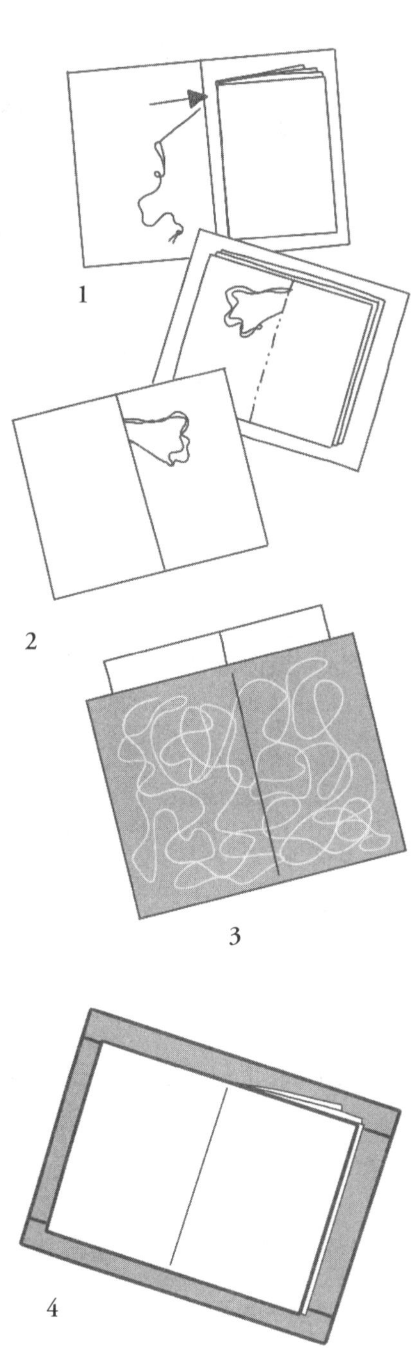

# The End of Napoleon

CHAPTER **33**

## Encyclopedia Cross-References

*UBWH 170-171 UILE 334-335*
*KIHW 538-539, 542 KHE 321, 328-329*

## NAPOLEON'S WARS (AND 1812 TOO)

### Review Questions

What two countries did the British convince to join with them in defying Napoleon? *The British convinced Austria and Russia to join with them in defying Napoleon.*

Who won the battle between Napoleon and the Austrian and Russian armies? *Napoleon won the battle.*

How did Alexander I stop Napoleon from continuing to attack Russia? *He signed a treaty, promising to give Napoleon part of Poland in exchange for peace.*

How did Napoleon decide to defeat the British? *He decided to starve them by cutting them off from European ports, and not allowing any countries of Europe to trade in their ports.*

Which European country defied Napoleon? *Portugal objected because they made a lot of money trading with the British.*

What did Napoleon do when Alexander I of Russia changed his allegiance? *Napoleon marched half a million men into Russia.*

What did he order the men to do to the countryside as they marched? *They were ordered to burn and destroy the countryside.*

What happened while Napoleon's army waited in Moscow to hear from Alexander I, the czar? *The air grew colder; winter was coming.*

Napoleon finally ordered his army to march back towards France. What difficulties did they face? List at least two. *Winter had come; the Russians had burned the bridges over the river between Russia and Poland; the French army was marching through the country it had burned on the march in, so there was no food.*

What had happened to most of his army when Napoleon returned from Russia? *Most of his army had died on the difficult march back to Russia.*

At this time, the United States decided to pick a fight with the British. Why? *The Americans were angry that the British had been raiding their ships for soldiers to fight Napoleon; and they were upset that the British had helped the Shawnee warriors rebel.*

Did Britain want to fight the United States? *No, the British were busy fighting Napoleon, but they sent ships to North America anyway.*

How did Tecumseh take advantage of this situation? *Tecumseh declared that the Shawnee would be allies of the British during the War of 1812.*

What happened to Tecumseh? *He was killed in a battle with William Henry Harrison.*

What important city did the British burn? *The British burned parts of Washington, D.C.*

How did the War of 1812 end? *Britain and the United States decided to sign a treaty and behave as if the war had not happened. The war achieved nothing.*

Whom did the French bring back to France to rule in Napoleon's place? *The French brought back Louis XVIII, the brother of the guillotined king.*

Where was Napoleon sent after he finally admitted defeat? *Napoleon was taken to the small, rocky island of Elba in the Mediterranean Sea.*

### Narration Exercise

Since there is a great deal of information in this chapter, use "directed narration." Say to the child, "Describe the War of 1812 for me." An acceptable answer might be, "While the British were fighting Napoleon, the United States declared war on Britain. The Americans were angry because the British made American sailors serve on British ships (OR The Americans were angry because the British had helped Tecumseh and the Shawnee warriors attack settlers). The British sailed ships into Lake Erie and Lake Michigan, and they also burned the Capitol Building in Washington D.C. But then the two countries signed a treaty."

Then, say to the child, "Describe what happened when Napoleon invaded Russia. Then tell me how the French felt about Napoleon afterwards, and what happened to Napoleon." An acceptable answer might be, "Napoleon marched half a million men into Russia. He told them to burn the countryside and to burn Russia. He expected the czar to surrender. Instead, the czar waited for winter to come. When Napoleon finally marched his men home, there was no food because they had burned the countryside. Many of the soldiers froze to death. Then the French turned against Napoleon. They brought back the brother of France's dead king. Napoleon was taken to the tiny island of Elba."

## WATERLOO!

### Review Questions

What did Napoleon do while he was living in Elba? *Napoleon bustled around his island, working in his garden and adding rooms onto his palace. He improved the roads, built bridges, and tried to make the fields bear better crops.*

Why did the people of France fear Louis XVIII? *The people began to fear that he would become a tyrant.*

To whom did Napoleon write letters? *He wrote letters to the soldiers of France; many of them wrote back and told him to return to France and chase the king away.*

How did people welcome Napoleon as he and his men marched towards Paris? *Because they were afraid of another tyrant in Louis XVIII, they welcomed Napoleon and did not stop him as he marched to Paris.*

What did the king's top general do, when he was sent to stop Napoleon? *He joined in the parade that followed Napoleon!*

When Napoleon reached Paris, he announced, "I have come to free the people of France from the slavery of the priests and nobles!" Had he actually freed the people either of the two previous times he had made this promise? *No, he had not brought freedom either time.*

What did England, Austria, and Prussia do when they heard about Napoleon's return? *They moved their armies toward the French border.*

Where did Napoleon's army meet the English army? *He met the English army at Waterloo.*

Who was the commander of the English army? *The Duke of Wellington was in command.*

Where did Napoleon plan on going, after his defeat? *He wanted to go to the United States and study botany.*

Where did the British decide to send Napoleon after his "Hundred Days of Power" were over? *They decided to send him to St. Helena—a small island far off in the Atlantic Ocean.*

What are two things that Napoleon did while in exile on the island of St. Helena? *He wrote a book about his life, read books in French and English, played cards, and sometimes gave small parties.*

What is written on Napoleon's tombstone? *It reads "Here Lies."*

### Narration Exercise

"Napoleon was supposed to run the island of Elba. But he was bored—and also embarrassed. Meanwhile, the king of France was behaving like the Revolution had never happened. So Napoleon left Elba with soldiers, gold, and guns. He landed in France and was welcomed by soldiers and by the poor people. But the English army didn't want Napoleon back in charge. The English army fought with Napoleon's army at Waterloo, and barely won. Napoleon was sent to another little island to spend the rest of his life. An English officer was supposed to follow him wherever he went!" OR

"Napoleon planned to sneak off the island of Elba and back to France. He wrote letters to French soldiers who encouraged him to come back! Finally he managed to sneak back to France with six hundred men. Many French welcomed him. Even the king's top general joined him! But England, Austria, and Prussia didn't want the "monster of Europe" to get his power back. Napoleon's army met the English army at Waterloo. He was defeated and taken prisoner again. His 'Hundred Days of Power' were over."

## Additional History Reading

*Napoleon* by Lucy Lethbridge and illustrated by Robin Lawrie (Usborne Pub. Ltd., 2005). This colorfully illustrated book chronicles the life of Napoleon from boyhood to his rise through the ranks of the French army and government to become Emperor of France. All his major battles, such as his fateful invasion of Russia and his final defeat at Waterloo, are included. (RA 1-2, IR 3-6)

*Dr. Jenner and the Speckled Monster: The Discovery of the Smallpox Vaccine* (Dutton, 2002). After Edward Jenner's discovery of the smallpox vaccine, Napoleon Bonaparte became one of the vaccine's most ardent supporters, sending his own doctors to study with Jenner, vaccinating the French army, and even creating an official medal for vaccinators. The chapter "Friends and Enemies" discusses their connection. (RA 3-4, IR 4-8)

*Pass the Pandowdy, Please: Chewing on History with Famous Folks and Their Fabulous Foods* by Abigail Zelz, illus Eric Zelz (Tilbury House, 2016). Delightfully alliterative chapter headings and fun illustrations help make this an engaging book about the eating habits of some famous historical figures, including Napoleon. (RA K-2, IR 2-5).

*James Madison: Fourth President 1809-1817 (Getting to Know the US Presidents)* by Mike Venezia. Entertaining book in the *Getting to Know the US Presidents* series; the author includes funny stories along with photographs and comic-book style illustrations to tell the story of our fourth president, who led the United States during the War of 1812. This author also has a great series about composers written in a similar style. (RA K-2, IR 2-4).

*A Picture Book of Dolley and James Madison*, by David A. Adler and Michael S. Adler, illus. Ronald Himler (Holiday House, 2009). A nice picture book about James and Dolley Madison's life and their contributions to the new nation. (RA 3, IR 4-5)

*Mr. Madison's War: Causes and Effects of the War of 1812* by Kassandra Radomski (Capstone Press, 2013). Good summary for kids on the important decisions and events related to the War of 1812. (RA 2-3, IR 3-5).

*William Henry Harrison: Young Tippecanoe,* by Howard S. Peckham. (Patria Press, 2001). This republication of a classic 1951 biography is now part of the *Young Patriots* series from Patria Press, and focuses on the youth of William Henry Harrison, up until the pivotal Battle of Tippecanoe. (RA 3, IR4-6)

*Dolley Madison Saves George Washington* by Don Brown (HMH Books for Young Readers, reprint 2015). Delightfully illustrated picture book about how Dolley Madison, wife of President James Madison, saves a famous portrait of George Washington from the White House before the British burn it down during the War of 1812. (RA K-2, IR 2-4).

*Fort McHenry,* by Charles W. Maynard (Powerkids Press, 2002). An easy-reader account of the building and defense of Fort McHenry, a centerpiece of the defense of Baltimore in 1814 and featured in Francis Scott Key's "The Star-Spangled Banner." Also appropriate for reluctant fourth-grade readers. (RA 1, IR 2-4) **LFA**

*The Star-Spangled Banner* by Peter Spier (Dragonfly Books, 1992). A beautifully illustrated book about the history of America's national anthem and its origins during the War of 1812.

*Long May She Wave: The True Story of Caroline Pickersgill and her Star-Spangled Creation* by Kristen Fulton, illus. Holly Berry (Margaret K McElderberry Books, 2017). The story of the 13-year old girl who helped to sew the flag that flew over Ft. McHenry during the War of 1812 and which became the inspiration for Francis Scott Key to write "The Star-Spangled Banner." (RA K-2, IR 2-4).

*Jean Lafitte: Pirate Hero of the War of 1812,* by Aileen Weintraub (Powerkids Press, 2002). The French-born soldier-pirate helps American soldiers fight the British at the Battle of New Orleans. Simple text, plenty of color pictures. (RA 1-2, IR 3-4) **OOP**

*The Battle of Waterloo* by Russell Roberts (Mitchell Lane Publishers, 2011). This book takes a detailed look at The Battle of Waterloo and focuses on the strategies used by both Wellington and Napoleon. (RA 2-3, IR 3-6)

## Corresponding Literature Suggestions

*The Count of Monte Cristo* by Alexandre Dumas, adapted by Rob Lloyd Jones and illustrated by Victor Tavares (Usborne, 2010). This is a "Young Reading Series 3" adaptation of the classic tale. It tells of a young French sailor who is framed for treason after an interaction with Napoleon. He is imprisoned for many years before making a daring escape (IR 3-6). For an audiobook, try the abridged version read by Jim Weiss (Well-Trained Mind Press, 2018).

*Russian Snows: Coming of Age in Napoleon's Army* by Scott Armstrong (CreateSpace Independent Publishing Platform, 2011). This is a story for older readers of a young teenage boy who enlists in the French Army. In 1812, he and his brother must take part in Napoleon's biggest, and most disastrous, campaign: the invasion of Russia. (IR 4-6)

*The Battle for St. Michael's,* by Emily Arnold McCully (HarperCollins, 2002). An engaging illustrated chapter-book novel, starring a young Maryland girl who carries messages between American forces during the War of 1812. **E-Only.**

*An American Army of Two,* by Janet Greeson (Carolrhoda Books, 1992). A fictionalized but fact-based easy-reader story about two sisters who scared off a British invasion during the War of 1812. (RA 1, IR 2-4)

*I Am Canada: A Call to Battle: The War of 1812* by Gillian Chan (Scholastic Canada, 2012). This novel for older children tells the story of a 13-year-old boy who wants to join the army after his older brother and father go off to fight the Americans during the War of 1812. He sneaks away from home to join the local militia and finds out how chilling war can be. (IR 4-6)

*Jeremy's War 1812,* by John Ibbitson (Kids Can Press, 2000). For good readers, the chapter-book story of a young boy from Canada who ends up in a British regiment during the War of 1812. (IR 4-8)

*Laura Secord: A Story of Courage* by Janet Lunn and illustrated by Maxwell Newhouse (Tundra Books, 2012). This story is about a young pioneer woman who makes a grueling trek through the Canadian wilderness to warn British troops of a surprise attack by the American army. (IR 2-4)

*Meet Caroline: An American Girl* by Kathleen Ernst (American Girl, 2012). The first book in the *American Girl: Caroline* series. Caroline's father is captured by the British at the start of the War of 1812. (RA 2-3, IR 3-5).

*Once on this Island* by Gloria Whelan (HarperCollins, 1996). The award-winning author of *Homeless Bird* tells this story about a young girl on Mackinac Island during the War of 1812. The first book in a series. (RA 2-3, IR 3-7).

*Salt: A Story of Friendship in a Time of War* by Helen Frost (Square Fish, reprint 2015). Anikwa, a member of the Miami tribe, and James, son of a trapper, are both twelve years old in 1812. They find themselves at Fort Wayne during a decisive meeting during the War of 1812. (RA 3-4, IR 4-7).

*The Town That Fooled the British: A War of 1812 Story (Tales of Young Americans)* by Lisa Papp (Sleeping Bear Press, 2011). Based on an actual event during the War of 1812, this is the story of a young boy who helps his town fool the British as they are sailing up the coast of the Chesapeake Bay. Simple but engaging picture book. (RA 1-2, IR 3-4).

*Time Warp Trio: Meet You at Waterloo* by Jon Scieszka (HarperCollins, 2007). Great series for reluctant readers. This funny story zaps three kids back in time, tasked with making sure that Napoleon loses the Battle of Waterloo. (RA 1-2, IR 2-4).

## MAP WORK

### Napoleon in Europe and Russia, and Britain's War With the US *(Student Page 122, answer 327)*

1. Find the area labeled "Napoleon's Empire" and color it red. Don't forget to include Spain (but do *not* color Portugal).
2. England convinced Austria and Russia to join with it against Napoleon. Find Great Britain, Russia, and the Austrian Empire, and lightly shade them blue.
3. Napoleon wanted to starve the British, so he said the British couldn't dock at any English port. Outline the coast of Europe, from Prussia all the way around to the Ottoman Empire, in purple. But do not outline the border of Portugal! They refused Napoleon's control, and allowed the English to dock at their ports.
4. Napoleon's army marched deep into Russia. Draw red arrows to the very right edge of your map (as they marched even further into Russia).
5. Napoleon's army was tired and cold in the middle of Russia. Napoleon heard rumblings of disappointment from the people of France and rushed back to Paris. Draw a red arrow from the edge of your map, back to "A" in Napoleon, as that is close to where Paris is.
6. Right at this time, the British took on the United States in The War of 1812. Draw a brown line between Britain and the United States.
7. Britain still had too much fighting to do with the French. Draw a brown line between Britain and France (yes, it will be a short line). Britain and the United States decided to stop fighting the War of 1812. Draw hash marks through the line between Britain and the United States.

8. Find Elba. This is where Napoleon was sent for his first exile. Underline Elba in red.
9. The British captured Napoleon and sent him to St. Helena—far away. Find the small island and underline it in red.

**COLORING PAGE** The Duke of Wellington defeated Napoleon at the Battle of Waterloo, but the battle was long and hard. This picture shows a part of the battle where Napoleon's cavalry (soldiers on horses) attacked the British army. *(Student Page 123)*

## PROJECTS

### CRAFT PROJECT Star-Spangled Banner Song

During the War of 1812, the White House was sacked and burned. The American Francis Scott Key was held by the British overnight, while the British planned to attack Fort McHenry, which guarded the town of Baltimore. That night, Fort McHenry endured intense bombing; but in the morning, Key looked out from the ship where he was being held and saw a huge American flag still waving from the fort. He wrote "The Star-Spangled Banner"—the song that later became our national anthem.

*Materials:*
- ☐ Student Page 124: Star-Spangled Banner words sheet
- ☐ item on to which you will decoupage the words, like a papier-mâché box, wooden plaque or large glass jar
- ☐ scissors
- ☐ white glue
- ☐ markers, colored pencils, paint (optional)
- ☐ polyurethane spray

*Directions:*
1. Choose which kind of base on to which you will decoupage the words. Paint that item. Allow it to dry.
2. Cut out the words to "The Star-Spangled Banner," leaving them grouped only in the verses. Glue the groups of words on to the project, and let it dry. For example, if you choose to decoupage on to a papier-mâché box, cut out the four verses and then cut out the title and "by Francis Scott Key." Glue the first two lines, title and authorship, on to the top of the box. Then glue each verse on to the sides of the box. Finish the box by painting a flag on the box.
3. Gently rub the edges of the glued words to see if any of the words are loose or lifting up. Add glue if needed.
4. Take outside or in a well-ventilated area and spray with polyurethane spray. This will seal the glued pieces onto the item. Put your project in a place where you can see it and remember one of the good things that came out of the War of 1812.

### MEMORY PROJECT The Star-Spangled Banner

Ask the student to read the first two verses of the Star-Spangled Banner (Student Page 124) out loud five times per day, until the verses are memorized. Add the third and fourth verses and ask the student to repeat those as well. Soon, you will find that all four verses have been memorized. Most people only know the first verse—now you can amaze your friends and family!

## CRAFT ACTIVITY St. Helena Island Salt Map

After Napoleon's surrender, the British announced that they were going to send Napoleon to Saint Helena, far off in the Atlantic—twelve hundred miles west of Africa. Napoleon was a prisoner, not permitted to go anywhere on the island without an English officer following him. His wooden bungalow had once been used for cattle stalls.

*Materials:*
- ☐ Salt Map Dough (recipe below)
- ☐ Student Page 125: St. Helena Map
- ☐ cardboard (11" x 14")
- ☐ blue acrylic or watercolor
- ☐ green paint or food coloring

*Directions:*
1. To Make the Salt Map Dough: Mix together 2 cups of flour and 1 cup of salt. Add 1 cup of warm water and stir with hands, mixing it together. Dough should be on the thin side so it is easy to manage. Add more water if needed. Also, if you would like to have the dough colored beforehand, add drops of food coloring to the warm water before you stir it in. Darker colors work best. A dark green for the continents and island is suggested.
2. Enlarge the map template to fit onto an 11" x 14" piece of paper. Color or paint all of the water blue. Glue the map on to the cardboard.
3. Put the Salt Map Dough on to the continent areas and St. Helena Island, raising the land up. Let it dry. (This could take up to a week depending on how thickly the dough was applied.)
4. Paint the map green, if you haven't colored the dough.

## MUSIC PROJECT Tchaikovsky's 1812 Overture

*Materials:*
- ☐ Recording of the 1812 Overture (try your library or YouTube)

*Directions:*

Listen for the different parts of the Overture, after reading the following:

In 1880, sixty-eight years after Napoleon's retreat from Russia, Moscow was planning a celebration in honor of the construction of the Cathedral of Christ the Savior. The cathedral had taken forty years to build, and it was going to be opened on the 70th anniversary of Russia's victory over Napoleon. Peter Tchaikovsky, a composer, was commissioned to write an overture for the festival. Although Tchaikovsky was not particularly inspired by the idea of writing the piece of music, he badly needed the money.

The overture took Tchaikovsky only five weeks to compose. It was a patchwork of other pieces of music including the Russian and French national anthems, a Russian folksong, a battle sequence that closely resembled an 1813 symphony by Beethoven, and even a theme from his own opera, *The Voyevoda*. Although Tchaikovsky thought the 1812 Overture was only so-so, today it is this great composer's most popular work.

The overture begins with the solemn Russian imperial anthem. Then in the stormy battle sequence, the Russian and French anthems battle for dominance. The end of the overture, symbolizing Napoleon's retreat and Russia's victory, is complete with the sounds of military bands, cathedral bells, and cannon blasts.

## ACTIVITY PROJECT Napoleon Invades Russia Snow Globe

Napoleon had the most powerful army in the world, but he couldn't overcome the frigid Russian winter. Make a snow globe of Napoleon. Shake it and watch Napoleon battle the snow.

Materials:
- ☐ Clear glass jar with smooth sides and a screw-on lid (ex. jam jar, small pickle jar)
- ☐ Water
- ☐ Silver glitter
- ☐ Plastic soldier
- ☐ Hot glue or strong craft glue

Directions:
1. Unscrew the lid and place flat so that inside portion of the jar lid is face up.
2. Glue the base of the plastic soldier to the jar lid with the hot glue (or strong glue). Let dry completely.
3. Once the soldier is dry, fill the jar with water until it is ¾ full. Screw on the jar lid so the soldier is in the water. Add more water until the jar is pretty much full once the top is on.
4. Add a spoonful of glitter to the jar. Screw the lid on and shake. Napoleon is trapped in the snow!

## Activity Project **Know Your Knots**

The sailors who sailed with different navies had to know a number of different knots. Some would keep the sails taut. Other knots could quickly be undone, to allow the ropes to slacken. The sailors had to know which knots to use in the right situation, and they had to be able to tie them under all kinds of conditions—at night, in storms, and in the middle of battle. Here is one knot that sailors had to know by heart.

Materials:
- ☐ 3 lengths of rope, each about 2 feet long
  The handle of a wooden spoon

The clove hitch is used to tie a rope to a post. To tie it, lay a piece of rope in front of you on a table. Make two loops, as indicated in the picture above. The loops should be a few inches across.

Without twisting the loops, pass the left loop over the right loop, so that the holes in the loops line up. Lift both loops, and place them over the handle of the wooden spoon.

Draw the two loose ends of the rope tight, as in the graphic above. Can you think of ways that you could use the clove hitch?

# Freedom for South America

CHAPTER **34**

## Encyclopedia Cross-References

*UBWH 185, UILE 344-345*
*KIHW 536-537, KHE 326*

## SIMÓN BOLÍVAR, THE LIBERATOR

### Review Questions

Where was Simón Bolívar born? *Bolívar was born in South America, in the Spanish colony of Venezuela.*

What was the difference between a creole and a peninsular? *A creole was born in the Spanish colonies, while a peninsular was a native of Spain itself.*

What did Francisco de Miranda try to convince other creoles to do? *He tried to convince them to drive the Spanish governor and soldiers from Venezuela.*

What did Simón Bolívar learn from his travels in Europe and from the books of Enlightenment philosophers? *He learned that other colonies had thrown off the power of the countries that founded them.*

What did Napoleon Bonaparte do that provided Venezuela with the chance to be free? *Napoleon marched into Spain and took the throne from Ferdinand. This fighting in Europe occupied many of the Spanish troops.*

What was one colony in South America that had already declared independence? *Paraguay and Argentina had already declared their independence.*

What did the creoles fighting for independence call their army? *They called their army the "Patriot Army."*

What did Bolívar and the other patriots do to Miranda when they found him ready to flee the fight with the Spanish? *They stormed into Miranda's house, took him prisoner, and locked him in his fortress.*

Where did Bolivar go when he was forced to flee Venezuela? *Bolivar went to New Granada and became a colonel in their army.*

What title was given to Simón Bolívar? *He was called El Libertador.*

How did the Spanish convince some of the creoles to fight **against** Bolivar? *They convinced the poorer men of the southern plains, who detested the wealth of Bolivar, to fight against rich Bolivar.*

Once Spain recovered control of Spain from Napoleon, and control of Venezuela from the creoles, where did Bolivar flee to? *Bolivar fled to Jamaica.*

### Narration Exercise

Because there is a great deal of information in this chapter, use "directed narration." Say to the child, "First, tell me two reasons why Simón Bolívar and other Spanish colonists wanted their colonies to be free from Spain." Acceptable reasons include:

"The colonists knew that the Spanish didn't think colonists were as good as 'real' Spaniards."

"Creoles weren't allowed to be generals or ministers of state in Spain."

"Simón Bolívar knew that other colonies had freed themselves from the countries that founded them."

"Simón Bolívar had read books by John Locke, and he knew about the revolutions in France and the United States."

Then, say to the child, "After Bolivar led the Patriot Army against Spain, the Spanish played a trick on Bolivar. Describe what happened." An acceptable answer might be, "Bolivar and the other leaders of the rebellion were rich men, with farms and big estates. The Spanish convinced the poor cowboys of Venezuela to fight against these rich men. Together, Spanish soldiers and cowboys defeated Bolivar. He had to flee to Jamaica!"

## FREEDOM, BUT NOT UNITY

### Review Questions

What plan did Bolivar include in his "Letter from Jamaica"? *He wrote about his plans for the South American colonies to become states, with elected congresses and presidents, who could join together into one country.*

Who did Bolivar want to run this one country? *He wanted a king—himself!*

Bolivar went to another colony and its leader for help. Who was glad to help him? *The emperor of Haiti was glad to help another colony rebel against its leaders.*

What was the name of another leader who wanted to help Bolivar take back Venezuela? *José San Martín helped Bolivar drive the Spanish out of Venezuela.*

In what colony was San Martín born? *He was born in Argentina.*

What was San Martín's plan to drive the Spanish out of South America? *He knew that the Spanish soldiers needed to be driven from Lima, Peru.*

The roads to Lima, Peru, were well guarded. How did San Martín decide to get there? *He decided to sail there.*

To sail to Peru, San Martín had to reach the coast of South America. What did he have to do to get there? *San Martín had to cross the Andes Mountains.*

How many states did Bolivar want to have in his new South American union? Can you name at least two? *The union would have three states in it: New Granada, Venezuela, and Quito (Ecuador).*

Did Bolivar's dream for a united South America come true? *No, it did not.*

San Martín thought he would convince his people he was a good leader by doing something bold. What was it? *San Martín thought that if he could get the port Bolivar had taken from Peru, his people would better respect him.*

Was he able to get the port? *No, he was not.*

What were two of the reasons South America was unable to unite? *There was too much fighting going on inside each country. The creoles insisted on ruling over the "Indians," the descendents of the Native American tribes who had lived in South America before the conquistadores came. The "Indians" quarrelled with the African descendents of slaves. South Americans who were "pure blooded" Spanish or Indian often fought with South Americans who were only part Indian, called mestizos, or part African, called pardos. And the landholders and army officers were too busy quarrelling with each other and grabbing for power to unite together under leaders who could make South America great.*

### Narration Exercise

Because there is a great deal of information in this chapter, use "directed narration." Say to the child, "Tell me at least four facts about José de San Martín." Acceptable facts include:

He was born in Argentina.

He fought for Spain, but he couldn't rise through the ranks because he was creole.

He planned to conquer Lima, the most important city in Peru.

He marched his army to the coast of South America by crossing the Andes Mountains.

He captured Lima by sailing up the coast in leaky cargo ships and besieging the city.

He lent some of his soldiers to Bolivar to help in the fight against Spain.

He had difficulty getting Peruvians to follow him.

He tried to get an important port away from Bolivar, but he failed.

He resigned because he thought that South Americans were not ready to be free.

Now, say to the child, "Tell me what Simón Bolívar wanted South America to become, and then tell me what really happened, both to South America and to Bolivar." An acceptable answer might be, "Simón Bolívar wanted the states of South America to each have a congress and a president. He wanted the states to then join together into one strong country with a king—and he wanted to be the king! But South American countries wouldn't join together. Many of them thought that Bolivar wanted too much power. Finally, he had to leave South America. He died of tuberculosis. South America was free, but it wasn't united."

## Additional History Reading

*Revolutionaries*, by Paul Thomas (Steck-Vaughn, 1998). Brief illustrated biographies of famous rebels, including Simón Bolívar, for strong third-grade readers or above; good for read-alouds. (RA 1-3, IR 3-6) **OOP**

*Simón Bolívar: Fighting for Latin American Liberation,* by Barbara C. Cruz (Enslow, 2017). For more advanced readers, a more detailed biography from the *Rebels With a Cause* series. LFA (IR 5-up)

*In the Land of the Jaguar: South America and Its People* by Gena K. Gorrell, illus Andrej Krystoforski. (Tundra Books, 2007). A broad overview of the history of South America with interesting illustrations, would be good for a read-aloud of pertinent sections. (RA 1-3, IR 4-6).

*South America (Rookie Read-About Geography)* by Hirsch Rebecca Eileen (Scholastic, 2012). Using colorful pictures, this book takes readers on a journey through South America's amazing rivers, waterfalls, and mountain ranges. (RA 1-2, IR 2-4)

*Venezuela*, by Kate A. Conley (Abdo & Daughters, 2003). A brief, readable guide to the country where Bolivar was born, with short sections on Venezuela's history; for advanced third-grade readers and older. (RA 2-3, IR 3-5) **LFA**

*Venezuela (Enchantment of the World)*, by Terri Willis (Scholastic, 2013). Reference book about Venezuela includes a chapter on the history of the country, including Simón Bolívar, Francisco de Miranda and the fight for independence. (RA 2-3, IR 4-6).

*Argentina (Enchantment of the World)*, by Jean F. Balshfield (Scholastic, 2015). Reference book about Argentina includes a chapter on the history of Argentina. Includes historical maps and drawings as well as maps and photographs of modern Argentina. (RA 2-3, IR 4-6).

*Bolivia (Blastoff Readers: Exploring Countries)*, by Lisa Owings (Blastoff Reader, 2014). This brightly illustrated book gives information on the geography, people, cuisine, holidays and culture of Bolivia. (RA 1-2, IR 3-6)

*Peru (Enchantment of the World)*, by Marion Morrison (Scholastic, 2010). Reference book about Peru includes a chapter on the history of Peru. This series also includes a historical timeline of the country alongside a broader world history timeline, helping to show how the country's history intersected with other world event. (RA 2-3, IR 4-6).

*This Place is High: The Andes Mountains of South America (Imagine Living Here)* by Vicki Cobb and Barbara Lavallaee (Walker Children's, 1993). From the Imagine Living Here series, this book gives some insight into the people, history, and culture of the Andes Mountains region, particularly Peru and Bolivia. (RA K-2, IR 3-4).

*Ecuador,* by Colleen Madonna Flood Williams (Mason Cres, 2015). Part of the Discovering South America series, this covers the early history of the former colony of Quito, as well as its current culture. LFA. (RA 3-4, IR 5-7)

*When the Slave Esperança Garcia Wrote a Letter* by Sonia Rosa, illus. Luciana Justiniana Hees, trans. Jane Springer (Groundwood, 2015). In 1770, Esperança Garcia wrote a letter to the governor of Piauí state, in Brazil, describing how she and her children were being mistreated. This picture book describes a slave's life in South America in the time immediately preceding the time covered in this chapter. (RA 1-2, IR 3-6).

## Corresponding Literature Suggestions

*The Emerald Lizard: Fifteen Latin American Tales to Tell in English and Spanish,* by Pleasant DeSpain, illus. Don Bell, trans. Mario Lamo-Jimenez (August House, 1999). These stories, from a number of different Latin American countries, are designed for reading aloud. (RA 2-3, IR 4-6) **E-Only.**

*The Gold Coin,* by Alma Flor Ada, illus. Neil Waldman, trans. Bernice Randall (Scott Foresman, 1994). Originally published in Spanish, this tale of virtue set in South America contrasts greed and kindness. (RA 2, IR 3-4)

*Patterns in Peru: An Adventure in Patterning,* by Cindy Neuschwander and illustrated by Bryan Langdo (Henry Holt and Co., 2007). Twins Matt and Bibi must use their understanding of patterns and sequences to locate the mysterious lost city of Quwi; and then find their way back again. (RA 1-2, IR 3-6)

*Tortillas and Lullabies,* by Lynn Reiser, illus. Valientes Corazones (Raylo Press, 1998). In this English/Spanish tale, four generations of Latin American women carry out the comforting routines of daily life; a good, gentle glimpse of another culture. (RA 2, IR 3-4)

*Up and Down the Andes,* by Laurie Krebs and illustrated by Aurelia Fronty (Barefoot Books, 2011). This book follows six Peruvian children, each using different modes of transportation, as they make their way to a winter solstice celebration. This book also includes notes on the history and culture of Peru. (RA 1-2, IR 2-3)

## MAP WORK

### Spain and Its Colonies in South America *(Student Page 126, answer 328)*

1. Ferdinand and Bolivar played tennis at the royal palace in Madrid, Spain. Find Madrid on the map and draw a red circle around the dot.
2. Argentina was one of the first countries to declare independence from Spain. Find Argentina, in South America, and color it orange.
3. Find Venezuela on the map and color it purple. Venezuela also wanted its independence. But Spain wasn't ready to give up on it so easily. Spain sent soldiers to the coast of Venezuela. Draw a yellow arrow from Spain to the coast of Venezuela.

4. When Ferdinand of Spain sent his troops to South America, Bolivar fled to Jamaica, owned by Britain. Find Jamaica and color it green.
5. Bolivar looked to Haiti for help. Haiti gave him ships and soldiers. Draw an arrow from Jamaica to Haiti.
6. San Martín knew that Lima was one of the key cities to Spain's hold on South America. Find Lima, Peru and underline it in blue. Then outline Peru in blue.
7. La Republica de Colombia was made of three territories—New Granada, Venezuela and Quito. Outline the border of this republic in orange (as these states, like Argentina, also wanted to be independent of Spain's control).

**COLORING PAGE** Simón Bolívar was called *El Libertador* ("the Liberator") because he helped South American countries win their freedom from Spain. *(Student Page 127)*

## PROJECTS

### GAME PROJECT Battle for South America! The Game

Read about the exciting life of Simón Bolívar as you play this game of *The Battle for South America*!

Materials:
- ☐ *The Story of the World, Volume 3*
- ☐ Student Page 128: The Battle for South America Game Board
- ☐ game pieces—beans, coins, buttons or small plastic toys to serve as player markers
- ☐ one or two dice, depending on how fast you want the game to go

Directions:

***Before the game:***
1. Enlarge the game board to fit on an 11" x 14" sheet of paper.
2. Color the board.
3. Glue Game Board on to cardboard or posterboard to add strength. (optional)
4. Cover with clear contact paper. (optional)
5. Select game pieces, one for each player.

***To play:***
1. All players begin at the place marked "Start."
2. Roll the die, or dice. The player with the lowest number gets to be first. Go clock-wise from the first player.
3. Follow the pathway to the end.
4. If you land on a circle with a ✥ then answer the question and follow the instructions.
5. The first one to the end who can answer the last question correctly wins the game.

### CRAFT PROJECT South American Cowboy

The South American cowboy was similar to the North American cowboy. Known as *gauchos*, these cowboys roamed the plains of Brazil, Argentina, Uruguay, and Paraguay. They hunted wild cattle and horses on the plains. Gauchos made their money by stripping off the hides of the cattle and selling those hides to Spain. They also played an important part in Simón Bolívar's victories by joining the battles at critical times. Here are two Gaucho outfits.

Materials:
- ☐ colored pencils or crayons
- ☐ scissors
- ☐ Scotch removable double-stick tape
- ☐ Student Page 129: Gaucho Paper Doll
- ☐ Student Page 130: Gaucho Paper Doll Outfits

Directions:

1. Color the Gaucho outfit, poncho and hat. The cowboys usually wore white blousy shirts and light-colored baggy pants. Their belts were made out of leather, and they had silver coins on them. Many belts were very elaborate. The vest, hat and boots were made of dark leather. Their poncho, which would also serve them as a blanket when they slept, was usually a red wool with black stripe on the bottom. After you've colored them, cut out the clothes.
2. Use the double-stick tape to attach the cowboy's outfits.

## COOKING PROJECT **Peruvian Rice Pudding**

This recipe originally came from the Middle East, and then became popular in Spain. Spaniards brought it to Peru, where it is still popular today. This is a big recipe, so it's good for feeding hungry revolutionaries (like Simón Bolívar and José de San Martín). For smaller revolutions, halve or quarter the recipe.

### *Arroz con Leche*

*Ingredients:*

1 cup orange juice
2 cups long grain rice
3 cups water
2 8-ounce cans sweetened condensed milk
2 cinnamon sticks
ground cinnamon for dusting
orange slices

*Directions:*

1. Bring all ingredients (except orange slices and ground cinnamon) to a boil.
2. Reduce heat, cover, and simmer for 15 minutes, stirring occasionally to prevent scorching.
3. Remove from heat and let cool.
4. Remove the cinnamon sticks, dust with ground cinnamon and garnish with fresh orange slices.
5. Invite your friends over and stage a revolution!

# Mexican Independence

## Encyclopedia Cross-References

*UBWH 185 UILE not covered*
*KIHW 536, KHE 326*

## THE CRY OF DOLORES

### Review Questions

What part of America was "New Spain" in? *New Spain was in Central America.*

What did the French philosopher Voltaire write about? *Voltaire wrote about the equality of all men, and their right to rule themselves.*

What was Don Miguel's job in the town of Dolores? *Don Miguel was the only priest in the town.*

What had Fray Estrada said that almost got Don Miguel into trouble with the Roman Catholic Church? *Estrada had said that Don Miguel taught strange, untrue beliefs instead of true Catholic doctrine.*

Were all men in New Spain treated equally? *No, they were not. Peninsulars born in Spain had much more power than the creoles and mestizos (half-Indians).*

How had Don Miguel helped the Indians of Dolores? List at least two actions. *He himself was a creole who owned two farms, so he had used his own land and his own money to teach the Indians skills. He had built a factory where the Indians could make valuable pots and bricks for sale. He had raised mulberry trees on his land, hoping that the Indians could make silk from silkworms. He had taught them to make wine from the vineyard planted outside the farmhouse.*

What did the Spanish soldiers do to Don Miguel's vineyard? What message were they sending him? *They slashed the vines and burned them. They wanted him to remember that the people of Dolores relied on Spain for everything.*

What was Don Miguel's speech—"The Cry of Dolores"—about? *The speech was about how hard their lives were because of the Spanish. The speech told the Indians and mestizos to act to gain their freedom.*

When Don Miguel became Captain-General Miguel Hidalgo of the New Spain Army, he led a mob towards Guanajuato. What did his mob do? *The mob killed over five hundred men and women.*

When Hidalgo and his soldiers reached Mexico City, what did Hidalgo decide to do? *He ordered his men to retreat.*

What happened when Hidalgo's army retreated? *The Spanish army attacked his army, defeated it, and captured Hidalgo.*

What did the Spanish army have to do before they could execute Don Miguel? *They had to have him "un-priested," or defrocked.*

What is September 16th? *It is Mexico's Independence Day.*

### Narration Exercise

Because there is a great deal of information in this chapter, use "directed narration." Say to the student, "Explain why Don Miguel rebelled against Spain. Be sure to tell me about the Cry of Dolores." An acceptable answer might be, "Don Miguel believed in the French ideas about equality. But in New Spain, the Spanish held much more power than the creoles and the Indians. Spanish soldiers even kept Don Miguel from helping the Indians with his vineyard. So Don Miguel told everyone who came to mass that they should rebel against Spain. He became a general and led them in an army against the Spanish."

Then say to the student, "Tell me about Miguel Hidalgo's army, and what happened to it—and to Hidalgo." An acceptable answer might be, "Hidalgo's army attacked a Spanish city. Even though Hidalgo didn't want them to, they killed everyone inside. So when the army reached Mexico City, Hidalgo stopped them. Instead, Spanish soldiers came out, defeated the army, and captured Hidalgo. They declared that he was no longer a priest, and put him to death."

## THE REPUBLIC OF MEXICO

### Review Questions

After Don Miguel's army failed to gain independence, what did Jose Maria Morelos Y Pavon do? *He led a second revolt against Spain.*

What was the group of army officers who claimed to be the true rulers of New Spain called? *It was called a junta.*

What did the Spanish do to Morelos when they captured him? *They put him to death.*

Who was the third rebel leader in New Spain? *Agustin de Iturbide was the third rebel leader in Spain.*

After fighting for Spain, Iturbide wanted to be honored with a special medal. Why did the Spanish refuse to give him this honor? *They refused because he was a creole and not a peninsulare.*

When Spain refused to honor him, Iturbide was angry. He started to write down some of his ideas, while continuing to serve in Spain's army. What were some of his ideas—"The Three Guarantees"? *He believed New Spain should become an independent kingdom, with its own king. All of its people would be equal, and Roman Catholicism would be its official language.*

What other rebel leader fought with Iturbide? *Vicente Guerrero and his army fought with Iturbide.*

Was Iturbide a good king? *No. He abused his power and threw leaders of the Mexican congress in jail.*

After a brief period with Iturbide ruling as emperor, the Mexicans decided to change their type of government to what? *They decided Mexico would be ruled as a republic.*

What general led the revolt against Iturbide? *Santa Anna led the revolt.*

After the republic was in place, how did Iturbide's enemies trick him? *They told him to return from Italy because the new government wasn't popular. Then they arrested him, put him in jail, and put him to death.*

### Narration Exercise

Because there is a great deal of information in this chapter, use "directed narration." Say to the student, "Tell me about the two freedom fighters, Morelos and Iturbide. Be sure to tell me what happened to each one of them." An acceptable answer might be, "Morelos was part of a junta that tried to rule New Spain. They wrote a constitution that said all men would be equal. Morelos was captured and put to death. Then Iturbide led a rebellion. Spain wouldn't give him a special honor because he wasn't a peninsulare, so he wrote out a new plan for New Spain called the Three Guarantees. This changed the name of the country to Mexico. Iturbide won the war for New Spain's freedom and became its emperor. But he was a bad emperor, so the Mexican people drove him away. Mexico became a republic. Iturbide's enemies tricked him into coming back to Mexico—and put him to death."

## Additional History Reading

*The History of Mexico*, by Amy Hunter (Mason Crest Publishers, 2002). A good chronological overview of Mexico's struggle for independence, with additional chapters on nineteenth and twentieth-century rebellions. (RA 2-3, IR 4-6) **OOP**

*Miguel Hidalgo y Costilla*, by Jan Gleiter and Kathleen Thompson (Raintree, 1989). A simple but complete biography, in the *Raintree Hispanic Stories* series. **LFA** (RA 2, IR 3-5)

*Miguel Hidalgo y Costilla: Father of Mexican Independence*, by Frank de Varona (Millbrook Press, 1995). An independent read for strong third-grade readers and older. (RA 2-3, IR 3-6) **OOP**

*Famous People of Mexico*, by Anna Carew-Miller (Mason Crest Publishers, 2002). A series of profiles of famous figures in Mexican history, beginning with the Olmecs and ending in the present day. (RA 2-3, IR 4-6) **LFA**

*Mexico: The People*, by Bobbie Kalman (Crabtree Publications, 2001). A brightly-illustrated, simple guide to the different people groups of Mexico and their origins. (RA 2, IR 3-5)

*In the Days of the Vaqueros: America's First True Cowboys* by Russell Freedman (Clarion, 2001). Beautifully illustrated book about the Central American cowherders who eventually shared their skills with the cowboys of the American west. (RA 3-4, IR 4-8).

*Let's Learn about Mexico: Activity and Coloring Book* by Yuko Green (Dover Publications, 2013). This book uses puzzles and activities to introduce kids to fascinating aspects of Mexican geography, language, food, arts, sports and festivals. (RA 1-2, IR 2-5)

*Mexico (Enchantment of the World)* by Liz Sonneborn (Children's, 2017). Reference book about Mexico; includes a chapter on the history of Mexico. (IR 3-5).

*Mexico ABCs*, by Sarah Heiman (Picture Window Books, 2003). Nice illustrations and brief, readable paragraphs about the history, culture, and geography of Mexico. (RA 1-2, IR 3-4)

*P Is for Piñata: A Mexico Alphabet* by Tony Johnston and illustrated by John Parra (Sleeping Bear Press, 2008). This colorfully illustrated book teaches about Mexico and Mexican culture using simple prose for young children and lots of interesting facts for older. (RA 1-2, IR 2-4)

*A Kid's Guide to Latino History: More than 50 Activities* by Valerie Petrillo (Chicago Review Press, 2009). This book features the history as well as more than 50 hands-on activities, games and crafts that explore the diversity of Latino culture. (RA 1-2, IR 3-6)

## Corresponding Literature Suggestions

*Adelita: A Mexican Cinderella Story*, by Tomie de Paola (Putnam, 2002). A delightful picture-book version of a very old story. (IR 2-4)

*When the Viceroy Came*, by Claudia Burr, Krystyna Libura, and Maria Cristina Urrutia (Groundwood Books, 1999). This simple picture book tells of the arrival of Viceroy Albuquerque in New Spain in 1702 from the point of view of one of his pages. (RA 1, IR 2-4)

*Juan's Sweet and Spicy Memory* by Hee Jung Yoon and illustrated by Christopher Corr (Tantan Publishing, 2017). This book teaches about Mexican culture and cuisine when a young boy helps a tourist family during the Cinco de Mayo celebrations. The story is aided by bright and colorful illustrations. (RA 1-2, IR 2-4)

*The Legend of the Poinsettia,* by Tomie dePaola (Puffin, 1997). This Mexican legend about how the poinsettia came to be is told through the wonderful paintings and engaging text of award-winning author and illustrator Tomie dePaola. (RA K-2, IR 2-4).

*A Library for Juana: The World of Sor Juana Ines,* by Pat Mora, illus. Beatriz Vidal (Alfred Knopf, 2002). In New Spain in the 1600s lived a girl named Juana who grew up to become a nun. Because of her love of reading and learning from a very early age, she is honored in Mexico today. This fictionalized story chronicles her early life. (RA 1-2, IR 3-4)

*Mystery of the Thief in the Night: Mexico 1,* by Janelle Diller and illustrated by Adam Turner (WorldTrek Publishing, 2014). A mystery book about a girl and her family who sail into a Mexican lagoon. When she meets a young girl, they soon find themselves enmeshed in adventure. This book is filled with Mexican culture, tradition, and even a bit of Spanish. (RA 1-2, IR 2-4)

*Meet Josephina (American Girl),* by Valerie Tripp, illus Susan McAliley (Pleasant, 1997). The first book in Josephina's series, the story is set near Santa Fe during the time when the area was under Mexican control, only a few years after the events of this chapter. (RA 1-2, IR 3-4).

*Nine Days to Christmas: A Story of Mexico* by Marie Hall Ets and Aurora Labastida (Dover Publications, 2017). This Caldecott Medal winner is a republication of a classic tale of a little Mexican girl's excitement at the approach of Christmas. This book perfectly presents a child's-eye view of Mexican culture. (RA 1-2, IR 2-4)

*The Princess and the Warrior: A Tale of Two Volcanoes* by Duncan Tonatiuh (Abrams Books for Young Readers, 2016). This book is about the legend of a princess, a warrior and how the volcanoes overlooking Mexico City, Iztaccihuatl and Popocatepetl, came to be. (RA 1-2, IR 2-4)

*The Tree is Older than You Are: A Bilingual Gathering of Poems and Stories from Mexico,* ed. Naomi Shihab Nye (Simon Pulse, 1998). A collection of stories and poems by 64 famous Mexican writers, in Spanish with English translations; excellent for reading aloud. (RA 2-3, IR 4-7) **OOP**

## MAP WORK

### New Spain and North America *(Student Page 131, answer 328)*

1. Outline the border of New Spain in green.
2. Don Miguel helped the Indians of Dolores. Remember his sermon, "The Cry of Dolores." Find Dolores and circle the dot that represents the city in blue.
3. The mestizos of Dolores marched toward Guanajuato and captured the city. Draw a purple circle around Guanajuato.
4. The small army then moved toward Mexico City. Draw an arrow from Guanajuato toward Mexico City.
5. An American ambassador traveled from Washington D.C. to Mexico City. Draw an arrow from Washington D.C. (the lone dot on the east coast of the United States) toward Mexico City.

**Coloring Page** Don Miguel led a large group of people (both Indians and half-Indian mestizos) to fight for the independence of Mexico (New Spain) from Spain. *(Student Page 132)*

## CRAFT ACTIVITY Independence Day Pinata

Mexican Independence Day is celebrated on September 16th of each year with a fiesta—a huge party! Make this traditional Mexican pinata for your own Mexican Independence Day celebration.

*Materials:*

- ☐ Large balloon
- ☐ Newspaper
- ☐ Typing paper
- ☐ Flour
- ☐ Water
- ☐ Large bowl
- ☐ String
- ☐ Masking tape
- ☐ Green, white, and red poster paint
- ☐ Candy or other treats

*Directions:*

1. Mix equal parts of flour and water together in the large bowl. (Note: in very humid areas of the country, the proportions should be closer to 1 measure flour to ¾ measure of water.)
2. Blow up the large balloon and tie the end. Tie the string to the end of the balloon.
3. Rip the newspaper into strips about 2" wide. Soak the newspaper in the flour/water mixture and plaster the strips over the balloon. Leave a bare spot near the tied-off end of the balloon!
4. When three layers have been added to the balloon, hang it up by the string until dry. When dry, repeat again, adding 3 more layers. Allow to dry thoroughly.
5. Repeat one more time, this time adding 3 layers of white typing paper strips.
6. When the final layer is dry, pop the balloon at the "bare spot." Pour candy or other treats into the pinata. Then cover the hole with masking tape and layer a few more strips of white papier-mâché over the tape. Let dry.
7. Paint the pinata with green, white, and red stripes—the colors of Mexico!
8. Hang the pinata up. Traditionally, children are blindfolded and try to break the pinata with a bat or stick so that the candy falls out. Be sure to do this in a large area! When the pinata breaks, yell the traditional words of fiesta: "Viva Mexico" and "Viva la independencia!"

## ART PROJECT Two Symbols of Mexican Independence

One of Hidalgo's followers, a grocer named Epigmenio Gonzales, drew this cartoon as a symbol of Mexican independence. The cartoon shows an eagle—the symbol of the Aztec people, the native peoples of New Spain—perched on top of a cactus. The eagle has the tail of a Spanish lion in his mouth. The lion, with his tail pulled by the eagle, is forced to cry out, "Long Live America!"

Here is another symbol of Mexican independence—the flag of Jose Morelos. The inscription means "She conquers equally with her eyes and her talons" and refers to the Aztec eagle, crowned with an emperor's crown and transformed into a symbol of Mexican rule.

Now, try to draw freehand one of the symbols above—or create your own symbol of Mexican independence. If you decide to draw your own symbol, show the Mexican eagle, dominant over a symbol of Spain (you can use one of the symbols on the Spanish coat of arms: a purple crowned lion, a gold castle, a golden chain, and a pomegranate with two green leaves). Make sure that you create an appropriate motto for your drawing!

## CRAFT PROJECT Mexican Flowers

The colors of the Mexican flag represent three concepts important to the Mexican people. Green stands for liberty; white stands for faith and the Church; and red stands for unity. These three colors are used on Mexican independence day to decorate for fiesta. Often, tissue paper flowers are used as well. Making flowers from tissue paper is an old Mexican tradition.

*Materials:*

- ☐ 12 sheets of tissue paper, about 6" x 12": 4 green, 4 white, 4 red
- ☐ three green pipe cleaners
- ☐ scissors
- ☐ ruler

*Directions:*
1. For each flower, stack four sheets of tissue paper together in a square.
2. Beginning at the bottom of the stack, make accordion folds about 1" wide. When finished, you should have a single, accordion-folded piece of paper, 1" wide and 6" long.
3. Round off all four corners with the scissors.
4. Twist a pipe cleaner around the center of the paper to serve as the stem. Twist the pipe cleaner back around itself firmly.
5. Carefully fan the four layers of paper out, pulling the folds gently outwards, one layer at a time, from the top down.
6. Repeat with the remaining two colors. When you are finished, you will have three Mexican tissue paper flowers, standing for liberty, faith, and unity!

## COOKING PROJECT **Mexican Breakfast**

The Spanish traditionally ate very light breakfasts—just rolls and coffee. But Mexicans were different than their Spanish rulers. They ate hearty breakfasts of eggs and meat. Try this traditional Mexican breakfast of hot chocolate and *huevos rancheros*; does it give you the energy to do plenty of schoolwork?

### *Huevos Rancheros*

*Ingredients:*
3 Tbs vegetable oil
6 corn tortillas
1⅓ cups refried beans
2 tsp butter
6 eggs
1½ cups shredded cheese
12 slices bacon, cooked and crumbled

*Directions:*
1. Mix beans, cheese, and butter; heat in microwave until thoroughly warm.
2. Heat oil over medium-high heat. Put tortillas into pan one at a time and fry until slightly browned, but not too crisp to fold. Drain on paper towels.
3. Fry eggs in the skillet, over easy (add extra oil if necessary).
4. Put tortillas on plates. Spread a layer of beans on top. Put a fried egg on top of the beans. Crumble two slices of bacon over each egg.

### *Mexican Hot Chocolate*

*Ingredients:*
three heaping spoonfuls of instant hot chocolate
generous squirt of chocolate syrup
½ tsp cinnamon
⅛ tsp chili powder
½ cup skim milk
½ cup water
cinnamon stick

*Directions:*
1. Combine milk and water in measuring cup; heat until just boiling in microwave.
2. Mix hot chocolate mix, cinnamon, chili powder, and syrup in the bottom of a mug. Pour milk/water mixture into mug and stir well with cinnamon stick.

## CRAFT PROJECT **Mexican Blanket Art**

In the mid 1800s and early 1900s, *saltillo* blankets in Mexico were used in many ways. People would sit on them when eating at low tables, they would use them like mats and sleep on them, and they would hang them in doorways to separate rooms! The colors on these blankets were rich and bold, and would include reds, blues, browns, and yellows. If a family had enough money, they would hire weavers to put a diamond shape in the center of their blankets.

In this activity, you'll make your own *saltillo* blanket, for use as a sitting blanket, as a sleeping mat, or as a door for your room!

*Materials:*

- ☐ White muslin, rectangle size of your choice (preferably 4' x 6')
- ☐ Markers or acrylic paint
- ☐ Paint brushes (if you're using paint)
- ☐ White string
- ☐ Four 3" x 5" index cards, any color
- ☐ Tacky glue or hot glue gun
- ☐ Newspapers to cover work space

*Directions:*

1. Make sure the muslin fabric is smooth and not wrinkled. Spread out the fabric on the workspace.
2. Using the paint or markers, make a striped design on your fabric. Allow it to dry.
3. If you want to make the (optional) fringe for the blanket, wrap the white string around the 3" x 5" card in loose loops. Then run a line of glue down the length of the end of the blanket, attach the loops to the glue so that they hang off the end, then cut the loops, so they make the loose string fringe. Repeat until both short ends of the blanket have their string fringe.
4. Hang your Mexican blanket up on the wall or in a doorway!

# The Slave Trade Ends

## Encyclopedia Cross-References

*UBWH 174 UILE 324-325*
*KIHW 543-545 KHE 322-323*

## THE WORK OF THE ABOLITIONISTS

### Review Questions

What was the main goal of the abolitionists? *They wanted slavery to be made illegal.*

What religious group in England had insisted that slavery should be made illegal? *The Quakers had long worked for the abolition of slavery.*

What had the Constitution of the United States said about slaves? *It had said slaves were not really people. When states counted their people, five slaves would count as three people.*

Why did northern delegates, who didn't own slaves, agree to this? *The northern delegates didn't want the slaves counted as whole people, because then the south would have many more representatives than the north in the House of Representatives.*

Why did farmers in the south want to keep slavery legal? *Many farmers in the south wanted slavery to stay legal so their farms would survive.*

Abolitionists in both England and the U.S. knew that something had to happen before slavery would become illegal. What had to happen? *Both countries knew that the slave trade had to be outlawed before slavery would become illegal.*

What did William Wilberforce ask of the British Parliament? *William Wilberforce asked the rest of Parliament to outlaw the slave trade, no matter what the cost.*

What law was passed in England and in the U.S. during the years 1807-1808? *Laws were passed that said that no English or American ships could buy slaves in Africa and then sell them in other countries.*

What happened to British planters when slavery was outlawed? *Soon after slavery was outlawed, many British planters went bankrupt.*

When planters began to go bankrupt, where did England buy sugar, coffee, cotton, and tobacco? *England bought these goods from the United States.*

### Narration Exercise

"Even though men were talking and writing about equality, slavery was still legal. The United States Constitution even said that slaves weren't really people! Abolitionists wanted slavery to be illegal. But they knew that, first, the slave trade would have to be outlawed. An abolitionist named William Wilberforce spent nineteen years convincing Parliament to make the slave trade illegal. Finally, slavery was made illegal in Britain. But it was still legal in America." OR

"Slavery was legal in both England and in the United States. In England, the Quakers were abolitionists (they wanted slavery made illegal). William Wilberforce worked for many years against slavery. In America, the south wanted slavery to be legal because the farmers needed slaves to help them grow cotton and tobacco. Northerners even agreed that slaves were worth less than a whole person, because they didn't want the south to have too many representatives in Congress! Finally, both countries made the slave trade illegal. Years later, Great Britain made slavery illegal too."

## Additional History Reading

*Amistad: The Story of a Slave Ship*, by Patricia C. McKissack, illus. Sanna Stanley (Penguin Young Readers, 2005). This is an account of the kidnapped Africans who took over the ship *Amistad* and tried to sail back to Africa and to freedom. Part of a leveled reader series, so it will make great reading practice, too, for young readers. (RA 1, IR 2-4)

*Courageous People Who Changed the World (Little Heroes)* by Heidi Poelman, illus Kyle Kershner. (Familius, 2018). A board book aimed at younger children, this book includes a brief introduction to, and famous quotations from, eight courageous people in history including William Wilberforce and Harriet Tubman. (RA K-2, IR 2-3).

*The Daring Escape of Ellen Craft*, by Cathy Moore, illus. Mary O'Keefe Young (First Avenue Editions, 2002). An easy-to-read account of Ellen Craft, who dressed like a white man so that she and her husband could escape slavery. After they gained freedom, they became involved with abolitionist work in the United States and in England. (RA 1, IR 2-4)

*Enemies of Slavery* by David A. Adler, illus Donald A. Smith (Holiday House, 2004). Thirteen profiles of Americans who fought against the institution of slavery in the United States, including John Brown, Lucretia Mott, Sojourner Truth, Denmark Vesey, and David Walker. (RA 1-3, IR 3-4).

*Freedom Song: The Story of Henry "Box" Brown*, by Sally M. Walker, illus. Sean Qualls (HarperCollins, 2012). This musical man escaped slavery by having himself mailed in a box to a free state in the mid-nineteenth century. Beautifully illustrated story of his life. (RA 1-3, IR 3-5)

*How Sweet the Sound: The Story of Amazing Grace* by Carole Boston Weatherford, illus by Frank Morrison. Moving picture book biography of John Newton, a slave ship captain who prayed for safety during a bad storm. After arriving safely at his destination, he eventually changed his ways and became a minister and an abolitionist, helping to end the slave trade in England. His passionate statements against slavery became well-known, but he is most famous for writing the hymn "Amazing Grace" (RA K-2, IR 2-3).

*If You Lived When There Was Slavery in America* by Anne Kamma (Scholastic, reprint 2004). A kid's-eye view of what slavery was like in America from Colonial times to the end of the Civil War. Detailed but simplified for younger readers. (RA 1-3, IR 3-5).

*Life on a Plantation*, by Bobbie Kalman (Crabtree Publications, 1997). Many illustrations and fairly detailed text compare the life of the plantation owner and his family with the lives of the enslaved workers in the cotton fields. (RA 2-3, IR 4-6)

*No More! Stories and Songs of Slave Resistance* by Doreen Rappaport, illus Shane W. Evans. (Candlewick, 2005). Beautifully illustrated book that shows many of the ways slaves resisted their own enslavement, including stories and songs from the early days of the slave trade through the Emancipation Proclamation. (RA 2-4, IR 4-7).

*Olaudah Equiano: From Slavery to Freedom*, by Paul Thomas, illus. Victor Ambrus (HarperCollins UK, 2007). An amazing account of a man kidnapped from eastern Africa for slavery. He eventually bought his way out of slavery and worked in England with the "Sons of Africa" to end the slave trade. (RA 1-2, IR 2-4)

*Only Passing Through: The Story of Sojourner Truth*, by Anne Rockwell, illus. R. Gregory Christie (Knopf, 2000). A picture-book biography of the famous African-American abolitionist, with historical notes and a timeline. (RA 2-3, IR 4-6)

*President of the Underground Railroad: A Story about Levi Coffin*, by Gwenyth Swain (Carolrhoda Books, 2001). Designed for third-grade readers and above, but contains some disturbing material; **parents should preview.** A Quaker in Indiana makes his home part of the Underground Railroad. (RA 2, IR 3-6)

*Sojourner Truth's Step-Stomp Stride*, by Andrea Davis Pinkney, illus. Brian Pinkney (Jump At the Sun Books, 2009). Beautiful book with bold illustrations of a bold abolitionist woman (she was six feet tall!). The illustrator is the son of the famed Jerry Pinkney, illustrator of many books about African-Americans over the years. (RA 1-3, IR 3-4)

*Sojourner Truth*, by Francis E. Ruffin (Powerkids Press, 2002). A simple-to-read, illustrated biography of the slave who was emancipated in 1828 and became a leading abolitionist. (RA 1-2, IR 3-4)

## Corresponding Literature Suggestions

*The Adventures of Huckleberry Finn,* by Mark Twain, adapted by Deidre S. Laiken (Abdo & Daughters, 2002). This adaptation, one of the *Great Illustrated Classics* series, tells the story of a young boy who drifts down the Mississippi in the company of an escaped slave. (RA 2, IR 3-5) **LFA**

*Africa Is My Home: A Child of the Amistad*, by Monica Edinger, illus. Robert Byrd (Candlewick Press, 2013). A fictionalized, beautifully illustrated first-person account of a nine-year-old girl taken as a slave onto the ship *Amistad.* While she longs to return home, she ends up waiting for more than two years to find out what will happen to her. **Parents should preview first.** (RA 2-4, IR 4-6)

*Amos Fortune: Free Man*, by Elizabeth Yates (Puffin Books, 1950). This Newbery-winning chapter book tells the story of a fifteen-year-old son of an African king, captured in 1725, and brought to Massachusetts as a slave, who finally bought his freedom as an old man. A family read-aloud for younger children; also look for the audiobook version. (RA 1-3, IR 4-5)

*Big Jabe*, by Jerdine Nolen, illus. Kadir Nelson (HarperCollins, 2000). A tall tale, set in the American South, about a Moses-like figure who leads slaves to freedom. (RA 2, IR 3-4)

*Day of Tears* by Julius Lester (Hyperion, 2007). This well-written book works as a read-aloud or independent reading for older or advanced students. It tells the story of the 1859 slave auction, the largest slave auction in US history. (RA 3-4, IR 4-6).

*Elijah of Buxton* by Christopher Paul Curtis. (Scholastic, 2009). Buxton is a settlement in Canada where run-away slaves lived, near the border with the United States. This story is told from the perspective of Elijah, the first child to be born there. The residents of Buxton have to grapple with the reality of slavery that still exists across the border. This is an engaging book, but the dialect can make it a challenge for younger readers. Listening to the audio version can help. (IR 4-6).

*Long Road to Freedom (Ranger in Time #3)* by Kate Messner (Scholastic, 2015). Third book in the *Ranger in Time* series about a time-traveling Golden Retriever. Can be engaging for reluctant readers; in this book Ranger sets off to help a young girl and her brother escape slavery and run to freedom. (RA 1-2, IR 2-5).

*My Name is Phillis Wheatley: A Story of Slavery and Freedom*, by Afua Cooper (Kids Can Press, 2009). A historical-fiction account of Phyllis Wheatley's life, from her childhood and traditions in Africa, to her slave journey to America, to the publication of her poetry; all told from her perspective.

*Sweet Clara and the Freedom Quilt*, by Deborah Hopkinson (Dragonfly, 1995). Set slightly later than the period covered in Chapter 36, this picture-book about a young slave seamstress is appropriate for younger readers. (RA 2, IR 3-4).

*The Talking Eggs: A Folktale from the American South*, retold by Robert D. San Souci, illus. Jerry Pinkney (Dial, 1989). This Caldecott-winning book tells a traditional tale passed along by African-American families in the American South. (RA 1-2, IR 3-4)

*The Village That Vanished*, by Ann Grifalconi, illus. Kadir Nelson (Puffin Books, 2004). A young girl watches as her mother and her grandmother plan to save their hidden village in Africa from slave traders who are coming. (This book is also in the Literature list for Chapter 7.) (RA 1-3, IR 3-4)

## MAP WORK

### The Slave Trade *(Student Page 133, answer 328)*

1. In England and in both Americas, there was much talk of the evils of slavery. William Wilberforce argued for the abolition of the slave trade. In 1807, England did outlaw the slave trade. Color Great Britain red.
2. English ships would no longer be traveling to the coast of Africa to buy and sell slaves. Remember the Triangular Trade Route from chapter 7? Use a pencil and re-draw those three arrows. Look back to the map from chapter 7 if you need help.
3. Remember that England outlawed the slave trade in 1807. Draw hash marks along the arrow that runs from Europe down to Africa. Then draw hash marks along the arrow from the coast of Africa to the West Indies.
4. England finally outlawed slavery in 1833. Plantations began to break up. But England could still get sugar, coffee, cotton, and tobacco from America. Outline the coast of America in green. Then draw an arrow from the United States to Britain and over the arrow, write the names of two of the four products that Britain bought from the United States.

### Coloring Page

Olaudah Equiano was enslaved and forced to cross the Atlantic Ocean shackled in a slave ship. He later gained his freedom and worked to end the slave trade by writing about how cruel and inhumane it was. *(Student Page 134)*

## PROJECTS

### Craft Project: Slave Ship Cutaway

The voyage made by slave ships coming from Africa to America was called the *Middle Passage*. The slave ships carried hundreds of Africans. Many slaves did not survive the journey in part because of the horrible conditions of the passage. The British Parliament discovered that one ship which was designed to carry only 451 passengers, was transporting over 600 slaves to America! The slaves' feet and hands were chained together, making it very difficult to move. Sickness sometimes caused as many as half of the slaves to die on the journey. Yet merchants made so much money that they did not change the conditions. This project gives a 3-D cutaway look at the slave ships.

Materials:
- ☐ brown Crayola *Model Magic* air-dry clay
- ☐ thick cardboard piece, cut the size of the construction paper you are using
- ☐ blue piece of construction paper
- ☐ Student Pages 135 and 136: Ship Side View, Ship Floor Drawings, Ship Bottom, and Ship Tops
- ☐ glue

Directions:

1. Glue the construction paper on to the thick cardboard.
2. In the middle of the paper, glue the cut out of the side view of the ship.
3. Using the clay, make a thin wall all around the ship's outline. It needs to be wide enough to encase the different levels of the ship that you will be portraying.
4. Fold down part B's tab on the side. Glue it down on to part A as indicated. Place a little brown clay under the bottom of the paper to hold it in place on the front of the ship and on the back. Also, note that the front ends of parts B and C are rounded. Fill in the sides with clay, if desired.
5. Repeat for part C, D and E.
6. Let the ship dry before sitting it upright.
7. *Optional*: Break a wooden skewer in half. Wrap a half of a white index card around the pointed end and glue the skewer to the top part of the ship as a sail. Repeat with the other half of the skewer.

## LITERATURE PROJECT Using the Bible to Support the Abolition of Slavery

Slave masters in the South encouraged Christianity among their slaves—they would tell their slaves that the Bible tells slaves to be good, hard, obedient workers. Slaves will be rewarded for their actions in heaven. Abolitionists also used the Bible to support their position of anti-slavery: pamphlets, posters, and newspaper advertisements containing Bible verses were everywhere.

Materials:

- ☐ Student Page 137: Abolition Poster
- ☐ Plain posterboard
- ☐ Markers or colored pencils
- ☐ Bible

Directions:

1. Read sections of "The Negro Woman's Appeal" on the Abolition Poster. This particular poster is targeted at white women. On this poster, a female slave prays on her knees. The picture and the poem were aimed to stir white women's sympathy. As you can see, several excerpts from the Bible are used as evidence of the injustice of slavery.
2. See if you can find several verses in the Bible that an abolitionist might use to support his or her position. Look for verses and key words that say, basically: "Do not be cruel to others." OR "Treat other people with kindness." Also look for verses about freedom and liberty.
3. When you have found several verses, write one on a small poster and hang it up. If you wish, illustrate your poster.

## CRAFT PROJECT Who Am I?

If you like the popular Guess Who? game, you'll enjoy this look at American and British slavery fighters, or abolitionists. They came from different backgrounds with various gifts and talents, which they used to help end slavery. With a few easy preparations, you'll be up and guessing in no time!

Materials:

- ☐ six 5" x 8" index cards
- ☐ Student Page 138: Who Am I? Game Card Templates

Directions:

1. This game requires two players. Copy the game card templates onto cardstock. Make three copies, using three different colors of cardstock. Then, cut out the cards.
2. Fold the index cards to form a tray that will hold the cards. Each player should have three trays, and all of the cards of one color. Place the cards on the trays facing each player, so that the opponents cannot see each other's cards.
3. Put the cards of the third color in a pile. Each player draws a card from the pile. The person on the card the player draws, is the person the player will pretend to be.
4. Each player is only allowed to ask yes or no questions to discover which person the opponent is. Players may ask questions like, "Are you a woman?" and if she says "Yes," then you know you can eliminate all of the male cards. The object of the game is to ask yes/no questions to discover who the other player is. The first person to figure out who the opponent is, wins!

## CRAFT PROJECT Early American Quilting and the Anti-Slavery Movement

Quilting has a long history in America, dating back to colonial times. If a piece of clothing had a stain or tear, the remainder of the fabric would be cut into scraps. Those scraps, along with scraps from other fabrics, were sewed together to make a quilt. The scraps were arranged into a pattern. These patterns had certain names like "log cabin," "lone star," and "wedding ring." Some people believe that quilts were used by abolitionists and others helping slaves escape, and that various patterns on quilts sent secret messages to escaping slaves. Try your hand at the log cabin squares. The instructions tell you how to make the squares with construction paper, but may use real fabric if you wish. You may choose your own colors for the strips, but the given colors make an interesting design.

### *Log Cabin Squares*

Materials:

- ☐ Student Page 139: Log Cabin Template
- ☐ 1 sheet construction paper, dark blue (or medium blue with black marker designs)
- ☐ 1 sheet construction paper, medium blue
- ☐ 1 sheet construction paper, light blue (or gray)
- ☐ 1 sheet construction paper, red
- ☐ 1 sheet construction paper, dark yellow (or yellow with brown marker designs)
- ☐ 1 sheet construction paper, yellow
- ☐ 1 sheet construction paper, cream
- ☐ 4 sheets plain paper
- ☐ Scissors
- ☐ Pencil
- ☐ Glue stick
- ☐ Tape

Directions:

1. Cut out the Log Cabin Template (do not cut out the individual strips yet—leave it as a square)
2. Trace the square onto four sheets of plain paper. Cut those sheets. You now have the backing to four squares.
3. Now cut the two strips labeled "D1" (for Dark Color 1) out of the template. Trace each of these strips four times onto the dark blue paper. Cut them out. You should have four strips of each size. Keep each size in a stack with its template strip.

4. Now cut out the two strips labeled "M1." Trace each of those strips four times onto the medium blue paper. Cut out and set in stacks as you did in step three.
5. Repeat this process for the remaining blocks as such:
   The two L1s: trace and cut four each from the light blue
   The two D2s: trace and cut four each from the dark yellow
   The two M2s: trace and cut four each from the medium yellow
   The two D2s: trace and cut four each from the cream
   The one C block (for Contrasting color): trace and cut four from the red
6. Now look at the mini pattern on the template page to remind yourself of the order of the strips. Take out the four backing squares and do the same for each square: Glue the longest dark blue strip to the far left of each square. Glue the other dark blue strip to the bottom of each square, etc. . . . Repeat this process for all the strips, working from the outside of the square toward the center piece (called the "chimney"—this is the patch that was traditionally black).
7. Once you have four identical, completed log cabin squares, make a quilt! Arrange the squares into a larger square. The dark blue corners should all face the center. Tape the backings of the quilt together and display your work on a wall!

# Troubled Africa

CHAPTER 37

## Encyclopedia Cross-References

*UBWH 179, UILE 346*
*KIHW 493 (picture), 506-507, 564 KHE 308-309, 343*

## THE ZULU KINGDOM

### Review Questions

What land was known to Europeans as "the dark continent"? *Africa was known to many Europeans as "the dark continent."*

Why do we know less about African history than about English history? *Because African tribes did not use writing to record their history, much of their history is lost to the West.*

Whose permission did the two English traders need before they could build a trading post? *The two English traders were brought to Shaka, King of the Zulus, to gain permission to build a trading post.*

What was the name of the trading post that the Englishmen built? *The English merchants named the trading post Durban.*

What did the two English merchants learn about Shaka? *They learned that he had caused trouble for many people of South Africa.*

Why did Nandi and her son, Shaka, move away from Nandi's family? *They were treated as though they were a disgrace, and were told by Nandi's family to leave.*

In his new kingdom of Mtetwa, Shaka learned to be a good soldier. What job did the king of Mtetwa give to Shaka after Shaka's father died? *When Shaka's father Sezangakhon died, the Mtetwa king sent Shaka to go and take over his father's kingdom.*

When Shaka seized control of his father's kingdom, how did he change the weapons the army used? *Shaka ordered the soldiers to fight with short stabbing spears instead of throwing spears, so that they would have to grapple with the enemy face to face.*

What are some of the other improvements that Shaka made to the army? *He sent them to walk on thorns with their bare feet, so that their soles would be tough enough to run over any rough land. He gave them uniforms to wear. He divided them into four sections and taught them to attack in the same order during each battle.*

With his new disciplined army, who did Shaka target first? *Their first target was the men from his mother's family who had thrown Nandi out.*

What did Shaka do when he returned to Mtetwa? *Shaka murdered the king.*

What did Africans call the period of ten years during which Shaka spread his rule throughout the continent? *The Africans called this the mfecane, or the Time of Troubles.*

What happened to Shaka when his mother died? *He went mad.*

Who eventually murdered Shaka? *His own half-brothers murdered Shaka.*

### Narration Exercise

"The Zulus were an African tribe. Their king, Shaka, caused trouble for all of South Africa. He became angry at his tribe because they had treated his mother badly. So he taught an army to fight with discipline and to use short spears. Then he attacked the men who had mistreated his mother! Shaka then set out to conquer the tribes all over South Africa. He destroyed many kingdoms. Two million Africans died! This is called the *mfecane,* or 'The Crushing.' Finally, Shaka was murdered by his own half-brothers." OR

"Two English merchants who built a trading post in South Africa met Shaka, King of the Zulus. Shaka and his mother were treated badly, and went to live in another kingdom, called Mtetwa. In Mtetwa, Shaka learned to fight. He built an army! He killed the king of the Mtetwa and spread his rule across South Africa. Tribes fled away from him and drove other tribes away from their land. Millions of people died! After his mother died, Shaka went mad. Finally, his own warriors turned against him and killed him. His half-brother became king instead."

## THE BOERS AND THE BRITISH

### Review Questions

What was the name of the Dutch settlement at the bottom of South Africa? *The name of the settlement was Cape Colony.*

What did the Dutch who settled in Cape Colony call themselves? *These Dutch called themselves the Boers—Dutch for farmers.*

What did the slaves do in Cape Colony? *The slaves helped the Dutch run their farms.*

What country had taken over the rule of Cape Colony? *The British took control of Cape Colony in 1820.*

What did the British do that angered many of the Boers? *The British outlawed slavery.*

Where did the Boers go when they left Cape Colony on their Great Trek? *They set off into the unknown depths of Africa, looking for another place to settle down.*

What did Dingane do that angered the Boers? *When the Boers went to make friends with Dingane's tribe, Dingane ordered them all put to death.*

How did the Boers ensure victory against the Zulus? *Boer leaders found out that one of Dingane's half-brothers, Mpande, hoped to be king. They promised Mpande that they would make him king of the Zulus if he would fight on their side!*

What did the Boers call their new settlement, near Durban? *They called it Natal.*

What eventually happened to the Boer settlement of Natal? *The British claimed Natal from the Boers, too.*

Can you remember one of the two other nations that the Boers established in Africa? *The Boers established the Orange Free State and the Transvaal Republic.*

### Narration Exercise

"The Boers were Dutch farmers who lived in South Africa. The British took over their colony, Cape Colony. The Dutch knew that they couldn't keep their slaves, so they packed up and travelled into Africa, looking for a new place to live. They decided to settle on the edge of the Zulu kingdom. The king, Dingane, didn't want them there. He put some of them to death! So the Boers promised the king's half-brother that they would make *him* king instead. They drove Dingane away and settled down in their new home, which they called Natal." OR

"The Boers were Dutch farmers who lost their colony to the British. So they started out on the Great Trek of the Boers. When they reached Shaka's kingdom, now ruled by his brother, they settled down. The king didn't want them there and fought against them. Their battles were so bloody that one of them even turned a river red. Finally, the Boers settled down in their new home, Natal. Four years later, the British took Natal too. The Boers travelled back into the center of Africa and established two more nations."

## Additional History Reading

*Shaka Zulu*, by Richard Spilsbury (Raintree, 2013). This book is written like a journal from Shaka's point of view. It tells stories from his life (including his childhood) and gives sketches of the people around him. **Parents should preview first—contains some descriptions that may seem gory to younger children.** (IR 3-6)

*The Zulu of Southern Africa*, by Christine Cornell (Powerkids Press, 1996). A very simple, easy-reader chapter book about King Shaka and the history of the Zulu nation. (RA 1, IR 2-3) **LFA**

*Zulu Warriors*, by Terri Sievert Dougherty (Capstone Press, 2008). Written in narrative style; this describes a battle between the Zulus and the British, the warriors' skills and training, and life in Zululand. Full of paintings and photos. (RA 1-3, IR 3-5)

*Zulu Warriors*, by Aaron Trejo (Bellwether Media, 2011). Same name as the Dougherty book above, but with a slightly different focus. Clear photos and large print make this book engaging. Gives detailed information about Zulu warriors, their training, and their weaponry. (RA 1-3, IR 2-4).

*If You Lived Here: Houses of the World*, by Giles Laroche (HMH Books for Young Readers, 2011). In addition to other houses around the world, learn about the decorated houses and their history in Pretoria, South Africa. Each spread includes interesting information about the materials, background, and unique facts. (RA 1-3, IR 3-5)

*Living in South Africa*, by Chloe Perkins, illus. Tom Woolley (Simon Spotlight, 2016). Follow young David as he talks about the geography, cultures, history, and modern everyday life of South Africa. Colorful illustrations and maps included. Excellent for beginning reading practice. (RA 1-2, IR 2-4)

*My Painted House, My Friendly Chicken, and Me*, by Maya Angelou, photos by Margaret Courtney-Clarke (Crown Books for Young Readers, 2003). A delightful book that follows Thandi, an eight-year-old Ndebele girl in South Africa. Photos also depict Ndebele women and their paintings (see decorated houses in the Laroche book above). (RA 1-3, IR 2-4)

*National Geographic Countries of the World: South Africa* by Virginia Mace (National Geographic, 2008). A reference book about South Africa, includes a chapter on the history of the country. Full of beautiful color photographs (RA 1-3, IR 4-6).

*S is for South Africa (World Alphabets)* by Beverley Naidoo, photo Prodeepta Das (Lincoln Children's Books, 2011). Beautiful photo alphabet book about modern South Africa. (RA K-2, IR 2-3).

*South Africa (Countries Around the World)* by Claire Throp (Heinemann, 2014). Reference book about South Africa, includes a chapter on the history of the country. (RA 2-3, IR 3-6).

*South Africa (Enchantment of the World)* by Ettagale Blauer and Jason Laure. (Children's Press, 2013). Reference book about South Africa includes a chapter on the history of the country. A bit easier for younger readers than the Throp book listed above. (RA 2-3, IR 3-6).

*South Africa: Modern World Nations,* by Vernon Domingo (Chelsea House, 2003). A detailed look at South Africa; chapters on the Dutch in South Africa and the Zulu could serve as read-alouds. (RA 2-3, IR 4-7) **E-Only.**

## Corresponding Literature Suggestions

*Shaka Rising: A Legend of the Warrior Prince (The African Graphic Novel Series)* by Luke Molver. (Story Press Africa, 2018). Graphic novel presentation of the story of Shaka, the powerful ruler of the Zulu Kingdom. (IR 4-9).

*Abiyoyo,* by Pete Seeger, illus. by Michael Hays (Aladdin, 1994). Folk singer Pete Seeger wrote and recorded this tall tale about an African giant, adapted from a traditional South African lullaby. (RA 2, IR 3-4)

*The Dove,* by Dianne Stewart, illus. Jude Daly (Frances Lincoln Children's Books, 2005). A flood comes to KwaZulu-Natal, destroying crops and animals that Lindi and her grandmother depended on. A dove arrives as the flooding subsides, inspiring them to create a new way of making their living until the next crop. Well worth finding through interlibrary loan and on the used-book market. (RA 1-2, IR 3-4)

*Galimoto* by Karen Lynn Williams, illus Catherine Stock (HarperCollins, 1991). Charming picture book about a young boy's quest to find enough wire and scraps of metal to make a toy. Set in the southeast African nation of Malawi (RA K-2, IR 2-3).

*Gift of the Sun: A Tale from South Africa* by Dianne Stewart, illus Jude Daly. (Farrar, Straus, & Giroux, 1996). Delightfully illustrated story from South Africa about a farmer who makes a series of trades hoping to reduce his workload, ending up with just a handful of sunflower seeds. However, these prove to be more useful than originally thought. (RA K-2, IR 2-3).

*The Herd Boy,* by Niki Daly (Eerdmans Books for Young Readers, 2012). Malusi must take care of his grandfather's herd animals on the South African grazing slopes, but he has aspirations for bigger challenges. A chance encounter brings him hope. Beautiful watercolor illustrations and words in Afrikaans and Xhosa included. (RA 1-3, IR 4-6)

*I Just Want to Say Good Night,* by Rachel Isadora (Nancy Paulsen Books, 2017). Gorgeous illustrations and captivating text depict young Lala on the southern African veld. It's Lala's bedtime, but she stalls by going around saying good night to everything and everyone. (RA 1-2, IR 2-4)

*Marriage of the Rain Goddess: A South African Myth* by Wolfson. (DeCapo Press, 1996). Inspired by a Zulu myth, this engaging story is presented as a picture book which will appeal to younger readers but the complex text should interest older readers as well. (RA 1-2, IR 3-5).

*Mufaro's Beautiful Daughters: An African Tale* by John Steptoe. (Puffin, 2008). Told with beautifully detailed illustrations, this is an African Cinderella story. (RA K-1, IR 2-3).

*Over the Green Hills,* by Rachel Isadora (Greenwillow, 1992). Especially good for reluctant readers or younger siblings, this picture book tells of a rural South African mother and her children who set off to visit the children's grandmother and trade for food and supplies along the way. (RA 2, IR 3-4) **OOP**

*Where Are You Going, Manyoni?,* by Catherine Stock (HarperCollins, 1993). Near the Limpopo River in southern Africa, Manyoni walks two hours to school every day. Watercolor illustrations beautifully capture the wildlife and vegetation Manyoni encounters on her route. The end of the book contains a key to the wildlife depicted and a list of unfamiliar words with their definitions. (RA 1-3, IR 4-6)

## MAP WORK

### English and Boers in Africa *(Student Page 140, answer 328)*

1. Find the dot with a "1" in the upper left corner of the map. The two English traders came from England (which is not on your map). Pick up their journey from the "1" and draw a red arrow from there, through the Atlantic Ocean, to Durban.
2. The king of the Zulus allowed the traders to build a post in Durban. With a red crayon, circle the dot that represents Durban.
3. The Dutch began to settle in Cape Colony many years before the British had come. Draw an orange circle in the center of Cape Colony.
4. The English gained control of Cape Colony. Outline the border of Cape Colony in red.
5. The English outlawed slavery. This angered the Dutch Boers because the Boers relied on slavery to farm. Many Boers left Cape Colony and moved north. Draw an arrow from the orange circle at the center of Cape Colony north (or east, depending on where your circle is) toward Durban.
6. Although the English were able to take Natal from them, the Boers were able to settle the Orange Free State and the Transvaal. Color both of these areas orange.

**Coloring Page** Shaka and his warriors terrified the tribes throughout the south and center of Africa. Some Africans called this the *mfecane,* or the Time of Troubles. *(Student Page 141)*

## PROJECTS

### Craft Project Zulu Beadwork Code

*Special thanks to Christina Kirk.*

The Zulu people had an intricate way of communicating with each other. They developed a code of colors that could be combined in different ways to create messages. These colors were often woven into patterns of geometric shapes that also contributed to the meaning of a particular message. Each color had a positive and negative meaning. For example, black had the positive meaning of marriage or regeneration. Negatively, black meant sorrow or death. Blue represented a request or marriage in the positive, and hostility or ill feelings in the negative. Yellow meant wealth or industry in the positive; it meant thirst or withering away in the negative.

Make your own Zulu code and send a string of beads with the key to a friend.

Materials:
- ☐ Assorted glass beads
- ☐ Elastic cord or *Stretch Magic* (at craft store in jewelry section)
- ☐ Colored pencils
- ☐ Unlined index cards or nice stationary paper

***Key:***
yellow = happy
light blue = cold
red = willing to help
orange = waiting for your answer
white = you
green = me

*Directions:*

1. Use your index cards and write down the "key" to your code. Decide what kind of project you want to make: necklace, headband, bracelet or ankle-bracelet. Choose the person to whom you will send a message, and then decide what your message will be. (For example, if you want to say, "I am happy. I am willing to help you. I am waiting for your answer," you would thread a green bead, a yellow bead, a green bead, a red bead, a white bead, a green bead, and an orange bead.)
2. Thread the elastic cord through your beads to create a message. When you complete the project, tie off the end of the cord.
3. Tie the two ends together and double the knot. Seal the knot with clear fingernail polish.
4. Wrap your project up and include your message key so your friend will be able to interpret your message.

## CRAFT PROJECT Make an Assegai Stabbing Spear

When Shaka took control of the Zulu tribe, he changed the soldiers' weapons. The Zulu army had used long spears that they could throw from a distance. They would throw the spears and attack once, and then they would have to run away! Shaka ordered his soldiers to fight with short stabbing spear, called an Assegai. This meant that his soldiers would have to grapple with the enemy face-to-face; there was no running away! Make your own Assegai stabbing spear.

*Materials:*

- ☐ Student Page 142: Assegai Spear Head Template
- ☐ A wrapping paper tube
- ☐ Stapler
- ☐ Raffia (the kind that is like twine, not in shreds) or yarn
- ☐ Thin cardboard or the face of a cereal box
- ☐ Aluminum foil or silver paint

*Directions:*

1. Cut the spear head template.
2. Trace the template onto the thin cardboard.
3. Cut the spear head out of the cardboard. Fold it in half.
4. Wrap the spear head in aluminum foil (leave the blunt end unwrapped) OR paint with silver paint.
5. Staple the two "tails" of the blunt end of the spear head to one end of the wrapping paper tube. Staple them to opposite curves of the tube.
6. Wrap that same end of the wrapping paper tube with the raffia or yarn (you should cover at least three inches of the end of the tube with yarn). Tie the end of the raffia and tuck it under the wrapped section to secure it.

## CRAFT PROJECT Make a "Traditional" African Pot

Use papier-mâché to make an African pot and decorate it with Zulu pottery designs!

*Materials:*

- ☐ ½ cup flour
- ☐ 2 cups cold water
- ☐ 2 cups boiling water (in saucepan)
- ☐ 3 Tbs sugar
- ☐ 1 balloon

- ☐ strips of newspaper (2" wide)
- ☐ cardboard strip (2" x 14"—or whatever fits your pot)
- ☐ masking tape
- ☐ acrylic paint
- ☐ paint brushes

*Directions:*

1. Mix cold water and flour. Squeeze out any lumps.
2. Add this to the boiling water in the saucepan, and bring back to a boil. Remove from heat and stir in sugar. Let cool.
3. Blow up a balloon. Dip strips of newspaper into the mixture and plaster onto balloon until covered. Leave an opening at the top of the balloon at its narrow end—this will be the top of your pot. Let dry for two days.
4. Once the papier-mâché is completely dry, pop the balloon inside. Gently shake out the balloon.
5. Make a "collar" out of the cardboard and masking tape. Set the closed end of the pot into the collar so the pot will stand up. Secure the pot to its base with masking tape.
6. Paint the pot with colors like dark brown, tan, orange, red, and yellow. You can paint with a Zulu pottery design.

# American Tragedies

CHAPTER **38**

## Encyclopedia Cross-References

*UBWH 174, 182-183, UILE 324-325, 350-351*
*KIHW 544-545, 556, KHE 322-323, 329*

## THE TRAIL OF TEARS

### Review Questions

American settlers who wanted to build houses on Native American land were supposed to do something. What was it? *They were supposed to pay for the land and sign a treaty explaining that the Native Americans had agreed to sell it.*

Which president of the United States signed the Indian Removal Act? *Andrew Jackson signed the Indian Removal Act.*

What did the Indian Removal Act say? *The Indian Removal Act said that the President could now take Native American land without asking for it or paying for it, as long as he gave the Native Americans who lived there an equal amount of land in the unsettled prairies of the west.*

Why did the American government think the Indian Removal Act was a good idea? *For over a hundred years, whites and Native Americans had quarreled, fought, and killed each other. Now, white settlers could live near each other, and the Native Americans could have their own part of the country, further away.*

Can you name three of the Five Civilized Tribes? *The Five Civilized tribes were the Chickasaw, Choctaw, Seminole, Cherokee, and Creek.*

Which group of Native Americans refused to go west? *The Creek Indians refused to go.*

What did the U.S. government do to make the Creeks move west? *U.S. soldiers came to their homes, chained them together, and forced them to move west.*

Which two tribes fought the hardest to keep their homes? *The Cherokee and the Seminole Indians fought the hardest to keep their homes.*

How did the Seminoles fight the U.S.? *The Seminoles picked up guns and fought for seven years in a war known as "The Second Seminole War."*

How did the Cherokee fight the U.S.? *They went to court, but the trials dragged on for eight years.*

Where were the Cherokee of Georgia forced to march? *They were forced to walk to the Oklahoma Territory.*

What do we now call this march that the Cherokee were forced to make to the Oklahoma Territory? *We call it the Trail of Tears.*

### Narration Exercise

"American settlers wanted to live on the land where Native Americans lived. So the President, Andrew Jackson, signed the Indian Removal Act. The Act forced Indians to leave their homes and go to live out west. Five of these tribes, the 'Five Civilized Tribes' had become very much like white settlers. But soldiers forced them out of their homes anyway. The Cherokee were marched to their new territory, eight hundred miles away. One out of every four Cherokee died. The journey became known as the Trail of Tears." OR

"The Five Civilized Tribes were Indian tribes who had begun to follow white customs. They owned land in the Southeast. But white settlers wanted these lands. So Andrew Jackson signed the Indian Removal Act, saying that the President could take this land as long as he gave the tribes land in the West. Some of the tribes agreed to leave. But the Seminole tribe in Florida fought a war against the United States for seven years! The Cherokee Indians went to court to keep their lands. But they lost. They were forced to march west on the 'Trail of Tears.' Many died on the journey."

## NAT TURNER'S REVOLT

### Review Questions

What group of people had even less freedom than the Cherokee Indians? *Slaves in the American south had even less freedom than the Cherokee Indians!*

Planters in the south heard stories that made them nervous. What were these stories about? *These stories were about the revolt on the island of St. Domingue.*

What did the white preachers tell the slaves on Sundays? *White preachers told their slaves they were to obey their masters without question.*

What did the slaves hear at their own church services? *They heard about a coming time of freedom when God would heal all the suffering of the slaves.*

What did Thomas Moore think that his slave Nat Turner was preaching about? *He thought he was preaching about the end of the world, described in the book of Revelation.*

What was Nat Turner actually preaching about? *Nat Turner's preaching was preparing the slaves to rise up and fight.*

What "sign" did Nat Turner see that led him to believe it was time to break free? *Nat Turner had seen the sky turn into an eerie greenish darkness during a solar eclipse.*

What did Nat Turner and his men decide to do when they met whites? *They decided to kill all that they met.*

Why did Turner's men fail to ride into Jerusalem, Virginia? *They had been drinking brandy and were moving more slowly.*

What happened when Turner's men were captured? *They were hanged.*

Who finally found Nat Turner? *A white farmer found Nat Turner as he crawled out of a ditch.*

How do we know about Nat Turner's side of the story? *Before he was hanged, Nat Turner told his story to his lawyer Thomas Gray. Gray wrote the story down and published it.*

What happened to the slaves as a result of Turner's rebellion? List at least three results. *Slaves were worse off than ever! Their owners were terrified of another revolt. Laws were passed keeping slaves from meeting together in groups of more than three. Black ministers were told that they couldn't preach to their congregations. Anyone who taught a slave to read or write would be punished by a year in jail. Free blacks couldn't own guns. They couldn't meet together at night unless three white men were there.*

### Narration Exercise

"Nat Turner believed that God had called him to lead slaves to freedom. When he saw an eclipse, he believed that the time had come. He chose six other slaves to help him. They killed more than fifty whites! Other slaves joined him. But armed slaveholders fought against Nat Turner and his men and captured them. Nat Turner hid for two months, but then he was captured and put to death. The slaveowners were afraid that another revolt might happen, so they passed laws to keep slaves from learning to read or write, from meeting together, or from owning guns." OR

"In America, slaves worked long hours and were treated very cruelly. Slaveowners who heard about the revolt in Saint Domingue were afraid that their slaves would revolt too! They sent the slaves to church, where white ministers told them to obey their masters. But black ministers were telling slaves that God would bring judgment to their masters. One of those ministers, Nat Turner, led a slave revolt. He and his followers killed over fifty whites. They were captured, but the slave revolt made slaveowners even more afraid. Slaveowners passed laws keeping black ministers from preaching. Slaves couldn't meet together in groups of more than three, or learn how to read and write. These laws were meant to keep another revolt from happening."

## Additional History Reading

*The Trail of Tears: The Story of the Cherokee Removal,* by Dan Elish (Benchmark Books, 2002). Designed for older readers, but very clear and readable with large text; also contains contemporary engravings and some rare photographs. Worth browsing, even for younger readers. (RA 1-4, IR 4-6) **OOP**

*Andrew Jackson: Seventh President 1829-1837* by Mike Venezia (Children's Press, 2005). A book about Jackson from a series of quirky presidential biographies. Does a good job of holding interest through cartoon-like drawings and interesting sidebar stories but doesn't gloss over key events in Jackson's presidency, including the Indian Removal Act. (RA 2-3, IR 3-4).

*Osceola,* by Santana Hunt (Gareth Stevens Publishing, 2016). This is an easily readable biography about Osceola, a leader of the Seminole tribe who fought against the removal of his people from their native lands. (RA 1-2, IR 1-4)

*Only the Names Remain,* by Alex W. Bealer (Little, Brown, 1996). Examines the long-lasting results of the forced march caused by the forced removal of the Cherokee. (RA 3, IR 4-7)

*Trail of Tears (Step Into Reading Step 5)* by Joseph Bruchac (Random House 1999). A good book for younger readers about the forced removal of the Cherokee Nation. (IR 2-4)

*American Indians: Fandex Family Field Guides* (Workman Publishing, n.d.). Fifty colorful cards introduce fifty famous American Indians and North American tribes; includes portraits, photographs, tribal symbols, and more. (RA 1-2, IR 3-5)

*North American Indian: Eyewitness Books,* by David Murdoch (Dorling Kindersley, 2005). Colorful two-page spreads with lovely illustrations and detailed text; includes information on the "Five Civilized Tribes," Southwest tribes, Arctic tribes, and much more. (RA 1-3, IR 4-6)

*The Cherokee: The Past and Present of a Proud Nation,* by Danielle Smith-Llera (Capstone Press, 2015). Using primary sources, this book tells of the Cherokee past, the Trail of Tears, and the development of the Cherokee into modern times. (RA 2, IR 3-6)

*Choctaw,* by Ada Quinlivan (PowerKids Press, 2016). An introduction to the history and present culture and customs of the Choctaw tribe. (RA 2, IR 3-6)

*Seminole,* by Gale George (PowerKids Press, 2016). An introduction to the history and present culture and customs of the Seminole tribe. (RA 2, IR 3-6)

*Nat Turner and the Virginia Slave Revolt,* by Rivvy Neshama (The Child's World, 2001). A clear, detailed, but simple biography with contemporary engravings. (RA 1-2, IR 3-5) **OOP**

*Nat Turner's Slave Rebellion (Graphic History)* by Michael Burgan, illus Richard Dominquez, Bob Wiacek and Charles Barnett III (Capstone, 2006). A retelling, in graphic-novel form, of the 1831 Virginia slave rebellion led by Nat Turner. (IR 3-4). **Parents should preview first.**

*Nat Turner and Slave Life on a Southern Plantation*, by Katie Schmid (Rosen Publishing, 2014). This graphic-novel depiction of the slave rebellion includes biographical sketches of the main characters, plus a timeline. (RA 1-2, IR 3-4)

## Corresponding Literature Suggestions

*Ahyoka and the Talking Leaves*, by Connie Roop, illus. Yoshi Miyake (Lothrop, Lee & Shepard, 2000). A fictionalized story about Ahyoka, daughter of the man who created a written language for the Cherokee. (RA 2, IR 3-5) **E-Only.**

*Cherokee Sister*, by Debbi Dadey (Yearling Books, 2001). In this chapter book for older or advanced readers, a white girl who lives at the edge of Cherokee land in Georgia is accidentally swept up in the Cherokee Removal. (RA 3-4, IR 4-6) **E-Only.**

*Cherokee Legends and the Trail of Tears*, by Thomas Bryan Underwood, illus. Amanda Crowe (Cherokee Publications, 1997). Underwood was a soldier assigned to guard the Cherokee people on their journey west; he recorded the legends he heard them tell, and his account is republished here. (RA 2-3, IR 4-6)

*How I Became A Ghost: A Choctaw Trail of Tears Story* by Tim Tingle (Roadrunner Press, 2015). Told from the perspective of a young Choctaw boy who does not survive the Trail of Tears, includes rich detail about Choctaw history and culture. (IR 4-7).

*On This Long Journey: The Journal of Jesse Smoke, A Cherokee Boy: The Trail of Tears, 1838*, by Joseph Bruchac (Scholastic, 2014). Part of the *My Name is America* series, this chapter book for slightly older readers takes the form of a diary kept by a Cherokee boy on the Trail of Tears. (IR 4-6)

*Soft Rain: A Story of the Cherokee Trail of Tears*, by Cornelia Cornelissen (Yearling Books, 1999). In this chapter book for slightly older readers, a nine-year-old Cherokee girl is taken away from her North Carolina village and sent west. (RA 3-4, IR 4-6)

*The First Strawberries: A Cherokee Story*, by Joseph Bruchac, illus. Anna Vojtech (Puffin, 1998). Watercolor illustrations and simple text retell a Cherokee legend. (RA 2, IR 3-4)

*Legends of the Seminoles*, by Betty Mae Tiger Jumper, illus. Guy LaBree (Pineapple Press, 1994). A treasure trove of information for adults about Seminole people and the scribing of these legends, this book contains stories that were passed down orally. The legends themselves are short and great for reading aloud to young children. (RA 1-4, IR 5-7)

*A Picture of Freedom: The Diary of Clotee, a Slave Girl, Belmont Plantation, Virginia (Dear America series)*, by Patricia McKissack (Scholastic, 1997/2011). Part of the *Dear America* series, this fictionalized diary of a real girl who was a slave in Virginia shortly after Nat Turner's revolt shows the risks that slaves had to take simply to learn how to read. A Historical Note at the end provides fascinating detail about the everyday life of enslaved people, their faith, their songs, and their efforts to win liberty.

## MAP WORK

### Native American Relocation *(Student Page 143, answer 329)*

1. Find the Oklahoma Territory and outline it in brown.
2. Lightly color the areas of Native Americans in green. (These areas are outlined on your map.)

3. The government forced Native American tribes to move to the Oklahoma Territory. Trace the dotted lines of the trails of the Chickasaw and Choctaw in brown.
4. The Creeks refused to go! But the government finally forced them to move. Color this dotted line in orange.
5. The Seminoles and Cherokee fought the hardest. The Seminoles fought for seven years before they were driven out. Soldiers forced the Cherokee to march during the winter—an event that would one day be known as the Trail of Tears. Trace both of these lines in blue. Then write Trail of Tears along the top of the Cherokee trail.
6. Nat Turner's slave rebellion took place in VA. Outline the state of Virginia in black.

**Coloring Page** The Cherokee people, as well as other Native American tribes, were forced out of their homes by the United States government and the state governments. Soldiers made them travel hundreds of miles to the new "Indian Territory" in Oklahoma. *(Student Page 144)*

## PROJECTS

### Craft Project — Cherokee Forest Pouch

Although many Cherokee Indians adopted white settlers' ways and settled in towns with stores and churches, some continued to live in the traditional Native American way. A Native American hunter might have used this game pouch to keep the results of his day's hunting nearby!

*Materials:*

- ☐ white piece of paper (8½" x 11")
- ☐ brown material, like suedecloth, fleece or felt (¼ yard)
- ☐ sewing machine, or needle and thread
- ☐ scissors
- ☐ jute rope

*Directions:*

1. Fold fabric in half and place the paper on it as a pattern. Cut two rectangles the size of the paper out of the fabric.
2. Turn fabric inside out and sew up the sides. Turn it back to the right side and press it down with pressure from your fingers, smoothing the seams.
3. Sew up the three inches from the bottom side, on the right side of the fabric. Cut fringe / strips into the bottom of it.
4. Make a drawstring casing on the top of the pouch by folding over the fabric about an inch. Sew along the top, with the folded side forming the pocket. Leave one part open about an inch to insert the drawstring.
5. Attach a safety pin to the end of the jute rope and slowly work it through the bag. Cut off the rope when you've determined how long you want it to be and tie a knot to the end, removing the safety pin. Fill your bag with treasures you may find on an adventure in a park, beach or your own backyard.

### Activity Project — Indian Sign Language

Native American tribes often used sign language to communicate with each other. Go on a walk in your neighborhood. Pretend that you are on a long march, and use the signs on Student Page 145 to communicate necessary information.

## ACTIVITY PROJECT **Tribal Face Paint**

Members of some Native American tribes would paint designs on their faces. These designs told you the person's membership and position in the tribe. The designs were also thought to provide spiritual protection. Depending on what tribe you were from, the colors and designs of the face paint were different. Make your own face paint (or use the store-bought kind) and decorate your face like a tribal warrior.

*Materials:* ☐ Face paint (in all the colors you will need for your design—see below).

*Directions:*

1. Decide which tribal warrior's design you would like to do. Here are some suggestions:
   *Comanche*: black lines smeared across the forehead and chin.
   *Crow*: red faces (with or without stripes) and yellow eyelids
   *Blackfoot*: circles, lines, and dots in blue, black, red, white, and yellow. A white line across the face, from cheekbone to cheekbone and across the bridge of the nose, meant the warrior was on a quest for vengeance. An all-black face meant a warrior had just committed a heroic deed.
2. Mix up the face paint recipe (make however many colors you need). Looking in a mirror, apply the face paint with a thin paint brush or your finger. If you need to change colors, rinse and dry your finger or the brush well. Excess water in the paint will make it runny.

***Face Paint Recipe:***

*For one color: Mix 1 tsp cornstarch with ½ tsp. water in a small dish. Add ½ tsp. cold cream or diaper cream. Add two drops of food coloring. Mix well. The face paint will wash off with warm water.*

# China Adrift

## Encyclopedia Cross-References

*UBWH 189 UILE 354*
*KIHW 568-569, KHE 344-345*

## THE FIRST OPIUM WAR

### Review Questions

As Chi'en-lung's reign drew to a close, to whom did he give power? *The old emperor gave more and more power to his favorite army officer, Ho-Shen.*

Why were people at court concerned that Ho-Shen was gaining power? *Everyone at court knew he was a corrupt liar.*

Why did the emperor give his throne to Pinyin Jiqing after 60 years on the throne? *His ancestor had ruled for 61 years, and he thought it would be disrespectful to rule as long as the greatest Manchu ruler.*

What did Pinyin Jiqing, now called Chia Ching, do to Ho-Shen? *He told him he would kill him, but allowed him to commit suicide.*

Chia Ching didn't get very far in cleaning up Ho-Shen's mess by the time he died. What was the biggest problem his heir, Tao-Kung, faced? *Tao-Kung faced the problem of opium.*

People from what country were smuggling opium into China? *People from Britain were smuggling opium into China.*

What was one solution to the opium problem, as suggested by one of Tao-Kung's officials? *He suggested that China make opium legal, so the money would stay in China.*

Why was Lin Zexu's nickname "Blue Sky"? *He was as pure as a cloudless summer sky.*

What was Lin Zexu's plan to wipe out the opium problem? *Lin Zexu went to the port of Canton and sent a message to the British whose ships sat at anchor. Unless all the opium on every ship in Canton was handed over, no trade would be allowed at all at any Chinese port—ever. And any British merchant found trading in opium afterwards would be arrested and put to death at once.*

What did Lin Zexu do with the opium that he recovered? *He had the opium dumped in three large holes near the water. The opium dissolved and was washed away.*

How did the British respond to the dumping of the opium? *They declared war on China and blocked all trade by sending battleships into all of China's harbors.*

What were at least two things the Treaty of Nanjing required of the Chinese? *China had to pay Great Britain twenty-one million dollars for the opium that had been destroyed. They had to agree to open up five more ports for British ships to trade in. The Chinese had to allow English merchants to build settlements and live in China year round! The whole island of Hong Kong, off China's southern coast, had to be given to the British! And China had to agree to make the same treaty with France and the United States.*

### Narration Exercise

Because there is a good deal of information in this chapter, use "directed narration." Say to the student, "First, explain how China's government became corrupt under the rule of Chi'en-lung." An appropriate answer might be, "When Chi'en-lung became old, he gave too much power to his favorite officer, Ho-Shen. Ho-Shen took bribes and forced officials to pay him money. When Chi'en-lung's son finally became emperor, he took away Ho-Shen's property and ordered him to commit suicide. But China's officials were corrupt and the treasury was almost empty."

Then say to the student, "Now explain why opium was such a big problem—and what the emperor Tao-kung tried to do about it." An appropriate answer might be, "Many Chinese were addicted to opium. They paid British merchants so much money for opium that China ran short of silver coins! So Tao-kung asked his official, Lin Zexu, to stop the opium trade. Lin Zexu threatened to put British merchants to death if they traded opium. He seized all the opium and dumped it into holes."

Finally, say to the student, "What did the British do to stop Lin Zexu—and why?" An appropriate answer might be, "The British wanted to keep selling opium, and making money. So they sailed steam battleships to China. They forced the Chinese to sign a treaty giving Great Britain twenty-one million dollars and Hong Kong. The treaty also let British merchants live in China and trade in Chinese ports."

## Additional History Reading

*See Chapter 28 for additional history titles.*

*10 Plants that Shook the World,* by Gillian Richardson, illus Kim Rosen (Annick Press, 2013). Excellent book that tells the story of ten plants and the impact they had on history and society. Several chapters in this book relate to important points in *The Story of the World, Volume 3,* including the chapter on cotton (New England mills, cotton gin and slavery) and the chapter on cinchona (Lewis & Clark expedition). The chapter about tea talks about how the English introduced opium to China in part to earn silver to pay for tea. The text is easy to read, with a lot of sidebar stories with interesting facts. The relevant chapters would make a good read-aloud to accompany each related chapter of *The Story of the World.* (RA 2-3, IR 4-8).

*Chinese History Stories: Stories from the Imperial Era, Volume 2,* by Renee Ting (Shen's Books, 2009). This book contains a section about Lin Zexu, the official who tried to stop opium from entering the country anymore. (RA 1-3, IR 3-5)

*Thomas Crapper, Corsets, and Cruel Britannia: A Grim History of the Vexing Victorians!,* by Peter Hepplewhite, illus. Tom Morgan-Jones (Gareth Stevens Publishing, 2016). This lively book has sections that describe opium use in Britain, as well as wars that Britain was involved in (including the Opium War) during the nineteenth century. (RA 1-2, IR 2-4)

*Cixi: The Dragon Empress,* by Natasha Yim, illus. Peter Malone (Goosebottom Books, 2011). Born during the time of opium smuggling, Cixi was the last empress of China. The narrative text is great for reading aloud and is accompanied by beautiful illustrations. (RA 1-4, IR 4-6)

*Great Ports of the World: From New York to Hong Kong* by Mia Cassany, illus. Victor Medina. (Prestel, 2018). Interesting book about various ports around the world, including Hong Kong. While this is a modern-day view of how shipping ports look, it can be a good way to start a conversation about how goods are delivered and have been delivered from country to country. (RA K-1, IR 1-2).

*Hong Kong (Enchantment of the World)* by Barbara A. Somervill (Children's Press, 2015). Reference book about Hong Kong, includes history from its beginnings thousands of years ago, through the Treaty of Nanjing and British rule to the present day. (RA 3-4, IR 4-8).

*D is for Dancing Dragon: A China Alphabet,* by Carol Crane, illus. Zong-Zhou Wang (Sleeping Bear Press, 2006). An English alphabet book that illustrates and explains China's history, customs, art, geography, food, music, wildlife, and more. (RA 1-2, IR 2-4)

*Decorative Chinese Designs Stained Glass Coloring Book*, by A. G. Smith (Dover Publications, 2006). The designs in this book are adapted from ancient Chinese art. Use it to incorporate picture study into history, or to simply relax with soothing coloring activity. Also check out the other Dover books about Chinese art, design, and fashion. (RA 1-4, IR 4-6)

*Happy, Happy Chinese New Year!*, by Demi (Knopf Books for Young Readers, 2003). A very colorfully illustrated book that explains the rituals of the Chinese New Year festivities. (RA 1-2, IR 2-4)

*Medicinal Plants Coloring Book*, by Ilil Arbel (Dover Publications, 1993). A Dover Nature Coloring book, illustrated by a botanical artist. The opium poppy is one of the plants featured, and each plant is captioned with information about it. This book would be useful for introducing children to how some plants have been used over time, for drawing practice, or for simple coloring fun. (RA 1-4, IR 4-6)

*Sea Queens: Women Pirates Around the World*, by Jane Yolen, illus. Christine Joy Pratt (Charlesbridge, 2008). One featured pirate is the fierce Madame Ching from 19th-century China. Other women pirates from the 1600's and 1700's are also described. (RA 1-3, IR 3-4)

## Corresponding Literature Suggestions

*See Chapter 28 for additional literature titles.*

*The Serpent's Children*, by Laurence Yep (HarperCollins, 2001). Told from the perspective of a young girl in mid-nineteenth century China, this is a story of a family's hardship during the time of the Opium Wars. Great for reading aloud; worth finding through interlibrary loan or on the used book market. (RA 1-4, IR 4-6)

*Spring Pearl: The Last Flower*, by Laurence Yep, illus. Kazuhiko Sano (Pleasant Company Publications, 2003). Created by the publishers of the *American Girl* series, these novels for older elementary students tell the stories of girls in other cultures. In this one, a young girl in Canton during the Opium Wars must work to save her master's household when her master is arrested. (IR 4-7) **OOP**

*The Adventures of Sherlock Holmes*, by Arthur Conan Doyle (Oxford World's Classics, 1994 and numerous other editions). In "The Man with the Twisted Lip," Sherlock Holmes infiltrates an opium den run by Chinese smugglers; older students will enjoy this fictionalized glimpse into the tangled Chinese-British opium trade of the nineteenth century. (RA 3-4, IR 5-adult)

*Ruby's Wish*, by Shirin Yim Bridges, illus. Sophie Blackall (Chronicle Books, 2015). Set at the turn of the century, this story of a large family with an ambitious youngest child shows the strength of Chinese family relationships. (RA 2, IR 3-5)

*Little Pear* by Eleanor Frances Lattimore (Odyssey, 2006). LIttle Pear lives in a small village in China around the early 1900s. Young children will enjoy and relate to his excitement for adventure and his tendency for mishap. (RA K-2, IR 3-4).

*Squishy Taylor and the Vase That Wasn't*, by Ailsa Wild, illus. Ben Wood (Picture Window Books, 2018). A funny mystery story to read aloud. Squishy and her "bonus sisters" decide to investigate when a Ming vase, apparently stolen during the Opium Wars, disappears from a locked apartment in their apartment building. (RA 1-3, IR 4-6)

*The Treasure of Ching Shih*, by John Gilgren (Promontory Press, Inc., 2015). Follow the scuba-diving Cali family on their dangerous journey to locate treasure hidden by the pirate Madame Ching in 19th-century China. (RA 1-3, IR 406)

## MAP WORK

### England and China *(Student Page 146, answer 329)*

1. Find England (Great Britain) on the map and color it red. Remember that England badly wanted to be allowed into China, but had been forbidden.
2. China tried to keep England and the West out. Outline the border of China in a thick brown line.
3. The English continued to smuggle opium into Canton. Find Canton and draw a red box around Canton.
4. The English smuggled opium through many ports on the coast of China. Draw three red arrows from the ocean, through the brown line on the coast of China, and into China.
5. Find Nanjing. The British forced the Chinese to sign the treaty of Nanjing, which was called the "unequal treaty." Draw a red box around Nanjing.

**Coloring Page** Lin Zexu was a Chinese government official, famous for his honesty. He used his soldiers and ships to try to stop foreign traders from bringing the dangerous drug opium into China. *(Student Page 147)*

## PROJECTS

### Game Project — Yellow River Race!

Tao-kung inherited an empty treasury. The dikes along the Yellow River were falling into the water. The dikes needed repair, but all the money for repairs was gone! See who can keep up the dikes.

*Materials:*
- ☐ 2 or 3 players
- ☐ Large, plastic tub (like one used to wash dishes in)
- ☐ Dirt
- ☐ Three pitchers of water
- ☐ Timer

*Directions:*

1. Fill the plastic tub half way with dirt.

2A. The object of the game is to build the dikes of the Yellow River up in the midst of the running water. If you have two players, then set a timer for one minute. While one player forms a dike (a wall of dirt that does not lean against the wall of the tub), the other player pours the water in the middle of the tub, but not on top of the dike. The person pouring the water should pour the water at a steady rate. If she runs out of water, have her fill up the pitchers again, and continue to pour until the timer sounds. If at the end of the minute the dikes are still standing, then the builder wins.

2B. If there are three players, place one player at each end of the tub. Each of these players will build a dike. When the timer begins, the third player pours water in the tub. The builders have one minute to keep the sides up as the third player pours water.

*Note:* This game may best be played outside or in the shower or bathtub area. It can get messy!

### Game Project — BRIBE! The Game

*Materials:*
- ☐ *The Story of the World, Volume 3*
- ☐ Student Page 148: Bribe Game Board
- ☐ Student Page 149: Game Card Template

- ☐ 40 pennies
- ☐ game pieces: beans, coins, buttons or small plastic toys to serve as player markers
- ☐ One die or two, depending on how fast you want the game to go

Directions:

***Before the game:***

1. Enlarge the game board to fit on an 11" x 14" cardstock. At that time, make two copies of the game cards onto two different colors of cardstock, making two decks of the cards.
2. *Optional:* Glue the Game Board onto cardboard or posterboard to add strength.
3. *Optional:* Cover the Game Board with clear contact paper.
4. Select game pieces, one for each player.

***To play:***

1. All players begin by placing game pieces in the center of the board where the name of the game is. The oldest player gets to start the game. Before the game begins, each player must decide if he is going to be the owner of the white squares or the black squares. Also, each player gets 20 pennies to put into his pot. (The players will spend the pennies in the game.)
2. The player may not begin the game until he rolls a three. Once he rolls a three, he may begin by placing his game piece at the starting square. He may not move forward until the next turn.
3. On each of his turns, the player will land on a white square or a black square. If he lands on a square that is his home color, then he may rest. But if he lands on his opponent's square, he must draw one of his opponent's cards. If he can answer the question correctly, then he may stay. If he does not know the answer, he must bribe the opponent to give him the answer by paying a penny. The opponent must give him the answer or look it up in the *Story of the World, Volume 3.*
4. The players each continue to move around the board. When he lands on the end of an arrow, he may slide to the end. If he slides past another player's piece, the player he passes is sent back to the center of the board. He remains there until he rolls a three.
5. If he lands on a square that is already occupied, the player who was there first is sent to the center of the board. He is stuck there until he rolls a three.

   END SQUARE—A player does not need to have the exact roll to finish on the *End Square.* Once there, he may choose a question from either pile. The winner is determined after everyone has passed the End Square. Whoever has the most pennies, wins!

## COOKING PROJECT **Poppy Seed Muffins**

There are many varieties of the poppy plant. Yes, opium is produced from a certain kind of poppy, but the poppy plant isn't all bad! Poppies have big, beautiful blooms and tiny seeds that we eat. These seeds are harmless—they don't contain opium! Make poppy seed muffins; they are delicious!

*Ingredients:*
2 cups all-purpose flour
2 tsp baking powder
¼ tsp salt
½ cup unsalted butter, softened
1 tsp grated lemon zest
⅔ cup sugar
2 large eggs

4 tsp poppy seeds
1.2 cups milk

*Directions:*

1. Combine flour, baking powder, and salt in a medium bowl.
2. In a large bowl, cream butter, lemon zest, and sugar until fluffy.
3. Add eggs, one at a time, to the butter-sugar mixture, and add milk. Beat well.
4. Stir poppy seeds into butter-sugar mixture.
5. Add the flour mixture to the butter-sugar mixture in three parts, beating after each addition. Do not overmix.
6. Spoon the batter into a 12-cup greased muffin tin. If desired, sprinkle the top of each muffin with additional sugar.
7. Bake at 375 degrees for 25 minutes, or until golden brown.

## GAME PROJECT **Shore Bombardment**

Materials:

- ☐ four tennis balls
- ☐ large cardboard box
- ☐ building blocks (wooden)
- ☐ four small throw or sofa pillows

The British forced the Chinese to surrender by sailing iron-clad battleships into Chinese ports and bombarding the Chinese from a safe distance! Experiment with this strategy.

Directions:

*Setting Up:*

1. Find a large cardboard box, large enough to sit in and peer over. This will be your battleship. Cut off the flaps; draw on the sides if you wish.
2. Build three towers out of wooden blocks. The towers can be any height; these will be your "port city" buildings.
3. Push your "battleship" to attack position, no closer than ten feet from the towers. The British had to stay in a safe position offshore to attack the ports! Climb into the box.
4. Your mother or father will play the part of the Chinese defenders. He or she will take up position behind the towers, holding the throw pillows.

*To Play:*

1. You have four chances to knock down the towers with your tennis balls. If you knock all three towers down, the British have won! Peer over the edge of your battleship to aim.
2. Whenever your parent sees your eyes appear over the edge, he or she can fire back. If a throw pillow hits you, your battleship is destroyed and the Chinese have successfully defended their ports.
3. If a throw pillow falls into your box without touching you, you may safely throw it back out again. This does not count as a hit.
4. If you don't knock over all three towers, the Chinese have repelled the British invasion! However, the British did finally conquer Chinese resistance. So you can collect your tennis balls and try again—until you win! How long does it take you? (The British fought three different "Opium Wars" to gain total control of Chinese ports!)

# Mexico and Her Neighbor

## Encyclopedia Cross-References

*UBWH 185, UILE 350-351*
*KIHW 562-563, KHE 342*

## REMEMBER THE ALAMO

### Review Questions

What two groups of people lived in the Mexican state of Texas? *Mexicans and "Anglos" lived in Texas.*

What was an empresario? *An empresario was an American settlement in a Spanish land.*

When an American settled in Mexico, what three things was he supposed to do? *He would become a Mexican citizen, convert to Catholicism, and obey Mexican laws.*

What was one reason Mexicans began to be annoyed with the empresarios? *More Texans spoke English than Spanish; many refused to convert to Catholicism or obey Mexican laws; many Americans brought slaves to Texas.*

When Santa Anna became dictator, what law did he pass that angered many Texans? *He said that no one in Texas could have a gun unless the Mexican government gave them permission.*

What was a garrison? *A garrison was a gathering of armed men.*

What happened when one of the garrisons found a cannon and loaded it with chains and pieces of iron? *The Mexicans demanded that they give it up. The Texans refused.*

After the Mexicans had come to take the cannon from the garrison, the Texans prepared themselves for war with Mexico. What quick-tempered frontiersman became the general of the new Texas army? *Sam Houston was voted general of the new Texas army.*

What message did Sam Houston send the Texans in the south? *He told them to hold out while he got an army together.*

What was the name of the fort that the 189 Texans took refuge in? *The name of the fort was the Alamo.*

What did William Travis do when the 4000 Mexicans led by Santa Anna surrounded the fort? *He stood firm and decided to fight.*

How many days did the battle last? Who won? *The battle lasted thirteen days. The Mexicans won the battle.*

### Narration Exercise

Since there is a great deal of information in this chapter, use "directed narration." Say to the student, "Explain why Mexico and the Mexican state of Texas started to fight with each other." An acceptable answer might be, "Mexico agreed to let Americans settle in the Mexican state of Texas if they would become Catholics, become Mexicans, and obey Mexican law. But many American settlers refused. So Mexico said that no more Americans could live in Texas. Then, Santa Anna became dictator of Mexico and decreed that no one in Texas could have a gun without permission. So the settlers in Texas decided to be independent. They drew up their own constitution and made Sam Houston their new general."

Then, say to the student, "What happened at the Alamo?" An acceptable answer might be, "Texans in the south of Texas were ready to fight against Mexican soldiers. When they realized that Santa Anna's army was close, they gathered in a fort that used to be a mission. This fort was called the Alamo. When Santa Anna arrived, he demanded that the Texans surrender, but they refused. After thirteen days of siege, the Mexicans climbed the walls and killed the defenders."

## THE MEXICAN-AMERICAN WAR

### Review Questions

Why was Santa Anna angry with American settlers in Texas? *Many refused to obey him.*

What did Santa Anna threaten to do? *He threatened to march to Washington and plant the flag of Mexico there.*

How did Sam Houston's men surprise Santa Anna and his men near San Jacinto? *He and his soldiers surprised them when Santa Anna and his men took a siesta.*

Why did some Mexican soldiers repeat "No Alamo"? *They didn't want the Texans to think they'd taken part in the siege at the Alamo.*

What did President Andrew Jackson propose that Mexico do with Texas? *He proposed that they sell it to the U.S.*

Sam Houston feared losing if Mexico attacked again. What was his solution? *He decided Texas should join the U.S.*

What was one objection some people had to Texas joining the U.S.? *Some people pointed out that Texas would be a slave-owning state; others said people in Texas were rough, crude, violent trouble-makers.*

What was the goal of the U.S. when it declared war on Mexico? *It wanted to gain not only Texas, but to drive Mexicans from North America.*

Who was the young Congressman from Illinois who opposed the war on Mexico? *Abraham Lincoln was the Congressman who opposed the war.*

At the battle near Mexico City, Santa Anna left the hills behind his army undefended. Why? *He thought no army could cross the high hills behind him.*

Who was the young U.S. captain that led the U.S. to victory? *Robert E. Lee led the U.S. to victory.*

What land did the U.S. gain from the peace treaty with Mexico? *The U.S. gained a piece of land where California, Nevada, Utah, Arizona, Colorado, New Mexico, and Wyoming now lie.*

### Narration Exercise

Since there is a great deal of information in this chapter, use "directed narration." Say to the student, "What happened to Santa Anna?" An acceptable answer might be, "Santa Anna and his men marched against Sam Houston's army. Santa Anna didn't think that the Texas soldiers were a threat, so his men took an afternoon nap. Sam Houston's men attacked them while they were sleeping! Santa Anna surrendered and was sent to Washington, D.C."

Now say to the student, "How did Texas become a state? Be sure to end your narration with the battle at Mexico City." An appropriate answer might be, "Sam Houston forced Santa Anna to make Texas an independent country. Sam Houston became President. But he didn't have enough money for an army, so Texans voted to join the United States—after ten years! Now the United States fought for Texas. American soldiers decided to invade Mexico and drive Mexico out of North America, so the U.S. army invaded Mexico and marched to Mexico City. Santa Anna and his men fought back, but Mexico lost and agreed to give up land in return for fifteen million dollars. Later, the United States paid another ten million dollars for even more Mexican land."

## Additional History Reading

*Alamo All Stars (Hazardous Tales)* by Nathan Hale (Amulet Books, 2016). Graphic novel, part of the *Hazardous Tales* series, tells the story of Texas history with humor and engaging illustrations. Complete with maps of the Alamo and major battles in Texas history, this book is an informative and fascinating look at the often-violent early days of the state of Texas. (IR 3-5).

*A Picture Book of Sam Houston*, by David A. Adler and Michael S. Adler, illus. Matt Collins (Holiday House, 2012). Adler's picture book biographies have been wonderful introductions to characters in American history. This one gives young children detail about Sam Houston, with lively illustrations. (RA 1-2, IR 3-4)

*Sam Houston: Standing Firm* (Texas Heroes for Young Readers series) by Mary Dodson Wade, illus. Joy Fisher Hein (Bright Sky Press, 2009). Excellent biography of Sam Houston that is written for younger children but would be enjoyed by all elementary school grades. Extremely detailed illustrations that younger children will enjoy looking at. (RA K-2, IR 2-5).

*Jim Bowie: Legendary Hero of the Alamo*, by Ann Graham Gaines (Enslow Publishers, 2015). A medium-difficulty biography of Jim Bowie, the Texas settler and soldier who died at the Alamo. (RA 1-3, IR 4-6)

*Davy Crockett: In Their Own Words*, by George Sullivan (Scholastic, 2001). This excellent chapter-book biography series includes plenty of quotes from the biographical subjects themselves. (RA 2, IR 3-4) **OOP**

*Davy Crockett*, by Marianne Johnston (Powerkids Press, 2001). Simpler than the Sullivan book listed above, this easy-reader biography has large print and many color pictures. (RA 1-2, 3-4) **LFA**

*A Picture Book of Davy Crockett* by David A. Adler, illus John & Alexandra Wallner (Holiday House, 1996). Illustrated biography of Davy Crockett covers his life from birth until his death at the Alamo. Includes a timeline to help situate his life into the larger picture of world history. (RA K-2, IR 2-3).

*The Alamo*, by Kristin L. Nelson (Lerner Publishing, 2004). An easy-to-read book about the Alamo. Contains a photo of the actual building. (RA 1, IR 1-4)

*Inside the Alamo* by Jim Murphy (Delacourt, 2003). Excellent and detailed book about the Battle of the Alamo, includes maps, photos, sketches, and drawings of the people and places involved. Includes several spotlight pieces on the major participants. Select sections would make good read-alouds and there are plenty of pictures and illustrations for younger children to look at. (RA 3-4, IR 4-8).

*Susanna of the Alamo: A True Story*, by John Jakes, illus. Paul Bacon (Gulliver Books, 1986). A wonderful picture-book account of Susanna Dickinson, one of the Texas women who was in the Alamo when it was captured by Santa Anna; she carried Santa Anna's victory message to Sam Houston.

*Jane Long: Texas Journey*, by Mary Dodson Wade, illus. Virginia Marsh Roeder (Bright Sky Press, 2009). Jane was a widow and a mother who, in later years, operated boarding houses where people such as Sam Houston and Stephen Austin frequented. She possessed a determined spirit and accomplished much in her eventful life. (RA 1-3, IR 3-5)

*Juan Seguin*, by William R. Chemerka, illus. Don Collins (Bright Sky Press, 2012). Biography about a Tejano (a Texan of Hispanic descent) who was deeply involved in many of the events described in this chapter. Despite recruiting soldiers to help the Texans, as well as signing the Texas Declaration of Independence, he ended up having to flee to Mexico for his life. (RA 1-3, IR 3-5)

## Corresponding Literature Suggestions

*A Line in the Sand: The Alamo Diary of Lucinda Lawrence, Gonzales, Texas (Dear America Series)* by Sherry Garland (Scholastic, 1998). A fictional retelling of the Texas Revolution as told through the diary entries of a thirteen-year-old girl. Despite the title, this book covers far more of the Texas Revolution than just the Battle of the Alamo. (RA 3-4, IR 4-6).

*The Battle of the Alamo: An Interactive History Adventure (You Choose History)* by Amie Jane Leavitt (Capstone Press, 2016). Experience this point in history as a Mexican soldier or a Texan rebel with this entry in the *You Choose History* series. (IR 3-4).

*The Boy in the Alamo*, by Margaret Cousins (Corona Press, 1986). Originally published in 1958, this classic tale of the siege of the Alamo has long been a young-reader favorite. (RA 2-3, IR 4-6)

*Defend Until Death!: Nickolas Flux and the Battle of the Alamo* (Nickolas Flux History Chronicles) by Nel Yomtov, illus Dante Ginevra (Capstone Press, 2014). As in previous books in this series, Nickolas gets zapped back in time, this time to the Battle of the Alamo. He begins by marching with the Mexican soldiers and later is with the rebels in the Alamo, giving a perspective of the battle from both sides. Includes plenty of factual information about the battle along with the engaging story. (RA 2-3, IR 3-7).

*I Remember the Alamo*, by D. Anne Love (Holiday House, 1999). An excellent chapter-book novel for good readers; two girls, one from Mexico and one from Texas, find their friendship complicated by the war over Texas. (RA 3, IR 4-6) **OOP**

*Outnumbered: Davy Crockett's Final Battle at the Alamo*, by Eric Fein (Rosen Publishing, 2004). Historical fiction for beginners, based on the famous battle. (RA 2, IR 3-4)

*Voices of the Alamo*, by Sherry Garland, illus. Ronald Himler (Pelican Publishing, 2017). Contains fictionalized firsthand accounts of events that led, over hundreds of years, to the events at the Alamo. Varying characters from those years speak almost poetically about their perspective. Paintings provide background for these quotes. (RA 1-2, IR 3-4)

*Remember the Alamo! The Runaway Scrape Diary of Belle Wood*, by Lisa Waller Rogers (Texas Tech University Press, 2013). Fourteen-year old Belle keeps a diary of her life in Texas. She chronicles her brother's death at the Alamo, and then her family's panicked flight to safety during the Runaway Scrape—an evacuation to escape the army of Santa Anna. This would make a great family read-aloud. (RA 1-3, IR 3-5)

*Blood in the Water: A Story of Friendship During the Mexican War*, by Pamela Dell (The Child's World, Inc., 2014). The war between Mexico and the United States interferes with the friendship between twelve-year-old Bonita and Carmen. The book contains photos and short explanations about the war, too. (RA 1-3, IR 3-5)

*Tucket's Ride*, by Gary Paulsen (Dell Yearling, 1997). A simple chapter book, telling the adventures of young Francis Tucket, who stumbles into enemy territory during the war between the United States and Mexico. For strong third-grade readers and above. (IR 3-5)

## MAP WORK

### Mexico, the Republic of Texas, and the US *(Student Page 150, answer 329)*

1. Mexico City was the capital of Mexico. Outline Mexico in green. Outline the border of the United States in blue.

2. Santa Anna made himself the dictator of Mexico. He made everyone who wanted to own a gun in Texas get permission from the Mexican government. Outline the border of Texas ("Original Mexican Territory of Texas") in green.
3. The Battle of the Alamo took place at San Antonio. Find San Antonio and circle the dot that represents San Antonio in green (because Mexico won the battle).
4. Santa Anna threatened to march to Washington D.C. and plant his flag there. Draw a green arrow from Texas to Washington D.C.
5. The Republic of Texas finally became part of the United States in 1845. Color Texas in blue (within the green border).
6. America forced the Mexicans out, then bought the land that is now California, Nevada, Utah, Arizona, Colorado, New Mexico, and Wyoming (and soon after, New Mexico). Find the area on your map, labeled Mexican Holdings, Sold to the U.S. in 1848. Outline the area in blue, then shade it in.

**COLORING PAGE** Vaqueros *(vah-KAYR-ohs)* were the cowboys of old Texas. Some were Mexican, and some were white or black Americans. They wore wide hats to protect them from the sun, and leather chaps over their trousers to protect their legs from thornbushes. *(Student Page 151)*

## PROJECTS

### GAME PROJECT Texas History Word Search

*Materials:*
- ☐ Student Pages 152 and 153: Early Texas History Clues and Word Search
- ☐ pencil

*Directions:*
1. Use *The Story of the World* to find the answers to the clues. Write out each answer on the Early Texas History Clues worksheet.
2. Now find the answers on the Word Search and circle them!

### ACTIVITY PROJECT Play Texas Ranger

The Texas Rangers were established in 1823 by Stephen F. Austin, the mastermind behind the agreement that allowed American settlers to settle in the Spanish territory of Texas. The Texas Rangers were to protect local people, homes, and businesses from outlaws, lawbreakers, and bad guys. Austin has a city named after him—the city of Austin, Texas. And he also left behind him the Texas Rangers, who still operate today.

*Materials:*
- ☐ Student Page 154: Texas Rangers Badge
- ☐ Colored pencils or crayons
- ☐ Safety pins
- ☐ Scotch tape
- ☐ Scissors

*Directions:*
1. Photocopy the student page as many times as necessary, so that you have one star for each player, minus one. Color and cut out the stars. Tape the safety pins to the backs of the stars
2. Elect one player to be the Outlaw. The other players are Texas Rangers. Each Ranger should put on a star.

3. Find a large playing area with a number of hiding places. Designate one place as Texas Ranger Headquarters. The Rangers should all go to Headquarters, close their eyes, and sing "Home on the Range." While they sing, the Outlaw should find a hiding place.
4. When "Home on the Range" is finished, the Rangers should spread out and look for the Outlaw. When a Ranger spots the Outlaw, the Ranger should shout, "Outlaw!" Then all the Rangers should run back to Headquarters before the Outlaw can tag them. Any Ranger tagged by the Outlaw must remove his star and join the Outlaw in the next round.
5. In the next round, the Outlaw will hide along with any captured Ranger. The game continues until there is only one Ranger left. This Ranger is the winner!

**Words to Home on the Range**

Oh, give me a home, where the buffalo roam,
Where the deer and the antelope play,
Where seldom is heard a discouraging word,
And the skies are not cloudy all day.
Home, home on the range,
Where the deer and the antelope play,
Where seldom is heard a discouraging word,
And the skies are not cloudy all day.
How often at night when the heavens are bright
With the light of the glittering stars,
Have I stood here amazed and asked as I gazed
If their glory exceeds that of ours.
Home, home on the range,
Where the deer and the antelope play,
Where seldom is heard a discouraging word,
And the skies are not cloudy all day.

*Note to Parent: This is not the Texas state song, but the Texas song is difficult to sing and unfamiliar to many students.*

## CRAFT PROJECT Defenders of the Alamo Flip Book

For twelve days and nights, the Texans fired at the Mexican army while the Mexicans shot cannonballs into the Alamo. On the thirteenth day of the siege, the Mexican soldiers made a final attack. They climbed the walls and poured into the fort. In less than half an hour, 189 Texans were dead. This activity will help you remember several facts about four of those 189 Texans.

*Materials:*

- ☐ Student Page 155: Alamo Flip Book
- ☐ scissors
- ☐ colored pencils or crayons
- ☐ Pencil

*Directions:*

1. Using the Alamo Flip Book page, fold on the line that goes the length of the paper. (Your paper should look as if it is "almost" folded in half.)
2. Using scissors, cut the paper on the remaining three lines. The paper should now have four sections.
3. Use the four people below—all defenders of the Alamo—and include three facts about each of them in your flip book.

William Travis

Commander at the Battle of the Alamo; one of his relatives moved to Jamestown in 1627; helped work on the family farm while growing up; moved to Texas in 1831 and set up a law practice; at first, he was able to recruit less than 30 men; directed the preparation of the San Antonio de Valera Mission, also known as the Alamo.

David Crockett

Born in East Tennessee; named his homestead "Kentuck"; elected to a seat in the TN legislature; fought in the Creek Indian War; nearly died from malaria, was reported dead, and astonished his family with his "resurrection"; set out to explore Texas in 1835; famous saying, "Be always sure you're right—then, go ahead!"

James (Jim) Bowie

His dad grew cotton and sugar cane on the family plantation; family tradition says that he caught and rode wild horses, rode wild alligators, and trapped bears; fought in the War of 1812; after the War of 1812, he became a slave-trader; used a larger butcher-like knife in the Sandbar Fight of 1827, and became famous for it; supposedly often told his fighters, "Keep under cover boys and reserve your fire; we haven't a man to spare."; before the Battle of the Alamo, he became sick with pneumonia or tuberculosis, and was found dead on a cot (when Santa Anna wanted to inspect his corpse).

William Carey

Was among the troops that marched to Gonzales during the fight for Gonzales' "Come and Take It!" cannon; he was a lieutenant, and called his company the Invincibles; during the battle of the Alamo, Carey commanded the fort's artillery.

4. Write "William Travis" on the left panel, on the bottom inch or so of the flip book. Flip the page up, and write three facts about this person (in complete sentences) in the available space. Then flip the page down, and choose a symbol for the person. For example, for William Travis, you might pick a cannon (because he answered the Mexican army with a cannon shot). You might use a fact from SOTW 3, or from the above information, as you choose your symbol.
5. Do the same thing for each of three more of the defenders of the Alamo. Be creative, and decorate your Alamo Flip Book with color!

## Cooking Project Gingerbread Alamo Façade

*Materials:*

- ☐ gingerbread dough (your favorite recipe, or ready-made mix)
- ☐ Student Page 156: Alamo Template
- ☐ cookie sheet
- ☐ table knife

*Directions:*

1. Roll out dough on to the cookie sheet so that it is about ¼ inch thick. The dough should be slightly larger than the size of the Alamo template.
2. Cut out the Alamo shape from the Student Page. Cut out the doors and windows. Lay the template on top of the dough.
3. Using the table knife, cut out the Alamo from the gingerbread. Be sure to cut out the windows and the doors.
4. Remove the template, and bake as directed. Take a picture before you eat it!

# New Zealand and Her Rulers

CHAPTER 41

## Encyclopedia Cross-References

*UBWH 176,181 UILE 274-275, 326-327*
*KIHW 236, 454, 572-573, KHE 88-89, 348-349*

## THE TREATY OF WAITANGI

### Review Questions

If a country has annexed land, what has it done? *It has taken that land for itself.*

Citizens from what country had settled in New Zealand? *British citizens had settled on the islands of New Zealand.*

The natives of New Zealand called the settlers pakehas. What did the natives call themselves? *They called themselves the Maori—the normal people.*

What did the Maoris receive in trade from the white settlers? *The Maoris traded for guns.*

What were two of the new diseases that Maoris caught from the settlers? *They caught smallpox, measles, and influenza.*

What did missionaries and English settlers beg the British to come to New Zealand and do? *They begged them to come and turn it into a law-abiding place.*

What was the solution the British proposed? *If the Maori would give New Zealand to the British, the British could make laws that would protect them from white invasion. The British promised that the Maori could keep all of their land, and that British soldiers would make sure that no settlers took it away.*

What promises did the British make to the Maori? *The British promised that the Maori could keep all of their land, and that British soldiers would make sure that no settlers took it away.*

The Treaty of Waitangi said Britain would protect the property and rights of the Maori. What would the Maori do in return? *The Maori would recognize England as their ruler.*

What animal did the British introduce to the South Island? *The British introduced sheep to the South Island.*

What did the governor tell the Maori when some of them tried to sell land? *He told them that they could only sell land to the British government.*

What did the Maoris realize about the Treaty of Waitangi? *It had many conditions the Maori were not aware of* OR *There were two versions of the Treaty.*

How did the two versions of the Treaty differ? *One gave the English the right to govern the land. The other gave them the right to take ("annex") the land.*

### Narration Exercise

"People from Australia came to New Zealand and settled there. The natives of New Zealand were called *Maori.* They bought guns from the Australians and fought with each other. The British said that they would come and keep the peace if the Maori gave them the right to govern the land. So the Maori signed the Treaty of Waitangi. They thought that the treaty gave the British government the right to *govern* New Zealand—but the treaty actually *gave* the land to Britain."

OR "The British came to New Zealand because the English settlers and the missionaries begged them to come. Farmers were fighting with each other, and the Maori were losing their land and drinking too much. So a British captain met with Maori leaders and signed a treaty that gave Britain the right to rule New Zealand. Many more settlers and many sheep came to New Zealand. But when the Maori tried to sell some of their land to the new settlers, they discovered that the British had claimed all of the land for themselves."

## THE NEW ZEALAND WARS

### Review Questions

On which of the two islands did most of the Maori live? *Most of the Maori lived on the North Island.*

What did Hone Heke decide to do? *He decided to take his country back.*

How did the British respond when Hone Heke cut the flagpole at Kororareka down? *They put it back up and finally stationed soldiers in front of it.*

The governor of New Zealand eventually became worried. What did he decide to do with his settlers? *He packed them onto ships that were anchored off New Zealand's coast.*

What did the Maori do when they saw a town emptied of its settlers? *They ran through and burned it.*

What two places did the settlers go to when they realized the town had been sacked? *Some went to Auckland; other went to Australia.*

What did George Grey finally convince the Maori to do? *He convinced them to make peace.*

After this peace, was the colony of New Zealand firmly in the hands of the British? *No, it was not.*

### Narration Exercise

"The English settled the South Island of New Zealand and wanted to settle on the North Island too. But the Maori were afraid that the British would take all of their land. Two Maori chiefs joined together to fight against the British. When the first war ended, nothing had been settled. The Maori and the British would fight for thirty years. The Maori people still protest against the British, even today!"

OR "A chief named Hone Heke was determined to fight against Britain. He kept cutting down the flagstaff where the Union Jack was flying. Finally, he and his followers burned the British settlement where the flag flew. The British fought back, but another chief named Kawiti joined with Hone Heke. Together, the two chiefs fought the Flagstaff War against the British. No one won the Flagstaff War, but eventually the British got almost all of New Zealand for themselves."

## Additional History Reading

*Aotearoa: The New Zealand Story*, by Gavin Bishop (Penguin Group 2017). This picture book story of New Zealand takes the reader through significant moments of the history of the islands. It is lavishly illustrated, and contains photos and Maori imagery.

*Fishing for Islands: Traditional Boats and Seafarers of the Pacific* by John Nicholson (Allen & Unwin, 2002). An interesting book about the lives and vessels of the early sailors in the Pacific. Includes a section on Maori war canoes. (RA 1-3, IR 3-5).

*Maori Warriors,* by Ray McClellan (Bellwether Media, 2012). An exciting book that explains the background, the training, and the equipment of Maori warriors. Vivid photos complement the text. (RA 1-3, IR 3-5)

*The Treaty of Waitangi*, by Ross Calman (Oratia Media Ltd., 2011). An explanation of the treaty between Maori groups and British settlers. It includes photos of the original documents, plus paintings and drawings of people and events surrounding the treaty. An older child could read the paragraphs to gain a better understanding of the interactions between the British and the Maori. (RA 1-4, IR 3-5)

*New Zealand (Countries Around the World)* by Mary Colson (Heinemann, 2012). A reference book about New Zealand, includes a chapter on the history of New Zealand. (IR 3-6).

*New Zealand ABCs: A Book about the People and Places of New Zealand*, by Holly Schroeder, illus. Claudia Wolf (Picture Window Books, 2004). Illustrations, interesting topics, and short paragraphs of text make this survey of New Zealand good for older reluctant readers. (RA 1-2, IR 3-5)

*T is for Taniwha: The Colouring Book for Kiwi Kids,* by Ann K. Addley (Ann K. Addley, 2015). Published in New Zealand, this ABC's coloring book beautifully illustrates concepts (such as the Haka dance), words, and objects in the country. Captions give more information about the picture on each coloring page. (RA 1, IR 2-4)

*Two Tuatara: A Kiwi Counting Book,* by Adrienne Body (CreateSpace Independent Publishing Platform, 2015). A colorfully illustrated counting book, featuring wildlife of New Zealand. The end of the book also has the numbers written in the Maori language, so young children can learn to pronounce them. (RA 1-2, IR 2-4)

*Welcome to New Zealand: A Nature Journal* by Sandra Morris (Candlewick, 2015). Beautifully illustrated guide to creating a nature journal that includes information about the flora and fauna native to New Zealand. This would make an excellent cross-over activity book for a science class, as the nature journal is appropriate for children no matter where in the world they live. (IR 3-6).

## Corresponding Literature Suggestions

*In the Beginning* by Peter Gossage (Scholastic New Zealand, 2006). Retelling of the Maori creation myth. (RA K-2, IR 3-5).

*Ka the Falcon*, by Bruce Gilberd, illus. Marco Dela Torre, maps by Joseph Morcom (Mackay Books, 2014). This picture book tells about the settlement of Aotearoa (New Zealand) through the eyes of a falcon named Ka. In addition to the story there is factual information scattered throughout the book. Maps are included, too. (RA 1-2, IR 2-4)

*Land of the Long White Cloud: Maori Myths, Tales, & Legends* by Kiri Te Kanawa and Michael Foreman (Arcade, 1990). Collection of 19 tales from the Maori. Illustrations are well done but some could be frightening for young children. (RA 1-3, IR 4-6).

*Taniwha*, by Mike Johnson, illus. Jennifer Rackham (Lasavia Publishing, 2016). The taniwha is a favorite mythical creature of New Zealand. This book poetically explores what the creature might look like. It has colorful illustrations, and it comes in English-only or in bilingual English and Maori. (RA 1-2, IR 2-4)

*The Weka-Feather Cloak: A New Zealand Fantasy*, by Leo Madigan (Bethlehem Books, 2002). This novel for slightly older readers features two young explorers who interact with a Maori artist and a mystery in present-day New Zealand. (RA 2-3, IR 4-6)

*Rata and the Waka,* retold by Jephson Gibbs, illus. Fraser Williamson (Clean Slate Press, 2016). This is a retelling of a tale from New Zealand, combined with gorgeous illustrations. "Waka" is the Maori word for "canoe." The book also contains information about Maori culture in New Zealand. (RA 1-3, IR 2-4)

*The Treasure of Mad Doc Magee*, by Elinor Teele (Walden Pond Press, 2018). Set in the town of Eden where memories of New Zealand's gold rush still exist, this story features twelve-year-old Jenny and her best friend Pandora. Threatened with having to leave Eden, Jenny sets out to find the large gold nugget rumored to have been hidden by Doc Magee, in order to save her family's farm. (RA 1-4, IR 4-6)

*The Whale Rider*, by Witi Ihimaera (Harcourt, 2003). For older readers or as a lengthy read-aloud; also consider watching the movie, directed by Niki Caro (Columbia Tristar, 2003). Tells the story of the granddaughter of a Maori chief, and the mythology that helps her find her role in her tribe; the movie and book are both frank about the Maori struggle with racism and violence. (RA 3-4, IR 4-6) Book is **E-Only.**

## MAP WORK

### Australia and New Zealand *(Student Page 157, answer 329)*

1. Remember that Great Britain had colonized New South Wales. Outline the border of New South Wales in red, then color it lightly in red.
2. Great Britain agreed to protect New Zealand from invasion if they could have the land. As soon as Great Britain had control, many settlers moved to the South Island. Color the South Island in red.
3. Great Britain and New Zealand fought about the North Island—who should have control over what part of the land? Find the North Island and outline it in red.
4. Auckland was the site of one of the major battles between the New Zealand natives and the British. Find Auckland and underline it in blue.

**Coloring Page** The Maori are the native people of New Zealand. They had lived on the islands of New Zealand (or *Aotearoa*, as they called it) for hundreds of years before the British came. *(Student Page 158)*

## PROJECTS

### Craft Project Maori Sweet Potato Garden

The sweet potato was one of the staple foods of the Maori in New Zealand. You can make a small Maori Garden with a few household items and a sweet potato!

*Materials:*
- □ Glass jar with a wide mouth—wide enough for sweet potato to fit in
- □ Three to four toothpicks
- □ Sweet potato
- □ Water

*Directions:*
1. Stick the toothpicks into the side of the sweet potato and place it, root down, into the jar.
2. Add water along the sides. It usually takes 10 to 14 days before you see white hairy roots start to sprout.
3. *Optional*: After your sweet potato has a good head of leaves and strong, thickish roots, transplant it in a terracotta pot that is big enough for you to completely cover the root. This beautiful plant will last a long time.

### Craft Project Make a Maori Pürerehua (butterfly)

Maori used pürerehua (butterflies) in their tribal ceremonies. The men would swing these over their heads and make loud noises, which would keep others away from their special meetings.

Materials:
- ☐ Ruler with a hole in one end (more than one hole is acceptable)
- ☐ Fine string (fishing line, dental string)

Directions:
1. Find a ruler with a hole in one end of it (more holes are okay, but use the one closest to the end).
2. Tie one end of a four or five foot length of fishing line, dental floss, or other fine string, through the hole.
3. Outside, swing the ruler around (like a lasso). As it spins through the air, it will make a sound like the Maori pürerehua.

## Activity Project Introducing Yourself in Maori—Pepeha

What is pepeha? Pepeha is the way to introduce yourself in Maori. To introduce yourself, you have to tell the story of how you arrived where you are now.

1. First, name your grandparents and your parents. Put your grandfather and your father first then your grandmother and mother. Make sure to use the women's maiden names. "My grandfather was/is (his name). My father is (his name)." And so on.
2. You must say where each parent and grandparent comes from. First, your grandfather; then your father; next your grandmother; and finally, your mother. "My grandparent came from (place)." And so on.
3. How did your parents come from where they were to where you were born? "My parent's were married in (place). They moved to (place)." And so on, until you tell how they came to the place where you were born.
4. How did you get from where you were born to where you are now? Or, have you lived in the same place since you were born? "I was born in (place) and lived there until I was (age). Then, I moved to (place) until I was (age)." And so on, until you get to where you live now.
5. Finally, you say who you are and where you are now: "I am (your name) of (place)." That is how you connect yourself to your ancestors in the way the Maori do.

## Activity Project The Treaty of Waitangi

The English and the Maori signed the Treaty of Waitangi. After the treaty was signed, the Maori found out the there had been two versions of the treaty, and that they were allowed to sell land only to the British.

Materials:
- ☐ Quarter (or some other coin, to represent a highly valued commodity)
- ☐ 5 cookies (or other desired "treat")
- ☐ 2 other participants (preferably one parent and one sibling)

Directions:

*Note: Before the game, give parent 1 cookie, and give sibling (or other participant) 4 cookies.*

1. You have a valuable, one-of-a-kind quarter. You know that your brother or sister would gladly give you four cookies for this rare quarter. (The Maori had valuable land. Settlers were willing to give the Maori much money for their land.)
2. As you are about to trade your valuable quarter to your sibling for four cookies, when you parent stops you and says, "Do you remember the agreement we made? You are allowed to trade your quarter only to me! I will give you one cookie for your rare quarter." (The British governor called the Maori in to remind them that they could only sell to the British, not to settlers. The Maori did not know about this when they signed the treaty.)

3. You really want the cookie, but you are not happy that you are allowed to trade only with your parent. You trade it anyway. (Remember, the Maori were allowed to sell land only to the British, who gave them a low price for their land.)
4. Your sibling now wants the valuable quarter. He is willing to pay your parent four cookies for the quarter. Your parent is willing to trade the quarter for four cookies. You parent enjoys eating the four cookies, and you are as upset as the Maori were. (The British government sold land to the settlers, and received much more money than they paid. This upset the Maori.)

# The World of Forty-Nine

## Encyclopedia Cross-References

*UBWH 183, UILE 350*
*KIHW 571 margin, 614, KHE 370-371*

## THE GOLD RUSH

### Review Questions

What are two jobs Jim Marshall did during his lifetime? *He was a soldier in the fight against Mexico. He was also a carpenter, farmer, and cattle rancher.*

What had Jim Sutter hired Marshall to do? *He hired him to build a sawmill on the American River in the Sacramento Valley.*

What did Marshall and his men find in the river? *They found gold.*

How did Marshall test the gold to see if it was real or if it was iron pyrite? *He hammered it out. If it hammered out smooth, it was real gold.*

What did Sam Brannan sell when he discovered there was gold at Sutter's Mill? *He decided to sell mining supplies—picks and pans.*

What was "staking a claim"? *Because California was a new state, people could drive a stake into the ground and claim the land as their own. This was "staking a claim."*

What were most newcomers to California hoping to find? *Most newcomers to California were hoping to find gold.*

Did all of the miners who traveled to California "strike it rich"? *No, many barely found enough gold to buy food and supplies.*

People came from many countries to find gold in California. Can you name three? *People came from China, England, France, Germany, Spain, Italy, Portugal, and Sweden.*

In what year did California become a state? *California became a state in 1850.*

### Narration Exercise

"Jim Marshall was building a sawmill in California when he found gold. Soon, over a hundred thousand people came to California to mine for gold. They were called "forty-niners" because they came in 1849. Many of them got rich—but others couldn't find anything at all. In 1850, California became a state."

OR "Thousands of gold miners came to California to mine for gold. They came from the United States but also from many other countries, like China and England. They got land for themselves by staking claims. Mining camps and towns called 'boom towns' grew up all over California. So many people came to California that California became a state in 1850. It was the richest state in the U.S.!"

## A WORLD OF UNREST

### Review Questions

Where did the Spanish dig their gold mines? *They dug gold mines in South America.*

Where did Americans dig their gold? *They dug gold out of California's rivers.*

The cities of 1850 had beautiful buildings at their centers—and what around their edges? *Cities had slums around the edges.*

What was happening in the new republics of South America? *Dictators and generals tried to take power away from the new constitutions.*

What two groups of people quarrelled in the United States? *Slave owners and those who didn't believe in slavery (abolitionists) quarrelled.*

Who fought against the English in Australia? *The Aborigines fought against the English.*

In New Zealand? *The Maori.*

The English also occupied parts of two other countries. Can you remember what they were? *The English were also in China and India.*

In Russia, who resented the riches of the czar? *Hungry peasants resented the riches of the czar.*

### Narration Exercise

"The world changed a lot in 250 years. The Spanish had dug gold in South America, but now Americans were digging gold in California. There were more factories, more cities, and more railroads. All over the world, people were unhappy with each other—in Australia and New Zealand and in South America."

OR "The English ruled over parts of Australia, New Zealand, India, and China—but the people in those countries wanted the English to leave. In South America, dictators and generals were trying to seize power. In the United States slaveowners argued with people who wanted slavery to end. The world was full of unrest!"

## Additional History Reading

*G is for Golden: A California Alphabet*, by David Domeniconi, illus. Pamela Carrol (Sleeping Bear Press, 2002). An alphabet book that offers a historical fact about California for every letter; for reluctant readers or younger siblings. (IR 1-3)

*The California Gold Rush (True Books)* by Mel Friedman (Scholastic, 2010). Good resource book for the California Gold Rush that is written at a level younger children can follow. Even the font is inviting. Includes pictures, maps and a glossary of important terms. (RA K-2, IR 2-4).

*California History for Kids: Missions, Miners, and Moviemakers in the Golden State (For Kids Series)* by Katy Duffield (Chicago Review Press, 2012). Interesting book about the history of California, includes a chapter on the Gold Rush and how California joined the United States as the thirty-first state. Each chapter includes instructions for a related hands-on activity. (RA 3-4, IR 4-6).

*Gold! Gold from the American River! January 24, 1848: The Day The Gold Rush Began (Actual Times)*, by Don Brown (Square Fish, reprint 2014). Engaging book even for younger readers, tells how the Gold Rush transformed California and the people who went there. Covers the hardships pioneers endured coming out West, as well as the discrimination faced by Native Americans, Chinese laborers, and women. (RA 1-2, IR 2-3).

*John Sutter and the California Gold Rush (Graphic History)* by Matt Doeden, illus Charles Barnett III and Ron Frenz (Capstone Press, 2006). The history of the Gold Rush, told in graphic novel format. Engaging comic book-style illustrations and easy to follow text make this a good choice for reluctant readers (RA 2-3, IR 3-6).

*Levi Strauss and Blue Jeans*, by Nathan Olson, illus. Dave Hoover, Keith Williams, Charles Barnett III (Capstone Press, 2007). A graphic-style biography about Levi Strauss (inventor of Levi's blue jeans), who went to California during the Gold Rush to market dry goods for his family business. (RA 1-2, IR 3-4)

*Life During the Gold Rush*, by Janey Levy (Gareth Stevens Publishing, 2013). This book details the difficult circumstances people (including immigrants and African-Americans) encountered—from tools used to the food eaten. (RA 1-3, IR 3-4)

*The Life of a Miner*, by Bobbie Kalman and Kate Calder (Crabtree Publishing, 2000). Good illustrations and interesting text describe mining techniques, mining towns, and the world of 1849. (RA 1-2, IR 3-5)

*Treasure Hunter's Handbook*, by Liza Gardner Walsh, photos by Jennifer Smith-May (Down East Books, 2014). A book for parents to read to their kids, this has a section on how to pan for gold in gold-bearing rivers! Lots of other fun family treasure-hunting activities included, too. (RA 1-4)

*What Was the Gold Rush?* By Joan Halub, illus Tim Tomkinson (Penguin, 2013). Another entertaining book in the *What Was* series, this book gives a good overview of the California Gold Rush and includes several pages of photographs and illustrations. (RA 2-3, IR 3-7).

*Dare the Wind: The Record-breaking Voyage of Eleanor Prentiss and the Flying Cloud*, by Tracey Fern, illus. Emily Arnold McCully (Farrar, Strauss, and Giroux, 2014). A biography of Eleanor Prentiss Creesy, who learned from her father how to navigate and sail ships. She and her husband made record time in sailing a ship from Massachusetts to California during the Gold Rush. (RA 1-2, IR 3-4)

## Corresponding Literature Suggestions

*The Adventures of Papa Lemon's Little Wanderers Book 5: The California Gold Rush*, by Lehman Riley, illus. Joshua Wallace (Matter of Africa America Time Corp., 2010). A multicultural group of time travelers head for the California Gold Rush to meet John Sutter and James Marshall. Contains colorful and quirky illustrations. (RA 1-3, IR 2-4)

*The Ballad of Lucy Whipple* by Karen Cushman (Clarion, reprint 2012) Twelve-year-old California Morning Whipple moves from Massachusetts to a mining camp in the Sierras during the California Gold Rush. There she changes her name to Lucy and helps her mother run a boarding house while trying to figure out how to get back to Massachusetts. This coming-of-age story includes plenty of gritty details of California in the 1850s. Good for advanced readers. (RA 3-4, IR 4-7).

*By the Great Horn Spoon!*, by Sid Fleischman (Little, Brown, 1988). Originally published in 1963, a classic young-reader adventure tale by a Newbery-winning author in which a twelve-year-old boy goes hunting for treasure during the Gold Rush in order to help out his aunt. (IR 4-8)

*Chang's Paper Pony*, by Eleanor Coerr, illus. Deborah Kogan Ray (HarperCollins, 1993). Chang and his grandfather immigrate to California in the mid-1800s to search for gold. Meanwhile, Chang dreams about having a pony so he won't be lonely. (RA 1, IR 2-4)

*Gold Rush Days: Hitty's Travels*, by Ellen Weiss (Aladdin, 2001). A simple chapter book about a doll who goes west with her young owner in 1849. (RA 1-2, IR 3-4) **OOP**

*The Legend of Freedom Hill*, by Linda Jacobs Altman, illus. Cornelius Van Wright (Lee & Low Books, 2003). In this picture book, two little girls find gold in California and use it to free African-American slaves. (RA 1-2, IR 3-4)

*Seeds of Hope: The Gold Rush Diary of Susanna Fairchild (Dear America Series)*, by Kristiana Gregory (Scholastic, 2001). For advanced readers, this story of a fourteen-year-old girl traces her journey from New York to Oregon and then to the California gold rush. (IR 4-6)

*Tucket's Gold*, by Gary Paulsen (Dell Yearling, 1999). A chapter book, telling the further adventures of young Francis Tucket, who discovers gold out west. For strong third-grade readers and above. (IR 3-5)

*Wagon Train*, by Sydelle Kramer, illus. Deborah Kogan Ray (Grosset & Dunlap, 1997). Simpler than the chapter books listed in this section, this beginning-reader story tells about a family travelling from Missouri to California in 1848. (RA 1, IR 2-4)

*When the Mission Padre Came to the Rancho: The Early California Adventures of Rosalinda and Simon Delgado (I Am American)* by Gare Thompson (National Geographic Children's Books, 2004). Written in the style of a diary, the book tells the story of the early missions in California and those who founded them in 1834. (RA 1-3, IR 4-6)

## MAP WORK

### The California Gold Rush and the Rest of the World *(Student Page 159, answer 330)*

1. California was the site of Sutter's Mill and the gold rush of 1849. Color California yellow.
2. People came to California to find gold. They came from countries such as China, Great Britain, France, Spain, and Portugal. Find these countries and color them orange.
3. Great Britain had control of land in India, Australia, New Zealand, and China. Color Great Britain blue. Then, outline the coasts of India and China in blue, and outline the borders of Australia and New Zealand in blue.

**COLORING PAGE** The possibility of finding gold in California drew miners from all over the world. *(Student Page 160)*

## PROJECTS

### ACTIVITY PROJECT Gold Strike!

The pebbles were pure gold! People from all over the world rushed to California to stake a claim on land they hoped would make them millionaires. Here is a chance to go on your own gold strike!

*Materials:*
- ☐ rocks and pebbles no bigger than what could fit in a child's hand
- ☐ gold paint or spray paint
- ☐ newspaper
- ☐ backyard

*Directions:*
1. Before you send your child or friend out to hunt for gold, gather some stones and paint them gold. Let them dry.
2. Before the "gold hunt," go out to a patch of your backyard and bury, or hide, the gold rocks. You might decide to make a map to help the gold hunter.
3. Send the gold hunter out, and after sending her in the general direction, give as little information as possible.

## Craft Project Sutter's Mill Waterwheel

Sutter's Mill was a waterwheel powered by the running water of the stream where gold was discovered. Make your own waterwheel to see how the mill worked.

*Materials:*
- □ cardboard
- □ empty spool of thread
- □ drinking straw
- □ quick-drying glue (rubber cement is best)

*Directions:*
1. Thread the spool onto the drinking straw. The spool should be loose on the straw, so that it turns easily. If the spool will not turn, replace the drinking straw with a thin pencil, a nail, or something with a smaller diameter (or find a larger spool).
2. Cut out four pieces of cardboard, each about 1 ½ inches long and ¾ inch wide. Put rubber cement along the short edges of each piece of cardboard, and attach to the spool at equal intervals, like the four spokes of a wheel.
3. Run water over the water wheel. When water hits the paddles, the wheel will turn!

## Activity Project Live In a Mining Camp

*Materials:*
- □ blankets
- □ chairs (or couches, to hold up the blankets while you make "blanket tents")
- □ miner food—choose from: beef jerky, beans, plain bread, coffee or tea
- □ your singing voice
- □ sleeping bag

*Directions:*
1. Many miners lived in tents. Make your own tent out of blankets. Use chairs and couches to hold up the blanket tent.
2. Miners often slept in blankets or sleeping bags—whatever they had at hand. Set up your sleeping bag in your tent. Remember, the miners would not have access to electricity, so do not use any electricity in your tent!
3. Very few women went west to mine, so there were many men mining during a time when, in general, men did very little cooking. There are even stories of men putting rice grains in a pan—without water—and wondering why, when they heated the grains over the fire, the product was not the white fluffy food they were used to eating!

   Some of the common foods the men ate were dried pork, potatoes, bread, beans, coffee or tea, and wild onions and garlic. Eat some of the beef jerky (dried pork), bread, and coffee or tea, for all three meals one day, and think about how boring the diet of the miners was.
4. The miners sang songs to entertain themselves and to take their minds off of their aching muscles. Below is "The Miner's Song." Sing the song to a familiar tune (the tunes to King Wenceslas or Greensleeves ["What Child Is This?"] work).

***The Miner's Song, by J. Swett***

The eastern sky is blushing red,
The distant hill-top glowing,
The river o'er its rocky bed
In idle frolics flowing;
'Tis time the pick-axe and the spake

Against the rocks were ringing,
And with ourselves the golden stream
A song of labor singing.
The mountain air is fresh and cold,
Unclouded skies bend o'er us;
Broad placers, rich in hidden gold,
Lie temptingly before us.
We need no Midas' magic wand,
Nor wizard rod divining;
The pickaxe, spade and brawny hand
Are sorcerers in mining.
When labor closes with the day,
To simple fare returning,
We gather in a merry group
Around the camp-fires burning,
The mountain sod our couch at night
The stars keep watch above us,
We think of home and fall asleep
To dream of those who love us.

5. Many of the men could survive all of the hardships of camp life—the meager food, the uncomfortable beds—because they thought of what they would do with their gold. Talk about what you will do with your gold when you hit "pay-dirt."

## MEMORY PROJECT **Poem**

The following is an excerpt from Thomas Hood's poem, "Miss Kilmansegg and her Precious Leg." Have the child read 4-5 lines out loud 5 times per day. Have the child add a few lines every day, until she has the poem memorized.

"Gold! Gold! Gold! Gold!
Bright and yellow, hard and cold,
Molten, graven, hammered and rolled,
Heavy to get and light to hold,
Hoarded, bartered, bought and sold,
Stolen, borrowed, squandered, doled,
Spurned by the young, but hugged by old,
To the verge of the church yard mold;
Price of many a crime untold.
Gold! Gold! Gold! Gold!
Good or bad a thousand fold!
How widely its agencies vary,
To save—to ruin—to curse—to bless—
As even its minted coins express:
Now stamped with the image of good Queen Bess,
And now of a bloody Mary."

**Additional State Study: How California Became a State**

*Note to Parent: This section is provided for California students who are required to do state history in third or fourth grade. Go over this information with the student, asking the student to repeat back to you the steps that California followed to become a state.*

California became a state in 1850. But before California could become a state, the leaders of California had to ask themselves several questions as they wrote their own state Constitution.

1. At the beginning of the process, California was run, not like a state or a territory, but as a military state; the army was in charge, and treated California like a conquered Mexican province.
2. Recent settlers from actual states complained because California was run like a military state, not like the states they hailed from.
3. The military governor, Brigadier General Bennet Riley, called the convention to draft the state constitution on June 3, 1849. Riley ordered the different California territories to elect delegates to this convention by August 1. People campaigned rapidly for election to the position of delegate!
4. The delegates met from September 1 to October 13. There were five issues of concern: slavery (would California be a slave or free state?); suffrage (who would get to vote?); the eastern state boundary (would it go all the way to the Utah territory?); whether or not married women could own property (in Mexico, married women could own property in their own names, but in the United States, their property belonged to their husbands); and whether duelling would be legal.
5. Decisions were reached: California would be a free state; only white men and some Native Americans would be allowed to vote; the eastern state boundary did not go all the way to the Utah territory; married women were allowed to hold property; and dueling would be illegal. The state capital was voted to be San Jose.
6. The constitution was signed on October 13. The delegates ran up the American flag, shot off guns, and signed the constitution.
7. Then the delegates had to petition Congress for statehood. Congress argued over California's statehood for ten months! John Calhoun of South Carolina and Henry Clay of Kentucky argued against admitting California, since this would give free states more votes against slave-holding states in the House. Finally, on September 9, 1850, President Millard Fillmore signed the resolution giving California statehood.
8. Because California was so far away, Californians didn't find out that they were now citizens of the U.S.A. until Oct. 18, 1850, when the steamer *Oregon* sailed into San Francisco Bay with a banner that said "California is a state" hanging from her rigging.

## Chapter 1: A World of Empires, *page 4*

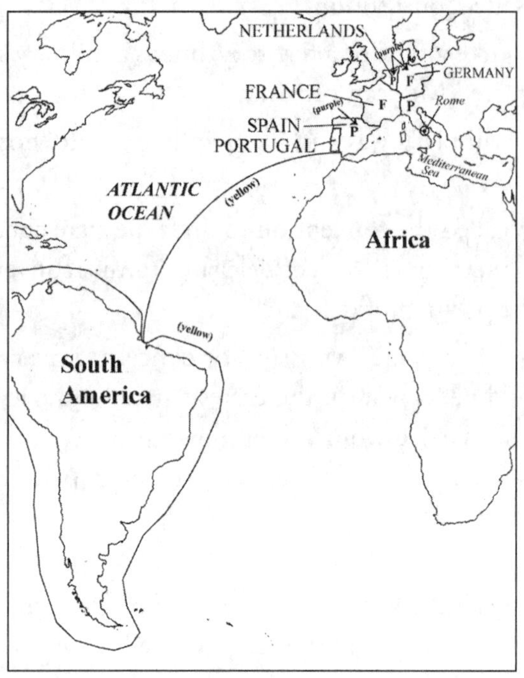


## Chapter 2: Protestant Rebellions, *page 11*

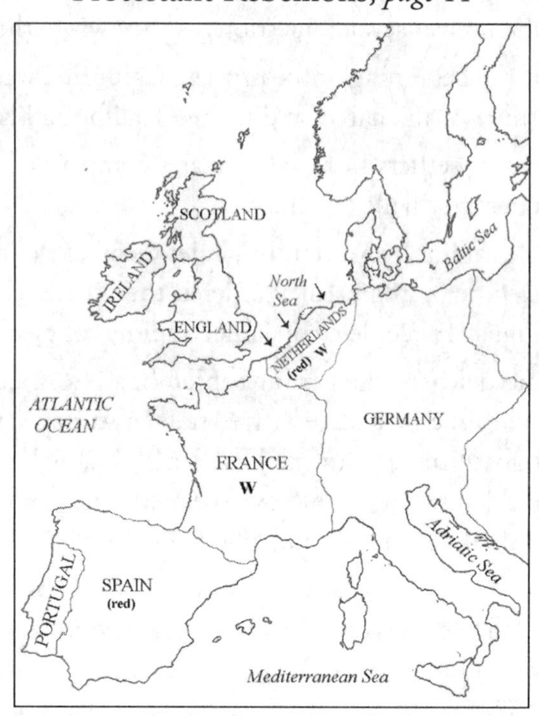


## Chapter 3: James, King of Two Countries, *page 17*

## Chapter 4: Searching for the Northwest Passage, *page 24*

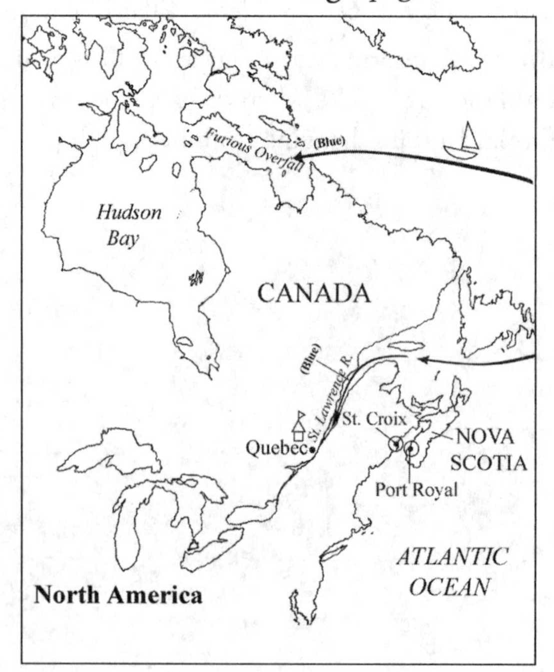

## Chapter 5: Warlords of Japan, *page 33*

## Chapter 6: New Colonies in the New World, *page 40*

## Chapter 7: The Spread of Slavery, *page 48*

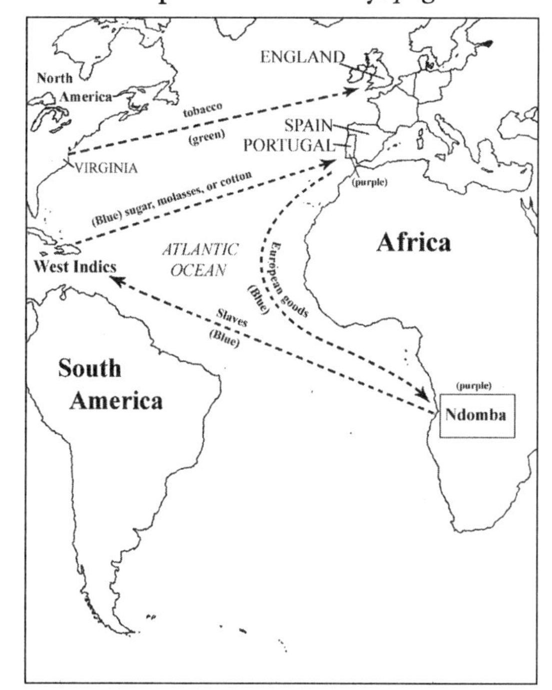


## Chapter 9: The Western War, *page 64*

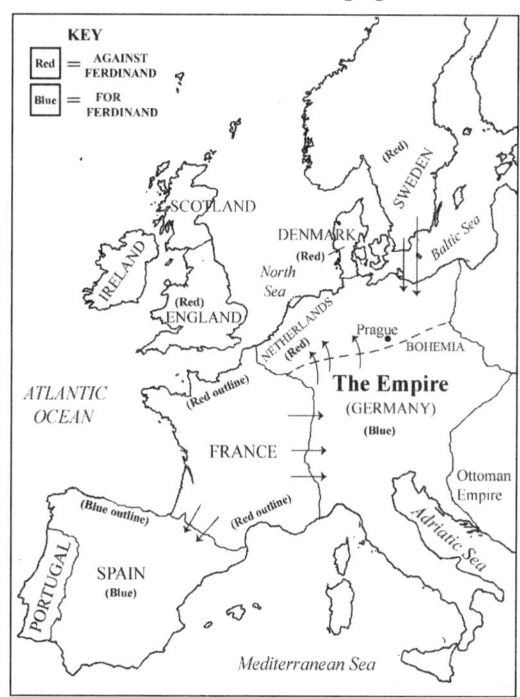

## Chapter 10: Far East of Europe, *page 72*

## Chapter 11: The Moghul Emperors of India, *page 80*

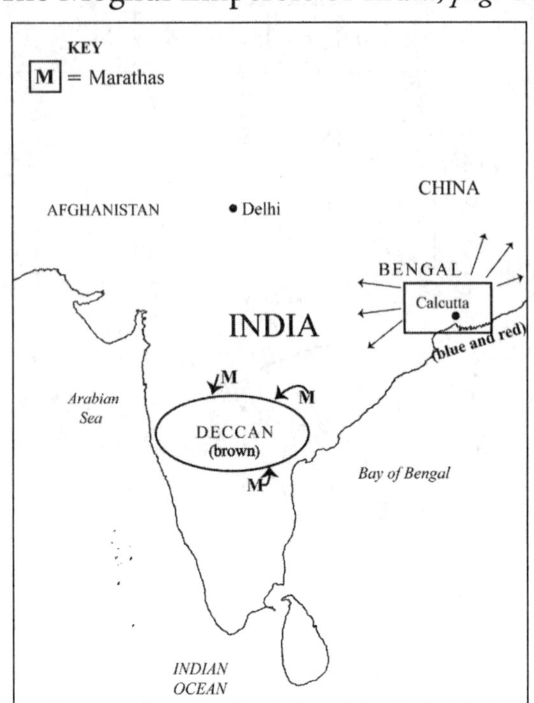


## Chapter 12: Battle, Fire, and Plague in England, *page 89*

## Chapter 13: The Sun King, *page 96*

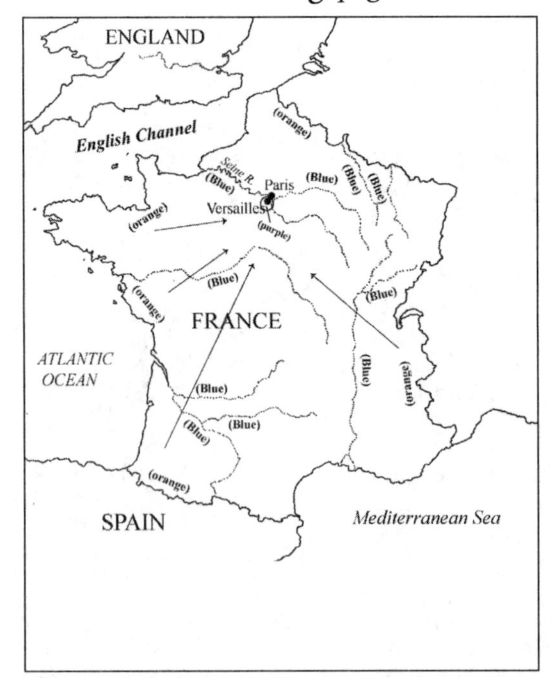

Chapter 14: The Rise of Prussia, *page 103*

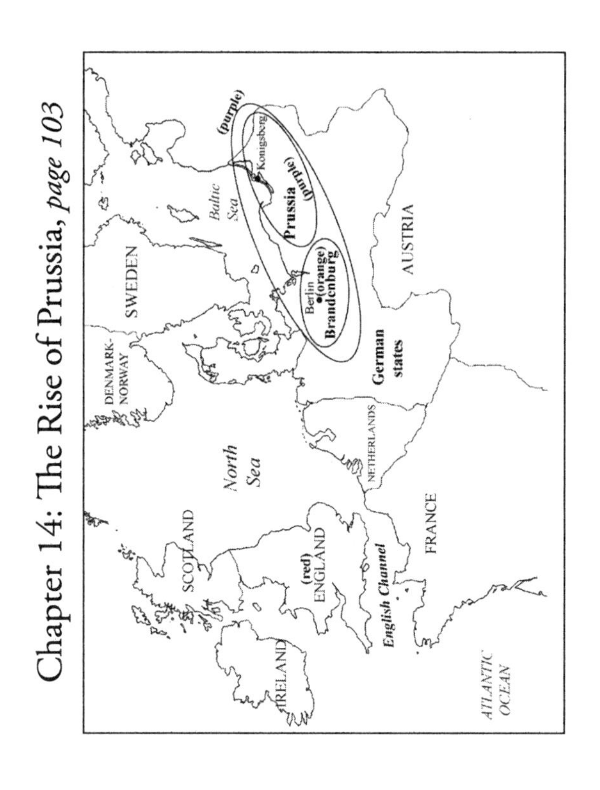


Chapter 15: A New World in Conflict, *page 112*

Chapter 16:
The West, *page 119*

Chapter 17:
Russia Looks West, *page 127*

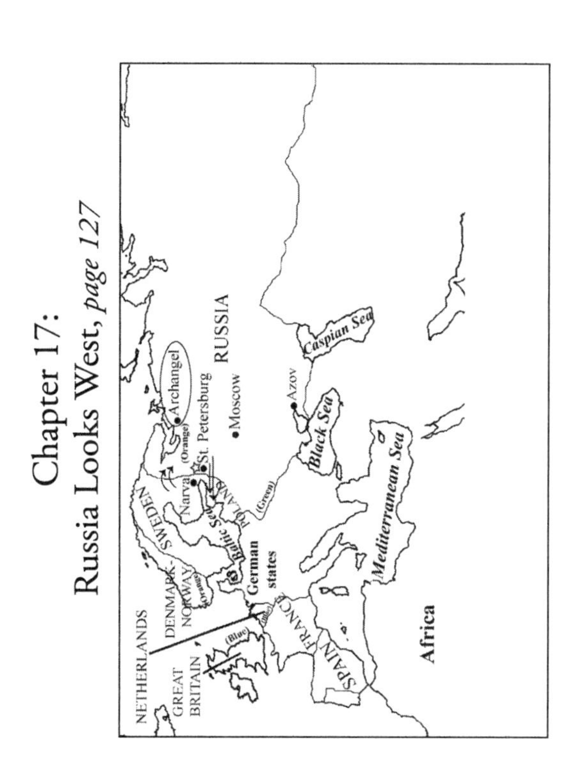

Chapter 18: East and West Collide, *page 133*

Chapter 19: The English in India, *page 139*

Chapter 20: The Imperial East, *page 148*

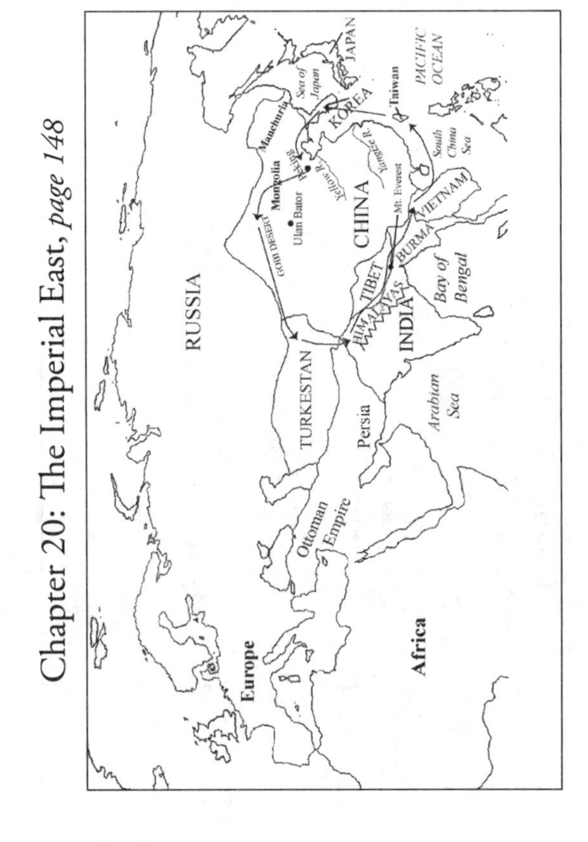


Chapter 21:
Fighting Over North America, *page 155*

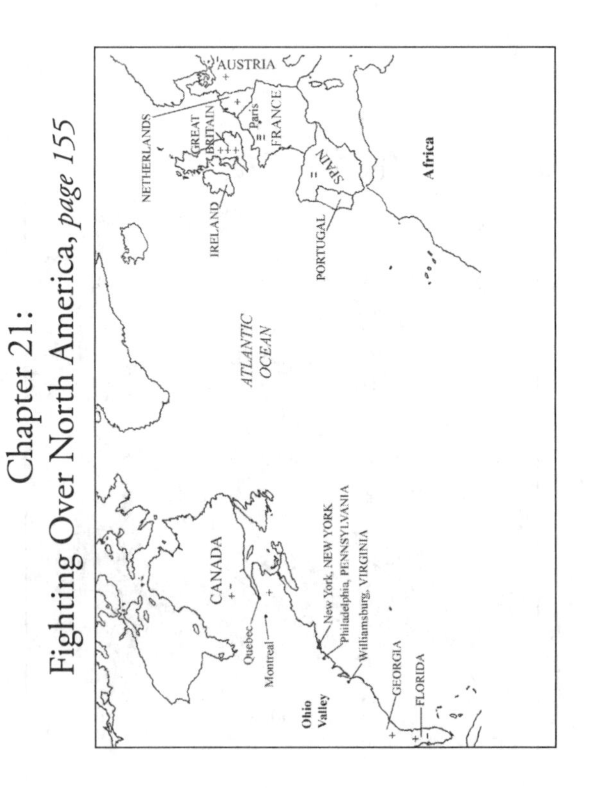

## Chapter 22: Revolution!, *page 165*

## Chapter 23: The New Country, *page 177*

## Chapter 24: Sailing South, *page 188*

## Chapter 25: Revolution Gone Sour, *page 195*

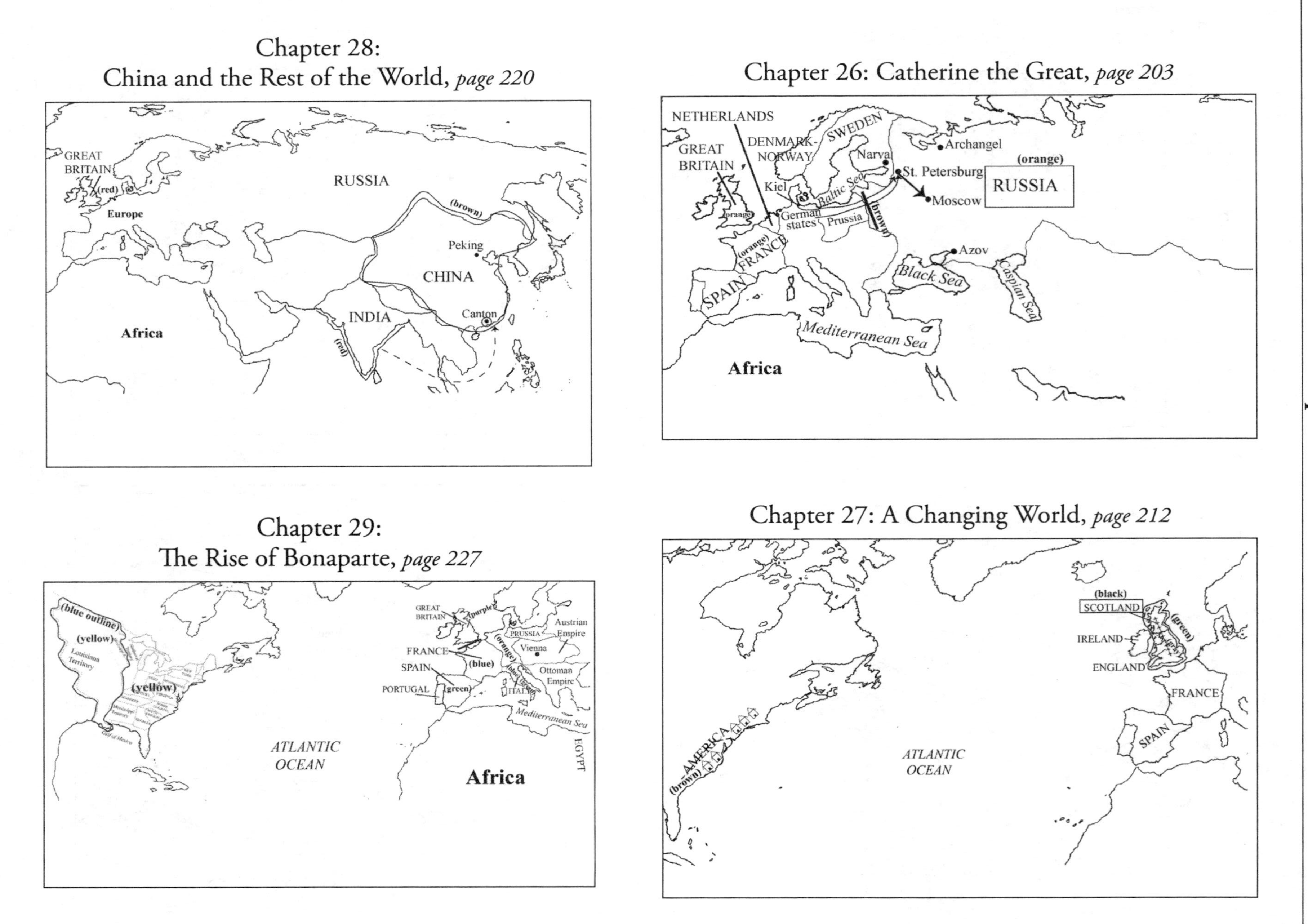
Chapter 28: China and the Rest of the World, page 220
GREAT BRITAIN
(red)
Europe
RUSSIA
(brown)
Peking
CHINA
INDIA
Canton
(red)
Africa
Chapter 26: Catherine the Great, page 203
NETHERLANDS
GREAT BRITAIN
(orange)
DENMARK-NORWAY
SWEDEN
Narva
Archangel
St. Petersburg
(orange)
RUSSIA
Moscow
Kiel
Baltic Sea
German states
Prussia
(brown)
(orange) FRANCE
SPAIN
Azov
Black Sea
Caspian Sea
Mediterranean Sea
Africa
Chapter 29: The Rise of Bonaparte, page 227
(blue outline)
(yellow)
Louisiana Territory
(yellow)
ATLANTIC OCEAN
GREAT BRITAIN
(purple)
FRANCE
SPAIN
PORTUGAL
(green)
(blue)
(orange)
PRUSSIA
Austrian Empire
Vienna
Ottoman Empire
ITALY
Mediterranean Sea
EGYPT
Africa
Chapter 27: A Changing World, page 212
(black)
SCOTLAND
(green)
IRELAND
ENGLAND
FRANCE
SPAIN
AMERICA
(brown)
ATLANTIC OCEAN

## Chapter 30:
## Freedom in the Caribbean, *page 233*

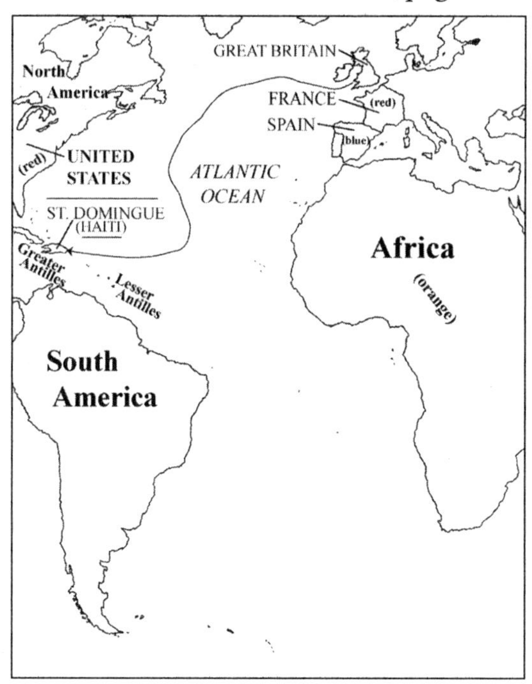


## Chapter 31:
## A Different Kind of Rebellion, *page 239*

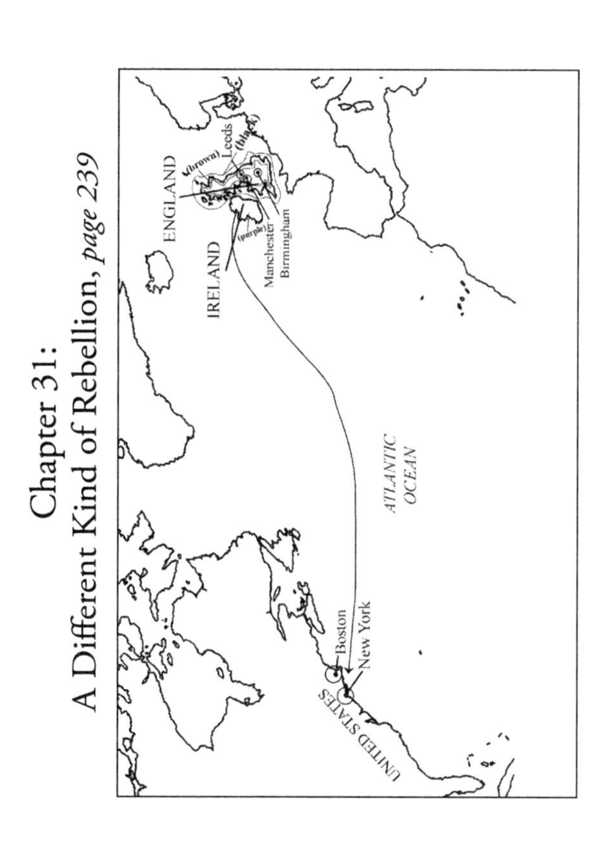


## Chapter 32:
## The Opened West, *page 246*

## Chapter 33:
## The End of Napoleon, *page 256*

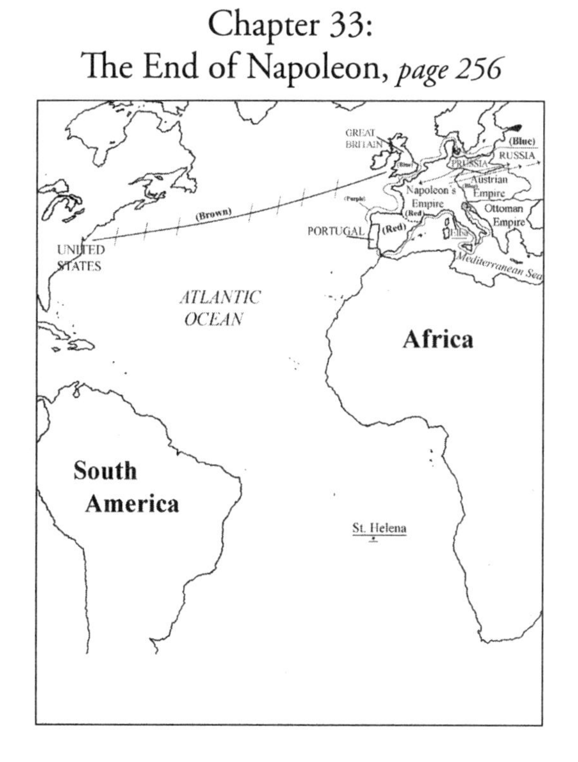

## Chapter 34: Freedom for South America, *page 263*

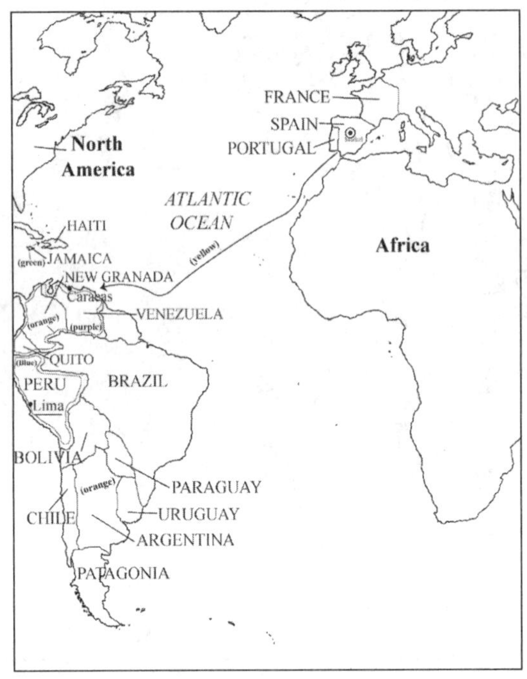


## Chapter 35: Mexican Independence, *page 269*

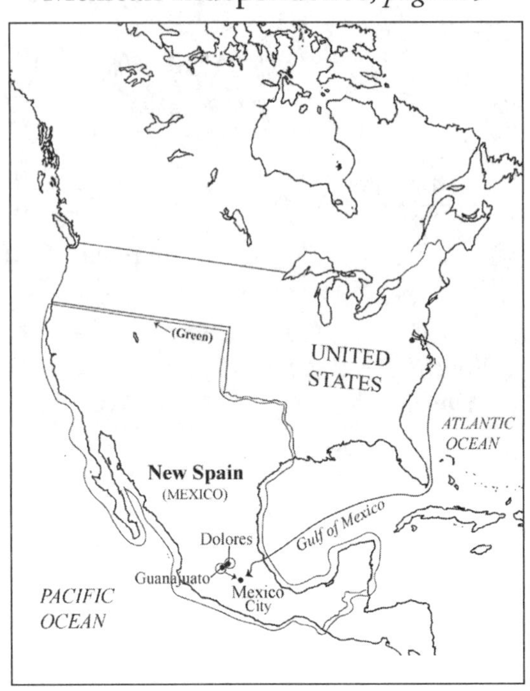


## Chapter 36: The Slave Trade Ends, *page 277*

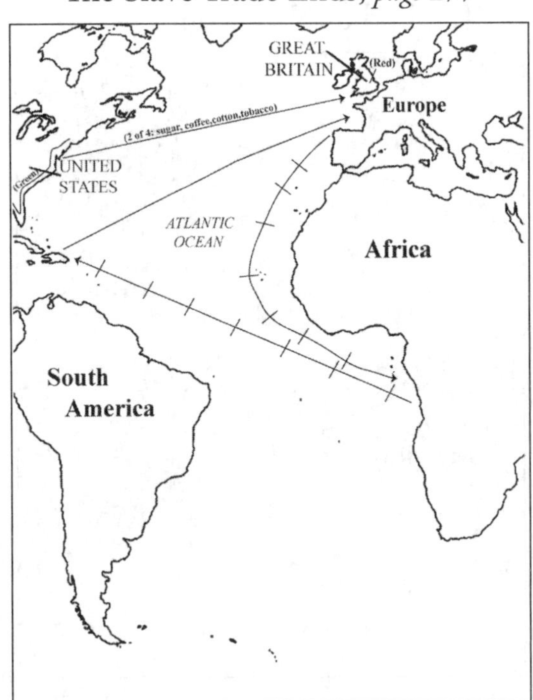


## Chapter 37: Troubled Africa, *page 285*

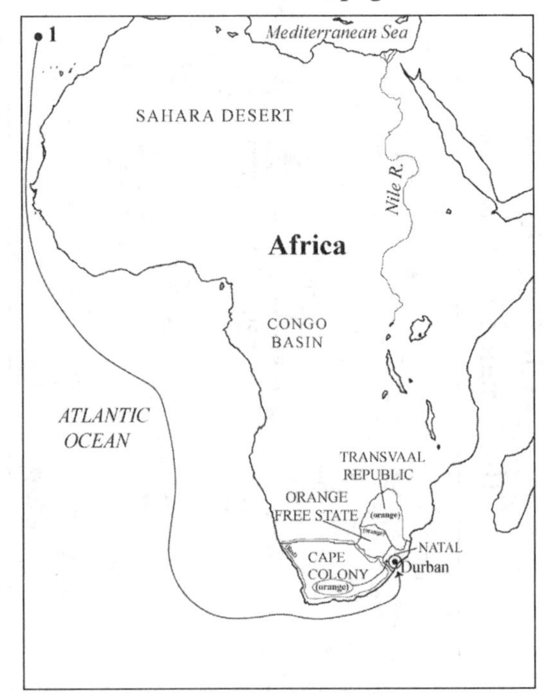

## Chapter 38: American Tragedies, *page 291*

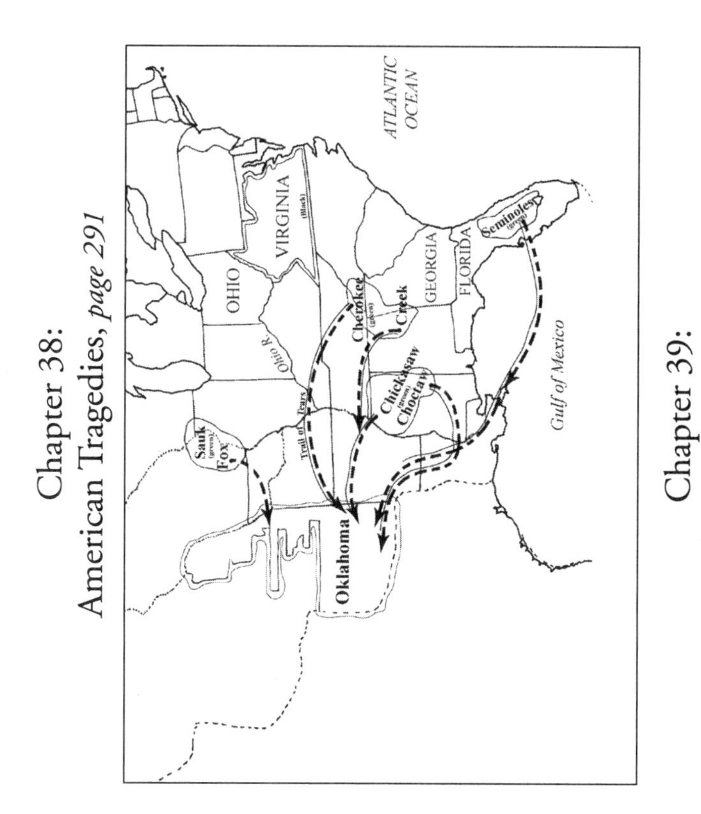


## Chapter 39: China Adrift, *page 297*

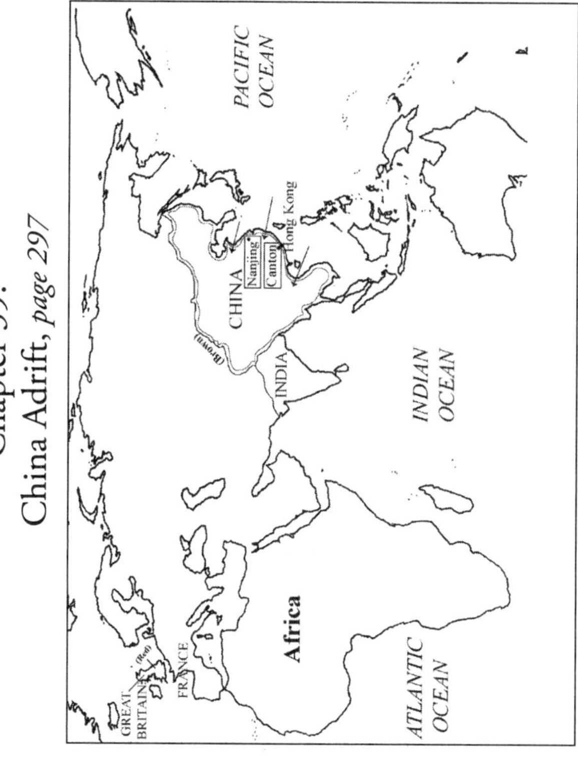


## Chapter 40: Mexico and Her Neighbor, *page 303*

## Chapter 41: New Zealand and Her Rulers, *page 310*

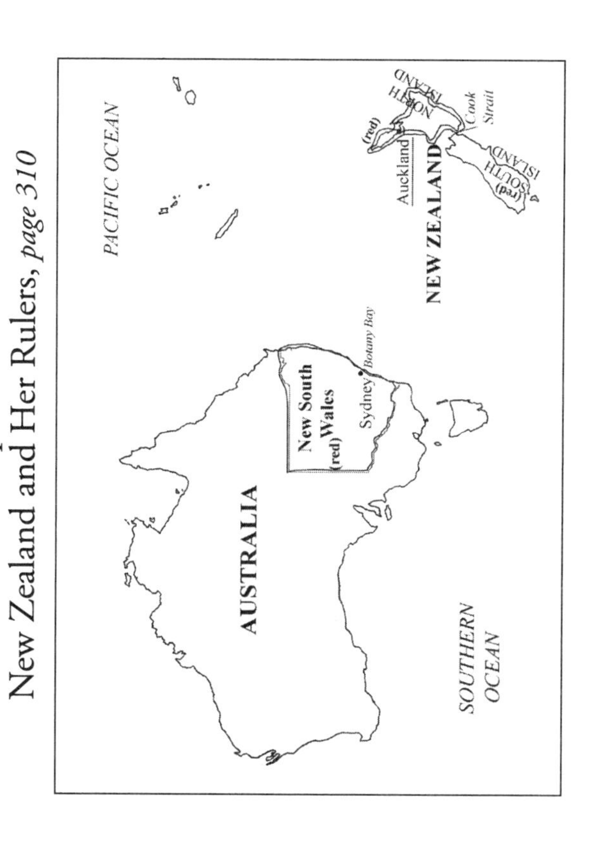

## Chapter 42:
## The World of Forty-Nine, *page 316*

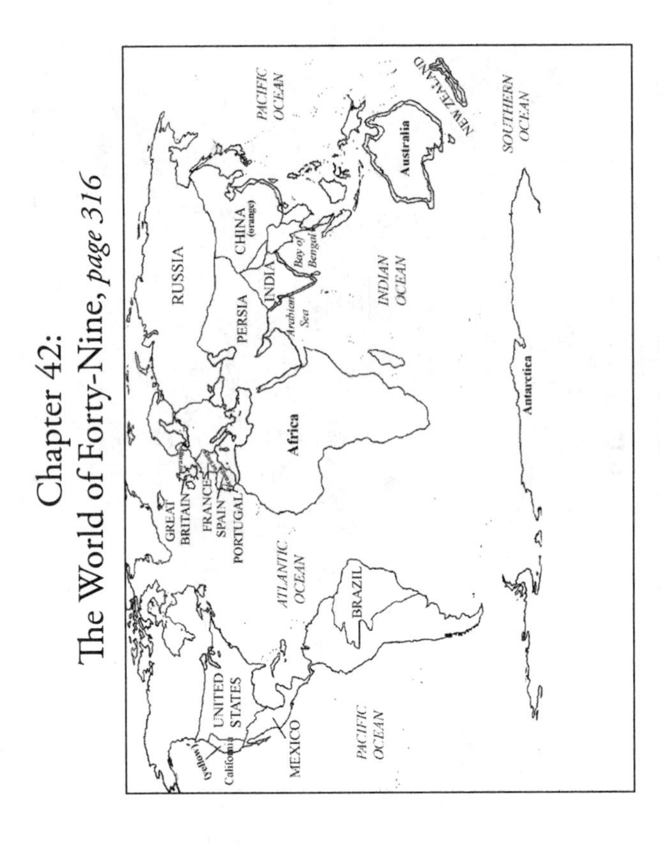

# The Story of the World

## Activity Book, Volume 3

## Revised Edition

# STUDENT PAGES

www.welltrainedmind.com

## PHOTOCOPYING AND DISTRIBUTION POLICY

The illustrations, reading lists, and all other content in this Activity Book are copyrighted material owned by Well-Trained Mind Press. Please do not reproduce reading lists, etc. on e-mail lists or websites.

For families: You may make as many photocopies of the maps and other Student Pages as you need for use WITHIN YOUR OWN FAMILY ONLY.

Schools and co-ops MAY NOT PHOTOCOPY any portion of the Activity Book. Smaller schools usually find that purchasing a set of the pre-copied Student Pages for each student is the best option. Other schools may purchase a classroom license ($100 per volume, per year) that allows duplication for school and co-op use. For more information, please contact Well-Trained Mind Press: e-mail support@welltrainedmind.com; phone 1.877.322.3445.



Reprinted by Bradford & Bigelow, May 2021

# Charles's Inheritance in Western Europe & South America

# Charles V

# Spanish Conquistadores

# 500,000,000,000

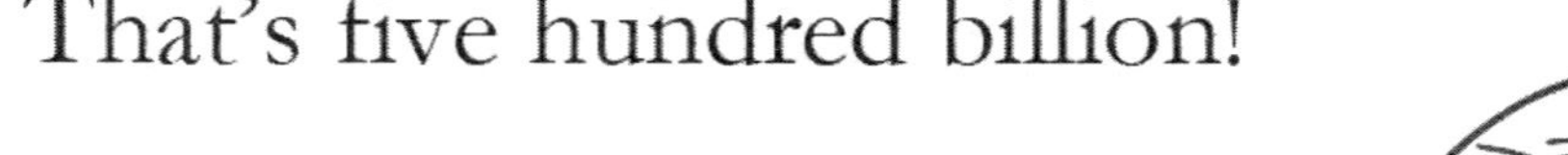

That's five hundred billion!

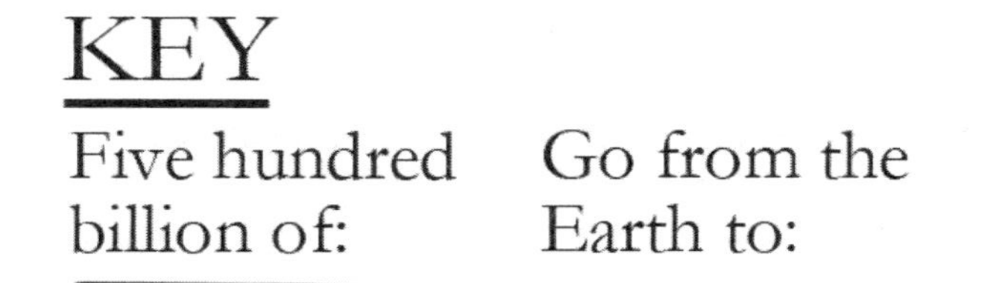

## KEY

| Five hundred billion of: | Go from the Earth to: |
| --- | --- |
| ☐ | = The Moon |
| ☐ | = Mars |
| ☐ | = Jupiter |
| ☐ | = Saturn |

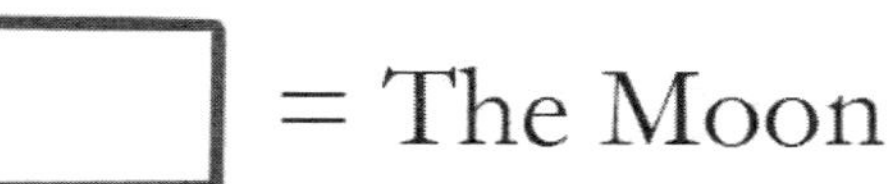

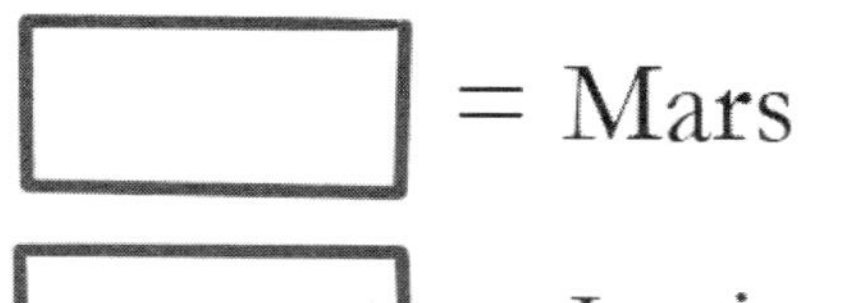

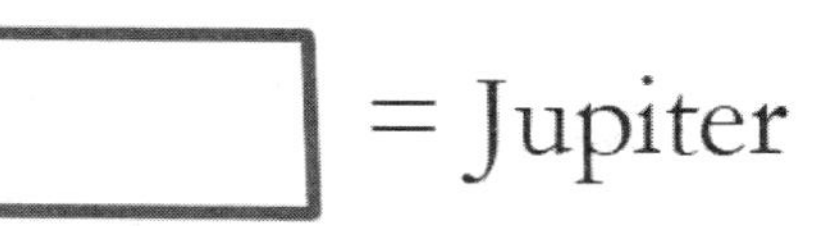

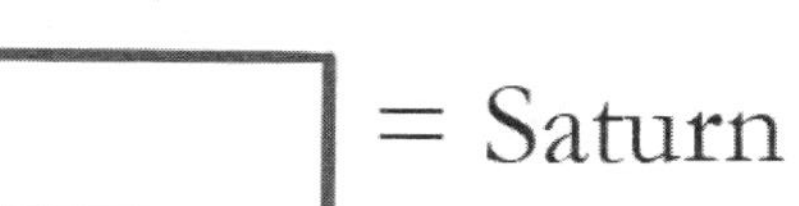

# Philip's Inheritance from Charles V: The Netherlands and Spain

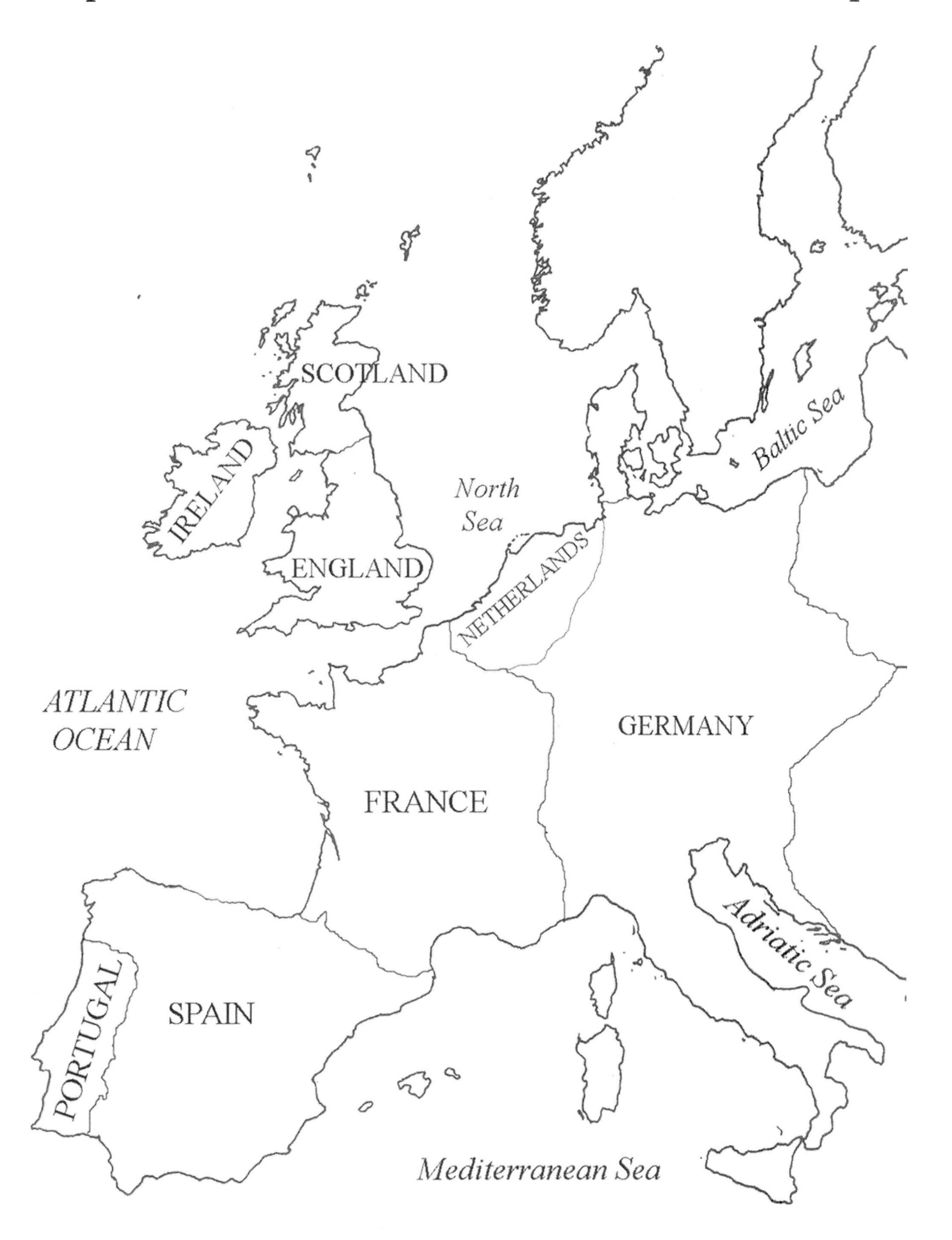

# Mary, Queen of Scots

# Marian Hanging

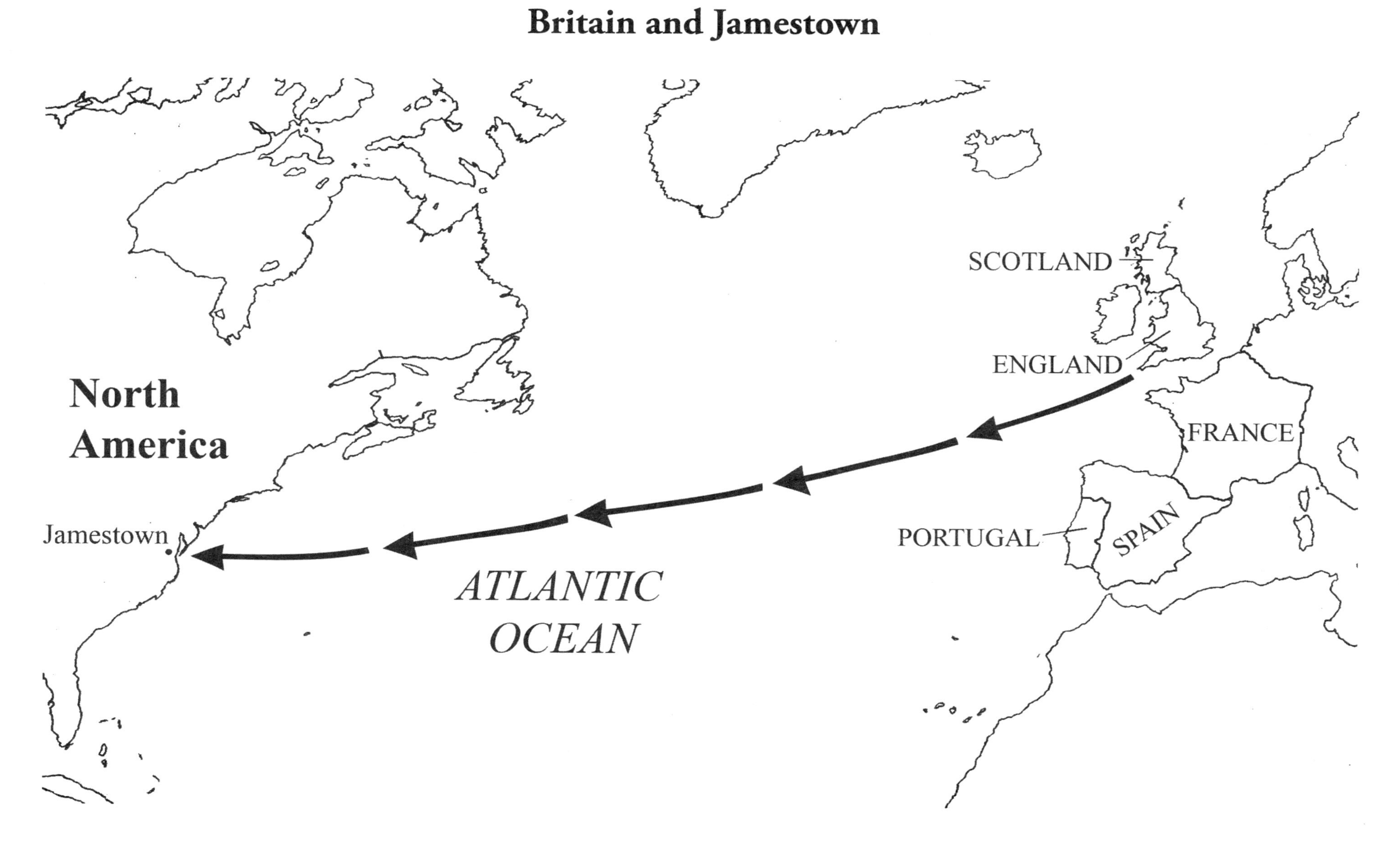
Britain and Jamestown
SCOTLAND
ENGLAND
FRANCE
PORTUGAL
SPAIN
North America
Jamestown
ATLANTIC OCEAN

# The *Susan Constant*

# Champlain's Exploration

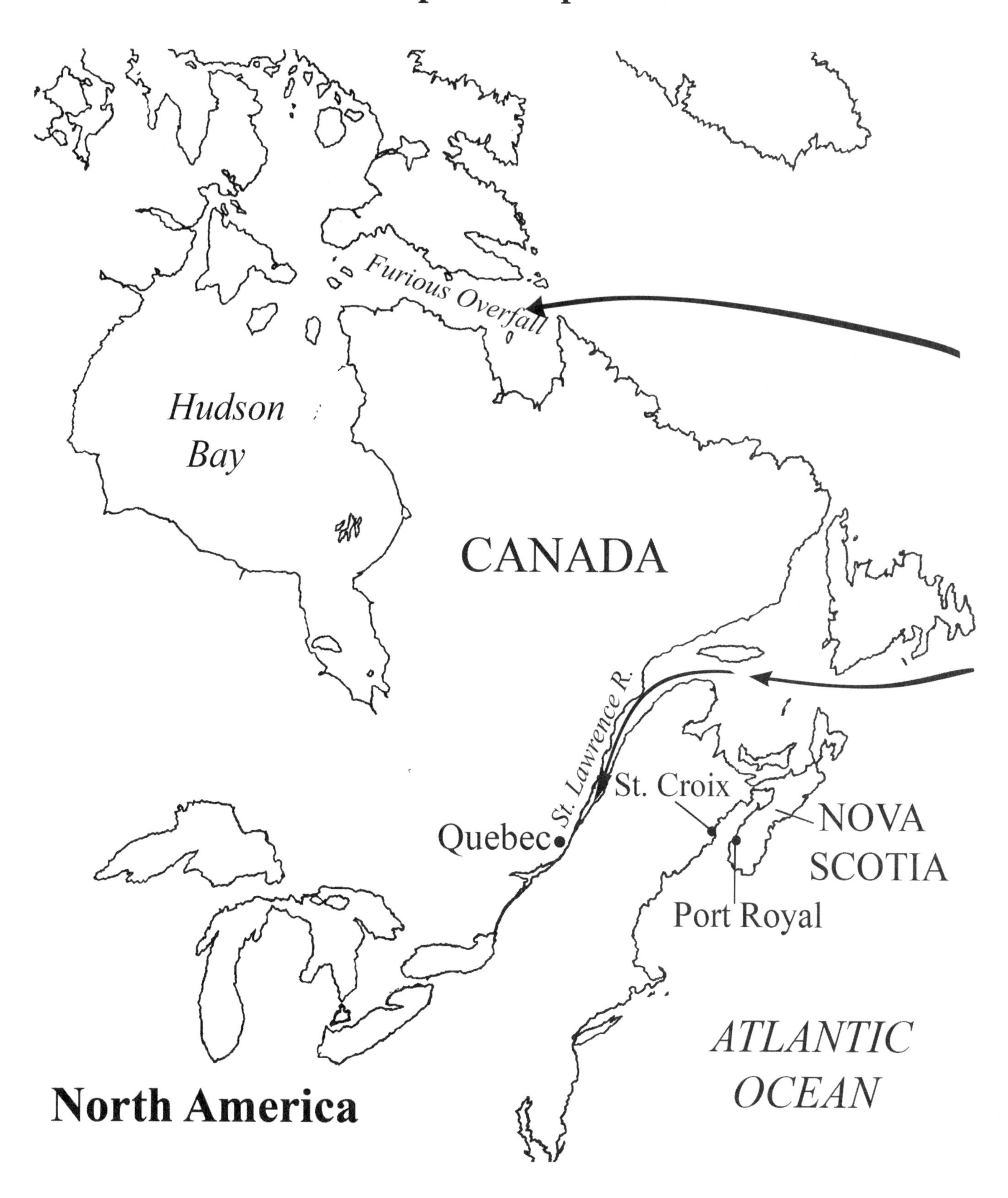

# Samuel Champlain on the Saint Lawrence River

# Floating Galleon Sail Template

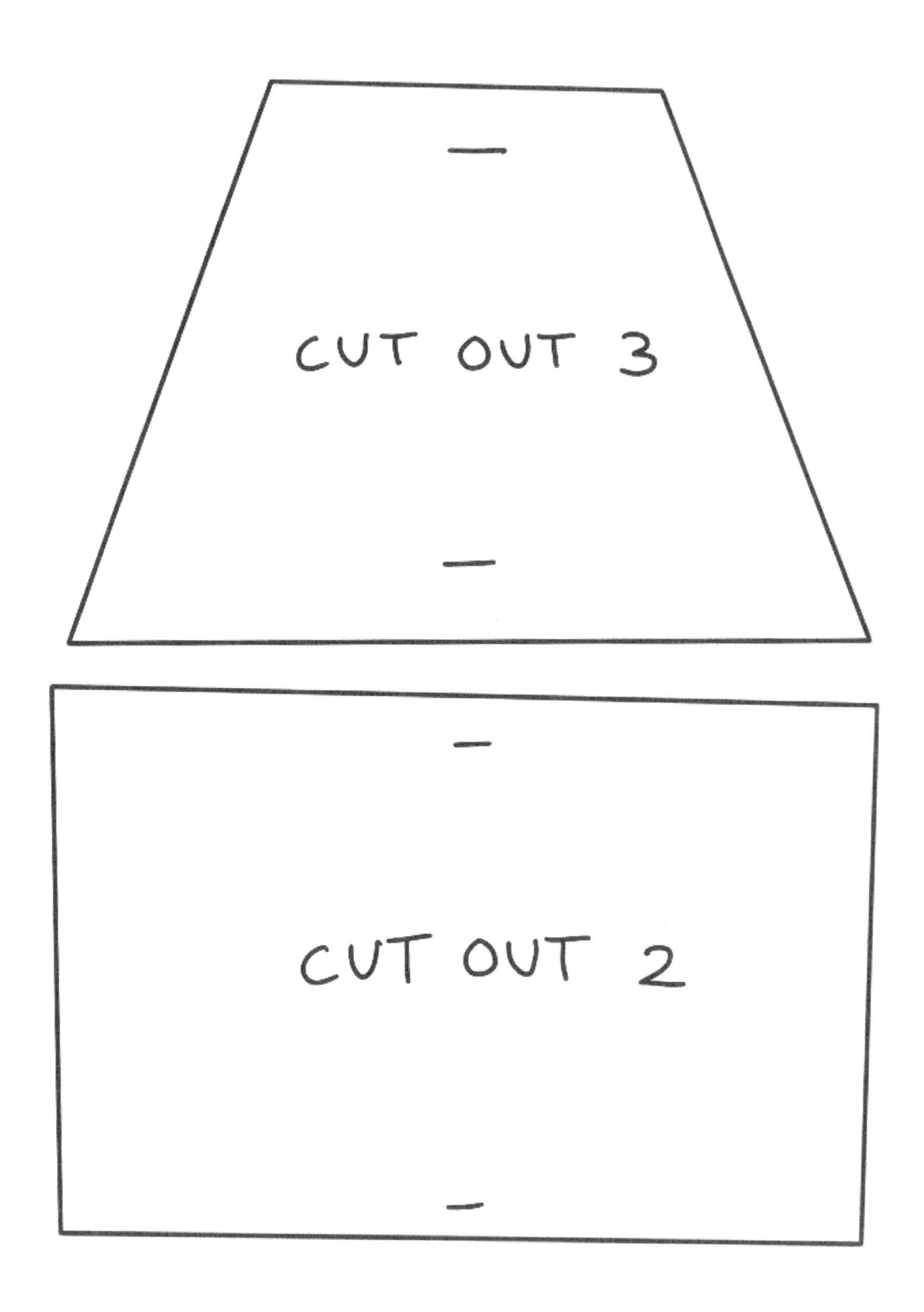

# Hideyoshi in East Asia

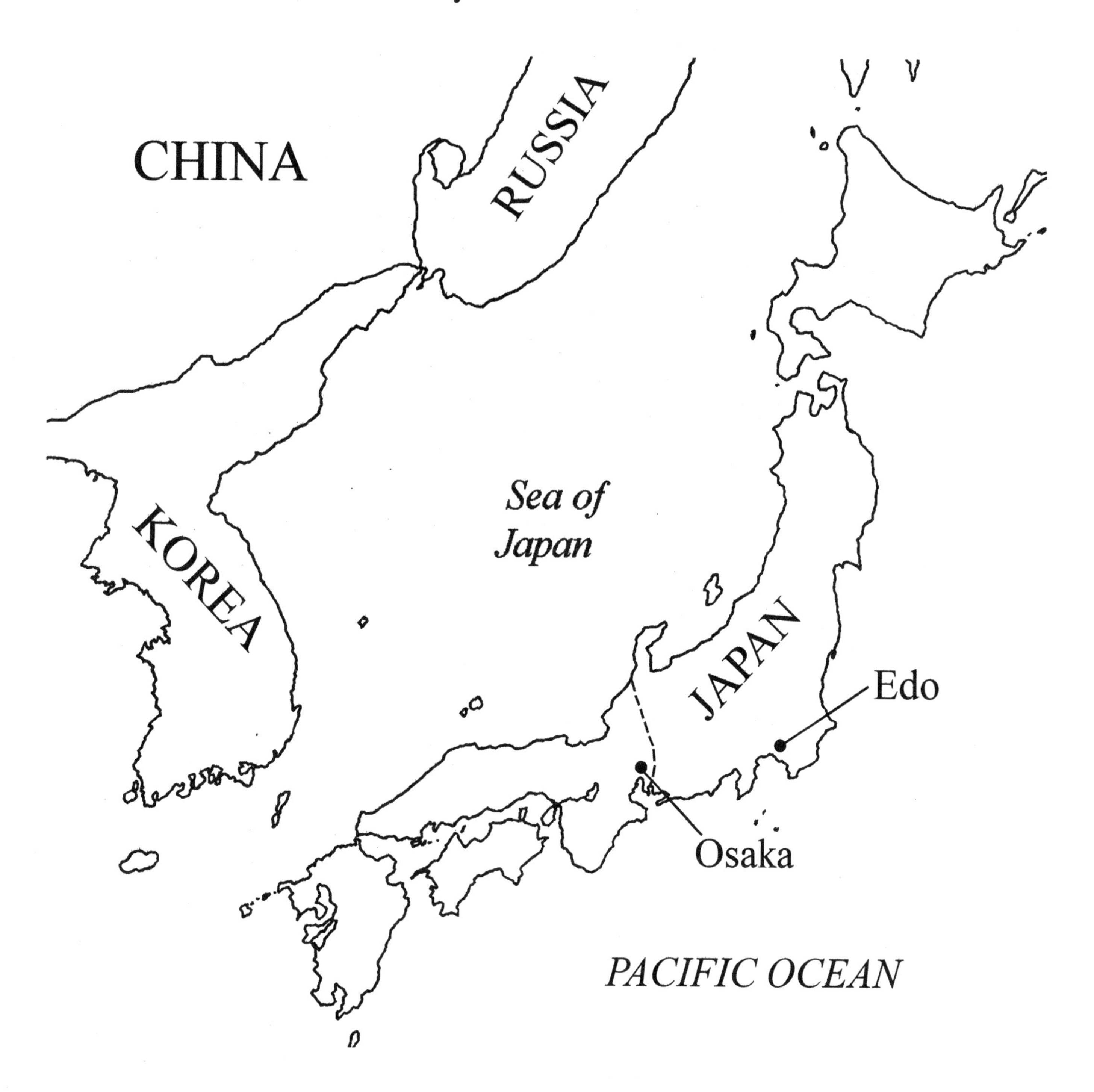

# Samurai

# A Korean "Tortoise Boat"

# Separatists in England, Holland, and Plymouth Plantation

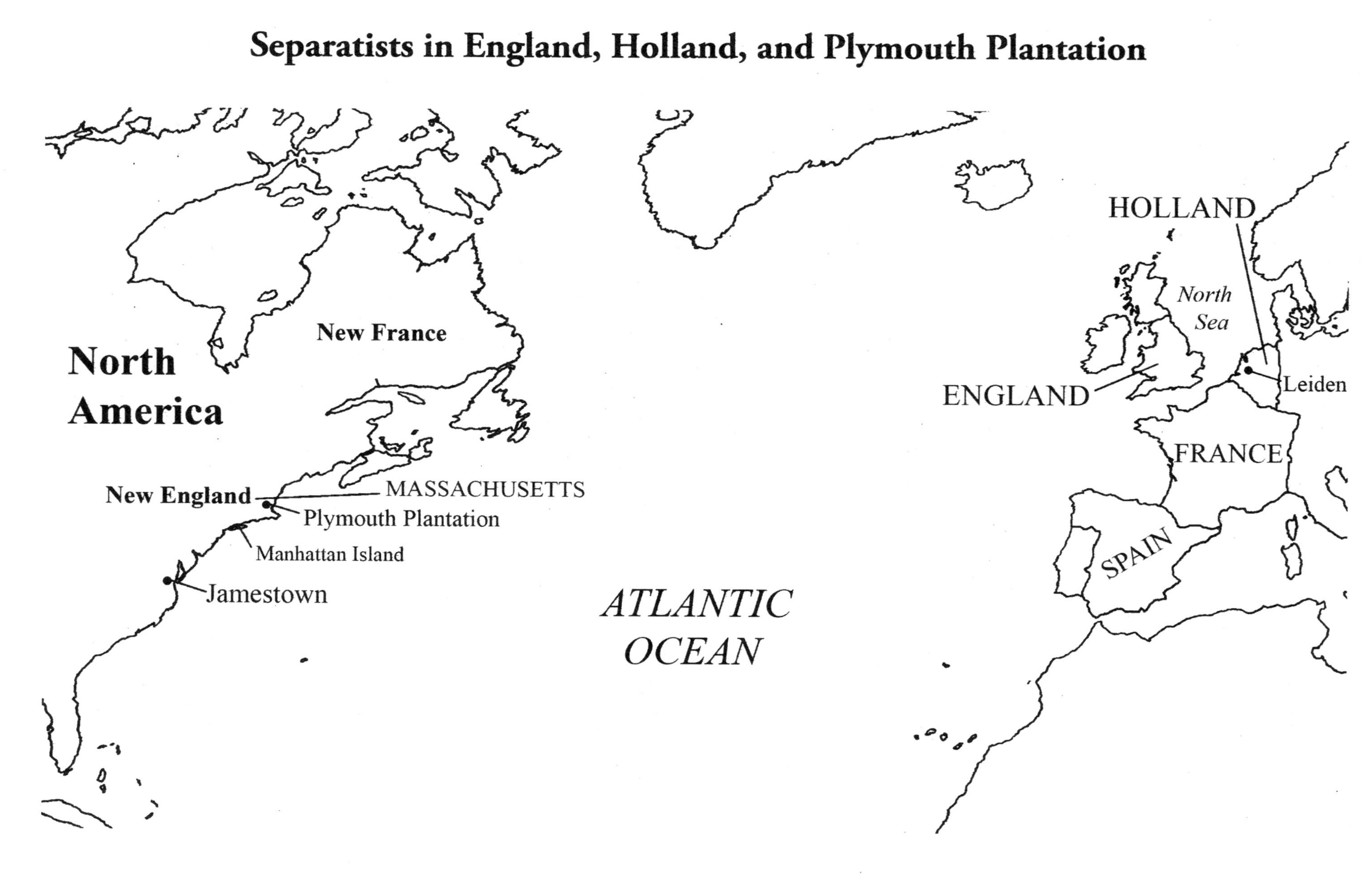

# Squanto Teaches the Pilgrims How to Plant Corn

# OUR MAYFLOWER COMPACT

In the name of God, Amen. We, whose names are underwritten,
the Loyal Subjects of our dread (1) ______________
(2)________________, by the Grace of God, of
(3)_________________________, etcetera.
Having undertaken to (5)_________________________________,
a (4)____________________________; do by these presents,
solemnly and mutually in the Presence of God and one of another,
covenant and combine ourselves together into (6)___________
_________________, for our better Ordering and Preservation,
and Furtherance of the Ends aforesaid; And by Virtue hereof to
enact, constitute, and frame, such just and equal Laws, Ordinances,
Acts, Constitutions and Offices, from time to time, as shall be
thought most meet and convenient for the General good of
(6)______________________; unto which we promise all due
submission and obedience.
In Witness whereof we have hereunto subscribed our names at
(7)___________________________ the (8) _______day of
(9)______________, in the Reign of (1)__________________,
(2)__________________________ of
(6)_______________________. Anno Domini,
(10)__________________.

## SIGNED

_________________________________________________

_________________________________________________

_________________________________________________

_________________________________________________

# THE MANHATTAN LETTER

## HIGH MIGHTY SIRS:

Here arrived yesterday the ship *The Arms of Amsterdam*, which sailed from New Netherland out of the Mauritius River on September 23; they reported that our people there are of good courage, and live peaceably. Their women, also, have borne children there, they have bought the island Manhattes from the wild men for the value of sixty guilders, it is 11,000 morgens in extent. They sowed all their grain in the middle of May, and harvested it in the middle of August. Thereof being samples of summer grain, such as wheat, rye, barley, oats, buckwheat, canary seed, small beans, and flax. The cargo of the aforesaid ship is:

7246 beaver skins, 178.5 otter skins,
675 otter skins, 48 mink skins,
36 wild-cat skins, 33 mink,
34 rat skins.
Many logs of oak and nut-wood.

Herewith be ye, High Mighty Sirs, commended to the Almighty's grace, in Amsterdam, November 5, Anno 1626.

## YOUR HIGH MIGHT.'S OBEDIENT.

# Triangular Trade Route

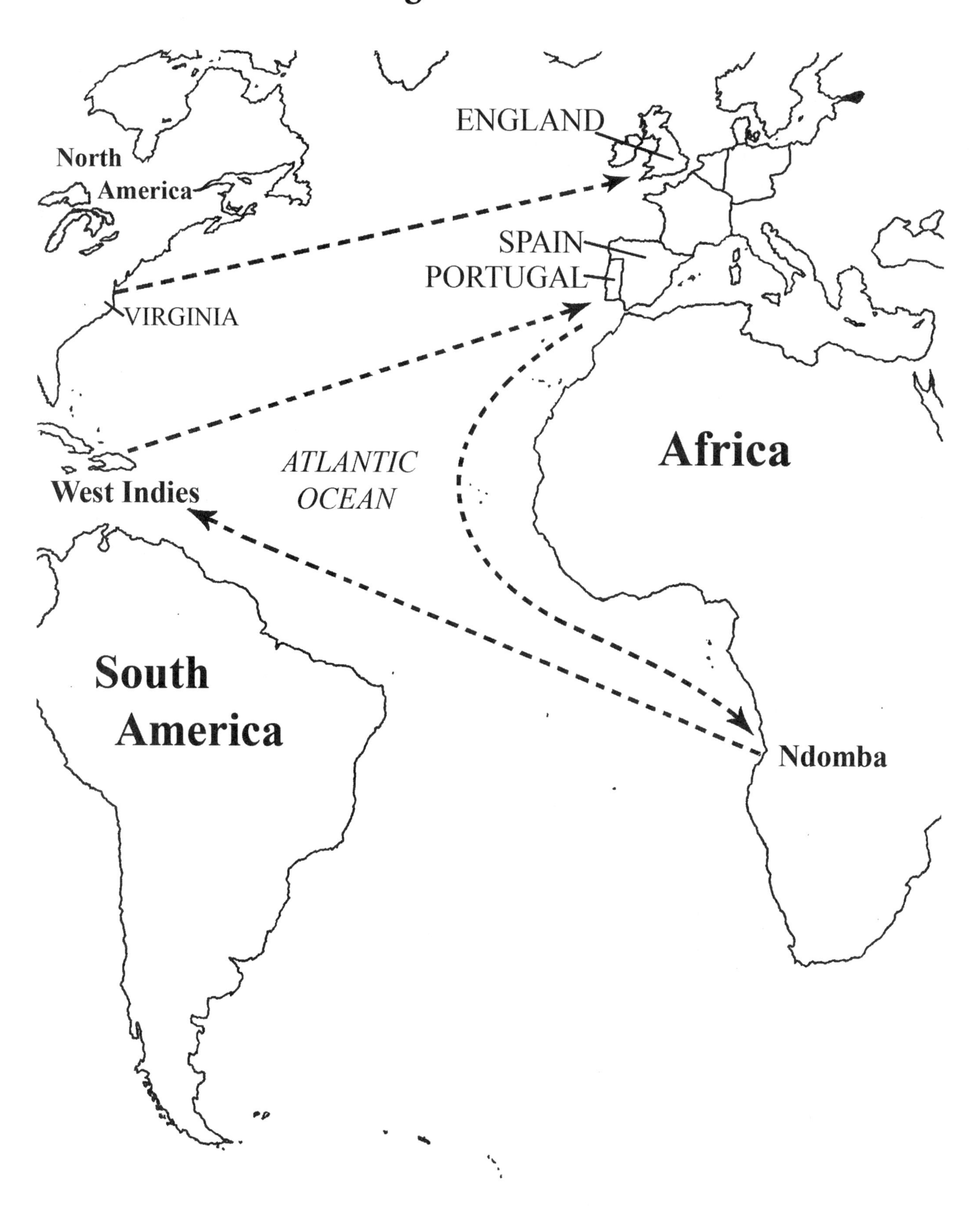

# Queen Nzinga

# Map of Persia

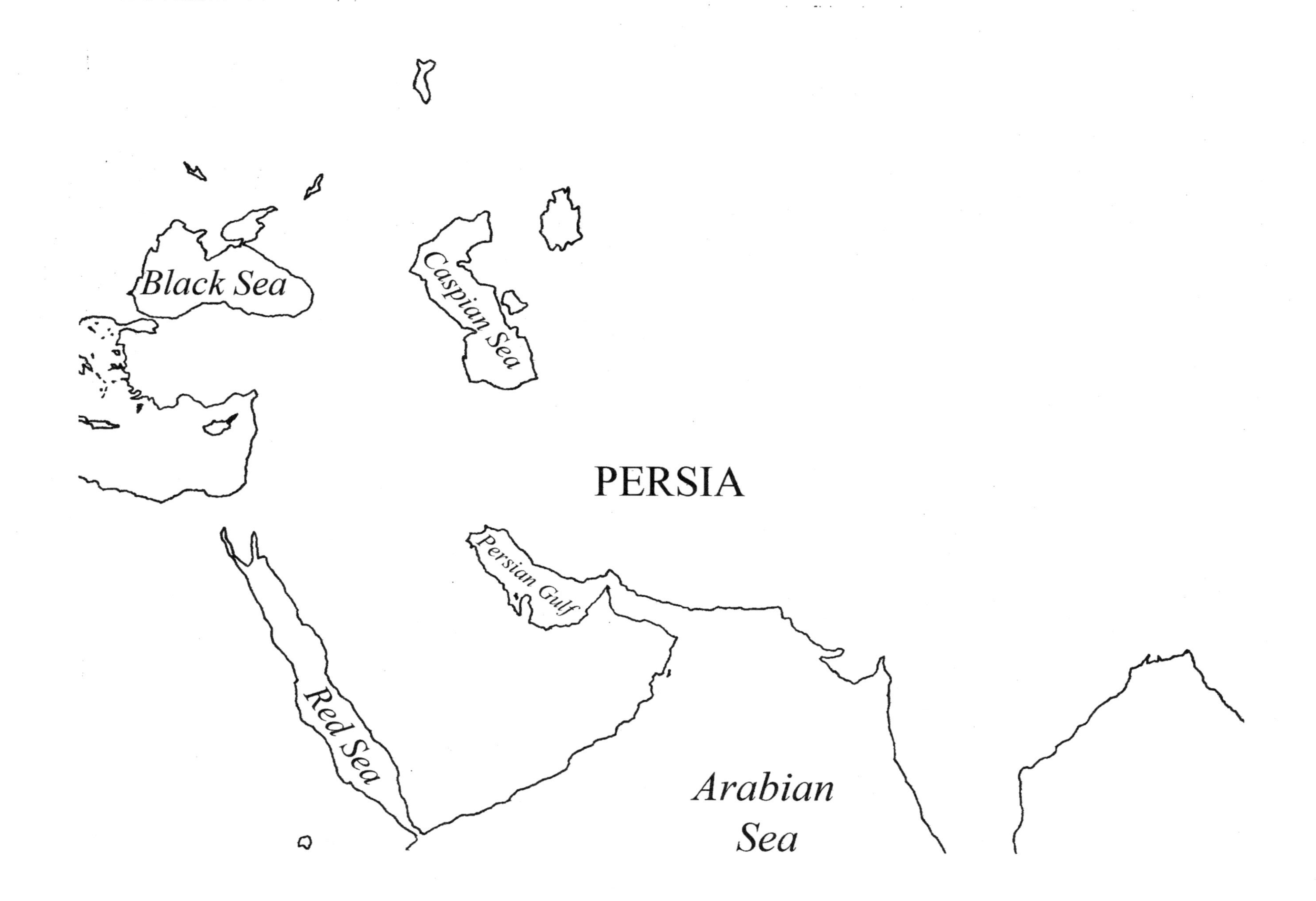

# Sultan Murad

# Poems of the Ottoman Turks

## To Sultan Murad IV

by Hafiz Pasha

Round us foes throng, host to aid us here in sad plight, is there none?
In the cause of God to combat, chief of tried might, is there none?
None who will checkmate the foe, Castle to Castle, face to face
In the battle who will Queen-like guide the brave Knight, is there none?
Midst a fearful whirlpool we are fallen helpless, send us aid!
Us to rescue, a strong swimmer in our friends' sight, is there none?
'Midst the fight to be our comrade, head to give or heads to take,
On the field of earth a hero of renown bright, is there none?
Know we not wherefore in turning off our woes ye thus delay;
Day of Reckoning, aye, and question of the poor's plight, is there none?
With us 'midst the foeman's flaming streams of scorching fire to plunge,
Salamander with experience of Fate dight, is there none?
This our letter, to the court of Sultan Murad, quick to bear,
Pigeon, rapid as the storm-wind in its swift flight, is there none?

## In Reply to Hafiz Pasha

by Sultan Murad IV (r. 1623-1640)

To relieve Baghdad, O Hafiz, man of tried might, is there none?
Aid from us thou seek'st, then with thee host of fame bright, is there none?
"I'm the Queen the foe who'll checkmate," thus it was that thou didst say;
Room for action now against him with the brave Knight, is there none?
Though we know thou hast no rival in vainglorious, empty boasts,
Yet to take dread vengeance on thee, say, a Judge right, is there none?
While thou layest claim to manhood, whence this cowardice of thine?
Thou art frightened, yet beside thee fearing no fight, is there none?
Heedless of thy duty thou, the Rafizis have ta'en Baghdad;
Shall not God thy foe be? Day of Reckoning, sure, right, is there none?
They have wrecked Ebu-Hanifa's city through thy lack of care;
Oh, in thee of Islam's and the Prophet's zeal, light, is there none?
God, who favored us, whilst yet we knew not, with the Sultanate,
Shall again accord Baghdad, decreed of God's might, is there none?
Thou hast brought on Islam's army direful ruin with thy bribes;
Have we not heard how thou say'st, "Word of this foul blight, is there none?"
With the aid of God, fell vengeance on the enemy to take,
By me skilled and aged, vizier, pious, zeal-dight, is there none?
Now shall I appoint commander a vizier of high emprise,
Will not Khizar and the Prophet aid him? guide right, is there none?
Is it that thou dost the whole world void and empty now conceive?
Of the Seven Climes, Muradi, King of high might, is there none?

# An Ottoman Pattern

# Protestant and Catholic Europe

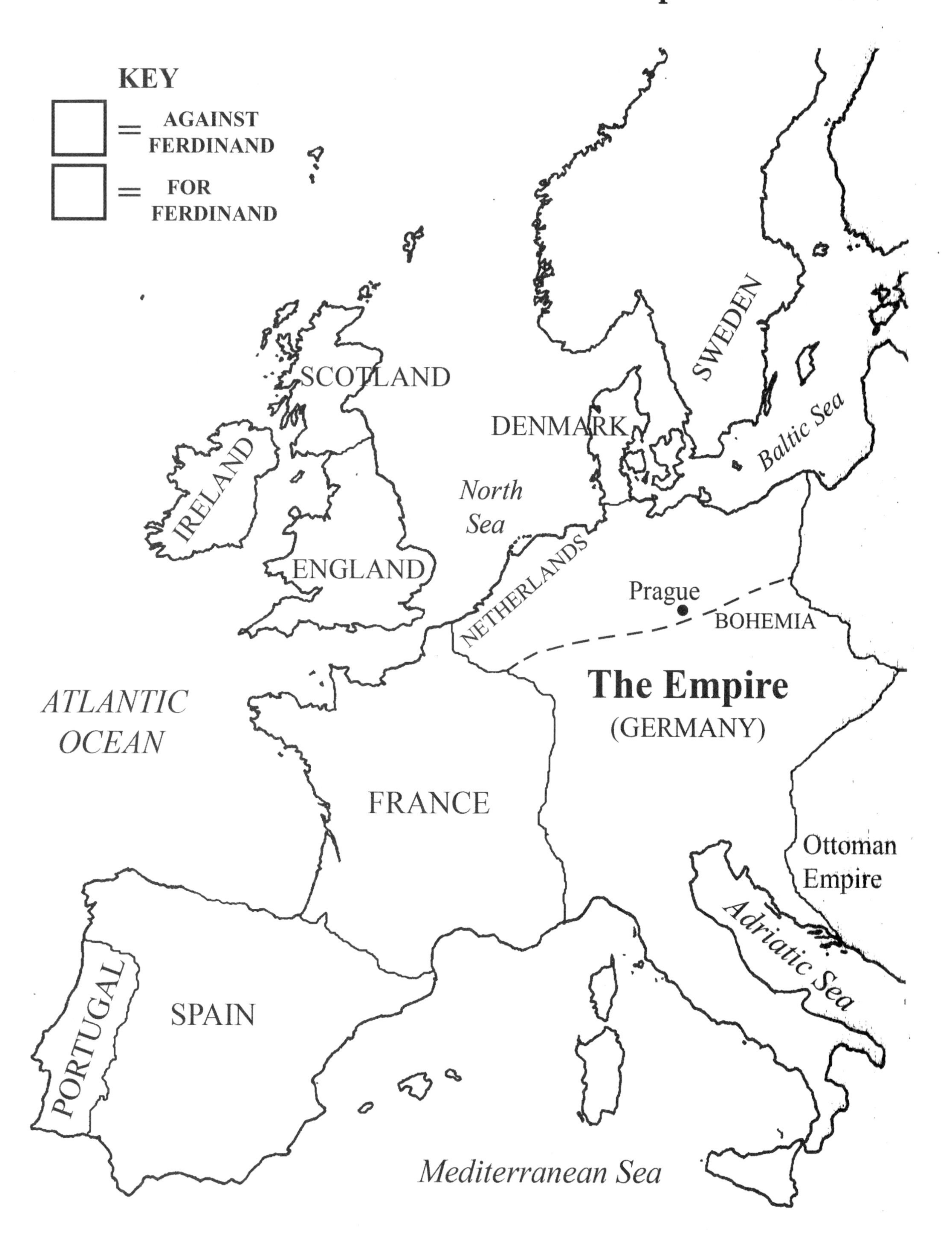

# Swedish Soldiers of the Thirty Years' War

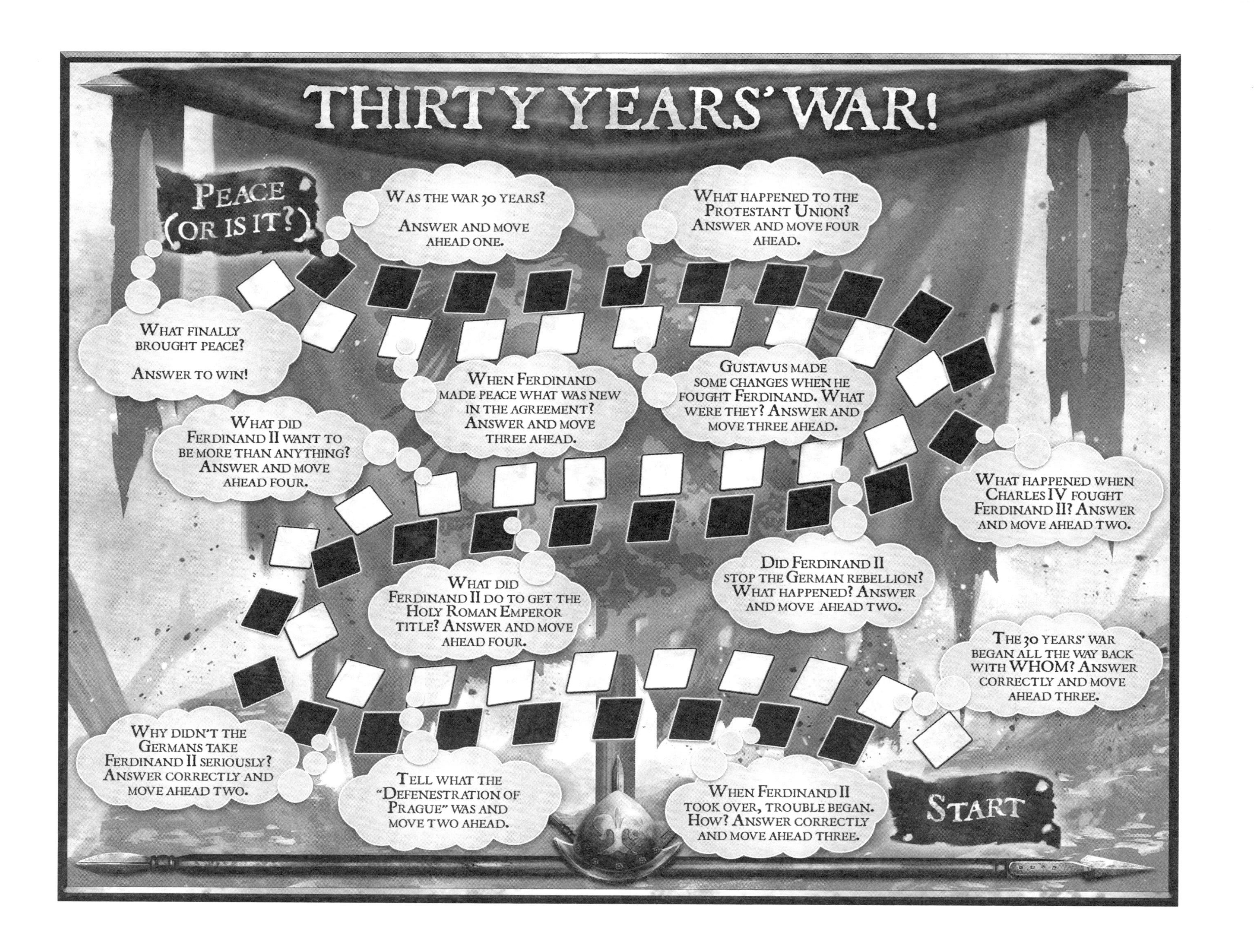
THIRTY YEARS' WAR!
PEACE (OR IS IT?)
WAS THE WAR 30 YEARS? ANSWER AND MOVE AHEAD ONE.
WHAT HAPPENED TO THE PROTESTANT UNION? ANSWER AND MOVE FOUR AHEAD.
WHAT FINALLY BROUGHT PEACE? ANSWER TO WIN!
WHEN FERDINAND MADE PEACE WHAT WAS NEW IN THE AGREEMENT? ANSWER AND MOVE THREE AHEAD.
GUSTAVUS MADE SOME CHANGES WHEN HE FOUGHT FERDINAND. WHAT WERE THEY? ANSWER AND MOVE THREE AHEAD.
WHAT DID FERDINAND II WANT TO BE MORE THAN ANYTHING? ANSWER AND MOVE AHEAD FOUR.
WHAT HAPPENED WHEN CHARLES IV FOUGHT FERDINAND II? ANSWER AND MOVE AHEAD TWO.
WHAT DID FERDINAND II DO TO GET THE HOLY ROMAN EMPEROR TITLE? ANSWER AND MOVE AHEAD FOUR.
DID FERDINAND II STOP THE GERMAN REBELLION? WHAT HAPPENED? ANSWER AND MOVE AHEAD TWO.
THE 30 YEARS' WAR BEGAN ALL THE WAY BACK WITH WHOM? ANSWER CORRECTLY AND MOVE AHEAD THREE.
WHY DIDN'T THE GERMANS TAKE FERDINAND II SERIOUSLY? ANSWER CORRECTLY AND MOVE AHEAD TWO.
TELL WHAT THE "DEFENESTRATION OF PRAGUE" WAS AND MOVE TWO AHEAD.
WHEN FERDINAND II TOOK OVER, TROUBLE BEGAN. HOW? ANSWER CORRECTLY AND MOVE AHEAD THREE.
START

# Soldiers of the Thirty Years' War Paper Dolls

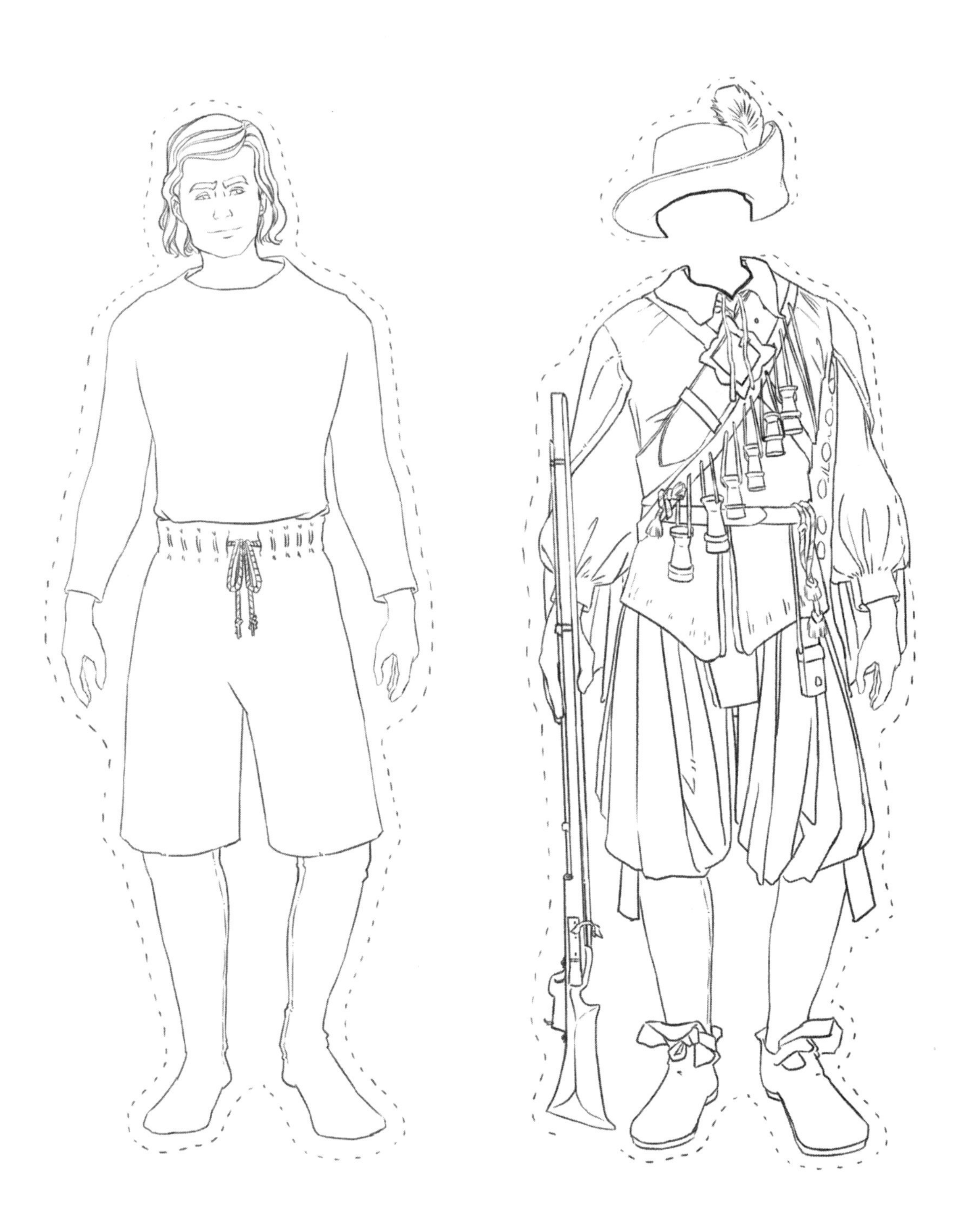

# Soldiers of the Thirty Years' War Paper Dolls

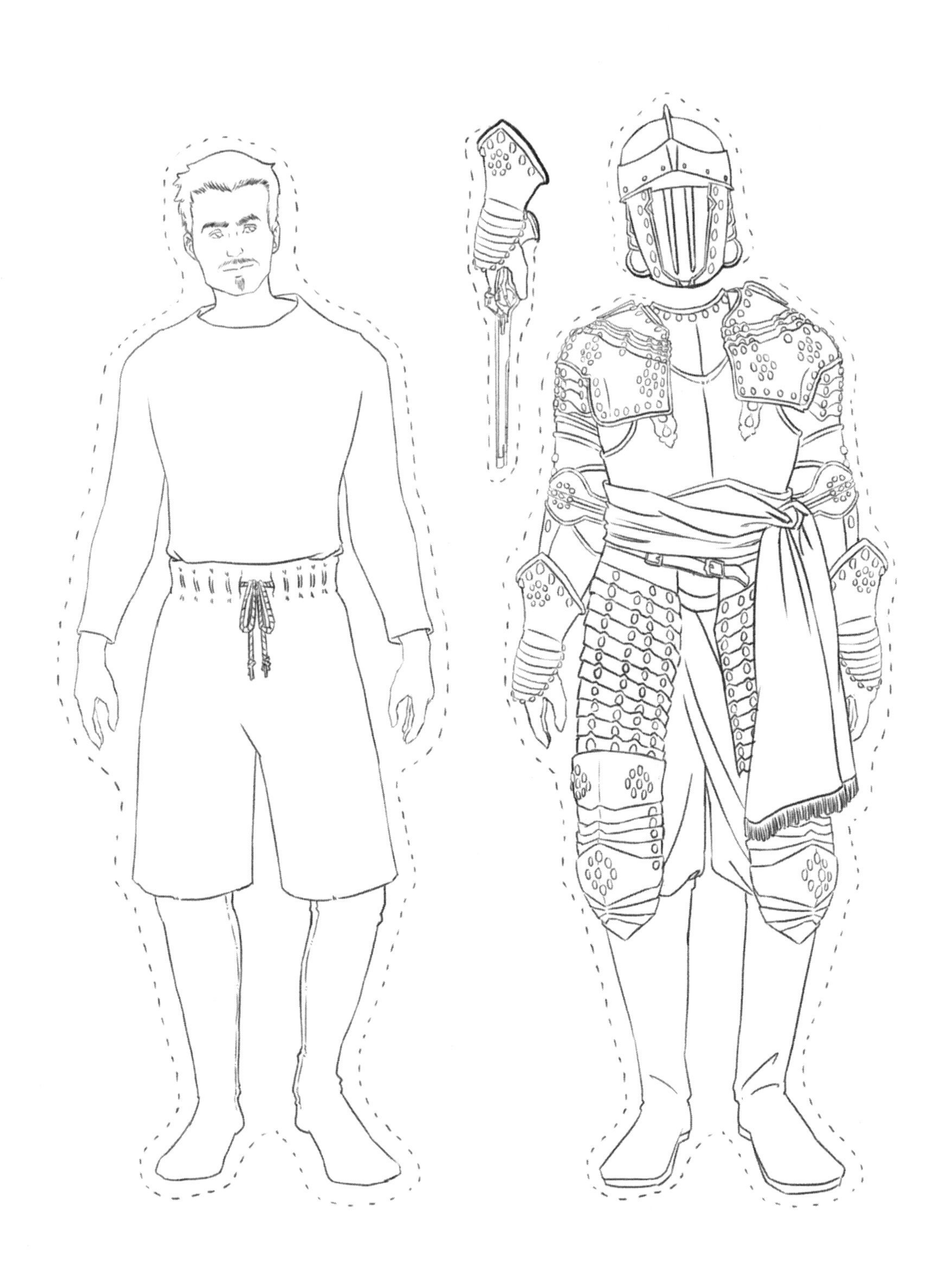

# Soldiers of the Thirty Years' War Paper Dolls

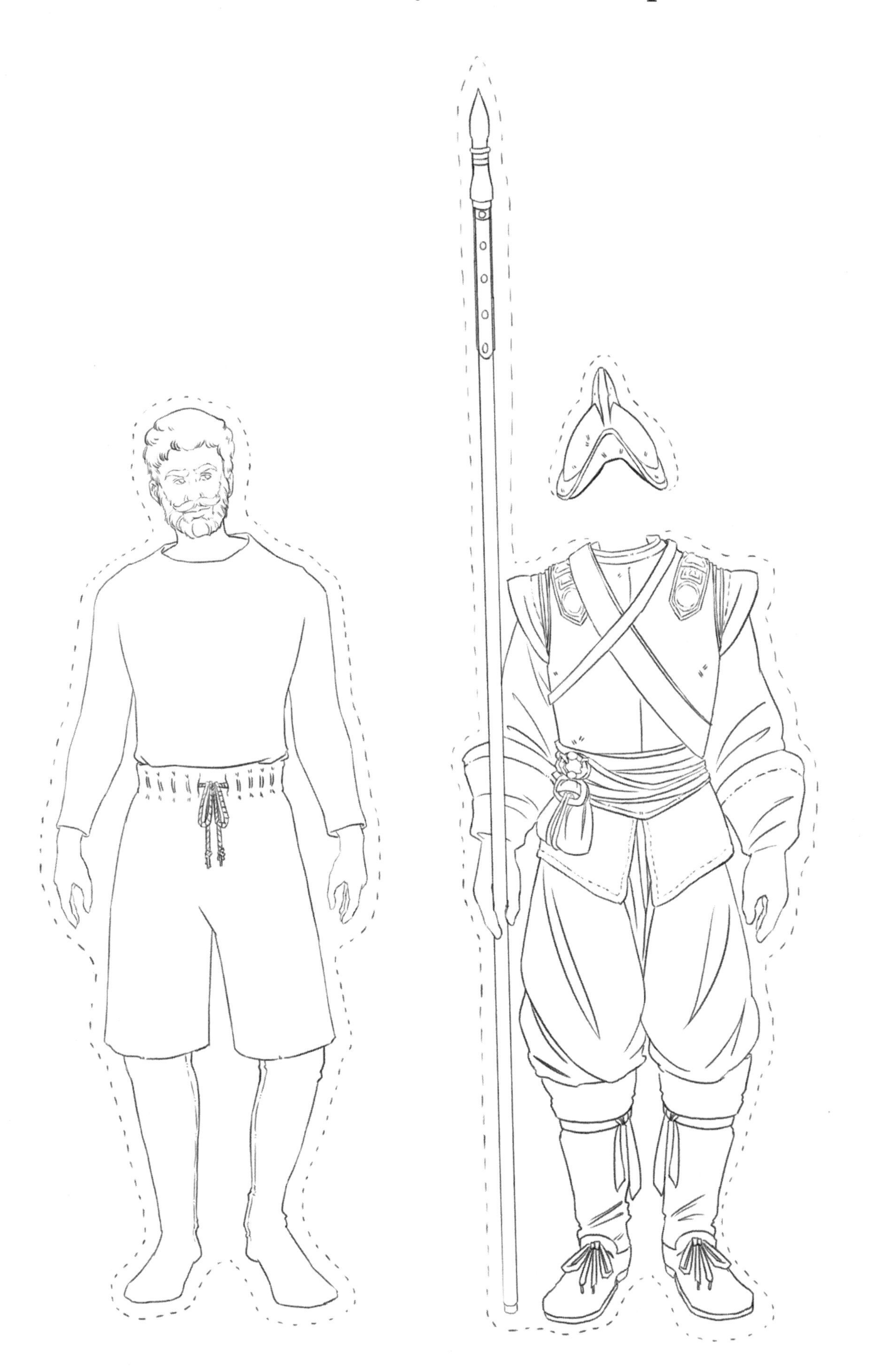

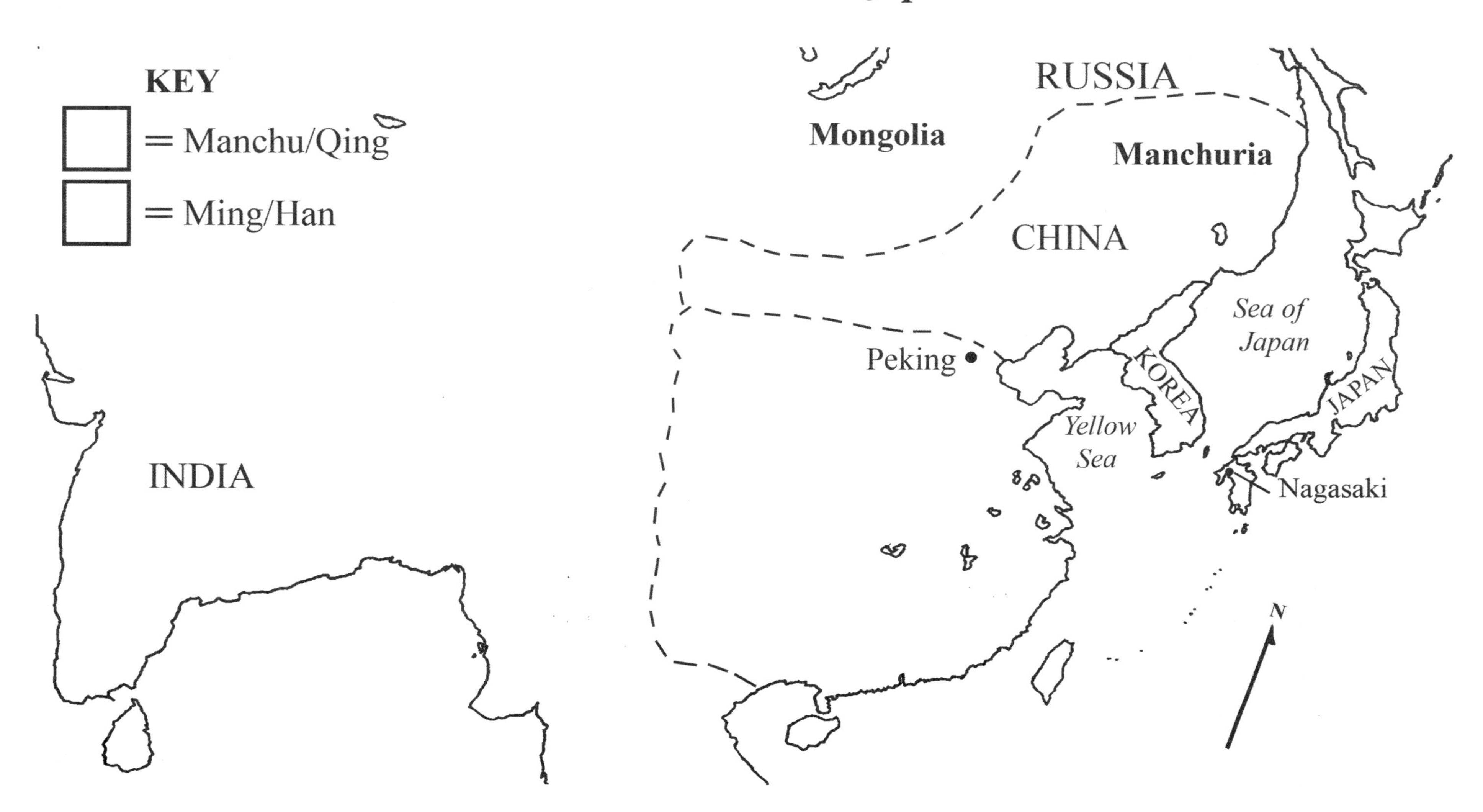
China and Iemitsu's Japan
KEY
= Manchu/Qing
= Ming/Han
Mongolia
RUSSIA
Manchuria
CHINA
Peking
Sea of Japan
KOREA
JAPAN
Yellow Sea
Nagasaki
N
INDIA

# A Zen Garden

# India

**KEY**

☐ = Marathas

AFGHANISTAN

• Delhi

CHINA

BENGAL

Calcutta

INDIA

*Arabian Sea*

DECCAN

*Bay of Bengal*

*INDIAN OCEAN*

# The Taj Mahal

# Peacock Throne Template

# Charles I's England

# The Great Fire of London

## France

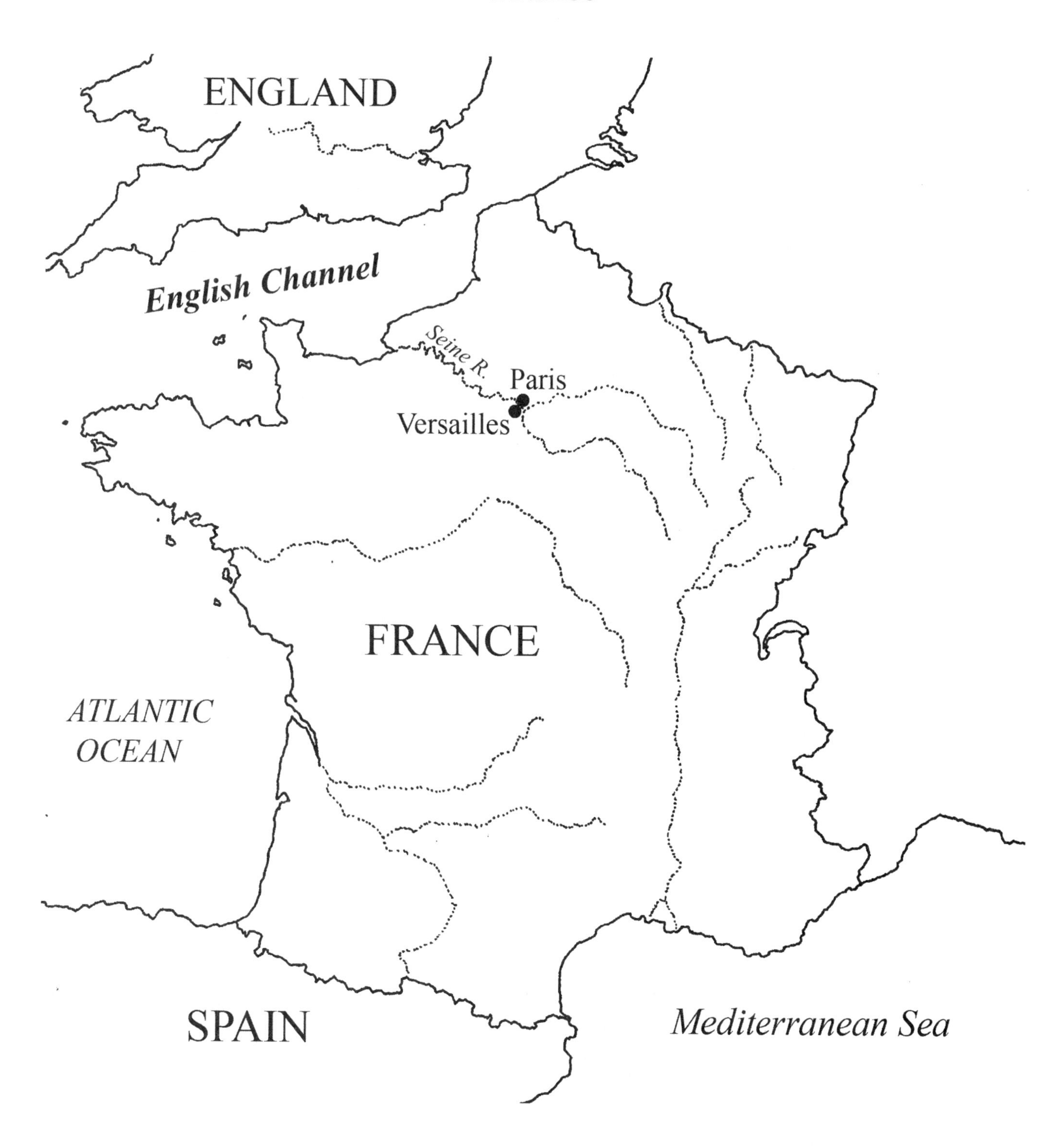
ENGLAND
English Channel
Seine R.
Paris
Versailles
FRANCE
ATLANTIC
OCEAN
SPAIN
Mediterranean Sea

# Louis XIV, The Sun King

## Versailles Mask

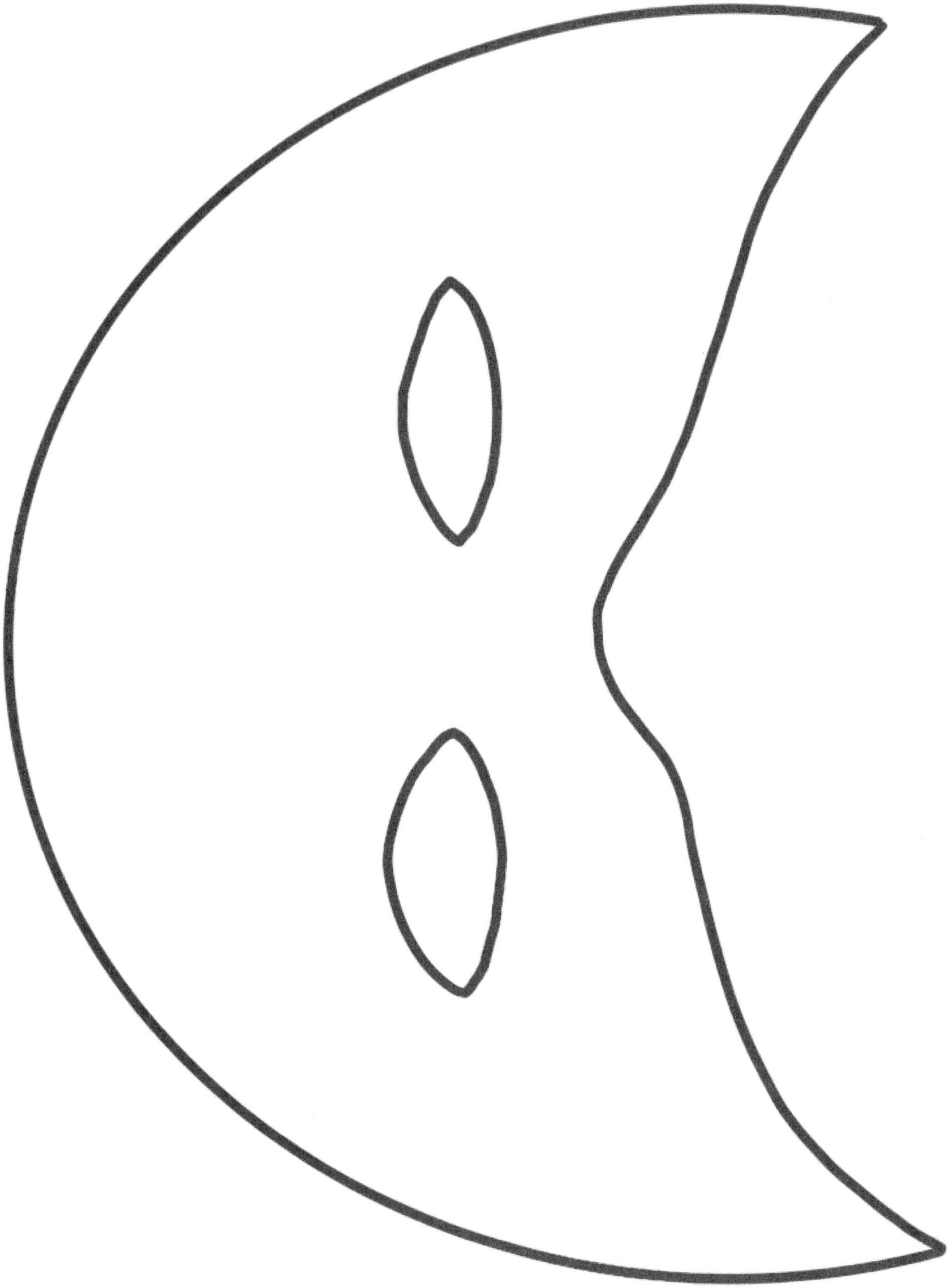

# The German States and Prussia

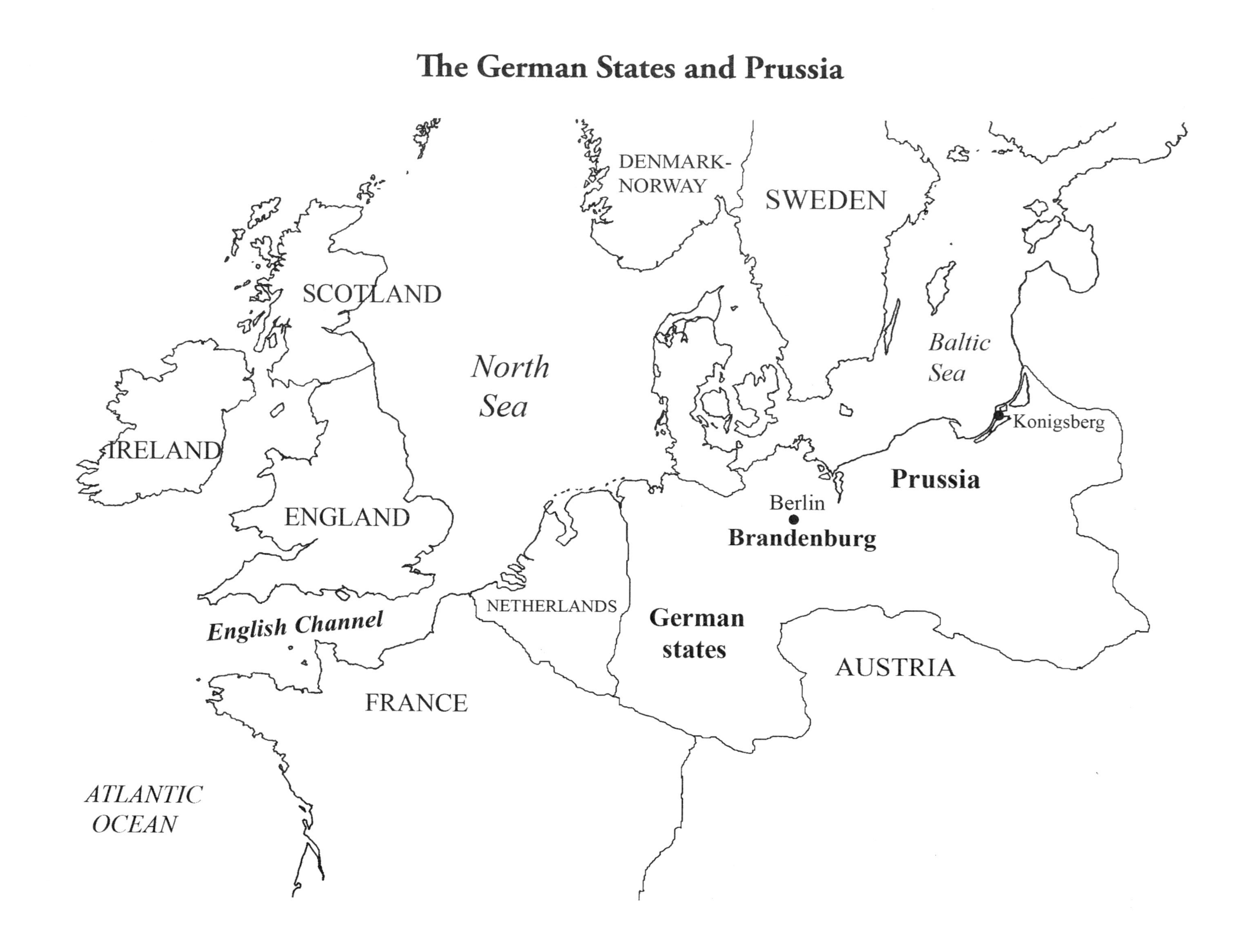

# The Linden Pathway in Berlin

# The Prussian Flag

## The Medal of The Order of the Black Eagle

## Colonizing North America

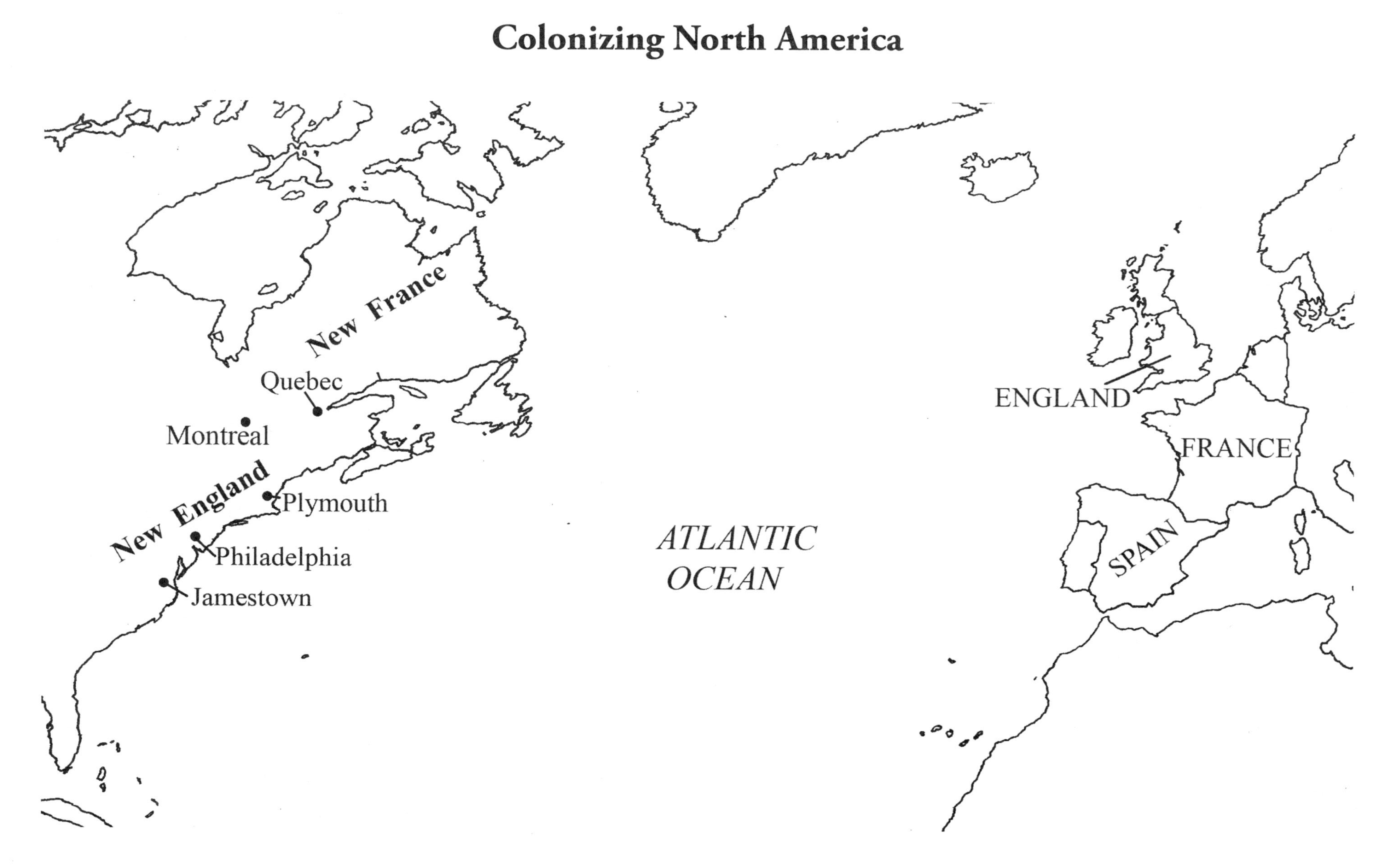

# Marie-Madeleine Defends the Fort

# England and the Netherlands

# New Kinds of Animals

# Peter and the West

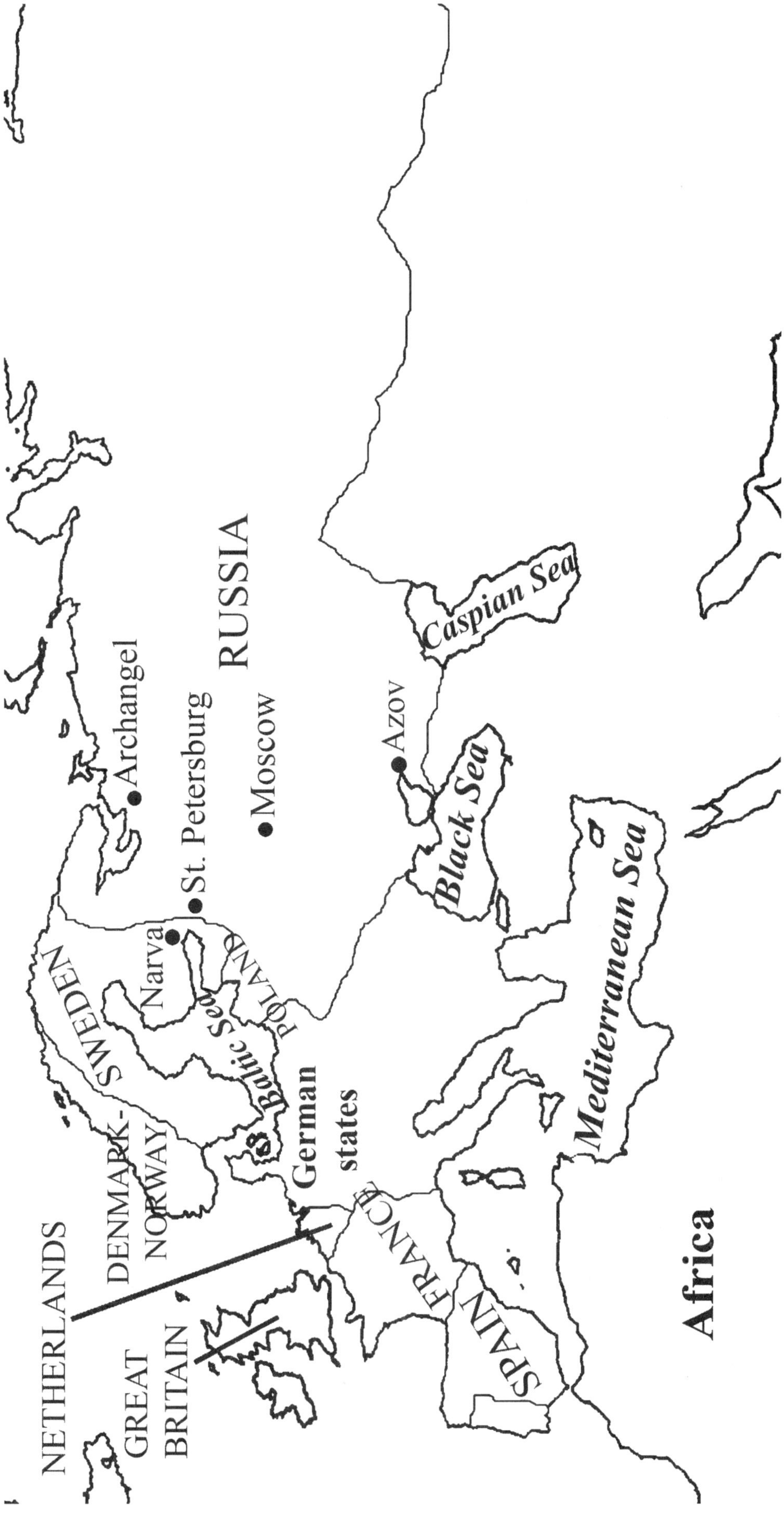

RUSSIA
Archangel
St. Petersburg
Moscow
Azov
Caspian Sea
Black Sea
Narva
SWEDEN
Baltic Sea
POLAND
German states
DENMARK-NORWAY
NETHERLANDS
GREAT BRITAIN
FRANCE
SPAIN
Mediterranean Sea
Africa

# The Peterhof Palace in Saint Petersburg

## Azov's Wall

# Peter the Great's Medal Template

Europe and the Middle East
NETHERLANDS
GREAT BRITAIN
DENMARK-NORWAY
SWEDEN
RUSSIA
Baltic Sea
POLAND
German states
AUSTRIA
Vienna
(HUNGARY)
FRANCE
SPAIN
Black Sea
Caspian Sea
Ottoman Empire
Mediterranean Sea
Jerusalem
Persia
Medina
Mecca
Arabia
Africa
INDIA
Arabian Sea

# A Tulip Party

# Ottoman Miniature Paintings

The Seven Sleepers

A Hunting Scene

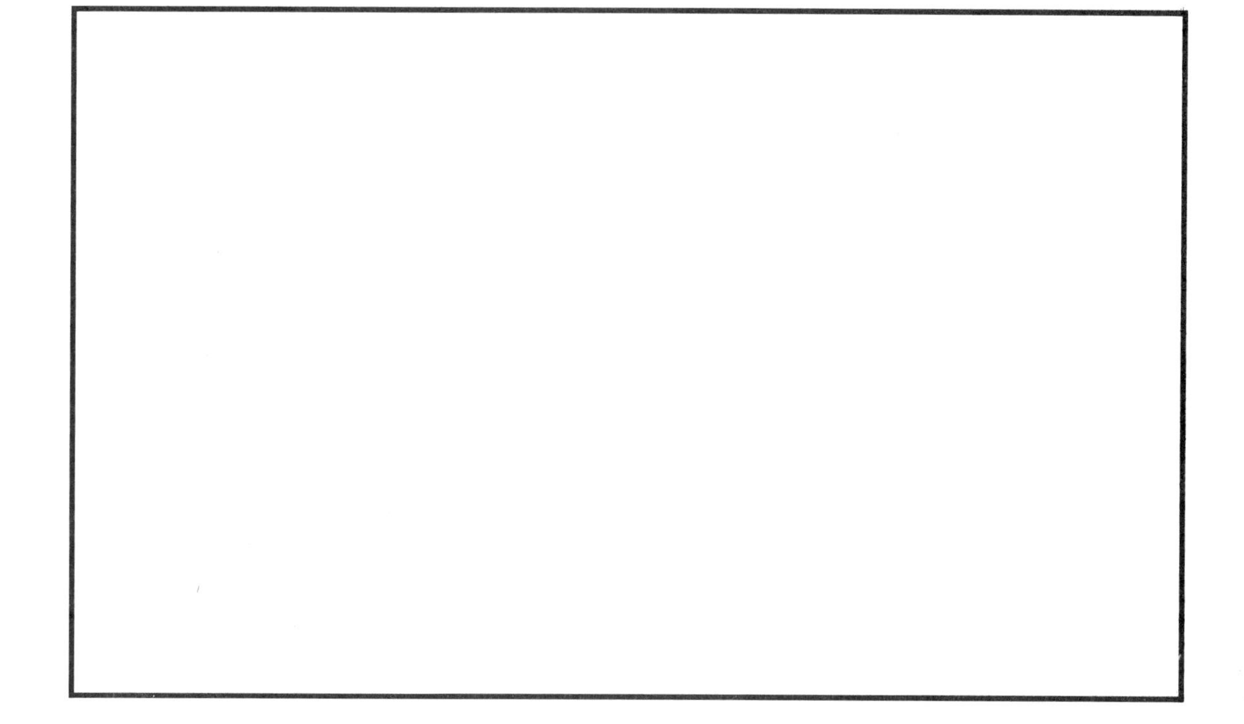

# Turkish Tent Templates

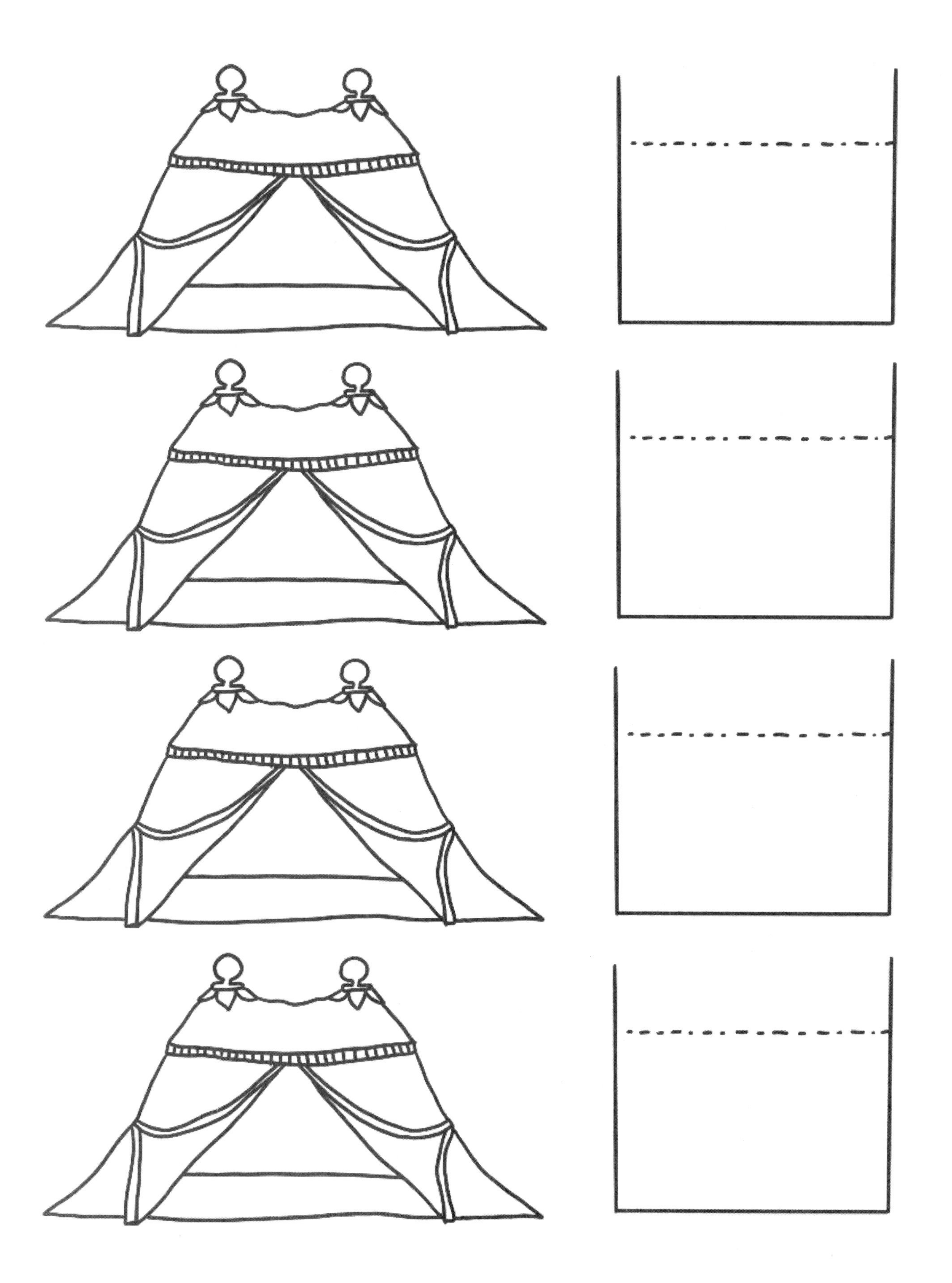

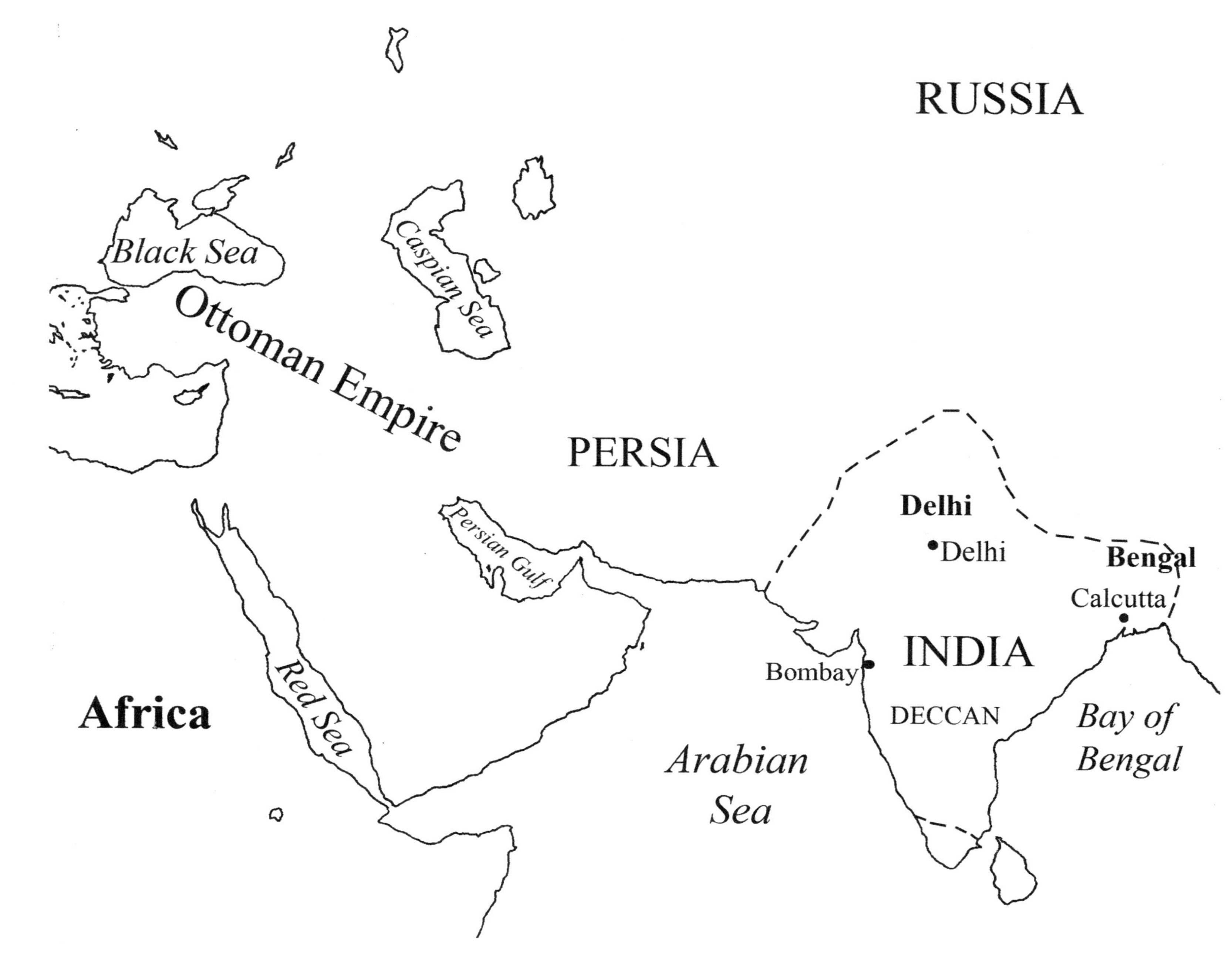
The Indian Kingdom
RUSSIA
Black Sea
Caspian Sea
Ottoman Empire
PERSIA
Persian Gulf
Delhi
Delhi
Bengal
Calcutta
INDIA
Bombay
DECCAN
Africa
Red Sea
Arabian Sea
Bay of Bengal

# A War Elephant of Bengal

# Samrat Yantra's Sundial

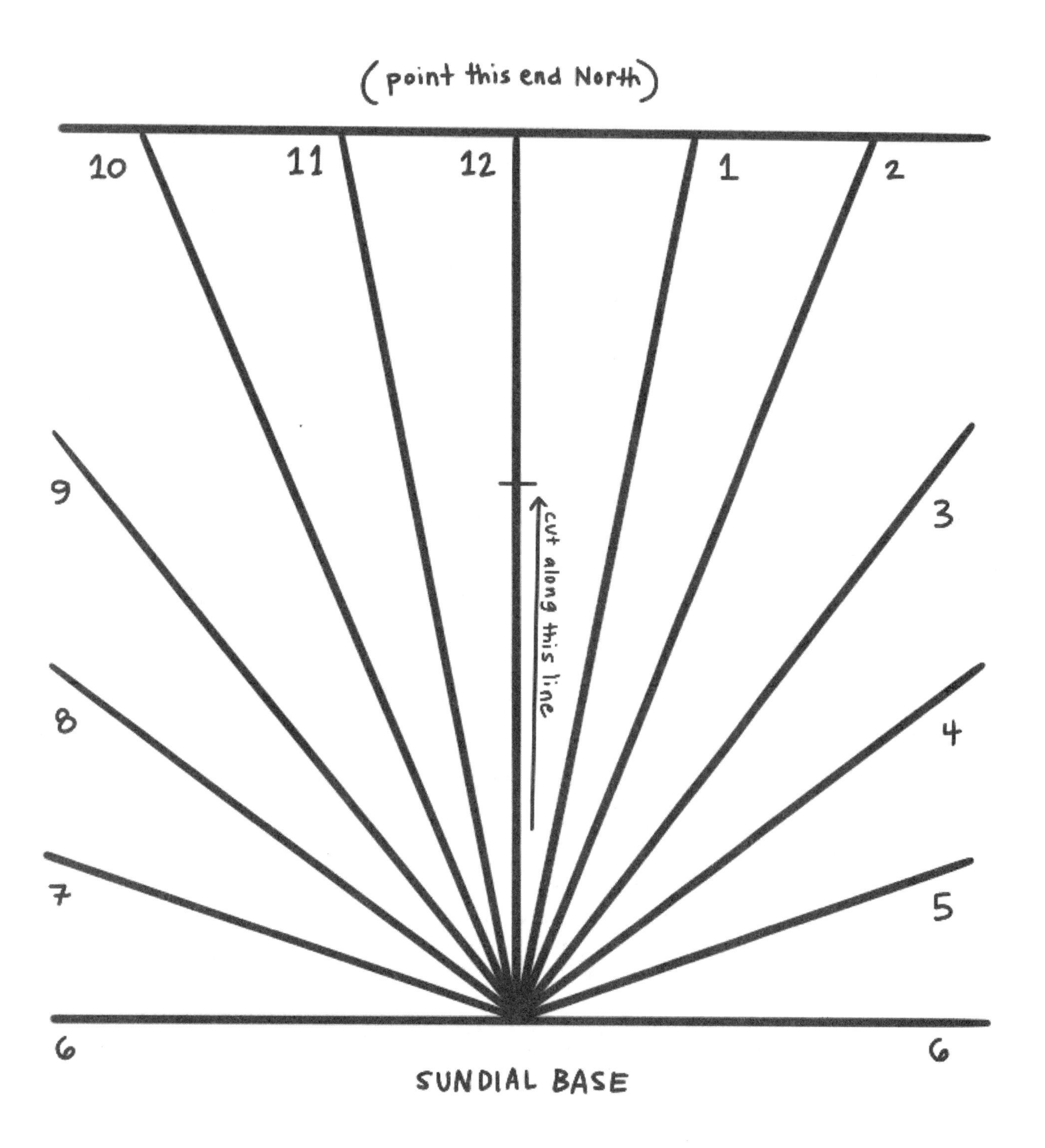

# Gnomon Template

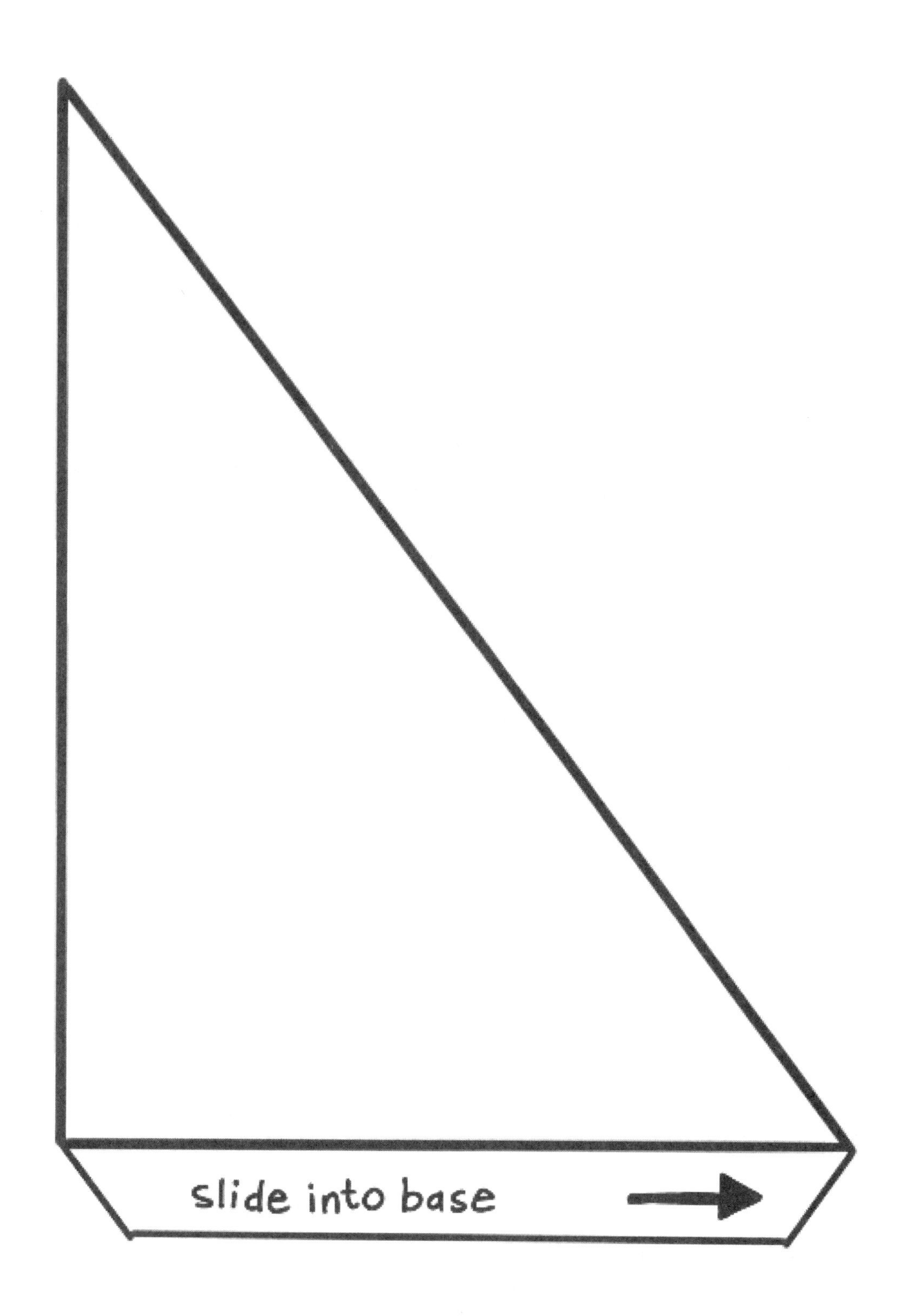

# Kirpan Template

# The Land of the Dragon

# A Chinese Dragon

# Three Pointless Wars

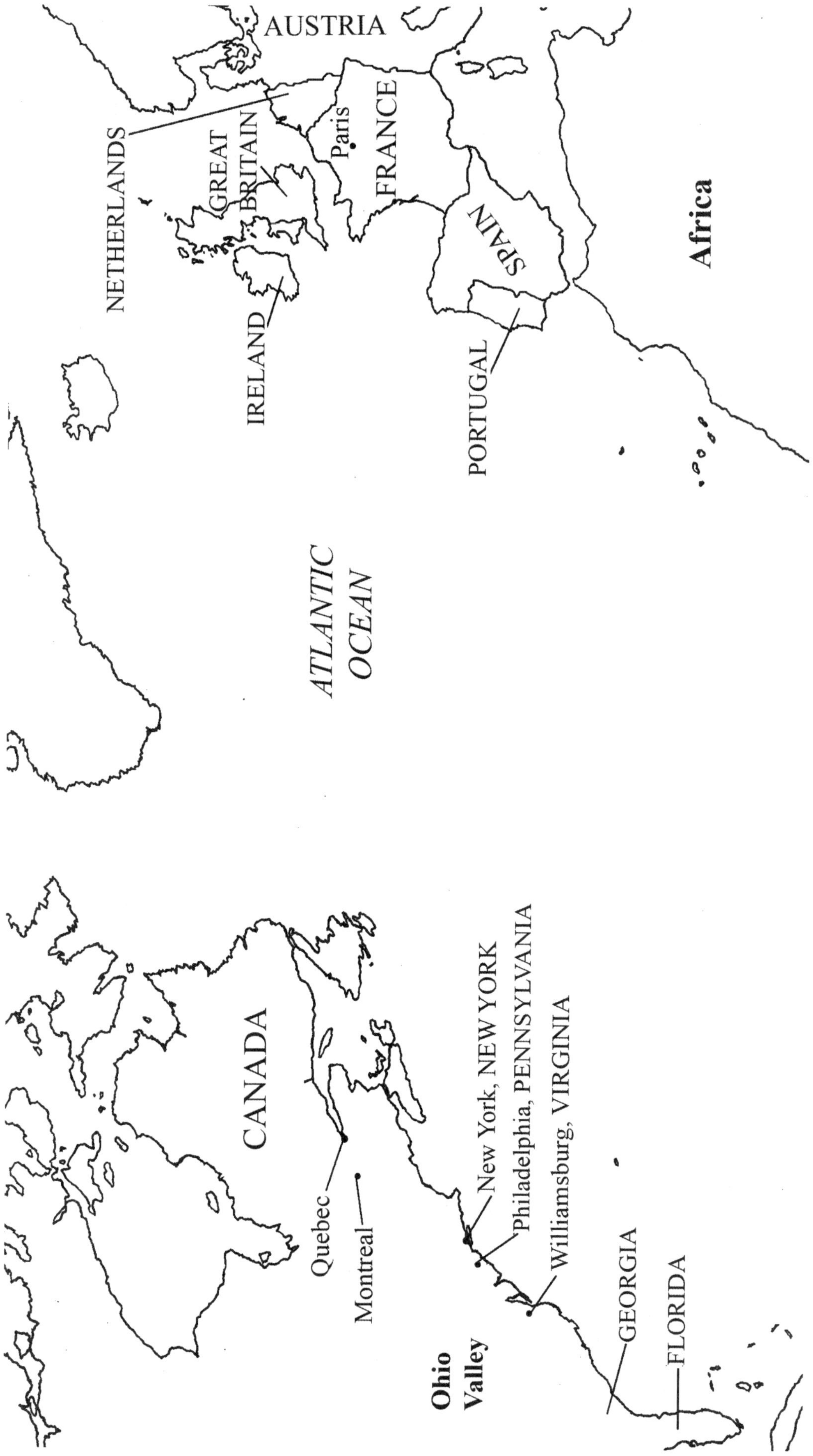

CANADA
Quebec
Montreal
Ohio Valley
New York, NEW YORK
Philadelphia, PENNSYLVANIA
Williamsburg, VIRGINIA
GEORGIA
FLORIDA
ATLANTIC OCEAN
NETHERLANDS
IRELAND
GREAT BRITAIN
AUSTRIA
Paris
FRANCE
PORTUGAL
SPAIN
Africa

# Iroquois and Seneca Warriors Surprise the British

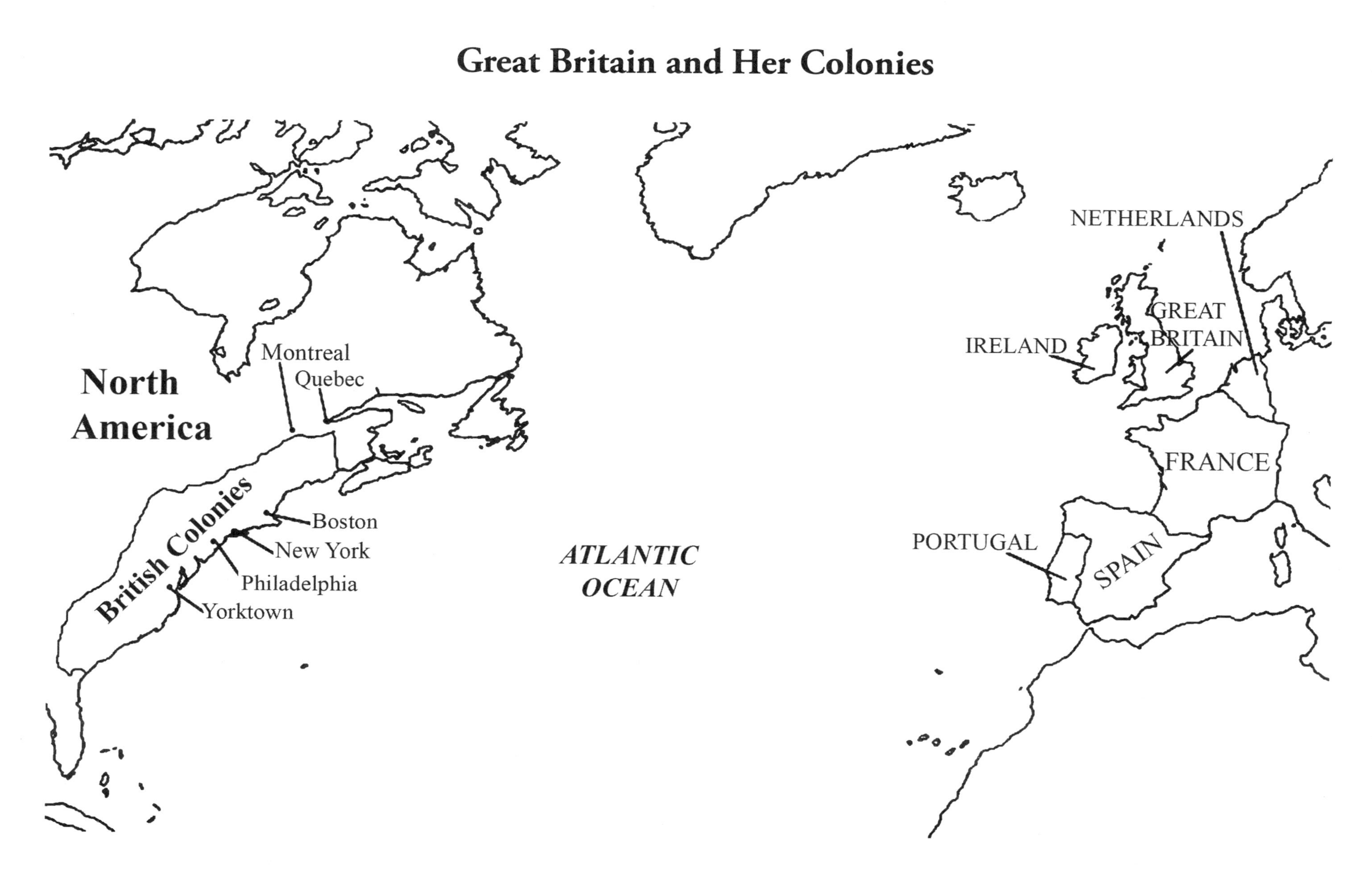
Great Britain and Her Colonies
North America
Montreal
Quebec
British Colonies
Boston
New York
Philadelphia
Yorktown
ATLANTIC OCEAN
NETHERLANDS
IRELAND
GREAT BRITAIN
FRANCE
PORTUGAL
SPAIN

# The Boston Tea Party

# American, British, and German Soldier Paper Dolls

# American, British, and German Soldier Paper Dolls

# American, British, and German Soldier Paper Dolls

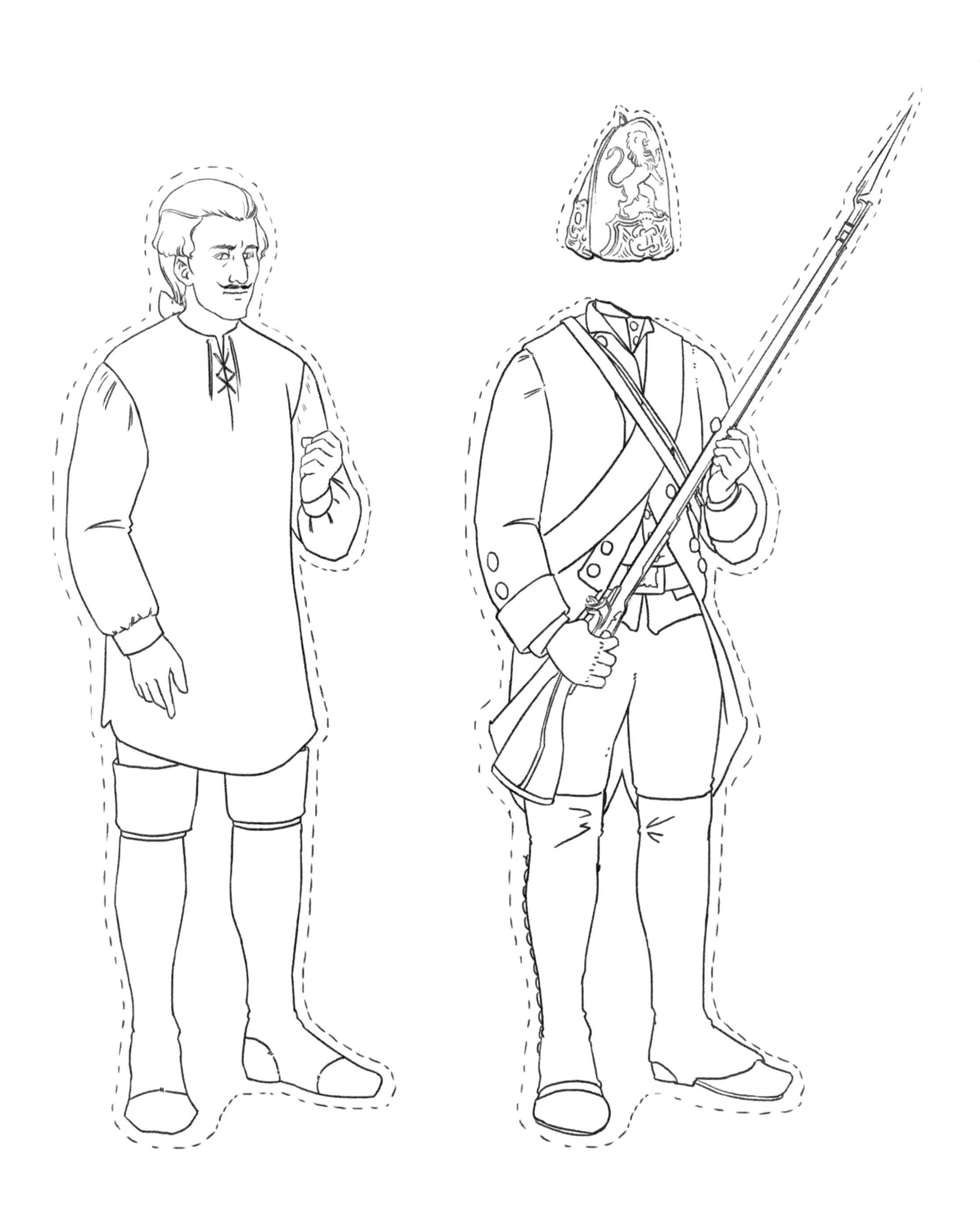

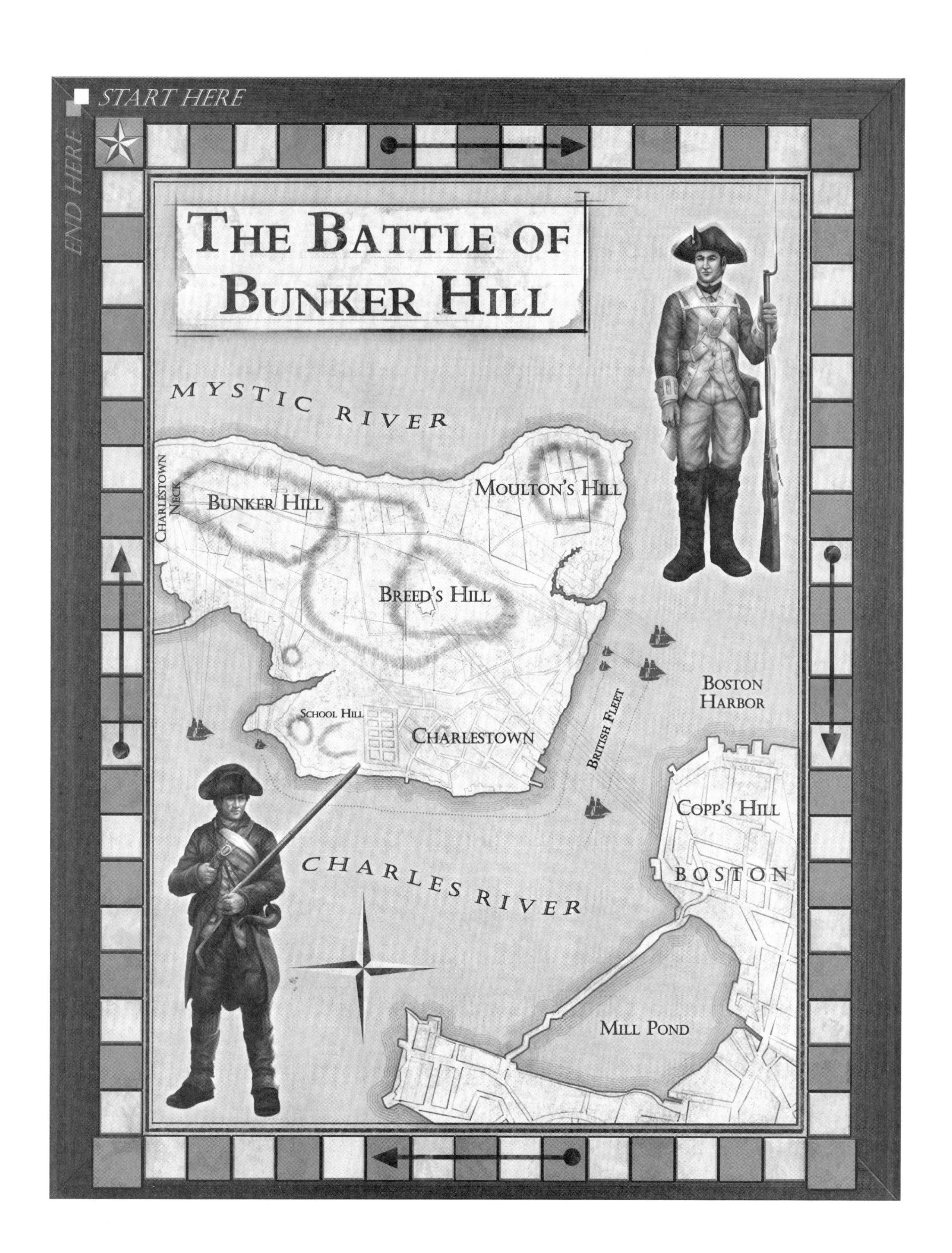
START HERE
END HERE
THE BATTLE OF BUNKER HILL
MYSTIC RIVER
CHARLESTOWN NECK
BUNKER HILL
MOULTON'S HILL
BREED'S HILL
BOSTON HARBOR
SCHOOL HILL
CHARLESTOWN
BRITISH FLEET
COPP'S HILL
BOSTON
CHARLES RIVER
MILL POND

| During the Seven Years' War, Britain spent hundreds of thousands of pounds defending the American colonies. The British wanted to increase American taxes to put some money back in England's treasury. | The British Parliament wrote new tax laws, called "Acts." The first was the Sugar Act. Americans had to pay extra money for all sugar and molasses that came into their ports—unless it came from Britain. | The second new tax law. Americans had to pay taxes on newspapers, pamphlets, dice, or playing cards. There was also a fee to get legal documents "stamped." | More Acts passed. Americans were ordered to provide rooms and food for British troops sent to North America—and to pay for those rooms and food themselves. | New taxes on glass, paper, paint and tea were passed. More money flowed into Great Britain's pockets. |
|---|---|---|---|---|
| The Americans argued about these tax laws in their General Assemblies—meetings of all the colony leaders. Many thought that Parliament should have asked the Assemblies to approve the new taxes before making them laws. | Patrick Henry argued that since no British citizen had to pay a tax unless his representative (a man elected to argue for his rights) in Parliament agreed, and since Americans had no representatives, the taxes were illegal. | "No taxation without representation!" became the cry of Americans up and down the coast of North America. | The new king of Great Britain, George III, agreed to repeal, or take away, some of the taxes. George's repeal of a few taxes didn't do any good—because Parliament insisted that the taxes on tea remain. | In March of 1770, some Americans in Boston were throwing snowballs at British soldiers. The soldiers panicked and fired, killing five people and wounding many others. For the first time, British soldiers had fired at their own colonists. |
| Resentment of Parliament grew and grew. American merchants decided to boycott all English tea. They refused to unload cargoes of tea. Tea parties became coffee parties. | In Boston, the governor insisted that ships be allowed to unload their tea. On the evening of December 16, 1773, sixty men dumped 342 chests of tea into Boston Harbor. | Parliament was furious at this "Boston Tea Party." It passed a series of laws, which the colonies called the "Intolerable Acts." Until Boston paid for the tea, the harbor would stay closed. | After Parliament closed Boston Harbor, leaders from every colony gathered in Philadelphia in 1774, in a big meeting called the First Continental Congress. | The Continental Congress wrote a petition to George III and Parliament, asking them to remove British soldiers from Boston, repeal the taxes, and reopen the port. |
| No one knew what would happen when the Continental Congress petition reached England. Many Americans were sure that war would follow. They began to collect weapons and bullets and to store them away. | Patrick Henry told the Virginia Assembly, "We have done everything that could be done. Is life so dear, or peace so sweet as to be purchased at the price of chains and slavery? I know not what course others may take; but as for me, give me liberty or give me death! | The petition to Parliament didn't bring peace. Instead, the British prepared to fight the Americans to keep their empire together. | The British could see young American men practicing with their weapons in fields outside of Boston. These men called themselves Minutemen, because they were ready to fight at a minute's notice. | On April 18, 1775, a troop of British soldiers marched out of Boston under the cover of dark. They planned to march most of the night and to arrive at Concord suddenly, surprising the Americans and taking the weapons away. |
| The Americans learned about the plan. Two men, Paul Revere and William Dawes, rode to Concord and warned the Americans there. They galloped all night, calling out "The British are coming! | Americans grabbed their weapons. Minutemen gathered together at Lexington, halfway to Concord, and waited for the British troops to march into view. | The soldiers arrived at Lexington early on April 19th—a cool and foggy morning. The chief British officer saw the Minutemen. He shouted: "Lay down your arms, you rebels, or you are all dead men!" | "Fire!" the officer shouted. Muskets sounded. Eight Minutemen fell. The rest retreated and regrouped in Concord. When the British arrived there, both sides fired. The war for independence began. | The news spread all through the colonies. Men got ready to fight. The Second Continental Congress met together and made George Washington the commander of the whole colonial army. |
| Washington wasn't sure he could turn his ragged collection of volunteers into an army ready to face the British! He didn't have enough weapons or food, and many of the soldiers had no shoes. | On June 17th, 1775, the first huge battle of the war took place. The British attacked the American soldiers camped on Bunker Hill, a high hill above Boston. | After three charges, the Americans were defeated, and the British were in control of the hill. But the British had lost three times as many men as the Americans. | Encouraged by the British losses, the Americans fought on. | |

# The 13 Colonies

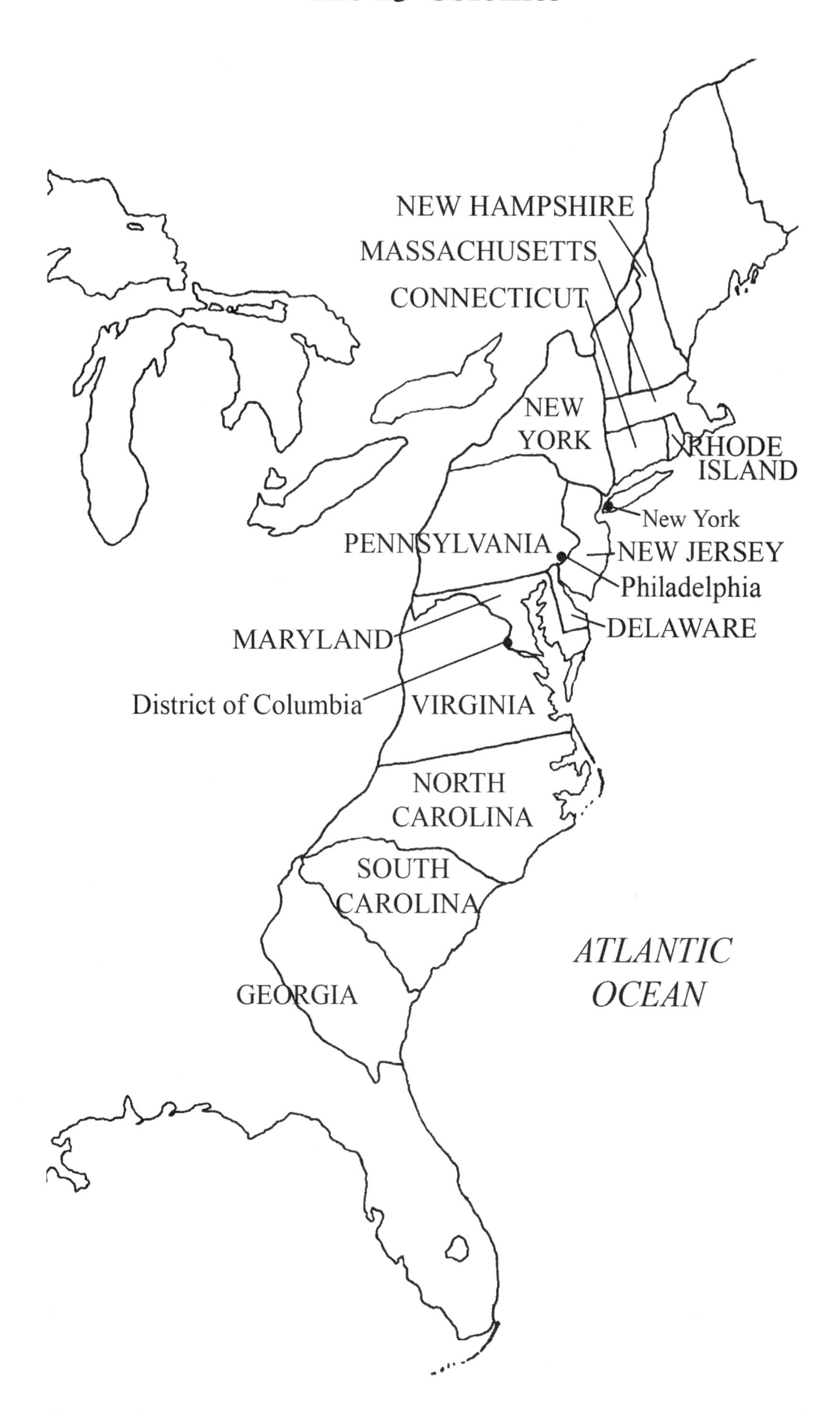

# Ben Franklin Goes to the Constitutional Convention

# Presidential Timeline
## 1789 - 1873

1789 1793 1797 1801 1805 1809 1813 1817 1821 1825 1829

1833 1837 1841 1845 1849 1853 1857 1861 1865 1869 1873

# 3 Branches Game Template

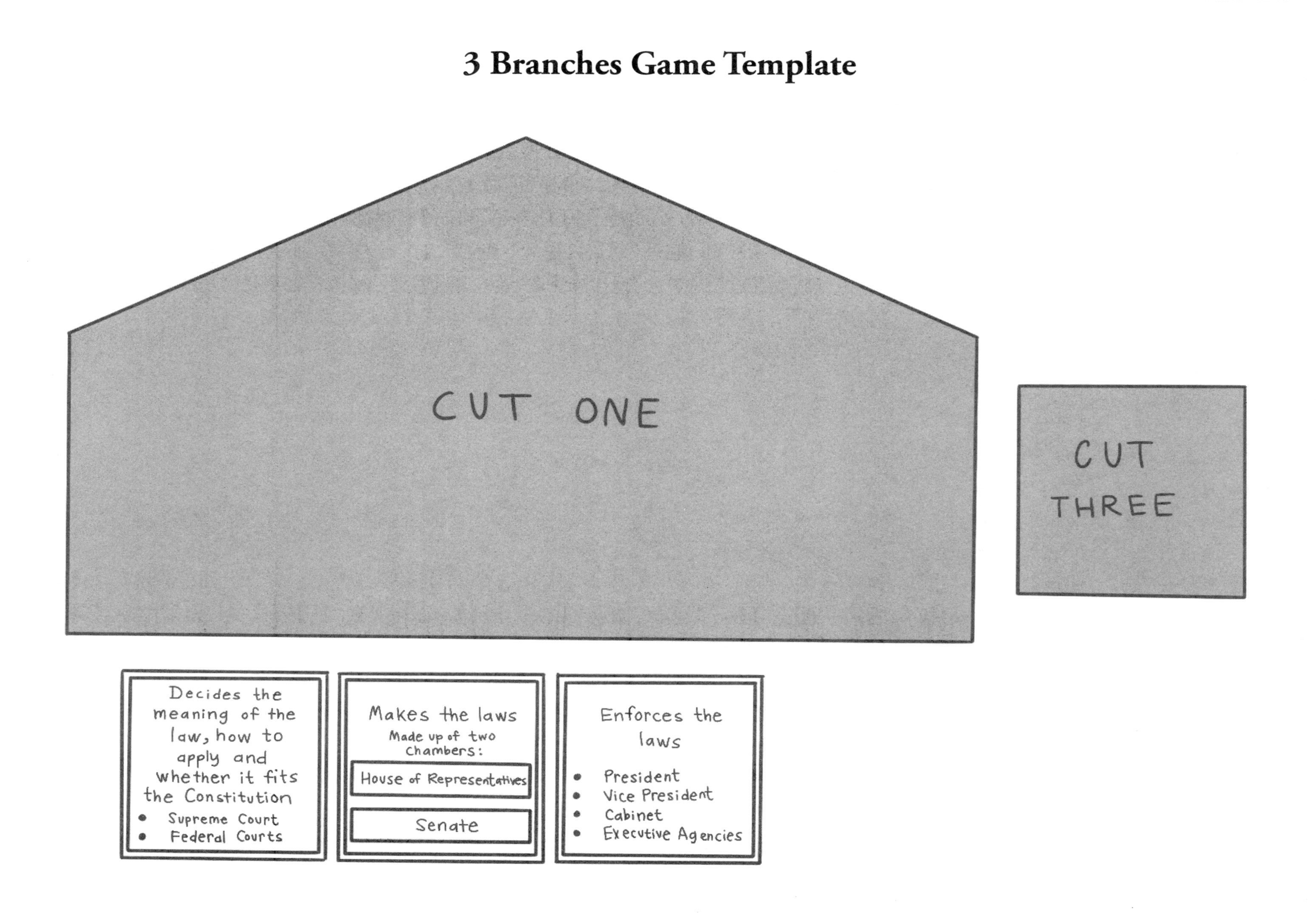

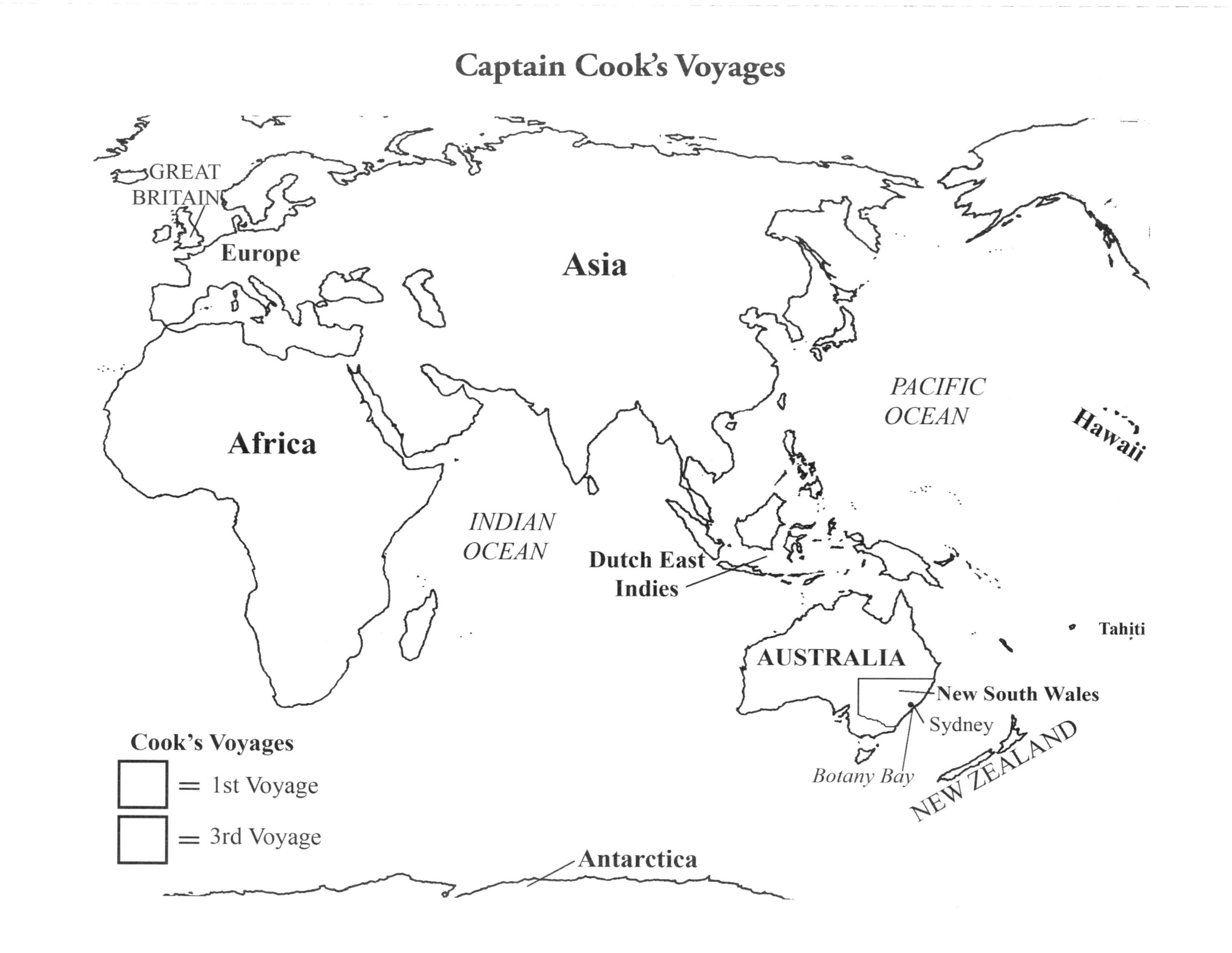
Captain Cook's Voyages
GREAT BRITAIN
Europe
Asia
Africa
PACIFIC OCEAN
Hawaii
INDIAN OCEAN
Dutch East Indies
Tahiti
AUSTRALIA
New South Wales
Sydney
Botany Bay
NEW ZEALAND
Cook's Voyages
= 1st Voyage
= 3rd Voyage
Antarctica

# The Hawaiians Meet Captain Cook

## Captain Cook Landing at Botany Bay

J A M E S B P H I S Q U A T T E R S
L I U B O P R I S O N C O L O N Y A
T B E Y U A Y I B A R B I I A W A H
K A Y A E V L Q T O L E L P C Y O U
K A N G A R O O D A S I S N A A P E
B O T A N Y B A Y H I R G E R C T P
S E N I G I R O B A O N L W R A F I
N O P U E C N O W W A V E S O E G L
C A P T A I N J A M E S C O O K J L
A D S H E H T O T V Y O J U T T A I
L U O O H I S T O R Y D Y T H I M H
C C T P Z P C C M E Z H X H A A E P
U K W E I Y Y S O T W P E W W T S R
T B R H E E T W I N G L Q A A I R U
T I S N N R E U A B P B N L I R U H
A L W D E N D E A V O U R E I B S T
Q L Y X R I J Y R Q L P E S R U E R
I S I M E O N G R E E N W A Y N O A

### Find the Following Words

| | | | |
|---|---|---|---|
| Hawaii | Aborigine | Britain | duckbill |
| Botany Bay | Calcutta | Sydney Cove | Captain James Cook |
| Squatters | kangaroo | Simeon Greenway | Endeavour |
| Arthur Phillip | prison colony | New South Wales | |

# Fighting in France

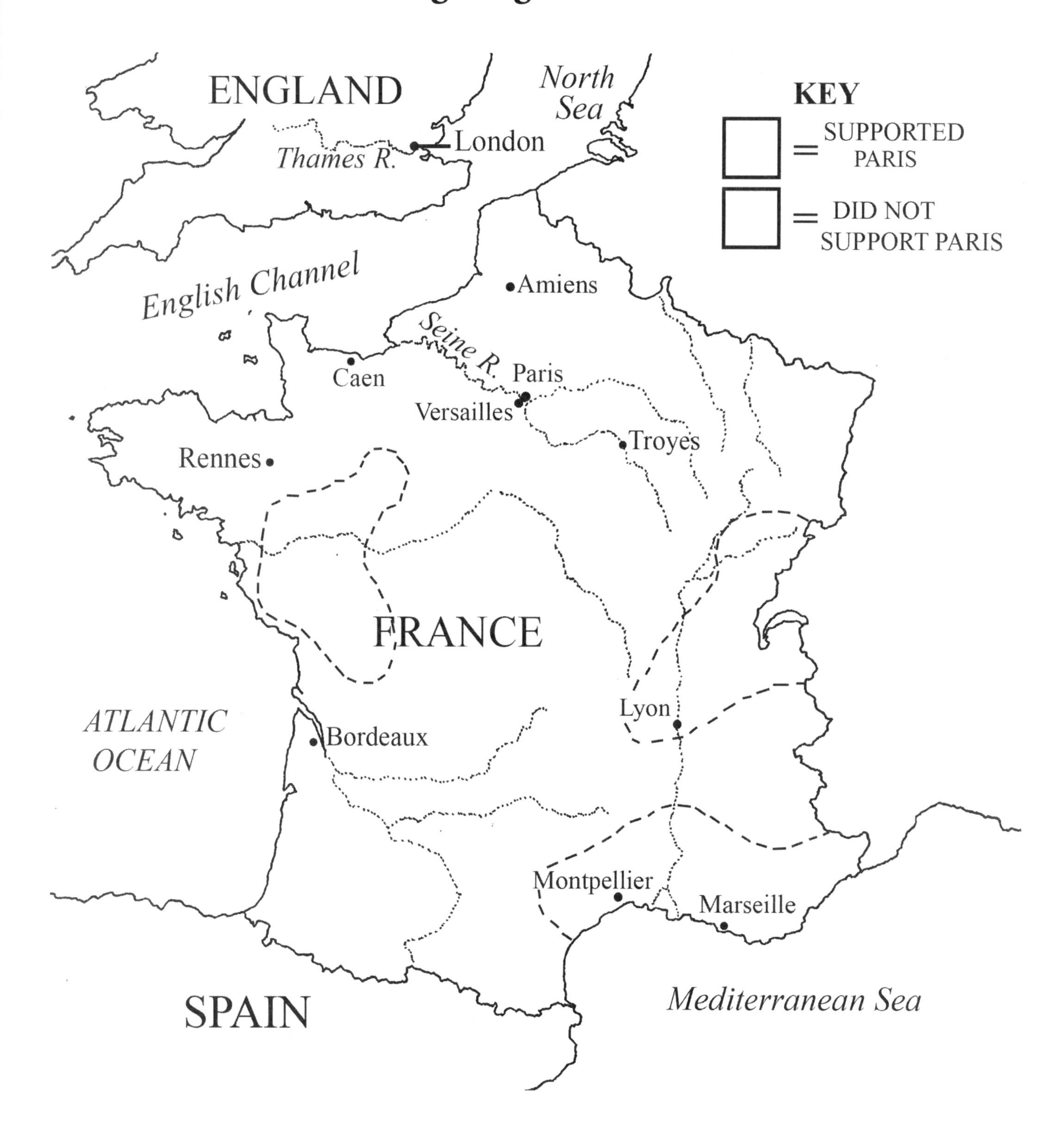

# Marie Antoinette

# The Bastille Fortress

START HERE
END HERE
STORM THE BASTILLE!

# Storm the Bastille! Game Cards

| | | |
|---|---|---|
| Chapter 25 is called "Revolution Gone Sour." Why? | What was the reaction by the people in France to America's *Declaration of Independence*? | Why did the Third Estate leave the meeting of the three estates at Versailles? |
| What kind of government did France have before the French Revolution? | What were a few of the reasons the French people started a revolution? | Tell something that you read about from the *Story of the World* this year so far. |
| Did the French Revolution happen before or after the American Revolution? | When the Third Estate was locked out of their meeting room, where did they go and what did they do? | When the people of Paris heard about the Third Estate's rebellion, what did they do? |
| Louis XIV had spent most of France's money building what? Do you remember what Louis was called? | What was "The Bastille?" | What is the day that the fall of the Bastille is celebrated in France? |
| The French were divided into three parts or "estates." Name the three estates. | What happened to the king and queen after the Bastille fell? | After the king and queen were killed, was everything peaceful? |
| Which "estate" had to pay taxes? | Who was Maximilien de Robespierre? | What were the people called who continued to support the king or at least the idea of a monarchy? |
| Which "estate" was the largest in France? | Louis, Marie, and the children had to escape! What happened? | The people got a stern message from the king of Prussia. What did this mean to them? |
| What did the noblemen of France spend their time doing? | Once Robespierre got the power, what happened to the revolution? | A British witness of the French Revolution said, "The guillotine was claiming both the innocent and the guilty…." What did this mean? |
| Who was the king at the start of the French Revolution? | What happened to Robespierre? | What is the Reign of Terror? |
| Who was the queen at the start of the French Revolution? | Tell something that you read about from the *Story of the World* this year so far. | Tell something that you read about from the *Story of the World* this year so far. |

# Hat Pattern

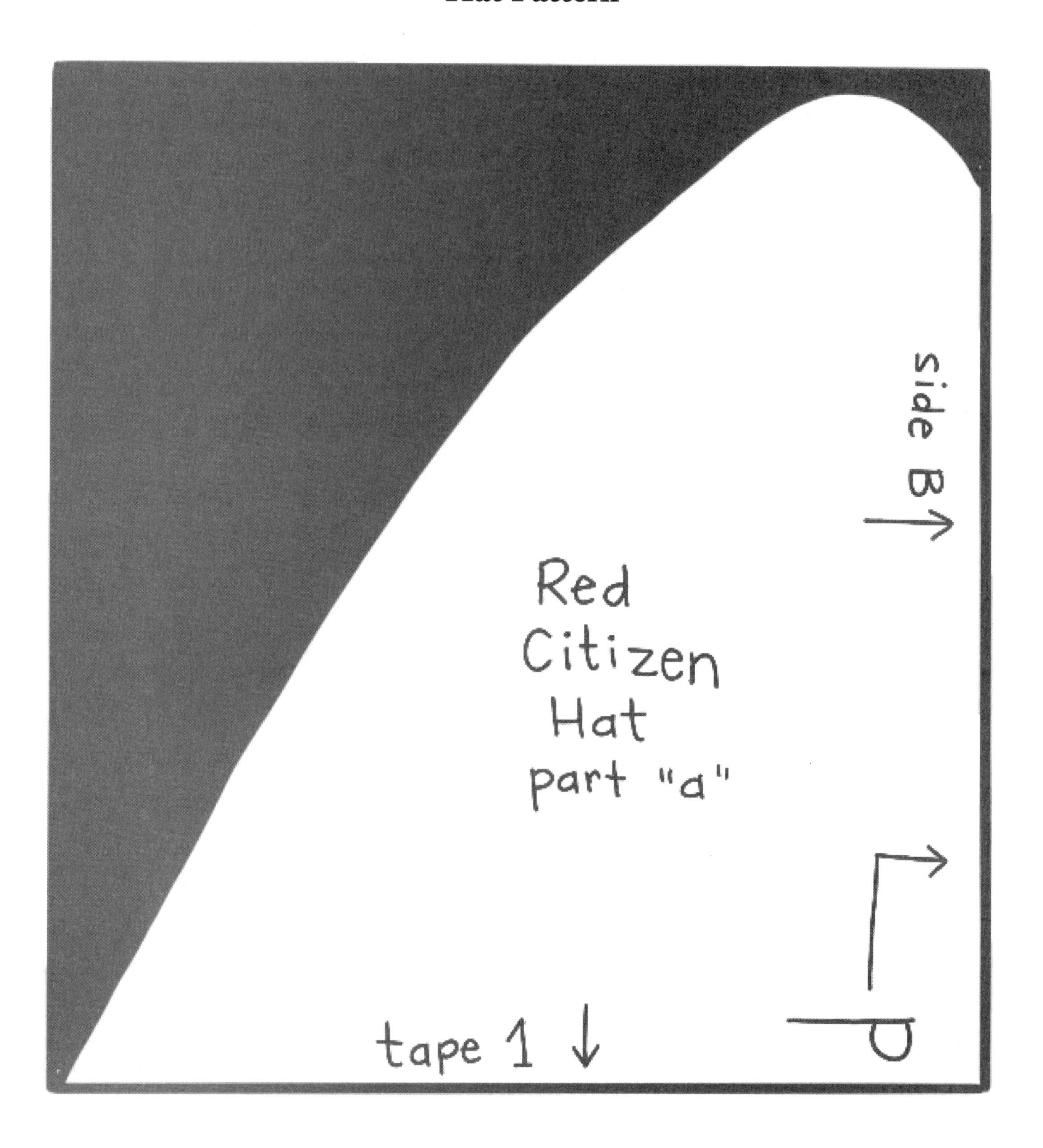

# Hat Pattern

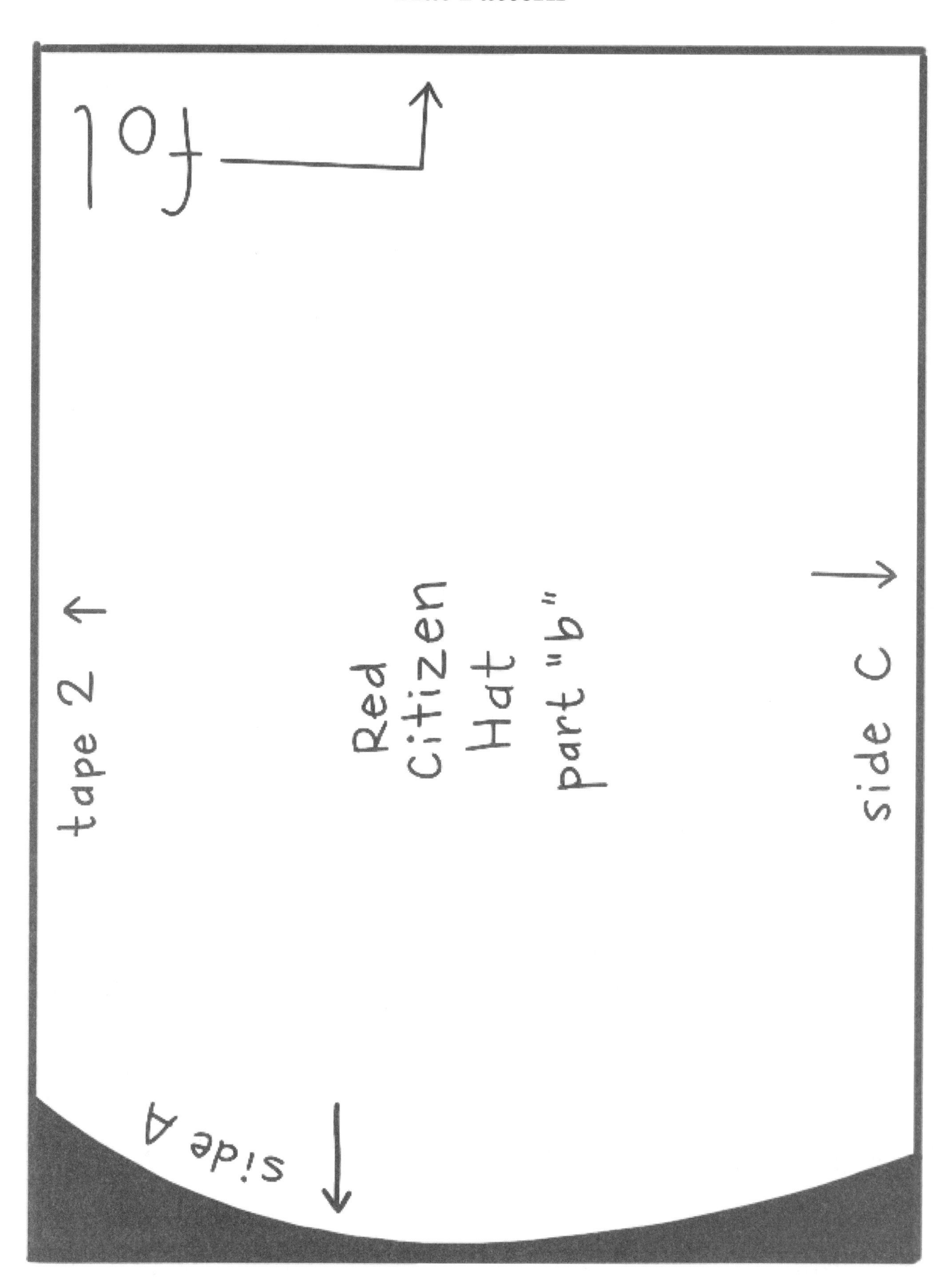

# The Declaration of Independence of the Thirteen Colonies

In Congress, July 4, 1776

The unanimous Declaration of the thirteen united States of America:

When in the Course of human events, it becomes necessary for one people to dissolve the political bands which have connected them with another, and to assume among the powers of the earth, the separate and equal station to which the Laws of Nature and of Nature's God entitle them, a decent respect to the opinions of mankind requires that they should declare the causes which impel them to the separation.

We hold these truths to be self-evident, that all men are created equal, that they are endowed by their Creator with certain unalienable Rights, that among these are Life, Liberty and the pursuit of Happiness.

That to secure these rights, Governments are instituted among Men, deriving their just powers from the consent of the governed, —That whenever any Form of Government becomes destructive of these ends, it is the Right of the People to alter or to abolish it, and to institute new Government, laying its foundation on such principles and organizing its powers in such form, as to them shall seem most likely to effect their Safety and Happiness. Prudence, indeed, will dictate that Governments long established should not be changed for light and transient causes; and accordingly all experience hath shewn, that mankind are more disposed to suffer, while evils are sufferable, than to right themselves by abolishing the forms to which they are accustomed.

# Declaration of the Rights of Man and of the Citizen

Approved by the National Assembly of France, August 26, 1789

The National Assembly recognizes and proclaims, in the presence and under the auspices of the Supreme Being, the following rights of man and of the citizen:

The representatives of the French people, organized as a National Assembly, believing that the ignorance, neglect, or contempt of the rights of man are the sole cause of public calamities and of the corruption of governments,

have determined to set forth in a solemn declaration the natural, unalienable, and sacred rights of man, in order that this declaration, being constantly before all the members of the Social body, shall remind them continually of their rights and duties;

in order that the acts of the legislative power, as well as those of the executive power, may be compared at any moment with the objects and purposes of all political institutions and may thus be more respected, and, lastly, in order that the grievances of the citizens, based hereafter upon simple and incontestable principles, shall tend to the maintenance of the constitution and redound to the happiness of all.

But when a long train of abuses and usurpations, pursuing invariably the same Object evinces a design to reduce them under absolute Despotism, it is their right, it is their duty, to throw off such Government, and to provide new Guards for their future security. —Such has been the patient sufferance of these Colonies; and such is now the necessity which constrains them to alter their former Systems of Government.

The history of the present King of Great Britain [George III] is a history of repeated injuries and usurpations, all having in direct object the establishment of an absolute Tyranny over these States. To prove this, let Facts be submitted to a candid world.

He has refused his Assent to Laws, the most wholesome and necessary for the public good.

He has forbidden his Governors to pass Laws of immediate and pressing importance, unless suspended in their operation till his Assent should be obtained; and when so suspended, he has utterly neglected to attend to them.

He has refused to pass other Laws for the accommodation of large districts of people, unless those people would relinquish the right of Representation in the Legislature, a right inestimable to them and formidable to tyrants only.

He has called together legislative bodies at places unusual, uncomfortable, and distant from the depository of their public Records, for the sole purpose of fatiguing them into compliance with his measures.

He has dissolved Representative Houses repeatedly, for opposing with manly firmness his invasions on the rights of the people.

He has refused for a long time, after such dissolutions, to cause others to be elected; whereby the Legislative powers, incapable of Annihilation, have returned to the People at large for their exercise; the State remaining in the mean

Articles:

1. Men are born and remain free and equal in rights.

2. The aim of all political association is the preservation of the natural rights of man. These rights are liberty, property, security, and resistance to oppression.

3. The principle of all sovereignty resides essentially in the nation. No body nor individual may exercise any authority which does not proceed directly from the nation.

time exposed to all the dangers of invasion from without, and convulsions within.
He has endeavoured to prevent the population of these States; for that purpose obstructing the Laws for Naturalization of Foreigners; refusing to pass others to encourage their migrations hither, and raising the conditions of new Appropriations of Lands.
He has obstructed the Administration of Justice, by refusing his Assent to Laws for establishing Judiciary powers.
He has made Judges dependent on his Will alone, for the tenure of their offices, and the amount and payment of their salaries.

He has erected a multitude of New Offices, and sent hither swarms of Officers to harass our people, and eat out their substance.
He has kept among us, in times of peace, Standing Armies without the consent of our legislatures.
He has affected to render the Military independent of and superior to the Civil power.

He has combined with others to subject us to a jurisdiction foreign to our constitution and unacknowledged by our laws; giving his Assent to their Acts of pretended Legislation:

For Quartering large bodies of armed troops among us: For protecting them, by a mock Trial, from punishment for any Murders which they should commit on the Inhabitants of these States: For cutting off our Trade with all parts of the world:

For imposing Taxes on us without our Consent:

4. Liberty consists in the freedom to do everything which injures no one else; hence the exercise of the natural rights of each man has no limits except those which assure to the other members of the society the enjoyment of the same rights. These limits can only be determined by law.

5. Law can only prohibit such actions as are hurtful to society. Nothing may be prevented which is not forbidden by law, and no one may be forced to do anything not provided for by law.

6. The security of the rights of man and of the citizen requires public military forces. These forces are, therefore, established for the good of all and not for the personal advantage of those to whom they shall be intrusted.

7. A common contribution is essential for the maintenance of the public forces and for the cost of administration. This should be equitably distributed among all the citizens in proportion to their means.
8. All the citizens have a right to decide, either personally or by their representatives, as to the necessity of the

For depriving us, in many cases, of the benefits of Trial by Jury: For transporting us beyond Seas to be tried for pretended offences:

For abolishing the free System of English Laws in a neighbouring Province, establishing therein an Arbitrary government, and enlarging its Boundaries so as to render it at once an example and fit instrument for introducing the same absolute rule into these Colonies:

For taking away our Charters, abolishing our most valuable Laws, and altering fundamentally the Forms of our Governments:

For suspending our own Legislatures, and declaring themselves invested with power to legislate for us in all cases whatsoever.

He has abdicated Government here, by declaring us out of his Protection and waging War against us.

He has plundered our seas, ravaged our Coasts, burnt our towns, and destroyed the lives of our people.

public contribution; to grant this freely; to know to what uses it is put; and to fix the proportion, the mode of assessment and of collection and the duration of the taxes.

9. No person shall be accused, arrested, or imprisoned except in the cases and according to the forms prescribed by law. Any one soliciting, transmitting, executing, or causing to be executed, any arbitrary order, shall be punished. But any citizen summoned or arrested in virtue of the law shall submit without delay, as resistance constitutes an offense.

10. The law shall provide for such punishments only as are strictly and obviously necessary, and no one shall suffer punishment except it be legally inflicted in virtue of a law passed and promulgated before the commission of the offense.

11. As all persons are held innocent until they shall have been declared guilty, if arrest shall be deemed indispensable, all harshness not essential to the securing of the prisoner's person shall be severely repressed by law.

12. Law is the expression of the general will. Every citizen has a right to participate personally, or through his representative, in its foundation. It must be the same for all, whether it protects or punishes. All citizens, being equal in the eyes of the law, are equally eligible to all dignities and to all public positions and occupations, according to their abilities, and without distinction except that of their virtues and talents.

13. Since property is an inviolable and sacred right, no one shall be deprived thereof except where public necessity,

He is at this time transporting large Armies of foreign Mercenaries to complete the works of death, desolation and tyranny, already begun with circumstances of Cruelty and perfidy scarcely paralleled in the most barbarous ages, and totally unworthy the Head of a civilized nation.

He has constrained our fellow Citizens taken Captive on the high Seas to bear Arms against their Country, to become the executioners of their friends and Brethren, or to fall themselves by their Hands....

legally determined, shall clearly demand it, and then only on condition that the owner shall have been previously and equitably indemnified.

In every stage of these Oppressions We have Petitioned for Redress in the most humble terms: Our repeated Petitions have been answered only by repeated injury. A Prince whose character is thus marked by every act which may define a Tyrant, is unfit to be the ruler of a free people.

Nor have We been wanting in attentions to our British brethren. We have warned them from time to time of attempts by their legislature to extend an unwarrantable jurisdiction over us. We have reminded them of the circumstances of our emigration and settlement here. We have appealed to their native justice and magnanimity, and we have conjured them by the ties of our common kindred to disavow these usurpations, which, would inevitably interrupt our connections and correspondence. They too have been deaf to the voice of justice and of consanguinity.

14. No one shall be disquieted on account of his opinions, including his religious views, provided their manifestation does not disturb the public order established by law.

15. The free communication of ideas and opinions is one of the most precious of the rights of man. Every citizen may, accordingly, speak, write, and print with freedom, but shall be responsible for such abuses of this freedom as shall be defined by law.

16. Society has the right to require of every public agent an account of his administration.

We must, therefore, acquiesce in the necessity, which denounces our Separation, and hold them, as we hold the rest of mankind, Enemies in War, in Peace Friends.

We, therefore, the Representatives of the united States of America, in General Congress, Assembled, appealing to the Supreme Judge of the world for the rectitude of our intentions, do, in the Name, and by the Authority of the good People of these Colonies, solemnly publish and declare, That these United Colonies are, and of Right ought to be Free and Independent States; that they are Absolved from all Allegiance to the British

17. A society in which the observance of the law is not assured, nor the separation of powers defined, has no constitution at all.

Crown, and that all political connection between them and the State of Great Britain, is and ought to be totally dissolved; and that as Free and Independent States, they have full Power to levy War, conclude Peace, contract Alliances, establish Commerce, and to do all other Acts and Things which Independent States may of right do. And for the support of this Declaration, with a firm reliance on the protection of divine Providence, we mutually pledge to each other our Lives, our Fortunes and our sacred Honor.

New Hampshire: Josiah Bartlett, William Whipple, Matthew Thornton

Massachusetts: John Hancock, Samuel Adams, John Adams, Robert Treat Paine, Elbridge Gerry

Rhode Island: Stephen Hopkins, William Ellery

Connecticut: Roger Sherman, Samuel Huntington, William Williams, Oliver Wolcott

New York: William Floyd, Philip Livingston, Francis Lewis, Lewis Morris

New Jersey: Richard Stockton, John Witherspoon, Francis Hopkinson, John Hart, Abraham Clark

Pennsylvania: Robert Morris, Benjamin Rush, Benjamin Franklin, John Morton, George Clymer, James Smith, George Taylor, James Wilson, George Ross

Delaware: Caesar Rodney, George Read, Thomas McKean

Maryland: Samuel Chase, William Paca, Thomas Stone, Charles Carroll of Carrollton

Virginia: George Wythe, Richard Henry Lee, Thomas Jefferson, Benjamin Harrison, Thomas Nelson, Jr., Francis Lightfoot Lee, Carter Braxton

North Carolina: William Hooper, Joseph Hewes, John Penn

South Carolina: Edward Rutledge, Thomas Heyward, Jr., Thomas Lynch, Jr., Arthur Middleton

Georgia: Button Gwinnett, Lyman Hall, George Walton

Louis XVI

European Ideas in Russia
NETHERLANDS
GREAT BRITAIN
DENMARK-NORWAY
SWEDEN
Narva
Archangel
St. Petersburg
RUSSIA
Moscow
Kiel
Baltic Sea
German states
Prussia
FRANCE
SPAIN
Azov
Black Sea
Caspian Sea
Mediterranean Sea
Africa

# Catherine the Great

# Catherine the Great Paper Doll

# Catherine the Great Paper Doll

# Catherine the Great Paper Doll

# Catherine the Great Paper Doll

# Be the Next Czar of Russia!

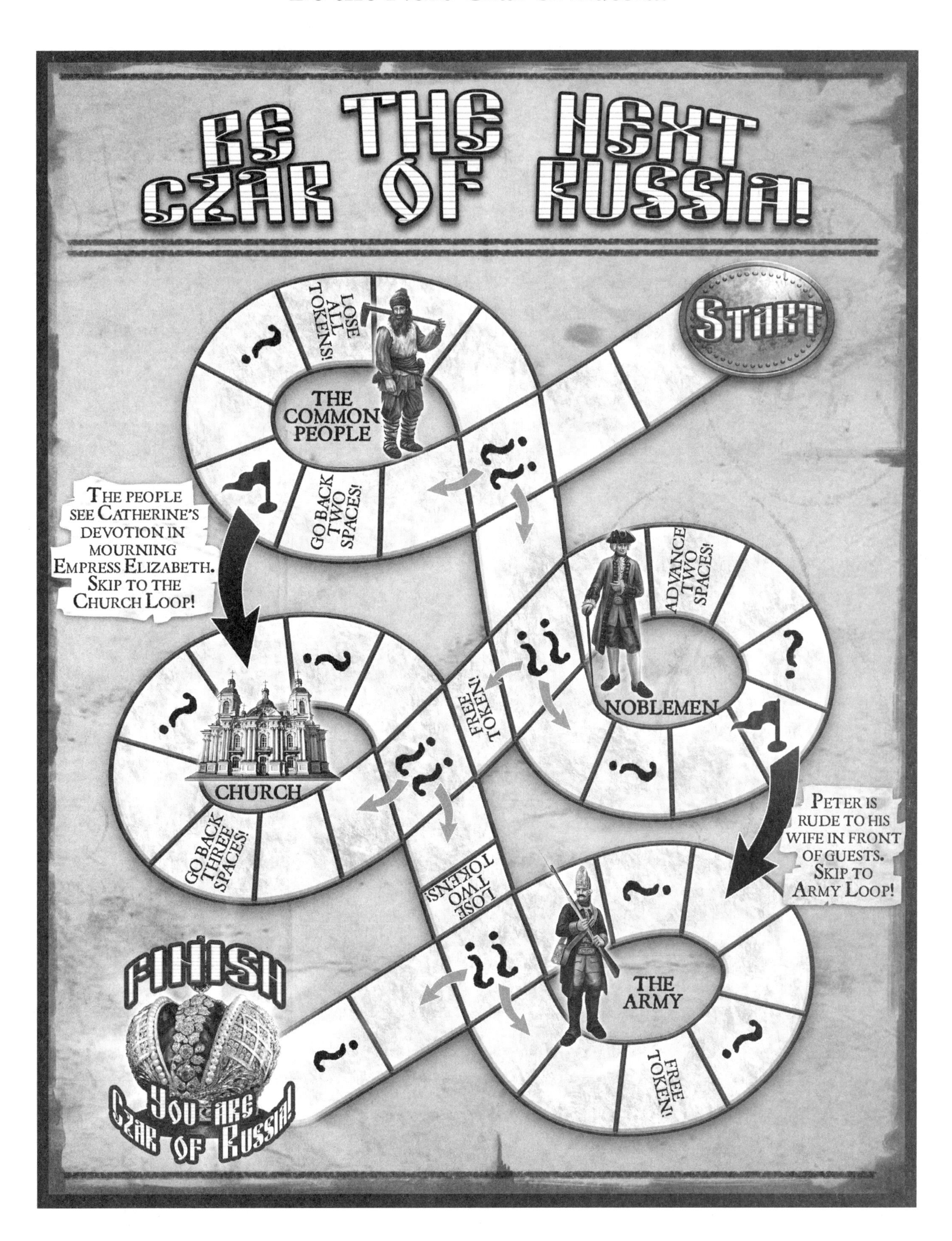

# Edward Jenner Administering Vaccinations

# Industrial Revolution in Britain and America

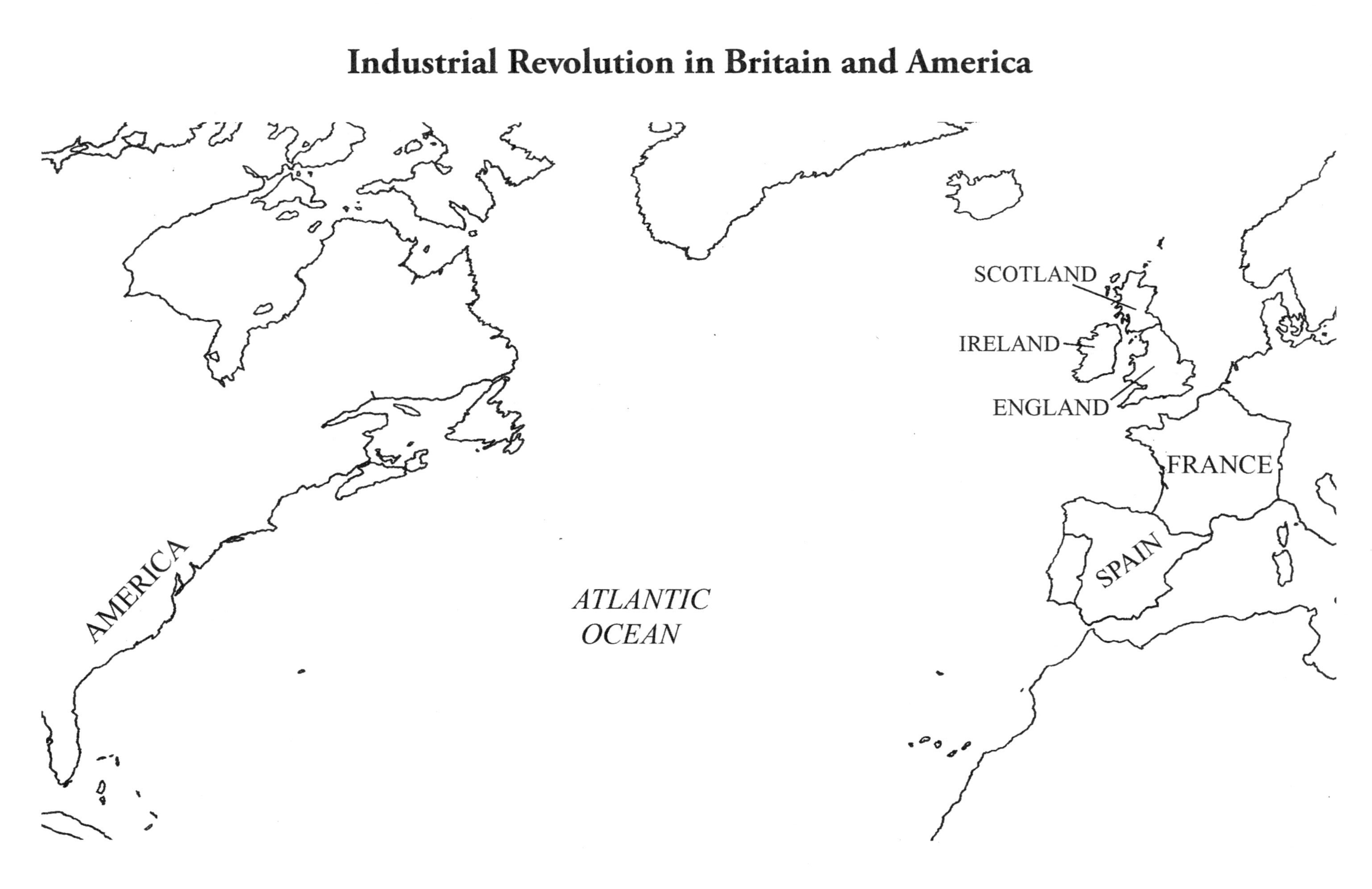

# A Steam Engine

# House of Interchangeable Parts BINGO!

| House of Interchangeable Parts | | | | |
|---|---|---|---|---|
| | | | | |
| | | | | |
| | | FREE | | |
| | | | | |
| | | | | |

| House of Interchangeable Parts | | | | |
|---|---|---|---|---|
| Mixer | Washing Machine | Oven | Drill | Vacuum Cleaner |
| Door Knob | Phone | Lamp | Piano | Garage Door Opener |
| Auto | Com-puter | FREE | Fridge | Water Faucet |
| Window | Lawn Mower | Pencil Sharpen-er | Bunk Beds | Blender |
| DVD Player | Freezer | Dryer | Printer | Dish Washer |

| House of Interchangeable Parts | | | | |
|---|---|---|---|---|
| Door Knob | Garage Door Opener | Blender | VCR | Com-puter |
| Dish Washer | Water Faucet | DVD Player | Radio | Oven |
| Printer | Washing Machine | FREE | Phone | Lawn Mower |
| Pencil Sharp-ener | Lamp | TV | Bunk Beds | Dryer |
| Drill | Mixer | Vacuum Cleaner | Fridge | Auto |

# Patent Application

DIRECTIONS: Sketch your invention in the space below. Be as detailed as you can!

DIRECTIONS: Answer the following questions in complete sentences on the lines given.

1. What does my invention do? How is it built? ____________________
________________________________________
________________________________________
________________________________________
________________________________________

2. What existing inventions have similarities to my invention? What makes my invention different? __
________________________________________
________________________________________
________________________________________

3. Will people find my invention useful? Why will they want to buy it? ____________________
________________________________________
________________________________________
________________________________________

# The Kingdom at the Center of the World

GREAT BRITAIN

Europe

RUSSIA

CHINA

Peking

Canton

INDIA

Africa

# The Chinese Emperor and the British Ambassador

# Napoleon, Europe, and North America

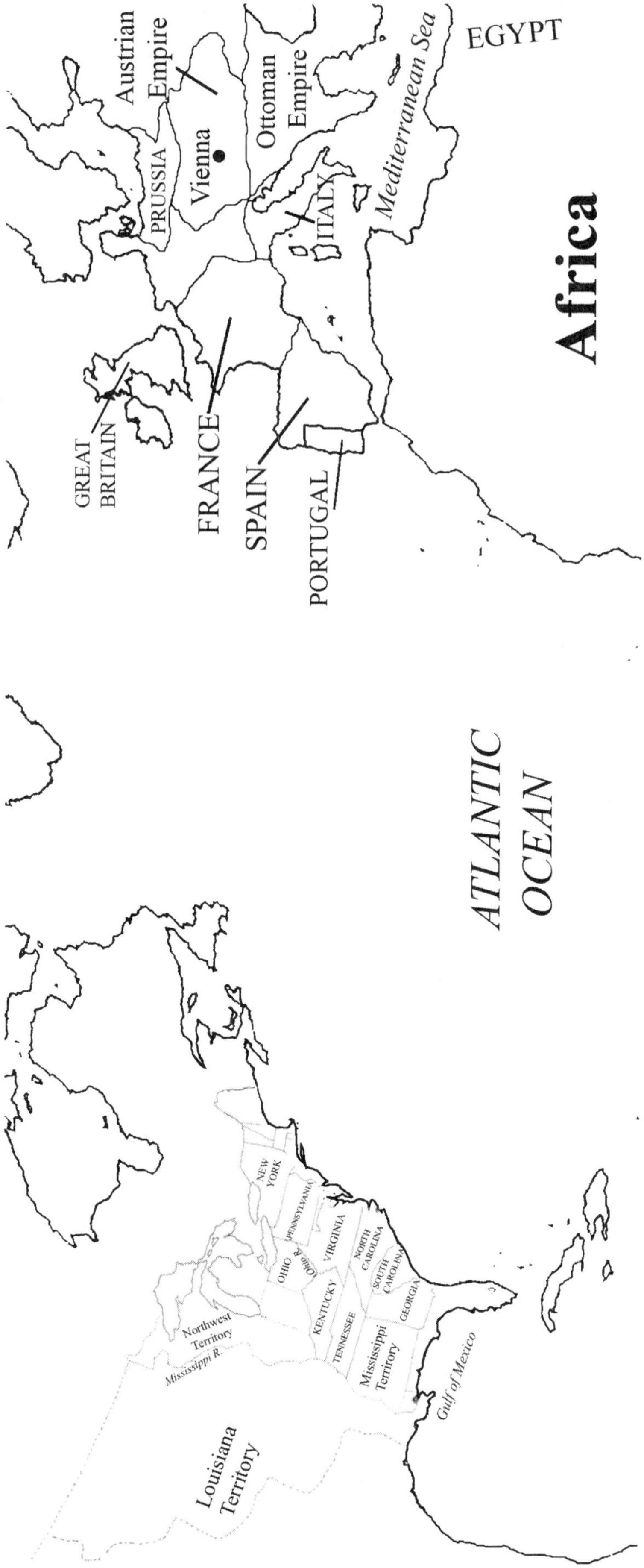

Austrian Empire
Ottoman Empire
EGYPT
PRUSSIA
Vienna
Mediterranean Sea
ITALY
GREAT BRITAIN
FRANCE
SPAIN
PORTUGAL
Africa
ATLANTIC OCEAN
NEW YORK
PENNSYLVANIA
OHIO
VIRGINIA
NORTH CAROLINA
SOUTH CAROLINA
GEORGIA
KENTUCKY
TENNESSEE
Mississippi Territory
Northwest Territory
Mississippi R.
Louisiana Territory
Gulf of Mexico

# Napoleon

CONQUER THE WORLD
THE FRENCH
THE BRITISH
FINISH
NAPOLEON BONAPARTE

# Conquer the World—French Cards

| | | |
|---|---|---|
| Tell everything you remember about Chapter 29.<br>Move ahead 3 spaces. | What was the response of the French people when Napoleon came back from Egypt?<br>Move ahead 1 space. | Napoleon urged the Council of Ancients to scrap the Directory and replace it with three Consuls, like ancient Rome. What did they do?<br>Move ahead 1 space. |
| What kind of government did France have after the French Revolution?<br>Move ahead 1 space. | Who fought at the "Battle of the Nile"?<br>Move ahead 1 space. | Tell something that you read about from the *Story of the World* this year so far.<br>Move ahead 2 spaces. |
| Did the French Revolution happen before or after the American Revolution?<br>Move ahead 2 spaces. | Who scoffed: "Do you suppose that I have gained my victories in Italy in order to advance the lawyers of the Directory?"<br>Move ahead 1 space. | Napoleon became the only Consul of France. What did the people think?<br>Move ahead 1 space. |
| How many men were elected to the Directory?<br>Move ahead 3 spaces. | Who said: "I have come to restore your rights and fight against the Turks who hold you captive!" and who did he say it to?<br>Move ahead 1 space. | Who said, "The French are infatuated [with the idea of liberty] but it will pass away in time...."<br>Move ahead 1 space. |
| France became an oligarchy. What is an oligarchy?<br>Move ahead 2 spaces. | The Directory agreed to Napoleon's plan to invade Egypt. Why?<br>Move ahead 1 space. | In Napoleon's new code of law, he ordered that each person be treated equally except a few. What were some of the exceptions?<br>Move ahead 1 space. |
| True or False? Austria was at war with France when Napoleon Bonaparte was called to help.<br>Move ahead 1 space. | Instead of invading Great Britain, Napoleon suggested invading where?<br>Move ahead 1 space. | What did Napoleon's new constitution say?<br>Move ahead 2 spaces. |
| Who said, "It is better to eat than be eaten"?<br>Move ahead 1 space. | Napoleon was told to invade Great Britain. What did he do?<br>Move ahead 1 space. | Napoleon needed money to expand his empire into Europe. Where did he get the money?<br>Move ahead 1 space. |
| Napoleon's troops were hungry and hadn't been paid, yet they were off to fight against the Austrians. What did Napoleon do?<br>Move ahead 1 space. | The 5 members of the Directory knew that Napoleon wanted power for himself. What did they do?<br>Move ahead 1 space. | Emperor Napoleon aimed at his old enemy. What country was that?<br>Move ahead 1 space. |
| When Napoleon fought the Austrians in Italy, who won?<br>Move ahead 1 space. | When Napoleon headed for Vienna, what did the Austrians do?<br>Move ahead 1 space. | What was Emperor Napoleon's plan to invade England?<br>Move ahead 3 spaces. |
| Who said, "Not all Frenchmen are robbers--but a good many sure are!"<br>Move ahead 1 space. | Tell something that you read about from the *Story of the World* this year so far.<br>Move ahead 1 space. | Who won between Emperor Napoleon and the British?<br>Move ahead 1 space. |

# Conquer the World—British Cards

| | | |
|---|---|---|
| Tell everything you remember about Chapter 29.<br>Move ahead 3 spaces. | When the British saw the boat building by Emperor Napoleon, what did they do?<br>Move ahead 1 space. | How many French ships were sunk against the British in the Battle of Trafalgar?<br>Move ahead 1 space. |
| What kind of government did France have after the French Revolution?<br>Move ahead 1 space. | How did the British get so many sailors to help fight Napoleon?<br>Move ahead 1 space. | Tell something that you read about from the *Story of the World* this year so far.<br>Move ahead 2 spaces. |
| Did the French Revolution happen before or after the American Revolution?<br>Move ahead 2 spaces. | What did the Battle of Trafalgar solve?<br>Move ahead 1 space. | What happened to the soldiers' boats that were waiting on France's side during the Battle of Trafalgar?<br>Move ahead 1 space. |
| What happened at the Battle of the Nile?<br>Move ahead 3 spaces. | Who was the commander of the English fleet in the Battle of Trafalgar?<br>Move ahead 1 space. | Who said, "The French are infatuated [with the idea of liberty] but it will pass away in time…."<br>Move ahead 1 space. |
| France became an oligarchy. What is an oligarchy?<br>Move ahead 2 spaces. | Who was Admiral Horatio Nelson and why was he such an enemy of Napoleon?<br>Move ahead 1 space. | What was the name of the decisive battle between the British and French Navies which was fought off the tip of southern Spain?<br>Move ahead 1 space. |
| True or False? Britain was an enemy of France.<br>Move ahead 1 space. | What did British Admiral Nelson do when Emperor Napoleon led an attack on Britain?<br>Move ahead 1 space. | Admiral Nelson saved England from the new Emperor, but what happened to him?<br>Move ahead 2 spaces. |
| True or False? After Napoleon became Emperor, he arrested all of the British citizens in France.<br>Move ahead 1 space. | What was Admiral Horatio Nelson's flagship named at the Battle of Trafalgar?<br>Move ahead 1 space. | Napoleon needed money to expand his empire into Europe. Where did he get the money?<br>Move ahead 1 space. |
| When Emperor Napoleon arrested all the British citizens in France, what did Britain do?<br>Move ahead 1 space. | Who said, "England expects that every man will do his duty!"?<br>Move ahead 1 space. | Emperor Napoleon aimed at his old enemy. What country was that?<br>Move ahead 1 space. |
| True or False? French and British ships prowled the seas, shooting at each other.<br>Move ahead 1 space. | How many British ships were sunk against Emperor Napoleon in the Battle of Trafalgar off the coast of Spain?<br>Move ahead 1 space. | What was Emperor Napoleon's plan to invade England?<br>Move ahead 3 spaces. |
| Who said, "20,000 men? I would lose that many in a battle anyway."<br>Move ahead 1 space. | Tell something that you read about from the *Story of the World* this year so far.<br>Move ahead 1 space. | Who won between Emperor Napoleon and the British at the Battle of Trafalgar?<br>Move ahead 1 space. |

# North America and Western Europe

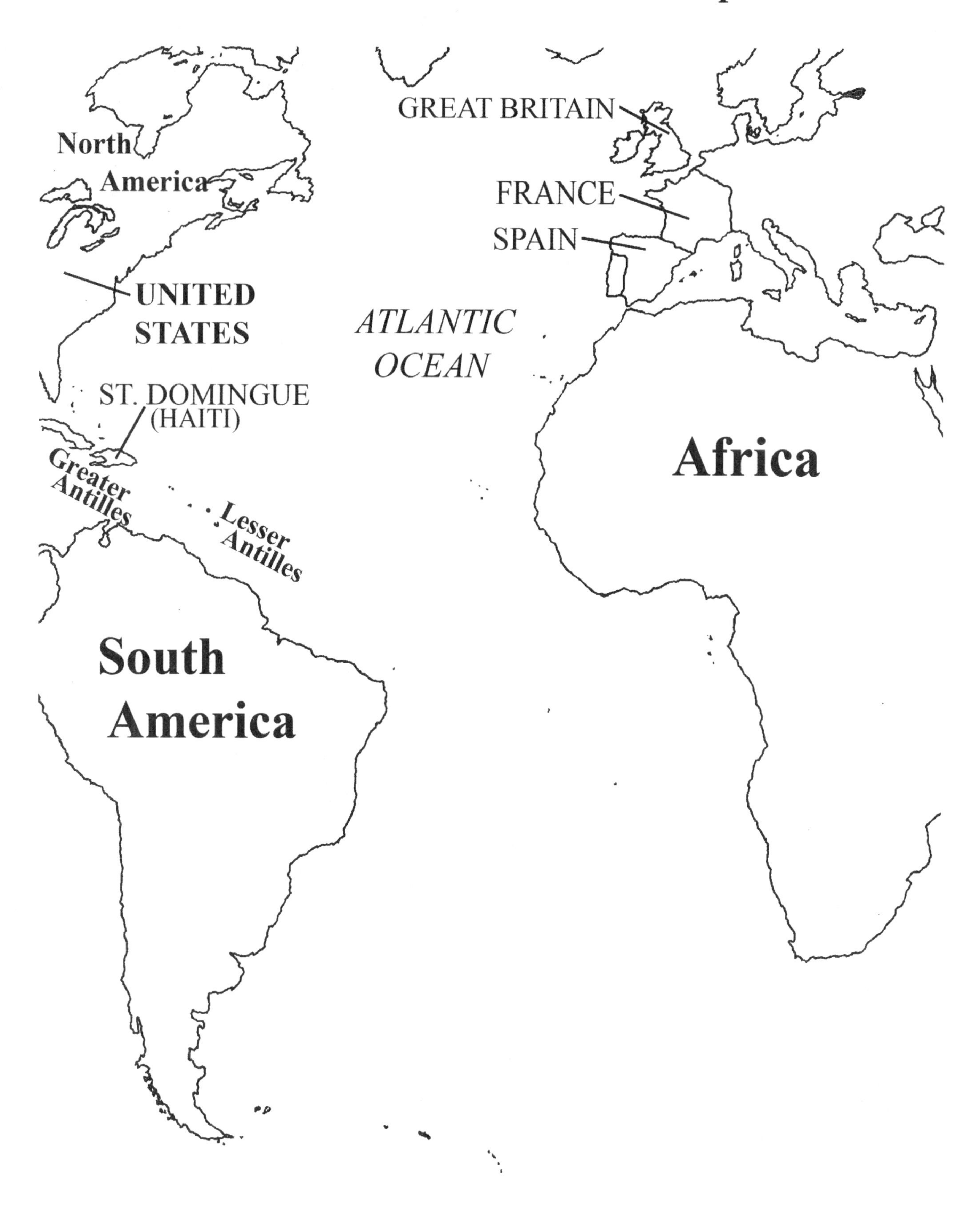

# Toussaint L'Ouverture

# Haitian Tree Stamp

# The Haitian Flag

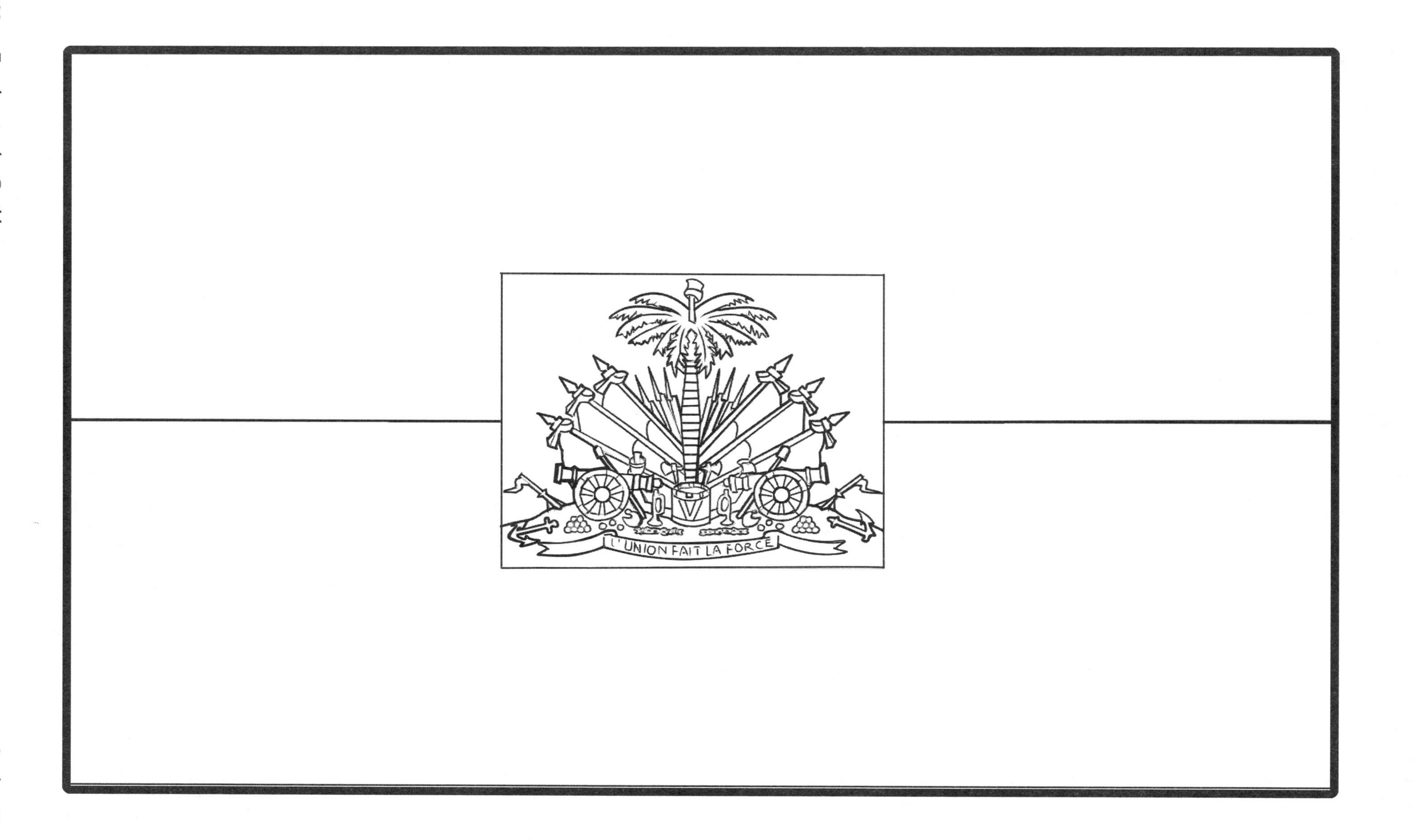

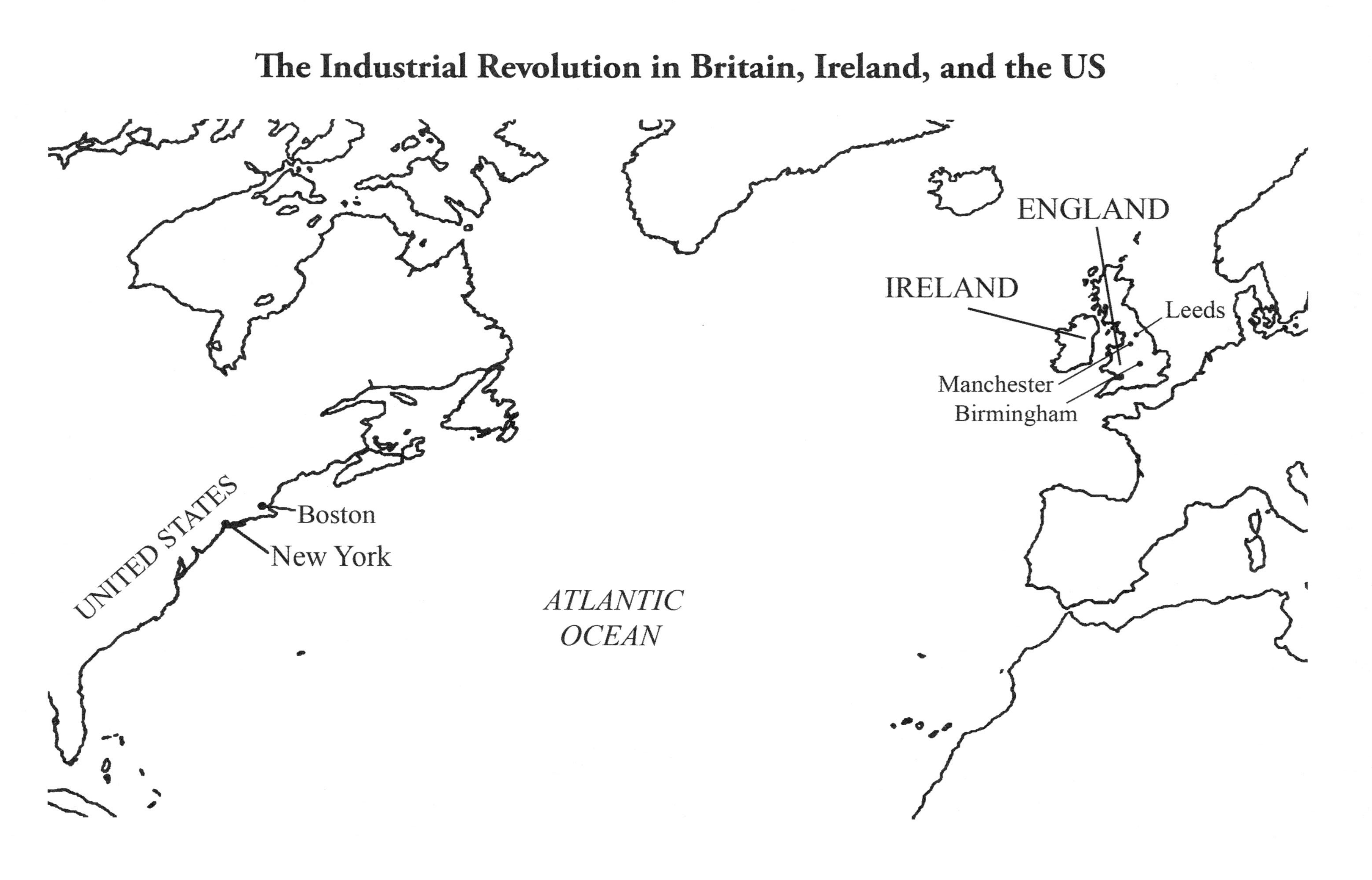
The Industrial Revolution in Britain, Ireland, and the US
ENGLAND
IRELAND
Leeds
Manchester
Birmingham
UNITED STATES
Boston
New York
ATLANTIC
OCEAN

# The Luddites Attack a Weaving Machine

# US Territories

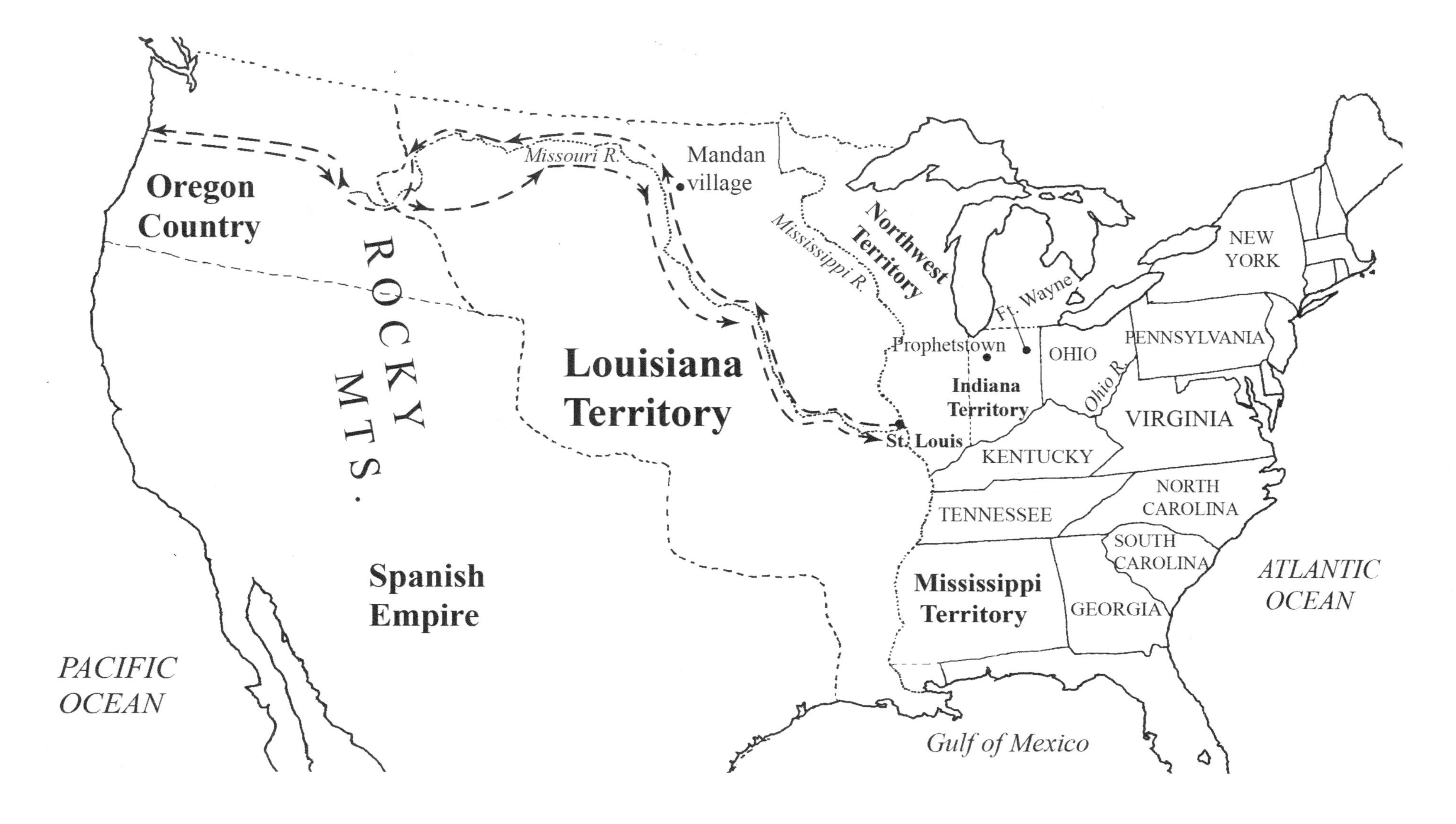

# Sacagawea and Her Son

# Jefferson's Secret Code

| | a | & | b | c | d | e | f | g | h | i | j | k | l | m | n | o | p | q | **r** | **s** | **t** | **u** | **v** | **w** | **x** | **y** | **z** |
|---|---|---|---|---|---|---|---|---|---|---|---|---|---|---|---|---|---|---|---|---|---|---|---|---|---|---|---|
| **a** | b | c | d | e | f | g | h | i | j | k | l | m | n | o | p | q | r | s | t | u | v | w | x | y | z | & | 1 |
| **b** | c | d | e | f | g | h | i | j | k | l | m | n | o | p | q | r | s | t | u | v | w | x | y | z | & | a | 2 |
| **c** | d | e | f | g | h | i | j | k | l | m | n | o | p | q | r | s | t | u | v | w | x | y | z | & | a | b | 3 |
| **d** | e | f | g | h | i | j | k | l | m | n | o | p | q | r | s | t | u | v | w | x | y | z | & | a | b | c | 4 |
| **e** | f | g | h | i | j | k | l | m | n | o | p | q | r | s | t | u | v | w | x | y | z | & | a | b | c | d | 5 |
| **f** | g | h | i | j | k | l | m | n | o | p | q | r | s | t | u | v | w | x | y | z | & | a | b | c | d | e | 6 |
| **g** | h | i | j | k | l | m | n | o | p | q | r | s | t | u | v | w | x | y | z | & | a | b | c | d | e | f | 7 |
| **h** | i | j | k | l | m | n | o | p | q | r | s | t | u | v | w | x | y | z | & | a | b | c | d | e | f | g | 8 |
| **i** | j | k | l | m | n | o | p | q | r | s | t | u | v | w | x | y | z | & | a | b | c | d | e | f | g | h | 9 |
| **j** | k | l | m | n | o | p | q | r | s | t | u | v | w | x | y | z | & | a | b | c | d | e | f | g | h | i | 0 |
| **k** | l | m | n | o | p | q | r | s | t | u | v | w | x | y | z | & | a | b | c | d | e | f | g | h | i | j | |
| **l** | m | n | o | p | q | r | s | t | u | v | w | x | y | z | & | a | b | c | d | e | f | g | h | i | j | k | |
| **m** | n | o | p | q | r | s | t | u | v | w | x | y | z | & | a | b | c | d | e | f | g | h | i | j | k | l | |
| **n** | o | p | q | r | s | t | u | v | w | x | y | z | & | a | b | c | d | e | f | g | h | i | j | k | l | m | |
| **o** | p | q | r | s | t | u | v | w | x | y | z | & | a | b | c | d | e | f | g | h | i | j | k | l | m | n | |
| **p** | q | r | s | t | u | v | w | x | y | z | & | a | b | c | d | e | f | g | h | i | j | k | l | m | n | o | |
| **q** | r | s | t | u | v | w | x | y | z | & | a | b | c | d | e | f | g | h | i | j | k | l | m | n | o | p | |
| **r** | s | t | u | v | w | x | y | z | & | a | b | c | d | e | f | g | h | i | j | k | l | m | n | o | p | q | |
| **s** | t | u | v | w | x | y | z | & | a | b | c | d | e | f | g | h | i | j | k | l | m | n | o | p | q | r | |
| **t** | u | v | w | x | y | z | & | a | b | c | d | e | f | g | h | i | j | k | l | m | n | o | p | q | r | s | |
| u | v | w | x | y | z | & | a | b | c | d | e | f | g | h | i | j | k | l | m | n | o | p | q | r | s | t | |
| **v** | w | x | y | z | & | a | b | c | d | e | f | g | h | i | j | k | l | m | n | o | p | q | r | s | t | u | |
| **w** | x | y | z | & | a | b | c | d | e | f | g | h | i | j | k | l | m | n | o | p | q | r | s | t | u | v | |
| **x** | y | z | & | a | b | c | d | e | f | g | h | i | j | k | l | m | n | o | p | q | r | s | t | u | v | w | |
| **y** | z | & | a | b | c | d | e | f | g | h | i | j | k | l | m | n | o | p | q | r | s | t | u | v | w | x | |
| **z** | & | a | b | c | d | e | f | g | h | i | j | k | l | m | n | o | p | q | r | s | t | u | v | w | x | y | |
| **&** | a | b | c | d | e | f | g | h | i | j | k | l | m | n | o | p | q | r | s | t | u | v | w | x | y | z | |

# Napoleon in Europe and Russia, and Britain's War With the US

# The Battle of Waterloo

# The Star-Spangled Banner

By Francis Scott Key

Oh, say can you see by the dawn's early light
What so proudly we hailed at the twilight's last gleaming?
Whose broad stripes and bright stars thru the perilous fight,
O'er the ramparts we watched were so gallantly streaming?
And the rockets' red glare, the bombs bursting in air,
Gave proof through the night that our flag was still there.
Oh, say does that star-spangled banner yet wave
O'er the land of the free and the home of the brave?

On the shore, dimly seen through the mists of the deep,
Where the foe's haughty host in dread silence reposes,
What is that which the breeze, o'er the towering steep,
As it fitfully blows, half conceals, half discloses?
Now it catches the gleam of the morning's first beam,
In full glory reflected now shines in the stream:
'Tis the star-spangled banner! Oh long may it wave
O'er the land of the free and the home of the brave!

And where is that band who so vauntingly swore
That the havoc of war and the battle's confusion,
A home and a country should leave us no more?
Their blood has washed out their foul footsteps' pollution.
No refuge could save the hireling and slave
From the terror of flight, or the gloom of the grave:
And the star-spangled banner in triumph doth wave
O'er the land of the free and the home of the brave!

Oh! thus be it ever, when freemen shall stand
Between their loved home and the war's desolation!
Blest with victory and peace, may the heav'n rescued land
Praise the Power that hath made and preserved us a nation.
Then conquer we must, when our cause it is just,
And this be our motto: "In God is our trust."
And the star-spangled banner in triumph shall wave
O'er the land of the free and the home of the brave!

# St. Helena Salt Map Graphic

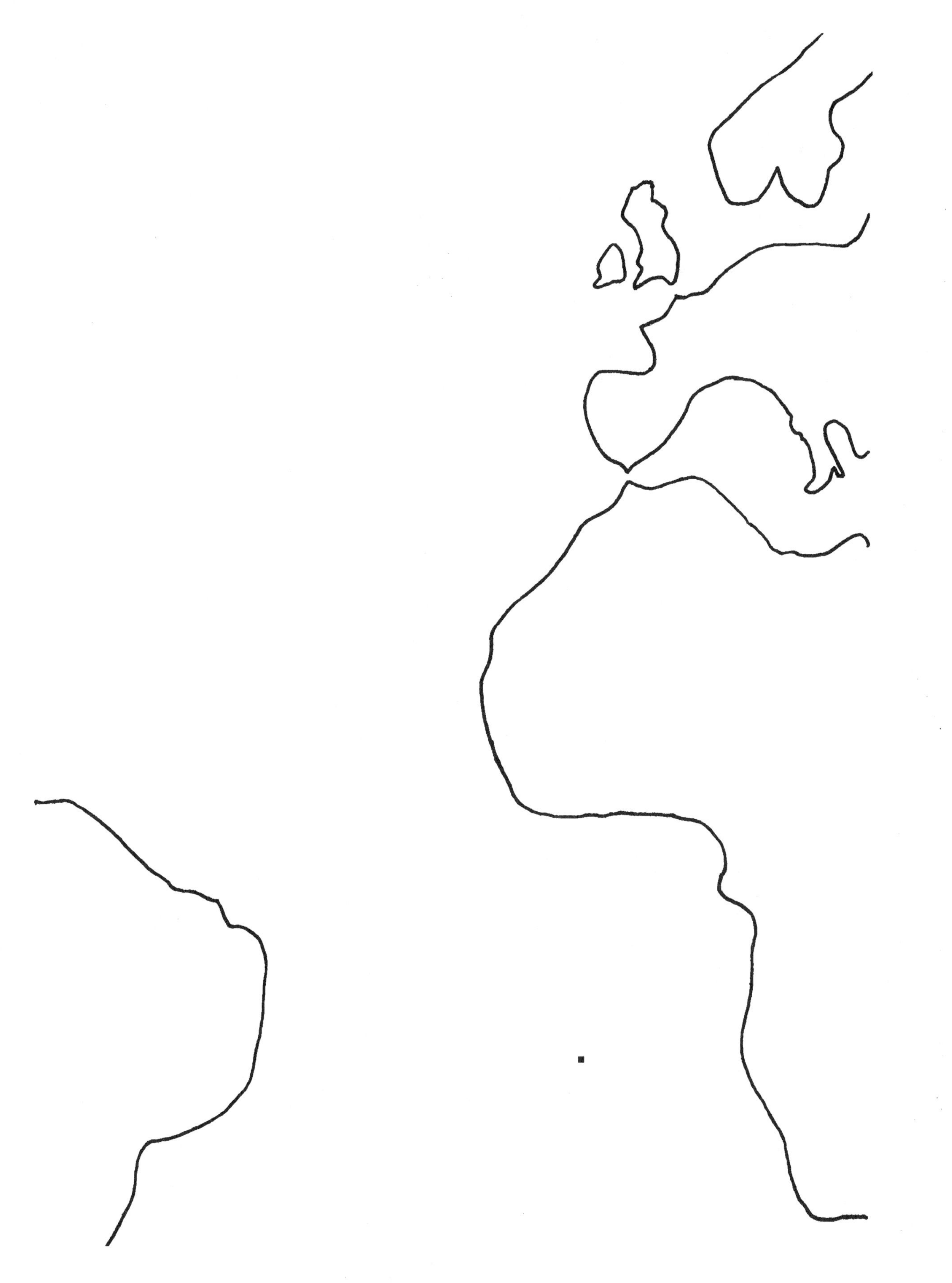

# Spain and its Colonies in South America

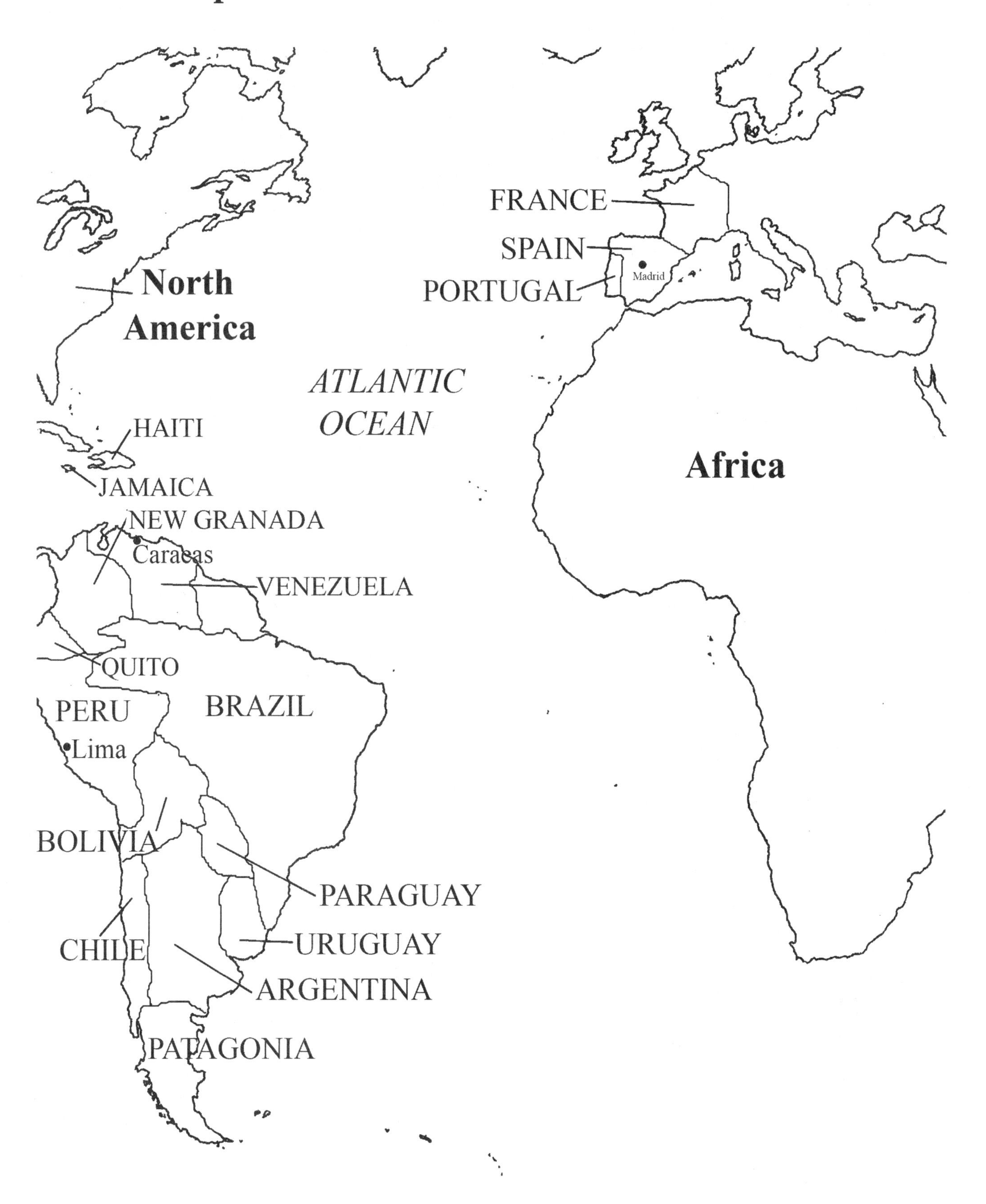

# Simón Bolivar, the Liberator

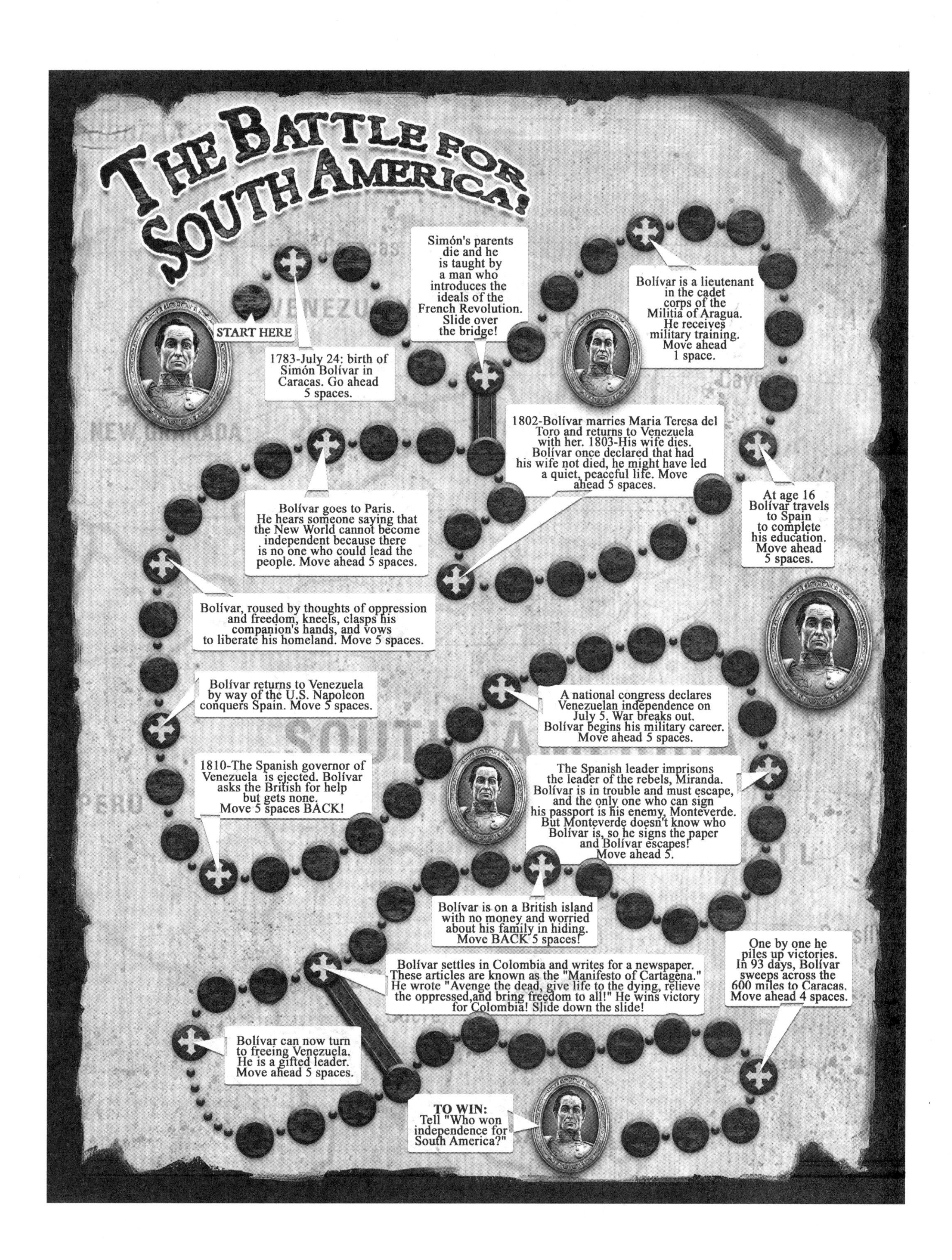
THE BATTLE FOR SOUTH AMERICA!
START HERE
1783-July 24: birth of Simón Bolívar in Caracas. Go ahead 5 spaces.
Simón's parents die and he is taught by a man who introduces the ideals of the French Revolution. Slide over the bridge!
Bolívar is a lieutenant in the cadet corps of the Militia of Aragua. He receives military training. Move ahead 1 space.
At age 16 Bolívar travels to Spain to complete his education. Move ahead 5 spaces.
1802-Bolívar marries Maria Teresa del Toro and returns to Venezuela with her. 1803-His wife dies. Bolívar once declared that had his wife not died, he might have led a quiet, peaceful life. Move ahead 5 spaces.
Bolívar goes to Paris. He hears someone saying that the New World cannot become independent because there is no one who could lead the people. Move ahead 5 spaces.
Bolívar, roused by thoughts of oppression and freedom, kneels, clasps his companion's hands, and vows to liberate his homeland. Move 5 spaces.
Bolívar returns to Venezuela by way of the U.S. Napoleon conquers Spain. Move 5 spaces.
1810-The Spanish governor of Venezuela is ejected. Bolívar asks the British for help but gets none. Move 5 spaces BACK!
A national congress declares Venezuelan independence on July 5. War breaks out. Bolívar begins his military career. Move ahead 5 spaces.
The Spanish leader imprisons the leader of the rebels, Miranda. Bolívar is in trouble and must escape, and the only one who can sign his passport is his enemy, Monteverde. But Monteverde doesn't know who Bolívar is, so he signs the paper and Bolívar escapes! Move ahead 5.
Bolívar is on a British island with no money and worried about his family in hiding. Move BACK 5 spaces!
Bolívar settles in Colombia and writes for a newspaper. These articles are known as the "Manifesto of Cartagena." He wrote "Avenge the dead, give life to the dying, relieve the oppressed,and bring freedom to all!" He wins victory for Colombia! Slide down the slide!
Bolívar can now turn to freeing Venezuela. He is a gifted leader. Move ahead 5 spaces.
One by one he piles up victories. In 93 days, Bolívar sweeps across the 600 miles to Caracas. Move ahead 4 spaces.
TO WIN: Tell "Who won independence for South America?"

# Gaucho Paper Doll

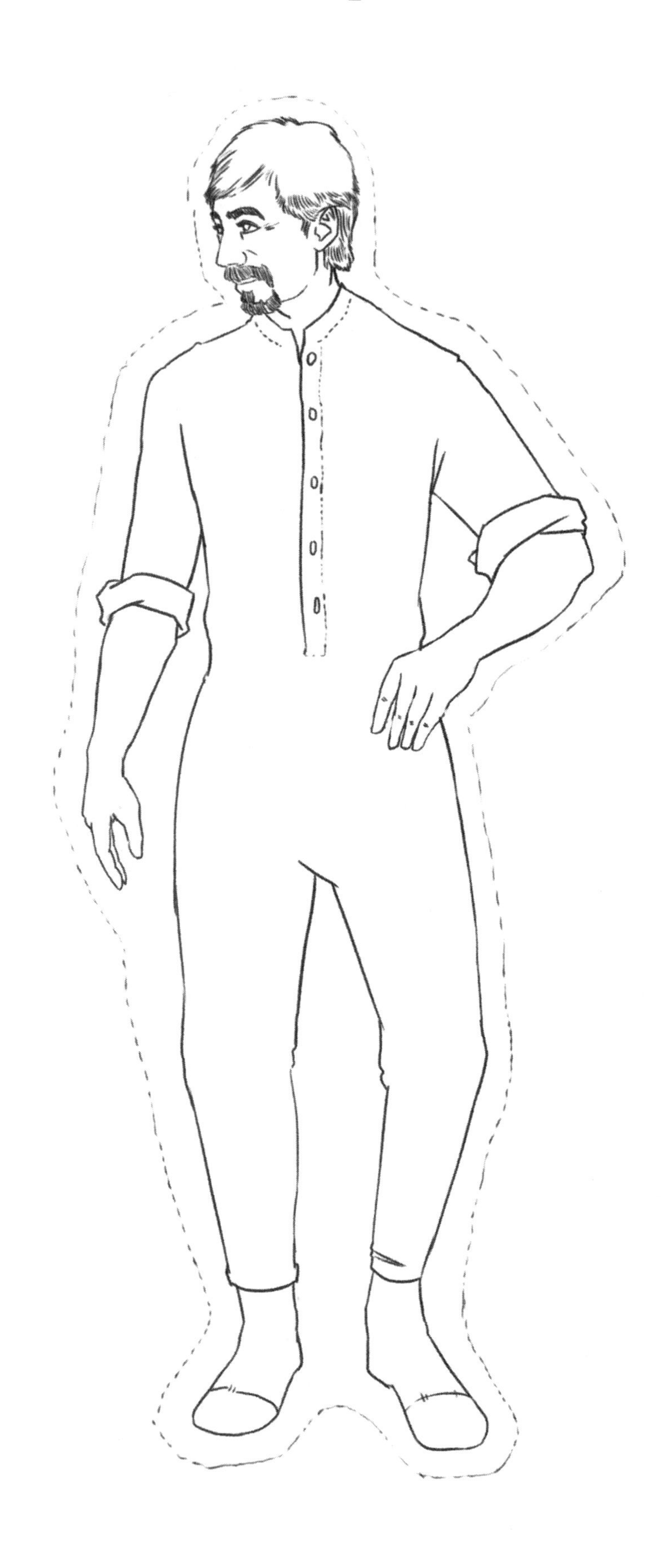

# Gaucho Paper Doll Outfits

# New Spain and North America

# Don Miguel de Hidalgo

## The Slave Trade

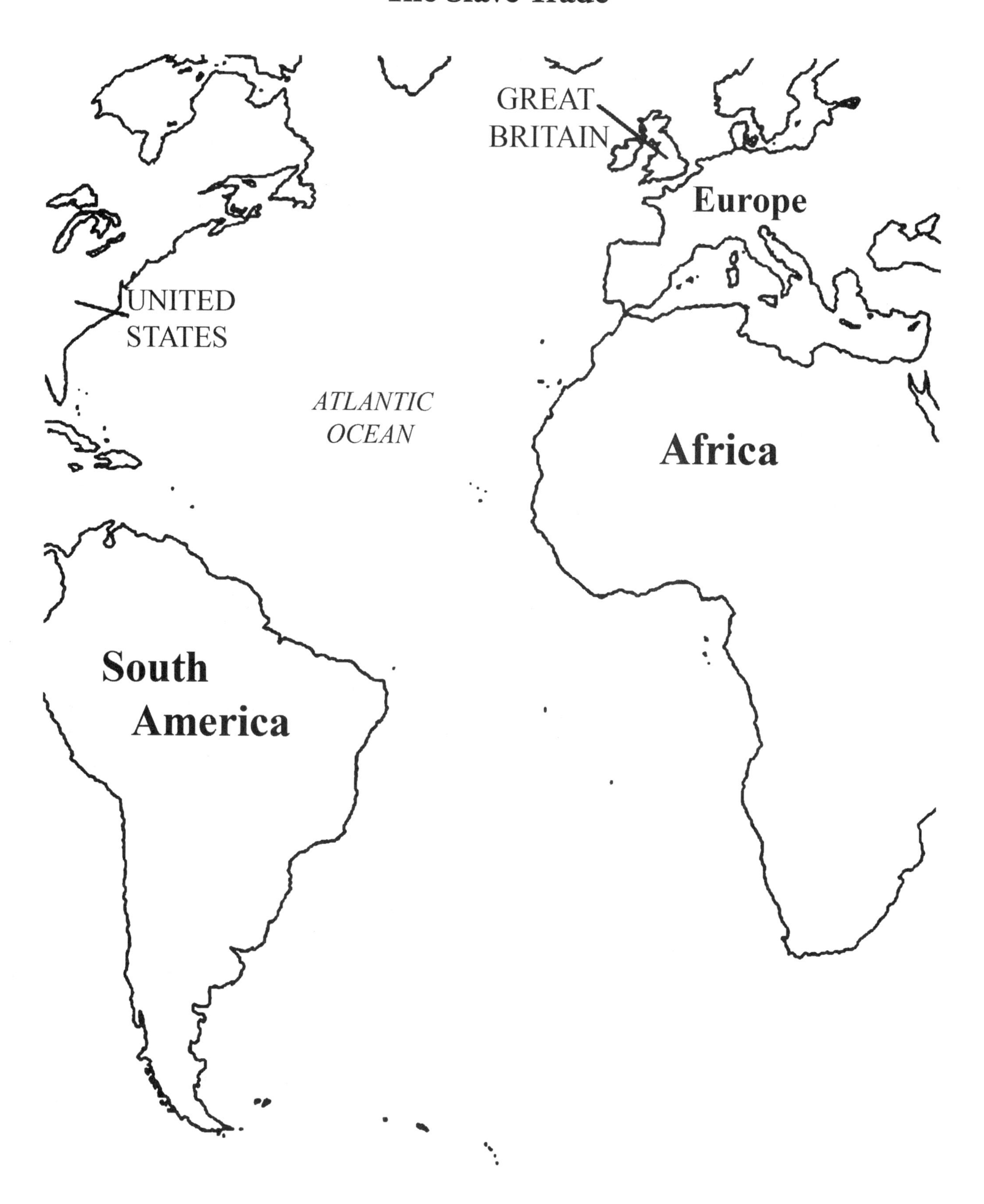

# Olaudah Equiano Writes About Slavery

# Slave Ship (Part A)

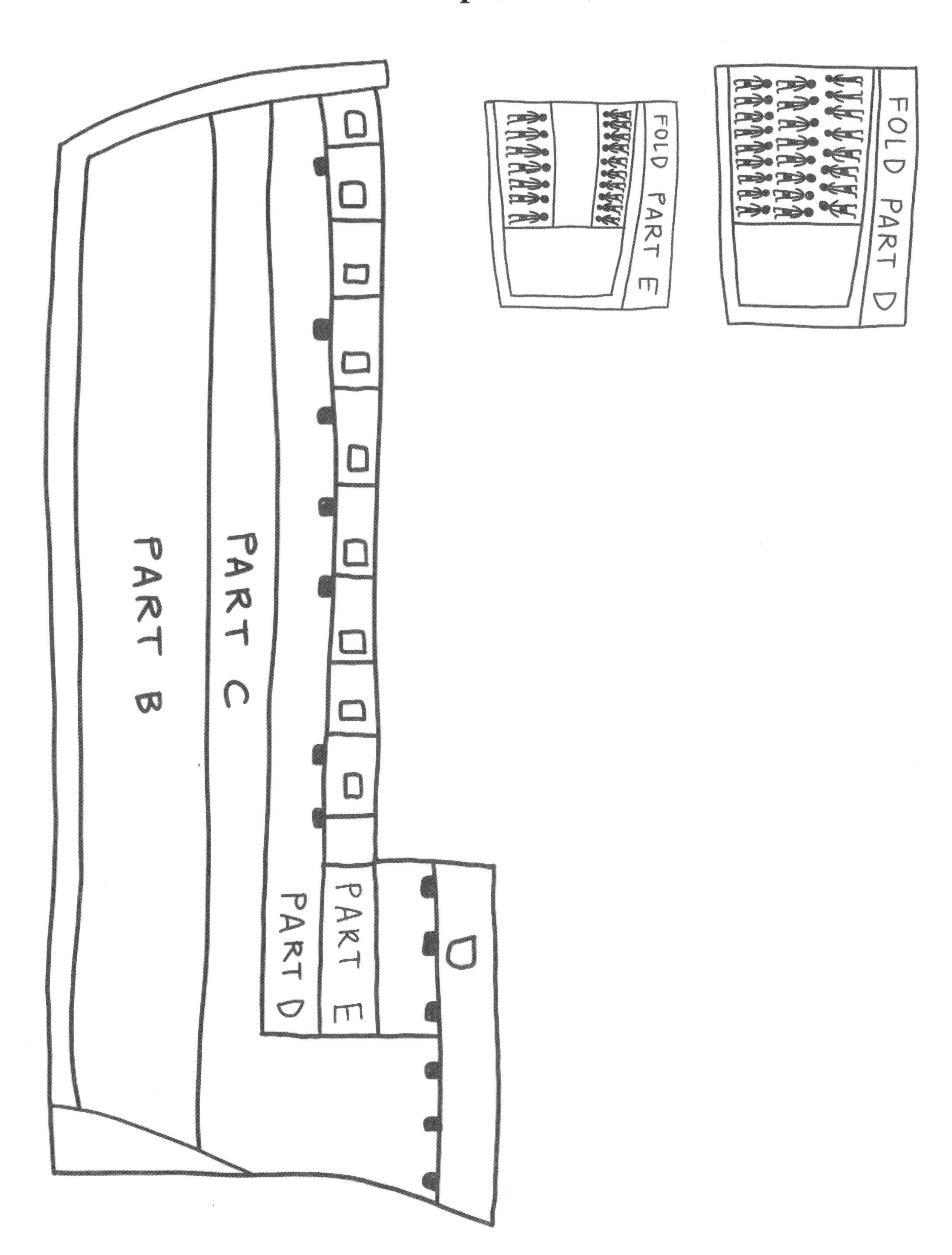

# Slaveship Bottom and Middle (Parts B and C)

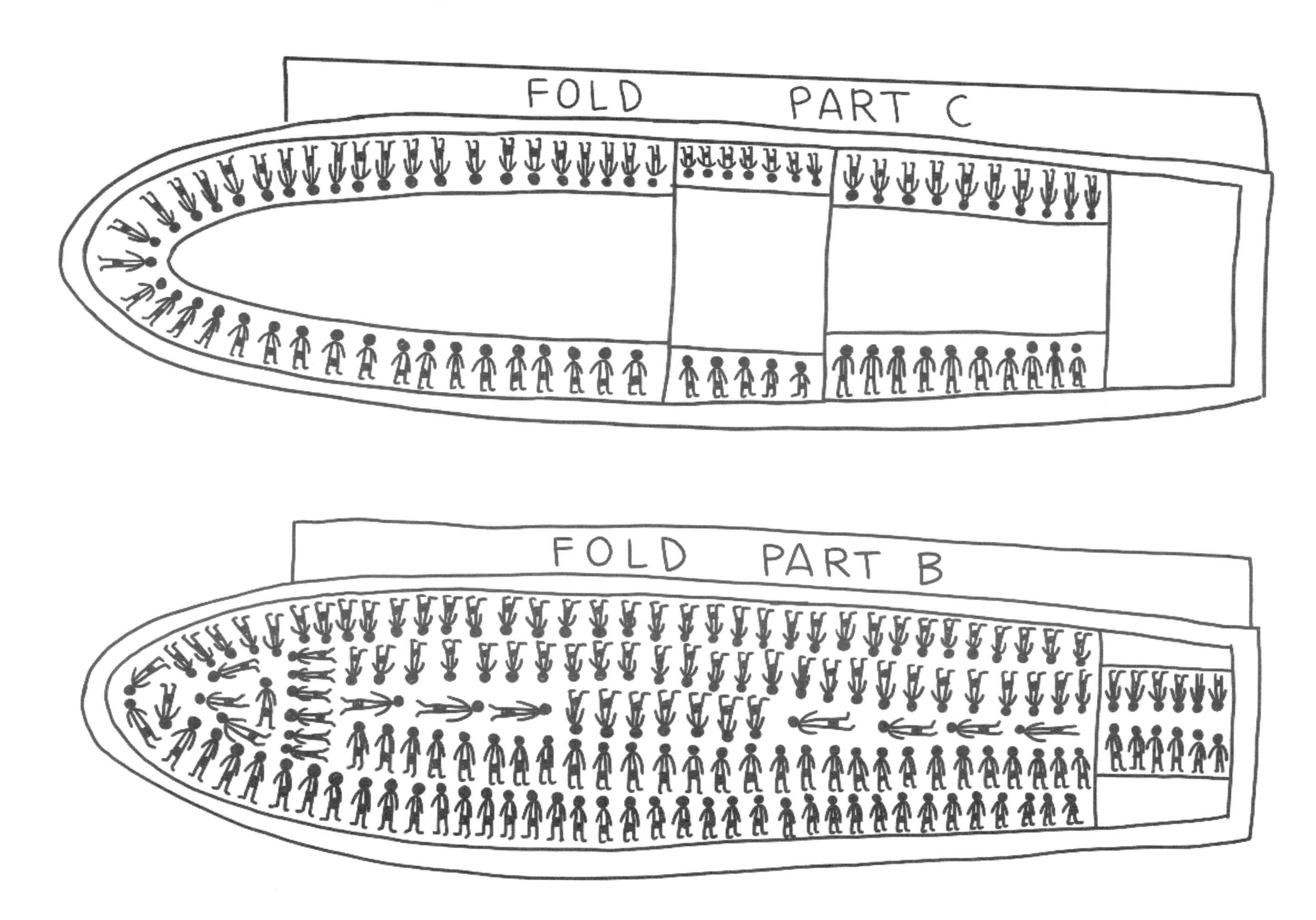

This Book tell man not to be cruel. Oh! that massa would read this Book.

# THE NEGRO WOMAN'S APPEAL
## TO HER WHITE SISTERS

Ye wives, and ye mothers, your influence extend—
Ye sisters, ye daughters, the helpless defend—
These strong ties are severed for one crime alone,
Posessing a colour less fair than your own.
Ah! why must the tints of complexion be made
A plea for the wrongs which poor Afric invade?
Alike are his children in his holy sight,
Who formed and redeems both the black and the white.
In the good book you read, I have heard it is said,
For those of all nations the Saviour has bled, —
No "respecter of persons" is he I am told,
All who love and obey him he ranks in his fold;
His laws, like himself, are both pure and divine—
Ah! why bear his name and his precepts decline?

"Do justly," I hear is the sacred command—
Then why steal poor Negro from his native land?
Can they violate this, and "love mercy?" Oh! no,
These claims, and these wounds, and these tears plainly show
That, assuming a power our God never gave,
The practice of sin will the heart more deprave.
That man, when rejecting his Maker's control,
His feelings and passions like billows will roll,
And spread desolation wherever he reigns
Behold it, alas! in this land of sweet canes.

'Tis the nature of crime so prolific its source;
To delude,—to mislead—and to strengthen their force;
Then pity dear ladies and send me relief,
This poor heart is breaking with sorrow and grief:
Could you see my affliction your tears they would flow,
For women are tender by nature you know.
In health and in sickness I daily must toil
From sunrise to sunset, to hoe the rough soil,
My fragile limbs torn, but I must not complain.
No voice of compassion its solace bestows,
If sinking with anguish I court some repose,
The wounds of fresh tortures will rouse me again,
For I must not one moment forgetful remain.
My babies are crying beneath the tall trees,
Their loud sobs come borne on the soft passing breeze,
To her whose rent bosom most keenly can feel,
Though she dare not her thoughts nor her wishes reveal,
While pierced with the knowledge they're roving alone, —
No hand to conduct them, and keep them at home—
To feed them—to sooth them, and hush them to peace
On that bosom of love, where their sorrows would cease.
Their smooth glossy cheeks, which as lovely I view
As are the mixed tints of the roses to you,
Are stained with the tears I would soon kiss away,
Could I see my sweet infants the long sunny day.
On their soft jetty locks hang the dew-drops of morn,
Which like pearls their bright ebony clusters adorn,
As they wander about round the green plantain tree,
Their little hands clasped, they keep asking for me—
Surprised that by her whom our nature has taught
To cherish and guard, they should now be forgot;
Alas! could they tell how my bleeding heart aches,
They would know that maternal love never forsakes:

The tide of affection that tinges your skin
With beauty's vermillion, proclaims it within;
But ladies believe me no warmer it glows
Because that through lilies and roses it flows.
The same holy hand which created you fair,
Has moulded me too in the hue that I wear;
No partial hand formed us, our title's the same—
'Tis inscribed on the Christian, whatever his name;
No sable can veil when his light from on high
Illumines the soul he has made for the sky,
To dwell in his courts, and be present with him,
When freed and redeemed from the bondage of sin.
Oh! fair Christian ladies, you bear a high name;
Your works of benevolence loudly proclaim
The mercy and kindness you show to distress;
Ah! Pity dear ladies, our Saviour will bless.

Richard Barrett, Printer, Mark Lane.

# Who Am I? Game Cards

(make 3 copies)

**Susan B. Anthony**
Helped in the *Underground Railroad* along with speaking out nationally against slavery.

**Henry Ward Beecher**
Presbyterian minister who used his nationally recognized oration skills to speak out against slavery.

**Angelina Grimke**
National speaker against slavery.

**James Birney**
In 1840, he was the Liberty Party's presidential candidate. Tried to end slavery politically.

**William Wilberforce**
British Parliamentary member who spent his life fighting to end slavery in England.

**Sojourner Truth**
Wrote her story and spoke all over the country against slavery.

**Harriet Tubman**
Guided over 300 slaves to freedom in the *Underground Railroad.*

**Olaudah Equiano**
Once free, he became a national speaker, describing the cruelties of slavery.

**Frederick Douglass**
Escaped slavery and became a national speaker against slavery.

**Henry Bibb**
Escaped from Native American masters and spoke against slavery with Frederick Douglass.

**Jane Cannon**
Campaigned against slavery and helped the *Underground Railroad.*

**Annie Burton**
Wrote life story, *Memories of Childhood's Slavery Days.*

# Log Cabin Quilt Pattern

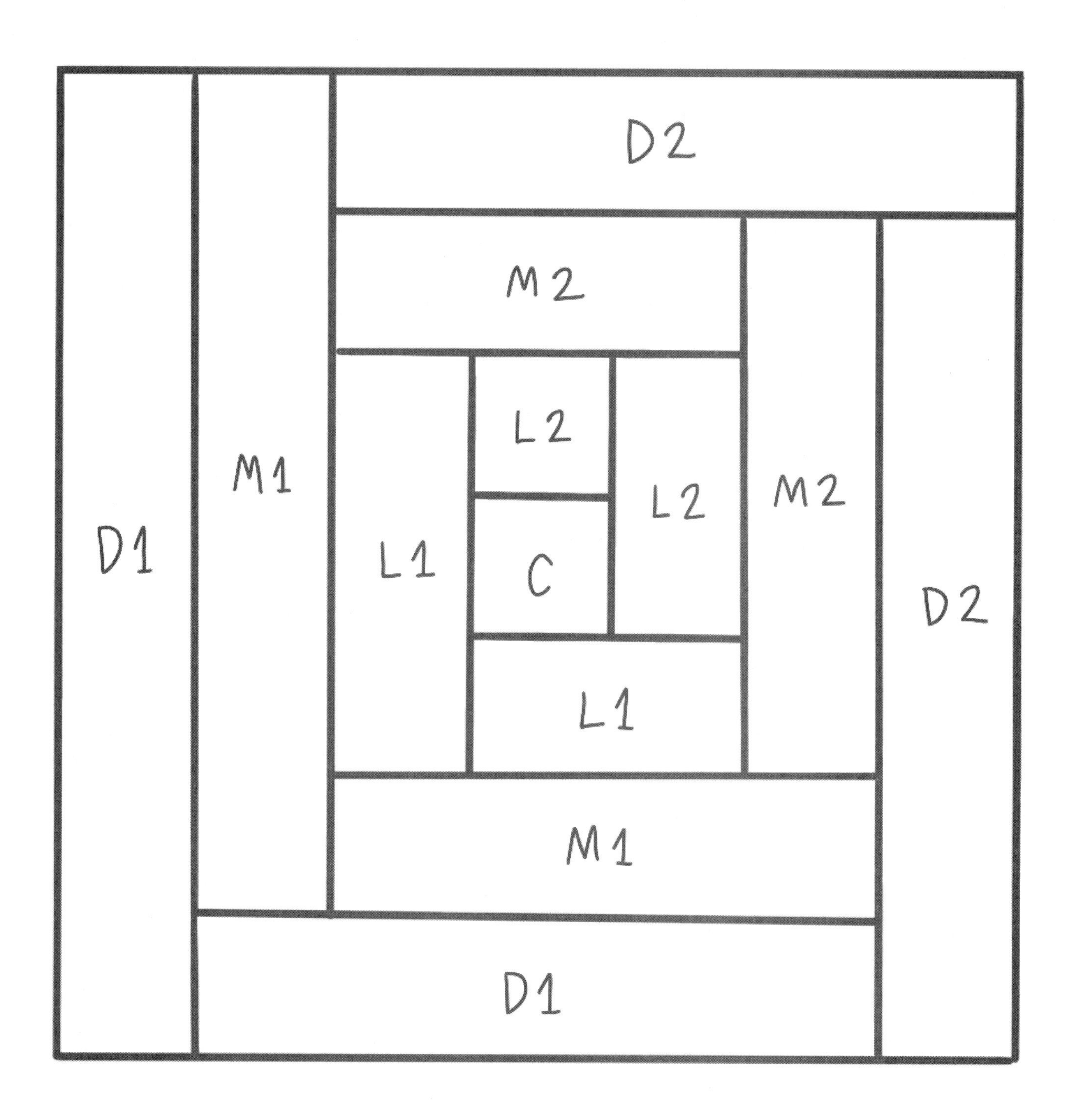

# English and Boers in Africa

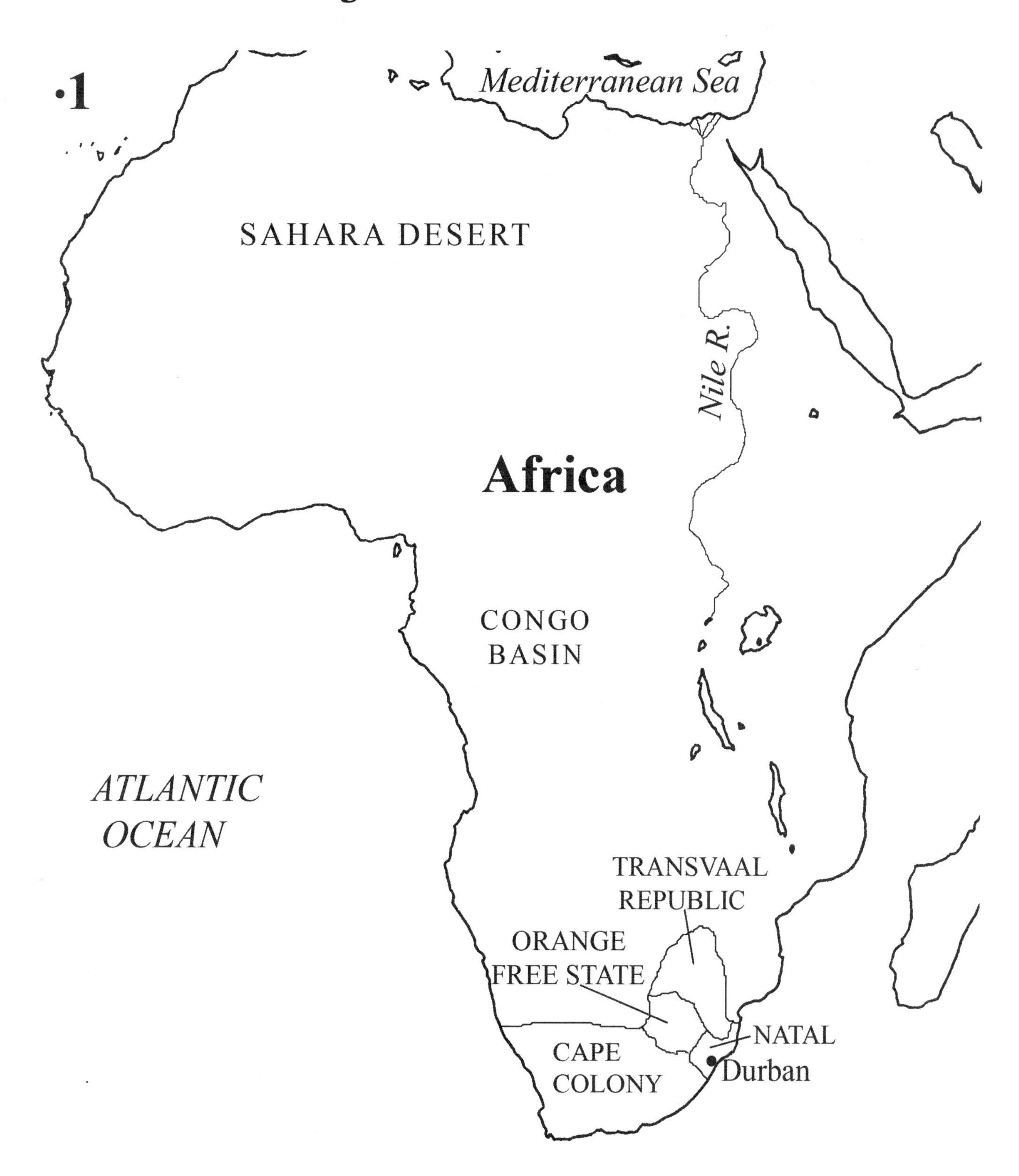

# Shaka Zulu

# Assegai Spear Head Template

Native American Relocation
Sauk
Fox
OHIO
Ohio R.
VIRGINIA
Oklahoma
Cherokee
Chickasaw
Choctaw
Creek
GEORGIA
FLORIDA
Seminoles
ATLANTIC
OCEAN
Gulf of Mexico

# The Trail of Tears

# Native American Sign Language

# England and China

# Lin Zexu and a Chinese Ship

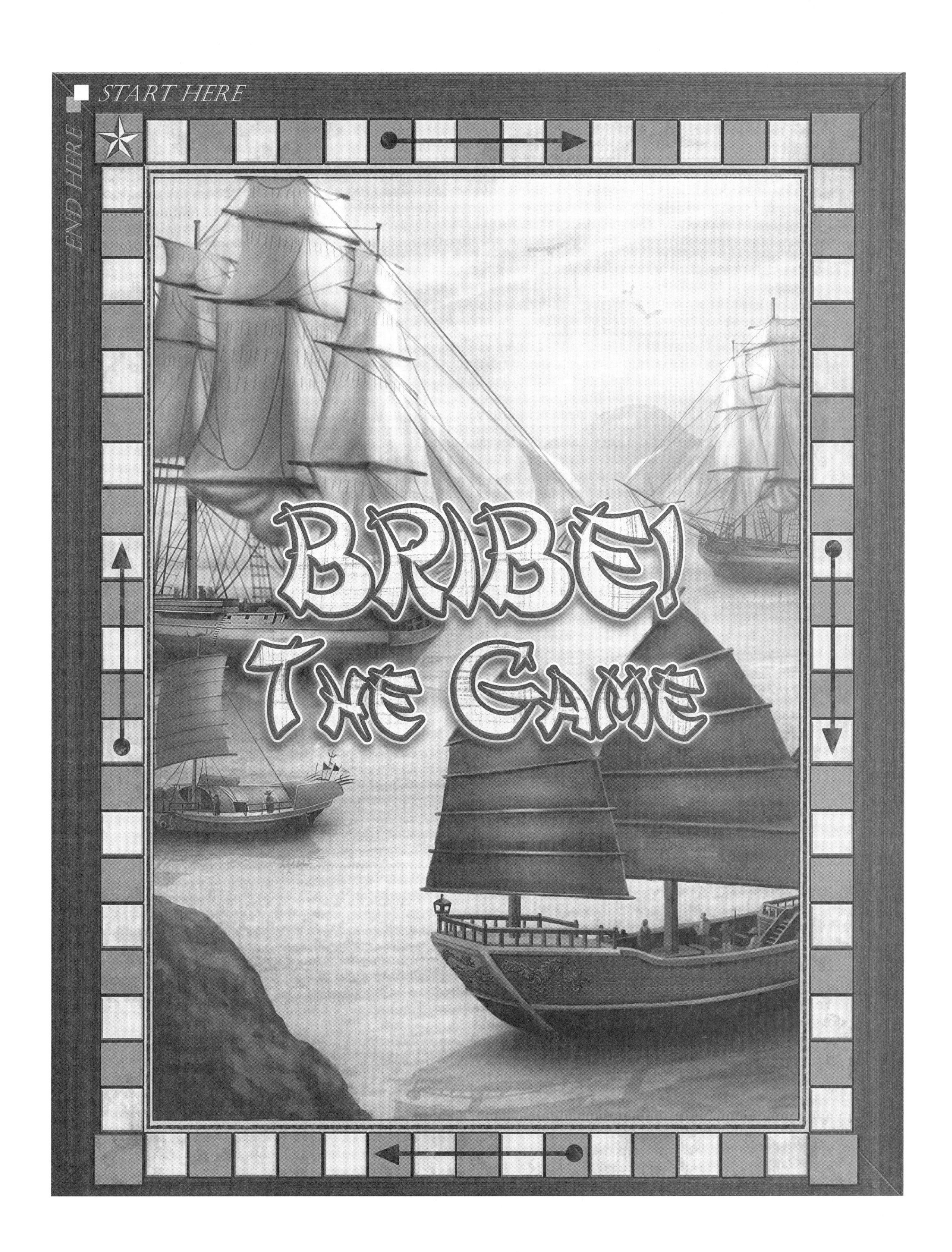
START HERE
END HERE
BRIBE!
THE GAME

# BRIBE! Game Cards

| | | |
|---|---|---|
| Who was Mary, Queen of Scots? *See Chapter 2.* | Who fought in the Opium Wars and why? *See Chapter 39.* | Who fought in the *Seven Years' War*? *See Chapter 21.* |
| Give a fact about King James, also known as James I of England. *See Chapter 3.* | How did the British gain and keep land in India? *See Chapter 19.* | Who were the *Luddites*? *See Chapter 31.* |
| What was Henry Hudson's quest? *See Chapter 4.* | The Ottoman Turks looked westward. Where did they attack and what happened? *See Chapter 18.* | Who did the Americans fight to gain their independence? *See Chapter 22.* |
| How did Toyotomi Hideyoshi help end Japan's long civil war? *See Chapter 5.* | What two ports did Peter the Great gain for Russia? *See Chapter 17.* | In the United States, what are the three branches of the government? *See Chapter 23.* |
| How did the pilgrims ensure the *Strangers* and the *Saints* followed the same rules? *See Chapter 6.* | Name one of Isaac Newton's ideas. *See Chapter 16.* | How did the British use Australia? *See Chapter 24.* |
| Who was Queen Nzinga of Angola? *See Chapter 7.* | What did William Penn do? *See Chapter 15.* | How did the French Revolution go sour? *See Chapter 25.* |
| What was the *Trail of Tears*? *See Chapter 38.* | What did Frederick do to become king? *See Chapter 14.* | Tell Catherine the Great's story. *See Chapter 26.* |
| What was the Thirty Years' War about? *See Chapter 9.* | Who was the Sun King? *See Chapter 13.* | What does *Interchangeable Parts* mean? *See Chapter 27.* |
| Who were the Manchu and what did they do? *See Chapter 10.* | Why did King Charles lose his head in England? *See Chapter 12.* | King George III sent an ambassador to China. What was China's reaction? *See Chapter 28.* |
| Name the three main early emperors of India during this time period. *See Chapter 11.* | Who led the Haitian Revolt? *See Chapter 30.* | How did Napoleon become emperor of France? *See Chapter 29.* |
| What did Lewis and Clark do? *See Chapter 32.* | How did Napoleon's life end? *See Chapter 33.* | Who was called the "Liberator" of South America? *See Chapter 34.* |
| How did the rebellion of New Spain begin? *See Chapter 35.* | Give a name of an abolitionist who fought to end slavery in either America or Britain. *See Chapter 36.* | Why was the Zulu Kingdom troubled? *See Chapter 37.* |

# Mexico, the Republic of Texas, and the US

# A Vaquero

# Early Texas History Word Search

Directions:

1. Solve the clues on the following page and write the answers in the spaces provided.
2. All the answer words from the clues are in the word search and run from left to right, top to bottom, and diagonally. Find them now.
3. Have fun!

```
L B J L T B N P L U M A E W A
I R O B E R T E L E E S M A S
N A N T X A C R A S L I P S U
C Z O H I Z H U A I T I R H P
O O J E C O R S B V I B E I E
L S I E S T A I I A I R S N S
N S M T R O R E P R U S A G U
D A B R N I G S A R D E R T R
R M O S E S A U S T I N I O R
S H W L Y O R L E C T I O N E
A O I N C L R L I M N M S D N
N U E X R A I I G E A I O C D
T S M A O S S W H X S D A Y E
A T P U C E O O T I O N K L R
A O R A K R N B E C M E W A Y
N N E B E P N M E O A G O A K
N E T D T M N A N C L R O K A
A R T G T E A S T I A A D Y A
```

# Early Texas History Word Search Clues

1. This American banker and his son made an agreement with Spain that allowed American settlers to live in the northern part of the Spanish colony of Texas. _ _ _ _ _   _ _ _ _ _ _

2. American settlements in the Spanish colony of Texas were called this: _ _ _ _ _ _ _ _ _ _ _

3. In Mexico City, the Mexican president was defeated in an election by a popular general. What was his name?
_ _ _ _ _   _ _ _ _

4. What was the name for a gathering of armed men? _ _ _ _ _ _ _ _ _

5. Many delegates from all over Texas met together to write a constitution for Texas. What was the name of the river on which they met? _ _ _ _ _ _

6. Who was voted to be the general of the new Texas army? _ _ _   _ _ _ _ _ _ _

7. What was the name of the brave man, famous for his hunting knife, who came to help the Texans fight at San Antonio? _ _ _   _ _ _ _ _

8. Who was the famous Tennessee frontiersman that came to help at the Alamo?
_ _ _ _ _ _ _ _ _ _ _

9. When Santa Anna and his army arrived at the Alamo, he ran up a red flag. This was a signal that meant:
_ _ _ _ _ _ _ _ _ without conditions!

10. Who wrote the letter that called for help, and ended with the famous saying, "Victory or death!"?
_ _ _ _ _ _

11. Santa Anna was angry that Texas was filled with American settlers who refused to obey him. He then threatened to march to what American city? _ _ _ _ _ _ _ _ _ _   _ _

12. What was the name the Mexicans gave to their usual afternoon nap? _ _ _ _ _ _

13. How many minutes did it take Sam Houston's soldiers to defeat the Mexicans at San Jacinto?
_ _ _ _ _ _ _ _

14. What was the name of the young Congressman from Illinois who objected when the US Army began marching toward Mexico City? _ _ _ _ _ _ _

15. Where was Santa Anna living when he decided to return to Mexico? _ _ _ _

16. What was the name of the young captain who defeated Santa Anna at a village near Mexico City?
_ _ _ _ _ _   _   _ _ _

# Texas Rangers Badge

# Alamo Template

# Great Britain, Australia, and New Zealand

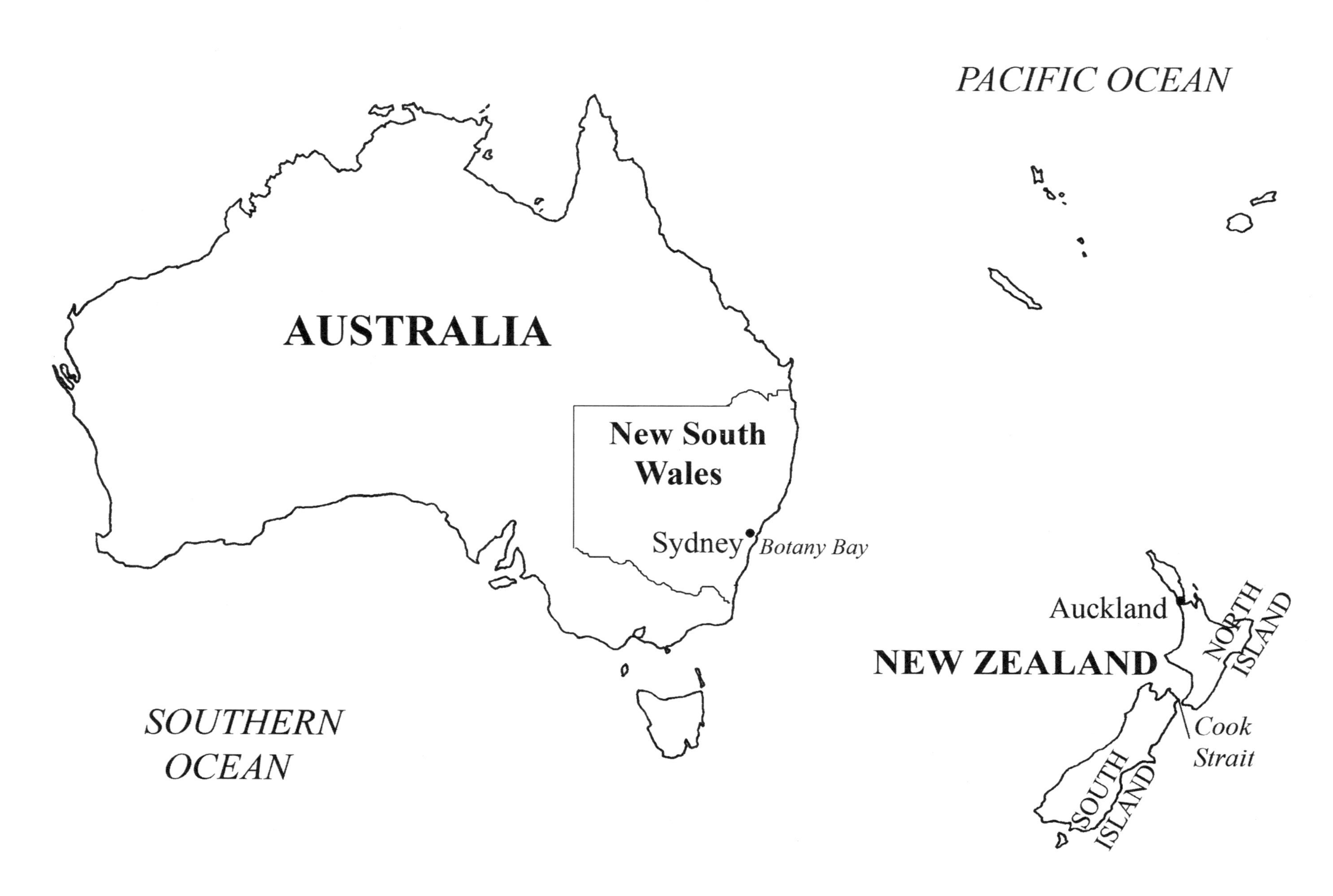

# Maori People

# The California Gold Rush and the Rest of the World

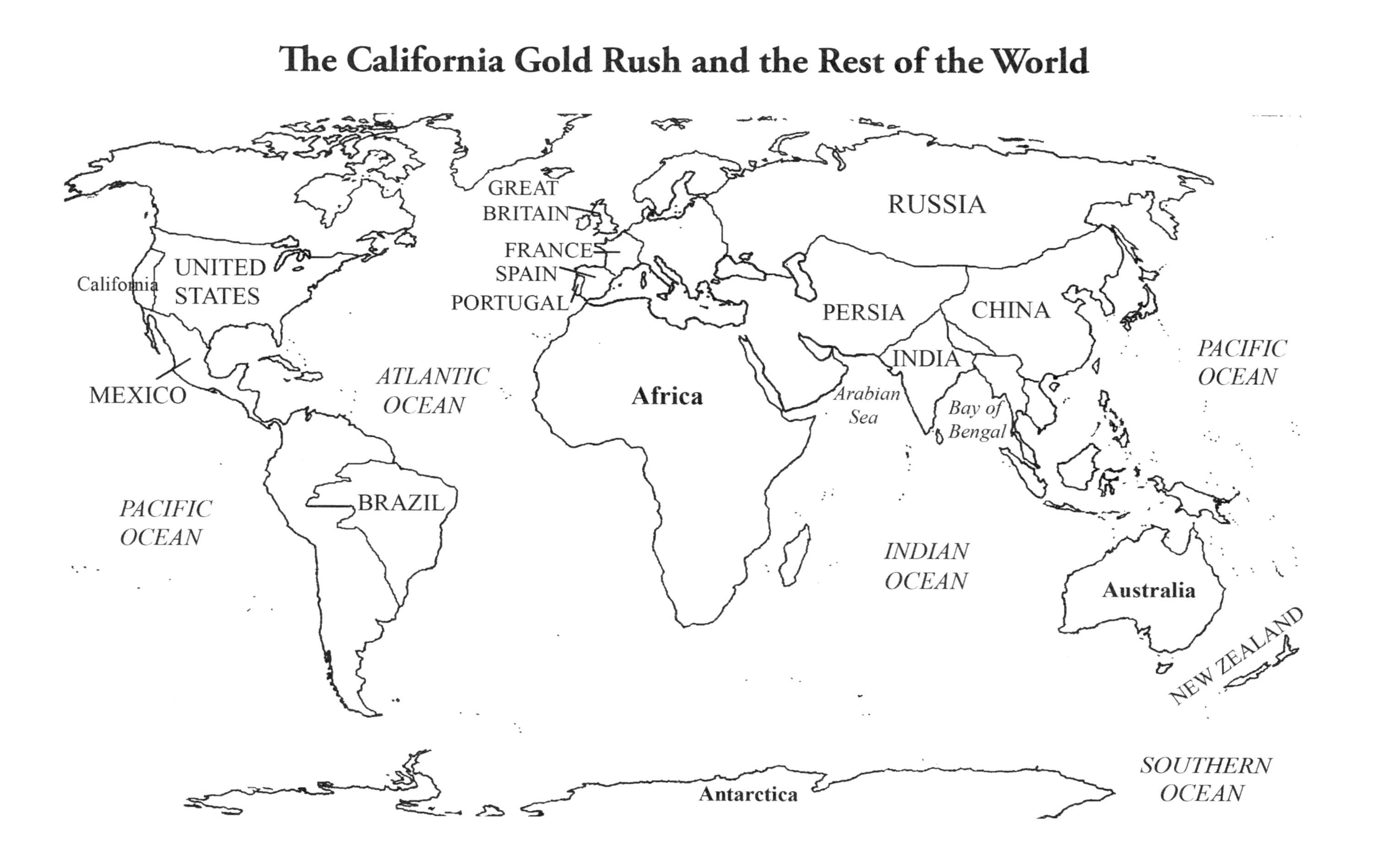

# California Miners

# Review Cards

## A World of Empires 1 SOTW3

When Charles was only 6, his father died and Charles became king of the Netherlands. When he was 16, his Spanish grandfather died and left him the throne of Spain. When he was 19, his German grandfather died and he became king over the German lands. Charles was still a teenager—but he was a teenager with three thrones.

But Charles wanted even more!

## Protestant Rebellions 2 SOTW3

Mary, Queen of Scots, inherited the throne when she was only 5 days old! Her mother ruled while Mary grew. She was a good leader, but she was Catholic—the Scottish noblemen were Protestant and didn't want a Catholic ruler. Mary spent her life dodging plots until she became a threat to Queen Elizabeth of England who imprisoned her for 19 years before executing her.

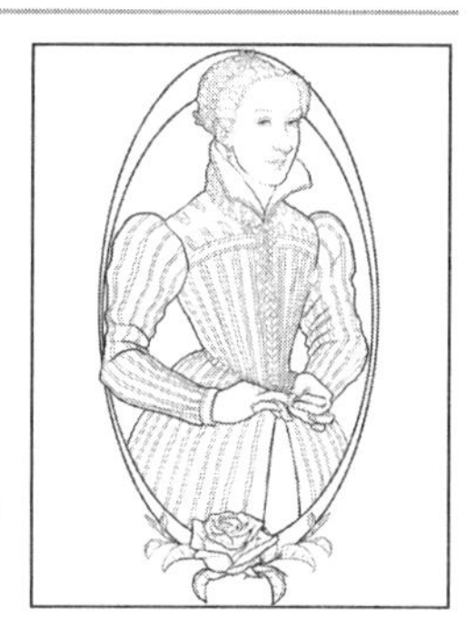

## James, King of Two Countries 3 SOTW3

James insisted that a king rules by divine right! He had gained his mother's throne in Scotland and Elizabeth's throne in England. During his reign he made enemies of the Catholics, Protestants, and even Parliament itself! But James is known for something he did right. During his reign, James agreed to make a brand-new English translation of the Bible, which is still used today!

## Searching for the Northwest Passage 4 SOTW3

King Henry IV of France hired a tough ex-soldier to try one more time to find the Northwest Passage. Unlike other explorers, Champlain saw his newfound Canada as a perfect place for a new French settlement. He returned with armloads of furs and vivid descriptions of the splendid land, convincing Henry to start a colony.

## Warlords of Japan 5 SOTW3

A great leader named Toyotomi Hideyoshi helped to end Japan's long civil war. He wasn't a prince or rich nobleman. His wife named him "The Bald Rat"! But he gained the attention of leaders as an energetic, loyal man, famous for his brilliant strategies in battle. When his warlord died, Hideyoshi won the title. Confidently, he made plans to expand the boundaries of Japan.

## New Colonies in the New World 6 SOTW3

After many miserable days at sea, the Mayflower sighted land. The Pilgrims had arrived! But before leaving the ship, the Strangers and Saints sat down and drew up a set of laws to make sure they all would follow the same rules. This "Mayflower Compact" said that all colonists must agree together before a law that all must obey was passed.

# Review Cards

**The Spread of Slavery** 7 SOTW3

One woman made it her life's work to fight against the Portuguese invaders. Princess Nzinga was born into the royal family of Ndomba, a kingdom on the western coast of Africa. All her life, Portuguese traders had been landing on the shores of her homeland offering cloth, jewelry, and rum in exchange for prisoners. She knew that once they boarded the ships, these prisoners were never seen again.

**The Middle of the East** 8 SOTW3

The Ottoman Turks thought that Abbas was afraid to fight. But Abbas had a plan! He hired an English soldier to train the disorganized Persian army. Sir Robert Sherley taught Abbas' soldiers to use muskets and other European weapons. After several years of training, the Persian army faced the Ottoman Turks and crushed them in battle! Abbas reclaimed his territory.

**The Western War** 9 SOTW3

Ferdinand's pursuit of the Holy Roman Empire's crown made him the enemy of the Protestants, since he captured their land and gave it to Catholics. One Swedish king, Gustavus, trained his soldiers carefully and paid them well so they would remain loyal during the fight against Ferdinand. He was the first European commander to put all his soldiers in the same uniform!

**Far East of Europe** 10 SOTW3

China had many problems. People were hungry and dissatisfied! One postman decided to attack the Ming emperor. His army marched right into Peking! So the Ming asked the Manchu to come help them out. The Manchu came right down into China and took over the throne! The first Manchu emperor treated the Han Chinese unkindly, but the second Manchu emperor let them have positions at court and treated them more fairly.

**The Moghul Emperors of India** 11 SOTW3

As soon as Shah Jahan became king, he made sure everyone knew he was just as powerful as his father. But he didn't rule alone. His wife, Mumtaz Mahal, traveled and helped him govern his kingdom. When she died, young Shah Jahan grieved severely. He built her a tomb, or mausoleum, that would show the world how much he loved her. It is called the Taj Mahal.

**Battle, Fire, and Plague in England** 12 SOTW3

Charles inherited the throne from his father, but from the start he made the people angry. Civil war broke out and he was eventually executed. Cromwell took over as "Lord Protector of England." But reform never came, and when Cromwell died, the Parliament wrote to Charles II, son of Charles I, to come back and rule England.

# Review Cards

## The Sun King 13 SOTW3

The French king claimed to be the owner of the country he ruled. The king was called a "visible divinity"—God's representative. Louis XIV ruled without opposition. He chose the sun as his emblem to represent his power and was called the Sun King. He built the beautiful Versailles with elaborate rooms. Hundreds of statues of Greek gods stood in the gardens, with Louis's face on every one!

## The Rise of Prussia 14 SOTW3

Until this time, people were loyal to a piece of land (like England) or to a monarch (like Louis XIV). But Frederick wanted Prussians to be loyal to a state. They learned to be loyal to an idea of a German kingdom, ruled by a German king. Frederick spent most of his reign building up this idea. And his son furthered his ideas. He connected the separate parts of the kingdom and made its army stronger.

## A New World in Conflict 15 SOTW3

The Iroquois Indian nation had not given up. They began attacking the towns and farms of French settlers in Canada. One 14-year-old, Marie Madeleine, heard gunshots and ran to the nearby fort. Her parents were gone, so she took charge of the fort's defense, along with her two younger brothers.

## The West 16 SOTW3

In western Europe, thinkers like Isaac Newton and John Locke tried to discover the laws that governed how everything worked—objects, planets, people, and governments. Locke wrote about the rights that every person had. Meanwhile, other people invented new methods of farming and better types of animals; this meant that people could grow more food than they had ever done before.

## Russia Looks West 17 SOTW3

Peter, who became Czar of Russia, had always been fascinated by the West. He wanted a warm port so his ships could sail all year round. He fought the Turks for Azov and fought the Swedes for a port on the Baltic. He planned a new city in a land that was swampy and filled with mosquitoes. It was named Saint Petersburg, and he built a palace there.

## East and West Collide 18 SOTW3

The Turks attacked Vienna because they wanted to make the West part of their empire. They camped around the city. But at last, French, Polish, and German soldiers attacked and defeated the Turks. The Turkish empire began to shrink. One Turkish ruler, Ahmet III, later tried to make the country more Western, but his army didn't let him. They threw him into jail.

# Review Cards

## The English in India 19 SOTW3

India was weak and divided, with rulers who didn't do a good job. Meanwhile, the English fought to protect their trading posts in Bombay, Bengal, and other parts of India. When the ruler of Bengal (helped by the French) tried to kick them out, the British East India company made its own army and took over Bengal!

## The Imperial East 20 SOTW3

In 1772, after Chi'en-lung had been on the throne of China for over 30 years, he decided to gather all of China's greatest literature together in one collection. The scholars traveled throughout China and gathered the great books. But while they were saving these books, Chi'en-lung ordered other books destroyed—especially those that were unflattering about the Manchu emperors.

## Fighting Over North America 21 SOTW3

France and England fought wars in Europe that also involved their colonies in North America. A young officer named George Washington was sent to tell the French to leave the Ohio Valley, but they refused. The English tried to attack the French, but were defeated by French and Indians who fought from behind trees instead of in lines. But eventually, the English drove the French out of North America. They took over Canada.

## Revolution! 22 SOTW3

Many of the American colonists were upset because the British taxed them without getting their approval. They didn't like the way the British treated them. Eventually this led to a war, and the 13 colonies declared that they were now their own country. The war was long and hard, but eventually the Americans, led by George Washington, won. They were now independent.

## The New Country 23 SOTW3

A group of men met in Philadelphia to make a Constitution—a set of rules for the new United States. It set up a government with 3 branches. The legislative branch (Congress) makes laws. The executive branch (the President) enforces those laws, but he can also stop those laws if they are unfair. The judicial branch (Supreme Court) decides if the laws are proper. George Washington was elected the 1st President.

## Sailing South 24 SOTW3

Captain Cook explored the Pacific, Australia, Antarctica and Hawaii, but was killed in an argument with the people of Hawaii. Later, the British made Australia into a colony for prisoners. They could work in Australia and make their own farms. The settlers did not treat the Aboriginal people well.

# Review Cards

## Revolution Gone Sour 25 SOTW3

The people of France were unhappy. They paid too many taxes, and the nobles, king, and priests paid little or nothing! The 3rd Estate (the group representing most of the people) wanted a new constitution where all people were equal. The people of Paris attacked the Bastille fortress to get weapons. France became a republic, and the King & Queen were killed. But the leaders of the republic were so afraid of threats that they started executing thousands of people.

## Catherine the Great 26 SOTW3

Catherine started out as a German princess who came to Russia to marry the heir to the Russian throne. But her husband was not kind to her. He wasn't a good ruler, and the church and the army didn't like him. So Catherine took over and became empress. As empress, she allowed some changes in Russia and some new ideas, but she held on to power, and the peasants' lives did not get better.

## A Changing World 27 SOTW3

Steam engines gave people new, faster ways to travel, and more power for machines. But the steam was produced by coal. Miners had to dig for the coal in dangerous mines. Meanwhile, Eli Whitney invented a cotton gin, which could get the seeds out of cotton much faster. This made more people in the United States want to grow cotton. Eli Whitney also made interchangeable parts, so that items such as guns could be produced more efficiently.

## China and the Rest of the World 28 SOTW3

George Macartney was Britain's ambassador to China. He was sent to ask the Emperor to allow Britain to trade with China. He brought the Emperor some of the wonderful items that Britain could bring to China. But the Emperor only saw these items as tribute. He sent a letter back to the King of England refusing all that he had asked. China, he said, didn't need anything that Britain had.

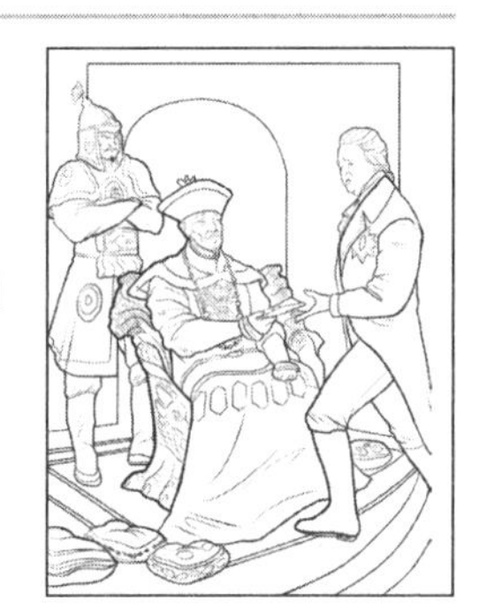

## The Rise of Bonaparte 29 SOTW3

An officer named Napoleon Bonaparte gained control over France, through defeating enemies and conquering other countries, and forcing the Council to give him power. He wrote new laws for France. He sold the Louisiana Territory to the United States. He wanted to invade Britain, but the British navy defeated France's navy at the Battle of Trafalgar.

## Freedom in the Caribbean 30 SOTW3

Saint Domingue was a French colony on an island just above South America. Rich French planters lived there—and so did many African slaves. The slaves worked hard, but were very badly treated. Finally, they revolted! Their leader, Toussaint L'Ouverture, organized them into an army and became the Lieutenant Governor of the island. But Napoleon sent a French army to reconquer the colony. Toussaint was captured and sent to prison—but the French caught yellow fever and had to leave. The newly free nation was renamed Haiti.

# Review Cards

## A Different Kind of Rebellion 31 SOTW3

When factories in England and America started to use steam power, goods like cloth became cheaper. People bought this cheap cloth instead of the more expensive hand-made cloth. Weavers who worked at home couldn't stay in business, so they had to go work in the factories. Factory owners could hire women and children more cheaply than they could hire men, so many men lost their jobs. Children worked long days, breathing dust and standing up for many hours. Some people in England, called "Luddites," tried to smash the factory machines.

## The Opened West 32 SOTW3

Thomas Jefferson sent two explorers to travel across the new Louisiana Territory and map it out. Meriwether Lewis and his friend William Clark built a boat and gathered a group of men. In 1804, they set out, traveling up the Missouri River. With help from Native Americans they met, they made it to the Pacific Ocean.

## The End of Napoleon 33 SOTW3

Napoleon conquered many countries. But then he invaded Russia, but failed and lost most of his army. He was sent into exile. Meanwhile, the United States and Britain fought a war because of the way Britain was treating American ships and sailors. They fought for 3 years. The British burned the President's House and the Capitol building. But eventually the two countries made peace, after gaining nothing from each other. In 1815, Napoleon came back to France and took over again. Several countries banded together to stop him. At the Battle of Waterloo, he was defeated. This time, he was sent to an island far out at sea, and was never allowed to come back again.

## Freedom for South America 34 SOTW3

Simón Bolívar was convinced that he could lead his country of Venezuela to independence from Spain. After that, he wanted to lead the rest of South America to freedom. After years of struggle, he and José de San Martín freed South America from Spanish control. But the South American countries could not agree to be united.

## Mexican Independence 35 SOTW3

Spain ruled Mexico, and didn't treat the Indians and half-Indians well. A Mexican priest named Don Miguel Hidalgo gave a speech, "the Cry of Dolores," demanding that Mexico get freedom from Spain. He failed, but other people started new uprisings. Eventually one of them, Iturbide, won independence for Mexico. But when he became the new king of Mexico, he did such a bad job that the army, led by General Antonio Lopez de Santa Anna, overthrew him and made Mexico a republic (like the United States).

## The Slave Trade Ends 36 SOTW3

Abolitionists knew that the slave trade had to be outlawed before slavery itself would become illegal. In England, Wilberforce asked Parliament to outlaw the slave trade no matter what the cost. "A trade founded in iniquity must be abolished...let the consequences be what they will." He argued for 19 years before Parliament agreed to make the slave trade illegal.

# Review Cards

## Troubled Africa 37 SOTW3

A young man named Shaka, who was a good fighter and leader, became the ruler of the Zulu people in southern Africa. He taught them new ways of fighting. Then he led them to attack other tribes, and these tribes fled to get away. Some Africans called this time the *mfecane*, or "crushing." Meanwhile, Dutch farmers called Boers were moving into southern Africa. They had African slaves, and when the British took over that area and declared slavery to be illegal, the Boers packed up and moved further into Africa to start their own countries there.

## American Tragedies 38 SOTW3

American settlers kept pushing into lands that were owned by Native American nations. This led to conflict. The American president, Andrew Jackson, signed the Indian Removal Act, which allowed the government to take away Native American land and give it to white settlers. The Native Americans were forced from their homes and made to walk to far-away lands in the West. Many of them died on the way. Meanwhile, black slaves in the American South hated being slaves, and one of them, Nat Turner, led a revolt. But he was captured and executed.

## China Adrift 39 SOTW3

The Chinese government wanted to stop the British from bringing the addictive drug opium into their country. A Chinese official named Lin Zexu drove away the foreign drug traders and destroyed their opium. But Britain fought a war against the Chinese and forced them to open their seaports to whatever Britain wanted to sell.

## Mexico and Her Neighbor 40 SOTW3

Many, many people from the United States came to the part of Mexico called "Texas" in search of cheap land. The Mexican government let them live there even though they had slaves (which was illegal in Mexico). But when Mexico tried to stop any more people from coming to Texas, and said they had to give up their guns, the Texans revolted. Some of them were defeated in a little fort called the Alamo, but eventually they defeated the Mexican general Santa Anna and became their own country. When they tried to join the United States as a new state, Mexico fought a war to stop this, but the U.S. invaded Mexico and took away much of its land, including Texas and several other areas.

## New Zealand and Her Rulers 41 SOTW3

The Maori people of New Zealand were having trouble with new weapons and diseases brought by the Europeans. They asked the British to come over from their colony of Australia and make laws to protect the Maori. But the agreement they signed actually gave all of New Zealand to the British...and no one told the Maori people about this until later! More and more British settlers came to the islands. A Maori chief named Hone Heke fought back, but after years of fighting, the Maori lost most of their land to the British.

## The World of Forty-Nine 42 SOTW3

A few miners went up to the American River to find gold—and returned to San Francisco with bags of treasure. A few hundred more arrived. Then a thousand followed them! By 1849, everyone in the United States knew about the gold at Sutter's Mill. 250 years earlier, the Spanish had been digging gold out of South American mines. Now, Americans dug gold from rivers!